Inside the Greens

Inside the Greens

The origins and future of the party, the people and the politics

Paddy Manning

To Milo Dunphy and Jack Mundey,
two Sydney heroes who were there at the start.

Published by Black Inc.,
an imprint of Schwartz Publishing Pty Ltd
Level 1, 221 Drummond Street
Carlton VIC 3053, Australia
enquiries@blackincbooks.com
www.blackincbooks.com

9781863959520 (paperback)
9781743820643 (ebook)

A catalogue record for this
book is available from the
National Library of Australia

Cover design by Kim Ferguson
Text design by Akiko Chan
Typesetting by Tristan Main
Images on inside covers: 'Liberty, ecology and disarmament' © Jack Carnegie;
'Welcome party on arrival at Upper River Camp' © Jerry de Gryse, courtesy NLA;
'Milne addresses Wesley Vale protest' © Tony Palmer/Newspix; 'Julia Gillard
and Bob Brown' © Alan Porrit/AAP; 'Richard Di Natale and Alex Bhathal'
© Mal Fairclough/AAP; 'Bob Brown at a Stop Adani rally in Sydney' © Alan Porrit;
Franklin River © Peter Dombrovskis, courtesy NLA

CONTENTS

Prologue   ix

PART ONE: THE LIFE OF A PARTY

CHAPTER 1   The World's First Green Party   3
CHAPTER 2   Democrats, Blockaders, Disarmers   29
CHAPTER 3   Green Independents   59
CHAPTER 4   Getting Together   91
CHAPTER 5   Breaking Through   121
CHAPTER 6   Picking Fights   161
CHAPTER 7   Turning the Corner   187
CHAPTER 8   Taking a Stand   215
CHAPTER 9   Into Power   259
CHAPTER 10   Milne Rebuilds   299
CHAPTER 11   The Real Opposition   331

PART TWO: THE CHALLENGE AHEAD

CHAPTER 12   Confronting the Climate Emergency   387
CHAPTER 13   Tackling Inequality in the Aspirational Era   411
CHAPTER 14   Pursuing Peace in the Age of the Strongman   429
CHAPTER 15   Cleaning Up Australia's Democracy   451

Notes   481
Acknowledgements   521
Index   525

FOREBEARS

On a crisp Saturday morning in the spring of 1966, almost a million people lined the streets of Sydney to cheer the leader of the free world, Lyndon Baines Johnson, the first US president to visit Australia. The prime minister of the day, Harold Holt, had declared Australia would go 'All the way with LBJ', and now it was time for a show of loyalty, with tonnes of tickertape, thousands of streamers and posters, and shop awnings decked out in pro-US banners. The official slogan was 'Make Sydney Gay for LBJ'.[1]

Anger at the Vietnam War was rising, however, and over the previous two days protests had erupted in Canberra and Melbourne, where a paint bomb had splattered the presidential limo. Now, as the motorcade headed down Anzac Parade towards the city, a hovering helicopter spotted protesters gathering at the University of New South Wales. The president's heavily armed Cadillac took a quick detour, hurtling down side streets at 80 kilometres per hour. As the motorcade came down Oxford Street and turned onto Liverpool, protesters broke through the crowds and lay down on the roadway. The Liberal premier of New South Wales, Bob Askin, travelling with Johnson, ordered: 'Run the bastards over!'

The protesters were dragged off by police, and the motorcade again abandoned the official route, bypassing the tickertape welcome at Town Hall, missing the floral carpet and the flight of homing pigeons at Queens Square, and heading straight to the Art Gallery of New South Wales for the state reception. Disappointed onlookers caught only a glimpse of the president, at best. Among them was a shy, conservative medical student from the country, Bob Brown, then 22, who many years later recalled that he was 'slightly irked by the fact that there were demonstrators who held up the cavalcade and then it went too fast so you couldn't see'.[2]

At Hyde Park, 15,000 protesters, rallied by student leaders, many wearing black, headed off in pursuit of the president. Then 15-year-old schoolgirl Lee Brown, daughter of well-known communists Bill and Freda, and later to become Senator Lee Rhiannon, remembers it vividly:

> That day was so exciting ... I can tell it moment by moment. The LBJ crowd were singing 'Yellow Rose of Texas', and blasting it out [through loudspeakers] over all of us, and some of the wharfies had wire-cutters, and they cut the wires. Then after they passed, we all ran across to the Art Gallery ... it was like we had taken over the city.

At the gallery, things turned ugly. The protesters mixed with the LBJ crowd, punches were thrown; mounted police were called in as reinforcements, and were pelted with black streamers and small stones. When a firecracker went off, the police, fearing a bomb, got heavy-handed. All up, there were 13 arrests. 'Wild Brawls in LBJ Welcome', blared the *Daily Mirror*. The US media reported that the president had experienced 'the most concentrated hostility in his career'.[3]

To this day, Bob Brown wishes he could have made contact with the anti-war protesters. 'I would have learned a lot,' he says. The young Bob Brown and Lee Brown, no relation to each other, and on opposite sides of the fence in 1966, would indeed meet up almost thirty years later, as members of a political party not yet imagined: the Greens. They would remain poles apart nonetheless.

That same morning, 22 October, *The Sydney Morning Herald* carried a full-page advertisement titled 'An open letter to the President of the United States of America'. It was signed by the maverick entrepreneur Gordon Barton, a self-made millionaire and sometime member of the bohemian 'Sydney Push' who had quit the Liberal Party years earlier in disgust at Robert Menzies' attempt to outlaw the Communist Party. Barton had forked out $1800 to publish his letter denouncing America's 'dirty war' in Vietnam and its 'kill and destroy' tactics.[4] The ad caused a sensation, especially among the large number of anti-war, small-L Liberals who could never vote Labor. Biographer Sam Everingham records that the telephone at

Barton's home, on Sydney's wealthy North Shore, rang off the hook from 5 am on the Saturday morning, and kept ringing all weekend. Letters arrived by the sackful – only eight of a thousand were hostile – and over the next fortnight hundreds of people pledged their support for an anti-war campaign.

When Holt called a snap election in November 1966, Barton agreed to fund independent anti-war candidates, running under the banner of the Liberal Reform Group – at this time he had no interest in standing for parliament himself. They had four key policy planks, designed to appeal to the disillusioned Liberal support base: loyalty to the throne and respect for the Constitution; support for anti-socialist principles; opposition to lottery-style conscription; and opposition to the war. Only eleven days after the open letter was published, the group advertised for respectable candidates who could not be perceived as hippies or communists. 'Suits and ties were in, beards were out,' writes Everingham. The group would preference Labor – in effect, a reversal of the tactics used by the anti-communist Democratic Labor Party, the third force in politics since its 1955 split with the ALP, which kept Menzies in power. The rebel Liberals made the front page of *The Australian* – and donations flooded in, large and small. By the close of nominations, the new party had candidates for 22 seats in New South Wales and Victoria.

Barton penned letters to the prime minister and world leaders, and an op-ed for *The Herald* urging Australia to adopt a defence policy independent of the United States. The day before the election, the group funded more full-page newspaper ads, featuring a graphic image of a mutilated Vietnamese baby. Holt won in a landslide, and opposition leader Arthur Calwell, who had opposed the war, was ousted by right-winger Gough Whitlam. Liberal Reform picked up a creditable 53,000 votes in its first outing – an average of just above 4.5 per cent in the seats it contested, and 6–7 per cent in safe suburban Liberal seats such as Bennelong, Mackellar and Parkes in New South Wales, and Balaclava, Deakin and La Trobe in Victoria.[5] The 1966 election marked the beginning of a new political party: the group was the kernel of the Democrats and, in many ways, a forerunner of the Greens, with its progressive-leaning challenge to the two-party system.

Immediately afterwards, Barton wrote a letter to members headed 'The election is over', in which he berated Liberal and Labor and called for a new approach – what he termed the 'missing alternative':

> We need a new humanitarian spirit, a concern for the human personality. We need a foreign policy based on faith, understanding and co-operation, instead of fear, ignorance and violence. We need a call to meet the great human and economic problems in our society ... Liberal Reform intends to stay in business as a permanent political organisation. It intends to stand for liberal, humanitarian and anti-authoritarian principles in society and government.[6]

As the 1969 federal election loomed, the party achieved instant national representation when Tasmanian independent senator Reg 'Spot' Turnbull decided, after secret talks with Barton, to join up as parliamentary leader of what was renamed the Australia Party. Australia was becoming 'a dictatorship', Turnbull declared, and the public was 'becoming every day more disenchanted with the Liberal Party, more disillusioned with the Labor Party, and more unhappy about having to vote for parties with sectional and sectarian interests'.[7] Yet the Australia Party polled poorly in the tight federal election of 1969, which Gough Whitlam almost won, with a big swing back to Labor, and Turnbull resigned.

Barton and rest of the Australia Party were undeterred. Policy work continued, driven less by Barton himself as time went on than by the Australia Party's 'egghead' membership, which research showed was heavily populated by middle-aged, middle-income-earning, tertiary-educated professionals.[8] A 28-page brochure outlining the party's 'principles and policy', produced in 1970, contained some genuine forward thinking, especially on foreign affairs. The party put no faith in the American alliance, and the flipside was a desire to develop Australia's own aircraft and shipbuilding industries. Apart from ending the Vietnam War, the party wanted Australia to adopt a scrupulous policy of non-alignment, to prohibit foreign military installations, to bring back all overseas troops, to replace treaties such as ANZUS with trade pacts, to give 1 per cent of gross national product to foreign aid, and to recognise China.

There was considered domestic policy too: a call for a Commonwealth takeover of education, government loans for university students, and the seeds of a needs-based schools funding policy that was sector-blind. With the White Australia policy already unravelling, the party wanted an end to all racial and religious discrimination in migration law. Under the heading 'Civil liberties', there was support for decriminalisation of homosexuality, the legalisation of abortion, and cannabis law reform. The party proposed national insurance and superannuation schemes. On parliamentary reform, it proposed multi-member electorates, extending the franchise to 18-year-olds, and abolishing compulsory voting.[9] On the third-last page was a rather staid 'conservation' policy, which mourned the squandering of Australia's heritage, and pointed out that our population was likely to double to 25 million by 2000. The five-point policy – a national conservation commission, more national parks, anti-pollution legislation – was better than the offerings of either side of politics at the time.

Attitudes were changing fast. A new wave of environmentalism had begun in the early 1960s with the publication of Rachel Carson's *Silent Spring*, which warned of the bioaccumulation of pesticides such as DDT. Soon afterwards in Australia, zoologist Alan Marshall's landmark book *The Great Extermination* delivered a frightful stocktake: platypus and koala populations decimated by the fur trade, and birds shot for the plume trade; seals and penguins boiled down for oil; prized timbers such as cedar and Huon pine wiped out commercially. Marshall called for a constitutional referendum to create a powerful new central environment authority like Britain's Nature Conservancy, 'to give a "new deal" to the fauna and flora of the nation as a whole'.[10]

Australians were beginning to fight for conservation. In Queensland, poet Judith Wright and others had founded the Wildlife Preservation Society in 1963, and spent years battling to protect the Great Barrier Reef from limestone mining and drilling for oil. Innovations included the first environmental bumper stickers – 'SAVE THE REEF' – which the society had made in 1968 and sold by the thousands. Their cause was boosted in January 1969, when an oil well blew out off southern California, covering 200 square kilometres of ocean and kilometres of sensitive coastline in thick crude. The Santa Barbara spill remains the third-largest in history, after Deepwater Horizon and Exxon Valdez. Soon afterwards, the Amalgamated Engineering Union put a resolution to the Australian Council of Trade Unions, imposing an immediate and total ban on all mining and oil extraction on the reef, which was shepherded through the 1969 conference by new ACTU president Bob Hawke. Wright wrote in *Coral Battleground* that the resolution was unprecedented: 'the first time, not only in Australian history but as far as we knew in world history, when the trades unions had taken a step that went so far outside their traditional boundaries of interest'.[11] Strongly backed by *The Australian* newspaper, the conservationists and the unions together stopped the project dead.

There were other groundbreaking campaigns. In Victoria, a campaign to stop clearing of fragile mallee scrub at Little Desert, in the Wimmera, for residential development led to the release of *Outline for a Bushlands Magna Carta*, positing the right to clean water and clean air, and to 'enjoy plants and animals in their natural habitats – and the duty not to eliminate them from the face of this earth'.[12] The bushlands Magna Carta was cowritten by Geoff Mosley of the newly established Australian Conservation Foundation, and adopted by a meeting of 1500 people at St Kilda Town Hall in 1969. The furore saw a big swing against the Liberal Victorian government of Henry Bolte in a December 1969 by-election. By the state election in May 1970, the notoriously conservative premier had a conservation policy written into his stump speeches for the first time, and the Little Desert National Park was declared.

In Western Australia, scientist Vincent Serventy, who had written the 1966 landmark *Continent in Peril*, and who was later dubbed the father of conservation, starred in Australia's first environment TV series, *Nature Walkabout*, aired on Channel 9 in 1967, in which he and wife Carol and their two young children travelled the outback for a year in a caravan and a four-wheel drive.

In New South Wales, Milo Dunphy, son of legendary bushwalker Myles, had been campaigning to save the Colong caves, in Sydney's Blue Mountains, from limestone mining, pioneering brazen new tactics like shareholder activism, protesting the annual meetings of the local subsidiary of the world's biggest cement company. Dunphy spied a political opportunity in the new Australia Party and, in a friendly takeover of sorts, joined up and proceeded to redraft its conservation policy, dragging it into the 1970s. In February 1971 he and two other members of the Colong Committee, representing 50 different conservation groups, stood for the Australia Party in the New South Wales state election. He was the first out-and-out conservationist to run for parliament anywhere in Australia.

Another key early influence on the Australia Party's environment policy was a medical research scientist from Adelaide, John Coulter, much later a Democrats senator. Coulter was secretary of the progressive Town and Country Planning Association, which published an open letter in mid-1971, signed by nearly 800 scientists, technologists and economists, warning that Western technological society was damaging the environment and reducing its capacity to support life. Coulter also talked about 'spaceship earth', and pondered the experiment we were running by burning so much fossil fuel:

> The 'she'll be right, mate!' boys mockingly say, 'you scientists can't even say whether the temperature of the world will go up or whether the CO_2 rise will cause another ice age' ... [but] simple calculation shows that the consumption of known petroleum reserves over the next few decades will liberate an amount of CO_2 equal to that now in the atmosphere and the burning of the much larger reserves of coal in the next two centuries will generate ten times the amount of CO_2 in the atmosphere. While it's true we don't know what effect this will have, it's equally true mankind is determined to find out because he is continuing this unique experiment as quickly as possible.

The growing pressure culminated in Liberal prime minister Billy McMahon appointing the first Minister for the Environment, Arts and Aboriginal Affairs, in 1971, carved out from his own department.[13] Nobody wanted the portfolio; the minister himself, Peter Howson, complained that he'd been given responsibility for 'trees, boongs and poofters'.[14]

* * *

As one new political party was forming, another was disintegrating. On Labor's left flank, the long Cold War decline of the Communist Party of Australia was well underway. The Labor national secretary, Laurie Aarons, hoped to give the party mass appeal by renouncing ties to Russia and embracing 'Eurocommunism'. In a painful split in 1971, CPA stalwarts Bill and Freda Brown formed the breakaway Socialist Party of Australia, with Russian support, and stayed loyal to the Soviet Union to the end.

Both had grown up in the Depression and, as Freda's biographer writes, 'believed they were living through the end of capitalism'.[15] Freda had grown up in Erskineville and watched police violently evict the poor from inner-city slums. Bill, an electrician by trade, had joined the army in 1943 and served in Borneo alongside left Labor luminary Jim Cairns, who described him as among the most honourable people he had ever met.[16] Freda was a trailblazer, co-founding the New Housewives Association in 1946 (until it was banned), and later the Union of Australian Women. From 1975 to 1990 Freda was president of the Berlin-based Women's International Democratic Federation, a role that vaulted her into global politics, and she worked alongside figures such as Indira Gandhi, Fidel Castro and Mikhail Gorbachev. Despite her feminist activism, when the women's liberation movement took off in the early 1970s, Freda was wary, if not hostile. She believed the feminists 'had some good ideas, but they thought men were the enemy instead of the class structure'.[17] Freda stepped up her focus on 'working class women's issues': childcare, equal pay, rising prices, maternity allowances and child endowment.[18]

Bill and Freda both stood for election on the CPA ticket. Freda ran for the state seat of Newtown in 1947 (decades later, the seat with the highest Greens primary vote in the country), winning 6.8 per cent of first preferences. Yet neither party ever enjoyed much electoral success. In the Senate, the communist vote peaked at 3.6 per cent in 1955 – meaning more than 160,000 voters had put the party first – but declined steadily thereafter, and by 1964 had fallen back below 1 per cent.

Communists had played a leading role campaigning for Aboriginal land rights, against apartheid and against the Vietnam War, but in Bill Brown's view many of the concerns of the so-called 'new left', who were disillusioned with socialism, were opportunistic and petit-bourgeois. Brown blamed the re-emergence of Trotskyism in the 1960s, and wrote that the movement, with its 'long record of an organisation based on the tactics of "enter, divide and destroy"', could not be 'considered a genuine part of the labor movement'.[19] Brown was not wrong about the modus operandi of 'the Trots'. It was Michel Pablo, general secretary of the semi-clandestine Fourth International (set up by Trotsky after he was expelled from Russia by Stalin), who coined the term 'entrism sui generis'. He thought mass radicalisation in advanced countries would take place through big traditional working-class parties, and Trotskyists should 'bury themselves alive inside such parties', not as an open faction but as a kind of sleeper cell, ready to guide the emergent left wing towards revolution when the time came.[20] Brown's charge of entrism against the Trots would echo decades later in both the Nuclear Disarmament Party and the Greens.

One such Trotskyist was the colourful Nick Origlass, a long-serving alderman and mayor of Leichhardt, in Sydney's inner west, described by his biographer Hall Greenland as the most expelled man in Australian political history – kicked out of his union twice, Labor twice, the Fourth International once and off council once. A blue-collar metalworker, self-taught in international socialism, Origlass twigged early to the rising importance of the urban environment, especially when Standard Oil proposed a refinery right next to a harbourside swimming pool, since named after Olympic champion Dawn Fraser. Origlass organised a petition of 700 residents and took the New South Wales government, which was backing the proposal, to court. The court approved the project, but on such strict conditions that it was shelved.

This was the first in a series of battles Origlass fought against industrial development on the Balmain peninsula, winning in most but not all cases. In 1966 Origlass wrote: 'the urge for a new "quality of life" is evidenced in the renewed interest in town planning. Communities of citizens are now indicated, and indeed are now emerging, concerned with the amenity of neighbourhoods.'[21] In 1968 he stood unsuccessfully as an independent Trot candidate for the state seat of Balmain, running on an urban environment platform. After the 1971 local elections, Origlass was narrowly elected mayor, and with

Issy Wyner set up the new 'Open Council', which gave every resident the right to turn up to council meetings and move a resolution. Origlass's mayoralty was short-lived – just two years – but ahead of its time. Origlass was one of Australia's original 'red greens'; his protégé, Greenland, then a radical student leader in the anti-Vietnam protests, would go on to play a significant role in the Greens.

The Green Bans, pioneered by Jack Mundey, grew out of the same militant industrial milieu. Mundey was born in Malanda, on Queensland's Atherton Tablelands, and grew up 'riding horses, swimming in streams and moving through the rainforest ... I never wore shoes.' But as his 1981 memoir continued:

> The cattle industry had been established by burning down the heavy stands of natural timber – maple, cedar, silky oak. This was still happening when I was young. It was nothing to look across at night and see hundreds of hectares being burnt off ... The subsequent erosion was the price paid for failing to appreciate the need to be harmonious with nature.[22]

Mundey moved to Sydney in 1951 to play three seasons for the Parramatta rugby league club, meanwhile working as a semi-skilled metalworker or labourer. After going to a 'ban the bomb' meeting in 1955, he also joined the local branch of the Communist Party. When Khruschev made his 'secret speech' the following year, Mundey writes that it 'shook me and many of my comrades to our toenails'.

> Khruschev revealed that twelve and a half million Russians had died in labour camps and elsewhere during Stalin's rule. Many of the dead had not been critics of their country or opponents of socialism, but they did not see eye to eye with the brutal methods of Stalin, the Secret Police and the group around the General Secretary. It was frightening what could happen to you if you stepped out of line in a 'socialist' country.[23]

Mundey stayed in the CPA for another twenty years nonetheless, even going on an official visit to Moscow in 1969 as part of a May Day delegation. He stood unsuccessfully for the party in half a dozen New

South Wales and federal elections over the decade from 1966 (Wentworth) to 1977 (Chifley); his best result was for the state seat of Canterbury in 1968, when he got 4.7 per cent of the vote.

By the time Mundey joined the Builders Labourers Federation (BLF) in 1957, Sydney was entering its first high-rise construction boom. Office towers soared, driven by new building technologies – elevators, concrete and glass – and enabled by relaxed planning controls. Suddenly there was a huge concentration of construction workers in the CBD. Mundey was appalled at the unsafe conditions, particularly for builders' labourers, who often died without compensation while doing dangerous work like night-time demolition, or 'riding the hook' of a crane as a 'dogman'. A former amateur boxer as well as a footballer, Mundey was fearless and stood up to the contractors, calling strikes and making a name for himself on building sites, where he was often barred as a troublemaker.

The BLF in New South Wales was run by a corrupt clique, and after a tense union meeting in 1961 the 'rank and file' team of Mundey and Bob Pringle were elected secretary and president of the BLF. They turned the union militant, and in a landmark 1970 strike brought the city's building industry to a standstill for five weeks, declaring site after site to be 'black banned'. The BLF used vigilantes to enforce its bans, shutting down sites to take on employers who would try to use 'scab' labour. Sometimes scuffles broke out and property was damaged, and the BLF was accused of resorting to violence – although they denied it – with its vigilantes dubbed 'Mundey's marauders' in the conservative press. It was these controversial, intimidating tactics, and the solidarity and pride generated among workers, that gave the 'bloody BLs' their power. As Mundey explained much later:

> Looking back, I can see that unless we had won this struggle, particularly for better conditions, and if we hadn't encouraged the rank and file to take a greater interest in control of the union ... [we would not have] gone on ahead to blaze trails in other social and ecological areas later on.[24]

The workers were fiercely loyal to Mundey, Pringle and Owens, who cut their own wages, as union officials, to the same level as that of the labourers, and took no pay at all, like the workers, when a strike was on. As union leaders, they were thoroughly, indeed radically, democratic. Workers were empowered to call a strike themselves, whether or not a union organiser was present. Most significantly, Mundey did not believe in entrenched union leadership; instead, positions should be rotated through limited tenure for all office holders, to stop the leaders losing touch with workers, hobnobbing with bosses and going soft or getting bought off. Mundey practised what he preached, going back on the tools and working on site after his term as an elected official.

Then Mundey and Pringle's BLF took a step that would reverberate around the world, and that remains electrifying in its potential to this day. In well-heeled Hunters Hill, on Sydney's lower North Shore, 12 acres known as Kelly's Bush – one of the last remaining pieces of natural bushland on the Parramatta River – were to be cleared to build three eight-storey towers and 40 townhouses. In 1968 the newly formed Hunters Hill Trust succeeded in electing nine pro-conservation candidates to the local council, which opposed the project. The developer AV Jennings lobbied the State Planning Authority and its friends in the government of Premier Bob Askin (who was later exposed for selling knighthoods to developers), and by 1970 the council had buckled, approving a scheme with no high-rise buildings, but more townhouses.

The development became an issue in the New South Wales election of February 1971, with *The Sydney Morning Herald* running a sympathetic story headlined 'The Battle for Kelly's Bush'. The government ducked and weaved, only to approve the development a few months after the vote. Thirteen local women incorporated a registered charity called the Battlers for Kelly's Bush and, encouraged by Mary Campbell from the National Trust, turned to the unions. As one of the battlers, Kath Lehany, later recalled:

> Mary said we could get the unions involved on our side if we ever got really desperate. She told us how the unions had saved the Great Barrier Reef from oil drilling and limestone mining and that they could refuse to work on building whatever Jennings wanted to put on Kelly's Bush.[25]

The Battlers wound up contacting the BLF, which issued a statement that 'as the workers had raised the buildings we had a right to express an opinion on social questions relating to the building industry'. Mundey, who affectionately described the Battlers as 'Upper-middle-class Morning Tea Matrons', wrote:

> They came to us and said that the time had come for us to put our theory into practice ... Our executive met shortly after their visit ... this was an issue that divided them. Some were rather blunt: 'Why should we save the bushland for these middle class shits?' Others said, 'Well, almost certainly we haven't got any builders labourers living in Hunters Hill. Why should it be our concern?' ... I summed up the discussion by saying what was the use of winning higher wages and better conditions if we lived in cities devoid of parks and denuded of trees? Our cities had to be for people, not for corporations to plunder and destroy. Kelly's Bush wasn't just for its neighbours, it should be public land and used by everybody who wanted to use it.[26]

The BLF agreed to impose a ban, on condition that the Battlers could demonstrate support for it among the locals more broadly, not just the fortunate few. Over 450 people turned up at a public meeting and it was clear that a large section of the residents of Hunters Hill wanted the place retained as bushland, not just for themselves but for posterity. The BLF's membership endorsed the ban, and when AV Jennings hinted it might use non-union labour to clear it, the workers called a lunchtime meeting on another of the company's building sites in North Sydney and passed a resolution: 'If one blade of grass or one tree is touched in Kelly's Bush, this half-completed building will remain for ever half-completed as a monument to Kelly's Bush.' Askin condemned the BLF, but the union succeeded in forcing AV Jennings to negotiate with the Battlers. Kelly's Bush remains a public harbourside reserve to this day.

It was only the beginning. In 1972 Mundey saw the possibility that the union could act in its members' long-term interests, as well as their immediate interests. Eighteen months later, in an interview with *The Australian*, Mundey had what has been called a stroke of genius, coining the term 'Green Bans' to describe the BLF's new form of activism. From Kelly's Bush, the BLF went on to impose Green Bans all over Sydney, saving the fabled Rocks precinct, Woolloomooloo, Centennial Park and more besides. At one point in early 1973 the BLF was holding up some 40 projects worth $3 billion. By the mid-1970s the property market had crashed, the post-war building boom was over, and by the time the next one came around in the 1980s a raft of planning laws to protect natural and cultural heritage had been established, and there was near-universal recognition that what the Green Bans had saved was worth saving.

When the German peace activist Petra Kelly came to Australia in 1977, she met Mundey and, the story goes, went home to found the German Greens ('Die Grünen'), setting off a worldwide political movement inspired by the Green Bans.

This is the story of how the Greens began and grew in Australia, of who they are now, and of where they are going.

The Life of a Party

CHAPTER 1

THE WORLD'S FIRST GREEN PARTY

The drowned beach at Lake Pedder in south-west Tasmania has a singular place in the history of green politics. Flooded for an unnecessary hydro-electric project in 1972, the beach still has wheel marks from the light planes of bushwalkers who once used it as a remote landing strip. The environment movement talks quite often about its wins, less often about its losses. Pedder is the exception, the movement's Gallipoli – a defeat from which was forged a new identity: the first green political party to contest an election, anywhere in the world.[1]

Pedder was unique. Geomorphologist Kevin Kiernan, who suffered the death of two friends that year in the battle to save Tasmania's wild south-west, says there was nothing like it in the scientific literature: a glacial outwash lake, 300 metres above sea level, with a pink quartzite sandy beach, saw-toothed 'mega-ripples' along the shallow water's edge, high dunes and over a dozen plants and organisms that existed nowhere else on Earth. 'It was a "oncer",' Kiernan says mournfully.

Why did such a globally significant political battle occur there and then? A dumb narrative would go like this: Pedder was so beautiful that, when it was threatened, conservationists got so angry that they set up the world's first green party to save it. A cooler-headed argument is that, amid a global environmental awakening, the emergence of a new post-material politics in Tasmania in 1972 was no historical fluke: Australia was arguably the richest nation per capita on Earth, and the only place where such extravagant wealth was colliding with such extraordinary wilderness.

Lake Pedder was meant to be preserved forever as the jewel in the crown of a national park, created in 1955 at the urging of the early conservationists. Tasmania's all-powerful Hydro Electric Commission, known simply as 'the Hydro', had its own ideas, and in the early 1960s a major road was cut into the south-west, funded by the Menzies government, putting conservationists on high alert. The Hydro was distinctly Tasmanian: a secretive government agency that was barely accountable to parliament.[2] 'Hydro-industrialisation', using cheap power from dams to attract heavy industry, had guided the state's development without challenge for most of the century. The Hydro's engineers planned to dam every major river in the state.[3] Their misguided ambition was to turn Tasmania into a 'Ruhr of the south'.

By the 1960s, Tasmania had been a Labor Party stronghold for more than three decades, corroding the state's democracy. In 1967, amid a drought-induced power rationing, Labor premier 'Electric' Eric Reece announced that Lake Pedder would be 'modified' under stage one of the $95-million Middle Gordon Hydro-Electric Scheme. 'Modified' was a euphemism: Pedder would be completely flooded to form the largest water storage in Australia, as part of a scheme much bigger than the Snowy Hydro, connecting three new dams and one new power generator. Only the top 1.5 metres of the new enlarged Lake Pedder would be used in the scheme; the rest would be dead water storage. The largest petition yet delivered to the state's parliament – according to the *Mercury*, with 7500 signatures it was 100 metres long and weighed 2 kilograms[4] – called for the lake to be saved, amid criticisms that the government was 'hydro happy'. A select committee of the parliament's upper house, while acknowledging the depth of feeling, rejected an alternative proposal that would have saved the lake at a cost of $11 million. Premier Reece rammed the enabling legislation through parliament, and thought that was the end of it.

The Middle Gordon scheme was just one of three big projects that Reece wanted to take to the 1969 state election. The others were the state's first woodchip mill, at Triabunna, and Australia's first casino, as part of Federal Hotels' Wrest Point development, at Hobart's genteel Sandy Bay. Dealings around the casino were questioned right from the beginning; the whiff of corruption would soon become a powerful stench.

In opposition, Liberal leader Angus Bethune wavered over Lake Pedder, describing it as a 'unique scenic gem' and warning that hydro development should not be allowed to become an obsession.[5]

In the 1969 poll, conservationists swung towards him, producing a hung parliament with one independent: Kevin Lyons, member for the northern Tasmanian seat of Braddon, who was thrust into the role of kingmaker. Lyons had created the Centre Party, modelled on the Country Party, when he quit the Liberal Party in 1966. He was courted by both sides and took 11 days to make up his mind, but ultimately backed Bethune to form a minority government; Lyons himself became deputy premier and tourism minister, responsible for Hobart's new casino.

Though Bethune's pro-conservation sentiments had helped him into office, almost as soon as he became premier he fell in lock step with the Hydro. Even some of his parliamentary colleagues were dismayed, such as upper-house Liberal Michael Hodgman (father of the state's current premier), who came out in favour of saving the lake, expecting that nuclear power would be widely available within 50 years.[6] He told the ABC: 'I hate to think what my great grandchildren are going to say of our generation for doing what we've done.'[7] For their part, the Pedder campaigners decided both major parties were a lost cause; one would later dub them the 'Laborials', and the tag stuck.[8]

*   *   *

The words 'conservation campaign' roll off the tongue now, but at the outset of the 1970s the campaigners in Tasmania were making it up as they went, and they were losing. As construction work accelerated, tensions grew. At a packed meeting in Hobart Town Hall in March 1971, campaigners formed the Lake Pedder Action Committee. Inaugural chairman Brian Proudlock recalled that the decision to hold the meeting came spontaneously to a group of bushwalkers on a busy weekend at Pedder:

> On a superb evening in late summer, just before the sun had set, the reality of this proposed act [of destruction] seemed to occur to all on the beach, watching the spectacle. We were shocked, fearful, then angry. We determined to save the lake by whatever means necessary. A public meeting was the first step and the Hobart Town Hall was booked.[9]

At the meeting, upper-house Liberal MP Louis Shoobridge called for a Pedder referendum, and a crowd of hundreds barged into parliament to support his private member's bill. Bethune refused. That autumn, more than a thousand people went on a 'pilgrimage', flying in or trekking five hours from Strathgordon to see the beach at Lake Pedder before it disappeared forever.[10] In the Legislative Council elections of May that year, the LPAC resolved to publicly support pro-Pedder candidates such as Shoobridge and former upper-house MP Ron Brown, the first chairman of conservation group the South West Committee, and to '[unseat] candidates who are opposed to conservation'.[11] Shoobridge still lost his seat, and Brown was not elected. By the end of the year there were LPAC branches across Tasmania and on the mainland, from Melbourne and Canberra to Brisbane and Perth. Some 50 petitions opposing the flooding of Lake Pedder were lodged in the federal parliament, representing a quarter of a million signatures.[12]

One way or another, the burgeoning campaign drew in many of the giants of the new green politics. Olegas Truchanas was a leading light. A Lithuanian-born engineer and amateur nature photographer, Truchanas had been the first person to raft Tasmania's remote Gordon River solo in 1958. After losing his negatives – and his house – in the devastating Hobart bushfire of 1967, Truchanas dedicated himself to documenting those wild places all over again, including the lake he called 'my Pedder'. It was risky, because Truchanas was a contractor for the Hydro. He began touring Tasmania, and later the mainland, giving spellbinding presentations about Lake Pedder: he talked in a matter-of-fact way, if at all, and preferred to let his slides speak for themselves, accompanied by the music of stirring composers like Sibelius. Over eight nights in Hobart, Truchanas packed the Town Hall to overflowing, with audiences often moved to tears. At an exhibition of paintings of Lake Pedder in November 1971, he said:

> Tasmania is not the only place in the world where long-term, careful argument has been defeated by short-term economic advantage. When we look round, the time is rapidly approaching when natural environment, natural unspoiled vistas are sadly beginning to look like left-overs from a vanishing world.

This vanishing world is beautiful beyond our dreams and contains in itself rewards and gratifications never found in artificial landscape, or man-made objects, so often regarded as exciting evidence of a new world in the making … If we can revise our attitudes towards the land under our feet, if we can accept a role of steward and depart from the role of conqueror; if we can accept the view that man and nature are inseparable parts of the unified whole – then Tasmania can be a shining beacon in a dull, uniform and largely artificial world.

Six weeks later, Truchanas was dead, drowned in the lower Gordon, which he knew was the next to be dammed, and so was determined to photograph as part of his efforts to save it. Putting a foot wrong, he slipped and disappeared underwater, trapped by a fallen tree. His sole companion on that trip was Kevin Kiernan, then a young speleologist who worked for the state government by day but whose real work was as voluntary secretary of the LPAC; he would go on to co-found the Tasmanian Wilderness Society. Kiernan was distraught, searching in vain for Truchanas before driving back to a nearby Hydro camp to raise the alarm.[13] It took three days to find Truchanas's body, after Hydro workers built a temporary dam upstream to lower the river.

As it would be in many green battles to come, the public face of the Pedder campaign was an otherwise apolitical woman, arts patron Brenda Hean, a piano teacher and church organist from Sandy Bay, who was a lifelong Liberal voter.[14] In television interviews, Hean came across as very proper indeed. This fed into government-fuelled stereotypes that the Pedder campaigners were a gentrified elite – who else could afford to fly in to enjoy the scenery? But Hean was not rich, and nor was she dabbling. She was convinced that Pedder was too beautiful to destroy, and her conservatism and stiff-upper-lip determination made her effective. When an ABC reporter asked her at what stage the campaigners would call it a day, she replied: 'Never! There's a lot of British spirit in us yet, you know.'[15]

If Brenda Hean was the soul of the campaign to save Lake Pedder, a Queensland botanist named Dr Richard Jones was the brains. Jones is a little-known figure outside green politics, but he has an important place in this story. Born in 1936, he was brought up near

Mackay, and studied science at the University of Queensland. Raised conservative, he became state vice-president of the Country Party, forerunner of the Nationals. Working as a high-school teacher, he met and married Patsy, also a teacher. The couple later moved to the University of Melbourne, where Richard obtained a doctorate in botany, and then to New South Wales, where he worked for the CSIRO and was elected to Deniliquin Shire Council as an independent. A serious, nerdy type, Jones was always politically active; according to Patsy: 'As far as he was concerned, if you wanted to do something there was really only one way to do it, and that was politically. And if you couldn't get anyone in the established parties to listen to you, you started your own party.' In 1970 Jones took up a lecturing post at the University of Tasmania, where he would set up a new centre for environmental studies.

Soon after he arrived in Hobart, Jones went to see Pedder for himself, and quickly got involved with the LPAC. For Jones, Pedder was symptomatic of a wider political problem; as he wrote in a 1971 lecture, 'concern for the environment is completely unrepresented in our governments'.[16] It was particularly true in Tasmania at that time, but the idea has since become fundamental to defence-of-nature activism everywhere: giving a voice to the voiceless biosphere. Jones feared an impending ecological collapse, and was impatient with hoary old ideological debates: 'There is no time for the luxury of revolution ... antagonism between the left and right is ludicrous in the face of the crisis confronting us.'[17] That sense of urgency has been a dominant theme within green politics, at least in Australia, ever since.

In 1971 the LPAC wrote to a number of conservation groups on the mainland, seeking help. One was the Myall Lakes Committee in Sydney, led by one of Australia's most radical conservationists, Milo Dunphy. Already a hardened veteran of numerous conservation battles, Dunphy needed no persuading to join the Pedder fight – he had walked there twice himself. Through the second half of 1971 he corresponded with Jones and Kiernan about the campaign. Kiernan's letters almost invariably signed off with a mopey flourish: 'Yours from the ecocide isle ...'

In some ways, outsiders like Jones and Dunphy were needed to save Tasmania from itself. The Hydro was an intimidating adversary, the biggest employer in the state. Dunphy believed that, coming from the mainland, he could go in harder than the Tasmanians, and told the LPAC so: 'You are concerned that [our strategy] may antagonise the engineers. Well, it is meant to! It is hard to see that we can stop "Australia's greatest environmental outrage" by being polite to its perpetrators.'[18] Looking back, Kiernan thinks locals needed the help from the mainlanders who were not so close to the places that were at risk: 'This is our home that's being fucked up, and it just tears your gut apart ... I think a lot of the locals were more than happy for people from elsewhere to take some of the leading roles.'

In November 1971 the LPAC and ACF held a conference in Hobart. A collection of transcripts from the 'symposium' was published immediately afterwards by the local bookshop under the provocative title *Damania*. Dunphy, more than anyone, stirred up the Hobart meeting, galvanising the campaigners, telling them it was never too late to win. He advocated 'guerrilla tactics', and his strategy was to target politicians; his motto was 'Surround the Bastards'. Speaking on the emergence of a new Australian environmental conscience, Dunphy noted that paid-up membership of conservation societies considerably exceeded the memberships of political parties, raising the question whether they ought to stand conservation candidates for parliament. Campaigners should forget their 'inbred Australian aversion to politics', he said. 'We rejoice in the fact that we are a democracy still; well, it is up to us to make it work. This will mean that you will run conservation candidates in forthcoming Federal, State and municipal elections.'[19]

As we have seen, Dunphy was not theorising: he had run for state parliament in the 1971 NSW election as the country's first green political candidate. But Pedder was an even bigger challenge: Dunphy described it as 'the first issue on which conservationists have spontaneously co-operated around Australia',[20] and 'a test of the total orientation of civilisation in Australia'.[21] The Hobart *Mercury* called him a 'crazed, left-wing conservationist'. Premier Bethune received a deputation from the LPAC, including Dick Jones and Brenda Hean, but dismissed the symposium's call for an inquiry.

Back in Sydney, Dunphy got a letter from Jones in early December. Written in a hurried scrawl, it brought ominous news: ahead of schedule, the Hydro had closed the gate on the partially complete Serpentine Dam. 'Water is now backing up to flood Lake Pedder,' Jones wrote. Given the heavy rains, he feared the flooding could be over in weeks, rather than the forecast six months. It was deliberate and unnecessary, Jones wrote, 'because the water being stored is useless until 1976'.[22]

It was true – the Hydro simply wanted to hand the conservationists a fait accompli. As the waters began to back up, the campaigners went into overdrive. And as the Pedder campaign heated up, other issues were boiling over. In its tumultuous term, the Bethune government had picked a huge fight with Federal Hotels, directing that the licence for a planned casino in Launceston must go to a competitor, and had riled bookmakers by proposing a state-owned TAB.

Behind the scenes, Federal Hotels began to cultivate the deputy premier, independent Kevin Lyons, whose relationship with Bethune began to fray. This presented an opportunity for the Pedder campaigners. Recognising that Lyons was in a position to save the lake, Jones, Kiernan and a few other LPAC members had joined his Centre Party in November 1971. Jones even got onto the party's executive. At a meeting of the state council in early February 1972, a motion was passed that recognised the 'growing wave of public opinion against the flooding of Lake Pedder', and called for work to stop until there was an independent investigation.

At the same time, Dunphy took a call from a Tasmanian contact, establishment figure Rod O'Connor, a seventh-generation wool farmer who had a tip-off. According to Milo's handwritten notes, O'Connor had 'had dinner with the Governor ... Lyons will cross the House on TAB in March'.[23] It was good oil.[24]

Dunphy now had early warning of the Bethune government's downfall, and started planning for the state election in earnest. At the next meeting of the Colong Committee in Sydney on 15 February, the balance of power in the Tasmanian parliament was discussed; the minutes recorded that one committee member said 'the conservationists should run candidates as a "total environment" party'.[25] This appears to be the earliest explicit written reference to the plan to form a new green party in Tasmania. Soon afterwards, when he launched the new Total Environment Centre in Sydney, Dunphy announced that the LPAC had asked him to fly down and help run an environmental political party's campaign in a coming state election.[26] As Patsy Jones recalls: 'Because Milo had been active in Sydney and been through it all, we paid for him to come down and be co-director of the campaign with Dick, and so that was a great learning experience. He knew how to run a political campaign.'

If Jones and Dunphy knew in advance that Lyons was about to pull the plug on the Bethune government, it seems very few others did. Bethune himself only found out on the day, 13 March, when Lyons declared that 'mutual trust' had broken down between himself and the premier, whom he accused of having a 'dictatorial attitude' and showing 'administrative incompetence'.[27] Bethune advised the governor to dissolve the parliament straightaway, and a snap election was called for 22 April 1972.

It was now or never, and the LPAC put ads in *The Mercury* for a public meeting at Hobart Town Hall on 23 March. 'Wanted: People who care. Lake PEDDER: The Quality of Government and Use of Resources.'[28] The ads featured the same stacked triangles – a visual cue for the 'mega-ripples' on the edge of the water at Lake Pedder – that would become the logo of the new political party. The LPAC's one-page agenda notice read:

This meeting has been called to form an action group to campaign future Federal and State elections to ensure that candidates elected in certain areas are sensitive to conservation issues of local and national importance. The temporary committee elected tonight will have the duty to organize a general meeting of all interested persons in the areas to be selected for the first campaigns as soon as preliminary investigations are completed.[29]

The committee was worried that opportunistic independent candidates would claim to represent the interests of conservationists and split the vote for Pedder. In a flyer distributed at the meeting, it asked: 'Can you see some effective way that a combined united group can be created who will attract all the available votes and thus demonstrate to the government of Tasmania and other States that they may in the future ignore environmental issues at their peril?'[30]

The Town Hall was packed to overflowing, and it was a fiery meeting, which the Hydro tried to stack with 200 of its engineers. Kevin Kiernan recalls:

> I had a phone call from a contact within the Hydro. I told Dick and Dick organized for front doors not to be unlocked until a minute beforehand so they couldn't occupy all the seats … so their plan was thwarted … but they were very disruptive throughout the meeting and attempted to drown everybody else out by shouting … it was pretty heated right from the start.[31]

There appear to be no minutes, but multiple witnesses recall that when Dick Jones put the final resolution to the meeting, he was shocked to hear noes drowning out those in favour. Another LPAC supporter, Chris Cowles, recalls:

> Dick suddenly realized the meeting was heavily stacked by Hydro workers and he thought 'oh, bugger this, I'm going to put the motion again' … When he did there was a huge shout – I mean, it almost lifted the roof off the place.

The landmark resolution was passed:

> In order that there is a maximum usage of a unique political opportunity to save Lake Pedder, now an issue of national and global concern, and to implement a national, well researched conservation plan for the State of Tasmania, there be formed a Single Independent Coalition of primarily conservation-oriented candidates and their supporters.[32]

After such a turbulent meeting, and with only four weeks to go until the election, Cowles remembers the Pedder campaigners had plunged into the unknown: 'We all thought, "now what have we done?" We hadn't formulated anything about how we were going to run the campaign.'

The new party was named the United Tasmania Group, and there was nothing lefty or radical about the first two candidates it selected, both of whom were former politicians of long standing.

Ron Brown, in his late fifties, apart from being one of the original Pedder campaigners, was secretary of the Apple and Pear Federation and had represented the rural constituency of Huon in the upper house for 16 years, while Sir Alfred White, a former agent-general in London, had been the Labor member for the state seat of Denison for 13 years. The remaining ten candidates, who would contest four of the five multi-member electorates, were all university-educated and respectable. As well as Hean, there was Norman Laird, an Antarctic scientist; Rod Broadby, a computer programmer; Ian Milne (no relation to Christine), who was in electronics; and Kelvin Scott, a lawyer working in the tax office. What bound them all was Pedder. Kiernan recalls that people like 'Norm and Brenda were really conservative folk ... there's no way these would've stood for a left-wing party'.

Milo Dunphy arrived in Hobart shortly after the Town Hall meeting, and spent most of the next three weeks either staying with Dick or at the university. He kept a relatively low profile, according to his biographer, cognisant of the Tasmanian suspicion of mainlanders. UTG opened up shop in Liverpool Street, and the buzz around the campaign office was something new. Jones and Dunphy churned out press releases, although these were often ignored.

The constant challenge, with a single-issue campaign, was to say or do something new. Dunphy was fearless and, inspired by US activist Ralph Nader's celebrated 'Nader's raiders', came up with some wild ideas. One was to find a conservation-minded 'patriot' who would bulldoze Premier Bethune's own front garden before the assembled media, and who would tell them, as he was arrested, that what he had just done was nothing compared to what the premier was doing to Lake Pedder. 'Apparently Nader gets away with this sort of thing,' Dunphy wrote.[33] The Pedder campaigners baulked at that one.

There was not enough time to organise a second mass pilgrimage to the lake, but one stunt went ahead. The Victorian branch of the LPAC had created a statue of Truganini, morbidly feted on her death in 1876 as the last Tasmanian Aboriginal. At a large open-air church service on Easter Sunday, the campaigners erected the statue on the beach at Pedder, with a plaque in her honour.[34] The gesture was meant to warn against a repeat of a historical error, but there was something alarming about what happened as the waters slowly rose to Truganini's shoulder, then her neck – must she die once more? Much later, after the flood, when the statue washed up on the beach, it was burned. The purported equivalence between a so-called 'eco-cide' and a real historical genocide was questionable at best.

UTG released just two policy statements during the election, including an eight-point, two-page economic program, which opened with the observation that 'Tasmania is in a crisis due to gross over-emphasis on hydro-economics', and warned that 'unemployment will continue to decline unless existing industry is supported and balanced by smaller diversified industries which can be developed from the environment'. It then listed some not-very-radical initiatives to promote a more diversified, 'new-life economy' based on tourism, a science-based woodchip and forestry industry, locally owned fisheries, alternative agriculture and so on.[35] The party also published a tabloid newsletter, *UTG Extra*, full of beautiful pictures of Pedder, as well as some interesting titbits: the very first issue promised a far-sighted 'new deal for Aborigines', including land rights on Cape Barren Island, rights to the muttonbird industry on the Furneaux Group, and employment in government Aboriginal programs, noting that Tasmania's Aboriginal people had been neglected for too long.

The Hobart *Mercury*, which received a large amount of advertising income from the Hydro, was implacably hostile. But Launceston's *Examiner* was more sympathetic, and there was firm support from the Melbourne-based Australian Union of Students. Not that UTG, or the broader Pedder campaign, was a student or even a youth movement. Tasmania was still an extremely conservative state. Jones was in his mid-thirties; Hean was in her sixties. Hobart's university campus was provincial, not as politically experimental as those in Melbourne and Sydney. As Kiernan wrote to Dunphy: 'Would you believe the uni students involved in this are rather anti-radical, and dead-set against stunts (me, a public servant, being accused of being too radical! What next!?)'[36] A young woman from Devonport, Christine Milne, who had enrolled in an arts degree at the University of Tasmania in 1971, recalls:

I wish I could say that the campus was on fire with environmental ideas, but unfortunately I have a clearer recollection of students burning tyres on the road to secure an underpass to the refectory ... [Lake Pedder's] fate was certainly not a subject for discussion. Nor did it feature in my political science course or as a subject for intercollege debating.[37]

With just two days to the election, UTG declared it would not allocate preferences, and this would remain the party's policy throughout its life. Dick Jones told *The Australian* that the major parties were 'just not worth' giving preferences to.[38] It was a strange decision, leaving votes to exhaust – a voluntary relinquishment of influence.

UTG raised as much money as it could for the campaign; the largest contributor, reportedly, was the Australian Union of Students, which donated $4000. The next largest was the Centre Party itself, which was folding with Lyons' retirement, and appears to have rolled its $300 bank balance straight over to UTG.[39]

The donation funds were needed. The biggest campaign expense was advertising. Like David and Goliath, UTG and the Hydro were fighting it out with paid newspaper adverts, arguing back and forth over the fate of Lake Pedder. The slugfest culminated in the first two-colour ad printed in the state, a full-pager in which the Hydro warned that a vote to save Pedder would lead to higher electricity prices. UTG later called for a royal commission over the Hydro's interventions in the election – the party reckoned the HEC had spent $20,000 during the campaign, an unusual, if not illegal, incursion for a government agency.

Eric Reece's Labor Party won the election in a landslide, winning 21 seats to the Liberals' 14. Tasmanians were fed up with the instability of a hung parliament, and rewarded Labor with a thumping majority. UTG did well on the day, although none of its candidates was elected. Statewide, UTG garnered a respectable 3.9 per cent of the vote – more than any other third party – and 4.9 per cent of the vote in the four seats it contested. Ron Brown, lead candidate in the Hobart seat of Franklin, where UTG polled 8 per cent, was very nearly elected, falling short of a quota by just 150 votes. Norm Laird also went close in Denison, where UTG got 6.9 per cent of the vote. It would be UTG's best performance.

Pamela Walker, who did a valuable honours thesis on UTG in 1986, wrote that 'in Tasmania the UTG was perceived as being indifferent to the material aspirations of working people and was charged with being anti-growth and idealistic'.[40] The gulf between the working class and the environmental movement is as much social as it is ideological. Geoff Holloway, who was secretary of the UTG from 1974 to 1976, also found that members were characterised by 'high educational achievement, professional occupations, high social mobility and concern for the realisation of non-economic values'.[41] Another way of categorising these people is the 'humanistic intelligentsia' – described as tertiary-educated, urban, relatively affluent, professional, often employed in the public sector.

UTG's strongest electorate, Denison, spreads from Hobart's inner-southern suburbs around the university (such as Sandy Bay and Taroona) to more working-class suburbs in the inner north (such as Moonah). UTG polled up to 12.5 per cent in booths in the south but only 3.1 per cent in the north. These voting patterns, already evident in 1972, are still reflected in the Greens' vote almost 50 years later. Denison, renamed Clark in 2017, is one of the handful of lower-house seats that have defined green politics nationally. Outside Hobart, with increasing rurality, the UTG vote plunged, and support was generally much weaker in the north of Tasmania. For Tasmanian academic Peter Hay, this has always been a fundamental problem for the green vote: 'If Green values have little attraction to either the conspicuously affluent or the traditional working class, the section of the community amenable to conversion would seem to be fairly small.'[42]

UTG was not discouraged – they'd achieved a lot in four weeks – and rolled without a break into the Legislative Council elections the next month, in which UTG candidate Noreen Batchelor won 8.6 per cent of the primary vote in Ron Brown's old seat of Huon. UTG really only got organised *after* the 1972 elections, when it was able to set up branches, enrol members and get a regular newsletter going. UTG was not even constituted yet, which has fed a fitful debate about whether UTG was really the world's first green political party or merely a loose grouping of independents campaigning on the issue of Lake Pedder.[43] As Jones wrote to one supporter: 'Our group does not operate as a party. We are an amalgamation of independents who are free to follow their conscience on matters other than our main platform.'[44] Still, in early 1973 the proposition 'that UTG should become a political party' was put to a formal ballot. The members voted a resounding 'yes', of course – to all intents and purposes UTG already was a party. That was certainly the view of Tasmania's electoral authority, which accordingly gave UTG a party group position on the ballot papers in its first election.[45]

In any case, the UTG had to keep going, because Pedder was not yet lost. A permanent vigil had been established on the beach and, soon after the election, the campaigners got a tip-off from an anonymous source, telling them to go straight to a certain senior counsel in Hobart and ask for an opinion on whether the legislation enabling the Middle Gordon Scheme was contrary to the original proclamation of the Lake Pedder National Park. The LPAC sought leave of the attorney-general, Merv Everett, to bring a case. The newly reinstalled premier, Eric Reece, blocked it, and Everett promptly resigned in protest. There was uproar, but with Everett out of the way, Reece simply rammed a so-called 'Doubts Removal' bill through parliament, reinforcing his bloody-minded determination that the dam would proceed.

*　　　*　　　*

As the Pedder campaign played out in Tasmania, a controversy with striking parallels was unfolding in New Zealand. A decade earlier, the conservative National government had proposed to raise beautiful Lake Manapouri, set in a national park at the south of the South Island, for a hydro scheme. Conservationists fought a decade-long campaign to save the lake, ending only in late 1971, when the government accepted the recommendations of a parliamentary inquiry and put the flooding off until there was a demonstrated need for the power. The Pedder campaigners were well aware of what was going on in New Zealand.

On 30 May 1972 a 24-year-old Wellington political science student, Tony Brunt, who had put together the platform for a new political party, launched it before a meeting of 'sixty curious souls'. At first he wanted to call it the New Zealand Youth Party – he couldn't imagine the ideas would be of any interest to anyone over 30 – but he decided on the name Values Party, of which today's Green Party in New Zealand is a direct descendant. If only for that reason, the Values Party is routinely described as the first national-level Green party in the world, being set up just a few months after the UTG – except it wasn't that green. New Zealand author Christine Dann, who examined the UTG and the Values Party for her 1998 doctorate in politics, described the party as 'humanist', and argued that concern for environmental quality was 'not the only – or even the main – issue motivating the Values Party'.[46] Brunt's original speech only contained four sentences on the environment; five years later, he conceded that he had never conceived of the Values Party as 'primarily an environmental or green party in the generally accepted sense of the term. It only became that in retrospective analysis.'[47]

The United Tasmania Group and the Values Party did not spring from nothing, of course; they were part of a global shift from materialist to post-materialist politics at the beginning of the 1970s, which included a new environmental awareness. The Australia Party certainly set an example for the UTG, and new parties were springing up elsewhere. In the United States, consumer activist Ralph Nader was approached to run for a new 'People's Party' in 1971; in the Swiss canton of Neuchatel, a short-lived Movement Populaire pour l'Environment was set up to fight against a toll road in late 1971.

Most powerfully, a loose grouping of academics, scientists and businesspeople called the Club of Rome published a short paperback, *The Limits to Growth*, which became the most popular environmental book in history. The heart of the book was MIT's then state-of-the-art 'world model' of five factors: population, agricultural production, natural resources, industrial production and pollution. Projecting economic and population growth rates current in 1970, the researchers modelled 12 plausible scenarios to 2000, and asked whether 'the momentum of present growth may not overshoot the carrying capacity of this planet' and considered 'the chilling alternatives such an overshoot implies for ourselves, our children and our grandchildren'. The Club of Rome was apolitical to a fault, pitching to audiences in both the Eastern and Western blocs, in developed and underdeveloped nations alike. The foreword to *Limits* stated up front that none of the Club members held public office or sought to express 'any single ideological, political, or national point of view'.

Nevertheless, there was an immediate and powerful backlash. On the right, *Limits* was dismissed for being too pessimistic about humanity's ability to solve problems with new technology. MIT's world model was smeared as 'pseudoscience', 'garbage in, garbage out' or 'the computer that printed out W*O*L*F*'. On the left, the book was criticised for failing to tackle the question of capitalism, power, class struggle, at all.[48]

Where *The Limits to Growth* tried to stay above politics, in the United Kingdom in January 1972 the newly launched *Ecologist* magazine published a 'Blueprint for Survival' for Britain, informed by the work of the Club of Rome and endorsed by prominent scientists, which advocated a return to deindustrialised, decentralised, self-sufficient communities as the only way of achieving a stable society. The *Ecologist* envisioned that a new stable society would be anti-consumerist, heavily regulated, taxed on polluter-pays principles and founded on respect for nature. Otherwise, the authors warned, 'the breakdown of society and the irreversible disruption of the life-support systems on this planet, possibly by the end of the century, certainly within the lifetimes of our children, are inevitable'. The alarmist language is alarmingly familiar today.

Crucially, the Blueprint argued for a new so-called 'movement for survival' to 'act at a national level, and if need be to assume political status and contest the next general election. It is hoped that such an example will be emulated in other countries, thereby giving rise to an international movement, complementing the invaluable work being done by the Club of Rome.'[49] If there was a moment when the idea of a new global green politics crystallised, at least in the English-speaking countries, this may have been it. The Blueprint was widely read – and often referred to by those in the UTG, which had 'Vote for the Survival Group' printed on fluorescent orange bumper stickers. Within months of its publication, both the UTG and the Values Party had been formed, and in February 1973 a new party was set up in the United Kingdom, calling itself simply 'People'. Within two years 'People' would be renamed the Ecology Party, and later the Greens.

On 12 and 13 June 1972 a stunning, privately placed advertisement appeared in *The Australian* and Tasmania's three daily newspapers, signed by one R.J.B. of Launceston. The ad took up a full page and pulled no punches:

TASMANIA – WORLD EPITOME OF MAN'S DESTRUCTIVENESS.

1804: First mass slaughter of Tasmanian natives.

1835: The authorities … 'scoured the bush and when the mobs were fallen in with … occasionally they were all shot or had their brains knocked out'.

1876: Last Tasmanian native, Truganini, dies. The only successful deliberate annihilation of any whole human race in history.

1888: Tasmanian government offers £1 bounty on Thylacine (Tasmanian Tiger). Settlers offer further bounty. Slaughter.

1930: Last recorded Thylacine killing … Thylacine extinct.

1938: Tasmanian government proclaims Thylacine 'protected'.

1968: Tasmanian government begins scheme to flood Lake Pedder deep under modern dam. Tasmanians (at elections) support lake's destruction.

1972: Lake Pedder submerges. A unique natural zone extinct.

BUT THE TRADITION LIVES ON … 400,000 PEOPLE EARNING HISTORY.

The Lake Pedder campaigners were mystified – who was 'R.J.B.'? Who was it who had spent £1000 for absolutely no gain? 'We were just gobsmacked,' recalls Friend. 'This was a full-page ad. It was unprecedented [and] hugely powerful.'

The *Examiner* traced the ad back to one Bob Brown, a medical doctor fresh from the mainland, doing locum work in the Launceston suburb of Mowbray. Brown, who needs no introduction now, had acted completely off his own bat. He had met the Pedder campaigners when they set up a caravan in Launceston, and had chartered a flight over the lake to see for himself. He recalls:

> When I flew over it, that day was particularly spectacular, there were sunshowers and sunbursts down the serpentine valley below the lake, and the lake was there underneath, and it's still very much burnt into my mind, but I'd also run into the people campaigning for Lake Pedder and I had an instant affinity with them, so there was, I guess, the environmentalist in me suddenly being treated with a watering-can and I was about to sprout and I didn't know how to! So that placing of the ad … I had a little bit of money, I felt very angry and frustrated … so I went off to do something as an individual.

A month later, in July 1972, Pedder Beach disappeared under the rising waters. But because the beach flooded every winter anyway, only to reappear in summer, the campaigners were convinced that any damage was reversible and the lake could still be saved. All someone needed to do was 'pull out the plug', as it were, at the Serpentine Dam. Bumper stickers were printed: 'Pedder Lives'.

On Friday, 8 September, tragedy struck. Brenda Hean had set off in a chartered World War II–era Tiger Moth with pilot Max Price, hoping to sky-write 'Save Lake Pedder' over Canberra. Flying low, the plane went missing over Bass Strait. Both were presumed dead. Disturbingly, Hean had called Kevin Kiernan just before the flight, to tell him of a strange conversation she'd had with an anonymous caller who had asked how the Pedder campaign was going; after she told him of the plan to fly to Canberra, he had signed off with a veiled threat: 'How would you like to go for a swim?' After the plane disappeared, it was discovered that the plane's hangar had been broken into, and its safety beacon had been removed. The police investigation was swept under the carpet. Many believe Hean's flight was sabotaged, but there is no proof. Kevin Kiernan, one of the last people Hean spoke to, doubts it was murder, but remains troubled by the cover-up.

Sometime in late 1972, the UTG decided to codify what it was all about, and adopted a short statement called the 'The New Ethic'. The statement is grandiloquent, beginning:

> WE citizens of Tasmania and members of the United Tasmania
> Group, UNITED in a global movement for survival, CONCERNED
> for the dignity of man and the value of his cultural heritage, while
> rejecting an view of man which gives him the right to exploit all of
> nature, MOVED by the need for a new ethic …

The statement moves through solemn undertakings to 'live our private and communal lives in such a way that we maintain Tasmania's form and beauty' and 'create aesthetic harmony between our human structures and the natural landscape', to land on extremely broad reform proposals, such as:

> CREATE new institutions so that all who wish may participate in
> making laws and decisions at all levels … CHANGE our society
> and our culture to prevent a tyranny of rationality, at the expense
> of values, by which we may lose the unique adaptability of our
> species for meeting cultural and environmental change … LIVE as
> equal members of our society to maintain a community governed
> by rational, non-sectional law …

Whether visionary or utopian (as the media saw it),[50] the New Ethic is an important foundational document. Christine Milne sees in the New Ethic the essence of the German Greens' four pillars. While the language is obviously dated, for Victorian Greens leader Greg Barber the key principles remain 'fresh as a daisy'. The contrast between the New Ethic and the Labor Party's 1891 platform, however, is stark: Labor focused on concrete reforms like the eight-hour working day and abolition of the *Masters and Servants Act.*

Authorship of the New Ethic is often attributed to Dick Jones, but it was more of a group effort, and it was the late Hugh Dell who both produced the first draft and polished up the final version, using his skills as a former journalist:

> They needed a set of ideas to work to, to give them a basis on
> which to go to the public … so I went home and I wrote it, I didn't
> edit it, I didn't correct it, I just sat down at the typewriter and
> wrote it … When I came back and saw [Dick] again – it was about

the third time I met him – he said we're going to publish that as a pamphlet ... I was amazed!

Everyone threw their ideas in, and Dell – who was put on a small retainer in November 1972, according to the UTG accounts – wrote it all up.

By then, campaigning for the federal election, to be held on 2 December, was on in earnest. In opposition, Labor's environment spokesman, Tom Uren, had shown he was onside with the Pedder campaigners. He had publicly called the decision to flood Lake Pedder a 'mistake', and ahead of the state election in April had urged Eric Reece to pause. During the federal election campaign, Uren gave a thoughtful speech in Hobart, recognising the rise of environmental concerns, promising an independent inquiry into Pedder if he was made environment minister, and pondering whether Tasmania had a historic opportunity to carve out a different, less environmentally destructive course than the mainland.

Heading into the election, the Australia Party targeted 15 lower-house seats, of which 11 were Liberal-held: Denison (Tasmania), Lilley (Queensland), Holt, Casey and La Trobe (Victoria), and Phillip, Mitchell, Parramatta, Macarthur, Lowe and Bennelong (New South Wales). The four Labor seats targeted were Sturt (South Australia), Forrest (Western Australia), Maribyrnong (Victoria) and Barton (NSW). Interestingly, these seats were not, by and large, in the inner-city suburbs that would poll best for the Greens decades later. In 1972 the gentrification of the inner cities had only just begun – they were not the bourgeois-yuppie-hipster enclaves of today. The Australia Party doubled its vote, to 2.4 per cent, marking its 'arrival in the big league', according to campaign director Fergus McPherson. Most importantly, Australia Party preferences were crucial to Labor's victory in four seats and influential in another three. Gordon Barton crowed: 'Since the ALP won only a net eight electorates and needed to win four to govern, it is clear Mr Whitlam's government exists mainly because of the Australia Party's efforts.'[51] The DLP had been negated.

On 2 December Gough Whitlam was swept to power in the 'It's time' election, ending 23 years of conservative rule. The Pedder campaigners were disappointed, however, when Whitlam decided to appoint Uren to urban affairs instead of the environment portfolio, which went to Moss Cass, about whom they knew nothing. Nevertheless, the Whitlam cabinet kept Uren's promise to hold an inquiry, which was set up as the new government's major decision on the environment, in January 1973. Here was a last chance to save Pedder.

A government source, however, told journalist Laurie Oakes: 'It will be more of an inquest than an enquiry.' Going by his report, the ministers had already agreed that it was too late to take action to preserve the ecology of the Lake Pedder area.[52] Though he fought hard within the government to save the lake at the time, Cass now concedes it was probably already too late.[53] The twists and turns of the Burton inquiry, which recommended that the Commonwealth bear the costs of a moratorium and proposed an alternative scheme that would save Lake Pedder, have been well documented. Hope came when, in late 1973, the Labor caucus overruled the cabinet, directing the government to make an offer to Tasmania to save the lake. Reece rejected the Commonwealth offer out of hand.

Towards the end of 1973, there was one last hope: a Green Ban. The LPAC had approached the Tasmanian Trades and Labor Council in 1971, proposing to institute a black ban against the Scotts Peak dam, part of the Middle Gordon scheme that would destroy Lake Pedder. They were given short shrift by the state secretary, Brian Harradine, later a long-time conservative independent senator, who was in lock step with the Hydro, which employed many union members.

There was no love lost between the unions and the environmental movement, as Kevin Kiernan wrote to Milo Dunphy in 1972: 'The very middle class nature of the conservation movement generally is giving [Jones] trouble with the labor bods.' By 1973, though, Mundey and his NSW Builders Laborers Federation had turned the Green Bans into a cause célèbre, and were holding up projects worth billions in Sydney, garnering nationwide attention. Mundey and the BLF didn't care who they offended. With the federal Labor caucus now opposing the dam, the Pedder campaigners tried again. 'Dick did a lot of talking with Jack Mundey,' recalls Patsy Jones, who remembers Mundey turning up at their Sandy Bay home. They may have even smoked a bit of pot – Mundey certainly did.

A public meeting in Hobart was organised, at which Mundey proposed a 'Blue Ban' to save Lake Pedder. Kevin Kiernan recalls that one of the other speakers was federal Liberal MP Edward St John, who was horrified at the thought of sharing a stage with a known communist, and refused. 'Right up until the whole thing started he wasn't going to come on,' says Kiernan, 'even though he was one of the key speakers, because Jack was there.' Somehow St John relented, and Kiernan says that, once proceedings got underway:

> ... they totally engaged. I can remember looking up at one point and seeing Jack and Ted, sitting up on the table side-by-side, close together, jointly trying to draft a statement, and thought 'this just shows how non-left-and-right this thing is'. You get the communist Jack Mundey and the extreme anti-communist Ted St John able to just throw away those divisions, and sit there working on the environment, and I think that's how the environment movement's been here forever.

Kiernan was at the subsequent meeting that carried the resolution to Harradine. 'He [Harradine] just sat there, and it was quite evident from the look on his face that nothing we were going to say was going to make any difference.'

*   *   *

The failure of the Pedder campaign became the failure of UTG, which contested 11 elections between 1972 and 1978, but began to trail after the 1974 federal election. In fact, the UTG became, for a while, a lesson in what not to do. The campaigners deliberately avoided direct action, in an effort to maintain respectability and electability. Dick Jones made a virtue of this, writing: 'At no time during the long years of the Pedder struggle has any action by campaigners for Lake Pedder been outside the law or in any way discreditable ... conservationists have maintained a dignity of purpose and action that is wholly creditable and praiseworthy.' After the loss of Pedder, many conservationists believed this was a mistake.

UTG did leave a legacy, and many old hands feel the forward-thinking policies of the party have come to fruition in the decades since, but by 1977 even the University of Tasmania student newspaper *Togatus* was taking UTG to task:

> They may take joy in being political amateurs but godammit they've been around long enough to be considered a political party, and not a crèche, and if their performance is as pathetic as it was in the last state election then it is time that their leaders ... get off their arses and either admit that they are effective as a lobby group and stick to that, or settle down to the ghost-like existence of third-partydom, doomed to twittering on the sidelines of politics.[54]

Contemporaries of Dick Jones say he often used, in conversation, a version of the slogan later adopted by the German Greens: 'Neither left nor right, just out in front.'[55] A very similar sentiment was embodied in the UTG slogan: 'Politics of the left and right versus politics of the future.'[56] It is abundantly clear, as author Richard Flanagan has written, that UTG found both left and right 'anathema and fundamentally the same'.[57] Political scientist Narelle Miragliotta similarly writes that the early Greens rejected both capitalism and communism and the tenets of unlimited economic growth.[58] In a piece for the party's newsletter, Jones explained:

> We are living in a period of imminent breakdown – social, economic, political, psychological and spiritual ... neither Left (Labor) nor Right (Liberal) are appropriate to this situation ... We do not believe in a future Heaven-on-Earth (the aim of the Left) nor do we pine for a lost Golden Age (the nostalgia of the Right) ...[59]

For Christine Milne, the basic fault line in pre-green politics, between left and right, 'came down to the same issue: how it would affect whoever already had wealth or made money, and how the proposal would influence how that money was shared'.[60]

The United Tasmania Group was born when the conservationists had no one else to turn to; rejecting an entrenched Labor government, they were let down by an unstable minority Liberal government, and finally stymied by the almost-certainly-corrupt independent, Kevin Lyons, who had sold out and quit politics. To save Lake Pedder, the campaigners felt they had no choice but to run for parliament themselves. Almost twenty years later, English researcher Sara Parkin said this was a familiar pattern:

> When Richard Jones and the UTG decided to take the damming of Lake Pedder to the polls in 1972, they assured themselves of a write-up on page one, and that feeling amongst the UTG, that they had been left with little choice but to take to electoral politics, has been felt by greens in different countries around the world ever since.[61]

Bob Brown made a second cameo appearance in the UTG story. After finishing his six-week locum assignment in Launceston in mid-1972, Brown left Tasmania to practise in Sydney's Sutherland Shire, but not before meeting the Pedder campaigners, who were touring the north of the state in a caravan. He was deeply moved – hence the newspaper ads he placed in June that year – but was gone before getting any more involved in the Pedder campaign. Brown was lured back to Tasmania by a quixotic search for the thylacine, organised by a mainland scientist and local farmer, which he helped fund and coordinate and which lasted months. In 1973, Brown was offered more work in the same suburban Launceston surgery as before, and bought a tiny old weatherboard on a small block at Liffey, 40 kilometres south of town, where he settled permanently.

By 1975, with the Whitlam government in crisis, Brown got a letter published in *The Examiner* decrying the major parties' failure to save Pedder, and their plans for more dams and woodchipping:

> [I was] saying that voting for the lesser of two evils – ie. the two big parties – was still voting for an evil, and people should look at options, and I got contacted by Dick Jones, through somebody else – I was out at Liffey – saying, 'Oh, we read that letter and we need somebody in the north of the state to stand with us, would you?' And that worried me greatly, because I was gay, and that would be a focus of very negative reportage and political commentary.

Next thing he knew, Brown was number two beneath Jones on the UTG's Senate ticket for the 1975 federal election.

Brown was a popular local doctor, but now had to reconcile his interest in politics and conservation with his homosexuality. Today we might think of it as a coming-out struggle, but Brown says things were different when homosexuality was a criminal offence. 'There was no way to come out, and people didn't,' he says. 'Nobody did. The only way is they got found out and jailed.' To go into politics, and also be true to himself, Brown would have to put his head above the parapet as a gay man. He knew that doing so would have consequences for those around him, and could rebound negatively on the UTG.

In 1975, his first campaign, Brown was not ready. The UTG's Senate vote nearly halved, compared with the 1974 result, dropping to 0.55 per cent of the statewide vote. Partway through the count, according to Brown's biographer, he looked up and saw that he'd received just two votes.[62] His final tally was 199. Afterwards, Brown wrote to one supporter: 'The UTG ideas are far-sighted and worthwhile to me – so passing setbacks are nothing more than that.'[63] Brown's journey in politics had begun.

In another private letter he wrote: 'Perhaps I have gained more from this campaign than the UTG did.'[64] He was right.

CHAPTER 2

DEMOCRATS, BLOCKADERS, DISARMERS

Recessions tend not to favour green politics. Inadvertently, the conservative governments that are often installed in hard economic times sometimes do. When Malcolm Fraser took over as prime minister in 1975, after provoking Australia's greatest constitutional crisis, the economy was in sharp recession.[1] The global recession was brought on by the 1973 oil shock, which sent petrol prices soaring, and ushered in years of 'stagflation' – high inflation and unemployment – and current account deficits, which were the essential preconditions for the rise of Thatcher and Reagan.

Malcolm Fraser became more moderate after politics, and he is now almost disowned by the Liberal Party. It is often forgotten how conservative the Fraser government was. Invited to dinner with US president Gerald Ford in 1976, and given the customary opportunity to pick any American as a dinner companion, Fraser chose the libertarian novelist Ayn Rand, cult author of *The Fountainhead* and *Atlas Shrugged*, and the arch-capitalist pseudo-philosopher beloved of almost all today's neoliberals.[2] Fraser did not undo every Whitlam reform – he kept the Heritage Commission, ensured there would be no going back on the Great Barrier Reef, and saved Fraser Island from sand mining. But his 'razor gang' austerity agenda, which included the abolition of Medicare, provoked outrage on the left.

Within the Liberals, the focus of discontent was Victorian Don Chipp, dumped from Fraser's front bench after the 1975 election. Chipp was a true small-L liberal, popular for rolling back censorship when he was John Gorton's customs minister. Chipp's resignation from the Liberal Party in 1977 caused a sensation, and he proceeded to set up a new 'centre-line' party, the Australian Democrats. Chipp's 1978 account of the birth of the party, *The Third Man*, stressed honesty, tolerance and compassion, a rejection of Fraser's 'law of the jungle' approach to social welfare and the principle of direct democracy. It did not make much of the environment, although Chipp was anti-nuclear, and a key reason for his resignation had been the Fraser government's handling of the Fox Ranger uranium inquiry. This had recommended more mining in the Northern Territory – setting the scene for the Jabiluka dispute 20 years later – even though it also found that the power industry was unintentionally contributing to the increased risk of nuclear war.[3]

The Democrats combined the New Liberal Movement out of South Australia – which did not have much of a platform – and the Australia Party. In 1973, flush with success, Gordon Barton had seriously predicted that the Australia Party could form government in Canberra in a decade, but a devastating result in 1974 proved the beginning of the end.[4] In his post-election review, Fergus McPherson wrote that the 'greatest shock' was the halving of the Senate vote, which fell *below* the lower-house vote despite the higher-profile candidature of Barton himself. He continued that the electoral 'mauling' should spark a reassessment of the Australia Party's future direction, and outlined four ways forward, which resonate today.

First, the party should aim to be 'pioneering' and adopt a 'radical and distinctive' mix of policies, regardless of whether they were likely to be taken up by the major parties. Second, it should be 'reformist', influencing the major parties to adopt more centrist policies through preferences; this was pretty much its strategy until now. Third, it should be a 'mass party' that aimed for government, and here McPherson threw down the gauntlet: 'If getting in and governing directly is the course of action we choose, then the Australia Party would have to consciously appeal to the economic interests of a large group in the community.'[5] This particular challenge, arguably, was never met by the Australia Party or the Democrats, nor yet the Greens. Fourth, it should be 'subversive' – if the Australia Party could not beat the major parties in the ballot box, it could at least infiltrate them.

None of this happened, of course. Barton stepped down as national convenor, to be replaced by progressive businessman John Siddons, later a Democrat senator for Victoria. Siddons, an 'economic nationalist' whose family owned the Sidchrome tool company,[6] went to work on a manifesto of the economic policies of the party he described as 'forward-looking, centre-based'.

Meanwhile the Australia Party's environment policies had become increasingly radical, and would be adopted by the Democrats holus-bolus. The party's 1973 policy platform sounded like a combination of *The Limits to Growth* and 'Blueprint for Survival', beginning: 'The Australia Party expresses its deepest concern for the imminent crisis of the natural resources and natural systems of the world. It regards this crisis as the greatest threat facing man and civilisation.'[7] Now, the party's policies included zero population growth, the 'plateau economy' and radical decentralisation, along with calls for a national environment commission, wilderness protection laws and other determinedly green measures. The party called it 'economics for survival'. Beyond the environment, the progressive policies added to the platform included a guaranteed minimum income, to be delivered through a negative income tax, as well as a capital gains tax. A draft election brochure for the Australia Party, produced ahead of the 1974 election, carried a new slogan: 'The AP is not on the left or the right ... the AP is out in front.'[8] Here was a genuine forerunner not just of the Australian Democrats, but arguably of the Australian Greens as well.

The Australia Party had a lasting impact through the Democrats' policy platform, and the many prominent party people who became Democrats Senators, such as John Coulter and John Siddons. Not a few Australia Party members wound up in the Greens. As the Democrats were forming, the United Tasmania Group, by now on its last legs, held talks about merging with it, but these went nowhere and the UTG fizzled.

The Democrats went from strength to strength. Chipp, who never imagined the Democrats would form government, outlined a very clear strategy at the launch of the 1977 election campaign:

Our first objective is to secure a Senate seat in every State. This will give us the balance of power, the balance of common-sense, the balance of reason in the Senate ... our role will be to restore the Senate to its proper function as a House of Review and a States House – not a party-political house.[9]

A few years later he would crystallise the party's raison d'être in an unforgettable line: the Democrats were there to 'keep the bastards honest'. It was a strategy that resonated with the electorate immediately: Chipp from Victoria and Colin Mason from New South Wales were elected in the party's first outing, with 16 per cent and 8 per cent of the primary vote in their respective states. Nationally, the Democrats polled over 9 per cent in the lower house, contesting 109 of 124 seats, and 11 per cent in the Senate. It was a stunning debut.

*   *   *

Bob Brown had not shed many tears at the fall of the Whitlam government, which he blamed at least partly for the loss of Lake Pedder (although he later acknowledged that Labor's accession to the World Heritage convention in 1974 was critical to saving the Franklin River), and which had given tacit approval for Indonesia's invasion of East Timor, the former Portuguese colony leaning towards communism. Now 31, however, Brown found that his politics were shifting. His parents had voted Liberal and he'd grown up admiring Menzies, and was an anti-communist. His first vote had been for the Country Party, and at one point he'd backed the New England New State Movement, which wanted to secede from New South Wales. As a young medical student, Brown intended to stand for the Liberals, and twice went along to the party's branch headquarters, in Sydney and Canberra, to join up. The first time the office was shut. The next time, it was just before 5 p.m. and he was asked to come back later, but he never did. A few years later, Brown turned out to cheer LBJ in 1966. He had not voted for Whitlam in 1972, scrawling 'Save Lake Pedder' across his ballot paper in protest. Nevertheless, a political awakening was gradually occurring: in the broadest terms, he was on a long journey from conservative to progressive.

After watching from the sidelines during the Pedder campaign, Brown began to get politically active. A liberating moment came in 1974, when, on holiday in the United States, he joined protesters at the University of Chicago, who were demonstrating against Secretary of State Henry Kissinger, who had backed a military coup in Greece and was speaking on campus. Brown had never protested before; all kinds of radical left-wing groups were rallying, and there were CIA types taking photos, but in a foreign country he found he didn't care. Brown identified with the protesters. 'They felt the same as me about the 19 students who had been smashed to death in Athens,' he would later say. 'That was my first involvement really in a political protest and I came away feeling in some way like I'd done a good thing … that was a breakthrough of sorts.'

Back home, as a UTG candidate during the 1975 election campaign, Brown mounted a lone protest on a Whitlam visit to Launceston, donning a three-piece suit and holding a placard stating 'Ban Uranium Sales'. Then, in January 1976, Brown was invited to raft the Franklin River by a near-stranger, conservationist Paul Smith, who realised the Hydro was about to repeat the Pedder experience and needed someone to make the dangerous journey with him. Brown found the two-week trip revelatory, life-changing, and the two rafters were shaken to find extensive Hydro works already underway at the bottom of the river. The trip, then rarely accomplished, got some media coverage, and Brown, determined that the Franklin must be saved, knew he was going to get active.

Brown's first hurdle was to come out as gay – otherwise, he felt he could not be honest with himself, let alone anyone else. He first told close friends, then his partners at the Launceston clinic, and then agreed to an interview for the ABC's *This Day Tonight* program, which was doing a story on homosexuality. Launceston's *Examiner* reported that Brown was the first Tasmanian to publicly identify as gay, and had done so to urge law reform. 'Politicians should look fairly at the law and remove discrimination on the grounds of sexuality from the statutes,' Brown told the paper. 'How can homosexuality between consenting adults be a crime when there is no victim?' It was a gutsy step, given homosexuality was still a criminal offence in the state. Brown's words were chosen to placate, rather than offend: 'I believe that being born homosexual is an unfortunate disadvantage for anyone … the fact that I am a homosexual gives me no feeling of pride.'[10] He still got hate mail, to which he replied politely, but there was more support than abuse. He was emboldened.

The last weekend in June, Brown held a meeting of conservationists at his home in Liffey, and they agreed to set up a new organisation, the Tasmanian Wilderness Society, that could roll from one campaign to another – from Pedder, to Precipitous Bluff, to the Pieman River, to the Franklin – without pause. Most present were members of the UTG, now resolved on taking direct action rather than pursuing party politics. Kevin Kiernan, who came up with the name, became the first director of the TWS. Bob Brown himself, still working part-time as a doctor, chipped in some money. His diary notes envisaged a non-bureaucratic campaigning organisation based in Hobart, with no hierarchy and a director who would be bound by branch decisions, but would otherwise be free to do as they pleased in the best interests of the TWS. Decisions would be by majority vote, on the voices, not consensus.[11] Meetings were free-wheeling – no minutes, no rules. It was the beginning of something big. Kiernan and Holloway sat down and drew up a map of the area they intended to save; many years later it would become Tasmania's World Heritage Area.

Towards the end of 1976, Brown took his most public stand yet. More than anything, he was worried about the prospect of nuclear war. On the radio at Liffey one day, he heard Premier Bill Neilson, who had replaced Reece in 1975, announce that the USS *Enterprise*, the world's first nuclear-powered aircraft carrier, would dock in Hobart for six days. With eight nuclear reactors, and armed with dozens of nuclear missiles, the *Enterprise* was not allowed to dock at Boston or New York. In 1971 Australia had imposed a temporary ban on nuclear warship visits for safety reasons, but the ban had been lifted by the Fraser government in 1976. The NSW government had banned nuclear warships from Sydney, however, and Brown decided to protest the *Enterprise*'s visit to Hobart by fasting for six days on top of icy Mount Wellington, sitting in a tent, literally freezing. He organised public meetings in Launceston and Hobart, paid for more advertising and attracted a lot of attention.

The protest was ignored by *The Mercury*, but Brown still got plenty of visitors. Some tried to support him or even feed him; others were abusive – 'You fucking commie!' they'd yell – and one night beer bottles were hurled at his tent. Surprisingly, the sailors themselves were sympathetic; one African-American told him, 'When we practise a scramble [to get the planes up off the ship within minutes of the start of a war with Russia], I think about the day it will be for real and I know I'll never see my wife and kids in Chicago again. I support what you are doing.'[12] Like putting an ad in the paper, Brown's protest was the defiant stand of a loner. But Brown developed a large enough profile that Dick Jones persuaded him to stand again for the UTG, this time in the state seat of Bass, which covered Launceston.

While up on the mountain, Brown was interviewed by a reporter from *This Day Tonight*, Dr Norm Sanders, and although neither knew it, the two were to live parallel lives for the next 15 years. Sanders recalled: 'We, we set up at night and we found his tent ... [he was] not weak but he was not full of energy.' As a reporter, Sanders was impressed with the clean-dressed physician, and realised the dramatic scene was made for TV: 'It was a boiling, red sunrise, with the clouds swirling around the peak. Bob spoke feelingly on camera about the sun being the bringer of life. He gestured at the dark shape of the *Enterprise* just entering the river. "And that is the bringer of death."'[13]

Sanders himself was an extraordinary character. A professor in geomorphology from Los Angeles, he had taken on the US oil industry after the Santa Barbara oil spill in 1969, heading up an organisation called GOO! (Get Oil Out!). Sanders was fearless – an accomplished mountaineer, bush pilot, sailor and motorbiker – and had become one of the best-known environmentalists in the United States, to the chagrin of the University of California bigwigs, who could not fire him but refused to promote him. In 1974, despairing of American politics after Watergate, and attracted by Whitlam, Sanders sailed to Tasmania – where in the 1960s he had done a doctorate while on a Fulbright scholarship – and married an Australian. After being interviewed about his sailing feat, Sanders was offered work as a reporter, and began to do edgy environmental stories, including on dodgy forestry practices as Tasmania's woodchip industry began to ramp up. When the ABC buckled under pressure from the forestry commission, telling him 'not to do any more stories like that', Sanders quit.[14]

Sanders helped Dick Jones set up his environmental studies centre at the University of Tasmania, and soon got involved with the TWS. For a year or so he took over from Kiernan, who felt burned out.[15] Sanders later recalled:

> We didn't have an organisation. We were just a guerrilla group
> and that's all it was ever meant to be … And so people started
> coming to our Monday night meetings. And more and more peo-
> ple came. And they became quite officious and then they wanted
> to have Monday afternoon meetings to set the agenda for the
> Monday night meeting. And then they wouldn't let us drink beer
> anymore because they were very serious greenies. And they didn't
> think we should write letters to the editors under assumed names.
> And, you know … so I just said, 'Well, to hell with it. I'm out of
> here' … I've always said you should never have a group any big-
> ger than three people.

In 1978 Brown took over from Sanders as the full-time director
of the TWS. He had found his true calling as environmental activist,
and would never return to medical practice. The campaign to save the
Franklin took off the following year, when Brown and a few others
crashed the opening of the Middle Gordon Power Scheme, which had
flooded Lake Pedder seven years earlier. Dignitaries from all over the
country turned up to see the generators switched on by former premier
Eric Reece, but what led the news that night was the impromptu demonstration: standing out the front of the power station, Brown carried
a sign reading: 'Wasted: $120 million timber under these waters'.
Others read: 'HEC generates massive debts' and 'Lake Pedder is dead'.

In the 1979 state election Sanders stood in Denison for the
Australian Democrats, having rejected approaches from Dick Jones
to stand for the UTG. It was the first general election that UTG failed
to contest. Sanders liked Don Chipp's approach, felt the Democrats
had better name recognition, and believed the party was fundamentally green. 'They were the first party at that time to start with the
knowledge that the earth needed help,' Sanders explained years later.
'The whole platform of the Democrats was about environmental
concerns.'

Sanders missed out narrowly, but there was uproar when certain successful Labor candidates were found to have overspent their
allowances under an obscure electoral law, and this triggered a by-
election in early 1980. Sanders stood again and this time he got up,
which made him the first out-and-out environmentalist elected to

any parliament in Australia. The state's tiny political establishment was in shock: suddenly they were being lectured by a tough, bearded greenie who turned up to parliament on a BMW motorcycle, and knew his engineering besides. Sanders needled the Labor government on the potential of wind power, which the Hydro had studiously ignored despite wind being Tasmania's world-beating resource, even going so far as to reject federal grants for research.[16]

*   *   *

In some ways the long campaign against the damming of the Franklin River was a repeat of the Pedder experience; the conservationists knew what was coming years before the Hydro announced its grand plans for another uneconomic dam. Both major parties in Tasmania locked in behind the Hydro, so the challenge was to raise support on the mainland, and around the world, to pressure the federal government to intervene. At key steps along the way, however, events took a different turn.

In 1981, Labor premier Doug Lowe – who was against the dam – succumbed to public pressure. His government had come up with a compromise, the Gordon-above-Olga scheme, which would have saved the Franklin River but dammed the upper Gordon. The legislation was blocked in the conservative upper house, which backed the Hydro's original Gordon-below-Franklin scheme. To break the deadlock, Lowe decided to put three options to the people: the Gordon-below-Franklin, the Gordon-above-Olga, and a 'No Dams' option, which Lowe had promised to Brown. Tasmanian Labor fatally undermined Lowe, forcing him to pull the No Dams option, and Lowe promptly resigned as premier and sat with Sanders on the crossbench. His last official act was to sign off the world heritage nomination for the Franklin, which he had included in a new Wild Rivers National Park; this would later prove crucial. Within a week Lowe and Sanders were joined by Mary Willey, a Labor member for Bass, who was outraged at the betrayal of Lowe and vowed to block any legislation that would flood the Franklin. The three crossbenchers held the balance of power in the lower house – although, as Sanders recalled later, 'You can only have a balance of power if there's any difference between the parties.'

The TWS debated how to campaign – should it boycott the referendum altogether? The society decided to urge an informal vote, encouraging voters to write 'No Dams' on their ballot papers. Volunteers doorknocked and leafleted every house in the state. Sanders told the new Labor leader, Harry Holgate, that if more than a third of voters wrote 'No Dams', he would bring down the government. Holgate said, 'Oh, no, you wouldn't do that, would you?' Sanders answered, 'I would.'[17]

And that is just what happened: the write-in was a stunning success. Precisely 33 per cent of voters wrote down 'No Dams'. The final informal vote was 35.5 per cent – apparently the highest informal vote in any referendum in the world.

Similar campaigns were mounted on the mainland the following year: in a February by-election in the federal seat of Lowe, in Sydney's inner west, 'No Dams' polled 9 per cent; mid-year, 25 per cent of voters in the ACT House of Assembly election wrote down 'No Dams'; in late 1982, 41 per cent of voters did so in a by-election for the well-off, semi-rural Melbourne seat of Flinders.

Premier Holgate simply prorogued the parliament, which did not sit for months, but when he could hold off no longer, Sanders immediately moved a vote of no confidence, backed by Lowe, Willers and the Liberals, and an election was called for May 1982. Brown, who had angsted over whether to stand in the 1980 by-election, stood in 1982 as a 'No Dams' independent in Denison. The general expectation was that the vote for the Franklin would be strong enough to elect both Brown and Sanders in that seat, as well as one or two pro-conservation independents in other seats. As Sanders recalled:

> Our thinking … was that with a 33 per cent no dams vote, we'd get a lot of people in, in Parliament … In fact, we were wrong. We didn't even get Bob Brown in. He was standing in Denison. I got re-elected mostly because of my motorcyclists. I had 800 motorcyclists behind me … So as a device to get a whole bunch of greens in, it didn't work, but it did get rid of the Holgate government and a Labor government that had been in power for … except for one term, for 40 years. And it shook things up … Robin Gray was a far, far better enemy than Holgate. I mean, he was just reprehensible.

Today, Bob Brown has no doubt that he lost because he was gay. Certainly he was the target of a nasty smear campaign by the company-backed Hydro Employees Action Team, or HEAT, which mass-printed the 1976 *Examiner* article – in which Brown had come out – with accompanying scrawls, and dropped it into letterboxes all over Denison. Brown recalled 35 years later: 'I won't tell you what they were letter-boxing but it wasn't very pleasant ... the opinion polls showed the slide in the vote for me standing as a Save the Franklin candidate. Norm, however, held his seat.'[18] Labor was decimated. Liberal premier Robin Gray's first act was to pass legislation for the Hydro's Gordon-below-Franklin scheme. Upper-house president Harry Braid said: 'No power on this earth will stop the dam now.'[19]

For years, Kiernan had been on a quest for sites on the Franklin that would be simply too precious to flood. In early 1981, with Bob Brown and journalist Bob Burton, Kiernan returned to a cave he had found years earlier. This time he found a midden, and ancient Aboriginal remains. Carbon-dating shortly afterwards showed the remains to be at least 20,000 years old; the cave would prove to be the most southern occupation of the earth during the last ice age. Kiernan named it Fraser Cave, hoping to attract the attention of the prime minister – this was an old trick of Milo Dunphy's, who had named Fife Cave in the Colong wilderness after the then mines minister, Wal Fife – but it was soon renamed Kutakina. Ridiculously, the Hydro proposed to continue the flooding, but to cover the cave in concrete to preserve the remains. Although his discovery was a critical part of saving the Franklin, Kiernan looks back with regret: 'I wish to Christ that I'd spent more time – some time even – talking to the local Aboriginal community because I think the fact that we launched straight into this stuff about protecting the wilderness really alienated some of those people.'

A key difference between the Pedder and Franklin campaigns was that politics had shifted in the decade since 1972, at least federally. Whereas Liberal prime ministers John Gorton and Billy McMahon had been deaf to the issues around Lake Pedder, Malcolm Fraser offered Robin Gray half a billion dollars in compensation if he would stop the dam. And in 1982 Labor's national conference resolved that, if elected, a federal ALP government would save the Franklin, recognising Australia's obligations under the World Heritage Convention, signed by Whitlam, which gave the Commonwealth a legal basis – the treaties power – for intervention. After the 1983 federal election was announced, Bob Hawke went all-out to get the Franklin vote, appearing with Brown during the four-week election campaign and pledging to save the river.[20]

Politics had also changed through the emergence of a new environmentally aware minor party. Democrats Norm Sanders, Don Chipp and his wife, Idun, rafted down the river with *Sydney Morning Herald* journalist Geraldine Brooks (later a Pulitzer Prize–winning author), whom Sanders described as 'our secret weapon'.[21] In the Senate, Chipp launched an inquiry into the Tasmania's south-west wilderness in 1981 – a young Graham Richardson was a member, and visited the river – and subsequently his colleague Colin Mason introduced a World Heritage Properties Protection bill, which passed after two Liberals crossed the floor, and which the Hawke government later rewrote and used to save the Franklin. (Some Democrats, such as Norm Sanders and Lyn Allison, believe Chipp's and the party's role in saving the Franklin has been written out of history by Greens supporters, who lionise Bob Brown.[22] On Don Chipp's death in 2006, however, Christine Milne was forthright in a Senate condolence motion: 'His contribution to the saving of the Franklin River is outstanding and was enlightened for its time – and I want to put that on the record. As that river flows free to the sea ... there is a little bit of Don in that fantastic ecosystem.'[23])

Last but not least, the greenies' tactics had changed. They were not just writing letters and signing petitions, but organising huge rallies all over the country, including the biggest ever held in Hobart, with some 15,000 people marching to save the Franklin. There was a sophisticated media strategy: the TWS campaigner Jill McCullough designed the triangular green 'No Dams' logo, which forms the basis of the Australian Greens' logo to this day, and the TWS ran a devastating advertising campaign on the eve of the 1983 election, placing double-page full-colour ads featuring the famous photograph of morning mist on the river's Rock Island Bend, by Olegas Truchanas's protégé, Peter Dombrovskis, under the heading: 'Could you vote for a party that will destroy this?' The TWS urged a vote for Labor in the lower house and for the Democrats in the Senate.

Most importantly, instead of mournful pilgrimages to Pedder, in 1982 the TWS launched the historic Franklin blockade. The precedent was northern New South Wales, where in 1975 the Forestry Commission had announced plans to log one of the last remnants of old-growth rainforest at Terania Creek. It was a small area near Nimbin, which had hosted the celebrated Aquarius Festival in 1973. It was not a docile community. In early 1979, the bulldozers started arriving. About 300 locals – mainly hippies who had retreated to the area – were invited to set up camp on a small farm abutting the forest, and decided to block off the road that the loggers' trucks would be using. It was a new tactic: non-violent, but putting your body on the line as a last resort, after talking had failed. In fact, 'tactic' may be too grand a word, for there was no plan at all. But the motley crew of hippies, with kids and guitars, sang songs like 'Will the Circle Be Unbroken?' and put on an improvised display of protest theatre.[24] The greenies sat high up in trees, to slow down loggers, and even spiked trees (hammering spikes in so the tree cannot be chainsawed safely) in an early example of 'eco-tage'. An inquiry was called, and ultimately a moratorium declared on logging there. Terania Creek was the first example of a successful blockade – a tactic which would become to green politics what the strike was to the labour movement.

The Terania Creek victory was part of the greening of Labor, which developed through the 1970s, and led straight to Hawke and Richardson. If it had continued, there may have been no need for a Greens party at all. The Wran Labor government had come to power in New South Wales in 1976, and Milo Dunphy got to work on the new premier immediately. In March 1977 Dunphy took Wran and his wife, publisher Jill Hickson, and a large entourage on a minutely planned bushwalk, camping overnight in the Colong wilderness. Dunphy could tell Hickson was sympathetic, as Wran observed sharply: 'Jill is a nature-lover and ... Milo could see she was completely involved in the bush. She got a lot of attention, the fattest sausage and the leanest chop.' Four months later the state government included the Colong in the Blue Mountains National Park.[25] As a response to the Green Bans, Wran's ambitious young environment minister, Paul Landa, would introduce the world-class *Environment Planning and Assessment Act* in 1979, bringing economic, social and ecological objectives into the law and giving the public the right to object to all development applications. In 1984 Landa died of a massive heart attack at just 43, and a young Bob Carr determined to continue his work. Carr, who took over the environment portfolio, came to learn that 'there had always been a light green tinge to Labor politics', from the party's first NSW premier, Jim McGowan, who passed the *Birds and Animals Protection Bill* in 1910, to the creation of the Kosciuszko National Park by Premier Bill McKell in 1944.[26]

Three years after Terania Creek, logging continued elsewhere in the region, and protesters, including later NSW Greens parliamentarian Ian Cohen, decided to mount another blockade, at what is now Nightcap National Park, to stop rainforest logging in New South Wales altogether. Cohen's memoir, *Green Fire*, is full of tales of dodging loggers and police. Occasionally things got serious. Many of the greenies had a 'fundamentalist hatred' of the logging machinery, he wrote, and sometimes there was vandalism: 'Once, after a particularly nasty altercation in the forest, I arrived back at camp to hear it gleefully reported that one participant had poured sand into the hydraulics of the dozer the previous day.'[27] Protesters chained cars together to block the road, even set them on fire. On one occasion a nightwatchman fired shots in Cohen's direction. One man, lying on the road in front of a truck, had his legs run over.

It was mayhem, but it worked. The land court granted a temporary stop-work injunction and Premier Wran announced he would save the rainforests. Later, Wran famously wrote:

> Terania Creek was to the natural environment what Green Bans were to the built environment ... when we are all dead and buried and our children's children are reflecting on what was the best thing that the NSW Labor government did in the 20th century, they will come up with the answer that we saved the rainforests.

One journalist later wrote that the Terania Creek protest and its outcome set the template for the preservation of almost a million hectares of rainforest, including the Washpool, the Hastings, Eden and

Coolangubra in New South Wales, the Daintree and later all the wet tropics in North Queensland, and the Franklin and the Lemonthyme in Tasmania.[28]

Back in Tasmania, the TWS agonised over whether to mount a blockade at all. Norm Sanders was sceptical at first – he feared the blockade would turn into a debate over law and order, which the greenies would lose, and distract attention from the river itself. He was also wary of the Quakers who were moving in on the TWS, who insisted on consensus and preached non-violent direct action. Sanders himself was no pacifist. He had served in the US Air Force and believed in standing up to bullies. Once, Sanders and fellow army veteran Peter Cundell (later host of *Gardening Australia*) fought back against hostile locals in Strahan who would occasionally intimidate or even beat up greenies.

The TWS and Bob Brown adhered to a non-violent philosophy, and to the consensus-driven approach, which was all set out in a 'Blockade Handbook', and the subject of training sessions for the recruits, who came from all over. Discipline was vital: any incident, even in the face of provocation, would be held against the protesters, and could turn public opinion against the blockade. But such discipline was foreign to the hippie types who came to join the Franklin blockade, fresh from wins at Nightcap, including Ian Cohen. Geoff Law, a TWS campaigner who coordinated national media from a base downriver in Strahan, found their subculture 'disconcerting'; he described one character, David Rainbow, as 'naked except for a loincloth, jungle-green face-paint, with a rainbow across his chest … [it] reminded me of *Lord of the Flies*'.[29] The TWS's answer was to send the ferals upriver, where they would be largely out of sight of the media. Cohen, for his part, wrote that the downriver types in the TWS office in Strahan would send commands by courier. 'Those upriver were frustrated by what was seen as out-of-touch guidance from afar.'[30]

The sharpest disagreement came when Bob Hawke's Labor Party won the federal election in March 1983. The TWS decided that the blockade should cease; the protesters upriver, who could see the Hydro already doing as much damage as it could, wanted to continue to observe and disrupt them. The TWS simply pulled out the communications equipment. 'Like [in] a nightmare, we watched as our life-support systems sailed downriver,' Cohen wrote.

Despite these tensions, the work of the Franklin blockade went smoothly. The aim was to disrupt the Hydro workers as much as possible, and to keep the national media interested, while enabling a steady stream of hundreds of willing volunteers to go upriver; they would get arrested for trespass and be brought back down to Strahan, to be fined or carted off to Risdon Prison, near Hobart. Miraculously, there was no major incident – no violence, no accidental drownings. In the end, 2613 people registered with the TWS at Strahan for the blockade. There were 1272 arrests and 1324 charges laid, but only 40-odd convictions. A clutch of later Greens politicians were there – Bob Brown, Christine Milne, Ian Cohen, Janet Rice, Penny Wright, Murray Matson and others. Milne was relaxed about going to jail – to a former boarder at a Catholic girls' school, the thud of a door shutting for the night, locking her in, was very familiar.

Above it all, crisscrossing the country, lobbying politicians, doing media, attending rallies and meeting international celebrities such as the botanist David Bellamy, was the charismatic figure of Brown. He had been the public face of the Franklin campaign from the start. He was not a natural frontperson, and loathed public speaking, but he radiated love for the river, and his conviction captured the hearts and minds of millions of Australians. In a 1980 documentary, *The Franklin Wild River*, Brown drifted down the Franklin on a li-lo, scruffy and wet, lost in the beauty of a deep gorge that most Australians would never see, but wanted to see saved. He was arrested and jailed on 16 December 1982, and was named Australian of the Year by *The Australian* on 1 January 1983.

At about the same time, Norm Sanders resigned his seat in the Tasmanian House of Assembly. He had returned from the blockade for a short sitting:

And the parliamentarians were mostly … it was an evening session. They were drunk and saying, 'Ah, bloody greenies, bloody greenies.' And I'd just been to dinner with these people who had just come out of gaol for their beliefs. And I looked at all of my colleagues in that Parliament and I said, 'I cannot sit in the same place with these people.' So I resigned right then and there. I got up and said, 'I resign.' And everybody said, 'You can't!' And I said, 'I'm doing it.' And the next day I got on my motorcycle and rode out to Government House and handed in my resignation, which freed me up for the next blockade.

Brown was elected on a countback under the Hare-Clark system, and went from prison to parliament in a day.

After his three attempts to get elected, and although his TWS supporters were urging him to continue the campaign, Brown was hesitant. Sanders tried to discourage him, as he recalled much later: 'I told him that anybody could be a politician, but that activists were rare creatures indeed. He decided to go for it anyway. I am pleased to say that I was wrong. He has been able to be an activist *and* a politician.' He later added: 'So that was the start of [Bob's] political career, when I resigned. He always comes along when I resign.'[31] Sanders stood unsuccessfully for the Senate in the 1983 election, when the Democrats polled just 6.8 per cent in Tasmania. Looking back, Brown admits that it was pressure from Sanders and Dick Jones that tipped the scales. 'I didn't quite know what to do, even though I'd stood and been through this whole debate within my own head just eight or nine months before.'[32]

The Franklin wasn't won with the 1983 federal election; the eight years of campaigning only succeeded with a bare 4–3 majority decision of the High Court in July that year, which not only decided the fate of that river but also upheld the ability of the Commonwealth government to intervene to protect the natural environment, where it was internationally significant. The environmental movement's greatest victory had been won without establishing a political party. But the Franklin campaign had vaulted Bob Brown into Tasmania's parliament, and there was no doubting that the new green politics had arrived.

*   *   *

The day after Hawke's Labor government was elected on 5 March 1983, the German Greens stormed into the West German parliament – the 520-seat Bundestag, then in Bonn – after their vote almost quadrupled in the federal election, jumping from 1.5 to 5.6 per cent, delivering them 28 seats. Germany was not the first European nation to have a Green party (as we've seen, the UK's People party was established in 1973), nor was it the first country to get a Green politician elected to the national legislature – that honour went to Switzerland, in 1979, followed by Belgium in 1981. But it was Die Grünen who put the world on notice.

The party's unofficial leader was Petra Kelly, born in occupied Bavaria in 1947 of a German mother and an American serviceman father. When she was 12, her family moved to the United States and she studied politics and campaigned for Robert F. Kennedy in 1968, and protested the Vietnam War. Kelly had worked for eight years in the European parliament, including as an adviser for Germany's Social Democrat Party (SPD, comparable with the ALP), but quit in disgust in 1979 when it acquiesced to NATO's infamous 'twin track' decision to deploy medium-range Pershing and cruise missiles in Western Europe.

Die Grünen grew out of the peace movement more than the conservation movement. After all, the Germans did not have pristine wilderness to defend – but they did have acid rain, runaway pollution and nuclear reactors to fight against. But it was not clear-cut; Die Grünen had different strands from the beginning, and holding right and left together was not easy. A key conference at Offenbach in October 1979 produced the famous 'four pillars', which have formed the basis of green politics around the world ever since. According to former UK Greens leader and author Sara Parkin: 'Most of the assembly wanted the new party to represent other possibilities to either socialism or capitalism, but the left-oriented delegates insisted on socialism and were reluctant about adopting non-violence as a fundamental principle.' According to one of the party's founders, August Haussleiter (reportedly a former Nazi[33]):

> ... there were 3000 people screaming their own positions in the convention hall. This person kept saying, 'Don't give up. Don't give up. They're getting tired.' Although agreement seemed impossible, I took a piece of paper and wrote four words on it: ecology, social responsibility, grassroots democracy, and non-violence.

Then I called [the leaders of the left and right] into the room where the journalists were and said 'Sign'. We then went back into the convention hall and announced, 'We have a programme.'[34]

Genuinely charismatic, Petra Kelly was one of the few people who could bring the different tendencies in Die Grünen together. In her 1984 book, *Fighting for Hope*, she argued that the political system was bankrupt. Die Grünen were the 'anti-party party' – although she later claimed this phrase was often misunderstood; it was not meant to describe a disorganised party, but one 'which always is able to distinguish between power and morality'.[35]

Quaker Peter Jones, who would work with Jo Vallentine in the Senate and later join the Tasmanian Greens, spent two years in Germany with Petra Kelly. He recalls her as 'a dynamo ... she spoke very, very fast ... she was very small, very fiery'. When she led Die Grünen into parliament, he recalled, 'They shocked the Bundestag, they stormed in, they took their seats they dressed very casually, they demanded to throw McDonald's out of the café, they horrified the CDU and the SPD, it was such fun.'

Die Grünen got traction in the 1980s, as Margaret Thatcher and Ronald Reagan waged a second Cold War. In 1984, speaking at the National Press Club in Canberra, Kelly was on fire, warning that Australia could not morally argue for non-proliferation while mining and exporting uranium, and could not lead a movement for a non-aligned, nuclear-free Pacific unless it stopped receiving British and American nuclear warships and closed its 30-odd military installations and bases. So-called communications bases like Pine Gap were certainly 'not harmless', Kelly said, because they gave the West a first-strike option. With such a large uranium resource, Australia was in a unique position to do something about it. 'You are at the source in starting and stopping the nuclear cycle,' she told the journalists, adding that Australia's excuse – 'If we don't do it, others will do it' – was 'not an ethical argument'. The parallels between uranium then and coal now are clear.

Pointedly, Kelly said that a small number of unions in Germany and Britain were refusing to work on certain energy systems, including nuclear, and she called on Australian unions to do the same; after all, '[t]he origin of the Green Ban movement … is here! The famous green ban movement that was a revolution for many people … and I believe it should take place also in the uranium industry.' As it happened, Jack Mundey had been elected as an aldermen to the Sydney City Council just weeks earlier. When Kelly was asked about the prospect of a national green party forming in Australia, she mentioned his election and said that was exactly how Die Grünen had begun – at the local level.

The German Greens were trailblazing, and were the first to confront the dilemmas that would beset green parties everywhere. As Kelly explained, with commendable honesty and foresight:

> The green party has had very bad problems internally … because power came rather quickly. Power in the sense that we were able to be the tip of the scale in many different regions – whether or not an SPD or CDU person would become minister or president. Second of all, many different streams of political life – on the left, in the women's movement, in the ecology movement – entered the green party. We have also a principle that you do not have to be a member to run for office. So we have in fact several non-members who are in fact members of parliament. That is the idea to bring in people who have been active in the grassroots and to give them also the chance to be holding office … but it also brings the problem of many people who say, 'I would rather have the greens become an old traditional left-wing party again', on the terms of old left-wingism which I think doesn't work any more because ecology is an entirely new concept, it is a completely revolutionary concept, where non-violence is an active part of that.

Of all the issues that would need to be negotiated before a new SPD/ Grünen government could be formed, Kelly wanted to insist on a clear 'no' to NATO:

> That will be the key question in 1987. So if the green sell themselves quickly, move towards power quickly, and get ministers rather quickly, I would see that to be the end of the green as a

radical party as I had hoped them to become and I think that is the big debate now within the green party, for we do have two strong sides to this.

Barely a year after entering the Bundestag, the split between Die Grünen's pragmatic wing – the realists, or 'realos' – and the ideological wing – the fundamentalists, or 'fundis' – was already opening up fast. Kelly, dubbed the 'peace angel', did not take sides, and worked to bridge the divide.[36] She was perhaps the only one who could.

*   *   *

Australia was waking up to the nuclear threat. The first Palm Sunday march was held in Brisbane in 1980, under the auspices of a new group, People for Nuclear Disarmament (PND), coordinated out of the office of anti-nuclear Labor senator George Georges. The rallies quickly spread to other capital cities, and soon exceeded the Moratorium marches, with more than 300,000 people rallying around the country in 1984. In November 1983, 700 women surrounded Pine Gap. Lee Rhiannon was there, and remembers that about a hundred women who jumped a fence and ran into the base all identified themselves, when challenged or arrested, as Karen Silkwood – the name of an anti-nuclear union whistleblower who was killed in 1974.

In Perth, the first Palm Sunday rally in 1982 drew a staggering 20,000 people. The peace movement was especially active in Western Australia, spurred on by the constant presence of nuclear-armed US warships. It is fascinating that two of the most frequently visited ports for nuclear warships in the 1970s and 1980s, Perth and Hobart, were also two of the first cities to set up green parties. Trish Crowcher, one of the founders of the Greens in Western Australia, remembers the time:

> The warships would come in every two to three weeks. You could see the cruise missiles from standing out on High Street, looking over the railway station. It was a very strong presence. There'd be four or five thousand sailors in town. So if you were opposed, it was very easy. Everyone knew at two o'clock on Sunday, come down to Fremantle, there'll be something going on.

A young peace activist, Jo Vallentine, was about to enter politics, although she did not know it yet. Born and raised in the West Australian wheatbelt, Vallentine was a mother, high-school teacher and Quaker who had started out as a member of the Young Nationals but wound up volunteering for Labor in the 1972 election, although she never actually joined the party.[37] A member of activist groups including Community Aid Abroad, the Campaign to Save Native Forests and the Aboriginal Treaty Support Group, she had not been very active politically until then Liberal premier Charles Court glibly announced in 1979 that Western Australia would be the first state to have a nuclear reactor, at either Breton Bay or Wilbinga, both north of Perth. 'Over my dead body,' thought Vallentine, and she joined the Campaign Against Nuclear Energy (CANE).

Bob Hawke had been elected on the 'no new uranium mines' policy adopted by Whitlam in 1977. Pro-mining forces in Labor had been pushing to abandon the policy, however, and by the end of 1983 there was intense speculation that Hawke would roll over. When he delivered the Curtin Memorial Lecture at the University of Western Australia in late September, Vallentine and co. erected a huge banner at the back of the hall reading 'What we need is a Labor government' and started singing peace songs. Vallentine confronted Hawke afterwards, warning that he was 'going to lose a lot of supporters' over uranium mining – to which Hawke replied: 'Who else are you going to vote for?'[38]

In June 1984, the ALP national conference in Canberra formally adopted the previously unofficial 'three mines' policy, giving the green light to uranium mining at Western Mining's Roxby Downs project in South Australia, later renamed Olympic Dam. The Nuclear Disarmament Party (NDP) was formed almost overnight by Canberra-based Dr Michael Denborough, who had identified that French atmospheric tests in the Pacific were having an impact on the thyroid glands of Australian sheep. To promote his party, he set up a card table in the lobby of the Canberra hotel in which the ALP conference was being held. People were leaving the conference room in tears, and Denborough told them they could join the NDP for just 50 cents and still remain members of the ALP. Looking back, Vallentine says the seeds of the NDP's undoing were sowed right there.

The NDP was the fastest-growing political party Australia had ever seen, attracting 8000 members between July and election day in December, and at one stage polling 17 per cent support.[39] With only weeks to launch the campaign, the West Australian peace groups canvassed some potential high-profile candidates, but all declined. 'So we thought, "It's got to be one of us,"' Vallentine recalls. The movement was heavily dominated by women, and when a university student put their hand up, they decided: 'No, no, that's not what we want – this is about mothers and children.' They turned to Vallentine, saying, as she remembers:

> 'You'll do' … because I could string a few words together and my commitment couldn't have been stronger. This is the one time in my life, I think, where it's helped to be a woman and one with young children because it fitted the bill, it fitted the narrative.

Almost no one expected Vallentine would be elected. The NDP candidate most likely to break into the Senate, everybody thought, was rock star Peter Garrett, who headed the NSW ticket. The Midnight Oil frontman and lawyer had released powerful anti-war hits like 'US Forces' and 'Short Memory', and performed at countless marches and rallies. He came very close, winning 9.7 per cent of the vote, but was done over by Labor, which, in a typical piece of skulduggery, preferenced the Liberals over the NDP in New South Wales. In his memoir, Garrett fingers Graham Richardson for directing the preference deal, but eschews sharper criticism. The Democrats also attacked the new party, which was a direct threat to them. Garrett wrote that the 1984 election was 'the first to see a haemorrhaging of two-party support', the beginning of a slide for the major parties that has continued to this day. Combined, the NDP and Democrats garnered 17 per cent of the vote.[40]

Vallentine got up with 6.8 per cent, helped to a quota by Labor preferences. The NDP campaign in Western Australia was more upbeat, she remembers: 'Even the logos were different … all green and white and positive; in other states it was the clenched fist and it was the mushroom cloud! We didn't want that kind of imaging.' Vallentine says that first original NDP campaign was the best she has ever been involved in, and the party was flooded with volunteers from all walks of life, especially lots of mothers, who had never done anything like it before. 'It was so cooperative and so life-affirming,' Vallentine recalls. On election night, as the numbers started coming in, Vallentine's campaign convenor, Annabel Newbury, observed prophetically, 'We've done too well.' They had meant to give Labor a shock and educate the public, not win a seat.

Vallentine credits Newbury, now a senior WA Green, with 'a stroke of genius' during the campaign. Newbury was approached early on by the Trotskyist Socialist Workers Party, who were keen to help the NDP's campaign. Newbury pointed out that the SWP was running its own candidates in the House of Representatives, and urged them concentrate on that: 'thank you but no thank you, we don't really need your help'.

The same arm's-length approach had not been taken in other states, and SWP members had occupied many of the key positions in the NDP. A fortnight after the election, when it was clear that Vallentine was the only person to have been elected, she and Newbury flew over to meet with the NDP officials from the rest of the country – and got a rude shock:

> There were a lot of SWP people in that meeting, we gathered, not really knowing everybody from other states at that point, but they were saying things like, 'Oh well, of course, your salary will be divided amongst all the different state groups, and we'd suggest these people for your office, and these are the campaigns we want you to work on' ... and Annabel and I were just sitting there thinking, 'Hooly-dooly, what have we walked into?'

Vallentine was worried that the SWP incursion would leave her and the NDP open to 'red-baiting'. For Vallentine, the SWP activists were simply too radical – for example, while she was happy to talk about getting American bases off Australian soil, she believed the public were not ready to hear about American imperialism generally, as the SWP wanted.[41]

The gathering storm erupted at the NDP's first national conference, in Melbourne in April 1985, before Vallentine had even taken up her Senate seat. Vallentine and a 17-strong contingent from Western Australia arrived at the conference, which was to deliberate on proscription and how to ratify the party's decisions. The West Australians wanted conference decisions to be ratified via Democrats-style secret ballots, with papers mailed to members, but found that their suggestion had not been circulated to members. The SWP wanted all NDP decisions to be taken at the branch level. Because consensus was impossible, the issue was put to a vote: 101 favoured ratification by branches, 78 by secret ballot. Suddenly, a group of almost 20 members, led by Peter Garrett and including Vallentine, Jean Melzer, number-two NSW candidate Gillian Fisher, Save the Franklin campaigner Judy Richter, and the maverick former Liberal member for Warringah Ted St John, who had drafted up the constitution for a new anti-nuclear party and was agitating to proscribe the socialists, walked out. The fastest-growing political party in Australian history was imploding in record time; its biggest stars, and its one senator-elect, had quit in less than six months.

Bitterness remains about the implosion of the NDP, and debates over the role of the international socialists and proscription have recurred constantly in the Greens. There is no doubt that the 1985 walkout was premeditated: Vallentine was surprised to find that a room had been booked in advance for the walkout group to go to. In a long 1993 interview with Gregg Borschmann, she described the process as 'awful' and felt that she had been set up.

According to Vallentine, Garrett's response simply was: 'How else could we have done it?' His memoir describes the SWP, or 'Trots', as a destabilising force who bedevil left politics to this day: for Garrett they were 'mainly young activists attracted to a virulent form of anti-capitalism', who 'saw the rise of the anti-nuclear movement as an ideal opportunity to further their specific aims, which I and many others did not share'.[42]

For the SWP members of the NDP, it was a rank betrayal of the party membership, by a minority of celebrities who could not win majority support for their arguments. Vallentine was accused of going against NDP policy – advocating multilateral disarmament (which achieved nothing but stalemate) rather than unilateral disarmament (i.e. by the West).[43] Against explicit accusations of SWP entrism, they argued accurately that there had been nothing covert about their membership of the NDP. Most of all, the NDP national executive, which by the end of the conference was dominated by the SWP-aligned members, tried to persuade Vallentine to stay in the party. 'If Quakers and socialists in Australia are unable to come together, how can we persuade the USA and the USSR to resolve their differences?' said a bitterly disappointed Michael Denborough.[44]

The full West Australian membership of the party – excluding the SWP – convened and voted. The result was an overwhelming validation of the walkout, in favour of disassociating from the NDP in the rest of the country. Vallentine, Garrett and the other dissidents set up a new advisory group to support her, called the Peace and Nuclear Disarmament Action Group (PANDA), but it did not last. Thenceforth Vallentine called herself a 'senator for nuclear disarmament'. She was the first federal parliamentarian elected solely on an anti-nuclear platform anywhere in the world.[45]

*   *   *

It is not generally known that the Greens – or at least *a* Green – contested the 1984 federal election. Historian, feminist and communist Daphne Gollan, who was in a long love affair with Nick Origlass, contested the seat of Sydney, held by ALP left-winger Peter Baldwin, and polled 5.5 per cent, pulling a few thousand votes for her campaign to demolish Sydney's ridiculous monorail.

Technically, Gollan stood as an independent in 1984, but she was a founding member of the Greens, which had already formed, although the registration was not completed in time for the electoral commission to include the party's name on the ballot papers. The party had been in gestation in Sydney since late 1983, when a group of ALP members – instigated by Tony Harris and based in the inner-west suburb of Annandale, and billing themselves literally as 'The Greens' – set up an 'open, democratic, environmentalist forum' to discuss books like *Socialism and Survival* by the East German dissident and 'fundi' Rudolf Bahro, and Labor luminary Barry Jones's *Sleepers, Wake!*

Harris was an economist and a teacher who joined the ALP in 1968 and became secretary of the Annandale branch in 1972. Harris had challenged the 'old guard' sitting federal member, the right-winger Les McMahon, for Labor preselection in 1981, offering himself as 'A Socialist for Sydney'. But Harris was also offering an alternative to the 'machine politics' of up-and-coming left-winger Baldwin, who unseated McMahon next time around and took over the federal seat in 1983. Perhaps there was no home in the ALP for Harris. A paper he wrote on the 'social chauvinism' of the inner-city branches in September that year analysed the changing composition of the party's membership – with tertiary-educated professionals moving in – and came to the withering conclusion that Labor was not changing with the times:

> The anti-authoritarian and collectivist ideas of meetings which emerged from the 60s and 70s movements, particularly the feminist critique of meeting practices, have had little impact on branch life. The involvement of women and the demands for affirmative action may not necessarily alter this … The grand irony about all the debating, branch stacking and throat cutting in the branches is that it takes place inside a structure that operates like a secret society. ALP branches are virtually invisible to the labor communities they represent … neither major faction [left or right] is addressing itself to the need to encourage wider participation in party affairs … the ALP remains, as it has for some time, the party of the bureaucrat, the ward heeler, the branch stacker and the go getter.[46]

It was a spirited encapsulation of the desire to do politics differently. Harris wanted to advocate the 'new politics' that had emerged from the women's and ecology movements. But the Labor Greens were not much more than a reading group until Harris, Hall Greenland and handful of others were kicked out of the ALP for handing out how-to-vote cards for independents Nick Origlass and Issy Wyner at the Leichhardt municipal elections in April 1984. A July *Sydney Morning Herald* report headlined 'ALP vote to expel seven "Greens"' noted both that the expulsion was supported by the federal member, Baldwin, and that the seven charged with disloyalty were 'members of a breakaway left-wing group informally known as the Labor Greens'. Greenland, the Origlass protégé who had served as Leichhardt alderman from 1980 to 1982, said the decision was a political death sentence and they would appeal.[47]

Harris did write to ALP state secretary Graham Richardson, who chaired the disputes committee that expelled the two men, although he says he has no memory of it now, and certainly had no idea he could inadvertently be creating a new political force that would threaten Labor's inner-city strongholds. 'These people were a big deal in a small pond,' he says. 'They didn't matter, and they never came to see me, which is pretty stupid anyway, because if you were a political activist in New South Wales in 1983 you had to have known that I was a pretty big influence in NSW Labor and federally. You had to know.' Richardson put no effort into getting the Labor Green renegades back into the fold. 'I always believed they'd come back home at an election, and that's what's happened essentially, even now.'

On 20 August 1984, by which time the NDP was also getting up and running, Harris convened a meeting at the Glebe Town Hall. The leaflet announced a 'Meeting to form a Green alliance: to run anti-nuclear candidates in the coming federal election', adding that the alliance could 'also campaign around other environmental, social and economic issues, including those abandoned by the ALP federal conference and the Hawke government'. 'A lot of work lies ahead in developing a Green political perspective for Australia,' the pamphlet declared, 'but in the meantime we have decided to adopt the four basic principles of the preamble to the German Green Party programme ...' These were: ecological sustainability, social and economic equality, grassroots democracy and disarmament/non-violence. An application for the registration of a political party, signed by Tony Harris and ten other founding party members, including Greenland, was filed on 3 October 1984. Harris nominated Gollan, who had attended every one of the Sydney Greens meetings, as a candidate for the seat of Sydney on 29 October, four weeks out from the election. The new party – simply "The Greens" – was officially registered on 24 January 1985.

A draft election platform called 'More Good Oil' was dated 15 October and opened boldly: 'The Greens in Sydney come from many backgrounds. Environmental and resident activists. Nuclear disarmers. Dissidents from the Labor Party who have witnessed betrayals by both wings of that party. Feminists. Anarchists. Those inspired by the German greens. Socialists of various kinds.' It was as good a summary of the origins of the party as has ever been written.

All in all, 1984 had not turned out too badly. With environmentalist Bob Brown in the Tasmanian parliament, peace activist Jo Vallentine in the Senate, Jack Mundey on the Sydney Council and the Greens registered as a national political party, the scene was set for the emergence of a new political force, one that would be more radical than the Democrats; it was not a 'centre-line' party like them, but had its roots somewhere on Labor's left. All they had to do was get it together. That very fraught process would take the best part of a decade.

CHAPTER 3

GREEN INDEPENDENTS

Getting into parliament is one thing; what to do when you get there is another. When Bob Brown entered the Tasmanian parliament in 1983, he did not go in as a fully formed, 21st-century Green. He had to learn on the job, and the Tasmanian House of Assembly in the 1980s was an exceedingly hostile place for a gay, green independent. Bob would later joke that the Risdon Prison was more hospitable, and that nothing in his later 16 years in the Senate came close to the ferocity of his decade in state parliament.

In early 1983 the Franklin Dam was still the single, all-consuming issue for Brown as he worked towards the federal election, and the High Court case that ended the dispute. For the first year Brown worked out of the TWS Hobart office, where he remained director. As he was an independent, the parliament gave him nothing but a windowless room and a phone – no staff, no photocopier, no computer. From this humble start, over the next six years Brown would build a team of Green Independents, taking his movement from one seat, to two, to five and the balance of power via the Labor–Green Accord. Then, just as importantly, Brown was able to keep that team intact in the 1992 election that delivered the voters' verdict on the incredibly tumultuous accord years.

It was a stellar political performance, one not explained simply by Tasmania's Hare-Clark system, or by the rise of green politics generally. It is important to understand why Brown was able to achieve what he did in Tasmania – becoming a rare national figure from state politics – because it laid a solid foundation for the formation of the Australian Greens. The key, paradoxically, is not the well-known environmental battles taken on by the Green Independents in the 1980s, from the King River scheme to Farmhouse Creek to Wesley Vale to resource security. Although each of these was an important battle, the Greens were doing what might be expected of them: fighting to stop dams, declare parks, stop woodchipping, stop a pulp mill. They won some and lost some, and they never sold out. The most important aspect – the surprise, perhaps – was how Brown and the independents were able to build trust in green representation among Tasmanians, and that arguably did not stem from the environmental issues.

There were few clues of what was to come in Brown's major stump speech ahead of the 1982 election. When he handed his files over to the state archives, Brown left a self-effacing, handwritten note to future researchers. The 33-page speech, he wrote, was 'an ORDEAL! ... I was beside myself to do this – so Dick Jones largely got it together.' The speech carried many of the same arguments the UTG had used against the flooding of Lake Pedder, was heavy on energy policy, and was even pro-coal in parts, as Brown sought alternatives to hydro-industrialisation. Tasmanian taxpayers were borrowing vast sums to provide heavily subsidised power to bulk users, despite declining demand, and paying again at the other end in the form of higher electricity prices for ordinary homes and businesses. Again, as UTG had done in the 1970s, Brown emphasised the potential of tourism in Tasmania, the need to properly price natural resources like timber, and the need to develop smaller businesses, especially in the services sector, rather than smokestack industries.

This would prove fertile ground for the independents over the next decade: a solid economic agenda, worked backwards, if you like, from a conservation imperative, whether saving Lake Pedder or the Franklin River. Brown didn't touch on this in his speech proper, but there was a potent agenda in the appended policy notes, buried under the label of 'improving the machinery of government': introducing freedom-of-information legislation, removing the power of Tasmania's Legislative Council to block supply, preventing gerrymanders. Just as the UTG had fought for Tasmania to finally introduce Hansard, Brown would expand on this better government agenda in parliament, and make it his own, so that even Tasmanians who might loathe greenies would send him appreciative notes. One unknown voter sent a clipping from the Burnie *Advocate* that reported on Brown's bill to open up local government meetings to public scrutiny; scrawled in capitals were the words: 'I get enthusiastic about

Dr Brown sometimes, our local council people still prefer a structure that's as secretive as the Masonic lodge.'[1]

The very first piece of legislation Brown introduced in 1983 was the Parliamentary Salaries and Allowances Amendment bill, to limit a scheduled pay increase for MPs to 3.5 per cent – in line with the rest of the state's public servants, rather than that of parliamentarians on the mainland. The legislation of Premier Robin Gray's government proposed a 21 per cent increase, which, Brown said, 'the state cannot afford and which totally fails to show restraint in difficult times'. No wonder the MPs hated him. Brown's bill also sought a permanent solution, backing opposition moves to appoint an independent tribunal to determine parliamentary entitlements.

This was just the beginning. In his first term in parliament, Brown introduced bills on freedom of information and disclosure of political donations, and a constitutional amendment to limit the power of the Legislative Council to block supply and force the government to an election – powers that had been used in 1924, 1948 and 1980, when the upper house had turned the Lowe government's Gordon-above-Olga legislation into Gordon-below-Franklin legislation. None of Brown's bills succeeded, but the public appreciated his efforts to hold both sides of politics to account. As one Launceston *Examiner* columnist noted in 1986:

> Dr Brown, who entered Parliament during the height of the Franklin dam debate as the guru of the greenies, has kicked on to become far more than just a single-issue campaigner. He asks more questions than any other member, is more attentive than most during debate and he canvasses a wide range of issues besides just environmental matters.[2]

Brown's 'machinery of government' agenda would continue in later terms, with bills to protect public service whistleblowers and to eliminate gerrymandering. One of the most progressive freedom-of-information laws in the country was finally enacted in 1992 as a condition of the Labor–Green Accord.

Alongside the plainly green bills – to ban battery farms, prevent cruelty to animals, make Tasmania nuclear-free, reform the Hydro, appoint a wildlife advisory council – there were socially progressive bills to remove landlords' ability to evict tenants due to 'distress', and to limit tobacco advertising. Brown and the Green Independents were also strong on Indigenous issues in Tasmania, backing land rights and slamming the Gray government's 'reckless, hateful' decision to cremate a significant collection of remains against the wishes of Aboriginal people. Brown personally went into bat for Kevin McDonald, a convicted Aboriginal murderer whose family were in Melbourne, pushing for him to be given a compassionate transfer from Risdon to Pentridge. After Brown's representations to the minister, the transfer was awarded. Many MPs would have ignored the whole thing.

Brown did not always get it right. In 1985, he pushed to allow councils to debate the addition of fluoride to drinking water – a nod to the anti-fluoride campaigners in the north of the state, including Di Hollister, who would soon stand as a Green Independent. During the 1989 election, when asked about cannabis, Brown replied as a doctor that the medical costs of alcohol and tobacco were already too high without legalising another drug. A few years later he was humble enough to admit he had changed his mind: 'Tasmania would be better off socially and economically by decriminalising the personal use of cannabis.'[3]

Most significantly, during the 1980s Brown introduced forward-thinking bills touching on three social issues that would loom large over Australian politics for the next three decades: euthanasia, gun control and homosexual law reform. Brown's approach in each case says a lot about his longevity as a politician. His 1986 Natural Death bill was intended to support patients who did not want their deaths to be prolonged by artificial means, such as being put on life support. As Brown explained in the second-reader: '[M]y bill does no more. It makes no provision for anyone to shorten the course of the natural dying process – in particular, it has nothing to do with mercy killing or euthanasia.'[4] It was a cautious rather than confrontational proposal, nudging debate along rather than mounting a full-frontal attack. Brown got a stream of supportive letters.

Brown first introduced a Dangerous Weapons bill to register firearms and ban rapid-fire semi-automatic and military-style weapons in Tasmania in 1987, after a spate of armed robberies; also relevant was the fact that Tasmania's was the only state government *not* taking part in a working group framing national gun control laws. 'Tasmania will be the only state that says, "we won't play ball",' Brown said, and 'it will bring us national publicity of the worst kind and it will cement the idea that Tasmania is over-gunned and under-governed as far as firearms are concerned.'[5] The day after the Hoddle Street massacre, 10 August, he moved unsuccessfully to debate his bill urgently, rather than wait on the government's own review, which would take at least a year. Brown was vilified as an opportunist, seeking political advantage from a tragedy, and leave was not granted. It was four years before Brown's legislation was finally debated. The bill was opposed by both major parties. Vindication, in the worst way possible, would take another five years.

Lastly, Brown took a 'softly, softly' approach to gay law reform, particularly the decriminalisation of homosexuality. He waited years for the right opportunity, which came in 1987. Tasmania's law reform commission had recommended repeal of the two sections that made it a crime, punishable with 21 years in jail, for two males to have sex in private. The Gray government rejected any such legalisation of homosexuality. Brown moved to repeal both sections of the code, and read out a Launceston *Examiner* op-ed that backed the decriminalisation: 'There is a belief among some, particularly among parliamentarians adept at transforming ignorance and prejudice into moral righteousness and votes, that governments have a right to be in the bedrooms of the community. They haven't.' Brown also read out a section that threw a sop to the homophobes: 'Homosexual acts do not have to be accepted or condoned by society; repugnance to such behaviours needs no apology.'[6] Then he framed the debate in terms of the lives directly affected: 'In a world beset with great crises this amendment may not be all-important, but it is important to many individuals in the Tasmanian community ...' Both parties voted against Brown's amendment. Attorney General John Bennett insisted that 'the criminal law has a role to play in condemning conduct which most people in this State continue to find offensive and morally reprehensible'.[7]

Tasmania was behind the rest of the country, which had begun the slow process of reform when Premier Don Dunstan of South Australia decriminalised homosexuality in 1976. The extent of the general prejudice is hard to imagine now, and it is correspondingly difficult to overstate the significance of Brown's stance as Australia's first openly gay parliamentarian (in fact, one of the first in the world). As a gay teenager growing up in rural Tasmania, activist Rodney Croome bought journalist Peter Thompson's 1984 biography, *Bob Brown of the Franklin River*, just to read the few paragraphs on his homosexuality. Croome literally hid the book under his bed. He likens the Tasmania of that time to a police state, actively repressive of gays and lesbians. At the first Gay Law Reform Group meeting he went to, Croome was told not to use his second name, as police could be outside taking down car registration numbers, adding to their list of 'known homosexuals'. Just by being an 'out' MP, Brown defied all that, whether he said much about gay law reform or not. A catalyst for change came in 1988, when police arrested the nine organisers of a gay rights stall at Hobart's Salamanca Place, who were getting together a petition on decriminalisation, and then arrested another 130 of the people who signed it. It was a fundamental attack by the Gray government, not only on gays but on freedom of speech.

The AIDS outbreak, and the federal government's famous 1987 'Grim Reaper' commercials, added to the impetus for reform because gay men would not come forward for testing while homosexuality was a crime. In the 1989 election campaign, activists rejected the advice of both Labor and the Green Independents that 'visibility would make matters worse', instead making sure that gay law reform was an election issue and gaining a significant increase in public support.[8] As we shall see, the Labor–Green Accord included a 23-point reform agenda, the last point of which was to decriminalise homosexual acts, but allow a free vote for ALP members. Anti-gay groups formed within weeks, with For a Caring Tasmania (FACT) and Concerned Residents Against Moral Pollution (CRAMP) staging rallies that were often fronted by government MPs.

Conservative forces have always tried to link the Greens with homosexuality and subversion, says Croome, and Brown personified everything they hated. The Green Independents knew what they were up against, hence their desire to move cautiously. In 1990, as Labor tried to wriggle out of its decriminalisation commitment under the accord, Croome issued an open letter to the Green Independents, urging them to introduce their own legislation. Tasmania's new, highly 'visible gay politics had taken its cue from the Green movement', Croome wrote, but 'we feel as if the movement which has fostered us has abandoned us. Twice the Green parliamentary office has promised to take the initiative on gay law reform and twice it has gone back on its undertaking ...'[9] In short, Brown and his colleagues had to be pushed. Milne records that the 1990 Legislative Council debate on decriminalisation was 'appalling, with calls to run homosexuals out of Tasmania, to reintroduce the death penalty for them and at the very least to jail them'.[10]

Brown got plenty of hate mail for his trouble. A thick file of 'Unfriendly Letters' in Brown's archives ranges from abusive – 'DOWN WITH DUNG PUSHERS' or 'YOUR A POOFTER BROWNIE A REAL ARSEHOLE I TELL YOU TRUE BROWNIE I WOULD SOONER FUCK A CAMEL THAN FUCK AROUND WITH YOU' – to threatening, like one with a spoof 'No Dams' triangle logo, for the 'SOCIETY FOR THE EXTERMINATION OF GREENIES AND POOFTERS'. Another was stuck under the front door of the TWS office in Launceston: 'I have my wife and kids to care for, you are trying everyday to put me out of a job. I know where Bob Brown lives and he knows that I know. I might surprise him with my chainsaw in the very near future.' Brown reported that threat to the police.

Brown's solid first term in parliament was rewarded in the February 1986 state election, after which he was joined in the House of Assembly by the British-born Dr Gerry Bates, an environmental law lecturer at the University of Tasmania who had campaigned against the Electrona zinc works in Hobart, and was a surprise winner in the seat of Franklin. Brown was easily elected this time, with a 7.4 per cent swing towards him, giving him the second-highest primary vote in Denison, at 16 per cent. Bates, whom Brown had recruited as a candidate, got 11 per cent and grabbed the second-last spot. Bates claimed he did only six hours of campaigning and won entirely on his reputation as a conservationist.[11] The Democrats did not bother running in either seat.

The overall 6 per cent swing to Robin Gray's government was crushing for Labor, at both the state and federal levels. In early 1986, federal secretary Bob McMullan and kingmaker Senator Graham Richardson urged the Hawke cabinet to do more on the environment, as Premier Neville Wran and his environment minister, Bob Carr, were doing in New South Wales. *The Sydney Morning Herald* reported that Richardson 'believes that in the long term it is also important that the ALP doesn't allow discontent to grow to the point where the now ad hoc fielding of independent green parties is replaced by a more organised green party as a force in Australian politics'.[12]

Tragedy struck on 19 March 1987, when Dick Jones fell from a ladder at his home in Sandy Bay and died, leaving his wife, daughter and son. Patsy Jones still cannot talk about the terrible, stupid accident. His old comrade from the Lake Pedder Action Committee, Kevin Kiernan, remembers Jones as the most strategic thinker he ever met: 'He was so good at being the chess master ... he really was an exceptional human being. Of all the people I've had association with in the conservation movement, Dick Jones stands head and shoulders above them all.' At a memorial service three days later, Bob Brown delivered the eulogy, describing the former UTG president as the 'foundation stone of Tasmania's environmental politics', a man who had 'great courage and determination – indeed, he had no reverse gear at all. I, for one, was drawn into environmental politics, given courage and direction, and had the course of my life altered by this man, my friend and mentor.'[13]

*　　　*　　　*

Tasmania's export woodchip industry, which commenced in the 1970s, took off in the 1980s. Fresh from its Franklin victory, the TWS had been powerless to stop the Gray government (backed by Labor) approving Hydro schemes to dam the King and Pieman rivers, and had rolled into a debate about logging the Lemonthyme and Southern forests for woodchips. Within days of the 1986 election, the Gray government sent in the bulldozers.

The pugnacious Alec Marr, a former bricklayer who had just joined the TWS and would soon become its spokesman, organised one of the state's first 'tree sits', at Farmhouse Creek, at the bottom of the Picton Valley, where logging had begun. It was the beginning of the TWS's first major blockade since the Franklin. In what would become famous as the 'Battle of Farmhouse Creek', the logging companies sent busloads of 'vigilante' workers in to smash the blockade, and things soon got dangerously violent. The police, under orders from the Gray government not to intervene, watched on as protesters were bashed and chainsaws wielded against them – one worker halfway-cut Marr's tree, which was swaying wildly in the wind, with him in it. Senator Norm Sanders was one of 37 people arrested, as was a young Nick McKim, later a Greens MP.

Newly re-elected, Bob Brown put his body on the line, lying down in front of the bulldozers. He was forcibly dragged away by the workers, who laid into him, breaking his glasses, ripping his shirt, punching and kicking him in the groin as police did nothing. It was all captured by the cameras, and a photographer snapped one of the most iconic images of Brown's career as he was manhandled by half a dozen workers in hardhats. It made news bulletins and front pages around the country. Two days later, Brown was shot at as he walked above the creek, with two companions:

> It was getting dark when a van of pro-logging vigilantes cruised past ... One of the men in the van yelled out, 'Are youse Bob Brown?' I did not reply and we kept walking; they drove downhill about 50 metres before stopping. A man got out, walked around to the back of the van, opened it up and took out a gun. He fired two shots in our direction ... after we reported this shooting to the police, the men were arrested and subsequently fined a couple of hundred dollars – for shooting on a Sunday! If it had been environmentalists who'd had the guns, there would have been lengthy jail terms.[14]

The furore prompted Graham Richardson to travel to Tasmania. Australian Newsprint Mills had already given Richardson a tour in late 1985, so the TWS and Brown said, 'All right, we'll fly over the Florentine Valley and show you what they didn't show you.' As they cruised over a clear-felled area where the smoke was still rising from the scorched earth, Richo asked the pilot, Nigel, what he thought of it all. As it happened, the pilot had dropped the incendiaries himself the previous day, and he went into a rage about the waste involved in such burning. It impressed them all. Then they flew over Farmhouse Creek, landed at idyllic Lake Sydney and, as the helicopter went off to refuel, they talked about the wilderness over soggy sandwiches.

Brown recalled that as soon as the party were back in Hobart, Richardson went into the TWS offices and used their phone to call the prime minister on the spot. In front of Brown, he said, 'Look, Hawkey, you've got to come down here and see this place.' As Brown recalled: 'That was the cementing of a strong relationship with the environment movement which was to be prodigious in its impact on protecting wild places in Australia over the coming three years.'[15] It was the same tactic Dunphy had used with Neville Wran a decade earlier, to save the Colong wilderness, and it worked again. Richardson was true to his word, organised a meeting between Brown and the prime minister, and subsequently protected both Farmhouse Creek and the Lemonthyme by including them in the World Heritage Area – although the federal government had to launch legal action against Tasmania to do so.

With a Labor powerbroker like Richo, who was much more influential than Cohen, onside and able to convince both Bob Hawke and treasurer Paul Keating, Brown was at the peak of his national influence. In the 1987 federal election, the TWS and the ACF launched a 'vote for the forests' campaign, urging support for Labor in 11 marginal federal seats, and helping to swing the poll for the government. When Richardson successfully lobbied Hawke for the environment portfolio after the election, the greenies were in their heyday.

Richardson's door remained open as North Broken Hill proposed a billion-dollar chlorine-bleached pulp mill at Wesley Vale in northern Tasmania. A former schoolteacher and the mother of two young kids, Christine Milne, born and bred on a dairy farm at Wesley Vale, set up Concerned Residents Opposed to Pulpmill Siting (CROPS) with a bunch of other locals determined to stop the mill, which would use native forest as feedstock. As we've seen, Milne had been jailed during the Franklin blockade, and had attended numerous conservation rallies. She had never been personally involved in politics, however, although having done a history honours thesis on Tasmanian tourism, she had led a low-profile campaign to help save the old Waldheim Huts in Cradle Mountain – even meeting Richardson, who had agreed to put money in. Stopping Australia's biggest manufacturing project, which started out with bipartisan support at all levels of government, was a completely different proposition. But Milne was defending her home – what she called (after Judith Wright) 'my blood's country'.

Milne proved a formidable spokesperson for CROPS, adept at forming alliances with abalone divers, doctors, farmers, trade unionists, scientists and conservationists, domestically and worldwide. She worked closely with both Brown and Bates, who raised the pulp mill in parliament. CROPS took chances, organising what Milne calls the first farmers' rally in Australia, where they drove their tractors into Devonport, letting off rotten-egg gas at a public meeting so everyone could smell the hydrogen sulphide, the same odour the pulp mill would emit.[16]

Driving her Datsun back and forth from Ulverstone, Milne was tailgated and run off the road. There were threats to burn her house down. Those in the media presumed that a housewife from rural Tasmania would be no match for Richardson, but Milne was persuasive in private meetings and worked well with him. Richardson quickly twigged that the farmers who were pissed off with the Gray state government over the pulp mill were lifelong Liberal voters who might swing to Labor in the 1990 federal election. Gray was so close to North Broken Hill that he famously issued a press release, concerning the recall of state parliament, on the company's letterhead. Richardson convinced his cabinet colleagues to impose the toughest pollution standards on the pulp mill, and the project was shelved. North's Canadian partner in the mill, Noranda, was under pressure from Greenpeace over dioxins and knew that if it accepted high standards at Wesley Vale, it would have to impose them everywhere.

When Premier Gray called a snap election in an attempt to get the pulp mill back on track, Brown got in touch with Milne and asked her to stand for her local seat of Lyons. Milne was reluctant, but as the face of the campaign – she had been dubbed the 'Boadicea of the Bush' – she felt obliged to run:

> I still wasn't interested in politics at all. It was the worst time in
> my life to even consider that … I had a two year old and a four
> year old, I lived on the north-west coast … all I wanted to do was
> stop the pulp mill and go back to a normal life, but having worked
> so hard to defeat the pulp mill, and with so many people having
> invested their heart and soul into stopping the pulp mill, to call an
> election on the pulp mill and not stand wasn't feasible.

Milne claims to have won the highest below-the-line vote in
the state parliament's history, gaining 16 per cent of first preferences.[17] She is clear about the significance of Wesley Vale. For many
Tasmanians, including her own dairying family, who did not have
time for bushwalks, the south-west wilderness was always somewhere 'out there'. She represented Tasmanians who were not directly
engaged by the fights over Lake Pedder, or even the Franklin. The
Wesley Vale battle was about preserving the clean air, clean water,
uncontaminated soils and rural vistas that were dear to many.[18]

The 1989 Tasmanian election over Wesley Vale was a watershed
for the Green Independents, who trebled their vote to 17 per cent –
a 12 per cent swing to them. They won five lower-house seats, one
in each state electorate, giving them the balance of power, with the
Liberals holding 17 seats, and Labor 13, in the 35-seat House of
Assembly. Brown got a massive 22 per cent of the primary vote in
Denison, up 6 per cent, while Bates won 18 per cent in Franklin,
up 7 per cent. There were two new MPs: Uniting Church minister
Lance Armstrong, who won 12 per cent in Bass, while Milne's fellow
anti–pulp mill campaigner Di Hollister won 10 per cent in ultra-
conservative Braddon. The Democrats, who ran candidates in every
seat *but* Braddon, were trounced.

As the head of the largest party, Gray tried to tough it out in
a minority government, claiming that Brown had often made
clear during the campaign that, if elected, he would not support a
no-confidence motion moved by anyone else. Gray invited the independents for an exploratory sit-down, and both sides exchanged
copies of their respective policy platforms. Milne remembers it as
one of the most awful meetings of her life – both sides were going
through the motions. From the Franklin to Wesley Vale, Gray was

a sworn enemy of the greenies – it was his signature politics – and he soon unilaterally withdrew from the negotiations. (The Liberals would shortly be implicated in an extraordinary but unsuccessful attempt to bribe Labor's Jim Cox to cross the floor and give the conservatives an outright majority: Cox revealed he'd been offered $110,000 by businessman and newspaper publisher Ed Rouse. After a Royal Commission, Rouse was prosecuted and jailed.)

In parallel talks, Brown and the independents were also negotiating with Labor leader Michael Field. Again, there was plenty of animosity and mutual suspicion to overcome. The first question for Brown and his colleagues was whether to enter into a coalition and demand a cabinet portfolio, at least for himself and Bates, as the most experienced independents, or whether to strike an agreement. They chose the latter, in what would become an important precedent for the Greens' deal to support Prime Minister Julia Gillard in 2010. As Brown explained years later:

> With hindsight, we made the right decision ... [our new MPs] were going to face a ferocious opposition from the Liberals ... I dismissed the idea of being caught up by a portfolio which would have demanded all the time and not allowed this essential building of cohesion amongst our own ranks and with our supporters. Remember, we didn't have a party, we were five Independents – and we were thrust right into the centre of the crucible.[19]

(The lack of a party proper had caused Brown and his colleagues some difficulty during the campaign, when the chief electoral officer sought an injunction to have their election materials pulled. Although commonly described as 'Green Independents', they had officially campaigned as 'The Independents'. The threat of an injunction was withdrawn after Brown released his own legal advice.)

The second question was how hard to push. In return for guarantees of confidence and supply, the Greens extracted a string of policy commitments from Labor. The talks dragged on for almost two weeks, and nearly collapsed. Labor had to go back and forth with the union movement, including forestry sector workers, who were extremely wary of a proposed deal with the greenies.

The independents, by contrast, were on their own – they had no party membership to consult, and only their own pre-election platform as a basis for negotiation. Christine Milne remembers a tense meeting over forestry with Michael Field and his deputy, Peter Patmore: 'We were arguing the point and Patmore leapt to his feet and chucked this chair up across the room. I remember sitting there thinking, "Is this how people behave in politics? This is very bad behaviour."' At one point, when talks were at a real impasse, the head of the premier's office, Alan Evans, walked Field off down a corridor towards the press gallery. Brown later recalled:

> I recognised that if they got to the press and said, 'It's all broken down; it's over on the final day', we would be over. I had to literally bolt down the other corridor and get to the press first and say, 'We're still negotiating … it's difficult but we're going to have another go at it.'[20]

The Green Independents had pushed as far as they could – so far, in fact, that they had to pull back. But they succeeded in getting many better government provisions in, such as commitments to fixed four-year terms, a pecuniary interests register and disclosure of donations, and – the very last item tacked on – the abolition of subsidised liquor for government ministers. As they walked out of the final meeting, Brown recalled Milne turning to him and saying, 'Bob, you done good.' 'We'd gone right to the line,' he recalled. 'We were getting everything we possibly could.'

Forests were the major sticking point, and accounted for the bulk of the Labor–Green Accord. Brown and Milne are proud to this day of the lasting achievements written into the agreement, which were delivered. First and foremost, there would be no pulp mill at Wesley Vale or anywhere else, and nor would the proposed Huon Forest Products chip mill go ahead; the area of World Heritage, including forests, was almost doubled – to 1.384 million hectares – and the new Douglas-Apsley National Park was created. Most significantly, there would be a ceiling of 2.889 million tonnes per annum imposed on annual woodchip exports – a figure based on the previous year's total.

This last condition proved too much for the union movement and the forestry industry, and would later lead to the undoing of the accord. Also, Liberal leader Robin Gray cried foul and, in another precedent for the Gillard years, was relentless in undermining the legitimacy of the Labor/Green government, moving no-confidence motions at every opportunity. The attacks were blatantly sexist, too: Milne and Hollister were called 'political sluts' for getting into bed with Labor.[21]

A more fundamental problem for the Labor/Green government was the parlous state of Tasmania's finances. The state was heavily in debt – secretly using the Hydro to borrow off-budget – and the interest was crippling. Bulk users in industry were getting power well below cost, while ordinary homes and businesses were paying high prices. Compounding the problem, resources like minerals, timber and fisheries were being sold off with inadequate or zero royalties, robbing the state of much-needed revenue. It all fed into the old UTG critique of the Tasmanian economy.

Because the state's debts had been hidden, neither the incoming government nor the independents had any idea of the budgetary situation during the election campaign, according to Milne:

> What undermined all of us and in my view destroyed the capacity to deliver a lot of what both Labor and we Greens had agreed in the Labor–Green Accord, was the financial state of Tasmania … Gray had pretended right into the election and all through the period before that the state finances were fine … and then after the election it became apparent that the state was broke, really broke.

Incoming premier Michael Field had to cut hard, including closing down dozens of small country schools. The independents – particularly Milne and Hollister, who were both teachers – had promised a lot of extra funding for public education. 'Suddenly we found, after the event, not only was there no money [for new schools] but there wasn't even enough to maintain what they had,' she recalls. At the beginning, says Milne, a Labor government with Greens holding the balance of power seemed the most exciting thing in Australian politics, and people were moving back to Tasmania from all over the country. 'Then suddenly, cuts, everywhere cuts, and cuts to the people we had made promises to. So that undermined the relationship between Labor and the Greens because we were all under such enormous stress.'

When the government produced a hit list of 28 country schools to close, a horrified Milne went around the state visiting as many as possible. Soon she put forward a private member's bill to save them, and a motion of no-confidence in the education minister, and deputy premier, Peter Patmore. The Liberal opposition swung in behind her, hoping to land a blow against the government. As Milne recalls: 'The media went wild, saying, "You can't do that, you'll be bringing down the government," and I said, "No I'm not, I have absolute confidence in the government, I've just got no confidence in this minister. I want this minister gone."' Field dug in behind Patmore, arguing that the closures had been signed off by cabinet, so a lack of confidence in the minister was a vote of no confidence in the government. Field's most senior advisers, including the head of the premier's department, arranged a meeting with the five independents and turned up very grave and in dark suits. 'They looked like funeral directors,' says Milne.

Brown left the negotiation to her, as the group's education spokesperson, and Milne proved she was no pushover:

> Of course this is the advantage of not having been in politics – I really didn't have a sense of what an enormous thing this was ... so around [the premier's advisers] come in their dark suits to say, 'This is it, if you do this, Michael Field is off up to Government House. We're not going to allow you to move this motion of no confidence and get the Liberals' support and bring the deputy premier down like this, we're off to Government House.' I said, 'Good, see you! OK, fine, off you go then.' So out they go, and we're all standing there thinking, 'Well, here we go, I wonder what's going to happen next?' About ten minutes later the white car leaves for Government House with Peter Patmore in the back to resign as education minister, and my private member's bill got up to save the schools, and all those schools were saved!

With recession looming, Tasmania's dire financial position in the early 1990s forced the Green Independents to do some hard thinking about the economic policies they wished to pursue. Milne in particular, with her farming background and knowledge of Tasmania's historical tourism industry, believed that the way forward was for the state to promote itself as a clean and green source of quality produce and wilderness experiences. As the Greens had long argued, the emphasis should be on high-value, low-volume goods and services. Natural resources, if they were to be developed, should be priced properly. It all came together in a landmark Green Independents Business and Industry Strategy, which Milne argues has been largely implemented 30 years later. There were other wins too, such as Lance Armstrong's successfully introduction of a bill to lower the voting age in Tasmania to 18; Brown later described this as 'the first Greens legislation enacted into law in Australia'.[22]

The instability of the Labor–Green Accord took a toll, however. At the March 1990 federal election, the Green Independents, with no party organisation behind them, decided to revive the name of the United Tasmania Group. As we shall see, despite a huge focus on the environment that year, this was a big mistake that contributed to a sense of fragmentation among green parties nationally. Where the Green Independents had won 17 per cent of the state-wide vote the previous May, they now polled just 5 per cent – well short of a Senate quota.

Ahead of a major election post-mortem in Launceston two months later, submissions highlighted a 'feeling of regression', 'poor identification with Green Independents' and a sense that 'United Tasmania Group does not have the same impact as Green'. The choice of the UTG moniker had not been debated at the grassroots level. What's more, the Australian Democrats had a complete set of green policies, whereas the Green Independents did not. Pondering why the Green Independents had lost so many supporters and campaign workers in just ten months, the report noted that 'Greens appear to have been ineffective and even disruptive', and 'public expectation of the Accord has not been fulfilled'.[23]

For some, like political scientist and former Greens convenor Stewart Jackson, Bob Brown and his fellow independents were

'MPs in search of a party'. Indeed, a 1990 memo from Brown's chief of staff, Michael Lynch, read: 'It is only now that [the Green Independents] have "real power" that we are questioning the need for some structure of our own.'[24] But what sort of party structure should they adopt? The UK Greens' international liaison officer, Sara Parkin, an authority on green parties around the world, wrote a short paper urging the Tasmanian Greens to clarify the purpose of their party:

> It is not an encounter group for lost souls, it is not the mirror image of the society we seek, it is not a servant of the [environmental] movement, it is not a movement, it is a POLITICAL PARTY, with the sole task of contesting elections on a Green programme.[25]

As talks to form a national green party accelerated through 1991–92, and coalesced around a draft model constitution, Bob Brown first formed the Denison Greens, which became a related party of the federally registered Greens in New South Wales, and then the Tasmanian Greens.

A brewing backlash against the forestry provisions of the Labor–Green Accord brought it undone. The state government began working on a new forest industry strategy in the wake of the 1990 federal election. Under growing leadership pressure, Hawke changed tack on the environment, replacing Richardson with Ros Kelly. When he took over as prime minister, Paul Keating was reported to have told a staff Christmas party that one of his achievements in his first year of office was 'putting the environment back where it belonged'.[26] On forests, 'resource security' was the mantra, and Brown knew that the mooted package threatened the accord's ceiling on woodchip exports. Brown went to see Premier Field privately. 'Michael, I don't know that we can stick with you in government if you pursue this resource security line, if you hand across the forests to the logging companies, if you up the export woodchipping quota,' he told the premier.[27] The warning fell on deaf ears: powerful currents were pulling Labor in the other direction, state and federally.

When the state legislation was duly introduced in 1991, it confirmed Brown's worst fears. The TWS letterboxed the whole state, and Brown was 'under intense pressure from environmentalists – my environmental friends – to be acting on the government and, in fact, one or two of them very stridently put it to me that I was doing the wrong thing by holding off, we should bring the government down'. Brown soon pronounced the Labor–Green Accord dead. Letters and faxes streamed in to his office from Greens supporters all over the country, congratulating him on his principled stand.

But if anybody thought that would be the end of the forest wars, they were wrong. The Green Independents honoured their pre-election commitment not to block supply, and the Field government limped along in minority until the January 1992 state election, which saw an overwhelming swing to the Liberals, led by Ray Groom. Now campaigning formally as 'The Green Independents', Brown and his five colleagues were all returned – a thumbs-up from voters, rather than a backlash. Premier Field swore Labor would 'never again' enter into an accord with the Greens. According to Milne, it was an 'absolutely stupid position' for the government to take, 'because theoretically they would never be in government again ... which is why it was the Labor Party that drove the process to cut the numbers in the Tasmanian parliament'.

Field would never lose the bitterness, telling the ABC a decade later that there was a fundamental problem with the way the Greens did politics: 'It seemed to me as Premier, daily, but it was probably monthly, there was a threat to bring the government down. So it wasn't actually conducive for harmonious relationships.'[28]

*　　　*　　　*

When Jo Vallentine went into the Senate in July 1985, no longer representing the Nuclear Disarmament Party, she was completely alone – as Bob Brown had been in the Tasmanian parliament in 1983. Vallentine had her staff and supporters in her home state, but that was it. Only the Tasmanian independent Brian Harradine was helpful; he wanted the crossbenchers to form a more influential bloc. Vallentine held off, and also resisted overtures from both Labor's Peter Cook and Liberal Fred Chaney; the newbie senator was polite but kept her distance. She also decided not to bother learning the ins and outs of parliamentary procedure, unlike Harradine, who knew it all backwards. She shelved her copy of *Odgers' Australian Senate Practice*, the bible of the Senate:

> It's a book about that thick, you know, nearly two inches thick … I thought if I spent all my time learning that I'm never going to get to talk about disarmament. So I thought 'Well, I'll just sort of plod on and make the most of the work in the chamber,' knowing that it was never going to be the focus.[29]

Vallentine put more than her fair share of questions to the government, and made lengthy adjournment speeches, but never got a bill passed, and for most of her time in parliament concentrated on the outside world, using the profile and staff and travel rights of a senator to continue her campaigning. It was a model that saw her dubbed the 'activist-legislator'.

For her first term, conscious that she had abandoned the party that had elected her (albeit with a retrospective mandate from NDP members in Western Australia), Vallentine stuck closely to peace and anti-nuclear issues, abstaining from voting on most other legislation, with notable exceptions like when she teamed up with the Democrats' Norm Sanders to back government legislation forcing oil companies to bid for exploration permits. At the end of 1985, *The Age* published extracts from Vallentine's diary, along with a picture of her meditating in a shawl on the front lawn of Old Parliament House. The peacenik Vallentine did not drink, smoke or eat meat, the article noted, and she took a weekly massage and had a quartz crystal for 'maximising energy'. The reporter wrote that Vallentine was resisting the temptation to take up a ragbag of community issues, feeling she had a 'moral obligation to others to remain very firmly single issue'.[30]

Vallentine's biggest impact, in her first term, was over warship visits. In early 1986, ahead of the West Australian state election, she launched a Franklin-style campaign encouraging voters to write 'NO NUCLEAR WARSHIPS' on their ballot papers. One in five voters did. A few months later, after the meltdown in Chernobyl, Vallentine got the biggest coverage of her first term as a senator when, after failing to get the state government to release its plans for handling a nuclear accident at the Port of Fremantle or naval base HMAS Stirling, a copy of the 54-page document fell off the back of a truck.[31] Vallentine told reporters:

> It is amazing, more for what it doesn't say. The sections on evacuation, issuing potassium iodate tablets and informing the public are blank pages marked 'to be prepared'. It is not a safety plan at all. Under this plan there would be chaos and confusion in the event of an accident. Who is responsible for getting rid of a leaking, radioactive ship?[32]

There were no answers, of course. Vallentine went on the front foot, warning that every household within a few kilometres of any Australian port visited by nuclear warships should have a stock of potassium iodate tablets, and a booklet outlining the dangers.[33] The powerful Senate Standing Committee on Foreign Affairs and Defence launched an inquiry into the safety procedures of nuclear-powered or nuclear-armed vessels in Australian waters.[34] Meanwhile, the West Australian government scrambled to update its own plan.

Two months later, Vallentine was thrown out of the state parliament. Having tried and failed to see Premier Brian Burke privately, Vallentine instead heckled him from the public gallery. Surrounded by 60 supporters, she got up during question time and shouted: 'As the elected representative of 52,000 West Australians, I ask the premier to release the port safety plan relating to the visits of nuclear-powered warships, because right now there are 12 nuclear reactors and dozens of weapons approaching Fremantle.' She wrote later it was a 'show-stopper!'[35] The speaker, Mike Barnett, asked her three times to cease disrupting the house, before ordering police to remove her from the gallery, to slow handclaps from her supporters. Vallentine alleged she was 'pressured, pushed and kicked from behind' by a plainclothes policewoman, and complained to the ombudsman.[36]

Vallentine upped the ante in her encounters with the law, and started getting herself arrested – just as Labor's George Georges had done at peace rallies in 1978 and 1985, as Bob Brown had done during the Franklin and Farmhouse Creek battles, and as Jim Cairns and other politicians had done at anti-Vietnam protests.[37] Vallentine had her own philosophy about it. A Quaker first and foremost, she describes her actions as 'holy obedience' rather than civil disobedience, because she believes she is obeying a higher law.[38]

On Mother's Day in 1987, after a parliamentary trip to Nicaragua, Vallentine was one of 800 demonstrators (actor Martin Sheen was another) arrested at a protest against underground nuclear testing in Nevada. Vallentine said the rally on Mother's Day was 'an important symbolic action to demonstrate the concern of women world-wide for the protection of mother earth and for the protection of their children'. In a patronising press release, Liberal senator Peter Durack chided: 'The fact that it was Mother's Day makes it worse. She could have better demonstrated her concern for children world-wide by setting a good example and spending Mother's Day at home with her own small children.'[39] Vallentine put out a press release asking whether men were always at home on Father's Day. Did they ask permission of their families before they went off to war? 'I'm trying to make peace here,' she recalls.

Ahead of the mid-1987 federal election, Vallentine sought a wider mandate, forming a Perth-based party that was initially called the New Movement, and would take in social justice and environmental issues, as well as peace and disarmament.[40] She soon renamed it the Vallentine Peace Group, trading on the high personal recognition she had with the public – at 28 per cent it was much higher, according to the party's polling, than that of any other federal politician from Western Australia.[41] Vallentine's campaign took out newspaper ads with the headline: 'Can you name the other eleven WA senators?' The ad continued:

> Er ... um ... er ... Difficult, isn't it? If you're having trouble, you probably know even less about how they performed in the last two years. But you *have* heard of *Jo Vallentine*. In two short years as a Senator, she has done the following: made 53 speeches; asked 57 questions without notice; given 34 notices of motion; participated in 20 divisions; presented 46 petitions ...[42]

The ad highlighted Vallentine's achievements, including her setting up of the national 'Lobby for Peace' network, and the Senate inquiry into the safety of nuclear warships visiting Australian ports. Peter Garrett launched the campaign, and the number two on her Senate ticket was Louise Duxbury, an environmental consultant (who later became a long-time organiser for the Greens). It was the 'Joh for Canberra' election, in which the Queensland premier Joh Bjelke-Petersen derailed John Howard's ambitions. Vallentine and her supporters cheekily purloined a bunch of Joh's stickers and blocked out the 'h'.[43]

Her primary vote dropped nonetheless, from the 6.7 per cent high of the NDP campaign in 1984 to just 4.8 per cent – which was below the share of the lead Democrat, Jean Jenkins. The NDP implosion had taken a toll, and fears of nuclear war had ebbed as Reagan and Gorbachev began disarmament talks. But the 1987 federal election, a double dissolution and the first for an expanded Senate (with 12 senators per state instead of ten), was extremely favourable for minor-party and independent candidates. Prophetically, Peter Bowers in *The Sydney Morning Herald* wrote that 'politicians will rue the day they increased the size of the Senate because it is only a matter of time before that house is controlled by an uncontrollable rabble'.[44] In the event, preference flows helped Vallentine into the 12th spot on Democrat preferences. Surprisingly, Vallentine flagged straightaway that she would not contest the next election: 'I think five years is the maximum a person should serve in parliament because after that it becomes easy to pick up some of the negative aspects about parlia-mentary life ... the lifestyle in parliament is not the best.'[45]

Vallentine was finally free to be her own politician, with her own mandate. A *Woman's Day* profile, published days after the election, showed her standing in front of the family's Kombi, emblazoned with a big peace sign; Vallentine had long golden hair and was dressed in bright purple from head to toe – hippy as. On her first day back in the Senate, she tried a new, more aggressive tactic: moving an amend-ment to the governor-general's address-in-reply, normally a set-piece speech to open the new parliament, proposing that Australia with-draw from the ANZUS Treaty. It led to a highly unusual two-hour debate, in which four Democrats supported her.[46] Vallentine found she had more credibility in the place; previously, she says, 'a lot of people thought I was a oncer'.

Vallentine lobbied hard for a seat on the powerful Joint Committee on Foreign Affairs, Defence and Trade, and was appointed in 1987; it was the first time a woman, or anyone from outside the major parties, had been included. Vallentine found the male-dominated committee daunting, and put up with more than her fair share of ridicule, but soon found there was a lot of forelock-tugging and lip-service paid to foreign affairs and defence personnel by members, who did very little of their own research and rarely probed witnesses. 'Honestly, they didn't have a clue,' she says. Vallentine used the position to challenge the defence experts who appeared regularly – over, for example, the political rationale for the hugely expensive Kangaroo '89 operation, the largest peacetime military exercise ever conducted in Australia, which covered almost the whole north of the continent, and was predicated on an 'unaccountable invasion by Kamaria (an imaginary foe to the north)'.[47]

Early on, Vallentine had turned up unexpectedly at the top-secret North West Cape communications base. Her presence was made known to the minister for defence, Kim Beazley, who ordered that she be given VIP treatment and a tour. 'I found all the technology mind-boggling and wished I could pull the plug on the lot,' her diaries recorded.[48] In her second term, her first major action was to get arrested at Pine Gap in October 1987, in protests timed to the expiration and likely renewal of the ten-year lease extension over the base, which had been struck in 1966.[49] It was a well-planned, week-long protest – not just by women this time – and there were strict rules for anyone planning to get arrested, which Vallentine had seen work in Nevada. No violence, of course, but also no drugs or alcohol, no swearing and, most importantly, no running, which might spook the guards.

Almost a thousand protesters gathered; the road to the base was lined with buses, vans and trucks. It started peacefully, with banners, streamers and balloons tied to the 'iron curtain' fence around the facility, and bongos, dancing and candles at night. At one point the protesters bounced a red rubber ball over the fence, inviting the Pine Gap authorities to stop playing war games and play ball instead. But two protesters went too far by supergluing themselves to a video camera tower and putting a hood over the lens. They were removed with acetone, while the crowd chanted, 'Close Pine Gap!' and 'Cease the lease!' Then it was time to go in. Wearing a 'Cease the Lease' T-shirt, and brandishing a mock eviction notice, Vallentine took off by herself. Many years later she recalled:

> [W]hen it came for the moment for me to go through the fence there were people stationed on the inside and I just went quite a long way along because actually I wanted some time away from the crowd and away from the cameras before I actually went in because it was really important for me to do this from a very centred space … so it was quite a while before anybody actually approached me. I mean I'd walked in fifty metres or so, I suppose, and a woman came up and said, 'Are you aware that you're committing trespass?' and I said, 'Yes.' And she said, 'Well, do you want to go back?' and I said, 'No,' and, you know, you've got this option or that, and I said, 'Fine.' And then she said, 'Well, I'm arresting you and what is your name?' and I said 'Jo Vallentine,' and she said, 'Oh, shit, this is my first arrest and it's a bloody Senator.'

Vallentine was charged with trespass, but pleaded not guilty, reading out her own six-page statement in court. She had deliberately chosen to commit civil disobedience, she said, but was not guilty of trespass because she had a lawful excuse: under the Nuremberg war crime principles, individuals were obliged to act if they believed that their government was preparing for acts of genocide, such as using Pine Gap to help the United States pinpoint nuclear targets in the Soviet Union – exactly what FOI documents had established was happening at the base. This international obligation overruled national law, Vallentine said. 'I think it is quite appropriate when we're considering the future of our planet to commit civil disobedience. From a moral perspective I felt obliged to take this action.'[50]

The magistrate found her guilty anyway and fined the senator $250, with $777 in costs. Of more than 100 others charged, most paid the fine, but Vallentine refused. 'That would be tantamount to admitting guilt,' she said. 'I have done nothing wrong.' About a dozen protesters did likewise, including one nun, and were sent to Alice Springs jail. When Vallentine got there, according to her mum, Sylvia, the warder said, 'There's only one other female prisoner here and we won't ask you to have the meal with her ... she is an Aboriginal.' Vallentine replied: 'Well, I won't have my meal unless I have it with her.'[51] Vallentine did three days' hard labour, gardening and cleaning dusty floors, in August 1988.

Vallentine used her arrest and jailing to publicise the cause, issuing a paper proposing an 'alternative security' agenda, which would move Australia from an offensive to purely defensive strategy, and her office organised two seminars around the concept 'Just Defence'. The options Vallentine envisaged were 'armed neutrality', like Sweden or Switzerland; a 'defensive defence' posture, which enabled a country to defend its territory without having the capacity to attack, or 'non-violent civilian-based defence', involving the withdrawal of work and services by civilians. 'The peace movement is no longer saying "no bases, no weapons, no uranium",' Vallentine said. 'We're going to get greater support for what we're saying when we have an alternative security agenda in place.'

From opposition, Liberal senator Fred Chaney proposed a highly unusual Senate motion, calling on the government to reaffirm its support for Pine Gap and the US alliance; it was supported by Labor, and so sailed through despite opposition from the crossbenches.[52] This led to one of Vallentine's most depressing moments in the parliament: a meeting with then foreign affairs minister, Bill Hayden, later governor-general. Vallentine was arguing that Australia should be more independent of the United States, in the manner of New Zealand, which had gone nuclear-free and banned warship visits. 'About 73 per cent of people in New Zealand were living in declared nuclear-free zones before the government actually made that declaration,' Vallentine recalled later, 'and I can remember saying to Bill Hayden, "We're going to get 70 per cent of people in Australia opposed to the bases here and we're going to get 70 per cent of the people in Australia opposed to the foreign warship visits."' Hayden replied that public opinion didn't matter – Australia was in too deep with the Americans. 'It won't work here,' she remembered him saying, 'we're too involved through those bases. You could get 80 per cent here and it won't work, we won't be able to get rid of them.'

Vallentine was absolutely crushed:

I didn't tell that to people in public because I thought, 'How deflating, what are we working for? What are we actually working for?' And I feel really upset just talking about it now. There was the foreign minister saying it wouldn't matter how much Australian people protested or made their … wishes known, that we wouldn't be able to get rid of them. I mean, I knew that actually Bill Hayden was on our side; I do believe that.[53]

In October 1988 in Fremantle, Vallentine handcuffed herself to the gangplank of the warship HMS *Edinburgh*, which had the Duke of York on board, carrying a placard that quoted Lord Mountbatten: 'Nuclear weapons serve no military purpose whatsoever – they merely take us closer to the final abyss.' She was charged with disorderly conduct and locked up again. In court, Vallentine wore a badge: 'I was arrested for peace.' The magistrate ruled that the gangplank was under the jurisdiction of the port, not police, and she had no case to answer.[54] All up, Vallentine was arrested five times in her seven-year parliamentary career.

Getting arrested wasn't all: Senator Vallentine would also turn up to press conferences to heckle the prime minister. It was unadulterated, joyous ratbaggery. On one celebrated occasion in 1989 she was suspended from the Senate for 24 hours for refusing to resume her seat after government and opposition senators walked out on her, denying a quorum for a debate on the use of the army to quell demonstrators at the US Nurrungar base, where there were 400 arrests. It was the first use of troops against civilian demonstrators on Australian soil; the *Sun-Herald*'s editorial sided with Vallentine, decrying the undermining of democratic process: 'A debate on a major issue of public concern was thwarted on the floor of the Senate.'[55]

Vallentine was described as a plague on the nation's conscience. After agonising over a decision for 18 months, in 1988 Vallentine abstained from voting on the Hawke government's war crimes legislation, which she described as 'selective revenge' against the losers of war, and opposed on the principle that war itself was a crime against humanity. In one of her most important speeches as a senator,

Vallentine acknowledged that failing to support the bill would put her 'alongside some people in our community who may be disguising guilt or their extreme right-wing political views and I feel uncomfortable in their company'.[56] But what about the Australians who had participated in the bombing of Dresden, she asked, or those Allied forces who bombed civilians in Vietnam? 'They are the architects of genocide,' she wrote, adding that those who planned the bombings, like Henry Kissinger, should be tried as war criminals. Most important to Vallentine was the threatened nuclear 'omnicide', or destruction of all humanity, and Australia's part in it:

> As a Quaker, pacifist and member of the War Resisters' International, I abhor the taking of life under any circumstances. Under the Nuremberg principles, to plan genocide is also a war crime. Therefore, Australia's involvement in US warfighting plans via Pine Gap, Nurrungar and North-West Cape, and nuclear warship visits, contravenes those principles.[57]

*   *   *

Using her profile as a senator, Vallentine was instrumental in bringing the various green political groups in Western Australia together. At the beginning of 1989, heading into the West Australian state election in January, there were four: the Vallentine Peace Group itself, another group called Green Development down south with Louise Duxbury and Lyn Serventy, a so-called Alternative Coalition that had as candidates the later Greens senators Christabel Bridge (later Chamarette) and Dee Margetts, and a group in North Fremantle who had been clever enough to form the WA Greens and affiliate with the federally registered Greens in Sydney. Vallentine and Newbury took a dim view of the people behind the WA Greens, whose leading figures included Kim Herbert, Nadine Lapthorne and later state Greens MLC Paul Llewellyn. Vallentine recalls they 'seemed like a mob of anarchists who decided that they were going to undermine the system by working within it, going through the Electoral Commission and having a go at electoral politics ... but, of course, we weren't unsupportive publicly'.

The WA Greens barely troubled the scorer, fielding 11 candidates in four of the Legislative Council's multi-member electorates and polling 3.2 per cent of the statewide vote.

After the election, talks began:

We had so many debates about the word 'Green', I mean whether it was the right one to go with. And with all of this interest in Green issues out there in television land we knew that was the word that was wanted; that was the one that was absolutely necessary. Not Rainbow Alliance, which is what they went with in Victoria because they thought that 'Green' was too extremist and that there were these impressions of the people before the bulldozers and the barricades and the forests and so on.[58]

The victory of Tasmania's Green Independents in May 1989 gave new impetus to the talks in Western Australia. Vallentine thought the Tasmanians were 'providing an interesting model for the rest of the country, perhaps for the rest of the world'. She attributed the community trust in the Green Independents there to 'the excellent record of integrity which Tasmanian environmental activist and politician Bob Brown has built up over many years', although she added: 'It remains to be seen whether a group of independents holding the balance of power in a state parliament is sustainable in the long run.'

In December 1989 the WA Greens merged with the Green Earth Alliance, and the Greens WA (which still exists today) was incorporated and called for candidates to contest the looming federal election. Personally, Vallentine was deeply ambivalent about recontesting her Senate seat. She found the internal wrangles 'debilitating', and refused to stand unless there was a unified green ticket. 'Sometimes I think we're not ready for that step,' she commented. In the end, Vallentine put her hand up for preselection, and emerged a clear winner with 90 per cent support. Second-placed was Christabel Bridge, while Gladys Yarran came third. '[It was] the first all-female Senate ticket in Australia,' Vallentine recalled, and 'the first Aboriginal woman to run for the Senate in Australia was on our ticket'.

Greens WA contested all 14 House of Representatives electorates, and won 7.5 per cent of the overall vote. In the Senate, the Greens won

8.3 per cent of the primary vote, slightly less than the Democrats, on 9.4 per cent, but once again Vallentine won on preferences after a lengthy count. For the first time, after winning the 1990 election, Vallentine got a full six-year term as a senator. 'Oh my goodness, suddenly I felt like it was a prison sentence,' she recalled later.

Vallentine's health began to deteriorate: the long trips from Perth to Canberra, then via Sydney or Melbourne, took their toll and she started to get increasingly frequent and severe migraines – debilitating two- and three-day events. While others could deputise for her at public functions, her Senate duties were an inescapable burden. It wasn't long before she was thinking about resigning. 'The getting out was planned a lot more carefully than getting in,' she says.

It is difficult to sum up Vallentine's achievements as the first Greens senator, especially because she was so self-effacing. Some of her best cut-through was achieved for off-the-wall causes. At the very end of her career, Vallentine launched a campaign against disposable nappies, which were more environmentally damaging than old-fashioned cloth nappies and were not 'disposable' at all, instead piling up in landfills.

In the lead-up to Christmas 1988, Vallentine launched a campaign against violence on television and introduced a private member's bill to ban the broadcast of any children's television program that was violent or promoted war toys.[59]

Vallentine's bill on war toys failed, as did a later draft law to set up a Peace Trust Fund, into which conscientious objectors could donate that proportion of their taxes which was spent on the military. A third private member's bill bore fruit, however. In her last speech to the Senate, Vallentine pointed out that there were 150 different secrecy provisions in various federal laws, and introduced a Whistleblower's Protection Bill to set up a dedicated agency with the power to conduct investigations and protect public servants who expose fraud and corruption. She was a lone voice in parliament.[60] In 1994 a Senate select committee, titled 'In the Public Interest', examined Vallentine's bill and supported many of its provisions. The Keating government rejected most of the committee's recommendations but agreed about the need to improve the system and signalled an intention to introduce whistleblower-protection legislation, but the Howard government abandoned it.[61] Although states and territories introduced various laws, reform at the federal level took another 20 years. For Vallentine, it was one of her crowning achievements. 'I really think I got that whole thing going,' she says. 'We had people who were whistleblowers and wanting to be heard [who had nowhere else to go] ... I'm pretty proud to have got that one started.'

Vallentine's legacy includes getting the ball rolling on the prevention of mining in Antarctica, which she campaigned against for years. A breakthrough came when Vallentine realised that her arch-enemy, West Australian Liberal senator Noel Crichton-Browne, had actually been to Antarctica:

> I thought, he's going to be for supporting an absolute ban on mining in Antarctica, and he was! He managed to get the Liberals to get a position before Labor! So I embarrassed Labor by putting up a notice of motion to the effect that we shouldn't be mining in Antarctica ... it forced the Labor Party's hand and they agreed.

'I liked the fact that I could wrangle something behind the scenes by talking to the Liberals and then Labor came on board,' Vallentine recalls. 'They would probably never admit to this, but I know that that's what happened.' Even the Democrats' environment spokesman, John Coulter, put out a press release headed 'Vallentine must take credit for Antarctic mining ban'.[62]

It was galling for Vallentine to find that, after seven years riding a huge wave of public support for peace and disarmament, which no doubt helped end the Cold War, she was required to argue in the Senate that Australia should not join a new war against a new enemy in the Middle East. 'I could not believe we were going to get involved,' she recalled later of the debate ahead of the Gulf War. 'That was particularly horrendous.'[63] She was arrested again, leading a sit-in in the Perth office of transport and communications minister Kim Beazley.[64] Crossing over from the Senate, Vallentine heckled Bob Hawke from inside the House of Representatives, reminding him of a promise he'd made earlier in the year that Australians would never again fight in a foreign war. 'Shame, shame, shame,' she yelled, and subsequently had to apologise to speaker Leo McLeay.[65]

There is no doubt that the first Gulf War added to Vallentine's frustration with politics. With her health failing – in 1991 she missed 48 days in the Senate – and her daughters heading into their teenage years, Vallentine resigned 'for body, family and soul reasons'. At the suggestion of deputy Senate leader Mal Colston, Vallentine claimed a parliamentary pension worth $33,000 a year because of poor health brought on by the job.[66]

When her resignation was announced and she was asked about her achievements in parliament, Vallentine mentioned changing attitudes to US bases, and cited her lobbying on Antarctica, but admitted there were no obvious successes she could point to. 'I cannot say that I achieved an enormous amount in terms of legislation,' she said, 'but then one person cannot expect to. Momentous change does not happen overnight.'[67] Reflecting on her career in politics, Vallentine wrote:

> [U]ltimately, it is in the community, rather than the parliament, where power really lies, with a fair amount of it also being in the bureaucracy. Apart from the executive, it is a mistake to credit parliament with too much power. It is a useful debating forum, as it should be, but I feel that there is too much pomp and ceremony accorded to it, helping to create an illusion of power. Illusions can be dangerous: politicians sometimes think they have power, and individuals often abdicate to those they perceive to be powerful.[68]

She sought 'power-with' the community, not 'power-over' it.[69] It was a profoundly green philosophy.

GETTING TOGETHER

The formation of a national green party seems inevitable now. It was not. The first steps towards it were difficult, there were defeats and reversals, and all involved still bear the scars. Bob Brown is one. For more than 30 years he has harboured a resentment that a clear path to growth for the Greens was not taken in 1986, when the idea of a national political party was mooted at a conference in Sydney, and rejected. Brown blames what he calls the 'old guard' in NSW, who have been 'blocking the growth of the national Greens as against the State Greens, all the way down the line'.[1]

As we have seen, Brown kicked off the process to form a national greens organisation just after Christmas in 1984, at a gathering of 50 friends – most of whom were veterans of the Franklin campaign – at his Liffey home. Petra Kelly had visited Brown there during the year, and urged him to form an Australian Greens party.[2] The group soon planned a major national conference, titled 'Getting Together', to be held at Sydney University over Easter 1986. It was not at all clear, though, that the Liffey group hoped to set up a party – in fact, the first minutes specifically 'reaffirmed our decision that the purpose of the conference was not to set up a political party but rather a movement'.[3] Gradually, the Liffey group pulled in speakers and support from all round the country. A crucial contact was with a young lecturer named Drew Hutton, who had set up the Brisbane Greens at the end of 1984 – the first such party in Queensland. Brown would first meet Hutton during these preliminary meetings and would say, many years later, that he, 'more than anybody, is responsible for the formation of the Australian Greens – and I include myself in that'.[4]

Hutton was born in Chinchilla, on Queensland's fertile Darling Downs, and sent to the state's most prestigious boarding school, Brisbane Grammar, where he was school captain (and was coached in athletics and tennis by a young Alan Jones). At university he was politicised by the Vietnam War and soaked up the new left politics of the late 1960s and early 1970s. He rejected the repressions of Joh's Queensland, and was interested in the same anarchic 'self-managed' socialist philosophy as the original NSW Greens. The year after Hutton set up the Brisbane Greens, he ran as a lord mayoral candidate for the Brisbane City Council, polling 4 per cent. He would run for the Greens nine more times over the next 30 years, in what is undoubtedly the party's toughest state, being conservative and having no upper house. The hostility to the Greens in his home state motivated Hutton to focus on the rest of the country.

In a newsletter distributed in March 1986 ahead of the 'Getting Together' conference, Hutton wrote that '[t]he stage would seem to be set for the emergence of a new political force in Australian society'. The only attempts to present viable solutions to the world's problems, he argued, were coming from outside the main political parties. Hutton posed a number of sensible foundational questions: what relationship should exist between the movement and the party? Should the party be based on ideology? What sorts of structures should be adopted? Should people from other political parties be allowed to join? To what extent do we accept the framework of parliamentary democracy?[5]

Meanwhile through 1985 the Sydney Greens held regular meetings at the inner-city Glebe Town Hall – to discuss the recent split in the NDP, for example, or talk about unions, or hear from Monash University's Alan Roberts on the 'nuclear winter', one of the subjects of his book *The Self-Managing Environment*. The culmination was a three-day October workshop to develop a 'Green Manifesto' for the new party, to be circulated among members. The draft captured the libertarian, 'anti-party party' ethos perfectly:

> We seek no benefits from this activity; the Greens are not interested in exercising power over people. In the event of widespread support for the Greens we are not a party interested in the government of people. Those interested in 'governing' or 'leading' already have an array of possibilities: all existing political organisations for starters. Our aim is to be an organisation of 'enablers'.[6]

Bob Brown's Liffey group process came out of the blue, lobbed over the top of this already bubbling green politics. In early 1986, Hall Greenland remembers thinking: '"Getting Together"? We'd already formed the Greens – what are they talking about? All they had to do was come and join us!' Greenland and Harris went along to the Getting Together conference nonetheless, among a dozen-odd interested observers from the Sydney Greens. On the eve of the conference, an article in *The Australian* headlined 'Towards the birth of a Green Party' gently ribbed the 'alfalfa fringe philosophies' of the organisers, and quoted Milo Dunphy saying that while he did not think a green party was necessary, 'there is definitely a momentum towards it'.[7] The turnout was huge, more than 500 people. Brown gave the opening speech: '[T]his is an age of crisis, and politics and parliament do need new directions.' A new force was emerging, Brown said, but he did not mention a Greens party.

The conference soon went off-track. Jane Elix from the Women's Electoral Lobby weighed in first:

> What has concerned me the most is the assertion that has been repeated over and over again in terms of moral righteousness that we can put our differences aside and work together to benefit us all. I think we're being terribly naive if we accept that without thinking about what it really entails. I see vast differences between feminist philosophies and other philosophies represented here. We cannot just gloss over our differences and in particular the difference between women-only groups and groups which include men and women.[8]

Another woman, peace worker Georgine Abrahams, chimed in: patriarchy was the problem, a culture against nature was a culture against women, and 'the number one battleground is ego, patriarchal ego'. Clearly, no leaders of the Greens were going to be smoothly anointed at this event. The friction was exacerbated by the organisers' failure to pay for professional childcarers. Peter Jones conceded it was 'a serious error'. Then the animal liberationists objected: animal rights were almost unrepresented in the program, and the wording of the credo, as it stood, tended to be 'eco-human centred';

more allowance needed to be made for non-human species. Things were going downhill.

There was broad support for a coalition of community groups, but when Drew Hutton's 'Green Party' session convened, the wheels fell off altogether. Hutton was almost apologetic: '[D]espite the fact we are talking about some degree of urgency, we are not wanting to foist a Green party on anybody.' Tony Harris took a different tack: any move should be bottom-up, not top-down; there were dangers in imposing a traditional party structure with secretariats, constitutions and so on. 'Let's just do it, let's take our desires for reality,' he urged. 'We could start that sort of movement now. Let's build it up with small groups operating in their desired fashion ... Certainly we oppose any attempt to form a single central green party or coalition at this conference.'[9] That was it, the nail in the coffin. The last plenary session was mayhem, with wild motions declared here and there.

In his summing-up, Bob Brown kept up a sense of optimism: 'What have we achieved this weekend? We have transplanted a seedling that was sown two years ago, a healthy seedling, well established, but still very much in need of careful nurturing.' Post-conference letters emphasised the lack of structural critiques of capitalism, the obvious gulf between the 'cosmic element/personal growth' and the more hardened political campaigners. Writing in ACF's *Habitat*, Joan Staples concluded:

> The conference overwhelmingly rejected forming a Greens Party now in Australia in spite of the considerable enthusiasm of a small number of individuals. The rejection appeared to be based primarily on the belief that the time was not yet ripe, that more groundwork needs to be done on a grassroots level ... While Getting Together did not actually 'get it together', it did have a sense of enormous possibilities for political influence if commonalities can be found and links made. Listening to some Broad Left people speak I found the jargon of socialism and Marxism grating. While some of the language may still be valid, and useful, the language speaks to a different era. There is a new political agenda, more complex than the dichotomy of capital and labour.[10]

The process of truly getting together would take another six years. Brown, a decade later, wrote that the delay was 'not entirely without benefits … it made it possible for the Greens to develop their own identity and differentiate themselves from the unstructured and vulnerable politics that had been so frustratingly evident in Sydney in 1986'.[11]

Whose fault was it? Greenland says the Sydney Greens were bystanders at Getting Together, and were certainly not responsible for the failure of the proposal for a Green Party:

> The delegates there were mostly from the peak groups – environmental organisations TWS, NCC, TEC, those kind of bodies – and they voted against it. We didn't block it, there were literally a handful of us there in a theatre of hundreds of people. I was there as an observer. I know that's hard to believe for some people that I didn't speak, but I didn't.

Ariel Salleh wrote a penetrating essay looking back on the Getting Together conference, titled 'A Green Party: can the boys do without one?'. 'The big question of course was whether a Green Party should be formed,' she wrote. 'Women favoured a looser, more organic coalition of movement organisations – wary, like sisters all over the world, of promoting any more patriarchal excursions into capital-P politics.' Women preferred working in collectives, she continued, with an informal rotation of roles and lateral decentralised network links:

> There is also a certain elitism about vanguard organisations, a symptomatically 'objectifying', patriarchal them/us split, quite out of touch with genuine respect and communication – that colonising tendency again. The worst excesses of this 'instrumental rationality', as the neo-Marxists call it, is demonstrated by party politics, which inevitably gets down to a manipulative scramble for numbers. Yet, many radical men still have a deep need for emotional gratification in terms of the old political paradigm. Ego is still smoothed by rubbing shoulders with other men in power. It is still massaged by the general cut and thrust of capital-P politics.[12]

Everyone retreated to lick their wounds, or simply did their own thing: it was the beginning of a very fractious, indeed tortuous, period. In the 1987 federal election, none of the budding Greens parties had momentum yet. The environmental movement, particularly the TWS and the ACF, for the first time took the novel step of endorsing Labor in eleven key marginal seats, on the strength of its commitment to save the Daintree Rainforest in Queensland. Also for the first time, donations from big business were on offer: the TWS reportedly accepted $70,000 from Perth-based developer Bond Corporation, to fund forest conservation (and pro-Labor) ads. There was an average 0.9 per cent swing to the government in those seats, against a national average 1.3 per cent swing away, meaning the environmental campaigners could claim to have generated a potent 2.2 per cent swing.

It was a controversial tactic, and there were claims that former Barry Cohen staffer Jonathan West, who was now heading up the TWS, was spearheading an elite group of activists fully embedded in the Labor machine, politicising the environmental movement and neglecting the grassroots.[13] The tactic left the Democrats smarting too, but their electoral support grew nonetheless. This was all the more impressive given Don Chipp's retirement the previous year; South Australian Janine Haines had taken over the leadership. In Tasmania, Norm Sanders was successful in his second tilt at the Senate, running at the top of the Democrat ticket there. In South Australia, former Communist Party member Bob Lamb got in touch with Harris and got permission to use the Greens' name, and his partner, anti-pesticide campaigner Ally Fricker, stood unsuccessfully.

In New South Wales, firebrand activist Ian Cohen was offered the top spot on the party's Senate ticket, becoming the first official Greens candidate in the country. As we saw in the last chapter, Cohen was a veteran of the Nightcap and Franklin campaigns, but had jumped to prominence in 1986, when, as part of the 'Peace Squadron', he paddled his longboard alongside the USS *Oldendorf* as it entered Sydney, and managed to grab the bow of the warship with an outstretched arm and surf its wave. He later wrote:

The hardest part over, I was positioned for the ride of my life up Sydney Harbour. I waved to police and protest craft alike, smiling from ear to ear. That is, until I sighted a boat ten metres in front. On board were cameramen with monstrously large lenses pointing at me. I pulled an excruciatingly intense face; after all, nuclear warships are no laughing matter.[14]

The resulting front-page picture for *The Sydney Morning Herald* launched Cohen's political career.

The election of 1987 was a double dissolution, which lowered the Senate quota to 7 per cent. As Cohen wrote later, this meant 'anything was possible'. Still, the Greens' Senate campaign could not have been more ratbag: Cohen's main tactic was to gate-crash the day's biggest election event, whatever it might be. He heckled Hawke over ocean outfalls, and Howard over the Franklin. He jumped back into the water with his surfboard to intercept the prime minister as he arrived by boat at Labor's Sydney Opera House campaign launch, and got arrested and charged for his trouble. He paddled out to take a water sample from the sewage outfall off Bondi, and with BUGA-UP (Billboard Utilising Graffitists Against Unhealthy Promotions) defaced tobacco advertising near the airport. It was 100 per cent stunt-driven. Cohen finished the campaign in jail, waiting for a $200 good behaviour bond to be posted.

For the party, the shoestring campaign was a raging success. 'After the Prime Minister and leader of the Opposition, The Greens were the most publicised political party in the elections,' wrote Cohen. He gained 31,861 primary votes, or 1 per cent, but 75 per cent of his preferences went to the NDP's Robert Wood, who had a primary vote of just 1.5 per cent but squeezed past far-right party Call to Australia's Elaine Nile to win the final, 12th seat. The party's election poster showed a leaf being placed into a ballot box – a cute idea ripped off from some European green party – under the slogan 'Green not Greed'. The named candidates – Cohen and his number two, Daphne Gollan – represented the two key tendencies within the movement: green-green and red-green. In New South Wales at least, both strands have been part of the Greens since the very beginning.

The NSW Greens did not run in the state election held eight months later, which ushered in the Liberal government of Nick Greiner. Instead, there were two competing nominally green tickets for the upper house in 1988. In its last years, the Labor government had sacked the Sydney Council, so Jack Mundey decided to have a crack at state politics, running atop a ticket of three left-leaning 'Community Independents'. Meanwhile, encouraged by Bob Carr, conservationist Milo Dunphy headed up a three-person 'Envirovote' team.

Dunphy genuinely believed he stood a chance. The two giants, both of whom had been at the birth of green politics in Australia 15 years earlier, and were on the executive council of the ACF, succeeded only in splitting the environmental vote: Mundey's team polled 1.7 per cent, and Dunphy 1.6 per cent. Mundey still might have been elected, except Dunphy preferred the Democrats above him, as did the NDP. Mundey was ropeable, and in a written statement took a swipe at Dunphy's 'political opportunism'. He finished on a sour note: 'Our votes could have elected a more effective representative.'[15] Ian Cohen recalls Dunphy telling him there was 'no way he could support a communist'. Mundey went off and joined the New Left Party, set up after the fall of the Berlin Wall by ex-Communist Party secretary Laurie Aarons. The Democrats scored the last upper-house seat, electing former Australia Party candidate Richard Jones, boosting the party's representation to two MLCs and giving them the balance of power.

Green Independents were popping up everywhere. Bob Brown, who had launched Milo Dunphy's campaign, was alert to this and busily cultivated a national network of green-tinged MPs, parliamentary candidates and local councillors. In late 1989 he sent out an invitation to a list of more than a hundred such people. It was a curious list: Mundey and Dunphy were on it, as were high-profile names Helen Caldicott and Bob Ellis, who would soon stand as independents themselves. Also on Brown's list were sitting senators Jo Vallentine and Irina Dunn, Drew Hutton, and state MPs Clover Moore, Ted Mack, John Hatton and others. But Ian Cohen and Daphne Gollan – who had actually stood for the Greens federally – were not. Clearly Brown remained extremely wary of the NSW Greens, after his 1986 experience.

The invitation was pure Bob Brown:

Many green representatives are more than independent. They are isolated representatives on councils or in parliaments dominated by the old materialist credo. This get-together is being held to share our experiences, problems and successes. It is designed to be relaxing, non-demanding, strengthening. It is specifically for people who have faced elections but who do not have the back-up of big party organisation. While we will be discussing the greening of the 'eighties', the prospect of the 'nineties' and the issues of the moment, the get-together is set to make acquaintances. It's not to organise elections or structures. Don't come if you see it as a step up the ladder ...[16]

The response was mixed; many were too busy preparing for the looming federal election. Jim Collins, an independent candidate for Eden-Monaro, replied in longhand, expressing his frustration with fringe groups hopping on the green bandwagon, and conservationists who didn't understand that politics was about 'getting up early, going to bed late, door knocking and ... people'. Collins complained that he was campaigning seven days a week, 12 hours a day: 'I am glad you are taking a "softly, softly" approach,' he wrote. 'Over recent months I have been to a series of "reform the whole world before breakfast" meetings.'[17]

Dunphy wrote back to Brown that he hoped a network of 30 to 40 Green Independents would stand in swinging seats in the coming federal election, to put the wind up the major parties and help get Labor back in. He continued that Green candidates for the Senate in New South Wales had proliferated, as an attempt by the Nature Conservation Council to set up a Green Electoral Network got bogged down:

The GEN just took too long. Halfway through the process Irina Dunn decided she could wait no longer and publicly announced her candidacy. The Democrats did likewise. A spurious Socialist Green group using the registered name Green Party has begun franchising the name (even in WA!) to individuals and groups who know little of the Socialist group's history. There is even an Australian Gruen party, basing its legitimacy on the sustainable agricultural practices of early German immigrants ... If the major four groups tightly exchange preferences we should seat a senator. But if the Socialist Greens and the multiplicity of 'Green' Groups confuse the voter, our interests may go down the tube. Personally I propose to vote for Irina and for the Democrats.[18]

Dunphy, like Brown, was obviously no fan of the Sydney Greens. In the event, Brown was forced to delay, twice, his planned meeting of Green Independents, then the federal election intervened. By 1990, green parties and candidates were popping up everywhere, often in competition with each other and with green-minded independents. The electoral commissioner complained to *The Australian* that he was being besieged by applications to use the term 'green', which was 'flavour of the month', and he was 'running out of fingers' to count the different parties.[19] Clearly, the wheat would have to be sorted from the chaff.

The Sydney Greens were responsible for a lot of the confusion, as custodians of the original federal registration of the Greens name. The group did not play a gatekeeper role; if anything, Tony Harris as the registered officer was too willing to afford local and interstate groups related party status under the Hawke government's new electoral laws. He would offer related party status to pretty much anyone who signed up to the four pillars – in some cases sight unseen.

From May 1989, Harris and the Sydney Greens held a string of conferences under the banner of the 'Green Political Network'. The whole point was *not* to form a traditional hierarchical party, but a 'horizontal network' of green parties. At a big meeting in September the network agreed to form a 'Green Alliance'. This would turn into a nightmare. Suddenly there was an explosion of groups, all with related party status, and all with the power, theoretically, to nominate Greens candidates in any federal seat in the country.

The Green Alliance was kept open to anyone who signed up to the four pillars, and soon key office-bearer positions were taken by members of the Socialist Workers Party. The SWP, run by brothers Jim and John Percy, was soon to be renamed the Democratic Socialist Party, after the collapse of the Soviet Union – which the Trotskyists interpreted as the defeat of loathed Stalinism. The renamed DSP launched a newspaper, the *Green Left Weekly*, a broader red-green paper to replace the party's journal of the two previous decades, *Direct Action*. Where mainstream media coverage of the emerging national greens party was inconsistent, *Green Left Weekly* wrote a huge number of articles about it.

DSP member Peter Boyle recalls, and Greenland confirms, that the party did not 'enter' but was specifically *invited* to join the Green Alliance:

> I was part of the DSP and a few of us had an informal catch-up with Hall [Greenland] and Tony [Harris], and that's where they pitched the idea that there might be an opportunity for the Greens to be a form of recruitment, because the whole eighties there had been so many attempts for various people all around the country to find a recruitment vehicle, because people were seeing there was a massive disenchantment with the major parties. A whole string of things happened – NDP was just one – literally, the eighties was one project after another being floated, most of which fell apart. The one that actually survived in the end was the Greens.
>
> Everybody was interested in a new start ... Then there's a shitfight, because you can imagine in the first few meetings, once it got going, different political forces started to show their hand and there were opportunists coming from everywhere – people who fancied themselves as politicians, put their hands up, it was like a string of weird people coming in and saying look at me, look at me. The pre-existing formations – you know, like Bob Brown's Tasmanian Greens – they all had little groups, they had fiefdoms ...

The Green Alliance was on an election footing within three months of forming, before any of these tensions could emerge. At the 1990 election, the Greens stood in 18 lower-house seats in New South Wales, with campaigns run by the local groups. Most encouraging were the eastern and inner-city electorates: Tony Harris polled 11 per cent in Sydney; a young ex-Labor lawyer from Bondi, Geoff Ash, polled 9 per cent in Wentworth, where he was up against Liberal John Hewson;

and Mark Berriman did as well in Kingsford-Smith, up against Labor stalwart Laurie Brereton. Labor took the incipient threat seriously, especially in Jeanette McHugh's seat of Phillip, where Greens candidate June Cassidy was followed home after an eastern suburbs Greens meeting was crashed by intimidating thugs, who made it clear they didn't want the Greens to run against the Labor MP. Cassidy told *The Telegraph* she was 'absolutely terrified' and withdrew the next day.[20] Generally, Greens preferences went to the Democrats, and in the lower house the majority of those flowed on to Labor.

The WA Greens ran in all 14 lower-house seats, and did better than the candidates in New South Wales, generally polling between 4 per cent and 9 per cent, but cracking double figures in Fremantle (10.6 per cent) and Curtin (10.2 per cent). Giz Watson, Robin Chapple and Dee Margetts – later MPs – all stood for the first time. Western Australia was certainly pointing the way forward. There were no Greens candidates for the House of Representatives in Victoria, or Queensland, where Hutton felt the party was "nowhere near ready". In Tasmania, Bob Brown was unwilling to access the federal registration and dragged the United Tasmania Group moniker out of deep-freeze, running in Denison and Bass. No lower-house candidates were elected.

In the Senate, apart from Jo Vallentine's triumph in Western Australia, the picture was even more of a shemozzle. In New South Wales alone, there were four competing notionally green tickets: Ian Cohen headed up the five-person 'official' team, coordinated by the Green Alliance, polling 1.9 per cent; Irina Dunn ran as an environmental independent, while the man she ousted, Robert Wood, had his last run for the NDP; finally, an oddball Illawarra scientist and black belt, Daniela Reverberi, stood for the Gruens. If there was a solid green vote in there somewhere, it was lost. Green Alliance candidates polled equally poorly in the ACT, South Australia and Victoria. In Tasmania, Bob Brown's chief of staff, Michael Lynch, stood in Tasmania, helping to elect the Democrats' Robert Bell. It was all small beer.

The bigger picture in 1990, dubbed the 'Green election', was the influence of the broader environmental movement, which backed Labor even more heavily this time around, helping the party overcome its worst primary vote since the war and saving Hawke from a resurgent Liberal Party under the moderate Andrew Peacock. The powerbrokers of the ACF – particularly, this time, Phillip Toyne – and the TWS decided that the green parties did not have a cohesive identity, and instead ran a $100,000 'Vote for the Environment' campaign, distributing 800,000 leaflets in ten key marginals, recommending the ALP in the lower house and a vote for the Democrats in the Senate, with two important exceptions: the UTG in Tasmania and Jo Vallentine standing as a Green in Western Australia. Greens and Green Independents alike were marginalised. Some 1.25 million Australians put the Democrats first in the Senate, where the party achieved its best-ever result of 12.6 per cent, enough to elect five new senators, which took their representation to eight and ensured they retained the sole balance of power.

In a column for *The Sydney Morning Herald*, journalist Robert Haupt vented his frustration at the 'How Green is my polly?' exercise going on in electorates around the country in the 1990 election, and excoriated Hawke and Richardson (and Peacock and Haines, for that matter) for giving the environmental movement an effective veto on investment projects, while 'concealing the economic cost from voters'. He called it the 'Big Green Lie', likening it to the Big Tariff Lie, which had protected Australian manufacturing jobs for decades but slugged consumers with higher prices and lower-quality goods. 'How much of our dismal performance is due to the green veto?' Haupt asked.

> We made progress against the Big Tariff Lie when our economic outlook was so diabolically grim that it had to be addressed. When unemployment re-emerges as our central economic concern (yes, you guessed it: after the election), our appetite for the truth may be sharper. Who knows? Maybe Senator Richardson won't have to do so much bushwalking.[21]

The 1990 election increased pressure for a consistent national approach, and the Green Alliance decided to freeze further applications. The effect was to ratchet up tension in the alliance, particularly between the original libertarian Greens like Tony Harris and Hall Greenland, and the DSP stalwarts. Harris now wrote to all federally registered green parties:

> It has become obvious that the DSP (SWP) has set out to aggres-
> sively colonise as much of the registration process as it can get its
> hands on; a clear double standard when one sets their own cen-
> tralist and authoritarian structure against what is supposed to be
> a decentralised grassroots process.[22]

Members dug out the clauses in the DSP constitution that required members to be loyal to the DSP and to 'reject any conflicting political loyalty, to place all of their political activity under the direction of the party'. Any work for non-DSP organisations and movements had to be at the direction of the DSP branch, and 'in accordance with the program, policies and decisions of the party'. Danny Bessel, one of the original Sydney Greens, wrote: 'The Greens in WA, SA, Sydney electorate and rural NSW now found themselves allied in name to members of an old-fashioned hierarchical Socialist Party, with a contrary world view, inhibiting our electoral growth.'[23]

The Green Alliance might simply have folded in on itself, collapsing under the weight of left sectarianism, but by early 1991 the environment movement was also pushing for a national greens party. Bitterly let down by Labor's resource security legislation, introduced in November, which gave loggers guaranteed, long-term access to huge swathes of old-growth forest, the ACF in particular believed that Hawke had broken a promise given in private to Phillip Toyne and president Peter Garrett.

Janet Rice, of the Conservation Council of Victoria, was another who felt let down. She had spent long days negotiating the terms of an agreement with Graham Richardson's office, and was promised a process that would have protected further East Gippsland forest areas if there were 'prudent and feasible alternatives' to logging. It was all set out in a letter from the Commonwealth to the Victorian government. 'I distinctly remember the phone conversation with Richo,' recalls Rice, 'with him telling me, "Don't worry, Janet, those national estate forests will never be logged," you know, "Trust me."' Straight after the 1990 election, however, with Richardson out of the environment portfolio, Rice had called the office, only to discover that 'this letter that we had been promised was only ever a draft, it had never been signed, never been sent'.

> I was devastated. He had lied to me. [So] of course it ended up
> there were no 'prudent and feasible' alternatives to logging this
> forest so we'll just go on and keep logging it and they're still doing
> it to this very day. It was a really pivotal moment for me and it
> came on the back of having put my faith in Labor politics and
> advocacy and trusting that Labor could actually deliver on sus-
> tainability … and being sold out. And I thought, well, we can't
> rely upon Labor to deliver …

For his part, Richardson says the greenies never realised how hard he had fought, inside the Hawke cabinet, for the forests, against the likes of Peter Walsh and John Button; if Rice felt betrayed, he told me bluntly, 'I don't care.' He had done as much as he could.

*   *   *

February 1991 marked the first meeting of what would become known as the Melbourne Group, which gave new impetus to the formation of a national green party. The secretive process was instigated by Drew Hutton, who had flown to Hobart to have dinner with Bob Brown the previous year. They'd agreed it was time to put behind them the bitter experience of the Getting Together conference five years earlier. The Melbourne Group began with 13 people, including Hutton, Brown, Jo Vallentine, Phillip Sutton from the Labor Party, and representatives from the ACF, the TWS and the Rainbow Alliance, a Victorian umbrella body convened in 1987 by influential political scientist Joseph Camilleri.

(Rather than contest elections, the Rainbow Alliance hoped to mount a broad challenge to the economic rationalism of the Hawke/ Keating ALP – which they dubbed 'Another Liberal Party'. The idea was not to compete with the emerging Greens, but to involve them. A cartoon in their newsletter captured it: 'Green is only *one* colour in our rainbow,' one guy says to the other, holding up a Rainbow Alliance banner.)

Bob Brown used the Melbourne Group to explore two quite different options: to try again to form a national green party, but if that didn't work, to unite the Green Independents with the Democrats. Brown's clear preference was for the latter. Weighing the pros and cons of this, a 1991 five-page memo by Brown noted that the Democrats had 'thoroughly Green policies across the board' but were 'thin on the ground and not well enough connected to the grassroots community groups'.[24] Part of Brown's thinking was that it would be better if Greens and Democrats did not stand against each other. At the February meeting of the Melbourne Group, Brown 'spoke of his recent talks with all eight Democrat Senators … [who] were all very keen for the Greens to merge with them'.

At an 'ecopolitics' conference in early April in Sydney, Brown made some widely reported comments along the same lines in a session with Janet Powell and the anti-nuclear activist Dr Helen Caldicott. Caldicott had formerly headed up a Green Labor faction, but quit in 1990 to stand in the northern New South Wales seat of Richmond as a Green Independent, where she'd polled a stunning 23 per cent. Brown was bullish: 'The question now, to me, is not whether we're going to have a cohesive national green force, but when,' he said, adding: 'The sooner, the better.' He also canvassed unification with the Democrats, which had adopted the four pillars of the German Greens into its charter. 'We have a green party which calls itself the Democrats,' he said, predicting that a national green party would emerge 'in parallel with the Democrats', and then would be followed by a 'merger of those two forces into a united green alternative for Australia'.

Brown had first approached Don Chipp about a merger between the Democrats, the Tasmanian Greens and the NDP in 1986, but was rejected outright.[25] Now he was trying again. Democrats leader Janet Powell and her deputy, John Coulter, went to Tasmania to talk with Brown and the other Tasmanian Greens, and came up with a plan for a plebiscite among both Democrats and Greens on whether to form the 'Green Democrats'. In 1991 Powell described the proposal as 'the major focus of my work this year'.[26] There were deep reservations on the Greens' side, however. Drew Hutton, who supported Brown, eventually decided the grassroots members 'just didn't feel happy about joining it … what it came down to was [that] most people wouldn't follow us'.

Any hope of a merger was effectively scuttled when Coulter deposed Powell as leader, in what he describes as one of the most difficult decisions of his life. The details of the change are murky, but it marked a distinct shift in direction for the Democrats, particularly as Queensland senator Cheryl Kernot was promoted to deputy leader. 'My leadership challenge wasn't [intended] to knock off the merger with the Greens,' recalls Coulter, 'but the effect of it was to bring Cheryl more quickly through the ranks.' When it came to a merger with the Greens, Coulter says Kernot 'didn't want a bar of it'. Coulter still believes it was a good idea: 'There might've been a split with the ideological left, and a stronger environmental party would've formed.' But after this, the relationship between the Greens and Democrats soured. From now on they would be out-and-out rivals.

Tony Harris could see that his vision for a decentralised party of the left was fading, and resigned as the NSW Greens' registered officer. What he sometimes called 'parliamentary cretinism' – blind pursuit of electoral success – had no appeal. He fired off a gloomy one-page letter to all green parties: renewed optimism about a national party was occurring 'at a time when I am personally questioning much about Green politics; and party and electoral politics generally'.[27] In another letter copied to all green parties, Harris wrote: 'Frankly, I have doubts as whether the word "green" can continue to be useful in describing my politics.'[28] Much of Harris's pessimism was driven by what was happening overseas: Die Grünen suffered their first major reversal at the 1990 elections, falling back under 5 per cent and losing representation in the Bundestag. The pragmatists were taking over, after years of internecine conflict between the realos and the fundis. For Harris, the party was over – literally before it had begun.

Bob Brown flew to Sydney and met Harris at his home, to make sure the DSP did not take control of the Greens. Harris handed over the registration and appointed Steve Brigham, a no-nonsense British psychologist from the Illawarra Greens, in his place, and bowed out altogether. Harris's sudden resignation and the appointment of Brigham as registered officer would soon be challenged internally, creating a giant legal headache for the party.

Brown, Vallentine, Brigham, Hutton and Greenland – who would become known as the five convenors – wrote to all registered green parties proposing a two-day conference in Sydney, not to debate *whether* to form a national Greens party, but *how*. As a starting point they attached an 11-page outline, 'Towards the Formation of a National Greens Organisation'. The rationale was simple:

> The last decade has seen the ALP largely abandon its tradition of progressive politics, leaving a power vacuum which has yet to be filled ... We therefore find ourselves with a convergence of factors representing the opportunity for a new broad-based green/progressive political organisation. Historically this is similar to the situation the labor movement was in at the turn of the [twentieth] century.[29]

First and foremost, a new organisation – to be called 'The Greens' – was needed to coordinate effective federal election campaigns 'within society as it exists' (a passing shot at the revolutionary socialists). It was not to be called 'The Green Party', as everyone felt the word 'party' smacked of establishment politics. Four structural options were considered: a loose network; a confederation, without overriding powers being vested in the national organisation, except by consent of the autonomous groups; a federation, which defined the powers of the national and constituent bodies; and a unitary organisation, in which constituent groups became branches. Brown, Hutton and Vallentine favoured the middle options – confederation or federation. The single most important issue was whether to proscribe members of rival political parties: 'We note that the broader movement has proved unwilling to countenance any green party which admits to membership the members of another party'.

The members reacted badly. There was particular concern, stoked by *Green Left Weekly*, at the private meetings of the Melbourne Group, whose attendees were anonymous and which did not issue minutes. How could an anonymous group be the source of any mandate, or given representation at a conference? The five convenors responded that the only reason certain names had been withheld was that 'they are, in the main, closely associated with non-party political organisations and are understandably cautious about being publicly associated with the possible formation of a political party'. This only fanned the speculation. Was Peter Garrett involved? Yes, as it turns out. A handwritten letter from Brown to activist Sue Arnold confirms Garrett was a member of the group, and went on: 'I've been talking with these people about the future of green politics since the early '80s and they must be included as we go along this path.'[30] Jack Mundey, too, went to an early meeting. According to the summary transcript, he stirred things up by observing that the 'weakness of ecologically oriented people is [their] failure to develop economic policy alternatives. MUST do this. Can't allow Trotskyist groups around the country to take agenda ... we have to grasp the nettle.'[31] Drew Hutton hoped Mundey would be a Greens candidate, sooner or later.

The May meeting date originally proposed by the Melbourne Group was badly timed too, clashing with the New South Wales election that same month, so it was deferred until August.

The election was a nailbiter. Eight green candidates ran in the lower house, polling between 4 per cent and 13 per cent and generally running third or fourth. The Greens' main game was in the upper house, where Ian Cohen polled 3.3 per cent, or more than 106,000 primary votes – 40,000 more than the NSW Greens vote in the Senate campaign a year earlier. Cohen wanted to run a grown-up (rather than stunt-driven) campaign, but as he wrote later, '[T]his presumption of sufficient political maturity ... fell flat on its face. Greens press releases piled high on every news desk but the media refused to show even the remotest interest.'[32] Cohen went excruciatingly close to beating the Call to Australia Party's Fred Nile for the last seat in the Legislative Council, and the count drew out for a month in what became known as 'the battle of heaven and earth'.

In early May, two weeks out from the New South Wales election, the five convenors proposed a new early August date to resume talks on a national green party, and called for options and a pre-meeting ballot on how many people should attend from each registered party, from the Tasmanian Greens and from the Melbourne Group, and how many votes they should each be entitled to. The DSP-aligned Green Alliance groups in New South Wales, the ACT and Victoria reacted angrily. In mid-June the five convenors called the entire process off, sending out a one-page letter:

These responses plus the coloured coverage give to the proposal to form a national green organisation in the DSP publication, *Green Left Weekly*, have led us to conclude that the August meeting in its proposed form would result in confrontation and a subsequent stalemate given the disproportionate presence of the DSP among the 14 registered green groups.

In a June article, Cassandra Pybus wrote that Brown was not about to climb into bed with elements of the doctrinaire left (specifically the DSP) who had recently metamorphosed into a rash of small green parties: 'He has not the time nor the inclination to engage in endless dialogue to find the organic political expression for the grassroots environmental movement while the planet is going down the gurgler.'[33] Jo Vallentine, still in the Senate, but fearing a rerun of the 1985 NDP national conference, wrote a plaintive five-page letter, explaining that 'some of the feedback from groups and/or individuals is disturbingly similar in terms of names, arguments and tactics to what I have experienced before':

> The NDP had always (except in WA) been open to all comers and the SWP (now the DSP) were in there, working very hard on the campaign in most states, while also still fielding their own SWP candidates. I didn't object to the SWP/DSP policies, and I admire the dedication of their members, but I object to their tactics of entryism ... Surely we should have learned the lesson of the NDP, which is that proscription should be absolute, across the country. How can members of another political party be loyal to a green political party?

Jim Percy himself responded with a two-page letter, published in *Green Left Weekly*, which confirmed the revolutionary objectives of the party, and revealed a lacklustre commitment to parliamentary democracy. Percy denied that the then SWP tried to make a takeover bid for the NDP, blamed Vallentine for the party's implosion and then moved on to why the DSP was involved with the Greens:

Firstly, unlike most (if not all?) other left parties in this country, our view of the ecological crisis is fundamental … we don't think either the planet or human society can be changed without a total transformation in the way we produce, consume and live. This will involve mobilisation of millions in action. Parliament, especially as presently controlled and run, is secondary to this. Nor will the struggle be single-issue. It can't win if it's limited to environmental questions as such. Human society and human oppression form a whole. It's this outlook that attracted us to the sort of thinking put forward by the German Greens, at least in their first decade. Our view was that if a similar party could emerge here, we would be part of it …

We can achieve lesser things – a few more seats, one or two reforms … but we'll still be back where we started. Forgive us if we reject such 'credible', 'effective' realism, we're still demanding the impossible.

Clearly, the DSP would not be backing down.

Nevertheless, the five convenors proposed a date to meet in mid-August. The invitation letter spelled out that all delegates should (a) be in favour of some form of national organisation and (b) agree to some form of proscription of members of other political parties. DSP members decided to turn up anyway, flouting the invitation. The very first motion was to kick them out, with a proposal 'that all delegates not be members of any nationally registered political parties which are not Green parties'. It was passed by a two-thirds majority – 21 for, eight against, one abstention. The meeting could not get past the issue.

Hutton describes the meeting, held at the Powerhouse Museum on the fringe of the CBD, as the 'worst two days of my life'. He got a migraine on the Saturday night and spent the whole of Sunday lying at the back of the hall, moaning. Hutton jokes that the NSW Greens, who favoured a decentralised network of autonomous local green parties, wanted 'a greens party in every shared household', and says it was impossible to get agreement on structure or anything else:

It was horrific, because there must have been at least a dozen, possibly more, groups, all with the name Green, all registered with the AEC, all representing totally contradictory elements. There was the green party in every shared household group, there were the Trots, there were the WA greens, there were the national greens – Bob and me and the others – so, four different groups represented in that meeting. To give Bob his credit, he stayed debating with them till the end of Sunday. I was, meantime, writhing with the worst migraine of my life.

The meeting put the original NSW Greens in a quandary. As Hall Greenland tells it, their view was that any national green party simply had to include the Tasmanians – the militants of the environmental movement who had saved the Franklin, stopped Wesley Vale and so on. But there remained a gulf between the NSW Greens and the Tasmanian Greens. According to Greenland:

> The bad blood existed, from my point of view, in the suspicions and hostility that came from people like Bob. Bob's not from a very political background – he's a country doctor, he's an environmentalist, from a small town, in a small state. We're big-city types from the labor movement, we're from Marxism, from the left, we're infighters, we're trench fighters, we've got an exotic political culture. Bob sees us as bomb-throwing extremists of some sort. We see him as someone who was a bit populist, a bit lightweight politically. That's why he wouldn't join us, [he thought] we were reds and weren't legitimate, from his point of view. We thought he was too moderate and not revolutionary enough and so on but, for god's sake, we knew the greens could not exist in Australia as a valid and effective force without Bob Brown being in it, in the 1980s and 1990s, and I think we were right.

Brown was negotiating from a position of much greater strength than in 1986, and the fallback possibility of a Democrats merger must have played on a few minds as well.

There were also principles involved. Geoff Ash, who was becoming a key organiser for the NSW Greens, recalls that Brown was effectively insisting delegates agree to form an Australian Greens party, with proscription, right there and then: 'It was extremely demanding and I was quite shocked because of course representatives didn't have authority to do that; they were there representing their groups ... Bob was demanding that basically those reps defy their local groups. It was actually quite stunning.' In fairness, that was the whole point of the meeting. In the end, a compromise was agreed by more than the required two-thirds majority: another meeting would be held in six months' time, on the basis that there would be proscription of members of other parties.[34]

The gauntlet had been thrown down, and Ash recalls that 'it caused the DSP to really react'. There came a point where Ash had to choose which side he was on. Green Registration Committee meetings had become utterly dysfunctional. The last straw came on 1 March 1992, when Ash and Doug Hine found themselves two of only three non-DSP members in a Green Alliance meeting of 19 that adopted a proposal assuming control of the state registration of the party. Outraged at such a blatant stack, both men walked out in disgust as soon as the first motion was put and they realised what was happening. It was all highly personal. Ash and Hine were walking out on branch members they knew well, some from their own branches, whom they had campaigned alongside but who had kept their DSP membership secret. Ash recalls:

> When they did that – when they took over the Green Alliance and stacked out a meeting – I realised there was entrism going on. At that point I decided they'd gone too far, and I did work hard with Steve [Brigham] and others to bring about proscription in the Greens, because I wanted to free the greens of the DSP from then on.

In a lightning move, Ash nominated the two co-secretaries as the Greens' registered officer with the commission. Both sides went straight to the commission, which, after submissions and a hearing, rejected the DSP's arguments. 'They decided we were the real greens,' says Ash.

The same battles were fought out state by state, group by group, as the Greens and the DSP disentangled themselves. Brigham wrote to the Australian Electoral Commission on 19 May and disaffiliated the DSP 'front' groups from the party, including the Green Alliance offshoots in the ACT and Victoria, plus a number of local Sydney groups, including the Western Suburbs Greens and the Greens in Lowe. Those branches would wither on the vine – grassroots members who were not DSP quickly worked out what was going on and resigned or stopped turning up. It took years, but most groups were ultimately deregistered for lack of members. Other groups that went on to unite under the Greens NSW banner decided to relinquish their AEC registration.

For those members of the DSP who had put so much work into the Greens, the adoption of proscription was a bitter pill. In one stirring letter, Brisbane-based journalist Karen Fletcher – who had stood for the Green Alliance in Breakfast Creek, and worked on Drew Hutton's lord mayoral campaign – complained that 'even the ALP tolerates the odd socialist in the branches. Bob Hawke used to say he was one, as did the current Governor General ... yet, in the "high profile" Green movement one cannot be a socialist.'

> Even on a pragmatic level this witch-hunt does not make sense ... green socialists were the driving force behind [the campaign] and have done the 'shitwork' on the ground for dozens of other green projects in Australia. The 'high profiles' know this to be true, and have been happy to give flowery speeches at fundraising dinners while the odious 'doctrinaire left' slave away in the kitchen and sell tickets at the door ... Alienation of the DSP and other left parties will not quicken the pace towards formation of a Green force in national politics. It will, rather, remove a whole layer of committed campaigners for a just and ecologically sustainable society from the 'official' movement ... It will not cause the masses to come flooding into an 'official' green party, ready to do the bidding of the Melbourne Group, profile or no profile. Formation of a party takes more than a few stars and a couple of articles in the Sunday Supplements. It takes a large group of committed people, a lot of work on the ground and, above all, a democratic process.[35]

Socialism per se wasn't the issue, of course – the problem was dual membership. Anyone was free to renounce their DSP membership and join the Greens, and plenty did. It was a significant but necessary battle, which paved the way for formation of the national party. For Jo Vallentine and Bob Brown, it was a straightforward reform, long overdue, and there would be no looking back. Steve Brigham just wanted to get on with it, as he wrote in one update: 'We will be, are, a political party ... Rightly or wrongly, we feel that it is worth giving the parliamentary politics system a "fair go" and that it may be possible for us to get the Green agenda through this notoriously unbending and unimaginative pillar of Establishment.'[36]

In Victoria, where energies had been diverted by the grand Rainbow Alliance, a state election was looming. Janet Rice was a key driver, working alongside Peter Christoff and Margaret Blakers. After her sharp disillusionment with Labor, Rice had joined the Democrats at the urging of Sid Spindler. In a 1991 circular from the Conservation Council headed 'Green State Election Strategy', Rice wrote that there was little support for a separate green party in Victoria, but some support for the Democrats to become the 'big green third force' and 'perhaps even second force!!'.[37] But her enthusiasm evaporated after leader Janet Powell was torn down. Rice felt the Democrats were too divided, between the progressives like Spindler and Powell, and those in the Don Chipp mould, who were small-L liberals. 'We needed the Greens!' Rice recalls.

The key meeting that agreed in principle to form a Victorian Greens did not take place until 7 November 1992 – and was held under a tree in the Darling Gardens, in inner-city Collingwood, because somebody forgot the key to the community centre. Before then the Victorians were fully focused on the October election, amid a major backlash against Labor that would sweep Joan Kirner from power and usher in Jeff Kennett as premier. Without time to establish a party, the focus was on setting up a 'Green Politics Network' to rate and potentially endorse candidates. The exercise was exceptionally rigorous: out of 70 questions put to all 444 candidates, Labor scored well with 60 ticks, the Coalition only 21, while the Democrats starred with 65. Two Green Independents stood: Jenny Saulwick, who was personally endorsed by Bob Brown for the safe Liberal country seat of Monbulk, and Colleen Hartland, much later a Greens MLC, in the western-suburbs seat of Footscray. Hartland was at first reluctant to join a Greens party that was so disorganised it had to meet under a tree.

A last-minute hurdle came with the lodgement of a claim for a review in the Administrative Appeals Tribunal (AAT) of the appointment of Steve Brigham as registered officer of the Greens, back in 1991. What hurt most was that the claimant, WA Greens member Chris Williams, a lawyer, was the partner of Christabel Chamarette, by now in the Senate. Chamarette was herself a delegated observer to the talks about a national green party, which put her in a difficult position – it was arguably bad faith.

In a personal note, Bob Brown wrote to Chamarette, saying it was 'ungreen' for Williams to have launched the action without contacting anyone first. 'We will have enough opponents throwing grenades into the Greens, without [more coming] from the inside,' he wrote.[38] The WA Greens said they could not force Williams to withdraw his action, which he'd brought in an individual capacity. Drew Hutton claims that Williams, who argued against proscription of the DSP, had a deal with Jim Percy to frustrate the formation of the Australian Greens. Earlier on, Williams had raised the resignation of Tony Harris and the appointment of Brigham with the Australian Electoral Commission. The commission had okayed the appointment but made an error, overlooking the fact that the Greens were already a parliamentary party in 1991, because they had representation in the Senate courtesy of Jo Vallentine, meaning they ought to be considered under different provisions of the electoral laws. Nothing whatsoever turned on this, but Williams tried to argue in the AAT that the commission's error meant not only that Brigham's original appointment was invalid, but also that the actions he had taken in his official capacity were invalid – including proscription of the DSP-aligned green groups.

It fell to Geoff Ash, himself a lawyer, to handle the Greens' drawn-out response to the claim. He did not mince words before the tribunal, calling Williams a saboteur. Bob Lamb of the Green Party SA joined in the action, backing Williams. The case deepened the divide between Western Australia and South Australia on the one hand, and the eastern states on the other. It was an exhausting and costly drag on the party, and it continued even after Brigham had quit as registered officer to run for the Senate in 1993. In 1995 the AAT finally ruled that the pointless case was vexatious.[39] Today, Brown describes it as 'a torpedo that, had it worked, would have exploded the Greens experiment, for good, in Australia'.

*   *   *

As the battles over proscription were going on throughout 1992, an Australian Greens Steering Group was meeting frequently, working up a draft constitution that had got to version six by the middle of the year. The possibility that the new prime minister, Paul Keating, might call a snap election at any time added urgency to the process. The structure envisaged was a confederation of state bodies, each guided by its own constitution, consistent and compatible with the national constitution. The Tasmanian Greens, led by Bob Brown, and the Queensland Greens, led by Drew Hutton, were aligned. Brown and Hutton originally wanted a strong national organisation and strong local groups, with state bodies in full control of state affairs, but merely a clearing house in national affairs rather than a power base. 'What we got in the end was a compromise, and it's haunted us really,' says Hutton. 'We ended up with the worst of all possible worlds: a confederation of state-based parties.'

On the New South Wales side, much of the negotiations were handled by Geoff Ash, who says that, without the largest and oldest state, 'it would've just been Tasmania and Queensland'. Ash wanted an Australian Greens established, but not on the model that Brown was putting up. New South Wales was constantly pushing for more power for the states. So the constitution eventually included a clause stating that 'within the Greens, state parties and their constituent groups will have the autonomy to make decisions relating to their own affairs'. Ash explains:

> We didn't want a top-down structure where a smaller body at the centre, or a smaller group of individuals at the centre, would be telling state parties what to do. We'd grown up, we'd been a state party effectively running our own race for a long time, and we wanted to retain that ... So we kept powers about membership, deciding preferences, preselecting candidates, control of finances ... all the key things.

By August 1992 the building blocks for the formation of the Australian Greens were almost in place, and planning was well advanced for a two-day meeting to formally establish the new party. There was one major sticking point left: whether or not Greens MPs should be allowed a conscience vote – as was the case in the Democrats, for example, and in the Australia Party before them.

For the Tasmanian Greens, it was almost an article of faith. In her memoir, Christine Milne writes that she:

> … had never been able to understand how people could stand in a parliament and vote against what they believed was right because the party said so. I would not then, nor would I now, join a political party that did not allow its elected members a conscience vote on every issue, because every issue has at its heart a values dimension.[40]

For the NSW Greens, the conscience vote was elitist, and completely at odds with the Greens' fourth pillar, grassroots democracy. If anything, the NSW view was more in line with that of ALP, which also binds its MPs – leading to Menzies' famous accusation that 'faceless men' held the real power in the party. It was a genuine difference in worldview: were the MPs delegates of the members, or representatives?

The standoff was not resolved until the Friday night before the weekend meeting, at a café in King Street, Newtown, where an awkward compromise was reached: there would be a carve-out. The conscience vote clauses would not apply to the NSW Greens, whose MPs would be bound to stick to the policies drawn up by party members, no ifs, no buts.

The compromise has stuck for almost three decades now, but it still rankles. Geoff Ash says the carve-out 'was quite a compromise for the Greens NSW. Many of us are still not happy that we can adopt national policy and MPs from other states can just run their own race and vote against it in Parliament, you know, that doesn't thrill us.' Bob Brown, who by 1992 had spent almost a decade in parliament, took a different view then and still holds it today:

Drew and I and our colleagues felt that ultimately in some matters there would be cases where people would need to exercise their conscience because they just could not go along with the dictates of their party, it would always be on issues of human ethics – abortion, sexuality, gene technology – they're examples. Ultimately we're all going to have some sticking point, whether children should be immunised [Brown thinks they should be], or whatever. There ultimately comes a time when a person has to be able to say, to the party, I cannot in conscience vote for this. You have to determine whether you want to keep me, or not.

With the final sticking point removed, the founding conference powered ahead. There were four delegates from Tasmania, led by Brown; four from Queensland, led by Hutton; and four from New South Wales, led by Brigham. Observers were not allowed to speak without permission. On the Saturday morning they got straight down to business: the charter and constitution were adopted on 29 August, as amended the night before; so too the next day's media release; a list of proscribed political parties was agreed upon; working parties were set up to steer the looming federal election campaign, policy and organisational development, and legal matters. Office bearers were elected the next day: Hazen Waller from Victoria was the first convenor, Doug Hine from New South Wales the first national secretary. A sliding scale of membership fees – from $5 for unwaged to $15 for high-waged – was calculated to meet an expected national expenditure of $30,000–$50,000 a year. An October date was set for the party's first national council meeting. On election strategy, Cunningham and Newcastle were considered favourable lower-house seats for the Greens in New South Wales. The minutes record an interesting note: 'It was stated that Peter Garrett was interested in standing for a house of representatives seat, possibly Manly.' Here was the culmination of 20 years' work, from the beginnings of the United Tasmania Group in 1972, via the Sydney Greens and the NDP flameout in the 1980s, to the creation, at last, of the Australian Greens in 1992.

Brown has often told the story: at 1 p.m. on the Sunday, at the community centre in Lavender Bay, North Sydney, at a press conference to mark a new era in Australia politics, not one television crew turned up.[41] The Sydney Harbour Tunnel was opening that same day, and it was front-page news. Flanked by Greens from six states, Brown told the grim bunch of journos that 'with 25 per cent of Australians telling the pollsters they want to avoid voting Liberal or Labor, we offer the electorate the choice of abandoning the two-party system which has failed us'. Brown announced that the party would not give a carte blanche on preferences to a particular party, but would instead allow individual candidates to decide which of the two leading parties to support.

The next day's coverage was modest: a few hundred words here and there on the inside pages. *The Australian* and *The Sydney Morning Herald* both led their stories with a bold claim by Drew Hutton, who said that with the great shift to the right in Australian politics, the Greens would put concern for ordinary people back into the equation. 'We are not on about developing a little niche in Australian politics,' he added. 'We expect that within the next decade there will be Green governments at various levels all around Australia.'[42]

The stake was in the ground.

CHAPTER 5

BREAKING THROUGH

Barely four weeks after the Australian Greens formed, the world's best-known Green, Petra Kelly, was shot dead by her partner, retired general Gert Bastian. He fired a single bullet from his service revolver into her left temple as she lay in bed, and then shot himself in the crown of the head. The gruesome mystery of Kelly's death – was it murder or a suicide pact? – has never been resolved.

The violence of Kelly's death shocked Greens in Germany and worldwide. It is no exaggeration to say that in the course of her eight fiery years in the Bundestag, Kelly inspired millions in her campaign against nuclear war and for ecology, including in Australia.

Bob Brown issued a press release lauding Kelly as a remarkable advocate for planet Earth, from Red Square to Pine Gap, and calling her a 'driving force for nascent green politics around the world'. Brown's archives hold touching, handwritten letters from the German activist, and photos from the time they spent together in Australia. In an obituary, he wrote that Kelly had 'enveigled [sic] us to get a Greens party going' in 1984. His last note from her, a postcard written a fortnight before her death, congratulated him on the formation of the Australian Greens, and talked about how she planned to run for the European Parliament in 1994. It did not read like a postcard from someone about to end it all.

The truth, however, was that both Kelly and the party she had founded were at a low point. In Germany's December 1990 election, the first held since reunification, the popular vote for Die Grünen had fallen from 8.3 per cent to 4.8 per cent, below the minimum 5 per cent threshold for the party list, meaning the party lost all 42 seats it held in the Bundestag. Only the Greens in Germany's new eastern states, a quite separate organisation, were successful, winning eight seats.

For Kelly, the 1990 electoral drubbing was both expected and well deserved. Her party was 'unable to stop its endless, internal power battles and quarrels and headed thus into political suicide'.[1] Kelly herself had no chance at a third term in parliament, despite being the highest-profile spokesperson. As she wrote to Brown, she had lost out in preselection 'because the Realo pro-SPD wing made quite sure that I would not get a safe seat because of my radical views on ecology, on human rights and on disarmament'.

In February 1991, as the first Iraq War raged, Kelly wrote a 12-page open letter to Die Grünen (and she later sent a translation to Brown, noting, 'Maybe it can help you in Australia not to make the same mistakes as we did.'[2] The letter opened: 'In the midst of a war in the Gulf it is very difficult to sit calmly at one's desk and mull over the Greens' past mistakes and omissions.' For Kelly, the war had proved her party right: the Greens had revealed criminal shipments of nuclear, biological and chemical weapons components to Iraq, warned about just such ecological catastrophes of war as the 1.5 million tonnes of crude dumped into the Persian Gulf, and published an 'almost prophetic peace manifesto' highlighting the 'devastating consequences of a lifestyle and manufacturing methods which are based on a steady flow of natural resources, squandering them recklessly and then resorting to violent appropriation of foreign raw materials'. The conflict was, for Kelly, a 'harbinger of further crises which will arise in future in the struggle for increasingly scarce resources'.

The question remained: why had German voters deserted the Greens, turning away from their far-sighted ecological policies just as the party was being vindicated, not just by the Iraq conflict but by recent developments including Chernobyl, Bhopal and the accelerating greenhouse effect? 'However much it hurts to say so, it was not that the voters failed to understand us,' Kelly wrote. 'On the contrary, we ourselves were to blame ... eight years of self-destructive and fruitless infighting among the various factions and their gurus paralysed our political activities and created an atmosphere steeped in jealousy and distrust.' Kelly wrote that the party needed to stop abuse of the fourth pillar, grassroots democracy: 'Grassroots is not merely a collective term defining the people who are present at a particular moment and consider themselves to represent the grassroots.'

Kelly harked back to the extraordinary damage done when a Greens branch in North Rhine–Westphalia managed to insert a proposal into the party platform to legalise sex between adults and children. It was a clear example of 'the dictatorship of a minority passing itself off as a "grassroots democracy",' she wrote. She also called on the party to professionalise its policymaking, by setting up a think tank of experts, and to appoint experienced and competent media spokespeople:

> We have to try to brighten up our party's image, because until now we have appeared unremittingly gloomy and intolerant. We are no longer able to laugh and show a bit of enthusiasm and zest for life. This is particularly evident at the national party conferences, and it is very depressing.

The core strategic dilemma for Die Grünen was whether to go into coalition with one of the major parties – generally, but not always, Germany's Social Democratic Party (SPD) – and this was the nub of the debate between the party's ideological and dogmatic fundis, and the compromising and pragmatic realos. Die Grünen were divided between those who wanted always to remain a party of protest and those who wanted to be a party of government, and the debate in Germany provided a template of sorts for green parties around the world, including in Australia. Although there was not initially a straightforward left–right split in Die Grünen, the fundi wing was eventually dominated by socialists, and the realo wing by those who favoured a reformist, green capitalism.

Right from the beginning, before entering parliament, Kelly had said that 'if the Greens one day start sending ministers to Bonn, then that's no longer the party I set out to build'.[3] Kelly always had grave doubts about joining a red-green coalition with the SPD, particularly if it meant supporting NATO, the clincher in the early 1980s. On that score, at least, she was regarded as a 'real fundamentalist', as Sara Parkin wrote in her 1988 book *Green Parties*, citing a typical Kelly rant:

> There is not a little bit of cancer or a little bit of malnutrition or
> a little bit of death or a little bit of social injustice or a little bit of

torture. It does not help us in any way if we begin accepting lower and safer levels of, for example, radioactivity, or lower and safer levels of, for example, lead or dioxin. We must speak out clearly, loudly and courageously if we know that there are no safe levels.[4]

The realo position was championed by Joschka Fischer, a former communist and student radical from Frankfurt, who was one of the first Greens elected to the Bundestag in 1983. Fischer became environment and energy minister in Germany's first red-green coalition state government with the SPD, despite what one historian describes as their 'notoriously cosy relations with "dirty" nuclear-power and pharmaceutical companies'.[5] This was hugely contentious inside Die Grünen. The fundis got organised in response to what they saw as Fischer's 'coup' and, galvanised by the 1986 Chernobyl disaster, passed a resolution to end all use of nuclear power and terminate the coalition. Fischer was ultimately sacked by SPD premier Holger Boerner, and the coalition was wiped out entirely in state elections in 1987, after what became known as the 'red-green chaos'. Fischer survived, publicly abandoning his earlier radicalism in a 1989 book which declared that 'ecological reform of the industrial system will be determined by the existing economic mode of Western capitalism'.[6] (As we shall see, he would later re-enter federal politics with spectacular success, rising to become Germany's long-serving foreign minister and vice-chancellor.)

Kelly wrote to Brown of her disappointment in Die Grünen, noting that all revolutions eat their fathers and mothers. She did not mean it of herself, but she may as well have. After her death, Brown was asked to pen a tribute for the ACF's *Habitat* magazine, and he dug out a 1986 quote from Kelly herself:

We are looking for a new power, power shared with others, not power exercised to gain control over them. Feminism, ecology and nonviolence belong together and are interrelated. But at the same time, we must be watchful that, while we struggle together against the big war, the little war in our everyday life is not forgotten – the little war being raged against the weak, the handicapped, the elderly, against children and women. All of us must be concerned with both levels: the big and the little war waged against us as individuals, against smaller countries, against the planetary environment, every single day. Resistance to war, to the use of nuclear weapons and nuclear energy, is impossible without resistance to sexism, to racism, to imperialism, and to violence as an everyday pervasive reality. There is a very profound relationship between the fact that many women and children are commonly attacked, beaten up, and raped, and that a nuclear war as well as a nuclear catastrophe threatens this entire planet Earth, which has no emergency exit.[7]

*   *   *

Back in Australia, the Greens were on an election footing from the moment their formation was announced at the end of August 1992. Two weeks later, asked by then opposition leader John Hewson why he wouldn't call an early election, Prime Minister Paul Keating famously replied: 'The answer is, mate, because I want to do you slowly.'[8] A campaign committee was set up, initially headed by the NSW Greens' Geoff Ash, and the party pulled together a 12-page election program summarising its principles and policies. 'The Greens have a long-term objective of "green" government,' the program declared, 'but in the meantime, Greens are a new force in Australian politics with the ideas, the people and the commitment to work with all Australians for major changes in direction.'[9]

As it is the first platform for the party's first federal election campaign, this document is worth picking over. The Greens' economic package was extremely broad-brush – it was a work in progress, really – and challenged 'the wisdom or policies of the old parties which are designed to achieve continuous economic growth', but crab-walked away from the old Australia Party wish for a steady-state economy, declaring: 'Greens want growth, measured in ways which include new quality of life indexes as measures of human progress.' Philosophically, the platform flagged a reversal of 'the 1980s shift towards minimal government intervention and reduced taxes', with the aim of reinvesting in 'an ecologically sustainable pattern of industry' and 'underwriting a national employment program which will

secure socially useful and rewarding employment for Australians'.
This included a new right to participate in paid employment. In other
words, there would be jobs for all. The Greens' centrepiece economic
policy, which *did* hark back to the ideas of the Australia Party, was a
Guaranteed Adequate Income scheme, although it was not universal:

> A Guaranteed Adequate Income (GAI) scheme is necessary to
> assist in overcoming problems of income and wealth distribution
> created by reliance on formal work at a time when this is becom-
> ing less available (in terms of total hours). The GAI will be paid
> to those who currently receive unemployment benefits, aged pen-
> sions, other pensions and income support schemes, and students.
> It will replace these benefits at least at the current rate.

The platform flagged the introduction of pollution taxes, resource
taxes on minerals, coal and woodchips, and promised a major review
of company tax, capital gains tax, sales tax and fringe benefits tax,
but flatly rejected a goods and services tax. The Greens would make
the personal income tax system more progressive by exempting low-
income earners, introducing a healthcare levy and reintroducing an
inheritance tax. In short, taxes would be going up, big-time.

The Greens' industry policy would 'remove us from the Age of
Quarry Australis, and towards an economy based on smart, clean,
green production of high-value-added manufactured goods and
services'. Favoured industries would get tariff and anti-dumping protection, and taxation assistance. A new Environmentally Sustainable
Industries Commission would develop plans for sectors such as
energy, tourism, chemicals, transport, whitegoods and wood products, which sounded like central planning.

Naturally, the platform had a thorough environment policy:
ecologically sustainable development, a National Biodiversity Act,
land-clearing restrictions, a 'cradle to grave' waste policy, a uranium
ban and a new Environment Commissioner. The last bullet point
was a short reference to the UN Framework Convention on Climate
Change, agreed at the Rio Earth Summit in June 1992. The platform
maintained the government's target to reduce greenhouse-gas emissions by 20 per cent by 2005, based on 1988 levels (a target that was

renegotiated under the Howard government, and, as of 2019, still has not been achieved). The Greens' energy policy proposed increased energy efficiency and greater reliance on renewable energy. There was no mention yet of carbon taxes, although the platform stated that, 'in the long term', the Greens would 'ensure that the price of energy fairly incorporates the full social and environmental costs of energy production and use', which was much the same thing. Effectively, by proposing to internalise the 'externalised' costs of fossil-fuel combustion, the Greens were anticipating a price on carbon.

On education, the Greens would increase resources for public schools, upgrade the TAFE system and develop a 'national workforce planning capacity … based upon the fundamental principles of social justice, sustainability and increased national self-reliance'. There was affirmative action for women, actions to reduce violence against women and to 'limit pornographic use of women'. The very last item, interestingly, was a 79-word population and immigration policy, which appeared deliberately vague. The Greens would 'introduce policies that bring human numbers and lifestyles into balance with nature's capacity, while at the same time encouraging technologies which enhance that capacity'. Certainly, the party steered well clear of zero population growth.

Just as their actual formation had attracted minimal coverage, the Greens could draw very little attention to their policy platform during the 1993 election campaign, which turned into a referendum on the Coalition's proposed goods and services tax, and became a presidential-style campaign between Keating and Hewson. Brown called the debate 'econobabble', and warned that the major parties were making a big mistake by ignoring the environment.[10] Rather more attention was given, just before Christmas in 1992, to the release of Mark 'Chopper' Read's first book, *Hits and Memories*, and the revelation that an elderly Tasmanian timber cutter had offered him $500 to knock off Bob Brown. 'I was a bit surprised to see that I was so valued,' said Brown, who dismissed the threat as 'pub talk', while calling for legislation to stop violent criminals from profiting from their memoirs.[11]

The newly founded Australian Greens had absolutely no money, and had to beg the branches for 'desperately needed' contributions, in proportion to their membership, which then totalled about 1500 people across four states. This was a structural weakness, albeit one common to the major political parties: the states collect the vast bulk of party funds, through their member fees, and the federal party is reliant on the branches for doling out those funds. Brown was tasked with writing letters to potential donors, sympathetic individuals and organisations, but he didn't have much luck: the party's first accounts show that a paltry $1275 was raised in donations in 1992–93. State contributions in the party's first year totalled $3600, raised from Tasmania ($1655), New South Wales ($1185), Queensland ($535) and the ACT ($225).[12] Arguably, the federal organisation did not have a huge need for funds: the party had a philosophical aversion to large expenditure on glossy campaign material anyway, and each state branch ran its own Senate campaign, while local groups ran the lower-house campaigns. In any case, the Australian Greens racked up an unfunded debt of $8000 in the 1993 election campaign.[13] It would flirt with insolvency for years.

The first Australian Greens campaign was run by Canberra-based Judy Lambert, the former Wilderness Society director who had been plucked out of environment minister Ros Kelly's office.[14] Helping out was Ben Oquist, a young communications graduate from UTS who had been elected as Australia's first green student union president in 1991, and who had met Brown when he travelled to Tasmania to join the Picton blockade early the following year. Already close to Brown, Oquist was gravitating to the centre of the Greens. He helped set up the party's first national office, in Sydney's Kings Cross, a tiny spare room offered by the magazine *Art Almanac*. (It was a choice between Sydney and Brisbane – the criteria were that the office must be in a state where the party was confident of getting 4 per cent of the vote, and where plenty of electoral funding was available.)[15] Brown did a national speaking tour, and the Greens produced a 30-second campaign advertisement and a five-minute policy statement that went to air on SBS. The ABC told the party it was not big enough to qualify for free airtime.

In the 1993 election the party contested every lower-house seat in Western Australia, Tasmania and Queensland, and a computer analysis was done to identify its best prospects in New South Wales and Victoria. 'A minimum of 15 marginal seats will be contested and that should determine the result,' the election campaign committee wrote.[16] As national spokesman, Brown predicted the Greens would win at least four Senate seats, and declared that through distribution of preferences in the lower house there was 'a high likelihood that the Greens will determine the outcome of the federal election'.[17]

Illawarra Greens veteran Steve Brigham was chosen to head up the New South Wales Senate ticket, while the Brisbane Greens' Drew Hutton was chosen to lead the Queensland ticket. The Greens were galvanised by the West Australian state election, where, as we shall see, Jim Scott was elected to the lower house. Bob Brown claimed the party had emerged as the third-strongest political force in the country. In Victoria, the Greens decided not to put up a Senate candidate but to back former Democrats leader Janet Powell, who was running as an independent. Dee Margetts topped the ticket of the Greens WA (still a separate party) and was seen as a likely prospect to join Christabel Chamarette, who had taken Jo Vallentine's seat on a countback.

The Tasmanian ticket was tricky – Brown was vacillating. His oldest friend, Hobart flatmate and fellow Sydney University medical graduate Judy Henderson, who had grown up with him in country New South Wales, was chosen to head up the Senate ticket. She was a solid, if low-profile, candidate: a veteran of the Franklin campaign who had spent a decade volunteering as a doctor in Nepal, and had then held a senior position at Community Aid Abroad. As his biographer James Norman wrote, for some years Brown had been wanting to write his definitive environmental book, *The Human Tragedy*, and would tell friends, 'I must go up to Liffey and write.'[18] Ten tumultuous years in state politics had taken a toll. At the beginning of 1993 Brown called his parliamentary colleagues together at Liffey, told them, 'I've had enough of this,' and resigned, effectively handing his state seat to Peg Putt on a countback. As Brown recalls it, Christine Milne was voted in as leader then and there. 'I had had it,' says Brown. 'I had really had the years of the Accord and the double-cross that occurred ... you know, we worked so hard on that Accord to make it work ... and I reasonably said to my colleagues, I can't keep going on this.'

Publicly, however, Brown ducked questions about whether he would run.[19] It was not until February that he declared his hand, confirming he would resign from the Tasmanian parliament and run in the federal lower-house seat of Denison. This was arguably the greenest electorate in the country, but was held by Labor's Duncan Kerr with a healthy 6 per cent margin. Brown says he had no expectation of winning and no real desire to get straight back into politics – his aim was to support Henderson's Senate tilt.

> But of course you can't stand and say, 'I'm just in this to bolster the Senate ticket.' I mean, you've got to mean it, that you're standing as a genuine candidate for the electorate as well, and so I did that. But had she not been standing, had we not had a chance [in the Senate], I certainly wouldn't have stood for Denison.

Brown's resignation came at a personal financial cost: if he'd stayed on for another term in state parliament, his payout would have been $900,000.[20] Once the risky move was announced, Brown put his best foot forward, telling *The Sydney Morning Herald*: 'I don't believe in waiting until you know you're going to win a seat, that's never been my way of operating. We have to break through the barriers and not be led by opinion polls.'[21] Brown refused to rule out a return to state politics if he failed. A Hobart *Mercury* poll in mid-February put Brown's primary vote at 15 per cent, trailing that of Kerr (41 per cent) and of Liberal Phil Ryan (20 per cent).[22]

Paul Keating's major pre-election environment policy statement had focused on 'brown' rather than green issues, like land degradation and soil and water quality. After he got a lukewarm reception, Keating complained that 'the problem in Australia is a lot of the greenies would like a rainforest in Pitt Street in Sydney and down Rundle Mall in Adelaide, while the Liberal Party would go and mine the Botanic Gardens in Adelaide and Hyde Park in Sydney'.[23] Labor made a desultory attempt to court the Green vote – mainly by being less disastrous than Hewson, with his vow to remove 'red, black and green tape'. When Bob Brown said he saw little difference between the two major parties, Ros Kelly objected: 'I would like to remind Dr Brown that if Labor had not been in power for the past ten years, the

Franklin River would have been dammed, the rainforests of the wet tropics would be stacked in a timber yard, and Kakadu would have been mined.'[24] Environment groups held back nonetheless, refusing to endorse Labor, as they had in 1990.[25]

Heading into the election, polls showed the Democrats' vote had plummeted. The Greens and the weakened Democrats agreed to exchange preferences.[26] At the campaign launch, Brown invoked Whitlam, saying the Greens were offering 'the most exciting, cohesive new direction espoused for an election since "It's Time" in 1972'. The Greens were not single-issue, but were offering 'an across-the-board policy platform; we want Australia to get away from the economic rationalism "leave it to the boardroom" approach of both the major parties'.[27] In an op-ed, Labor's former finance minister Senator Peter Walsh – on his way out of politics – lashed out at Bob Brown's green 'snake oil':

> According to the Brown Green from the South they are for a 'guaranteed adequate income scheme', but this and other proposals will not be 'costed to the last dollar' because the Greens 'are not going to form government'. The need for an 'guaranteed adequate income' will certainly be enhanced if green policy for 'labour-intensive small business' (and consequential subsistence wages) is adopted ... Like everyone else who believes in motherhood, Greens are for value-adding, tariffs, 'directed trade', 'directed protection', and enhancing 'the competitive advantage of Australian industries in the world market, not to featherbed inefficient industries in the domestic market'. A prize clutch of mutually exclusive propositions ... even if Greens didn't have a record of trying to close down our most competitive industry (mining) as well as forestry and blocking every viable proposal to add value to their products.[28]

Two days out from the election, Judy Henderson's chances in Tasmania – arguably the party's best Senate prospect – went up in smoke when a Tasrail worker found what appeared to be a bomb at a railway line next to a logging yard at Black River, in the state's far north-west. Two passing motorists told police they had seen a sign reading 'Earth First', the name of a US eco-terrorist group. Premier Ray Groom took it up in the state parliament: '[I]t is most regrettable that some more extreme elements of the conservation movement may be willing to use violence to pursue their cause ...' The next day the Burnie *Advocate* ran a front-page story with the headline 'Railway bomb: environment group linked', and on election eve the TV news bulletins across Tasmania showed police scouring the area for evidence. In her 2017 memoir Christine Milne wrote:

> The 'bomb' was found to be ammonium nitrate, used by local farmers and loggers to blow up stumps in land clearing. A second device nearby had wires and batteries bound by cloth tape, but could not have been detonated. The Earth First sign was written on a sheet and without their trademark exclamation mark.

Years later, a freedom-of-information application revealed that Tasmanian police thought the device was 'an elaborate hoax and they have not ruled out the possibility that it may have been placed there by loggers in an attempt to discredit the Green movement'.[29]

The Greens polled 6.7 per cent of first preferences, their best performance in the eastern states, and well clear of the Democrats' 1.6 per cent, but a long way behind independent Brian Harradine, who took 10.4 per cent. In the final count, Labor's Shayne Murphy easily beat Henderson into the sixth spot.

In New South Wales and Victoria, the Greens faced competition in the Senate from Trotskyist Green Alliance candidates.[30] The Greens polled 2 per cent, just beating the Green Alliance (1.6 per cent), but well behind the Democrats (4.9 per cent). In Victoria, the left-progressive field was even more split, and the major parties hoovered up all six spots. In Queensland, the Greens' Drew Hutton polled 3.2 per cent, behind the Democrats' John Woodley, who got 93 per cent of Greens preferences and was elected. A ray of hope for the Greens came in the ACT, where Kerrie Tucker received 5.9 per cent of the primary vote – a pointer to the future. Tucker worked at the Canberra environment centre, putting out the *Bogong* newsletter, and had been involved in the ACT Greens from the beginning. Asked to stand as a candidate, Tucker was reluctant and asked to meet Brown himself. She recalls that she told him she felt she was not the right person and Brown said simply: 'They're the best sort, the ones you drag in kicking and screaming end up to be good politicians'. Brown was wary of anyone who wanted to run for parliament as a career move. The real bright spot, of course, was Western Australia, where the state party polled 5.5 per cent, beating the Democrats (4 per cent); helped by a strong flow of Liberal preferences, lead candidate Dee Margetts was elected to the Senate. She would share the balance of power with Christabel Chamarette, whose partner, Chris Williams, had run in the number-two spot, even though he was suing the party federally. But the Australian Greens could draw little comfort from the performance of Greens WA; they had little to do with the campaign and were structurally separate entities.

In the lower house, Bob Brown was easily the best performer, the only candidate to get a vote in double figures, polling 14.2 per cent in Denison. Labor's Duncan Kerr was elected without going to preferences. On the night, Brown told one paper: 'I said right at the outset that the odds were tilted against me but it is a very handsome vote for the Greens.'[31] In New South Wales, the party got over the 4 per cent hurdle in nine of 14 seats, with Sydney topping the list at 7.4 per cent, followed by Newcastle, Grayndler and Wentworth, in that order. In Victoria, young biologist Rebecca Wigney debuted on 4.5 per cent in the eastern Melbourne seat of La Trobe. Greens WA polled best in Curtin, the safe Liberal seat in suburban Perth, gaining 9.5 per cent of the primary vote.

In short, the party's first outing was a fizzer. The Greens' own post-election analysis noted that in a 'highly polarised' election that focused tightly on the leaders and the GST, the Greens had polled an average 4.5 per cent of the vote in the lower-house seats it had contested, and in the Senate averaged 2.9 per cent. The Greens directed preferences to the ALP ahead of the Coalition in all but three seats, but their impact on the result was debatable. The party's strongest claim was that Greens preferences, which flowed 72 per cent to the ALP, determined the outcome in 12 seats – that is, those in which the winning margin was smaller than the amount of Green preference votes. 'If fewer than 1500 green voters in the eight most marginal seats had changed their preferences to put the Coalition ahead of the ALP, the election outcome would have been reversed,' the report noted.[32] The preference flows to Labor were not reciprocated: in some instances, Labor preferences went to the Democrats before the Greens.

Candidate quality was an issue. The analysis noted that a 'philosophical emphasis on local decision-making and action led to local selection of candidates with a strong local commitment, but in many cases little state or national profile'. The entry of Bob Brown into the campaign had provided a much-needed boost, meaning 'the media (with its strong emphasis on "personality politics") was more willing to take the Greens seriously'. The Greens had not had the kind of support the environment movement, particularly the TWS and the ACF, had given to the cause in 1990, and which the party estimated was worth between 1.5 per cent and 2.5 per cent in its targeted electorates. This was even though a Morgan poll had showed the environment was the most important issue in the election for approximately 21 per cent of voters, the same level of concern as Medicare or health. The Greens had not really capitalised on the 7 per cent swing against the Democrats.

In a press release issued in May, Bob Brown put a brave face on the result, saying the Greens had 'proved their electoral viability as an emerging third force in national politics by outpolling the Democrats in seats contested by both parties in four out of five states'; the exception was Queensland. With Keating re-elected as prime minister and moving early to appoint his Republic Advisory Committee – headed by Malcolm Turnbull – Brown tried to put a green spin on the debate, saying the 'the key issue in this debate must be whether a republic will support ecological sustainability'.[33]

It was a hard time, as Ben Oquist told James Norman:

That '93 election was very polarised. If you were a progressive, you were against Hewson and voting with Keating. There was very little space for the Greens. We did expect to do better; we had high hopes. We thought we were offering a whole new set of ideals that weren't being offered by the Labor Party. But we just didn't get any airspace.[34]

Brown would spend the next few years building up the party, but also working on his writing, even describing himself as a philosopher. They were lean years for the Greens.

*   *   *

When Jo Vallentine resigned at the beginning of 1992, she was replaced in the Senate by Christabel Chamarette. A staunch Anglican who had done missionary work in Bangladesh, Chamarette had been a psychologist in Fremantle's maximum-security male prison for a decade, an experience she described as radicalising and also got her involved in Indigenous advocacy: she set up the Aboriginal Driver Training Program. Aboriginals were severely over-represented in the WA prison system, and a large number had been incarcerated simply for driving without a licence. Raised by conservative, apolitical parents, Chamarette was a Liberal voter for many years until, appalled at their support for the death penalty, she switched to Labor, then abandoned them for the NDP when Bob Hawke adopted the 'three mines policy'. Chamarette did not come to the Greens through environmental activism; by her own admission, she hardly had an environmental bone in her body, and became increasingly sceptical of the benefits of many campaigns, which set her apart from the rest of the party.

Chamarette's first major challenge in the Senate came when Labor immigration minister Gerry Hand introduced legislation requiring the mandatory detention of asylum seekers who arrived in Australia by boat. It was the beginning of a quarter-century of advocacy for compassionate and principled treatment of refugees, which has marked the Greens out from both Labor and the Coalition.

The early-1990s debate is uncannily familiar. The first rickety boats had begun to arrive in Australia from Vietnam, Laos and Cambodia in 1976, fleeing communist regimes including Cambodia's Khmer Rouge, which killed two million people before Vietnam invaded in 1978, ousting the murderous dictator Pol Pot. The Fraser government was sympathetic, accepting some 2000 refugees. There were few asylum seeker arrivals through the 1980s, until a second wave of boats began to sail from war-torn Cambodia, and to a lesser extent China, in 1989. The major centre for accommodating immigrants, the former migrant hostel at Villawood, in Sydney's west, was on the wrong side of the country, and so in 1991 a former BHP workers' camp at Port Hedland, in Western Australia, was repurposed as a detention centre. The second wave of boats triggered a public outcry, although only around 400 people arrived on them. In the federal parliament, the Liberal immigration shadow Philip Ruddock described the Cambodians as 'queue jumpers' (even though there was literally no queue in Cambodia, where Australia was leading a UN peacekeeping effort), and slammed Labor's 'abysmal failure to maintain control of entry to Australia', insisting that 'the government of the day should have the right to determine who shall, or shall not, be able to enter Australia and settle permanently'.[35] Although Labor protested it was a 'myth' that immigration led to unemployment, Ruddock argued that 'in the middle of the worst recession in 60 years, it is clear that the Australian economy cannot sustain a large influx of new migrants'.[36]

For years boat people had been detained under the *Migration Act* on a discretionary basis, but when a group of Cambodian refugees, who had been awaiting processing since 1989, challenged their detention in the Federal Court in 1992, the government rushed to amend the migration legislation before the case could be heard. On 5 May, Hand announced the new policy: 'I believe it is crucial that all persons who come to Australia without prior authorisation not be released into the community ... the government is determined that a clear signal be sent.' The detention was meant to be limited to nine months, and the whole policy was described as an interim measure. The government had the strong support of the opposition – Ruddock's only complaint was that the measures did not 'go far enough or quickly enough'[37] – and the bill sailed through the lower house that day.

When the bill reached the upper house that evening, Chamarette reacted as a Christian might, with compassion, and took her lead from fellow crossbench senator Brian Harradine, the Father of the Senate, whom she had chosen to sit next to on the government side of the chamber, rather than alongside the Democrats. Harradine spoke powerfully against both the legislation itself and the unholy rush to pass it ahead of a court case. He and Chamarette objected on the grounds that mandatory detention was a breach of human rights and Australia's international obligations. Said Chamarette:

> It would seem that these people are having their right of habeas corpus removed after they have already spent two years in custody ... [W]hy is the government seeking to make conditions more punitive and more distressing for people who have left their home country with nothing or next to nothing, often in fear of their lives, than it does for people who come on a visitor's visa and choose to overstay and then apply for residency?[38]

The crossbenchers voted against the legislation, which passed regardless. Warning that Australia would have to 'bear the diagnosis of history', given that it was well-placed to offer assistance to refugees from our region, Chamarette expressed her moral outrage: 'It is a sad indictment of this government's immigration policies that it is the lot of some 450 refugees to carry the full weight of punishment and bear the brunt of Australia's fear of a flood of boat people.'[39]

At a seminar to mark Refugee Week in mid-1992, Chamarette delivered a paper exploring alternatives to detention, and deploring the philosophy of deterrence:

> General deterrence, where you impose some kind of regime to influence other people is, by definition, patently unjust. If we detain people in order to deter others, we may be violating justice, morality, and even legality. It violates international covenants and conflicts with some Australia state laws which regard imprisonment as a measure of last resort.[40]

Chamarette also put her finger on the idea that what would later be called 'push factors' – the threats forcing people to leave their home country – outweighed the 'pull factors' luring refugees to Australia: 'In a world riddled with local conflicts of greater and lesser magnitude, it would seem more than a little naive to think that any policy Australia may have of detaining refugee claimants will deflect such people when a genuine crisis arises.'[41]

In Chamarette's four years in the Senate, the Greens, Democrats and Harradine voted against every single amendment to the migration legislation, but were defeated by the major parties voting together every time. Well before September 11 and the wars in Afghanistan and Iraq, Australia was on its way towards the *Tampa* crisis and the Pacific Solution. There was even an early, successful turnback, when immigration officials raced up to Christmas Island to interview a boatload of Chinese, avoided the whole question of asylum and persuaded them to head back north. With Chamarette setting the precedent in 1992, there was little doubt where the Greens would stand.

After the 1993 election, Dee Margetts joined the Senate. An environmental economist and former teacher from Fremantle, Margetts had come to the Greens through the peace movement. Labor would regret that its preferences had put her into the Senate ahead of the Democrats: the government did not have the numbers in the 76-seat chamber, and the crossbench was a mess. The Coalition had 36 seats, Labor 30, the Democrats seven, Greens WA two, and then there was Harradine. To get its bills through, Labor first needed backing from the Democrats, then both the Greens, or one of them plus Harradine. Margetts and Chamarette divvied up legislation between them, but did not feel bound to vote together. The shared balance of power would prove a nightmare for Keating, who had famously described the Senate as 'unrepresentative swill', and for the government's leader in the upper house, Gareth Evans.

From the outset, Margetts took a strong stance on economic policy and globalisation, using her first speech to attack 'the lunacy of a blind faith in the benefits of financial and economic deregulation' and the 'cargo cult of multinational investment or trickle down to such an extent that we are celebrating the export arms industry as a potential growth sector'.[42] A concrete test came with the budget for 1993–94, presented in mid-August. Having run the mother of all scare campaigns against John Hewson's GST, Keating and Treasurer John Dawkins proceeded to hike almost every indirect tax, including, most controversially, wine and petrol taxes, to get the deficit under control, and delayed promised company and income tax cuts. The budget was a stinker: the indirect tax hikes were seen as regressive and were hugely unpopular within the union movement, which described it as an 'act of bastardry'. Margetts spooked the government by refusing to rule out blocking supply, as the Democrats had done. The two Greens dug in, wanting compensation for low-income earners facing higher taxes, and were prepared to work with the Coalition to oppose certain budget measures outside the appropriation bills.

Suddenly three women – Kernot, Chamarette and Margetts – were in the news every day, exercising real power over the fate of the nation. Commentators marvelled that Keating would not be able to bully his way through this one. Labor was used to dealing with the Democrats, and quickly reached a compromise with leader Cheryl Kernot, but Gareth Evans admitted the two Greens were 'on a different wavelength'. He added: 'If they had an identifiable program that they were keen to implement, that would be a basis for some kind of rational negotiation.'[43]

As the weeks dragged on, the Greens came under real pressure, described sometimes as 'political ingénues', 'zealots' and 'wildcards'. The dollar dived to a seven-year low as uncertainty over the budget increased, on occasion forcing the Reserve Bank to intervene to prop it up. It was a crisis: at one point an early election was on the cards, but the Greens backed away. Chamarette recalls journalist Laurie Oakes accusing her of provoking a constitutional crisis, comparable to the blocking of supply in 1975, which she flatly denied. Bob Brown rang and argued with Chamarette for half an hour over the phone, urging her to pass the budget in exchange for a deal to save Tasmania's forests. But Chamarette insisted the Greens would not cross-trade on issues, the way the Democrats did. Today she regards that as the most important stance she took in the Senate: 'If I had said yes, Keating would have said, "Ha, see! They don't really care about the social justice of the budget, they just want their agenda."' Brown was decidedly unimpressed.

Chamarette and Margetts vacillated and backflipped on occasion, and once voted against each other by accident in a debate on a budget bill. A final deal took a record 64 days to negotiate, and the Greens won significant concessions – principally, a $144 million compensation package for low-income earners including increases to family payments and the job search allowance.[44] By then it was

October, and after the saga Dawkins moved future budgets to May, before the fiscal year began.

Looking back, Bob Brown put the handling of that 1993 budget down to inexperience, with both senators having less than 18 months combined. John Howard, installed as opposition leader in January 1995, believed the 1993 budget negotiation was the moment the Keating government lost its legitimacy. Labor pondered Senate voting reform, including single-member electorates in the upper house, to avoid a repeat experience. Howard was vehemently opposed to what he saw as an attack on the Senate. Years later, Margetts said:

> [I] did try to make the issue of the social and environmental impacts and potential problems of globalisation one of the major themes of my term in the Senate for six years. At the end of that I felt, in that I had wanted to make people understand what those issues were, that I had failed.[45]

The budget was only the beginning of Labor's woes with the Greens. There were two big-ticket items Labor wanted to get done by the end of the year: industrial relations and native title. Industrial Relations was held over into 1994. Native title would prove one of the defining achievements of the Keating prime ministership. Chamarette describes it now as 'the reason I was there – from a spiritual point of view, I was meant to be there for that'.

In June 1992 the High Court had handed down the *Mabo* decision, overturning the legal doctrine that Australia was an uninhabited land – terra nullius – when the British took possession of it in 1770. The case affirmed the existence of native title, but spelled out that it was extinguished by the colonisers and only survived where Aboriginal people could demonstrate a continuing association with the land. After Keating gave his landmark Redfern speech in December 1992, acknowledging the history of Aboriginal dispossession, the government moved to create a legal framework to recognise native title and resolve disputes. Negotiating passage of the *Native Title Act* through the Senate went down to the wire.

Chamarette, with her background in Indigenous activism, handled the talks for the two Greens, and she held out the longest, almost voting the bill down. She consulted with every Aboriginal community in Western Australia. She also got legal advice from a string of experts, including the New South Wales Aboriginal Land Council and Gary Corr, who had butted heads with Evans before, and was later to be the partner of Christine Milne. Believing every group *but* traditional owners was being given certainty by the bill, Chamarette pushed for a Senate inquiry that would delay the whole process until the following year.

She came under terrific pressure. The major Aboriginal peak bodies had been in close consultation with the government, felt they had done the best deal possible and accused the Greens of putting the entire reform at risk. The president of the Human Rights and Equal Opportunity Commission, former High Court judge Sir Ronald Wilson, came to see Chamarette to personally urge her to pass the bills.

Chamarette's refusal was so obdurate that she began to receive supportive letters from racist groups opposed to any recognition of native title. 'I got all the precursors of Pauline Hanson's kind of group, saying "you're fantastic!",' says Chamarette. But the two Greens were holding out for more native title, not less. 'Nobody understood our position,' she admits now. Whenever people came to see her, she'd first ask whether they'd read the draft legislation. 'No one had.' At one point, the Tasmanian Aboriginal activist Michael Mansell acknowledged that 'these two white women in Canberra are asking more for Aboriginal people than Aboriginal people are asking for themselves'.[46]

Chamarette says it was a choice between the lesser of two evils, and she went into the Senate in tears on the day she supported it, because she feared she was selling out the Aboriginal people. The Greens secured a string of amendments, which for the next six years made it easier for traditional owners to claim native title, until John Howard effectively undid them all as Liberal prime minister with his '10-point plan' following the *Wik* case. 'We created a window,' says Chamarette now. 'Some claims got through.' The Greens could have voted it down, and Chamarette says, 'I almost did.' Almost 25 years later she can still see both sides: given the extreme difficulty traditional owners have had establishing native title through the Native Title Tribunal, there is an argument that voting it down may have been the better course. But the fear was that Aboriginal people would have ended up with nothing.

A cartoonist dubbed Chamarette and Margetts the 'gumnut twins' early on in their term, and the tag stuck. There is no doubt the two West Australian Greens were widely misunderstood. Their contribution in parliament was hit and miss – at one point, Chamarette was estimated to have missed 47 per cent of votes – and they were often winging it on legislation, without the guidance of a policy platform. The dilemma was particularly acute when they held the balance of power. 'If we didn't know whether we agreed with a change or not, we went with the status quo,' recalls Chamarette. 'If we agreed with the change, we went with the change.' Other senators noticed, telling reporters they were convinced there were occasions when the Greens did not have a clear understanding of what it was they were voting on.[47]

They backed the government's landmark industrial relations legislation, which ushered in enterprise bargaining. Margetts voiced her 'considerable doubts' at Labor's motivations – 'just as financial deregulation caused as many ills as it cured, so may inappropriate labour market deregulation' – but focused on protecting women and other groups that had the weakest bargaining positions in the workforce.[48] The two Greens also got stuck into Labor over East Timor, for example, and on human rights.

At one point Chamarette got a letter from Gough Whitlam commending her on a speech in the Senate.

> We realised he used to spend every day reading the Senate Hansard and the Reps Hansard. He often used to ring me up and suggest follow-up questions to questions I'd asked in the parliament. He really didn't like what Keating and Hawke had done, you know, and so in things like his ratification of the International Covenant on Civil and Political Rights, it hadn't been followed up as speedily as he wanted, so he'd suggest 'you *could* ask the Government *this*', and I would! I was his decoy questioner in the Senate, and there was a guy in the Reps as well.

With Labor slipping rightwards, Whitlam was fighting a covert rearguard action to protect his legacy, in this case via the Greens. After a few months of back and forth, Chamarette and Whitlam celebrated over dinner at a Brisbane steakhouse.

As the relationship between the Keating government and the two WA Greens deteriorated, they voted increasingly with the Coalition. Throughout 1995, of 67 divisions in which Labor and Liberal were opposed, the Greens voted with the Coalition 33 times, and their relationship was described as 'cosy' on issues like native title and racial vilification, with Chamarette leading the opposition to criminal sanctions under the *Racial Discrimination Act* – especially section 18C, which would prove controversial two decades later. Some stands they took were strange. Margetts, whom Labor described off the record as an 'unreconstructed Trotskyite', nevertheless opposed measures introduced by Labor treasurer Ralph Willis to properly tax private trusts that were trafficking in losses.[49]

*   *   *

There should be a special place in Greens history for the trailblazers who broke into parliaments and held the fort on their own, dealing with a torrent of legislation with no or minimal staff, and no precedent to guide them: Bob Brown was alone for three years in the Tasmania legislature from 1983, and Jo Vallentine did almost seven years solo in the Senate from 1985. Over two years from 1993, the Greens broke into parliaments in Western Australia, the ACT and New South Wales. More than any other issue, it was the intensifying forest wars that propelled the first Greens into legislatures around the country, as the Keating government tried to get forests off the federal political agenda and off the front pages.[50]

In early 1992 the Resource Assessment Commission delivered a 1300-page report recommending a permanent forest estate. The Commonwealth and all states and territories except Tasmania committed to set aside a 'comprehensive, adequate and representative' network of high-conservation value forests, while providing resource security for loggers. When the states dragged their heels, Keating came up with the idea of using the Commonwealth's annual export woodchip licencing as a bargaining chip, threatening to reduce volumes by 20 per cent a year for five years, all the way to zero, unless the states developed 20-year Regional Forest Agreements.

The negotiation of those RFAs through the rest of the 1990s would prove as contentious as the blockades and rallies of the 1980s had been, and it is no coincidence that the four states with a woodchipping industry – New South Wales, Victoria, Western Australia and Tasmania – also tended to be the first to have Greens representation.

At the beginning of 1993, Jim Scott was the first Green elected in WA, where the south-west forests were under threat. Scott had grown up in Doodlakine, in the wheat belt. Knowing that salinity was destroying the land and seeing country towns collapse under Premier Charlie Court's 'get big or get out' mantra for farmers impelled him towards politics:

> I always still have an image in my mind, when I was younger, seeing my first movies ... they always started off with these pictures of landclearing with a ball and chain between two bulldozers, tearing down the bush, and I think it had some sort of psychological impact on me. I always felt really bad about it.

Scott joined the Greens in 1990 and threw his hat in for preselection for the upper house in the 1993 state election, which he won when Dee Margetts suddenly pulled out to run for the Senate. Liberal premier Richard Court defeated Labor's Carmen Lawrence, and, unusually, Scott won at his first attempt, surprising the pundits; he went on to serve 12 years in the state parliament. Scott attributes his win that year to a lingering aversion to Labor in the wake of WA Inc scandal, and to 'a really big push on the forests'. He had been down to lie in front of the bulldozers himself, and the Greens helped organise rallies to save native forests in Perth that grew to 40,000 people. Scott says the government was giving timber away, 'losing money on it, but still doing it'. Among his achievements, Scott busted the minister's department flagrantly doctoring maps showing how much jarrah forest was left. By himself, however, Scott could not make much difference to legislation in his first term.

In 1995 the political pendulum really started to swing against Labor nationally. By threatening to cut export woodchip licences, Keating had provoked the fury of the forestry division of the Construction, Forestry, Maritime, Mining and Energy Union, led by

Michael O'Connor. What followed would go down as one of the dirtiest episodes in Labor history: loggers descended on Canberra from all over the country at the end of January, surrounding Parliament House with their trucks. The optics were terrible for the government, and the salt in the wound was that the demonstration was led by a Labor-affiliated union. Enraged, Keating considered calling in the army. Judith Ajani, author of *The Forest Wars*, described the blockade as a curtain-raiser for John Howard's return to lead the opposition that same week, and wrote that 'Australian voters witnessed the first display of Howard's "battlers" versus Keating's "special interest elites": the core of a meticulously crafted election strategy to capture more of the 1990s middle-class vote'. The Greens, who had been on standby for a snap election since 1994, hinted that when it came, they might direct their preferences to the Coalition. One article quoted Tasmanian Greens leader Christine Milne: 'It is really extraordinary how far back we are meant to remember in order to be grateful to Labor. How long are they going to make us remember the Franklin River?'[51]

The first election for the year was in the ACT, a fortnight after the blockade. The Liberals' Kate Carnell won a swing of 11.5 per cent, and was able to form government with the support of crossbenchers including two ACT Greens, who had made a stunning electoral debut, winning 9 per cent of the vote, with Kerrie Tucker taking Molonglo – which would prove to be one of the safest Greens seats in the country – and former TWS volunteer Lucy Horodny successful in Ginninderra. The election was the first under the Hare-Clark system, with three multi-member electorates returning 17 members to the Legislative Assembly. The Liberals won seven seats, Labor six, the ACT Greens two, plus progressive-leaning independent Michael Moore and former Raiders footy star Paul Osborne. Combined, Labor, the Greens, the Democrats and Moore won 52 per cent of the vote; Labor, the Greens and Moore could have formed a government.[52] There was consternation inside the Greens that Tucker and Horodny would back the Liberals, and a meeting of members debated it at length, but ultimately Moore sided with Carnell and, when it came to a vote, the two new Greens followed suit. Tucker's first move was to tell the Assembly 'our decision to allow Mrs Carnell to work as Chief Minister is by no means an endorsement of the

Liberal policies. We intend to work in this place issue by issue. We also look forward, quite probably, to working on many occasions with Labor in opposition and with the other Independents.'[53]

The ACT Greens' strong showing encouraged Bob Brown, who claimed it was a sign that the federal government was taking the wrong path on the environment. Keating pooh-poohed the ACT result, saying it was a 'basically a municipal election'.[54] Not so easily dismissed was Labor's resounding defeat at the by-election for the federal seat of Canberra six weeks later. Liberal Brendan Smyth was elected, sounding the death knell for Keating's government.

In the lead-up to the by-election, the TWS's Alec Marr and the Greens candidate James Warden had met with the Liberal Party's federal director, Andrew Robb, and told him that although conservationists believed Labor was out of touch and wanted to teach the government a lesson, the Coalition should not take the green vote for granted. If Robb ran the right campaign, the conservationists would do whatever was necessary to damage Labor. Robb agreed, and the TWS distributed leaflets reminding voters that the federal Labor government had not fulfilled its promise to protect the ancient forests, and urging them to 'vote Green and send a message to Canberra'.[55] The small-G greens would not preference Labor. Marr told the ABC later that year: 'It was quite historic really, in that that was the first time that major groups have run television advertising campaigns against the Labor Party since they've come to power.'[56] There was no doubt that environmental issues, including the government's bungling of the woodchip licences and the truckers' blockade, heavily influenced the by-election vote; Labor's own officials conceded as much.[57]

In New South Wales, Labor's Bob Carr bucked the national trend, beating Premier John Fahey in March 1995. After the bitter disappointment of 1991, lead upper-house candidate Ian Cohen was determined. Ahead of the election, Labor pursued a secret deal to secure Greens preferences, which it hoped would shore it up in a string of key marginal seats. The Greens held out for guarantees from Labor on woodchipping, ocean outfalls, pollution controls and wilderness expansion. Cohen was successful this time, winning a seat in the Legislative Council on a 3.8 per cent first preference vote. Entering state parliament to negotiate with Carr, Cohen told

The Sydney Morning Herald: 'I see this as just a continuation of my campaign. I'll do whatever it takes, hang off a warship or wear a suit in parliament. It's all part of the same struggle.'[58]

The Greens' prospects were made easier by the success of a 1991 referendum that cut the size of the Legislative Council from 45 to 42 MPs, and with half the reduced chamber up for election, the quota fell slightly. The Greens were up against the single-issue No Aircraft Noise party, set up after the opening of Sydney's infamous third runway in late 1994. In the seat of Marrickville, NAN candidate Kevin Butler won 24.6 per cent of the primary vote, easily beating the Liberals and Greens, and finishing with 40 per cent of the two-party preferred vote, while in Port Jackson Hall Greenland, who had by now drifted away from the Greens, polled 20 per cent primary and 36 per cent after preferences.[59] Perhaps the inner west was no longer rusted on to Labor. (Sylvia Hale, later a Greens MLC, got elected for NAN in Marrickville Council in September that year.)

The Queensland state election held on 15 July 1995 proved a crucial turning point in the history of the Greens. The Goss Labor government had been in power for six years, after voters had finally turfed out the corrupt government of National Joh Bjelke-Petersen in 1989, and had a bumpy relationship with the environmental movement. Goss was popular and had a majority of 19 seats. But many were on a slim margin, and polls showed that Labor was neck-and-neck with the Coalition opposition, under Rob Borbidge. It was clear that preferences from the Greens could play a decisive role.

Drew Hutton flagged publicly that Labor could not take the Greens' support for granted. One Greens party source said: 'You can bet your boots no party will get across-the-board preferences.' The looming issue was a proposed toll road from Brisbane to the Gold Coast, which would cut through Australia's largest koala habitat. The Goss government was originally opposed, but back-flipped after receiving advice that Queensland's population growth demanded the road be built, so it proposed an expensive compromise: a $50-million-plus, cut-and-cover tunnel under the state forest. Conservation groups, and many voters in the affected electorates, preferred that the toll road was not built at all. The Coalition promised to shelve the project completely.

Both sides put considerable effort into wooing the Greens; as one wag put it, Labor's state secretary, Mike Kaiser, 'donned the koala suit' to negotiate preferences with them. Among other measures, Labor promised a massive new Cape York wilderness area, as large as Kakadu. For national environmental groups such as ACF and the TWS, this was enough to justify advocating a vote for Labor. But not for the local green groups, who accused the peak bodies of being 'Labor stooges', and certainly not for Hutton or the Queensland Greens, who decided to recommend voters preference the Coalition in three marginal seats and 'put Labor last'. The environmental movement split, bitterly, and the accusations flew thick and fast.

Whatever deal had been negotiated, it was the first time in Australian history the Greens had directed preferences against Labor and in favour of conservative parties. If the intention had been to give Labor a scare, the plan worked better than expected. The Coalition won all three marginal seats with Greens preferences, and a hung parliament was returned, with devout Christian independent Liz Cunningham in Gladstone – also elected on Greens preferences – holding the balance of power. Goss only just retained government: the last contested seat, Mundingburra, went to Labor by 16 votes, partly due to preferences from the Green candidate, who had polled over 11 per cent. Hutton did best, polling 24 per cent in Mount Coot-tha, laying the foundations of a Greens win there two decades later. One newspaper editorialised that the Greens had got the outcome they were hoping for:

> [Their] decision, it seems, has not resulted in the defeat of the Labor Government; it has resulted in the 'greening' of the Coalition; it will result in the achievement of several objectives of the Greens (such as abandoning the tollway between Brisbane and the Gold Coast and the creation of the Cape York wilderness zone); and it has put the environment firmly back on the agenda for the Federal election.

Others were bemused. Alex Mitchell wrote that the Queensland Greens were a 'peculiar outfit' under Hutton, with 'strange ideological bearings': 'Anyone with even a passing knowledge of the

Queensland Nationals will be aware that their environmental vandalism has been utterly horrendous … they would have sunk oil wells on the barrier reef given half a chance.'

Australian Greens leader Bob Brown, who had toured Queensland during the campaign, squarely backed the Hutton strategy, and warned Keating that the next federal election could see a repeat performance. The TWS's forests campaigner, Virginia Young, said Goss had offered one of the most significant environmental packages ever seen. Her colleague Greg Sargent, who had worked on the Cape York proposal, wrote a searing memo:

> In 1983 the Wilderness Society advocated a vote for the federal ALP on the strength of a promise to protect one wild river in south west Tasmania. In 1995 the Wilderness Society advocated a preference for the Queensland ALP on the strength of a promise to protect twenty wild rivers in Cape York, along with a platform of a wilderness zone covering 1200 km of the eastern side of the Cape, no export woodchip industry, a Great Southern Queensland Forest Park system, accelerated movement of the timber industry into plantations, statutory tree clearing guidelines, a continuous system of marine parks from the Gulf of Carpentaria to Moreton Bay, and legislative protection of wilderness … Our [TWS] largest concern was that if any party came up with the biggest environmental reform agenda in Australia's history, the Green Party decided to shaft them anyway, and the conservation movement just stood on the sidelines, then what kind of message are we sending to federal political parties?[60]

The Greens insisted they had a broader social agenda, one which was antipathetic to the economic rationalist ALP. The serious question raised was whether the Greens' political objectives might sometimes conflict with – or even trump – their environmental objectives.

It did not take long for the gloss to wear off the election result. The winning margin in Mundingburra was so narrow that the result was challenged, and when Labor lost the resulting by-election in early 1996 – with no Green candidate running this time – the parliament's balance-of-power independent, Liz Cunningham, backed opposition leader Borbidge to form a minority government. Queensland Labor – and particularly the then head of the cabinet office, one Kevin Rudd – would never forget the Greens' role in the downfall of Goss.

As premier, Borbidge did not keep faith with his commitments to the Greens, and they soon had a litany of grievances: the Cape York plan was abandoned, the Port Hinchinbrook development near the Great Barrier Reef was back on, funding for the environment department was slashed, a process to control land clearing was shelved, and so on. Within a year Hutton was conceding that his strategy of 'greening up' the Coalition had failed, and by 1997, with a new state election looming, he had completely renounced the 'unholy alliance', arguing he had been misled.

*　　*　　*

After losing in Denison in 1993, Bob Brown retreated to his Liffey home. His lifelong friend Judy Henderson recalled that 'income was an issue for him in those years. People had told him that he would have no trouble getting on to the lecture circuit, and that it would be an income-generating activity. In fact that didn't happen.'[61]

Brown was far from idle, however, and found a willing writing collaborator in one of Australia's greatest moral philosophers, the Melbourne-born and Oxford-educated bioethicist Peter Singer, whose 1975 book *Animal Liberation*, which espoused veganism and opposed animal experimentation, had attracted worldwide acclaim, and who controversially supported abortion and euthanasia. Singer had joined the ALP in the 1970s, but quit as it swung right under Hawke and Keating, and in 1992 had been one of the original founders of the Victorian Greens. In 1994, when former Coalition opposition leader Andrew Peacock quit politics, Singer had won a stunning 28 per cent of the primary vote in the safe Liberal seat of Kooyong, in Melbourne's inner east.

Over the following year, Brown and Singer co-wrote *The Greens*, and the book was published in 1996. It was not an official party manifesto or platform, but their personal guide to the new force in Australian politics. The book is unique – no other Australian political party has a foundational text co-authored by someone of such intellectual weight – but it is rarely cited 20 years on, even by Greens.

This is a pity, because *The Greens* is readable and full of insight, and still perhaps the most coherent exposition of Brown's political philosophy.

Brown and Singer's main charge was that the Greens represented 'the most profound worldwide transformation of politics since the rise of socialism more than a century ago'. The book's preface plants a stake in the ground: 'The Australian Greens are not a ginger group seeking to win just a few seats, or to persuade the old parties to adopt a green tinge. The Greens aim to transform politics and bring about Green government.' The book first outlines why the Greens are needed, setting out the threats to the global atmosphere and climate, rivers and oceans, soils and forests. 'We are already living in the greenhouse,' the authors state early on. A stark picture emerges of the destruction of the Australian environment: the early 1990s drought, the thousand-kilometre algal blooms on the Darling, 800-kilometre storm fronts blowing away millions of tonnes of topsoil, and runaway species loss, including the worst rate of extinction of mammals anywhere on the planet.

The book defended the still-raw decision by the Queensland Greens to give some preferences to the Nationals:

> As long as Labor parties believe that they will always get Green preferences, they have no incentive to get serious about dealing with environmental and social problems. They can always say, 'You'll still have to give us your preferences, because we are not as bad as the conservatives.' And in the same way, if the conservatives can never hope to win Green preferences away from Labor, they have no incentive to develop better social or environmental policies. After the 1995 Queensland election, no party can take Green preferences for granted.[62]

Centrally, the book tackles consumerism and economic rationalism, attacking the Hawke and Keating governments as 'the worst of all Labor governments' for turning their backs on their party's traditional socialist values and making inequality worse, after 12 years, than it was when they came to power. The Greens challenge the dominant ethic of maximising 'what is good for *us, now*,' asking readers to see themselves 'in universal terms ... from an ethical perspective it is not the fact that I gain or lose by some action I am considering, but that *someone* gains or loses'.[63] That 'someone' could include future generations, and non-human animals. Brown and Singer reject the idea that human beings are determinedly, naturally selfish.

Although they railed against the stranglehold of economic rationalists, Brown and Singer's alternative 'green' economics remained a work in progress. Like all Greens, they did not believe that infinite economic growth is possible on a finite planet, and called for an alternative 'index of sustainable economic welfare' that would value natural assets and account for their reduction from pollution or exploitation. The Greens wanted to limit the power of the market, restoring democratic control – which was code for re-regulation after years of steady deregulation. They wanted fair trade rather than free trade, and here they become frankly protectionist, attacking Keating's APEC and complaining about the threat to Australian labour, safety and environmental standards.

On the social side, there was clear support for the decriminalisation of marijuana and heroin, which would provide plenty of ammunition for tabloid attacks over the years. In places, Singer's controversial ethical positions came to the fore – on health funding, for example, where the writers noted opposition to the idea that 'because modern medical technology *can* prolong life, it *should* do so'. In other places, the authors are surprisingly conservative, supporting recognition for same-sex relationships, for example, but stopping short of support for gay marriage, or equivocating on voluntary euthanasia, observing that 'greens differ'.

At a personal level, Brown found other building blocks falling into place in these quieter years. He found a life partner in Paul Thomas, a sheep farmer and human rights activist who also worked in community-based care. A professional relationship with Ben Oquist, which began when Oquist was the Greens' national media officer in the 1993 election campaign, was cemented when Brown appointed him to his staff in 1996, and would last two decades.

Brown was preselected very early on for the next Tasmanian Senate campaign – in December 1994. All the following year, the party was preparing for a snap election, and hopes were high. In one memo, national federal election campaign team coordinator Andrew Parratt joked that the party's goal was to 'win four Senate places and attain an overall vote of 10%'. The party was not in great shape financially, however, despite pledges at the third national conference – held in Healesville, Victoria, in August 1995 – that states would pay contributions to the Australian Greens quarterly. 'Unfortunately these remittances have been irregular, which in turn renders the National body close to insolvent,' wrote party secretary Robert Rosen in December 1995, and he predicted that the organisation would run out of money altogether by February.

Earlier in 1995, a memo had been circulated reminding party members that Bob Brown was shouldering his own costs:

> I think we ought to be fair to Bob and realistic about his value to all the Greens' campaigns. By way of illustration, today he is going to speak to the Bastille Day in Sydney where he is likely to get national media coverage … in advertising terms, this sort of coverage has a value of several thousand dollars. Yet he has to personally fork out $500 for getting up there and he has no income (not even the dole!) and his personal finances are dwindling. He does what he can to get his costs covered by the event organisers – virtually to the point of begging. I am aware that this problem causes Bob some continuous stress and I think the Greens should be careful not to presume his commitment is there for the taking.[64]

Before the March 1996 federal election, the Greens contested a state election in Tasmania. After the tumultuous Labor–Green Accord years, and despite keeping its five seats, the party had lost a degree of influence in the lower house, being sidelined under the Liberal majority government of Ray Groom. Greens leader Christine Milne, who had slotted straight into Bob Brown's position with no party process whatsoever, kept faith with the electorate by taking a strong stand against a hugely unpopular 40 per cent pay rise for parliamentarians. She also tried to advance gun law reform but, like Brown before her, was blocked by both parties. Through 1995, however, the major local issue for the party was again the forests, in particular a proposed road through the Tarkine wilderness, in the north-west of the state.

Brown, Milne, Di Hollister and Peg Putt were all arrested at the end of 1995, protesting against the construction of the road, and Brown refused to apply for bail, spending another night in Risdon, the same prison in which he had been locked up during the Franklin blockade. Behind the scenes, the party was terrified that his arrest would jeopardise his candidacy for the Senate.

The issues of MPs' pay and the forests helped drive a backlash against the Groom government in the election, although the Greens also suffered a 2 per cent statewide swing against them under Milne – partly due to the rise of a pop-up party, the 'Extremely Greedy 40% Extra Party', opposing the pay rise for MPs. The Reverend Lance Armstrong (author of *Good God, He's Green!*) lost his seat of Bass after introducing a censorious private member's bill to restrict the advertising or display of soft-porn magazines like *People* and *Playboy*. Despite the loss, the Greens' four seats could have united with Labor's 14 to reach a majority of 18, and Milne expected to go into negotiations with opposition leader Michael Field. In perhaps the only example of a political party actively denying itself power, Field refused to deal with the Greens and chose to remain in opposition.

Like Field, Premier Ray Groom had promised to govern in majority or not at all – he had described the Greens as the Liberals' 'arch-enemies' – but after the election the Liberals' self-interest kicked in and he was replaced by Tony Rundle, who *was* willing to govern in minority. So an unpopular Liberal government limped on after 1996. Under Milne's leadership the Greens were able to rack up wins on legislation by collaborating – gun reform in the wake of Port Arthur, the decriminalisation of homosexuality after gay rights activists took the state to the UN and the High Court – and joining in the Tasmanian parliament's historic apology to the stolen generations. Notwithstanding these achievements, both major parties were determined to reform the lower house, reducing the number of seats, in a stitch-up expressly designed to rid the parliament of the Greens once and for all.

*   *   *

Although Brown and the Greens publicly defended the preference decisions taken by Drew Hutton in the 1995 Queensland election, behind the scenes the party was determined at all costs to 'avoid the fracas over preferences which has happened in Queensland' in the looming federal election.[65]

The Coalition, and particularly campaign director Andrew Robb, made a year-long effort to woo both the Greens and the environmental movement generally. The key was John Howard's announcement, in early 1996, that the Coalition would set up a $1.1-billion Natural Heritage Trust, funded from the sale of a third of Telstra. It was clever politics: the then executive director of the Australia Institute, Clive Hamilton, described it as a hand grenade lobbed into the environmental movement. The TWS's Alec Marr was convinced Labor were done for, and was fighting bitterly with them behind the scenes, as Pamela Williams' book *The Victory* records:

> The Labor Party went absolutely feral, screaming down the phones at us. People talk about the Liberals having a 'born to rule' mentality, but I have never seen arrogance the like of which we saw in the Labor Party after 13 years. They told us we had nowhere else to go and that it didn't matter what we advocated, that our people would run over us and vote Labor anyway.[66]

The split put the capital-g Greens in a bind. Brown described Howard's Natural Heritage Trust as 'a quantum leap forward for the Liberal Party – the best environment policy the conservatives have come up with', but he refused to trade it for Telstra.[67] In the Senate, the Greens agreed to swap preferences with the Democrats, and to rank the ALP over the Coalition, but Brown flagged that in the lower house they would struggle to make a recommendation. Ultimately, decisions in individual House of Representatives seats were left to local and state Greens groups; they preferenced the ALP over the Coalition in 60 out of the 92 seats they contested.

Unlike in 1993, the battle over environmental policy was a key feature of the 1996 campaign, and the Greens got plenty of attention. The official launch of Brown and Singer's book helped, although the reviews were predictably negative, with the Sydney Institute's Gerard

Henderson describing the party's agenda as 'economic moonbeam material'.[68] Peter Singer's own Senate candidacy generated a lot of interest, good and bad. Perhaps the worst moment for Singer came at a communications union rally in Melbourne, opposing the sale of Telstra, at which he and Democrats leader Cheryl Kernot were invited to speak. Singer discovered that he'd been dropped from the bill because Kernot was refusing to share a platform with him. Before the rally he confronted her publicly, demanding loudly to know why she had excluded him from the debate and, in scenes that looked terrible on the news that night, pursuing her through the crowd as she refused to answer. An upset Kernot asked him to 'show some human decency ... just leave me alone'.[69] TV viewers were appalled.

With polls showing the Democrats and Greens neck and neck, with about 6 per cent each, the tensions between the parties were on open display. On the *Sunday* program, Kernot branded Chamarette and Margetts as 'feral obstructionists', and warned the Greens were 'much more radical than the Democrats ... We're not into stunts or rhetoric – we're into being engaged constructively in the parliamentary process with whomever wins government'.[70] In tight Senate contests, it would all come down to whichever party benefited from the major parties' surplus and preference flow-on. 'Our party's future is not really in our hands anymore,' a senior Democrats strategist said. 'If the ALP and the Liberals wanted to shut us out, they could do it in every state except South Australia.'[71]

A week out from polling day, Brown gave his first address to Canberra's National Press Club, marking the looming election as the first in which 'everyone in Australia will be able to vote green'. He talked in general terms about the 'thin green line' of green parties around the world – including Ralph Nader's tilt at the US presidency for the Greens that year – and the revolutionary shift from thinking about 'us, now' to 'them, later'. Brown announced the Greens' 'democracy charter', which included a call for proportional representation in the lower house (also then being mooted by UK Labor leader Tony Blair) and freedom-of-information legislation. When asked about the GST, Brown answered he would only support taxes on luxury items. On supply, Brown ducked and weaved, saying that he could not foresee any circumstances in which the Greens would block supply, but also that he would not weaken the party's bargaining position by committing to never block supply, as the Democrats had done. Brown was unequivocal on the sale of Telstra, which the Greens argued would reduce service in rural areas, raise prices for consumers and cost the budget some billion dollars a year in lost revenue. He ruled out any kind of deal – 'categorically, under all circumstances, we will not vote for the sale of Telstra' – and condemned what he called a 'hollow prospect': the idea that 'we've got to flog off one part of the national estate … to protect another'.

When the question of preferences came up, Brown launched into both Labor and the Democrats. Labor could lose the election over the forests, he predicted, at least partly because the Greens had opted not to direct preferences to the party. Typically, when the party recommended it, some 75 per cent of Greens voters gave their preference to Labor, but that proportion dropped to 60 per cent when the Greens issued a split ticket. That difference alone could cost Labor six to eight marginal seats, he predicted, including Bass. Brown also slammed the Democrats' preference allocations, which had put far-right groups like Call to Australia or Australians Against Further Immigration above the Greens.

Howard campaigned as though the election was close, adopting his famous 'small target' strategy, and by election day it was clear the electorate was well and truly tired of Labor and Keating after 13 years. The result was a landslide. Most stunning was the Coalition's well-planned victory in blue-collar areas like Sydney's western suburbs, traditionally a Labor heartland, now home to 'Howard's battlers', working-class people who felt alienated by Keating's embrace of issues like APEC, native title and republicanism. Far-right winners included the disendorsed Liberal Pauline Hanson in Oxley, in Queensland. The election gave Howard a thumping mandate, although he was soon quibbling over what had been 'core' and 'non-core' promises, and would backflip on his 1995 declaration that there would 'never, ever' be a GST.

Critically, the election split the environmental movement, both internally and from its natural political allies within Labor and the Greens. The movement's warm relationship with the Howard government did not last long, and there was a strong view that the TWS, in particular, had been tricked. Behind the scenes, Robb had struck a side deal with the forestry industry, whose workers agreed to keep quiet ahead of the election and trust that Howard would do nothing to hurt them. They were not disappointed.

Brown was narrowly elected as a senator for Tasmania, polling 8.6 per cent and just pipping the incumbent Democrat, Robert Bell, who scored 6.9 per cent, in what was undoubtedly a turning point for the Greens. Years later, Ben Oquist told biographer James Norman that the Australian Greens may not have survived if Brown had been rejected by the electorate a second time: 'I'm not sure the Greens would have been able to get off the ground at all. I remember thinking at the time, when the count was on and it was close – what would we do if he didn't get in?'[72]

Outside Tasmania, it was a very different picture: the Democrats, under Kernot's leadership, had put the 1993 collapse behind them and come roaring back with primary support of 10.8 per cent, three times the Greens' vote nationally, which won them five seats and gave them a total representation of seven senators, with the loss in Tasmania offset in Victoria. The Greens' star candidate for a Victorian Senate seat, Peter Singer, polled 2.9 per cent on primary votes, and was trounced by Democrat Lyn Allison (10.8 per cent); he would not contest again. Christabel Chamarette fell well short of a quota with a primary vote of 5.6 per cent, and she was easily beaten by the Democrats' Andrew Murray. Her political career was over too – she had never won an election in her own right – and she fell out of involvement with the party, going back to community work and her doctoral research on the psychopathology of parliament, which was never completed.

In South Australia, the old Greens party had withered but was re-formed in 1995 by Environmental Defenders Office solicitor Mark Parnell, who had moved to Adelaide from Melbourne with his wife, Penny Wright (who herself had been arrested at the Franklin), and their young family. Parnell tried and failed to get a Greens SA branch going again, when local conservationists – many of whom were actively involved with the Democrats – decided it would simply split the progressive vote. On Parnell's second attempt, Bob Brown turned up and persuaded the meeting that the Greens were part of an international movement, much bigger than the Democrats. 'Bob's the difference,' says Parnell. 'He's a very charismatic character.' At their first election, however, the reformed Greens SA got a disappointing two per cent first preference vote, compared with the Democrats on 14 per cent.

Among the Greens' lower-house candidates in the 1996 federal election, Parnell in Boothby, Shane Rattenbury in Namadgi, Kim Herbert in Stirling and Jamie Parker in Bennelong would all later represent the party in state and territory parliaments. In the party's first tilt in the Northern Territory, euthanasia advocate Dr Philip Nitschke polled well with 6.3 per cent.

The post-election report by the Australian Greens' campaign coordinator, Andrew Parratt, was blunt: 'Clearly we failed to achieve the representation we all were hoping for in this election campaign.' Parratt blamed a lack of policy detail, scarce resources, and a lack of support from environmental groups. In Queensland, the TWS had gone so far as to back the Democrats over the Greens. Most importantly, however, Parratt blamed the lack of a preference strategy. Outplayed by the Democrats' 'weird and wonderful' preference deals, and their decision to abandon split tickets, the Greens were ignored by the major parties and 'avoided like the plague in most instances':

> If we had been willing to disclose or decide most of [the] marginals earlier we could have had preferences from both Lab and Lib … at the next election the choices for us will be more clear with regard to preferences; in pragmatic terms, if we deal we will get more, if we don't we will get less.

In the main, this came down to a question of how much autonomy local groups should have in determining preferences for lower-house seats. If the party wanted Labor's preferences in the Senate, it had to be able to offer its own preferences in the lower house, but these were decided locally. This played into Labor's hands, Parratt felt, especially in New South Wales and Queensland:

> The strong Labor orientation within the Greens is of considerable benefit to the ALP … they have sufficient supporters within the Australian Greens and environment greens to influence and

determine the majority of our decisions. 'Why should we give you any help in the Senate [when] we can negotiate in the HoR with the local groups.'

On the plus side, Parratt noted that the party's membership had risen by half during the campaign, it had contested in a record number of seats, and its vote in both the lower and upper houses was comparable. Together, this demonstrated that the Greens represented a 'real political alternative, rather than simply seeking the balance of power in the Senate'.

We are not a lobby group, we are not a wing of the conservation movement ... Other political parties perceive us as a party, unionists perceive us a political party, community groups perceive us as a political party, the voting public perceives us as a political party; at times it seems to me that the only people having problems perceiving us as a political party are our own members. If we continue down this track we will not fulfil our potential destiny, we will satisfy no one.

CHAPTER 6

PICKING FIGHTS

It took less than a month for the greenish tinge to wash off the Howard government. Before the 1996 election, the Coalition had promised to abolish Labor's three mines policy, and North Ltd had signalled it would dust off plans to mine the Jabiluka deposit, next to the Kakadu National Park. It was one of the main reasons the ACF had swung behind Labor in the election campaign. An application to develop the mine was made straightaway.

When Howard sat down with 3AW's Neil Mitchell in Melbourne for his first interview as prime minister, the first issue raised was Jabiluka, and whether it might cause the government trouble with the Democrats and Greens in the Senate. Howard was typically guarded, arguing that the only part of the Jabiluka project that encroached on Kakadu was the access road, and if environmental safeguards were met it should go ahead, given the jobs that would be created: 'What the government is going to do is strike a balance … no time is a good time when you have groups in the community that will always oppose mining developments of this character.'[1]

The Howard government soon increased export woodchip quotas, and, in the lead-up to the Kyoto climate talks in 1997, took an even more jaundiced view on greenhouse-gas emissions than the Keating government had done. Bob Brown said the TWS had been 'duped' and declared that it would be a generation before the environmental movement would be prepared to trust the Coalition again. Brown was soon describing South Australia's Senator Robert Hill as the 'minister *against* the environment' and 'shifty', the Natural Heritage Trust as a politicised 'slush fund', and the Howard government's environment policy as a 'fraud'.[2]

In Victoria, the Greens had to roll straight into a state election at the end of March but, being short of the necessary 500 members, could not contest it as a political party. Liberal premier Jeff Kennett was comfortably returned. Seven Greens members stood as independents: Jenny Henty did best, in Hawthorn, with 8.8 per cent of the vote after preferences; Greg Barber did nearly as well, in Northcote, with 8.4 per cent, while Gurm Sekhon polled 6.6 per cent in Melbourne. Even this early, the potential support in Melbourne's inner north was becoming clear, and there was no doubt that the results were hurt by the absence of the party name on ballot papers. Yet the successive elections – and particularly the failure to crack 4 per cent in the Senate, and so gain federal funding – almost bankrupted the Victorian branch. The dire situation reinforced the party's need to recruit members by establishing more local branches; only 15 were up and running.

After the dust settled, Barber and party electoral analyst Stephen Luntz, a former Democrat, sat down and analysed the Greens' vote in the 1996 federal poll. They found that the party's best lower-house seats – like Melbourne – got eight times their vote in the worst. It was a bit like the situation of the Nationals – highly concentrated support – and completely different to that of the Democrats, which had a ratio of three times, meaning their support was more diffuse. 'At the time, people thought the Democrats would crush the Greens,' says Barber, 'but we realised they weren't even trying in the lower house.'

Interestingly, the Greens' best electoral prospects were not in the areas where the membership of environmental groups was highest. People used to hold Greens meetings out in outer-eastern suburbs of Melbourne, recalls Barber, places like Dandenong and Ringwood, but the voting patterns told a different story, suggesting that the most fertile ground was in the inner city – especially suburbs like Carlton and Brunswick. 'It was not hard to predict which seats would fall, and in what order,' he says. The Barber and Luntz analysis in 1996 marked the beginning of a 'bite and hold' strategy that would start to bear fruit 20 years later. Lindsay Tanner, a luminary of the Labor left who won the seat of Melbourne in 1993, was early to spot the trend.

Barber also surveyed voters countrywide, asking them who they'd voted for in the last federal election. The results were striking: 30 per cent had voted Green; 28 per cent hadn't voted at all (some hadn't ever voted), 23 per cent had voted ALP, while just 5 per cent had voted for the Democrats, another 5 per cent for the Liberals, none for the Nationals, and around 10 per cent other. Barber wrote: 'Not surprisingly, we didn't take many votes from the Dems. Further evidence that we are not really in competition with the Dems, directly, for votes. We took a shitload of our vote from the ALP.'[3]

The paper sparked a furious argument, as Barber recalls. 'I was one of the raw youngsters of the party back then,' he says, '[and] people a few years older than me were veterans of environmental battles, but to me it was just mathematics.' The paper also did some rudimentary analysis of the Greens vote, by age and education. Like voters for the Democrats and the Australia Party before them, Greens voters were highly educated: fully one-quarter of the Greens voters were university-educated and under 35 years old – a major over-representation of students. For Tanner, the tendency of the tertiary-educated to vote Green was the most ominous statistic. Even now, he maintains it is the single biggest predictor of the Greens vote.

On Sunday, 28 April 1996, eight weeks after the federal election, Martin Bryant shot dead 35 people at Port Arthur, in what was then the worst massacre by a single shooter in history, shocking Australia and the world. The most profound shock was felt in Tasmania, of course, where everybody knew someone who had been there or knew how easily they or their loved ones could have been among the victims.

The next day, the new premier, Tony Rundle, called an emergency cabinet meeting with the opposition leader, Michael Field, and Greens leader, Christine Milne, who recalls: 'They had to decide how to respond to it, because we not only had the Tasmanian media, we had the world's media there. Their discussion was basically fiddling around the edges. I said, "No, we have to have gun law reform, we have to ban these weapons."' Six months earlier she had reintroduced legislation first moved by Bob Brown to ban exactly the kind of military-style semiautomatic rifles used by Bryant, only to have both major parties vote it down 30–5, as always. With the world's media waiting, Milne issued a veiled threat: she would go straight outside, hold a press conference and say the Tasmanian parliament had blood on its hands. 'It was all a bit uncomfortable, until they agreed,' she says. 'It then became a tripartite decision.'

A ban on rapid-fire rifles was announced – just 24 hours after the tragedy – and an all-party committee set up to sort out the details. When the tripartite committee met a week later, the Greens, counselled by lobby group Gun Control Australia, got the ban they were looking for, although they did not succeed in banning semiautomatic handguns.

The tougher job, politically, fell to the new prime minister, John Howard, who had called for stricter gun laws nationally before the election, warning that Australia must not go down the American path. On 1 May, at the state memorial service in Hobart, Howard said: 'This is an event that has shaken the core of the country in a way that no individual crime has done in my lifetime.'[4] He meant it, and acted decisively to bring not only his own party but his Nationals colleagues onside, as well as the police ministers of all states and territories. In his autobiography, *Lazarus Rising*, Howard wrote that he took an uncompromising approach, and felt 'elated' by the support he received from all sides of politics, including many non-Liberals who approached him on the street and urged him to persevere. The National Firearms Agreement was struck on 10 May – it had taken less than two weeks from go to whoa – and there have been no mass shootings in Australia since.

Howard's autobiography makes no mention of the Greens' role in gun law reform after Port Arthur, observing only that Tasmania's gun laws were weaker than those of other states and were tightened. Milne is more forthcoming:

> I have no time for Howard on virtually anything, especially after the Iraq war, but I absolutely acknowledge his national leadership on gun law reform ... *but* he would not have been able to do it nationally if the state in which the massacre had occurred had not come out and said that that state was going to ban these weapons. It enabled him to have the moral authority to take it on nationally and that's what he did.

The Greens never did hold a press conference to say 'we told you so' after Port Arthur, or seek party-political advantage from the tragedy, and Milne says that was deliberate: '[It] comes back to, do you want outcomes or do you want votes? Do you want the credit for it, or do you want the outcome?'

From the outset, it was clear that getting the numbers in the new Senate was going to be dicey for Howard. Of 76 seats, the Coalition held 37, two votes short of the majority it needed to pass legislation, while Labor held 29, the Democrats seven, the Greens two, plus independent Brian Harradine. This gave Howard two routes to a majority: either the Democrats or the Greens.

Howard was very courteous with the Democrats' leader, Cheryl Kernot, a real powerbroker, but wary of the two Greens. There were two major reforms he was hoping to fast-track: legislation for the sale of a third of Telstra, to raise an estimated $8 billion, and the Coalition's Workplace Relations Bill, which sought to introduce individual contracts for employees, limit the powers of the Australian Industrial Relations Commission, and ban secondary boycotts.[5] Howard courted Kernot, giving the Democrats an advance copy of the bill and sidelining the Greens. He did not meet with Dee Margetts or senator-elect Bob Brown until early August, a week out from the government's first budget.

Brown and Margetts reiterated that they were implacably opposed to the sale of a third of Telstra, and pushed for a Senate inquiry. On industrial relations, Brown came away wary: 'Red lights are flashing on that.'[6] The Greens had campaigned strongly on industrial relations in the 1996 election, especially in Victoria: a flyer for Melbourne candidate Gurm Sekhon spelt out that the Greens were the only party that included the right to strike in their policy platform.

On budget day, Tuesday, 20 August, Senator Mal Colston quit the Labor Party to sit as an independent, and was elected as deputy president of the Senate in a secret ballot, 38 to 34, tilting the playing field dramatically in the Coalition's favour. Just one vote short of a majority, the government could now pass legislation without the support of Labor, the Democrats or the Greens. Colston would go down in Labor history as the worst 'rat' of all time.[7] Congratulating him, Dee Margetts observed it was 'important to note that it is possible or should be possible in this chamber for the position of President to be held by someone who is not of a major party'.[8] Three days later, Margetts confirmed that she had split with Brown and voted for Colston, who had helped her in the past; she too was now an independent.

Bob Brown's first speech to the Senate was on 10 September. First up he acknowledged Jo Vallentine and Christabel Chamarette, who had 'pioneered the entry of Green politics into this, the national parliament'. He warned against population growth, and linked it with the likelihood of future mass migration by environmental refugees. He put global warming up in lights, referring to predictions of a one-degree temperature rise by 2025, and went on:

> [I]f we do not rein in the greenhouse gas phenomenon one billion people on this planet will be displaced if the oceans rise by a metre at the end of the next century ... if we do not bring our warming gases under control, each hectare of forest being logged on this planet is of a value between $1,000 and $4,500 for its ability to contain carbon alone – something never written into the equation, so far as I am aware, in the debate over the value of Australia's forests, one which has been raging in this country.

The temperature rise, of course, has happened much faster than scientists were predicting even as recently as 1996.

Brown also flagged the Greens' broader agenda: challenging economic rationalism, pushing for proportional representation (preferably Hare-Clark), introducing freedom-of-information laws, restoring foreign aid, supporting euthanasia (which had just become legal in the Northern Territory). As the first openly gay man in the federal parliament, Brown declared happily: 'Some 20 years ago I, as that young doctor in Launceston, made it public that I am homosexual. Now 20 years down the line much has changed but I, naturally, have not.' Brown depicted the ten Greens sitting in Australian parliaments as part of a global wave, and in conclusion commended Howard on the forthcoming visit by the Dalai Lama: 'I say this about his holiness: he has said on one occasion that were he able to vote he might vote for an environmental candidate; were he able to stand, we might welcome him very much to stand as an environmental candidate.'[9]

Coincidentally, at the same time Brown rose to give his first speech in the Senate – 5.15 p.m. – the Greens' polar opposite, Pauline Hanson, was delivering her first speech in the House of

Representatives. Hanson moaned about 'reverse racism', warned that Australia was being 'swamped by Asians' and called for the abolition of multiculturalism. Hanson got all the coverage and, within a year, would go on to found One Nation.

*   *   *

Politics was changing. The emergence of right parties had shifted the ground, and half a dozen of the Greens' deeper thinkers laid out a ten-year strategy for the party in a prescient 1997 discussion paper.[10] The starting point was the rosy possibilities opened up by voters' growing impatience with the two-party system and rejection of economic rationalism. The Greens saw fertile ground and cited author Michael Pusey's Middle Australia Project, which found that two-thirds of the middle 70 per cent of income earners were unhappy or angry about politicians, and believed business elites had too much power. They thought government should 'row a little, not just steer'. Eighty per cent of middle Australians believed the gap between rich and poor was getting too wide, but only 13 per cent blamed freeloaders and 7 per cent blamed migrants. 'There is no need to assume that Australian decency is played out,' the Greens' paper noted. They recognised they could not rely on ecological catastrophe to drive voters towards them, and that the values-based movements of the previous 25 years – environmental, peace, feminist, gay and so on – would only ever provide a support base of 10–15 per cent of voters. What to do?

> The reality of a growing gap between the rich and corporations and the rest of us, the decline of the middle class incomes and securities, and the *awareness* of it restores class. Populism has always been that, a resurfacing of class into delimited agendas. What a pity if it is captured by the right. The Greens represent the possibility of integrating both fields of action, issues and class, and presenting explicit and democratic choice to the voters. But how do we look to them? To the extent they are aware of us it is as an interest group representing a narrow point of view and an exclusive ethic, that is, part of a system from which they feel alienated.

The authors posited that 'we are at the beginning of a reconstruction of ideas for a just society which will eventually overcome neo-liberalism; just as the neo-liberals set themselves up to undermine the post-war neo-Keynesian consensus and succeeded'. The Greens had to take advantage.

With 800,000 people unemployed, and another 600,000 under-employed, the Greens needed to flesh out their work policies, which expressly supported the principle of full employment but gave no detail on how this would be achieved. Two-thirds of Greens voters were under the age of 35, and the Greens had the highest proportion of very-low-income voters of any party, given the large number on Austudy or the dole. (This was in stark contrast with the Democrats, who had the wealthiest voters of any party.) With tax reform expected to dominate the next federal election, due by 1999, the authors believed that environmental reform did not have the breadth of popular support to ensure the Greens were not ignored, as they had been in 1993.

> The last thing anybody expects is for the Greens to take on jobs. It will catch everyone flat-footed: journalists, the other parties, business – all our traditional enemies. If we can just get them to attack our employment generating policies, and to say how they cannot work under neo-classical economic assumptions, then we will be off and running … we could come out from behind the ALP shadow, the ALP which put industry policy and Senator Button to bed over ten years ago.

A Greens jobs policy would be underpinned by environmental and infrastructure job creation funded by ecological taxes and low-interest RBA loans, an industry policy that picked winners, and redistribution of work through (for example) shorter working hours, as in France. It was a potent formulation, in many ways ahead of its time.

A core question was the relative position of the Greens, who generally polled around 3 per cent, and the Democrats, on 10 per cent. The authors wrote that the 'time has come to differentiate ourselves. Their lead is so great at the moment that if we are not to focus on our unique value we will be seen as just a somewhat weird version of them and eventually not seen at all.' The relationship between the Greens and the Democrats would steadily deteriorate. A crucial divide came when the Democrats negotiated 500 amendments to the government's Workplace Relations Bill, after two months of talks behind closed doors.[11] As the legislation was debated, Brown quoted *The Australian*'s economics editor, Alan Wood, who'd written that the bill was better than Peter Reith expected to get, 'although he cannot afford to say so because he still needs Kernot's co-operation to get it through'. Brown went on: 'In other words, Kernot was fooled.' Kernot's interjection was not recorded in *Hansard*.

In October that year, Kernot stunned her party and the political establishment by announcing she would defect to Labor. At an intensely emotional press conference, she said: '[H]aving long been a champion of a third party alternative ... I have found it increasingly difficult to stand in the middle, trying to be endlessly fair to both sides when I have grown so alarmed by the kind of politics being played out by the Coalition.' Her shock defection was the first of a series of blows from which the Democrats would not recover.

Howard continued to pick fights. One was over climate change. Howard disappointed the scientific community and the environmental movement, who wanted Australia to take the lead, by opposing mandatory uniform greenhouse-gas reduction targets for developed countries, and arguing instead that targets should be 'differentiated' for countries like Australia, which was fast-growing, 94 per cent reliant on fossil fuels for energy, and effectively incurred emissions on behalf of other countries due to its exports of coal, agricultural commodities and energy-intensive manufactures like steel and aluminium. During 1997, in the build-up to the UN's critical Kyoto climate talks, the goal of which was to come up with a legally binding framework to control global emissions, Dee Margetts said Howard's position was an international embarrassment:

We have already faced criticism during international conferences in Geneva and Berlin and now we will go to the next major international conference on greenhouse issues with another pathetic excuse for our inaction on this crucial issue. This is analogous to a chain smoker seeking an exemption from anti-smoking bans because they are addicted to nicotine.[12]

Bob Brown introduced a bill for a Sun Fund, to promote solar energy, which went to a committee and died. In November, just weeks before Kyoto, the government unveiled a significant package of measures including a proposal for a mandatory renewable energy target and a boost for the tree-planting and revegetation programs in the Natural Heritage Trust. The government would support UN efforts to set up an international emissions-trading scheme. Brown accused the government of cynicism and hypocrisy.[13]

When the talks began in Kyoto, Dee Margetts led a small Australian demonstration, which jostled Robert Hill on his entrance to the main summit hall, which was half-empty when he spoke.[14] But Hill played hardball and came back with a stunning win: Australia was one of only three developed countries allowed to *increase* its emissions (alongside Iceland and Norway), in our case by up to 108 per cent of the 1990 baseline, in the first commitment period of 2008–12. What's more, Hill insisted on a special 'Australia clause', which allowed a reduction in carbon emissions from avoided land clearing to be counted towards the Kyoto targets. Australia had got off almost scot-free; Labor's then environment spokesperson, Duncan Kerr, compared our task to a 'three-inch putt'.[15] It was a measure of vindication for Howard, but even though Australia had signed the protocol, the government refused to ratify it.

Another fight was over the Constitutional Convention to settle on a republic model to put to the people in a referendum. Howard decided that the convention would be half-appointed by various governments and half-elected by voluntary postal ballot. Labor saw the ballot as a stalking horse for the abolition of compulsory voting generally, and opposed the 1997 legislation setting up the convention, as did the Democrats and the Greens, amending it to make voting compulsory and sending it back to the Reps. The Coalition refused to buckle, and when it appeared likely that it was to be a voluntary vote or the convention would not be held at all, Brian Harradine and Bob Brown backflipped and supported the vote.

Brown recalls that the night of his decision was the first time the Greens' Quick Decision-Making Group, set up to consult party members and advise MPs when the platform did not give enough guidance, was put to the test. Brown was in a café in Manuka, ducking in and out to make calls:

> I said to every state I need to know within 24 hours what I should do here … anyway the final decision came through all of them: 'We don't know. We want you to make up your mind.' This is the party, you know, put on the rack over a difficult decision with multi-factorial plusses and negatives.

Brown held a press conference announcing he was voting 'for the republic, not for the government', and confessing that 'this decision hasn't come easily'. There had been no deals, no trade-offs. Brown said the Greens were rock-solid supporters of compulsory voting but the idea that it was the thin end of the wedge had been overdone: 'this is not a vote for a parliament, it's a vote for a consultative convention'.[16]

The Greens ran a ticket in most states and territories. Tasmania did best, with 10 per cent support, and New South Wales worst, with just 1 per cent – but, perversely, it was only there that a candidate was elected, party convenor Catherine Moore, on a loose party ticket called 'Greens, Bill of Rights, Indigenous Peoples'. They favoured a two-thirds majority of parliament appointing a president – but used the debate to push for wider constitutional reform, including recognition of the First Australians, equal representation for women, environmental responsibility, a bill of rights, recognition of local government, proportional representation in the lower house and fixed parliamentary terms.[17]

The Greens' leader in Tasmania, Christine Milne, was one of the state's three parliamentary delegates to the convention (along with the premier and opposition leader), and on day one spoke strongly in support of a motion that two of the ten days be set aside for a wider discussion:

> We are here to talk about whether we want to move to a republic
> and what sort of republic we would want for a democratic republic

of Australia. In talking about what sort of republic we want, we cannot ignore issues of Indigenous Australians. We cannot ignore issues of rights to clean air and clean water, or rights to equality in our Constitution ... it's imperative that we expand the agenda.[18]

The motion was lost, and discussion of any wider reform agenda was confined to the drafting of a new preamble to the constitution. Milne and Moore were bit players, not on a party ticket – they took slightly different positions on the codification of the reserve powers – and split towards the end. Milne went along with the compromise ARM model adopted by the majority of republicans, while Moore abstained from a number of votes on the model, half-siding with the direct-electionists. Both voted, however, in favour of the crucial resolution by which the convention agreed to put the ARM's favoured bipartisan appointment of the president to the people at a referendum.

Howard's most dramatic fight was on the waterfront. On 7 April 1998, some 1400 workers were locked out overnight by Patrick Stevedores, after months of simmering industrial dispute. Former soldiers hired by the National Farmers Federation, secretly trained in Dubai, stormed the docks in balaclavas and with guard dogs, to intimidate workers and unload shipping containers at Patrick's terminals. The shock tactics were planned over a year, and Howard's employment minister, Peter Reith, had been involved and supportive.

Such thick plotting between government and a corporation to crush a unionised workforce was shocking to many Australians. Thousands joined pickets in support of the MUA, among them a young student, Sarah Hanson-Young, who later remembered she 'helped turn sausages & feed the brave workers standing up against Howard's ideological IR warfare'.[19] Bob Brown spoke at one demonstration in Melbourne, and the Greens ran newspaper ads supporting the MUA and reminding everyone the party had strongly opposed the 'Reith-Kernot Workplace Relations Act' that had allowed the sackings, including the draconian secondary boycott provisions.

Both sides of the waterfront dispute claimed victory: the Federal Court reinstated the MUA workers, but they went back on a new enterprise agreement that enabled Patrick to increase productivity.

In all the mythology woven around the dispute, the Greens' support for the MUA is often forgotten.

*   *   *

Another fight the Howard government picked was over the Jabiluka uranium mine, which had been simmering as the project wound its way through the federal assessment process. Uranium prices were back up, and Jabiluka was the first of an expected 25 new uranium mines in Australia. The $14 billion project was being developed by Energy Resources Australia, then majority owned by North Ltd, the same company the Tasmanian Greens had fought over the pulp mill at Wesley Vale. ERA claimed the mine would take up less than 20 hectares of land. Bob Brown said the whole Kakadu area was magnificent, and 'to say that it will only take up 20 hectares is like saying a scratch won't matter on a Beethoven record'.[20] A worldwide coalition of green groups called for Kakadu to be listed as World Heritage in Danger in August 1997, but two months later the energy and resources minister, Warwick Parer, announced the project would go ahead.[21] The Aboriginal community split, with the Northern Land Council supporting offsite milling but opposed to the construction of a mill onsite, while the Gundjehmi corporation, representing the Mirarr, opposed the project outright. The scene was set for confrontation.

The Jabiluka campaign began to build around the country, including in Western Australia, where the Greens were on a roll. At the state election at the end of 1996, which returned Premier Richard Court's government with an increased majority, the Greens had picked up two extra seats in the upper house on a modest swing, and shared the balance of power with two Democrats in what would become a protracted arm wrestle. Giz Watson and Christine Sharp joined Jim Scott, taking up their seats from 1997 and hoping to take on a veritable shopping-list of causes, working in cahoots with the opposition. Born in England, Watson had grown up in Perth and studied environmental science before working as a carpenter and builder, and was the country's first openly lesbian MP. Going into Parliament was like entering a gentleman's debating club, she recalled later: 'This chamber had been conservative-dominated for I think it was 103 years, ever since it was established, and when you look at the history of the Legislative Council it was the sort of landed gentry who set it up'.[22] The MPs' new offices would soon become a drop-in centre for anti-Jabiluka activists in Perth, including a young graphic designer called Scott Ludlam, who gave the photocopiers a flogging.

In mid-1997, a group called the Gaia Foundation – whose spokesperson, Kate Vallentine, was the daughter of the former Greens senator – announced a 40-day tour of Australia's major uranium projects, starting in Perth on Hiroshima Day, going via Kintyre to Jabiluka and then on to Olympic Dam in South Australia. Hearing Vallentine interviewed on Perth radio just before Christmas that year, Ludlam had taken his first actively political step and turned up to an anti-nuclear rally – he was so nervous, apparently, that he took his mum along. She had handed out for Jo Vallentine in the 1980s, but, thinking back, Ludlam believes he voted Democrat in the 1990s, notwithstanding there were WA Greens candidates by the time he reached voting age. 'I'd never heard of them,' he says. After the anti-Jabiluka rally, Jo Vallentine, who'd spoken to the crowd, spotted the quiet young man hanging around and invited him for a cup of tea and a debrief with the other organisers.

Ludlam had never been involved in any form of protest before, but was compelled by the struggle of traditional owners, the Mirarr people, against the Jabiluka mine: 'This mob is confronting the mining company that owns their town, the global nuclear industry, the commonwealth government, the NT government, and the mining sector more broadly, and 90 per cent of the commercial press – that's who they're going up against. Everybody thinks they're going to lose.'

As a designer, Ludlam had done a bit of consulting work with mining companies. 'I'd been at the PR end of the industry and had a certain affection for it – not hostility; I know how they think and how they talk.' Over the summer, he started volunteering for the anti-Jabiluka campaign – designing newsletters, posters and web pages – while also reading voraciously, and writing an anti-nuclear play called 'Atomic Oz'. A bit of street theatre, the play was performed on a map of Australia, with all the nuclear sites marked out. Jo Vallentine played Mrs Mop, trying to clean up the nuclear waste;

'This ash is so fine, you can't clean it up,' she would complain. Ludlam was dipping his toe into green politics.

Momentum increased from February 1998, after the Federal Court ruled against a legal challenge brought by Mirarr elder Yvonne Margarula, effectively giving the mine the final go-ahead. Thousands marched at rallies on the east coast in April. Speaking at the Melbourne demo, Bob Brown warned the government that Jabiluka would be a watershed confrontation, comparing it to the Franklin campaign of 15 years earlier. 'Having come through the Franklin campaign where there were 6,000 who went to the blockade, 1,500 arrested, 500 jailed, I think this is going to be bigger,' Brown said.[23]

Traditional owners blockaded the access road to the Jabiluka site, 200 kilometres east of Darwin, and called for protesters from around the country and internationally to join them. Jo Vallentine told Ludlam he should go up and get himself arrested. Ludlam recalls that when he told one of his mates what he was about to do, 'he was like, "Mate, they've already made their minds up. It's already decided." It wasn't hostile, it was incomprehensible – why would you go and get flattened on this thing you know you're going to lose?' But hundreds of protesters began to arrive, from all over the country. Ludlam turned up alone, straight off a coach, and like all newcomers was immediately made aware he was a guest on Aboriginal land and this struggle was about land rights:

> We got a passport when we arrived, from the Mirarr, that said, 'These are the rules, you're welcome here, but if you fuck up you're on the next bus back down south.' I was nervous about being there, I felt completely out of my element … being in a camp full of hippies, the camp politics, there's some really wonderful people there but also by then there's some crew who've been up there for months who are in their own tribe of direct action, doing hardcore shit, and then the new kid turns up and it's like 'go and dig the toilets, mate' … which I did.

In a 2007 doctoral thesis on the blockade, a Queensland university sociologist argues that the Jabiluka campaign was beset by conflict and eventual schism, because there was tension between the 'movement of crisis' of the Mirarr people, for whom the project had immediate personal consequences, and the 'movement of affluence' of environmentalists, who faced none.[24] Ludlam, who was arrested for trespass at the blockade alongside 150 other protesters, makes a very similar point:

> We were in the lockup in Jabiru for a couple of hours because we'd refused to give our names – we were all John Howard that day – but the lockup was hilarious fun, it was just 150 people drawing on the walls and running amok. That's what I mean about arrest privilege. For the mob up there, being thrown in the Jabiru lockup can be a matter of life or death.

With a federal election looming, the opposition, led by Kim Beazley, was inclined to oppose the mine but was accused of obfuscating, saying an incoming Labor government would only allow Jabiluka to operate if it was already by then an existing mine. Brown said the ALP was positioning itself 'to say before the election that they will stop the mine and say after an election victory it will have to go ahead'. Environment minister Robert Hill said Labor was 'leaving the door open for mining to try and woo Northern Territory voters, while telling green groups down south they are opposed to the mine'.[25] Beazley rejected a call from the Greens to announce that Labor would stop the mine going ahead if it won government, even if the final contract had been signed:

> The Labor Party has never repudiated contracts and never will when we come into office; that is a formula for presenting yourself internationally in a way that nobody ever wants to put another cent into your country. We do not repudiate contracts in the Labor Party, but having said that we don't think there are going to be any contracts in place, of a meaningful nature, between now and when the next election occurs and if that is true we would not support the go-ahead of the mine.

ERA said it did not know what a 'meaningful contract' meant, but was soon pointing to sale contracts for the yellowcake.[26] The parallels with Adani's Carmichael coalmine, more than 20 years later, are obvious. By mid-1998, ERA had got all the heavy equipment it needed onto the site and construction began. The World Heritage Committee in Paris sent out a team of inspectors, and the Greens and Democrats renewed calls for work to stop, pending their report. Thirty-one people were arrested when they locked on to ERA's bulldozers and trucks, but all charges were dropped. The numbers at the camp had swelled from 40 in March to 300 by July, but a steady stream of media commentary suggested Jabiluka had not captured the public imagination the way the Franklin had done. Peter Garrett, as president of the ACF, told *The Australian* Jabiluka was starting to bite, but 'it's a difficult issue for us to campaign on because it involves some logistical difficulties in getting people there'.[27] Garrett, Tom Uren and musicians Vince Jones and Regurgitator went up. Numbers continued to build.

Ludlam was only a foot soldier at Jabiluka, but another later Greens senator had a higher profile: Sydney-based activist Kerry Nettle, then working as environment officer for the student union at the University of Technology. Nettle spent four months at Jabiluka, working as a communications officer. On the day Garrett visited, she did so many interviews she didn't know who she was talking to and hung up on Sydney shock jock Stan Zemanek, who'd asked, 'And what have you been smoking, love?' Nettle did a lot of liaison between traditional owners and the blockade, and confirms the tensions. 'There were crazy hippies carving Buddha statues into termite mounds,' she says. 'You get mad hippies at everything.'

The blockade was packed down in August as the wet season approached, and amid hopes that Labor would win the coming federal election. The future of the mine itself would hang in the balance for another five years. 'I think of Jabiluka as the Franklin of my generation,' says Nettle, 'in terms of the people who were politicised, the people who were subsequently involved, the people who I still know who are active.' Ludlam remembers meeting Nettle there, and says his takeaway from the blockade was that, even in the face of apparently insurmountable obstacles, 'you're not automatically going to lose':

Sometimes you're going to win ... I can remember the day they arrested Yvonne for trespass. That's a profound thing to happen to

an Aboriginal elder on her own country and I can remember that
kind of washing back through the entire campaign, you know, this
is not just about a uranium mine, really, is it?

*   *   *

Jabiluka was the biggest environmental issue of the 1998 election but,
unlike in 1996 or 1990, the environment hardly figured in the broader
debate this time around. Instead, as in 1993, the goods and services
tax dominated, with Howard and Costello unveiling a major economic reform: a new tax system, with a broad-based consumption
tax of 10 per cent replacing the existing wholesale sales tax and a
range of other indirect and state taxes.

Just weeks out from the poll, Democrats leader Meg Lees signalled that her party could support a GST that excluded fresh food,
and services such as health and education. This might have opened
up campaign space for the Greens, who were steadfastly opposed to
the regressive consumption tax. But, once again, they struggled to
get attention.

Bob Brown, who was not up for re-election in 1998, publicly
predicted that the Greens would win at least two Senate seats: Dee
Margetts would be re-elected in Western Australia, and former
Antarctic base leader Louise Crossley would get over the line in
Tasmania. In the lower house, party strategist Stephen Luntz identified Melbourne as 'a winnable seat when the ALP is in government',
and described Fremantle as 'one of the most winnable seats in the
country for us, but the prospects are certainly lower than returning
Dee so it is probably not worth focussing on'. The party's highest pri-
ority was to garner preference flows to support Margetts' re-election,
Luntz wrote. 'We need to unite to pressure the ALP, and possibly the
Nats or Libs, to preference to Dee. We should be willing to sacrifice
preferences in states where we will not win for this.'[28]

A complication was that the Australian Greens and the WA
Greens remained separate parties, which did not help with the preference negotiations, and a 1997 proposal to finally unite had become
bogged down over how to align the two constitutions – amendments
would be required on both sides, meaning all states had to agree,

which of course they didn't. Worse, coming into the election, the Australian Greens were still scratching for funds from the states, and were completely reliant on volunteers.

For the first time, in 1998 the Greens did some focus group research, among those aged 18 to 30 who were committed Greens voters or potential Greens or Democrats supporters. Two groups in Hobart and Melbourne, with students and the unemployed over-represented, nominated unemployment, education and privatisation as the hot issues for them, and worried that the Liberals were turning Australia into 'an uncaring, selfish, short-sighted society' and 'there'll be nothing left for us'. The environment was a secondary issue, even though participants recognised it was ignored by the ruling parties and 'our future depends on it'.

Almost universally, the Greens/Democrats voters loathed the Liberals as ruthless and destructive, while recognising that they 'get things done'. They felt Labor was tired, cynical, divided, shifting rapidly towards economic rationalism, 'less apt at governing', but were nevertheless the 'better of two evils'. They were split on the unpredictable Democrats, particularly post-Kernot, with some saying they had shifted to the left, into the space vacated by Labor, while others perceived them to be 'Liberals in frocks'. They also had some frank criticisms of the Greens, who were people of integrity and 'about the future' but were also perceived as a single-issue party, 'emotionally charged (utopian, impractical, irrational)', 'narrow, fringe' protesters who opposed everything and 'produce nothing', and who lacked business skills or political nous. Even among these people there were real barriers to voting Green: 'they don't care about people like me', they 'consist of "hippies" and unemployed', 'there's no point voting for people who won't ever get into power ... it's a wasted vote, really'. One participant asked: 'Do they know how to govern?' As another put it: 'If the Greens got into power you'd be pretty worried because all their policies would be environmental and that is it.'

Most depressingly, perhaps, for a party that had been around for a while now, there was very low awareness of the Greens. Few knew what the 'balance of power' was, for example, or that the Greens had held it at state level. The pollsters summed up that prospective voters supported the ideology and long-term vision of the Greens, but needed reassurance that their vote would count and that, if voted in, the Greens could bring about change. They wanted examples of past successes, actual achievements, not just things the Greens had opposed. A particular test for the Greens was to balance the politics of confrontation, which could be alienating, with the art of compromise and 'shady' deal-making. Two campaign slogans tested well: 'Rescue the future' and 'Thinking locally, acting globally'.[29] They chose the first.

After the party's national conference in Healesville in August 1998, the Greens announced that Pauline Hanson and the GST would be their prime targets in the coming election. Bob Brown said members would demonstrate at more One Nation rallies in protest over the party's 'dangerously anti-environment' stance.[30] The strategy was reflected in the choice of young Gunditjmara woman Charmaine Clarke to be the party's lead Senate candidate in Victoria. A reconciliation advocate, a member of the Stolen Generations and a former ABC Radio journalist who had been prominent in anti-racism protests, she would have been the first Indigenous woman in the federal parliament if elected. Clarke was quickly endorsed by former independent Phil Cleary, who announced in September he would not run for the Senate, boosting the Greens' slim chances. As a 'black green', Clarke joined an anti-Jabiluka protest outside the Melbourne headquarters of North Ltd, saying that 'black and green have never stood together with such determination'.[31]

The Greens' national campaign was run out of Melbourne, coordinated by Dan Cass, son of the former Whitlam environment minister, Moss. Cass had worked on the party's Victorian campaign (starring Peter Singer) in 1996. Right from the start, the campaign was dominated by the GST reforms, which Howard announced in mid-August. Brown denounced the GST as 'anti-green', because it would increase the price of organic fruit and vegetables but lower the price of pesticides and diesel; he also warned it would increase the divide between rich and poor.[32] The Greens made mileage out of the Democrats' conditional support for the regressive consumption tax, which was tantamount to having a bet each way. In a release pitching for union support, Clarke trumpeted: 'We are more Labour than Labor. The Greens are the only party in the Parliament radical enough to have the right to strike in our policy. Working people should remind themselves that the Democrats caved in to Coalition pressure and passed the worst industrial relations laws in the country.'[33]

Despite the campaign barbs, Bob Brown and Meg Lees did a preference swap deal. The Greens had been the first party to declare they would put One Nation last in the federal election, after the party had stormed the Queensland parliament in June, winning 23 per cent of the vote and 11 seats in a stunning debut. But the Greens' still-shambolic preference processes came back to bite the party: the tiny Northern Territory branch somehow missed the mail about putting One Nation last, and decided to put the Country Liberal Party last instead. This turned into a national news story, generating negative publicity and scotching the Greens' chance of getting preferences from the anti-racist Unity Party, which was campaigning against One Nation. In the lower house, the Greens made a show of weighing up the major party platforms,[34] but it was clear the flirtation with the Coalition was over: they wound up recommending Labor in 60 out of 66 marginal seats.

*   *   *

Coming before the federal election, the Tasmanian election of 1998 was the Greens' first major reversal in Australian politics. Liberal and Labor (led by Jim Bacon) had cooked up a plan to eliminate the Greens by reducing the number of state MPs from 35 to 25, increasing the quota required for election from 12.5 per cent to 16.7 per cent.[35] In *The Canberra Times*, journalist Crispin Hull described the conspiracy between the major parties to do in the Greens as a 'democratic outrage', and warned that there could well be a repeat performance at the Commonwealth level, and there need not be a referendum. 'Do not be surprised if the major parties push through a change to the Senate voting system to favour themselves,' Hull wrote.[36]

In her memoir, leader Christine Milne writes that when the reform went through, without debate, she knew 'it was over for the Greens. We would all lose our seats. I knew what it meant for us, for Green politics, and what twenty-five members meant for the quality of government in Tasmania.' She went back to her leader's office and cried. After a dispiriting campaign – for the first time, the party struggled to fill the Hobart Town Hall for the official launch – the Greens were very nearly wiped out of the parliament altogether. Statewide support held up reasonably at 10.2 per cent (down 0.9 per cent) – One Nation were not organised enough to register – but the new quota was just too high. In her memoir, Milne records that as she walked to the tally room to concede defeat on election night, she told her advisers to go ahead and tell the Greens who were there to meet her that they should 'not approach me, embrace me or make eye contact until after my speech: kindness would have been my undoing. They did as I asked and I gave one of the most memorable speeches of my life, predicting that the Greens would be back.'

Remarkably, however, Brown's successor, Peg Putt, defied the old party stitch-up and clung on in Denison, polling 10.5 per cent. The Labor and Liberal parties were so confident of eliminating the Greens that they had gone to the trouble of literally removing the cross benches in the House of Assembly. When the House reconvened, Milne recalls, Putt brought her own folding aluminium and plastic picnic chair: 'she walked in, calmly set it up where the cross-bench used to be and proceeded to take her place. It was such an inspiring gesture of rebuke, resilience, persistence and hope ... it screamed "never, ever give up".' Milne treasures the chair, which was later picked up by author Richard Flanagan at an auction, to this day.

Although Bob Brown was not running, he remained the key national figure in the Greens' campaign, with mixed results and very little cut-through in the mainstream media despite a national tour and the usual blizzard of press releases. Brown's first burst of publicity came from a court appearance in Melbourne. He had been arrested and charged with obstructing a lawful logging operation at a protest in the Goolengook forest, in East Gippsland, the previous year. Remarkably, the charge had been dismissed by a magistrate in early 1998 because the state government could not prove the logging was lawful. The Supreme Court ruled the magistrate had erred in law, but the judge reserved his decision. (Three weeks after the election, Brown was vindicated and the charges were thrown out.)[37]

In the second week of the campaign, Brown was involved in an anti-woodchipping protest outside a Liberal Party fundraiser in

Hobart, which turned ugly when Prime Minister Howard and his wife, Janette, were reportedly jostled as they arrived. There were about 80 protesters, including a costumed quoll who threw herself under the wheels of the Commonwealth car, yelling, 'Howard, you rapist!' Brown himself also stood in front of the car, shouting, 'Save the forests!' A nine-year-old girl, protesting with her mum, was shoved up against a wall by security guards, and a press photographer fell into a pram with a baby in it.

'I do not regard it as intelligent protest to bring young babies into protests,' Howard said afterwards. 'I have no objection to anybody lawfully demonstrating. It's part of Australian politics. The Australian public will make a judgement as to the maturity of a senator who stands in front of a Commonwealth car routinely to get his photograph in the paper.'[38]

There were no arrests, but the TV footage was very negative. According to one report, Brown made no apology for the protest, saying the atmosphere would have been different if the prime minister had stopped to talk to them, and he was untroubled by the Liberal claim that he was 'a stunt a day man'. Brown replied: 'It's not as bad being a "stunt a day" person as being a thousand stumps a day as the Liberal Party are.'[39] Plenty of Greens supporters, however, were disappointed and rang the Tasmania campaign office to say so.[40]

Criticised in *The Australian* for taking it to the streets rather than sticking to his day job in the Senate, Brown penned a strong letter complaining that his many speeches on forests were never covered, and pointing out that Howard had refused repeated personal invitations to visit Tasmania's threatened forests. 'It would be easy for a Green senator to sit on his hands in the cosy confines of the Senate while the destruction escalates. I cannot.'[41]

There was more bad publicity when two Molotov cocktails were thrown through the window of ERA's Darwin office at 2 a.m. – the culprits were never found – and an anti-Jabiluka protester chained himself to the door of Nationals' MP Doug Anthony's office in Tweed Heads, in the northern New South Wales seat of Richmond, and threatened to blow himself up. Brown said the Greens had nothing to do with either action and abhorred violence.[42] By contrast, the Greens' national campaign launch in Hobart, where Louise Crossley unveiled the centrepiece eco-tax package – including a carbon price of $25 per tonne of CO_2 – got almost no coverage.[43] A morale boost came four days out from polling day, when Die Grünen in Germany stormed to the balance of power, led by Joschka Fischer. Brown said: 'We are looking to winning the balance of power in the Australian Senate next weekend.'[44]

It was not to be. In the Senate, One Nation polled a strong 9 per cent on debut, and its high vote knocked down support for all other parties. Howard lost seats, but held enough to retain government. On election night Brown was confidently predicting that Crossley would get over the line in Tasmania, having won 5.7 per cent of the primary vote – paradoxically helped by One Nation, which had directed preferences away from Brian Harradine, who had robbed them of the opportunity of a race election. Brown steadfastly denied that the Greens had done any preference deal with One Nation in Tassie, as Democrats candidate Robert Bell had accused them of doing, but did not deny that the preference flow, which turned out to be 73 per cent, would help.[45] Years later, Brown would describe the preference dealing as the most distasteful aspect of the job.

As the count wore on, Harradine, with a primary vote of 7.9 per cent, regained the lead over Crossley, helped by Liberal preferences. In Western Australia, Dee Margetts won 5.7 per cent of the primary vote but was beaten by the Democrats' candidate, gay activist Brian Greig, who polled 6.3 per cent. Margetts, who remained in the Senate until mid-1999, was philosophical and would later re-emerge in state politics.

The Greens' overall vote in the Senate was disappointing, at 2.7 per cent. The Democrats' vote held up well, given the Kernot defection and equivocal support for the unpopular GST, with the party winning primary support of 8.4 per cent and nine senators in the new Senate, enough for them to hold the balance of power outright. In the lower house, the Greens contested 115 seats and won primary support of 2.6 per cent across the country, topping the 4 per cent funding threshold in 30 seats: ten in New South Wales, ten in Western Australia, five in Tasmania, four in Victoria and one in Queensland. The candidate in Newcastle, Carrie Jacobi, got the best result in the country, with 9.4 per cent of the primary vote.

The Greens' post-election review was pretty scathing, beginning with the observation that the party has 'never had a national political strategy, which is increasingly an impediment to our development', and noting that, with regard to the stated goals of increasing the primary vote and Green representation in the federal parliament, 'we failed'.[46] The review pondered why cooperation should be so hard to achieve. Preferencing remained poorly understood, and the review slammed the Northern Territory branch's decision not to put Hanson last, which gave ammunition to the Democrats and cost the Greens the preferences of Unity in Victoria and New South Wales. The review described Unity as a Labor front that cost the Greens tens of thousands of dollars by keeping their vote under the crucial 4 per cent threshold. 'The fact that they preferenced against Charmaine Clarke was one of the more morally bankrupt incidents of the whole Federal Election and personally hurtful to her.'[47] The review proposed an informal five-point strategy for future campaigns: '1. Get smaller left groups support over the Democrats. 2. Do a preference swap with the Democrats before major parties. 3. Convince the ALP to preference us over the Democrats. 4. Preference the ALP over Coalition. 5. Place One Nation last.'[48]

A potent observation was that, under a Liberal federal government, Greens voters tended to drift back to the mainstream parties – the ALP and, to a lesser extent, the Democrats:

> When the ALP is up for re-election, the Greens chance of winning is 6:1, whereas when the Liberals are in government it is even-Stephen. That would suggest that people are quite likely to consider voting Green when the ALP is in, but when they are not in, the contest is more difficult for us.

A winning trend appeared to have reversed in the Howard years:

> [Our] wins were all between 1982 and 1996 whereas the losses have been from 1996–98. We would expect the opposite trend to be the case given that the party has increased in size approximately three-fold between 1995 and 1998. Our profile has also increased, as has our reputation among progressives. Yet despite these positive trends we have gone from good to bad electorally.[49]

A definite hindrance was the environmental movement, which 'contributed nothing formally to the Greens at this election', despite numerous high-level approaches by Bob Brown and his office. 'Our recommendation to the party is that we cease to see relations with the movement in personal or even electoral terms.' The original vision of conservationists such as Milo Dunphy and Geoff Mosely, who had hoped to convert the vast memberships of environmental organisations into an electoral force, had crumbled before the Greens. Far more useful and cost-effective were connections with unions, who were taking a real interest in the Greens: after the party's strong stand on the industrial relations debates and the waterfront dispute, unions had contributed some $4200 out of a total $10,000 in donations received; some, including the National Tertiary Education Union and the National Union of Students, had gone close to endorsing the party.

After five years as a confederation in which it had contested three elections, at the end of 1998 the Australian Greens were little stronger than they had been at the beginning: they had one senator, had been almost wiped out in their home state of Tasmania, were estranged from the environmental movement, had burned their bridges with Labor, and their primary vote was falling. The next election, when Bob Brown's Senate term was up, would be do or die for the party.

Despite the gloomy situation, the review reached an eerily prescient conclusion about the party's prospects at the next election:

> We could have an early onset of the next wave of environmentalism or perhaps an equivalent 'future angst' in the form of millennial anxiety. In this situation, Bob Brown would shine as the most credible politician in Australia on the big-picture millennial angst questions and could plausibly carry the Greens to a surge of support (say 4–4.5 per cent).

Which is exactly what happened – although of course nobody could know it yet.

CHAPTER 7

TURNING THE CORNER

If, at the national level, the Greens were hanging on by the skin of their teeth during the 1990s, something very different and more organic was happening at the grassroots, especially in New South Wales. In Tasmania and Western Australia, the Greens had grown from the top down. There were Green members of parliament, like Bob Brown and Jo Vallentine, before there was a party structure, or a grassroots membership. In New South Wales, by contrast, the Greens grew more slowly, from the bottom up, assisted at the local level by a proportional voting system for council elections.

In 1991, John Sutton in Newcastle and Bruce Welch in Marrickville were the first Greens elected to councils anywhere in the country, and representation jumped through the decade, spreading to inner-Sydney councils like Leichhardt, Waverley and Randwick, then into the suburbs and to regional councils such as Illawarra and Byron shires. In the 1995 council elections, the Greens won 19 seats, and by 1999, there were 27 representatives sprinkled across the state. As Marrickville councillor Sam Byrne wrote, 'local government is an important rung on the grassroots democracy ladder, and I believe our best chances for lower house breakthroughs will come through local government when future Green mayors run'.[1]

A little later, the same pattern was evident in Victoria: the state's first Green representative was David Risstrom, elected to Melbourne City Council in 1999; Gurm Sekhon was the first Green anywhere to win an outright majority in a single-member electorate, in a Yarra City Council by-election in 2001, and Greg Barber became the country's first Green mayor there in 2003. Tasmania caught on at much the same time: Bob Brown's partner, Paul Thomas, was elected to the Huon Valley Municipal Council in 1996, first as an independent and then as an official Greens candidate in 1999.

In South Australia, ex-communist Joy O'Brien was elected to the Burnside City Council in 2000, becoming that state's first Greens representative.[2] Western Australia might have been strong – and there were dozens of independent councillors who considered themselves greenish – but the party didn't nominate official candidates. The Australian Greens Local Government Network was formed in 2001; by the following year there were 37 Greens councillors around the country, mostly in New South Wales, giving voters a taste of the party and forming a political talent pool that would include many future MPs.

New South Wales was catching up at the state level, too. Labor's premier, Bob Carr, an old friend of Milo Dunphy's and from the environmentally friendly Wran school, was genuinely interested in conservation. In consequence, lone NSW Greens MLC Ian Cohen's first term got off to a good start in 1995. In shades of Bob Brown and Richo, Cohen found himself inside the tent, working with Carr under an informal accord. Carr had gone to the election promising to declare 24 new national parks, which helped secure the green preferences that gave him his narrow win. He kept his promise, cutting logging quotas by 30 per cent in 1996. His government declared 403,000 hectares of new wilderness or national park, and deferred logging of 816,000 hectares of old-growth forest, as a precursor to more comprehensive assessments that would underpin 20-year regional forest agreements with the Commonwealth.[3] Cohen described it as a 'historic step':

> I was a protester at the Washpool National Park, the south-east forests, Chaelundi State Forest and the Richmond Ranges ... Time and again I have accused the government of mirror and smokescreen legislation. That has been a major problem. [But] we must look at the big picture ... The government has attempted to work out a balance in difficult circumstances.[4]

Looking back, Cohen believes it was Carr who made the difference: 'You can work the system at all levels – legal, direct action and political – but [things happen] when you've got someone at the head of the political system who is really genuinely onside.'

On the crossbench, Cohen worked increasingly closely with Democrats defector Richard Jones, a former Australia Party environmentalist. Cohen and Jones both supported government moves to decriminalise recreational marijuana use, and were pilloried as potheads in parliament and the tabloid media; the jokes fell flat when they responded by calling for drunken MPs to be breathalysed.[5] Cohen went hard against the M2 freeway through Sydney's north-west, which included an outrageous clause preventing the government from building competing public transport links during its 30-year life. Cohen revealed that the Roads and Traffic Authority was propping up the company with $24 million of taxpayer funds, and under parliamentary privilege accused the company of misrepresenting its accounts, and the federal government of corruption for failing to act.[6]

Cohen's supportive relationship with the Carr government didn't go full-term, however. The first fractures came in late 1997, over amendments to the *Environment Planning and Assessment Act* that allowed community consultation to be bypassed. Then, when the forest assessments were finally released in late 1998, Cohen cried foul. Instead of protecting the 816,000 hectares the conservation movement had hoped for, or the 620,000 hectares the forests minister had proposed, the government would save just 380,000 hectares, a number much closer to the industry and CFMEU position. The decision was widely seen as an attempt to save the marginal northern New South Wales seat of Clarence, which had three sawmills, and which Labor had won from the Nationals in 1995.

Cohen may take a more moderate view nowadays, but at the time he unleashed: 'To hell with you, Bob Carr ... your government has sold us out and you are not going to get away with it.'[7] Carr was unapologetic: having declared 151 new national parks since 1995, he claimed 'the greenest credentials of any government in Australia's history'.[8] Cohen immediately flagged that the Greens would withhold preferences in the looming state election, and the battlelines were drawn.

The Greens had preselected their lead candidate, Lee Rhiannon. Rhiannon had changed her name after her 1989 separation from electrician and journalist Paddy O'Gorman. (For the record,

Rhiannon's new surname, which was suggested by a friend, had nothing to do with the Fleetwood Mac song.) At some point Rhiannon's membership of the Socialist Party of Australia lapsed, and she joined the Greens in 1990 at the urging of NSW Greens stalwart Geoff Ash. When her membership form came through, both Hall Greenland and Tony Harris raised their eyebrows, muttering, 'Lee Brown's joined!' Harris observed that Rhiannon did have a botany degree – she had graduated with honours from UNSW, doing a thesis on water and nutrient stress in banksia species. Rhiannon had kept up her activism through the 1980s, working as a freelance journalist for unions including the Maritime Union of Australia, joining the board of the Rainforest Information Centre, setting up AID/WATCH, and building up a national profile as convenor of the Coalition for Gun Control, set up in 1988. She was even arrested in 1999, at a protest to save urban bushland at Manly Dam from developers.

Ian Cohen had met Rhiannon at university in the 1970s and had no qualms about backing her for preselection. 'I voted for Lee, and that was potentially a mistake, you know, in hindsight,' says Cohen now, 'although the fact is, if she hadn't gotten up then, she was determined, she would have gotten up sometime.' At the time, Cohen had faith in their past friendship, respected her activism and 'didn't really have any real, proper understanding of her quite hardline communist views'. It was when he took Rhiannon on a tour to introduce her to senior conservationists and progressive businesspeople from the New South Wales north coast – greenie movers and shakers – that the alarm bells went off. 'I got quite a bit of complaint about her afterwards, from people who met her, who were pretty astute political operators, saying, "What the hell are you supporting her for?"' Rhiannon dismisses Cohen's comments as 'another of his unsubstantiated slurs against me'.

With Labor and the Greens facing off over the forests, and the Coalition pitching a $25 billion electricity privatisation that could fund a vote-buying spree, Cohen and Rhiannon knuckled down. The 1999 election in New South Wales was the notorious 'tablecloth' election, with an upper-house ballot paper carrying the names of hundreds of candidates for often misleadingly badged micro-parties.

It was the first election in which Glenn Druery harvested preferences to get a candidate elected: four-wheel-driver Malcolm Jones, from the Outdoor Recreation Party, who got in with just 0.2 per cent of the primary vote. The 'preference whisperer' Druery would go on to cruel the Greens' chances at a number of federal elections.

In the preference negotiations, Rhiannon pushed for a new tactic. Bob Brown's strategy, she recalls, was to wait for that one moment of the campaign when the media would ask the Greens which party they were intending to favour in marginal seats, and try to leverage that into the best possible deal for the environment – exchanging 'preferences for policy'. In the 1999 state campaign, however, Rhiannon pushed for a new approach: exchanging 'preferences for preferences'. The Greens would favour Labor in the lower house in exchange for Labor preferences in the upper house.

The strategy caused some tension between Rhiannon and Brown, but it worked. The Greens opposed electricity privatisation, and supported Labor in the tightest marginal seats. They did not preference the Coalition anywhere. Rhiannon got elected with just 2.9 per cent of the primary vote – a 0.8 per cent swing against the party compared with the 1995 result, but a respectable result given all the front parties and the sheer number of candidates. The Greens did very well in inner-city seats such as Port Jackson and Marrickville, coming second in both with a primary vote of 29 per cent. There is no doubt Green preferences helped Carr, but there was a small swing to Labor in any case, and he had a thumping win, adding five seats. Still, with two MLCs, the Greens now were an official parliamentary party in New South Wales. It was a boost to the party nationally, just five months after a disappointing 1998 federal election result.

Rhiannon's first speech in the Legislative Council acknowledged her communist past:

I particularly wish to thank my parents, Bill and Freda Brown. My parents were members of the Communist Party of Australia. I was raised surrounded by people whose driving conviction was how to work to make this world a fairer, healthier, more peaceful place for all. Being raised in a household steeped in political campaigns leaves one with many proud moments. One of those was the night my father and Jack Mundey became the first people arrested in Australia for protesting against the Vietnam War. I find these days when I explain my background some people are surprised by my acknowledgement. I am certainly proud of being part of a tradition of optimistic social activism ...

Rhiannon attacked Labor's sell-off of Walsh Bay, the historic public wharves at Millers Point on the western fringe of Sydney's CBD. In a stirring speech, she rattled off the list of donors to Labor, including Carr's mates at Transfield and Mirvac, signalling her interest in what would become a potent area of focus for the Greens. She put the work of the parliament into context:

> If the bill passes the House, the battle to save Walsh Bay will not be over. Just behind Millers Point lies The Rocks, the birthplace of the green bans. It was from this movement that my party, the Greens, derived its name ... this Parliament makes the laws, but it is the people who make history. The Greens will fight all the way with the people of Walsh Bay to ensure we have a city for people and a history of which we can be proud.

After a slow start, the Greens in New South Wales were becoming a force to be reckoned with, both inside and outside the party. Rhiannon hired onto her staff a like-minded NSW university lecturer, John Kaye, who had a doctorate in electrical engineering from the University of California, Berkeley, and would go on to have a significant career in the party. Kaye was a committed socialist and proud member of the National Tertiary Education Union, who had joined the Greens two years earlier. From Rhiannon's office he would prove a relentless campaigner for free education – becoming the state party's often-quoted spokesman before he was elected – drafting so-called 'Robin Hood' legislation to wind back public subsidies for elite private schools. As Hall Greenland would say years later, 'many of us thought John was the brightest person in the party, not just in NSW but in Australia'.[9]

*   *   *

Overseas, too, green parties were gathering momentum. In Germany, Die Grünen had re-entered the Bundestag in the 1994 federal elections, and in 1998, informally led by Joschka Fischer, the party formed a red-green government with the Social Democratic Party. Previously in Europe, lone Greens MPs had been invited to become environment minister, for example. In 1998, by contrast, the SPD *needed* the Greens to form a majority in the Bundestag: the coalition was a direct result of the party's electoral strength. It was a huge milestone for green parties worldwide.

The experience of national government quickly turned traumatic, however, and Fischer's role as foreign minister again divided the party when civil war broke out in the former Yugoslavia, and Germany joined in NATO-led air strikes intended to protect civilians in Kosovo. The strikes killed hundreds, and a number of Greens MPs voted against them – but enough held firm to enable the government to continue. Bob Brown often says of Die Grünen that 'the realos won', but it was in some respects a pyrrhic victory: for many German pacifists, the party's support for even a so-called humanitarian war was a final betrayal of green principles.

Nevertheless, Die Grünen were once again showing the way. It is no coincidence that after New Zealand adopted a German-style mixed-member proportional electoral system in 1996, three Green MPs were elected there for the first time. In the 1999 election, polling 5 per cent of the vote, they got seven MPs elected, including party leader Jeanette Fitzsimmons, who won the single-member electorate of Coromandel – the world's first victory for a Green in a first-past-the-post ballot. It was enough to give the party the balance of power.

Greens co-leader Rod Donald wrote that Labor and the social-democratic Alliance party were not interested in striking a formal agreement, so there was instead:

a de-facto understanding that Greens may exchange information with those ministers who care to share, and that in normal circumstances the Greens will support the government. This gives the Greens 'all care/no responsibility', which may be preferable to an agreement ... [we] are free to examine each issue on its merits, and to vote with any other party, as we see fit. We have been able

> to force changes to government legislation [and] appear to have
> had more influence on legislation than has the Alliance.[10]

The New Zealand Greens were able to get up a royal commission into genetic modification, pass their first bill, on energy efficiency, and get a $15 million green package to fund legal aid for environment groups, the certification of organic foods and other measures.[11]

At their 1997 national conference, held in Canberra, the Australian Greens agreed to host a global gathering of more than 70 green parties over the Easter weekend of 2001, timed to celebrate the centenary of federation.[12] The event would prove bigger than Ben-Hur, and fell to party stalwart Margaret Blakers to organise. It was not easy to persuade cash-strapped Greens from all over the world to come to Australia, and Christine Milne travelled to the European Greens Party conference in 1998 to argue the case. Nor was it the first international get-together of green parties. An informal conference had been held at the 1992 Rio Earth Summit, and in 1999 some 150 Greens from 24 countries met in Oaxaca, Mexico. Milne went there, too, and discovered they were about to gazump the Canberra event and launch a global greens network on the spot. She persuaded them to put out a 'millennium statement' instead.[13]

Strange as it seems in hindsight, given what was to come that year, the theme of the 2001 Canberra conference was 'optimism'. Bob Brown described the Global Greens as the 'positive face of globalisation'.[14] The backdrop was growing anti-globalisation sentiment, which reached a crescendo with the 1999 'Battle of Seattle' protests against the World Trade Organization. A harbinger of the Occupy movement, the Seattle protests went global, and had a new energy: a protest on the net – police brutality live – with unionists and environmentalists on the same side.[15]

At the time, Christine Milne wrote that the Seattle protests were the 'birth scream of a newly emerging global consciousness'.[16] In Australia, the Greens joined in the 'S11' blockade against the World Economic Forum meeting at the Crown Casino, Melbourne, in 2000. Half a dozen Greens MPs were there, and issued a joint statement slamming the WEF as an 'ally of the rich', alongside the WTO, the IMF and the World Bank.[17] Despite (or because of) intense security, the blockade was marred by violence, with mounted police and the riot squad attacking protesters around the building. Bob Brown stood up for the blockaders, depicted as thugs by the mainstream media. West Australian premier Richard Court was trapped in his car as he tried to force his way through, with protesters jumping on the roof, spray-painting the vehicle and letting its tyres down. Brown blamed Court, calling him 'spoiler/bully of the day' for trying to force his way through a peaceful blockade rather than using another entrance like the rest of the dignitaries.[18] Ben Oquist, who was there alongside Brown, wrote that it was probably the most significant protest since the Franklin, and described the protesters as 'true internationalists, keenly aware of problems outside Australia, eager to promote global solutions to the planet's and humanity's crises'.[19]

The turnout for the Global Greens conference continued to build, and with 800 delegates attending from 72 countries, the venue was shifted from Old Parliament House to the Canberra Convention Centre. An historic scene-setter came with November's US presidential election, in which George W. Bush beat Al Gore by the slimmest of margins; Gore was not helped by the Green-endorsed campaign of Ralph Nader, who was making his second tilt at the presidency: Nader's vote in the key state of Florida was much greater than the difference between the two frontrunners, arguably costing Gore the presidency. As soon as he was inaugurated, President Bush scotched any notion that the United States would sign up to the Kyoto Protocol. Nader, who had been billed to speak at the Global Greens conference, pulled out late in the piece; a Swiss delegate speculated that perhaps he had not come to Canberra because he was afraid of the critical questions he would receive.[20]

Still, Nader had his supporters at the conference: one pointed out that it was not long ago, under President Bill Clinton, that the US Senate had rejected Kyoto, voting 95–0. London's *The Guardian* backed Nader, pointing out that Clinton had wrecked the previous year's climate talks in The Hague. A searing essay in *American Prospect*, titled 'Green Herring', argued that the party consisted of dangerous spoilers who had no chance of getting elected, who mainly took votes from Democrats, and who, if they kept growing their vote, could deny the Democrats victory and propel the Republicans to control of both houses of Congress, giving them 'a supermajority with which they could gut not only environmental legislation but probably most of the New Deal as well'.[21] After 2000, the Greens' vote in US presidential elections ticked down and has never recovered.

Conference host Bob Brown opened proceedings to a standing ovation, declaring that 'since the collapse of communism, materialism or economic rationalism – the rule of money over values – has had full rein … we Greens are the balancing factor, the natural reaction to this divisive ideology from the big end of town'. Among the speakers, the most stirring response was for Colombian Greens senator Ingrid Betancourt, an anti-corruption campaigner who had taken on the drug cartels and, despite death threats against her and her children, was running for president the following year. Betancourt nearly broke down as she spoke about her struggle:

> Let us not list our weaknesses but rather claim our strengths … we are not entitled to be a marginal political option … we should aim for power and obtain it … We are flying the modern flag of the new humanism. Our fight is for the salvation of the planet … to be Green in this millennium, we have to take on the uniform of the new Samurai, to defend our values, our principles, our ideals, above everything, even above our own life, because without those values, without those principles, without those ideals, life becomes a condemnation … The first thing we should defeat is our own scepticism.

She, too, got a standing ovation. Betancourt was not exaggerating: ten months later she was kidnapped while on the presidential campaign trail, and held captive for six years.[22]

The main business of the conference was to adopt a Global Greens charter, drafted by Louise Crossley of the Tasmanian Greens, based on the 1992 Earth Charter, and the charters and constitutions of green parties around the world – including the UTG, whose 'New Ethic' was heavily reprised in the preamble. After hours of amendments, with Christine Milne in the chair, the final 19-page document was adopted by acclamation. The conference also agreed to form a new organisation, the Global Greens, and to reconvene in Africa within six years.

It would be easy to dismiss the Global Greens conference as a talkfest, but the new organisation did give the parties a sense of common identity and purpose. Arnold Cassola of Malta, secretary-general of the European Federation of Green Parties, marvelled:

> Thirty years ago or so, when the first greens started harping on the neglect of the environment, [the] establishment looked down upon us and even snubbed us … twenty years ago there were just a handful of green parliamentarians. Ten years ago there were no green ministers. Today, we can boast of thousands of local Green councillors and hundreds of national parliamentarians all over the planet, not to speak of the ever more influential Green ministers in six European and two African countries.[23]

Bob Brown, waving the charter in his right hand at the podium, closed the conference with an optimistic statement of intent: 'We are going to change the world *radically*.'

The conference was a shot in the arm for the Australian Greens – all part of the plan in an election year – and in the burst of publicity it generated, the party predicted it would win two to five seats in the Senate.[24] Another boost came from a dramatic state election result in Western Australia, where the Greens picked up two more upper-house seats on the back of a major public shift on saving the south-west old-growth forests. The WA Greens ran perhaps their best ever campaign, helped by a surge of more than $70,000 in private donations.[25] They averaged 8 per cent in the upper house, outpolling the Democrats, and gained the sole balance of power, with five seats in the Legislative Council – more than One Nation, which won 9 per cent of the primary vote but took only three seats due to unfavourable preference flows. The Liberal vote collapsed as a chunk of its base broke away to form a new group, Liberals for Forests, which contested eight seats and won one. One LFF candidate, in Albany, was the later Greens MLC Diane Evers. Copycat groups soon sprung up around the country, including Doctors for Forests and Lawyers for Forests. The new MLCs were Robin Chapple, representing the

Mining and Pastoral region in the upper house (she is still perhaps the only Greens parliamentarian ever to have worked for BHP), and former senator Dee Margetts, in the Agricultural region. Suddenly the Greens were consulted on everything.

The Greens' big win in Western Australia was followed by a decent result in the Queensland state election, with the party averaging 7 per cent of the vote in the 31 seats contested – a 50 per cent increase – and outpolling the Democrats. More significantly, in the federal by-election held in Ryan soon after, the Greens polled 6 per cent, helping Labor take the safe Liberal seat and rocking the unpopular Howard government, which even supporters were coming to regard as mean and tricky. The Greens had given Labor preferences in return for an agreement to halt land clearing. Ben Oquist emailed all party MPs: 'In one deal for preferences in one seat the Greens we have achieved more than the Democrats have achieved in five years of deals with the Howard government. It is fantastic that the Greens and Labor can work together to achieve real wins for the environment.'[26] The Queensland Greens felt they were odds-on to win a Senate seat.[27]

In the lead-up to the 2001 federal election, in short, something was going right for the Greens, and the party realised it was on a roll. A new national treasurer, Greg Buckman, got the finances into shape, noting formally that past practices such as failing to submit audited annual returns were 'unethical, and almost illegal ... and could have led to de-registration'.[28] The spirit of optimism was reflected in the party's new glossy national magazine, *Green*, published three times a year and taking over from the *Daily Planet* newsletter out of Tasmania. There was a minor sticking point: the New South Wales branch wouldn't circulate the magazine among its members, being concerned about both the content and shouldering the cost of printing and distributing it. It was a small sign of the internal cracks already appearing, even as the party's strength was building, particularly between the Australian Greens and those in New South Wales.

There was tension, for example, when Lee Rhiannon introduced a draft education policy that proposed to strip public funding from elite private schools that charged more than $8000 a year. The Queenslanders thought the Greens should support diversity in schools; Christine Milne did not want the party to attack private education; Margaret Blakers thought there should be more emphasis on 'increasing the cake, rather than redistributing funds from a few wealthy schools'. Such disagreements on policy carried over into process, too. There was a long debate on whether the office used by the Global Greens should become the Australian Greens' national office; eventually the consensus was yes, but New South Wales abstained (as it increasingly would). At the December 2000 council meeting, the Greens' national policy coordinator complained that certain states had a tendency to block consensus 'purely on their inability to organise effectively ... the NSW Greens have difficulty getting the Australian Greens national business to all local groups, thereby creating "grass-roots democracy" problems and slowing down Australian Greens policy making'.

National secretary Stuart Cook tried to tackle the simmering 'us and them' attitude: 'Of most important note [sic] is the lack of trust between the states, especially NSW and Tasmania, and the Australian Greens, most obvious in the desire of these states to not share their membership databases with Australian Greens.'[29] Cook pointed out that this was a legal requirement of federal registration, and all states agreed to send their member lists in – but it seems they never did. Around this time, party stalwarts such as one-time convenor Cath Moore from the Southern Highlands recalls getting a surprise when she turned up to the national conference and found the New South Wales delegates sitting in a tight bloc. Instead of the freewheeling, hippy meetings of old, there was caucusing going on.

*　　　*　　　*

None of this behind-the-scenes grind was apparent to the outside world, of course, and the Greens' membership Australia-wide jumped by 60 per cent between 2000 and 2001, according to one newsy titbit in *Green* magazine.[30] Helping out was the softening support for the Democrats, who were mildly invigorated when the young South Australian senator Natasha Stott-Despoja toppled Meg Lees as leader, but the party had yet to recover from its support for Howard's GST. Bob Brown had always had his doubts about Lees' strategy, having once told Drew Hutton:

> The Democrats are going to destroy themselves because their tac-
> tic is wrong. If you're going to hang in close to the Liberal Party
> and mitigate their policies, rather than hang in close and mitigate
> Labor's, you're actually starting from such a low base on things
> like the GST or industrial relations that you're going to get your-
> self in trouble.[31]

It was a crucial observation, albeit second-hand, which went as close
as Bob Brown has ever come to admitting that the Liberal and Labor
parties are not equally contemptible. In truth he could not afford to
go much further, politically, without conceding that the Greens
should simply side with Labor and change them from within.

In the lead-up to the 2001 election, Brown told the party that
it was the 'most propitious, potential-filled election for the party
since 1990 – when we weren't ready (WA was)'.[32] It was do-or-die
for both the party, which stood to lose all its federal parliamentary
representation, and Brown's own political career. As the party's pre-
eminent national figure, his own pre-selection was not challenged,
but Brown was very concerned to spend enough time in his home
state that he would be 'owned by Tasmanians'. The Greens NSW
were so concerned that the Australian Greens could end up with no
federal representation that they organised a huge fundraising dinner
for Brown in Sydney. More than $30,000 was gifted to the Tasmanian
Greens for their Senate campaign. Brown felt the party needed different candidates, with an established profile – tennis star Pat Rafter was
a possibility in Victoria. Choosing candidates always and only from
among the branch members was a 'perennial prescription for losing',
he said. Brown was also keen on a gender balance: student activist
Cate Faehrmann won Senate preselection in South Australia; high-
profile conservation council director Rachel Siewert was preselected
by the Greens WA. (On the other hand, organics federation president,
farmer and anti-GE campaigner Scott Kinnear was handpicked by
Brown over the candidate preselected by Victorian members, midwife
Sally-Anne Browne.) Having stood unsuccessfully in 1993 and 1998,
Drew Hutton decided not to run in Queensland in 2001, and the
lead candidate spot went to Toowoomba-based farmer Sarah Moles.
In New South Wales, Jabiluka veteran Kerry Nettle narrowly beat

Ben Oquist into first place – one of a series of preselection disappointments for Brown's right-hand man.

At the May National Council, the Greens decided to make forests, global warming and education the main issues – in that order. New South Wales wanted it recorded that they 'did not wish to block consensus but they are not satisfied with this outcome'.[33] Whatever the party hoped, the issue dominating politics that year was refugees. The number of asylum seekers arriving by boat had jumped tenfold in 1999. Many came from East Timor, which had descended into violence during its historic August independence referendum. The convenor of the Greens' tiny Northern Territory branch, Andy Gough, wrote firsthand of the police-run tent city housing thousands of refugees in Darwin, and wound up working in the refugee support network and travelling to Dili on the Royal Australian Navy's huge catamaran, HMAS *Jervis Bay*. The Greens had always backed Timor Leste: one of Brown's successes in his first month in the Senate was to get a motion passed supporting self-determination by the former colony, which caught the Howard government napping and shocked the Indonesians.[34]

After Indonesian president B.J. Habibie announced that an independence referendum would be held in East Timor, Brown says, the Greens were the first to call for the Australian army to intervene to keep the peace; he gives an account of how things unfolded in his book *Optimism*. Howard's own memoir gives a quite different account of what he regards as one of his government's finest moments. He admits that as reports of violence escalated in the lead-up to the referendum, there was pressure for Australia to send in peacekeeping troops, but maintains, having raised the idea in a private meeting with Habibie, that the Indonesians would never have tolerated foreign troops on their soil. Brown writes of a meeting with Alexander Downer, just two days before the East Timorese referendum, at which the then foreign minister – who had access to more information and intelligence than anyone else in Australia – assured him there would be no bloodshed. '[He] could not have been more dangerously or irresponsibly out of touch,' Brown writes.[35]

Within days of the vote, which was overwhelmingly pro-independence, some 1400 East Timorese were killed by Indonesia-backed militias. After Habibie's imposition of martial law failed,

United Nations secretary-general Kofi Annan formally asked Australia to intervene. Howard's memoir states that this request came after he had made clear that Australia was prepared to make a major contribution, but expected to lead the operation. According to Brown: 'We read how John Howard intervened … he did nothing of the sort. He did nothing of the sort. The UN had moved for intervention, and President Habibie in Indonesia had called for it because he, good-hearted man, couldn't stand what was going on.' Two months later, Brown moved a Senate motion calling for self-determination for West Papua.[36] Two years later, another Brown motion called on the Australian government to ask the United Nations to appoint a war crimes tribunal to investigate crimes against humanity during the Indonesian occupation of East Timor.[37] He was nothing if not persistent, and the same applied for his actions regarding Tibet.

Notwithstanding Australia's successful peacekeeping role in Timor, the boats kept coming, mainly carrying refugees from war-torn Iraq and Afghanistan: 3000 people in 2000, 5500 in 2001.[38] Early that year, Pauline Hanson, galvanised by One Nation's strong showing in Western Australia and Queensland, said Australia should turn the boats back: 'We go out, we meet them, we fill them up with fuel, fill them up with food, and we say "go that way".'[39] David Marr and Marian Wilkinson's masterful account of the 2001 election, *Dark Victory*, tells how the Howard government sought to balance its legal and moral obligations with its desire to win re-election that year. With the benefit of hindsight, the *Tampa* crisis, which broke just as an election loomed, presented a perfect opportunity.

Media reports on Monday, 27 August 2001 suggested that a Norwegian container ship, the MV *Tampa*, had rescued some 433 Afghan refugees from their distressed fishing boat and proceeded to take them to the closest suitable port, Merak in Indonesia, as the law of the sea required, but the refugees had threatened that they would jump overboard unless the captain took them to Christmas Island, which was much closer but did not have a wharf big enough for the *Tampa* to dock at. Howard refused to allow the *Tampa* to enter Australian waters, and sent the HMAS *Manoora* and SAS soldiers to board the ship if needed.

Labor leader Kim Beazley's reaction, on the day the crisis erupted, was to inform the House during question time: 'We support the government's actions in regard to the motor vessel *Tampa* ... they seem to us to be appropriate and in conformity with international law.'

Bob Brown recalls getting an urgent message from Oquist:

Ben calls me out of the most important issue confronting the Senate ... and he's saying, 'This ship's come in,' and I said, 'What?' and went back with him and sat in our lounge while he explained what was happening, and he said, 'I think we should put out a press release,' and I said, 'No, Ben, I think we should hold a press conference.'

Howard had effectively embraced Hanson's turnback policy, Brown stated, and he warned that such a stance would damage Australia's reputation in the Asian region. 'It's harsh, it's inhuman, and it is going to create a rising resentment with other governments, as well as many people who are more humanitarian within the Australian community.'[40] As Oquist wrote later, 'no other politician that day said anything in support of those on board the stranded container ship'.[41]

It was a historic moment for the party. Many Greens supporters to this day describe themselves as 'Tampa Greens', such as Melbourne social worker Alex Bhathal, a member of the Darebin branch who has spent nearly 20 years campaigning for the party in the federal seat of Batman:

I can remember the moment at which I joined the party, and I paid up my membership the next day. I was sitting on the couch in my lounge room in Preston and I was breastfeeding my oldest son, who's now 15, and the footage came on of the 438 men lying on the open deck of the MV *Tampa*, the container ship, and some of them were unconscious; they were in a terrible state, they were literally caught in a life and death situation because of the Howard government, but the Howard government had the full complicity of Kim Beazley and the ALP ... so I saw that footage, and I was just horrified, and then immediately there was an interview between Kerry O'Brien, I think, and Dr Bob Brown, the leader of the Australian Greens, and Bob stood up for the Australia that I believed in, that I thought I belonged to.

International anger mounted, with the United Nations High Commissioner for Refugees, the Red Cross, Amnesty International and international groups governing shipping and trade urging Australia to let the refugees land. But the polls quickly showed Howard was on a winner, and over the next few days he dug in, introducing an extremely harsh Border Protection Bill, which was blocked in the Senate by the Greens, the Democrats, Brian Harradine – and Labor. Instead, Howard came up with the 'Pacific Solution', this time largely supported by Labor, under which offshore islands were excised from Australia's migration zone, and asylum applications would be processed offshore.

Brown, who condemned Labor as 'gutless', kept up a barrage of questions in the Senate. So did the Democrats' Andrew Bartlett, who recalls suggesting that after two weeks of silence from his leader, Natasha Stott-Despoja, perhaps she might put out a press release? Brown wrote later that anyone surprised by his reaction to the *Tampa* crisis should read the Global Greens charter; he was simply defending human rights, and Australia as a humanitarian country. The immediate reaction, he added, was a barrage of abusive mail, including bullets and pictures of nooses, 'and then, three months later, a doubling of the Greens vote across the nation'.[42] Brown still describes it as:

> a real turning point for the Greens, because a lot of people voted for the Senate in the ensuing election ... people who I least expected would vote Green kept coming up to me and saying, 'I voted Green in the Senate this time because of the stand on *Tampa*.' And you know, it's an across-the-board thing, it's not a Liberal, Labor or Green thing, it's decency towards other human beings, it's there right across the spectrum.

Within a fortnight, the September 11 attacks in the United States changed everything, and if the moral imperative was clear-cut to Brown in the *Tampa* crisis, things now got harder. President Bush declared a 'war on terror', and Howard promised Australia would back the United States to the hilt.

Supporting a condolence motion for victims of the terrorist attacks, Brown tried unsuccessfully to move amendments urging calm and ensuring that any military retaliation was done in accordance with international law and led by the United Nations.[43] Any Australian involvement should be debated in parliament, he said, and warned: 'I pick up from Australians a great deal of concern that the blank cheque being offered by Prime Minister Howard has written into it the lives of young Australians … Australia is an independent nation and it must act as one.'[44]

Within weeks, however, the Americans invaded Afghanistan. Australia sent special forces and air support, the beginnings of a military adventure that has yet to end, eighteen years later. Just as the formal election campaign was getting underway, Brown warned against civilian casualties and decried the lack of an exit strategy, but stopped short of opposing the war outright. Many years later, he wrote that the initial invasion of Afghanistan on 6 October was 'justified', given that then Taliban leader Mullah Omar was sheltering al-Qaeda leader Osama bin Laden. When it came time to put boots on the ground, though, and with Australia sending 1500 troops, Brown was opposed, and as the United States' cluster-bombing campaign started, he came out strongly, urging a winter break to let aid into the country and calling on Howard to 'demand an immediate halt to cluster bombing which itself is a form of terrorism against civilian populations'. For that, the *Herald Sun* accused Brown of siding with the Taliban.[45]

*   *   *

The new war on terrorism was confronting for Greens everywhere, but especially in Germany, where foreign minister Joschka Fischer was about to send 3000 troops – his country's first foreign deployment since World War II – and the party contemplated dropping the non-violence pillar. In Australia, the Greens wrote a 'please explain' letter to their German counterparts. Here, the party's slogan was 'vote green, not khaki'. Headline writers called it the first election since the Vietnam era to be held to the sound of distant gunfire.

The Howard government deliberately conflated the two issues – boats and war – stoking fears that the asylum seekers may themselves be terrorists. Under Beazley, Labor's hopes faded and the government was returned with a small swing towards it, although almost no seats changed hands. The Greens tried to draw attention to the environment, and got some unexpected help in Tasmania from the well-timed resignation of Labor senator Shayne Murphy, a former CFMEU forestry division official, who was outraged at the state forestry agency's blinkered determination to maximise woodchip exports. Announcing he would continue to sit as an independent, Murphy endorsed the Greens policy and said he would campaign for Bob Brown and other independents ... as it turned out, he didn't.[46] Labor promised to ratify the Kyoto Protocol, in an effort to win preferences, but the Greens withheld them in key lower-house seats such as Beazley's own seat of Brand, which was extremely marginal, as punishment for his stance on asylum seekers. More broadly, unsurprisingly, the environment hardly rated a mention in 2001.

For the Greens, the most decisive electoral contest was with the Democrats, who had outmanoeuvred them by doing a deal to gain Labor preferences in the Senate. Brown had been approached by Labor's Laurie Brereton in early 2000, who told him, 'We need your preferences' – to which Brown replied, 'Yes, we need the forests.' Having held out for an environmental policy win, Brown was appalled that the Democrats and Labor did a deal instead, with no policy concessions extracted. Brown said the Democrats were now themselves 'the bastards', excoriating the party for selling out their former environmentalist credentials, as well as supporting the Coalition's GST and industrial relations legislation.[47]

As Stott-Despoja (along with Andrew Bartlett) had voted against the GST, she was able to deflect some of the anger at the party, but she admitted to reporters it was the Democrats' biggest test, with five of the party's nine senators up for re-election. In her first election campaign as leader, Stott-Despoja's mixed messages on the war and refugees did not help, but the party did better than expected, winning four seats and losing just one, in Queensland. Despite a 1 per cent swing against them, the Democrats still polled 7 per cent, beating the Greens, whose vote in the upper house nearly doubled, to 5 per cent. The Democrats trounced the Greens in South Australia and Queensland, and squeezed past them in Western Australia and

Victoria. One Nation preferences were decisive: in Western Australia they elected Democrat Andrew Murray over Rachel Siewert, even though she had pipped him by 0.1 per cent on the primary vote; but in New South Wales Kerry Nettle on 4 per cent was able to sneak past One Nation on 5 per cent and, with their preferences, leapfrog the Democrats' Vicki Bourne, on 6 per cent. The Greens put One Nation last everywhere, and no side deal was done in New South Wales, according to Nettle, who says someone in her office was civil one day when One Nation called up, and the Greens wound up above the Democrats. It would not have taken much: the Democrats' whole campaign pitch in 1998 was to oppose One Nation.

The Greens were helped for the first time by a late surge in donations – the Australian Manufacturing Workers Union contributed $10,000, for example. This enable them to buy advertising in the gay press and on SBS, which worked wonders as sections of the ethnic vote swung behind the party.[48] The strongest gains were in the inner suburbs of the two largest cities, where the party cracked double figures in eight seats: in Victoria, which overtook New South Wales for the first time in terms of statewide support, Melbourne topped, with 16 per cent, followed by Batman (12 per cent), Melbourne Ports and Kooyong (11 per cent each). In New South Wales, the Greens did best in Sydney (15 per cent) and Grayndler (13 per cent), followed by the Northern Rivers seat of Richmond (10 per cent). Denison in Hobart rounded out the list with 10 per cent. The story of the Greens has in some ways been defined by this handful of prize electorates ever since.

In *The Australian*, Liberal Party federal director Lynton Crosby was reported to have said privately that there had been two conviction politicians in the 2001 campaign: 'One was John Howard. The other was Greens senator Bob Brown.'[49] Commentator Hugh Mackay wrote that Brown and the Greens were providing the electorate with a 'new moral compass'.[50] The party's own post-election review noted the Greens were 'finally recognised as "not just a one issue party"'.[51] For all the moral support the Greens received in 2001, however, the party was disappointed to get only one new senator elected.

Brown circulated a frank memo to the national council that included a bald admission: 'Our policy stand won us votes but lost us seats.' He proposed a new way to handle preferences, which would combat the strategy employed by the Democrats, who had traded Senate preferences for House preferences without regard to policy. 'Had the Greens been given Labor's preferences we would have won seats in WA, Victoria and Queensland,' he wrote. While the Greens were unlikely to ever get Liberal preferences, Brown continued:

> Labor is different. It has no policy principles but is keen on trading Senate preferences for House preferences. It happily gave the Democrats, with their anti-Labor record on industrial relations and the GST, Senate preferences over the Greens with our strong (stronger than Labor) record on these issues. How do we keep our scruples but not lose out to this unprincipled dynamic?

Brown proposed that Senate and House preference negotiations be done at the same time – the Greens generally did them separately, with responsibility split between the state branches and the national campaign – and that the party adopt an across-the-board policy of not directing preferences in the reps except in exchange for policy outcomes.

Brown also proposed an allocation of the $1.6 million windfall in public funding the party was about to get from the Australian Electoral Commission, having exceeded the magical 4 per cent threshold in the upper house everywhere but the Democrat strongholds of South Australia and Queensland, and in 76 lower-house seats around the country. Brown proposed that the states keep all funding for the lower-house campaigns, but donate half the funding from the Senate campaigns into a national pool that would fund the Australian Greens, global outreach and a Green think tank, and help the struggling South Australian and Queensland branches. 'This is a golden opportunity for the Australian Greens,' he wrote. 'While Labor laments its structure and factional divides, we have a clear slate to build upon and should quickly decide the best way forward, sharing the public funding across the nation.'

Perhaps unsurprisingly, with so much money at stake, an almighty blue broke out. Treasurer Greg Buckman resigned in 2002, circulating an email complaining about the New South Wales branch generally, which was dragging the chain on its federal contribution, and Lee Rhiannon in particular. Buckman was ultimately persuaded to stay on – crisis averted – but the dispute dragged on well into 2003. Geoff Ash says the Greens NSW had 'worked hard for six federal elections to finally achieve Senate funding, and was not about to be told by Brown how it should be spent. The NSW party would democratically decide that, and that would include monetary assistance to poorer states.' Ash saw Buckman, from the Tasmanian Greens, as a consistent Brown supporter.

There was more tension early in Howard's third term when Bob Brown floated the idea of a 'Telstra for trees' deal. Senator Shayne Murphy had flagged he was open to selling off the remaining 50.1 per cent of the telco, which put the ball in motion. Brown, responding to a journalist's query, said he would go to the Greens' national council meeting the next day and propose backing the sale in return for government undertakings to end land clearing, particularly in Queensland, and logging of old-growth forests. 'We are a democratic party and I will follow what the party says,' Brown said.[52] Former senator Dee Margetts weighed in, opposing the idea. Greens convenor Gurm Sekhon said he expected the national council to confirm its opposition, and it did.

When the media got to senator-elect Kerry Nettle, she also ruled out any support of Telstra privatisation by the Greens in the future. 'Bob Brown, myself or any future Greens senator will not be voting for the privatisation of Telstra,' she said.[53]

Although the furore was short-lived, it went down in Greens folklore as a huge test for the party, which was suddenly at odds with its charismatic co-founder and leader; many a minor party has come a cropper at such moments. For Lee Rhiannon, the moment Nettle stood by the platform was the moment she knew that the party had a strength that was greater than any individual. Brown still remembers it as 'the most contentious moment' of his leadership:

In a moment of talking to a journalist just inside the door of the Senate I said yes I'd talk to Howard about the sale of Telstra if it would save Tasmania's forests. Huge. We had a conference straight after that where I had to humbly back down and a motion was put forward censuring me for venturing such an idea and

[I had to] back down in front of the national media and took it all on the chin – no shouting, no screaming – and that's *the* most contentious moment of my leadership. The Murdoch media went for it in a huge way, with the NSW Greens prevailing if you like, but I was quite content and afterwards watched Telstra being sold and the Tasmanian forest logged. But that's what you do when you're in a leadership position. You put your case and then you accept the verdict and I always did, without exception.

Despite the emerging divisions, the Greens were on the march. In July 2002, the Tasmanian party, led by Peg Putt, pulled off a stunning comeback, polling 18 per cent statewide, getting Putt re-elected in Denison and electing three new MLAs: Nick McKim in Franklin, Kim Booth in Bass, and Tim Morris in Lyons. The dirty Liberal–Labor attempt to wipe out the Greens by reducing the size of the lower house had backfired. After sitting on her own for four years, Putt had brought the party back from the brink. The Greens' gains were all at the expense of the Liberals, so Labor retained its majority, but the voters' verdict was clear. Four seats was enough for the Greens to regain parliamentary party status – in fact, they were officially designated one of two opposition parties. The major parties had to accept that the Greens were no aberration and were there to stay.

The Democrats, however, never won seats in the Senate again. Soon after the election, former leader Meg Lees waged a scorched-earth war of retribution against Stott-Despoja, ultimately bringing her down in 2002, but destroying the party in the process. The polls captured one aspect of it. Bob Brown reckoned Newspoll consistently under-represented support for the Greens, but it was nevertheless indicative: the Greens overtook the Democrats after the 2001 election, and from then on regularly recorded primary support in the 5 to 8 per cent range – in chartspeak, there was a new floor under the Greens.

Popular memories of a 'Democrats moment' are hazy. In truth, the minor party took three body blows over a five-year period: Cheryl Kernot's defection to Labor; Meg Lees' backing of the GST; and, nine months after the 2001 election, Lees' tearing down of charismatic young leader Natasha Stott-Despoja. Individually they might have been recoverable, but arriving in succession they proved fatal.

At the end of 2002, in his column for *Green* titled 'Bob's Back Page', Brown recalled how, two years earlier, the party was 'wowed' if its polls jumped from the usual 2–2.5 per cent to 3 per cent. Post-*Tampa*, the party had polled 5 per cent. Now, the latest Morgan poll had the party on 10 per cent, and its membership had soared to more than 5000 around the country. 'This, in turn, worries some folk,' Brown reflected.

> Will the influx weaken our policy base? Will we get too big? How can we handle such growth? While we do need to build the party structure rapidly, I relish this growth. We are succeeding because we are sticking to our policies. Our mission is to supplant economic rationalism with humane values and we can only succeed one way – by winning the support of more people than support the ecocrats [sic]. We must not fear popularity.

Writer Amanda Lohrey described the rising support for the Greens in the early 2000s as a 'groundswell', arguing that a new ecological constituency had emerged – not out of the blue, but after decades of grassroots activism and hard politicking at the local and state levels. True, but that story is inseparable from the demise of the Democrats.

As public support rose for the Greens, and membership more than tripled from 2100 to 7500 in the first three years of the decade, so did the stakes rise internally. The interminable arguments continued about the party's structures and processes (or lack thereof), and distribution of money between the federal and state bodies. The flare-up between Brown and the party over the sale of the rest of Telstra in 2002 reignited older debates about the relationship between the members and the parliamentarians – were they representatives, trusted to exercise their own judgement, or delegates who abide by decisions of the membership. To stop these tensions boiling over, the party decided that, a decade after it came into existence, it was time for a proper structural review. This would be led by party stalwart Margaret Blakers.

Christine Milne wrote a blistering two-page submission that left no doubt where the Tasmanians stood. When the original local and state green groups were formed in the 1980s and 1990s, little or no thought had been given to setting up nationally or globally. 'The problem we now inherit,' she wrote, 'is the legacy of not thinking big enough when we came to organising ourselves.' Given that the party platform called for Australia's states to be abolished in favour of a strong national government, and for local government to be restructured across bio-regions, why shouldn't the party adopt that same structure? As things stood, the party was dividing into rich states, New South Wales and Victoria, and poor states – 'the haves and have nots, the exact opposite of what Greens aspire to', as Milne put it. At the centre was a poorly funded, weak national organisation that was a mere 'puppet of the states'. Milne wanted the state parties abolished, and a national office established with a national member database. This would become a familiar refrain. Opposed to corporate sponsorship, Milne proposed a tithe, not just on MPs, but on better-off members. 'If everyone with an above-average income contributed 1% per annum,' she wrote, 'we would raise $500,000 per annum.'[54]

Milne's memo was a red rag. Some state parties, particularly New South Wales, believed the federated structure gave them necessary and valuable autonomy, and were concerned that Milne's proposal would lead only to the concentration of power in a far better resourced national body. In a draft discussion paper, one submission argued there should be no direct contact between members and national office-bearers, and the Australian Greens 'should remain a "secretariat" for the state/territory parties'.[55]

Aware that the structural review could reopen old wounds, Margaret Blakers came up with an idea. She would conduct a 'Grand Green Tour', visiting each state to meet the party's grassroots members. The national council agreed to cover her petrol costs, and Blakers set off from Hobart in her Subaru. Blakers had her own barrow to push: she wanted to see continued funding for her two pet projects, the Global Greens and the Green Institute think tank set up in late 2000 to host the Rio +10 international greens conference in Canberra.[56] Over two months that winter, she travelled 15,638 kilometres, up to Melbourne, across to Adelaide, inland to Mount Isa, across to Cairns, and then all the way back down the coast through Brisbane and Sydney, and through Victoria back to Tassie. Blakers held 35 meetings, attended by nearly 500 people. She finished with a slipped disc in her back after so much time spent driving. What struck her, more than anything, was that the members had no idea the Australian Greens existed. 'They knew about Bob Brown, of course, but otherwise all they knew about was their branch.'

After all that, the Grand Green Tour and the 2002 structural review resolved very little. On the key questions of the constitution and funding, the review effectively restated a series of options that were already in the too-hard basket. The upshot was 17 uninspiring recommendations, calling for further reviews or discussion.[57] At the party's national conference in September 2002, Bob Brown congratulated the party on ten years of progress and its increased representation, with two senators, eight MPs in state parliaments and 40 local councillors around the country. Then the conference hit a brick wall over the structural review. Given continuing disagreement over the sharing of party funds, the idea of extra dollars for the Green Institute was dismissed early on, and the body was soon wound up. A modicum of progress came in 2003 with the creation of the Australian Greens Coordinating Group, a quasi-executive body for the party that met monthly. Also that year, finally, an overwhelming 80 per cent of Greens WA members voted to join the Australian Greens. At last the party was truly Australia-wide.

Although it was unable to fix its deep structural flaws, the party was changing rapidly. Greg Buckman, who would go on to write a book about Australia's environmental battles, laid out a five-point plan for a truly national party organisation, which would have a permanent office, a national enquiry service, including a website and phone number, a national magazine going to all members (the New South Wales and Queensland branches were still not distributing *Green*), a web-linked national membership database, and a single membership fee. More than fifteen years later, the national membership database still doesn't exist, but the other four items on Buckman's agenda were slowly ticked off.

Most significantly, and of necessity, the new members that flooded into the party from 2001 onwards changed it. Old hands had mixed feelings about this. At the party's national council in early 2003, a workshop was held on the topic; it was titled 'New members – opportunity or threat?'[58] One-time convenor Stewart Jackson found that a fifth of the joiners after 2001 were ex-Labor, disgusted at their party's abandonment of principle, particularly on *Tampa*. 'I joined the Greens because of Kim Beazley,' one staffer told Jackson. '[He] was appalling as a version of the opposition, and I thought if there's no decent opposition then we must be doing something to create an opposition and therefore I joined.'[59] New members came from the Democrats and the Liberals as well, of course, and going by Jackson's survey, they were broadly more right-leaning: 'Those that joined most recently (2001–2008) strongly disagreed with moving the party to the left ... [they] do not see being "left-wing" as a positive move for the party.'[60] Many new members were less radical than the early Greens, and were used to and expected to join a centralised hierarchical party organisation.[61] The Greens had begun a slow transition from an activist-led, social movement group to a centralised, professional electoral party.

CHAPTER 8

TAKING A STAND

A loud voice for peace was never more necessary in Australian politics than during the slow descent into a senseless war in Iraq during 2002, proving the lessons of Vietnam had not been learned. Labor leader Simon Crean, who had taken over from Kim Beazley after the 2001 election, did not provide it, dragging his heels when it came to Labor's support for a US-led mission, and denying MPs a conscience vote in any parliamentary debate on the war. The Greens, by contrast, were clearly opposed from the outset, and Bob Brown was constantly quoted in the press and a prominent speaker at the rallies happening all round the country. Brown pressed repeatedly for parliament to have the final say on whether Australia would join the war. Brown and his fellow Greens senator, Kerry Nettle, were at the forefront of a 500-strong coalition of unions, churches, community groups and politicians who issued a joint statement against joining the United States in a pre-emptive military strike on Iraq.

After the Bali bombings in October, which killed 88 Australians, Brown was lambasted by right-wing media for making a link between Australia's support for a new war in Iraq and a heightened threat of terrorism. Andrew Bolt accused Brown of 'fishing in bile' and '[using] the bombing to condemn Howard'. In fact, as Matt Price pointed out in *The Australian*, Brown had done nothing of the sort. Brown condemned the Bali attack as 'inexcusable hatred' and, when invited by reporters to connect it with Howard's support of the US, answered that 'there is no indication that this has anything to do with Iraq', and insisted he was 'not going to be part of any political finger pointing'. What Brown did say, when pressed, has stood the test of time:

We have to review the direction we're taking to concentrate on regional security, rather than being involved in the global adventurism of President Bush … there is a real concern that I have, and many Australians share, that if we take part in an invasion of Iraq, it will simply heighten the risk of repeated acts of this variety.'[1]

The director-general of ASIO, Dennis Richardson, soon made exactly the same point.

When Australia was poised to 'forward-deploy' some 2000 troops to the Persian Gulf, even as the government insisted war was not inevitable, Brown said Howard had clearly decided to join the United States in invading Iraq.[2] He would be proved right about that too: an ABC exclusive in late 2018 confirmed that Howard had already dispatched a group of defence personnel to Florida to begin planning the invasion, but had informed neither the rest of the defence force nor the public.[3] Through the second half of 2002, the Greens improved in the polls. The majority of Australians did not support an invasion of Iraq unless it was backed by the United Nations.

An October by-election in the federal electorate of Cunningham, on the New South Wales south coast, became a test of public sentiment on the war. The combination of a bitter Labor preselection stoush and the absence of a Liberal candidate in what had been a safe ALP seat gave the Greens a good chance. The Greens preselected Michael Organ, a resident anti-development activist and archivist at the University of Wollongong.

Local issues aside, coverage of the by-election focused on the war and the implications for Crean of a defeat in Labor's industrial heartland. 'The spectre of Iraq hangs right over politics in Australia,' Bob Brown told the ABC, '[and we will be] going very strongly to let the people of Cunningham know that they have an alternative to the John Howard and Simon Crean point of view.'[4] The United States' embassy was concerned enough to interview one of Organ's campaign workers, Dan Cass, about what was motivating anti-war sentiment in the Greens and among local voters.[5] The Greens finished second in the primary vote and overtook Labor on preferences, winning 52 per cent of the two-party vote. Breaking into the lower house was a historic win for the Greens – and the first time an independent minor party had won a seat since Federation (not counting former NSW premier

Jack Lang, who was elected for Lang Labor in 1946). Brown warned that Labor history could be repeating itself, recalling the 1955 DLP split, when members fled in a trickle, then a flood.[6] Stunned at his own victory, Organ's first achievement was to get barred from entering parliament for wearing a 'NO WAR' T-shirt under his sports jacket.

The Greens' momentum carried through to the Victorian election of November 2002. Standing in the Greens' most promising lower-house seat of Melbourne was Richard Di Natale, a former VFA footballer and medical doctor who had worked in Aboriginal health in the Northern Territory. Di Natale was not your stereotypical greenie, telling the *Australian Financial Review* he was tired of being asked to pose next to trees. 'Those stereotypes are a bit dated now,' he said. 'I don't think those images do justice to what we represent. There's been a huge influx of intellectual capital into the party since the federal election.'[7]

The Greens vote jumped eightfold, to 9 per cent, in the election that delivered a landslide victory for Labor's Steve Bracks. Although no Greens member was elected, five inner-Melbourne seats were now Labor/Green marginals, with the party winning a primary vote above 20 per cent in each. Most significantly, the win by Labor meant Bracks could deliver on his promise to introduce proportional representation in the state's upper house, knowing full well it would give the Greens a foothold in the state parliament. Things were finally looking up in Victoria.

As the Greens surged, federal Labor was torn. Around this time, frontbencher Mark Latham recorded in his diaries that Crean was 'bleeding to death' on Iraq. 'Bob Brown is killing us on this issue through the power of a simple, commonsense message: Bush is an imbecile and Australia should not be part of his war.'[8] In December, former West Australian premier Carmen Lawrence resigned from the federal shadow cabinet and went to the backbench, complaining the party was poll-driven under Crean and shifting too far to the right. 'I'm trying to capture the next generation of young progressive people,' she wrote.

The Greens can't do it. The Greens aren't the solution. The Greens are a third party, a minor party. It's about the Labor

Party taking stock of the future, grabbing that new generation
and asking serious questions about human values, about sustainability of the environment and a range of issues that I know they
all care about.[9]

In a shock announcement in South Australia at the end of January,
left-wing state Labor backbencher Kris Hanna quit and applied to
join the Greens, declaring the ALP had 'lost its soul'. It was a blow to
the minority government of Premier Mike Rann, who had scraped to
victory the previous year with the support of a former Liberal independent, beginning 16 years of Labor power in the state. Hanna
committed to supporting Labor on confidence and supply.

For Hanna, as for Lawrence, the final straw had been the party's stance on asylum seekers, but he also said he had been subject
to 'intimidation' by Labor colleagues over his opposition to the
looming war with Iraq and anti-terrorism laws that breached civil
liberties. Hanna predicted more would follow him out of Labor: 'I
think there will be a trend based on the frustration that backbenchers
feel around the country. Other people, like me, will probably end up
finding that you can actually change more outside rather than inside.'
As well as high principle, there was also some base politics involved:
two months earlier, Hanna had been overlooked for a cabinet post,
in favour of an independent who was supporting Rann.

Ahead of his defection, Hanna had held talks with Brown, who
welcomed him as a 'great asset to green politics'. Hanna said the
Greens were 'the only party going anywhere in Australia today and
it's because of their integrity and idealism. Bob Brown is one of the
few politicians in Australia today showing true leadership.' At the
Greens' state conference, Hanna got a standing ovation and members voted overwhelmingly to accept his application, with just two
votes against.

The warm reception would not last long. In the media, reaction was mixed. Polls showed statewide support for the Greens
at 10 per cent, suggesting an upper-house seat was a certainty
at the next election. Hanna was well regarded in his electorate,
but there were calls for him to resign from parliament – as Cheryl
Kernot had done, for example – and contest a by-election as a Green.

The Age editorialised that the Greens were 'not entitled to his seat' and branded him 'a fraud upon the voters' who must resign.[10] In the short term, nonetheless, Hanna's defection was a shot in the arm for the South Australian Greens, who had polled just 2 per cent in the 2002 election, and so far had failed to make much of an impact politically in the Democrats' home state.

The build-up to war intensified. John Howard, who addressed the National Press Club to justify his decision to send 2000 troops, allowed two days of parliamentary debate but did not himself speak. In the Senate, Labor, the Democrats and the Greens passed a motion of no confidence in Howard's handling of 'this grave matter', the first time in the 102-year history of the Australian parliament that the upper house had censured a serving prime minister. But when Brown moved a motion opposing Australia's involvement in any attack on Iraq, Labor went to water, siding with the government to vote it down.[11]

On the weekend of 15–16 February 2003, more than 600 peace rallies were held all over the world. In Australia, at least half a million people marched through state capitals and regional cities – numbers larger than the protests against the Vietnam War. Victorian Peace Network organiser Damien Lawson, later chief of staff to Adam Bandt, recalls that the campaign, which had collected mobile numbers for the first time, sent out tens of thousands of text messages. More than 150,000 people turned up on the Friday night at Melbourne's Federation Square. A huge cheer went up for Bob Brown, the top-billed politician on the day, who told the crowd that the huge turnout showed Howard had 'no mandate ... at all', and said 'this war is not Australia's war'. He concluded: 'We, Mr Howard, insist: turn the ships around, bring our 2000 Australians good and true home; get us out of this war, give us the peaceful option.'[12]

*   *   *

A month later, voters in New South Wales went to the polls. Polling about 6 per cent, the Greens hoped to pick up a third upper-house seat in the state election, which Brown said would be a referendum on Iraq. *The Herald* editorialised that state elections should be about state issues – Brown's idea was 'as silly as it gets' – then launched into the party that cast itself as 'high-principled incorruptible progressives'. Some Greens were 'leftovers of Australian communist activism' who had 'successfully infiltrated fledgling green organisations and recast themselves ... as guardians of the natural environment'.

With his eight-year term up, veteran Ian Cohen faced something brand-new for the minor party: a tough preselection contest. The New South Wales branch had always been fractious, but this preselection marked the opening of a deeper divide. While working together well enough in parliament, relations between Cohen and Lee Rhiannon had soured. Cohen was an anarchic 'green Green', open to working with either side of politics in the pursuit of green outcomes. He says his own green politics are neither left-wing nor right-wing, but 'the whole bird'. Rhiannon, by contrast, was a 'red Green', a highly disciplined, hard-left campaigner.

As the end of Cohen's term neared, Rhiannon and her supporters pushed for the introduction of limited tenure for MPs, proposing rule changes that were not explicitly aimed at Cohen but which he took as an attempt to get rid of him. In a letter to members, Rhiannon wrote that a limit on the number of terms for MPs would discourage careerists from exploiting the party, and her experience as a Greens member of the NSW Legislative Council had convinced her that 'one term, which in the Upper House is eight years, is what we should be adopting for our elected representatives in this House'.[13] Cohen also had to fend off a challenge from Brown's right-hand man, Ben Oquist, this time having a crack at state parliament after being beaten by Nettle for the 2001 Senate race.

Cohen prevailed, and a push to require the state delegates council to approve a member running for a second term was defeated. (Years later the party did adopt new rules on tenure: MPs could not run again after 13 consecutive years in the Legislative Council or Senate unless they had 75 per cent member support.[14]) Under the 'zipper' principle used in New South Wales, which ensures alternating spots on the party ticket for men and women over successive elections, the second spot went to lead female candidate Sylvia Hale, the Marrickville councillor and book publisher from Hale & Iremonger who had joined the Greens from the No Aircraft Noise party. Oquist was relegated to the unwinnable third place, and dropped out. In the lower house, the Greens ran a serious campaign to get Leichhardt deputy mayor Jamie Parker elected in the Labor-held inner-west seat of Port Jackson, taking in Balmain. Parker was a colourful character – by day a PR man for herbal outfit Naturopathica, which sold dubious products like Horny Goat Weed and Fatblaster.

Having hoarded their electoral funding, resisting demands of the national organisation and poorer state branches, the NSW Greens went into the 2003 state election relatively cashed up. But the party was not prepared for what came next. As Oquist had predicted, the rising strength of the Greens drew intensifying attack. Three weeks out from polling day, *The Sunday Telegraph* was splashed with the sensational headline 'ECSTASY OVER THE COUNTER – REVEALED – THE GREENS' HIDDEN POLICY'. So-called party drugs such as ecstasy and speed would be sold in licensed drug shops, the paper reported, and registered addicts would receive free heroin for use in safe injecting rooms across the state. Parker, as spokesman, defended the policy, saying 'prohibition isn't working'. The policy was readily available on the party's website (and had been for months), but the *Telegraph* claimed readers had to 'scroll down a long way' to find detail about legalising hard drugs, which was effectively 'hidden' because it wasn't included in official election campaign material.

In the ensuing furore, Liberal opposition leader John Brogden ruled out any preference deal with the Greens – scotching any real chance Parker had of getting elected – and called on Premier Bob Carr to do likewise. Bob Brown was cautious in his defence, telling ABC Radio that the harm-minimisation policy was the 'courageous but proper way to go', while qualifying that 'the Greens are not going to get into government' and calling for more research.[15] The *Telegraph* kept up the attack, highlighting what it called 'off-beat' policies like a four-day working week, a tax on deceased estates worth more than $1 million, a ban on caged birds and a ban on political donations from property developers. The Greens were undeterred: Rhiannon released a database of political donations, the kernel of what would later become the watchdog website Democracy4Sale, consolidating a potent agenda for the party at state and federal level.[16]

A week after the *Telegraph*'s attack, a Herald/AC Nielsen poll showed the Greens' primary vote had gone *up*, from 8 per cent to 10 per cent.[17] Two days before the poll, the US-led invasion of Iraq began, and Australian SAS troops went into action. The Greens milked it, putting out a press release on election eve: 'A vote for John Brogden is a vote for John Howard.'[18] The Greens got a 4 per cent swing in the lower house and turned their three most prospective lower-house seats into Labor–Green marginals: in Port Jackson and Marrickville, with a first-preference above-the-line vote of 29 per cent, and in Keira, with 19 per cent. The upper house result was unpredictable, as it was the first election to use optional preferential voting – abolishing group voting tickets, instead allowing voters to allocate preferences to parties above the line. It was a system Rhiannon had put forward as the Greens negotiator on electoral reform, and was taken up by the Carr government in 1999. The NSW reform was a key win for the Greens – Rhiannon said it would 'finally ensure that people will be able to allocate their own preferences, rather than having to worry about the presence of front parties or vote funnelling' – and would later serve as a precedent in the Senate and elsewhere, as parliaments tried to rein in so-called 'preference whispering'.[19] In the 2003 vote for the Legislative Council, the Greens got a primary vote of 8.6 per cent – an almost 6 per cent swing – and Ian Cohen and Sylvia Hale were comfortably elected. Cohen hailed the result: the Greens had arrived and were knocking on the door of lower-house seats.[20]

*   *   *

Iraq and the War on Terror continued to shade Australian politics through 2003. In the Senate the two Greens were the only dissenting voices on legislation giving ASIO new powers – the beginning in earnest of a 15-year trend towards ever more draconian surveillance law. Brown told the ABC the opposition had agreed to a proposal that would allow innocent people to be hauled off the street and locked up for a week without charge. 'What is the point of having an opposition to this Howard government if you are left with the ALP?' he said. 'It is an astounding and an astonishing sellout by the Labor Party. Doc Evatt would be turning in his grave.'[21] As weapons of mass destruction failed to appear in Iraq, Brown called for another inquiry, this time into the pre-war intelligence.

Hoping to appear statesmanlike ahead of a looming federal election, John Howard invited President Bush to address the Australian parliament on 23 October. Politics as usual would be suspended for the day. All senators were invited into the House of Representatives for the Bush address, in a joint sitting, which was to be followed the next day by an address by the visiting Chinese president, Hu Jintao. Only Prime Minister Howard and the opposition leader, Simon Crean, would speak. Howard must have sensed trouble was brewing; his memoir records that he warned Bush to watch out for 'a Green named Brown'. Brown gives a good account of his decision to interject in his own book, *Memo for a Saner World*, published the following year: 'I knew that if we spoke up during either president's speech, it would bring a storm of denunciation down upon us. But if we stayed silent, or simply refused to attend, then we would feel worse.' When it came to the Bush address, top of mind for Brown was the plight of the two Australians, David Hicks and the completely innocent Mamdouh Habib, both of whom had been detained for almost two years without charge or legal representation in the US prison at Guantanamo Bay.

On the eve of Bush's speech, Brown planned what he would say, meeting Nettle in her Sydney office, with Michael Organ on the line from Wollongong. Nettle decided she would also interject, to denounce the US–Australia free trade agreement, then under negotiation. Brown went off to address a 5000-strong anti-Bush protest at the Sydney Town Hall, and drove to Canberra later that evening. Though the public was banned, each MP was allowed a guest, so the Greens had three. For the Bush address, they chose Hicks' lawyer, and Habib's wife and son; for Hu's address, they planned to bring a Chinese dissident and two Tibetans. As they arrived, Brown's heart was pounding, he wrote, 'accompanied by a feeling of impending failure of nerve'.[22]

Once seats were taken, and the address begun, Hansard records only that as Bush was mid-sentence ('Today, Saddam's regime is gone, and no-one—'), he was interrupted, and the speaker, Neil Andrew, intervened:

The SPEAKER – Senator Brown, I warn you.

The SPEAKER – Senator Brown will excuse himself from the House. The serjeant will remove Senator Brown from the House.

What Brown said was not recorded for posterity, but according to his book he said: 'Mr Bush, this is Australia. Respect our nation.' Pointing to his guests in the gallery, Brown continued: 'Return our Australians from Guantanamo Bay.' As Bush paused and government MPs started groaning and hurling accusations his way, Brown went on, 'Respect the laws of the world and the world will respect you,' finally adding, 'We are not a sheriff!'[23] When the serjeant-at-arms came to escort Brown from the chamber, he refused, because as a senator he could only be removed by a vote of senators. 'Read the standing orders,' Brown told the serjeant, who backed off.

Meanwhile, Bush resumed his speech, and when he got to the free trade agreement, Nettle piped up:

The HONOURABLE GEORGE WALKER BUSH – ... Our nations are now working to complete a US–Australia free trade agreement that will add momentum to free trade throughout the Asia-Pacific region while producing jobs in our own countries.

The SPEAKER – Senator Nettle will resume her seat. The President has the call.

The SPEAKER – Senator Nettle is warned.

The SPEAKER – The serjeant will remove Senator Nettle. The President has the call.

The HONOURABLE GEORGE WALKER BUSH – I love free speech!

Standing, Brown and Nettle called out, 'So do we!'

At the end of Bush's speech, Tony Abbott – at the time the Leader of the House – moved that Brown and Nettle be suspended from the service of the House for 24 hours. It was agreed on the voices, although there were definite noes. Brown tried to call for a proper division, but was ignored. Nettle then tried to reach Bush to hand over the Habibs' letter and was met by a phalanx of Coalition MPs, who blocked her from reaching the president. At the forefront was Howard himself, arms out wide as a barrier. There was ugly jostling on the floor of the House – acting Senate president Ross Lightfoot later admitted that Brown and Nettle could have 'walked into my elbows', and he allegedly hissed 'die' to Nettle.[24] Brown managed to get to Bush and shake his hand – 'a double thumb-wrap handshake from him', he wrote – and asked again for the Australians to be returned home. Bush gave a noncommittal reply about 'looking at it' and was off.

The heckling of George Bush was broadcast round the world, but Brown says it was nothing of the sort: 'I got up and spoke to him, straight, fair dinkum, across the way, there was no heckle in it.' Brown maintains there was a flagrant breach of parliamentary procedure that day: 'The Speaker had zero right to tell me to do anything. I was a senator, and could only be directed by the President of the Senate. The House speaker had no authority over senators in a joint House sitting. The clerk of the Senate, Harry Evans, was quite clear on this. There's never been a joint sitting since and will never be one again, and nor did George Bush ever address a parliament again.'

The Greens' phonelines immediately went into meltdown, and Brown recalls that as he went outside to a press conference, there was 'this new young member of parliament from Queensland jumping up and down, shouting, "You are outrageous, you are disgusting," and I said to the media, "Just hold on a moment … would the puppy please sit down?" And he did. He went quiet. That was Peter Dutton, fresh from the constabulary, [he'd] just been elected.' As the media went on the attack, demanding to know *why* Brown had heckled Bush, no one from the gallery asked Brown what he said. 'Only CNN in London asked, "What did you say to the president?"'

The effect of the dubious 24-hour suspension moved by Abbott was that the two Greens were prevented from a repeat performance when Hu addressed the parliament the next day. Brown later obtained an opinion from the clerk of the Senate, Harry Evans, that the speaker's use of three bulky security men to block him and Nettle from entering the chamber for Hu's speech 'may be judged illegal if it were taken to the High Court'.[25]

The government went on the attack in the Senate: Territorian Nigel Scullion described Brown as a 'political terrorist' and Queensland's Senator George Brandis went right over the top, waxing lyrical on how the 'commonalities between contemporary Green politics and old-fashioned fascism and Nazism are chilling'.[26] The faux outrage, blanket headlines and shock-jock bile passed quickly, however, as Brown reflects:

> I get these days a lot of friendly comments from people ... and that's the issue that's brought up the most: 'I particularly liked it when you stood up on George Bush.' Yet at the time it was just a total tirade. A week or two later the progressive voices start writing letters, they've sat back and considered it all, but the nooses and the white powder and the death threats and things are instant from the right.

The Greens' protest that day remains a true expression of the party's spirit, remembered often, on all sides of the party. The Bob Brown who turned up to cheer President Lyndon B. Johnson in 1966 had completely transformed, 27 years later, into the only Australian political leader with the guts to challenge President George W. Bush.

*   *   *

Labor leader Simon Crean continued to drag in the polls as infighting consumed the party, culminating in a leadership challenge in December 2003. The surprise victor was Mark Latham, the brash third-way guru who had described Howard as an 'arselicker' for toadying to George W. Bush, and the Coalition as a 'conga line of suckholes'. It was the beginning of a roller-coaster ride for the opposition. In the first months of 2004, an election year, Latham struck a blow that hurt the Greens, making a captain's call to preselect then ACF president Peter Garrett for the safe Labor seat of Kingsford-Smith, in Sydney's south-east. Latham was a Garrett fan, and so was NSW premier Bob Carr, the member for Maroubra, and both worked to smooth his entry to the party.

In his 2015 memoir, *Big Blue Sky*, Garrett gives his own account of his decision to join the ALP, which he knew would disappoint many greenies:

> I was too much of an economic dry and too allergic to utopianism to side with the Australian Greens ... Sanctimony sucks, and while there were a number of people involved with the party whom I liked and had worked with in the past, including Bob, I couldn't envisage years of playing a dishonest song to the bleachers, promising a nirvana that couldn't be delivered and castigating everyone else as moral inferiors ... In their eyes, Labor and Liberal were indistinguishable from one another ... As a way of slicing votes, it was effective rhetoric, but a long way from the truth. On environmental issues like climate change, the differences were great, which explained why, in nearly all cases, the Greens would exchange preference votes with Labor, the party they spent most time attacking. They wanted Labor to stay in power but they also wanted to enlist the support of left-oriented Labor supporters – it was a deft double act but not one in which I wanted to participate.[27]

In an article for *Green* at the time, Brown wrote that Garrett would be 'a great asset' to the ALP:

> ... but I do worry about Peter. He is going to have a hard time of it in the Labor Party. He is a very ethical man. He has been a real values person, a beacon of values in Australia ... I can't think of anybody else who has as much potential and strength of character to be able to change a party from within ... [But] I don't expect much change. The Greens build politics outside the old politics because, when it comes to ecological wisdom or social equity, the old parties have long since gone off track and will not reform. No one individual, no matter how good, can change that. The ALP, now it has Garrett, needs to deliver ... Peter would be much better off with the Greens ... Our values on social justice, on the environment, are issues that Peter has been espousing very much through his music over many years.[28]

To get his nomination cleared by the ALP, Garrett faced a sobering test: an aggressive cross-examination by the head of the CFMEU forestry division, Michael O'Connor, a member of the party's powerful executive, who asked whether he would use the party to further an environmental agenda. Garrett responded he would be a team player, 'but I'd argue for better environmental policies every step of the way'.[29] Both Garrett commitments would be sorely tested in a few years.

At the beginning of 2004, Latham had accepted an invitation from Bob Brown to visit the Tasmanian forests. Latham was no greenie, but had the view that a solid left-of-centre campaign should focus on three Es: education, the elderly and the environment. In his *Diaries*, Latham wrote how much he liked Brown: 'other than economic policy, our beliefs are quite similar ... it's a shame that people like Bob Brown have been lost to the [Labor] Party'.[30] Brown tried again what had worked with Richardson some 20 years earlier. He took Latham on a helicopter flight over the Styx Valley – the Labor leader scored it five out of ten, only the northern half worth saving. After a walk through the neighbouring Valley of the Giants, however, Latham was stunned, rating it 'ten out of ten'. Afterwards, Brown told journalist James Button he was dismayed at Latham's response, which was 'studied, desultory ... he was not responding to me. It was as if he was saying, "I am not going to be shown to relate" – not just to me, but to the forests.'

The federal–state relationship fractured further with the mid-year death of Tasmanian premier Jim Bacon – which moved Latham to tears. Paul Lennon, a former adviser to Brian Harradine who was fervently anti-Green, took over as premier. Lennon was close to woodchipper Gunns Ltd, and had a very jaundiced view of Latham's negotiations with Brown. Tasmanian Labor gave no help to Latham on forests whatsoever, and he would soon be dramatically undermined by the forest unions. The stakes got higher when Gunns announced a feasibility study into a new pulp mill in Tasmania. Latham immediately supported the idea, effectively handing the Greens a new campaign plank. Christine Milne, working as an adviser to Brown, had already been endorsed as the Greens' lead Senate candidate for the state. Brown said Gunns' pulp mill proposal boosted Milne's chances of winning a second Tasmanian Senate seat for the party. 'She's already fought off one of these [mills],' Brown told one reporter. 'She's an expert.'[31]

Unlike Labor, the Greens also campaigned hard on Iraq through 2004. The party got a lift at the beginning of 2004 with a healthy 4 per cent swing in February's Queensland election, which boosted their statewide vote to almost 7 per cent, although it was not enough to win any seats. A real kicker came when intelligence whistleblower Andrew Wilkie joined the party, signalling he could seek preselection in New South Wales for the looming election; the party's Senate ticket had already been chosen, but a lower-house endorsement was still possible. Wilkie, who confessed he had joined the Young Liberals while at the Duntroon military college, told *The Sydney Morning Herald* he had initially approached Labor, but 'the more I researched the parties' platforms I realised that it was the Greens that was my natural home'.[32] Brown was supportive, and Wilkie was soon linked with John Howard's own seat of Bennelong. He would be a thorn in the prime minister's side all year, attracting steady media coverage from local rag *The Northern District Times* to *The New York Times*.

By mid-2004, Labor had gone to water on same-sex marriage, ceding more high moral ground to the Greens. The opposition had been taking a softly, softly approach to reform, championed by left-winger Anthony Albanese, steadily removing discrimination against same-sex couples, starting with superannuation law in 1996.[33] In mid-2004 two gay and lesbian couples from Victoria applied to have their overseas marriages recognised by the Family Court. The Howard government moved immediately to prohibit same-sex marriages, enshrining in statute the common-law definition that marriage could only occur between a man and a woman.[34] With an election looming, Labor baulked, voting in favour of Howard's amendments. So the country took a huge step backwards, kicking off a campaign to legalise same-sex marriage that would continue for more than a decade.

Inside Labor, supporters like Albanese and Senator Penny Wong began agitating for change. The Greens, meanwhile, used their position in the federal, state and territory parliaments to good effect. In the House, Michael Organ introduced a private member's bill – the Same Sex Relationships (Enduring Equality) Bill – to 'remove discrimination to ensure people in same-sex relationships receive the same rights as people in heterosexual relationships in all areas of the law (including marriage)'.[35] It was never debated, but the Greens kept up the pressure, reintroducing bills for marriage equality in 2007, 2008, 2009, 2010 and through the ensuing decade.

That was all to come, however, and with neither major party interested the issue did not loom especially large in 2004. When Howard announced the election in August, he deftly shifted the goalposts, dodging the moral quagmire of war and terror and tapping straight into the hip-pocket nerve. 'This election is about trust,' he declared. 'Who do you trust to keep interest rates low?'

Bob Brown, as usual, was hugely ambitious for the party and freely told reporters the Greens were set to win a million votes at the election. 'I have a feeling that this electorate's on the move,' he said. 'There's very much a 1972 feeling about the place, but with a more confident and informed electorate this time and with more choices.'[36] Given neither he nor Kerry Nettle was up for re-election, the Greens were in the luxurious position that they could only go forward. Brown (and most pundits) thought Christine Milne a near certainty, likely to get a quota in her own right, and there was already commentary that she was a possible natural successor as the Greens' figurehead.[37] The party's expectations were high for Western Australia, Victoria and New South Wales, while Queensland, South Australia and the ACT would be tougher. The lead Senate candidates were all Greens heavyweights: in Western Australia, conservation council stalwart Rachel Siewert, having her second tilt after coming so close in 2001; in Victoria, serving Melbourne city councillor David Risstrom; in New South Wales, Rhiannon staffer and academic John Kaye; in Queensland, party co-founder Drew Hutton; in the ACT, the popular Kerrie Tucker, resigning after nearly a decade in the territory parliament. Most analysts predicted the Greens would win the minimum five seats required to achieve parliamentary party status – and the Democrats would lose it. In the lower house, Brown trumpeted the Greens' best prospects: Cunningham, where he hoped Michael Organ could hold on; Melbourne, where National Tertiary Education Union official Gemma Pinnell was running against Lindsay Tanner, having had a good crack at the corresponding state seat two years earlier; and Sydney, where a young Amnesty International campaigner, Jenny Leong, put Tanya Plibersek on notice.

The Greens headed into the election with a well-rounded 170-page policy platform, the product of two years' development, which was boiled down to a 24-page booklet that was professionally printed and freely distributed. Left-leaning University of Queensland economist John Quiggin described the party's economic policy as 'one of the most coherent and intellectually defensible documents of its kind ever put forward by an Australian political party', comparable in rigour to the Coalition's 'Fightback!' document in 1992. Quiggin commended the Greens' determination to raise revenue to fund spending commitments, and observed that the party had stepped away from their anti-growth philosophy. The stated policy objective now was to 'maintain and enhance the collective net wealth of the nation, including non-monetary economic and social assets', which implied economic growth. 'Anyone who decides to vote for the Greens on the strength of their support for the environment and opposition to war should be encouraged to know that they are also choosing a party with a policy that is economically as well as socially responsible,' Quiggin wrote.[38] The Greens were turning respectable. With a campaign budget of more than $750,000, the party could suddenly even afford print advertising, if not TV.[39]

The Greens were heading into a storm, however, that would blow the campaign completely off course and undo years of hard work on the platform and strategy. The tone was set in the first week, when Prime Minister Howard told shock-jock John Laws that the Greens portrayed themselves as 'warm and fuzzy' on the environment but had 'a whole lot of other very, very kooky policies in relation to things like drugs and all of that sort of stuff and new taxes and whatever, which people never talk about'.[40] The next day, Melbourne's *Herald Sun* ran an exposé which led with the sensational claim that 'ecstasy and other illegal drugs would be supplied over the counter to young users in a radical policy framed by Senator Bob Brown's Greens'. The article, which ran in the News Corp tabloids nationally, 'revealed' other 'extraordinary' Greens plans for Australia including: 'Laws to force people to ride bicycles more often and eat less meat. Driving farmers from their land. Medicare funding for sex-change operations. Capital gains tax on the most expensive family homes. An open door policy on asylum seekers.' It was a repeat of the attacks of the previous year's NSW election. Brown accused Rupert Murdoch and his minions of a 'get the Greens' strategy.

The party soon complained to the Press Council. The very thrust of the story was wrong: the Greens' policy was for the decriminalisation of personal use of illicit drugs, for a start, not the legalisation of trafficking or supply. The rest of the article was riddled with errors, with some claims downright fictitious, based on material directly supplied by the Liberal Party.[41] Six months later, the Press Council upheld the Greens' complaint, in what was reportedly one of its harshest rulings, criticising the *Herald Sun* for 'irresponsible journalism' and finding the newspaper should have checked its facts with the party.[42] Brown told reporters he had no doubt the story cost the Greens 'hundreds of thousands of votes and very probably seats in the Senate'.[43] It was all too late by then, of course.

The tabloid hit job was followed in quick succession by attack ads from an unexpected quarter. In 2002 the TV networks' industry body had decided it would no longer seek substantiation for statements made in political advertisements. Brown had described the change as a disaster for democracy, amid general fears that Australian politics was being further Americanised.[44] Come the 2004 election, the Family First party, which had debuted in South Australia two years earlier with the election of Assemblies of God pastor Andrew Evans, had built up a $1 million war chest and launched TV ads claiming the Greens were 'giving my kids easy access to marijuana'. Brown got legal advice that the ads were defamatory – implying that he was actually handing out drugs to children – and the Greens complained to the Australian Electoral Commission. The commission did not intervene, but the ads were subsequently withdrawn.[45]

In print, where the truthfulness of election ads had never been regulated, fundamentalist politician Fred Nile, who was running for the Senate in New South Wales, placed a *Sydney Morning Herald* ad headlined 'Good News For Paedophiles' and sub-headed 'The Greens want to Classify Teenagers as Adults', which would 'bring a smile to child-abusers in every suburb'. Brown's adviser Ben Oquist wrote afterwards that 'surprisingly, it was those parties professing to promote "morality" and "values" that sunk the lowest'.[46] Tasmania's forest industry got in on the act too, with ads attacking the Greens not just over logging but also over their policies on drugs and even vegetarianism.[47] The attacks cast a pall over the Greens' campaign. The worst blow, however, was yet to come.

Only in the final weeks of the campaign did it become clear that both the Democrats and Labor had done preference deals in the Senate with minor parties on the religious right, notably Family First, that would cruel the Greens' chance of winning new Senate seats in most states. Christine Milne said the Democrats' decision was 'almost spiteful', given the party's policy positions were diametrically opposed to those of Family First on Iraq, asylum seekers and same-sex marriage; it was especially bizarre in Western Australia, given that sitting Democrats senator Brian Greig was openly gay.[48]

In the lower house, it was a different story. Competing against Labor in their best prospects of Cunningham, Melbourne and Sydney, the Greens hoped they could run second in their primary vote and garner preferences from the third-placed Liberals. Treasurer Peter Costello pointed out that although the Greens' policies were too extreme for the Coalition, 'we always put Labor last'.[49] Elsewhere, the Greens finally agreed to preference Labor over the Liberals in most marginals – mainly over Iraq, support for signing up to the Kyoto Protocol and – the clincher – protecting Tasmania's forests. But the forests debate was about to turn against both Labor and the Greens.

After months of shadow-boxing, Latham chose Greens preferences over Tasmania's forest industry, announcing an $800 million package to stop old-growth logging and retrain workers.[50] In the final week of the campaign, in a brazen repeat of the 1995 Canberra blockade, the CFMEU's Michael O'Connor organised a rally of 2000 forest workers in high-vis to welcome John Howard on a flying visit to Launceston to announce a modest conservation package with no net job losses. The optics were perfect for Howard, who was cheered as a blue-collar hero. From the back of the packed Albert Hall, *The Australian*'s Matthew Denholm reported, one burly timber worker yelled, 'You're the best f..king Prime Minister we've ever had.'[51] Brown predicted an 'absolute slaughter' of the forests if Howard was elected. But it was a decisive win for Howard, literally embraced by unionists, which would haunt Labor for years. It was arguably the moment Howard clinched the election – much more substantive than his infamous handshake with Latham. Brown would later finger the prime minister and O'Connor over a $4 million donation to a CFMEU training fund, allegedly a gift in exchange for the union's political support. Howard denied it.[52]

The Greens did boost their national vote in the Senate, up 3 per cent to almost 8 per cent, but apart from that it was all downhill. It was soon clear that the party would not retain Cunningham, nor would it take Labor to preferences in Melbourne or Sydney. Worse, it was obvious that David Risstrom would fall short in Victoria, even though he had polled 8.7 per cent of first-preference votes in the upper house. Family First, on a primary vote of just 1.8 per cent, would overtake him in the final round. For the Greens, it was simply appalling that Labor would prefer to have a pretender from the religious right, with no mandate, potentially holding the balance of power in the Senate, rather than a genuinely progressive candidate from a party with much policy affinity and a real constituency behind him. Risstrom condemned Labor's tactics: 'I think Labor has betrayed its heartland by preferencing to Family First.'[53]

Rachel Siewert won in Western Australia, the one state where Labor had given the Greens preferences in the Senate, and Brown claimed victory for Christine Milne – prematurely, as it would turn out. The party was well short of his million-vote mark, and Brown feared the majority of voters 'want people behind razor wire, they want the East Timorese done out of their royalties, they want to see the drift of funding to the public sector away from the private sector, they want to see Indigenous Australians doing badly in the health stakes. That is a statement of Australia 2004.'[54] Democrats leader Andrew Bartlett blamed the Greens for Howard's re-election, likening Brown to Ralph Nader in the 2001 US presidential campaign. Bartlett said the Greens–Labor preference deal may have forced the ALP too far to the left for voters on issues such as forests. 'The Greens basically becoming the far-left wing of the Labor Party has potentially pulled Labor too far to the left and left more ground for John Howard,' Bartlett said.[55]

The ensuing three-week Senate count would prove excruciating for the Greens, however. Milne had fallen just short of a quota with 13.1 per cent of the primary vote, and the slow tally of postal and absentee votes brought Family First's Jacqui Petrusma back into contention, and then made her the favourite, although she had won just 2 per cent of first preferences. Brown was scathing:

> On all past form, Christine would be home and hosed with Labor and Democrat preferences, but this time both parties directed preferences to Family First ahead of the Greens. They fell prey to a nationally orchestrated pro-Howard blitzkrieg to divert preferences from the Greens and get them across to Family First [to] assure government control of the Senate.[56]

Milne was saved by the tendency of Tasmanians – especially, in this case, peeved Labor and Democrats supporters – to ignore the party ticket and vote below the line, and beat Petrusma soundly in the end.

An even more agonising wait lay ahead for Drew Hutton in Queensland, in his tenth tilt at politics; he was in an unpredictable six-way contest for the last seat, against Pauline Hanson herself, anti-paedophile campaigner Hetty Johnston and neophyte Nationals candidate Barnaby Joyce, among others. The count quickly boiled down to a runoff between Hutton, the favourite this time despite being dubbed Queensland's 'greatest political loser', and Joyce, considered an outside chance.[57] After the electoral commission failed to deliver 1359 postal ballots in outback Queensland, forcing the governor-general to give those voters an extra week, the Nationals flagged a challenge in the Court of Disputed Returns, which could trigger a fresh half-Senate election.[58] The stakes were enormous: if Joyce was elected, the Howard government would win a historic outright majority in the Senate, with 39 seats out of 76.

As counting continued, Joyce pulled ahead due to preferences from the Fishing Party, to which the Nationals had promised a review of angling prohibitions on the Great Barrier Reef. Hutton slammed the secret preference deal as a 'conspiracy'.[59] When the result came through, Nationals leader Ron Boswell rang Howard with the news and told reporters the prime minister was 'over-joyed … this is the icing on his cake because he's now got something that we haven't been able to achieve for 25 years'. Hutton said it was a sad day for Australia: 'I predict one of the first things John Howard will do with his absolute power over both houses of parliament is to change the voting rules for the Senate to make it impossible for smaller parties to ever get elected again.'[60] He wasn't right, but Joyce's fateful victory over Hutton would have huge ramifications for the country over the next 15 years.

*　　*　　*

The Greens had increased their vote in both houses of parliament, and doubled their representation in the Senate at the expense of the Democrats, who won none of the seats they were contesting and were clearly approaching the end of their three decades in Australian politics. It was a watershed election, confirming the Greens as the third-largest political force in the country.[61] Despite this, the Greens had been rendered all but irrelevant by Howard's majority in both houses. New senator Rachel Siewert confronted the challenge of trying to wield influence without having the power to do anything concrete, like establish a Senate inquiry.

The Greens would nevertheless have an impact: Brown successfully moved an urgent motion calling for a rollout of non-sniffable Opal fuel across the Central Desert region; Siewert was the first parliamentarian to call for an inquiry into AWB Ltd (formerly the Australian Wheat Board); in the debate over controls on the sale of abortion drug RU-486, Kerry Nettle attracted massive publicity by wearing a T-shirt into the Senate imploring then health minister Tony Abbott to 'get your rosaries off my ovaries'.[62]

The disappointing result in the federal election was compounded a week later by a lacklustre Greens showing in the ACT. Although Kerrie Tucker had polled 16 per cent in her unsuccessful Senate contest, the Greens' best primary vote in any state or territory, the party garnered only 9 per cent in the ACT election, electing a single MLA: East Gippsland forest activist and ANU scholar Deb Foskey, who won in Tucker's old electorate of Molongo. The party had hoped to win two to four seats in the 17-seat assembly, and retain at least a shared balance of power. Instead, the government of Labor's Jon Stanhope was returned with a majority, sidelining the Greens for the next four years.

In February 2005 the Greens had another poor result, this time in Western Australia, a reckoning after four years wielding the balance of power outright in the upper house, during the first term of Labor premier Geoff Gallop's government.

The WA Greens' foremost achievement was working with Labor to save the last of the old-growth forests in the south-west, reserving an additional 87,250 hectares on top of the regional forest agreement.[63] As the country's LNG boom took off with the approval of Chevron's massive Gorgon project on Barrow Island, Jim Scott claims the Greens were first to call for a strategic energy policy, ultimately adopted in the government's 2006 decision to reserve 15 per cent of the extracted gas for domestic use. 'The Premier and the Prime Minister have said what a wonderful thing it is that we are selling billions of dollars worth of natural gas to China,' Scott told state parliament in 2003. 'However, absolutely no thought is being given to putting in place a strategic energy use plan for the future of this State. People have the idea that it will keep coming from somewhere. However, that is not the reality.'[64] The Greens were also able to work with Labor on groundbreaking gay law reform, identifying 200 pieces of legislation that discriminated based on sexuality, and drafting amendments to equal-opportunity legislation that gave same-sex couples equal rights to de facto couples – to adopt, to access reproductive technology, to superannuation and so on. The age of consent for gay men was lowered from 21 to 16. For Giz Watson, the resulting 2002 legislation was a crowning achievement for the Greens: Western Australia leapfrogged other states and went from having 'some of the worst laws to some of the best laws'.

The most vexed issue throughout the Gallop government's first term, however, was the electoral reform designed to introduce 'one vote, one value' in Western Australia, which had the worst malapportionment in the country. The votes of rural constituents had twice the weight of Perth voters in the lower house, and three times as much in the upper house. Labor, having suffered conservative control of the upper house for over a century, was determined to fix the malapportionment once and for all, and took up the issue as soon as it got elected. Three of the Greens' five upper-house members were from rural divisions, however, and although the party had an in-principle commitment to one vote, one value, the party room found it very difficult to get consensus among its own MLCs.

MLC Chrissy Sharp, who did most of the work on the issue, was herself from the country, living on a farm near Balingup in the south-west. Labor finally reached a compromise with the Greens: one vote, one value would be applied in the lower house, with a variation of 10 per cent and adjustment for about half a dozen big remote electorates; in the upper house, there would be six regions – three urban, three rural – that elected six representatives each (taking the total number of MLCs from 34 to 36), despite their wildly varying populations. The result was that malapportionment favouring country areas actually got worse, and it has continued to worsen as country areas depopulate.

The Greens argued that the new upper house would be like the Senate, which gives Tasmanian voters 13 times more weight than those in New South Wales, and would reflect the interests of non-metropolitan areas in Western Australia, one of the most geo-graphically centralised populations on Earth: its land covers half a continent, but almost three-quarters of the population live in Perth.

Defending the 'state Senate' model, Sharp told one newspaper: 'We support continued malapportionment in the Upper House so we can provide for a Parliament that is better grounded in natural resource management.'[65] The debate was acrimonious both inside and outside the party room, and it took a long time for the Greens to reach a consensus position. The two Perth representatives, Giz Watson and Jim Scott, backed one vote, one value, but they were opposed by the rural representatives, particularly Chrissy Sharp and Dee Margetts.

The reform had a torturous passage into law: 2001 legislation was struck down by the High Court in 2003 and had to be renegotiated in a rush after the 2005 election, before the new upper house was to sit. In the second round of negotiations, Bob Brown intervened strongly in favour of one vote, one value and against the vote-weighting model the WA Greens were pushing for. Sharp recorded later:

> It was the only time I am aware of that Bob tried to intervene in
> [WA] Greens affairs. All five Green MLC's rejected Bob's interfer-
> ence. Although I remained firm under Bob's considerable pressure
> of emails and phone calls, nevertheless it contributed to my con-
> cern that perhaps I could have got it wrong.[66]

Sharp subsequently conceded that the new model was 'slightly to our
disadvantage', and that has proven to be the case in subsequent elections, where it has most helped the Nationals and One Nation. Labor
allowed the Greens to wear the public opprobrium associated with
the persistent malapportionment, and blamed them for the associated
cost of another two MLCs, and there is no doubt the debate contributed to the Greens' poor 2005 result, even if the reforms themselves
did not take effect until the 2008 election.[67]

Stalwart MLC Jim Scott felt the Greens had handled the negotiations poorly, and ahead of the election resigned to run in the party's
most promising lower-house seat of Fremantle, up against Labor's
Jim McGinty. Scott placed third, polling 15.8 per cent, and quit politics altogether. Sharp also retired in 2005, burned out after eight
years. The Greens copped a small statewide swing against them in
the upper house, down 0.5 per cent to 7.5 per cent, but it counted
against them heavily in terms of representation, with the loss of seats
held by Chapple (Mining and Pastoral), Margetts (Agricultural) and
Scott. Watson held onto her seat of North Metro, and Paul Llewellyn
replaced Sharp in South West.

It was enough for the Greens to retain the balance of power in the
upper house, where the numbers were finely balanced, with Labor and
the Coalition split on 16 seats each. Yet there was no hiding that the
WA Greens had suffered another setback. A decade later, the Greens
admitted the 2005 deal was unfair and offered to work with the
government of Premier Mark McGowan to fix the upper-house malapportionment and abolish group voting tickets as well. MLC Alison
Xamon said her party now supported a one vote, one value system,
'but we also want to support the voice of regional Australia ... the
Greens are always open to talk about how we can do governance better
and certainly open to having discussions with the Labor Party about
how we might want to look at reforms of the Legislative Council.'[68]

Today Giz Watson says the decision was a bad mistake: 'It makes it harder for us to get elected in the council [which] continues to be dominated by country conservatives. If I was to put my finger on one thing that we shouldn't have done, that would be it.'

*   *   *

Within weeks of the 2004 federal election, woodchipper Gunns Ltd filed shock legal proceedings in the Victorian Supreme Court seeking $6.4 million in damages from three organisations – The Wilderness Society, Huon Defenders and Doctors for Native Forests – and 17 individuals, including the Greens' Bob Brown, who personally faced a $1.7 million claim, and Tasmanian leader Peg Putt, up for $1.5 million. The defendants were accused of disrupting Gunns' logging business at protest actions from 1999 to 2004, as well as 'corporate vilification', as part of an overarching conspiracy. The case, which would be known as the 'Gunns 20', was Australia's first major 'strategic lawsuit against public participation' (or SLAPP suit), and was often compared to the UK's decade-long 'McLibel case'. When the proceedings were filed, Brown later said, 'I knew better than to call the lawyers. The first thing I did was to call a press conference. Within 24 hours we had a candlelight vigil for democracy, in Hobart. We jangled keys like in the Prague Spring.'[69]

The analogy is flawed – many died during the Prague Spring, of course – but there was no doubting the gravity of the Gunns 20 case. The targeting of the Greens' leaders in Hobart and Canberra represented a serious threat to the party. Brown and Putt were on high parliamentary salaries, but neither had huge assets behind them; if either was bankrupted, they could be unseated. With the state government and the corporation working in concert, Tasmania's democracy was vulnerable. Author Richard Flanagan told the Hobart vigil the case was an assault on free speech: 'There is now fear abroad in Tasmania. Who is to get the next writ? Who is next to have their lives destroyed because they cared enough about their beautiful island home to say something, to do something?'[70] Brown and Putt taped their mouths shut at the vigil in protest.

A struggle against apparently overwhelming odds was not new territory for the 20 defendants. There was some precedent: North

Forest Products had threatened to sue Putt in the mid-1990s, after she had gone to Japan as a Greens MP to target the paper makers who bought Tasmanian woodchips, and to raise awareness among consumers, leading to accusations of treachery; the Liberals' Michael Hodgman dubbed her 'Tokyo Peg'. 'They were wanting me to go to court over whether or not North Ltd had ever damaged the environment,' Putt recalls. 'I thought, "Okay, let's do that!" At some point someone sort of tapped them on the shoulder and said, "Hey, this is a bad idea," and they backed out.'

The Gunns lawsuit was part of a bigger strategy: two days after the writs were issued, the company announced that the site of its new pulp mill would be Bell Bay, in the Tamar Valley. Taken together, the Gunns 20 case and the new pulp mill marked a dramatic escalation in Tasmania's forest wars, which would loom large over green politics for the rest of the decade.

The story of the rise and fall of Gunns has been well told, and cannot be charted in any detail here; suffice it to say the SLAPP suit would prove a huge and costly mistake by CEO John Gay, one among many. The lawsuit generated enormous sympathy for the conservationists' cause. Even the Hobart *Mercury* – no friend of the Greens – called it intimidation and a threat to freedom of speech, and warned that Gunns would 'live to regret it'.[71] In the Tasmanian parliament, the Greens' Nick McKim tabled a Protection of Public Participation Bill, giving courts the power to strike out legal actions that were unlikely to succeed and were intended to prevent public debate; three years later, the ACT would later become the first jurisdiction to pass such laws, introduced by Greens MLA Deb Foskey and strongly backed by the Labor government. Brown spoke at rallies calling for donations to help fight the case, and support came from some unlikely quarters.[72] Federal independent politician Peter Andren, the member for the rural NSW seat of Calare, helped raise money among well-heeled conservative country folk, and moved a motion in the federal parliament, seconded by fellow country independent Tony Windsor, decrying Gunns' case.[73] In 2005 all states did adopt common defamation laws that prevented companies with more than ten employees from suing.

Gunns' first and second writs were rejected as 'embarrassing' by Justice Bernard Bongiorno in the Supreme Court of Victoria in

July 2005; his overall impression was of 'a collection of very general allegations of wrongdoing by a large number of people over an approximately five-year period'.[74] The same judge threw out a third revised claim in August 2006; as Brown described it, the judge had taken a 'chainsaw' to Gunns' claim.[75] In November 2006 Gunns filed a fourth claim, which dropped the overarching conspiracy allegation, and also dropped the claims against Brown, Putt and three other defendants. Brown told the ABC the withdrawal proved Gunns had no case against the politicians: 'It's a real victory in particular for free speech and for the right of parliamentarians to advocate the protection of Australia's great forest heritage in Tasmania and elsewhere.'[76] For the rest of the Gunns 20, the saga would carry on for three more years. The eventual toll on the TWS was immense, nearly ripping the organisation apart. Brown said he and Putt would seek advice to reclaim more than $1 million of their legal costs; two years later, they won.[77]

*　　*　　*

It had never mattered before, but the swearing-in of two new Greens senators in mid-2005 raised a question: should the four-member-strong federal parliamentary party appoint a leader, or carry on with Bob Brown as its unofficial national spokesman? Brown and his three Senate colleagues in Canberra had adopted a set of 'Party Room Rules' which included a vote for leadership and other Party Room positions. Appointing a leader was not straightforward, given the Greens' historical roots as an anti-party party whose motto was to 'do politics differently'.[78] The example of Die Grünen was salutary: in federal elections that year, the Red–Green coalition with the SPD was voted out, leading to the formation of the 'grand coalition' between the SPD and centre-right Christian Democratic Union, which installed Angela Merkel as Chancellor. A drop in the primary vote for Die Grünen was partly blamed on lax issue of visas by leader Joschka Fischer as foreign minister. Charismatic leadership had been good and bad for Die Grünen, as Ludger Volmer, secretary of state in the Red–Green coalition government, wrote afterwards: 'The party and the parliamentary group became a chorus of applause for Joschka Fischer … the media appointed him as the only leader and the Greens didn't want to destroy that image.'[79] Die Grünen would not return to power at a national level, but the legacy of its seven-year coalition with the SPD – in which a green environment minister, Juergen Trittin, kickstarted Germany's world-leading 'Energiewende', passing the 2000 Renewable Energy Act – still inspires Greens worldwide.[80] At the time it was described as a flawed Die Grünen compromise, but looking back it has created 350,000 jobs and spurred more than EUR200 billion of investment.[81]

In New Zealand, tragedy struck in early November when, two days after an election, the party's co-leader Rod Donald died suddenly of a heart attack at 48. The Greens had won six seats on a primary vote of five per cent and, although outside the Labour-led coalition government, the two co-leaders were made spokespeople on energy efficiency and buying Kiwi-made products. Brown lauded Donald as a 'magnificent Kiwi', and a tribute in *Green* magazine acknowledged his leadership of the successful campaign to adopt proportional representation: 'Consequently, he changed the face of New Zealand politics, breaking the monopoly of the two big parties and allowing smaller parties like the Greens to achieve parliamentary representation.' In the same issue, Brown set out a determined agenda for the Australian Greens, the same as for Greens in New Zealand or Germany: 'we are, and always have been, on our own way to government'. Brown acknowledged that as the party grew there would be more diversity of views. 'Maybe that means factions. Whichever party avoided them? Rather than fearful avoidance we should foster tolerant accommodation of differences under the Charter.'[82]

Inside the party, those differences were sharpening. The debate over leadership came to a head at the party's national conference in Hobart that November. In an atmosphere described as 'bitter and contentious', the conference failed to reach a consensus on a leadership model, so Brown put it to a vote – and the right of the party room to decide its rules was ultimately affirmed. NSW delegates voted against it, according to Rhiannon, because limits on the powers of the leader had not been set out. 'They still haven't been,' she says. 'The Greens NSW however accepted the national decision to have a leader and have never tried to reverse it.' Two weeks later the federal party room duly elected Brown as leader, unopposed, with

Rachel Siewert as the federal Greens' first whip. Announcing his appointment, Brown told journalists: 'We are a very cohesive and happy group, leading the advocacy of humanitarian and ecological policy on Capital Hill.'[83]

The Greens' state branches would gradually adopt their own positions. In five state elections over the 12 months from March 2006, the party broke into South Australia and gained a fourth upper-house MP in New South Wales, taking them to a higher level of combined representation in commonwealth, state and territory parliaments than the Democrats had ever had.[84]

Ten months out from the South Australian election, sitting Greens MP Kris Hanna announced he would seek preselection for the upper house, rather than go up against his old party, Labor, in the lower-house seat of Mitchell, in inner Adelaide. Hanna had been an effective Greens MP, but had never felt beholden or accountable to the party. He was challenged and beaten by Mark Parnell. Hanna, after falling out with the Greens, declared he would stand as an independent – leading *The Australian* to brand him a 'double rat' – and won the seat, largely due to Liberal preferences. The Greens polled just 4 per cent in the upper house, amid a massive 19 per cent swing to Nick Xenophon. But Parnell was elected on half a quota due to a collapse in support for the Democrats. He would share the balance of power on a crowded crossbench.

The Greens did well in Queensland, polling 8 per cent of the primary vote, but the most significant election of 2006 was in Victoria in November, the first to be conducted after Premier Steve Bracks reformed the upper house to introduce proportional representation. It was always a mystery why the Greens did not catch on more quickly in the country's most progressive state – a mixture of bad luck, the unfavourable electoral system and a hostile preference strategy from Labor explains it. The 2006 election marked the beginning of the slow ascendancy of the Victorian Greens, led by Greg Barber.

Barber was something new and different for the party. As a young biologist, he was inspired to mount a one-man campaign in the old-growth forests of the Central Highlands.[85] He would go on to work for a string of non-government organisations, including the Conservation Council of Victoria, the Tenants Union and

Bicycle Victoria, and joined the Greens in 1993. Inspired by the anti-globalisation protests in Seattle, Barber decided to enrol in an MBA at the University of Melbourne while day-trading to supplement the family income. 'It was almost like I was volunteering to be infected with the capitalism virus in order to develop a cure,' he says.

Barber was a new breed of pro-market environmentalist; to the left radicals of the NSW Greens, these were 'neoliberals on bikes'. Barber was a strategic thinker, however, who built up the Victorian Greens' branch network and masterminded a 'heist' on Labor's inner-Melbourne local government stronghold. When he stood for the City of Yarra Council in 2002 he won a thumping primary vote of 47 per cent. Becoming chair of the council's finance committee, Barber put his MBA to use. He fixed up the cash management, and put more money into tree planting, bike paths and a beefed-up open space program. Ratepayers loved it. The following year, the council elected Barber to the mayoralty, making him the first Greens mayor in the country.

When Bracks introduced proportional representation into the Victorian upper house in 2003 – establishing eight regions of equal population with five members each, meaning the required quota was 16.7 per cent – it was clear that minor parties might finally get a foothold. Barber did not run for Yarra Council at the local elections of 2004, preparing instead for a crack at the Northern Metropolitan region, the most prospective for the Greens, covering Carlton, Brunswick and Northcote. The party's other target was Melbourne's Southern Metropolitan region, covering the wealthy inner city south of the river from Prahran to St Kilda and out to Brighton.

Barber signalled early on a willingness to deal with the Liberals on preferences. The Greens actually copped a small statewide swing against them in the upper house, but managed to elect three MLCs. Barber got a quota in his own right in Northern Metro. Sue Pennicuik, an environment officer for the AMWU, also got elected in Southern Metro on a solid 15 per cent of first-preference votes. The surprise victor was social worker Colleen Hartland in Western Metro, covering Melbourne's western suburbs. After a short stand-off between Barber and Pennicuik, he was confirmed as the state leader; each of the three Greens would go on to sit in the upper house for more than a decade. Barber recalls that Labor MPs would heckle them: 'You're only here because of us!'

The Greens' belated surge into the Victorian parliament was a shot in the arm for the party nationally. In New South Wales that year, preselection was underway for the upcoming state election, set for March 2007. Lee Rhiannon was up for re-election after completing her first eight-year term. Because she had campaigned internally in 2003 on the desirability of a form of limited tenure, it was unclear whether Rhiannon would stand again. When Rhiannon called Brown to tell him she had decided to run, he and Ben Oquist flew to Sydney the next day to urge her not to. Rhiannon was reduced to tears. Brown does not resile from the fact that they delivered a blunt message – namely, that it would be highly hypocritical for Rhiannon to renominate. According to Rhiannon, Brown's real agenda was for Oquist to run in New South Wales, get a profile in state parliament and then go federal. Regardless, Rhiannon turned out to have the overwhelming support of the branches: she won 574 votes, with John Kaye second at 299 votes, and Oquist third at 165 votes. Neither Brown nor Rhiannon went public over the tensions, or the heated meeting.

Despite the widening rift inside the party, the Greens in New South Wales were on a roll and, outwardly at least, working well with their national colleagues. A case in point was the privatisation of the iconic Snowy Hydro scheme, sprung upon the people of the state in late 2005. With a cash-strapped Labor government proposing to sell the state's majority 58 per cent share to fill a budget black hole, Victoria and the Commonwealth had little choice but to follow suit, and work began on a share-market float, led by federal finance minister Nick Minchin. The sale upset the public, however, particularly in country New South Wales areas that were dependent on the scheme for power and irrigation water; the idea that it would fall into foreign hands was alarming.

NSW Greens MLC Sylvia Hale successfully moved a motion calling for the production of papers relating to the proposed sale, which turned up 40 boxes full of embarrassing documents. Hale told the ABC they showed 'there is a vast number of members of the Labor Party who are desperately unhappy about the sale'.[86] When it emerged that the state Treasury had destroyed some documents, the government of Morris Iemma was on the back foot.

Meanwhile, in the federal parliament the Greens and three Democrats were the only Senate votes against the sale. Bob Brown gave a speech that fired up a doyen of the press gallery, *Sydney Morning Herald* columnist Alan Ramsay, beginning: 'There was movement at the station, for the word had passed around, that Beijing and Tokyo and Chicago and Paris were on their way ... And they have got more than a £1000 in their pockets.'[87] Brown obtained advice that the proposed sale would be illegal, and within a week Howard did an astonishing backflip and canned the sale.[88] The Greens claimed a significant win.

Another Greens agenda item gaining traction was political donations, particularly after the Howard government lifted the disclosure threshold to $10,000 in early 2006. The Green's democracy4sale.org database collated NSW and national funding disclosures by party and donor – an enormous labour of love led by retired academic Norman Thompson and other volunteers working out of Lee Rhiannon's office – and exposed the increasing reliance of the NSW Labor Party on donations from developers in particular. The Greens' transparency website won cred across the political spectrum. 'It's a sad fact that government in this state involves a business model based on a legal form of payola,' wrote *The Sydney Morning Herald*'s Michael Duffy. 'Any readers concerned about this might like to have a look at democracy4sale.org. It makes harrowing reading.'[89] Years later, Rhiannon's tireless efforts to shine the light on developer donations during Labor's darkest years would be lauded by Independent Commission Against Corruption counsel Geoffrey Watson.

For all the inroads that the Greens were making, however, Labor entered the state election with a comfortable buffer – left over from the last campaign, led by Bob Carr – and with a soft opponent in Liberal leader Peter Debnam. The Greens had a chance at taking the inner-city seats of Balmain and Marrickville, but after *The Daily Telegraph* reprised its attacks on the Greens' drug policies, the Liberals again decided not to preference the minor party, extinguishing any real prospect of their victory.

In the end, the Greens won a small swing towards them, polling 9 per cent statewide. Both Rhiannon and Kaye were elected, making the Greens the first minor party in the state to win two quotas. The Democrats, One Nation and other micro-parties left over from the 1999 'tablecloth' election were wiped out. With Labor holding 19 out of 42 seats, the Greens now held the balance of power in the upper house.

It was a significant victory. Rhiannon put the win down to climate change, and Kaye signalled he would be a vigorous campaigner on the issue, adding that Premier Iemma was misguided to put his faith in 'clean coal' technology. 'He's an emperor with no clothes on when it comes to climate change,' Kaye said. 'It's also Peter Debnam, and I must say Kevin Rudd and John Howard, [who] are living in a fantasy land when it comes to "clean coal".'[90] In his maiden speech, Kaye issued a stern warning: 'We are in the first decade of the greenhouse century. For at least the next 100 years, if not longer, every decision, every choice and every consequence will be tempered by our impact on the climate, and its impact on us.'[91]

*   *   *

As the Howard era ground towards its conclusion, the four Greens in the Senate did their best to keep up the pressure – on Tassie forests, on the Coalition's contentious WorkChoices industrial relations legislation, on whaling, on right-to-die legislation, against deployment of more troops to Afghanistan, and on bringing home David Hicks, who by now had been held in solitary confinement at Guantanamo Bay for five years without charge. At the beginning of 2007 an electoral commission investigation at the request of Bob Brown revealed that a company linked to the Exclusive Brethren religious sect had, ahead of the 2004 election, spent some $370,000 on election advertising supporting the return of the Howard government, and attacking the Greens – without disclosing it. 'It is a highly deceptive and global campaign which is being slowly, slowly brought out into the light of day,' Brown told journalist David Marr.[92]

For the first time since the 1990 federal election, the environment was smack-bang in the middle of the national agenda. The millennium drought worsened through 2006, then the driest year on record, and Australia's climate anxiety ratcheted up. Polls at this time showed that Australians were the most concerned population about the impact of climate change of any surveyed around the world. By early 2007, 76 per cent of people asked considered it a 'major problem', only 5 per cent thought it was 'not a problem' and 77 per cent indicated they were 'prepared to pay more … if it would help reduce greenhouse gas emissions'.[93]

John Howard, in his memoir *Lazarus Rising*, wrote that between the drought, Al Gore's film *An Inconvenient Truth* and the United Kingdom's Stern Review, he faced a 'perfect storm' on climate change.[94] Howard had stuck by President George W. Bush in refusing to sign the Kyoto Protocol (even though his government had negotiated an extremely favourable deal in 1998), while declaring that Australia would meet its targets anyway. It was a nonsensical position, barely supported even within his own cabinet, and Labor leader Kevin Rudd made easy political yards by committing to sign Kyoto if elected. Realising he needed to do something, Howard added the environment to Malcolm Turnbull's duties as water minister, and tasked him with developing a 'cap and trade' emissions-trading scheme. For the first time in Australia, and perhaps the world, climate change was a significant election issue, and domestically there was bipartisan consensus about how it might best be tackled: with a price on carbon.[95]

Bob Brown and Kerry Nettle were up for re-election. Having developed a proper national strategy, the party took a more professional, evidence-based approach to the 2007 election. There was a fundraising strategy, for example, aiming to raise $750,000 for the federal campaign, of which $600,000 would come from 'high net worth' individuals. The strategy bore fruit: donations to the Australian Greens kicked up in 2007–08, falling just short of the target with $745,639, a new high – and there were some interesting names. Wealthy Sydney-based bookmaker Greg Beirne, outraged by the Gunns 20 case, gave $200,000 to the Tasmanian Greens; in Western Australia, stalwart Ruth Greble, who had been donating to the party since 1999, dug deep and kicked in $123,500. Unions that had been lukewarm supporters since the Greens went in to bat for workers in Howard's early IR reforms and the waterfront dispute donated almost a quarter of a million dollars this time, dominated by the Electrical Trades

Union ($169,506), whose maverick secretary, Dean Mighell, saw the potential jobs for his members in renewable energy, particularly rooftop solar, followed by the CFMEU ($40,000) and the AMWU ($30,000). The CFMEU's donation was a shock, given its history with the greenies.

Roy Morgan research was used to analyse the Greens' voter base, identify those non-Greens voters most likely to switch, and work out what issues were most likely to appeal to them. A confidential internal paper by national officer Mark Jeanes provided a fascinating snapshot of the party's supporters. Demographically, the results were unsurprising. Compared with the rest of the country, Greens voters were younger, better educated (they were twice as likely to have a degree) and had higher income (although they were under-represented in the highest-income bracket, over $100,000 a year). There were caveats to the 'young inner-city trendy' stereotype, however: more than two-thirds of Greens voters were partnered or had children.

Most interesting were the 'Greens voters vs all' comparisons of attitudes to a dozen political issues in order of importance. Greens voters were more than three times likelier than the broader population to be concerned about the environment, of course, but they also ranked education twice as highly, and gave much more weight to open and honest government. Greens voters cared far less than the rest of the country about managing the economy, business, law and order, and defence – which was at the bottom of the list. And Greens voters were at odds with the rest of the country on a handful of issues: a two-thirds majority agreed that 'terrorists deserve the same rights as other criminals', whereas a two-thirds majority of Australians did not; a similar proportion of Greens agreed that 'homosexual couples should be allowed to adopt children', while a majority of Australians did not; less than a third of Greens agreed that 'obedience and respect for authority are the most important values children should learn', while more than 60 per cent of Australians agreed.

At the same time, there were issues hugely important to Greens voters that also struck a chord with a majority of Australians. While 96 per cent of Greens agreed, predictably, that 'if we don't act now we'll never control our environmental problems', so did 89 per cent of Australians. There was similarly overwhelming support for propositions that 'the gap between rich and poor is growing' (94 per cent of Greens vs 87 per cent of Australians); 'Aboriginal culture is an essential component of Australian society' (87 per cent vs 69 per cent); and 'globalisation brings more problems than it solves' (67 per cent vs 60 per cent). Clearly, there was a mass constituency for many of the Greens' dearest policy positions.

Based on Morgan's value segments, the research identified two groups of non-Greens voters who were likely to switch – 'young optimists' and the 'socially aware' – noting that 75 per cent of them were Labor voters. Jeanes' note boiled it all down: the Greens' highest priority target group were 300,000 to 400,000 'educated young Labor' voters around the country, with Victoria in particular having 'large potential'. Winning over all these voters, Jeanes wrote, 'would lift our primary vote from 8 per cent to 11 per cent'. The non-environmental issue with the most appeal to those voters, he noted, was education funding. It was a hip-pocket issue that would directly affect educated young Labor voters, and it was an easy area in which the Greens could differentiate their policy – to abolish the HECS system of government student loans – from Labor's.

The Morgan research was backed up by focus groups in Melbourne, Sydney, Canberra, Hobart and Launceston, and the feedback from the consultant DDR – marked 'highly sensitive and confidential' – was harder to swallow:

> The Greens are caught between a rock and a hard place. They are seen to be a single issue party, and that issue is the environment. This both defines them and undermines them. Certainly for the first time the environment is on the voting public's agenda – so in one sense the Greens' time is now (and many see this as the make or break election for the party) ... BUT both Liberal and Labor are on the bandwagon ... The Greens need to ensure they remain in the debate and are seen as the reliable voice on the environment ... The Greens are seen to lack any policies or experience outside of the environment. They are also seen to be verging on the extreme in many of their views ...
>
> Bob Brown is both a plus and a minus for the party. Much of the perceptions of honesty and integrity and passion are derived from

> Bob, but so too are the perceptions of extreme. Some of the younger voters (on the mainland) were actually unaware of Bob or felt he was not relevant to them – too old; too conservative looking … Almost nothing is known of the other Greens senators (although Christine Milne is known in Tasmania) – and the pictures of the group together hardly inspire interest or excitement in the party.

For most people, the authors wrote, 'Bob *is* The Greens party'. Terms like 'heroic' and 'idealistic' were used to describe him, and some voters recalled him standing up to George W. Bush. Younger voters, however, did not remember the Franklin, and some thought Brown came across as dour, was 'always on a pile of logs' or looked like a 'boring preacher' or 'happy country Dad'. At least he wasn't seen as a 'traditional old hippie'.

More encouraging was the voters' recognition of the important role the Greens played in the federal parliament:

> The main point of resonance for The Greens appears to be their ability to step into the gap left by the Democrats. Voters want to see some sort of check and balance in the Senate, and The Greens are ideally placed to take on that role given they are seen to be a party of integrity, principle and honesty. We heard continual references to:
>
> The Greens being the conscience in the Senate
>
> The Greens providing a voice in the Senate
>
> However, talking about winning back or rescuing the Senate *does not work*, as these terms do not reflect the role people want the party to play.[96]

This finding posed a difficulty for the party, which had planned a Senate-focused campaign with just this theme. Driving the strategy was research analysing state-by-state those voters who put the Greens as their second preference, which showed that on top of the 7–10 per cent of the population who indicated they intended to vote Green, there was an additional 14 per cent of the population who said they would consider voting Green if they were given a compelling reason to do so. 'The Greens' policies and principles are attractive to around 20% (one in five!) Australians,' wrote the National Election Campaign

Committee, and accompanying charts showed the percentages were even higher in the hotspots of inner Perth, Melbourne and Sydney, western Adelaide and Brisbane, and (perhaps surprisingly) the regional centres Geelong and Wollongong.

Taking all this research in, the Greens resolved to campaign on climate change first and foremost, followed by industrial relations, health and education. At the same time, tired of the ritual tabloid pre-election beat-ups, Brown fought internally to rein in the Greens' drug policies, dumping calls for the regulated supply of 'social drugs' like ecstasy and the 'controlled availability' of cannabis. The new policy still advocated removal of criminal sanctions for personal drug use, but would allow regulated use of cannabis for medical purposes.[97] The more radical Greens weren't happy.

On climate change, Bob Brown caused a furore early in 2007 by calling for a plan to completely phase out coal – both for domestic use and for export. Cue sensational headlines that the Greens wanted to shut down the coal industry within three years: the *Courier-Mail* declared Brown had 'LOST THE PLOT', while the *Daily Telegraph* blared that the Greens would 'SACK 50,000 AUSTRALIANS'. Brown had been verballed. What he meant – and the Greens' policy outlined – was that a plan would be developed and committed to within a single term, although the actual phase-out would take much longer, possibly decades. But the distinction was lost in the media coverage, and Brown was pilloried for making 'policy on the run' that would wipe out Australia's largest export industry, worth $25 billion a year.

The Greens had a bigger problem getting traction through 2007, however. The rise of the Kevin Rudd and Julia Gillard 'dream team' to the Labor leadership sucked up much of the political oxygen on the progressive left. It was the eternal problem for the Greens: the party always did better under a Labor government, when they could peel off disenchanted progressive voters, than they did under a Coalition government, when progressives not understanding the preference system, mistakenly believed voting 1 Greens then 2 Labor might somehow help the Coalition win, so they had better stick with Labor. The Greens call it the wasted vote myth, and it dies hard.

*　　　*　　　*

The Greens had their own generational challenge, of course, and in one media interview Bob Brown, then 62, let slip that his third term in the Senate would likely be his last. Apart from Brown and Nettle, the lead Senate candidates for the 2007 election were the coming generation of Greens politicians, for whom Brown had been a lifelong inspiration, not a peer.

In Tasmania, just below Brown in second place, there was Andrew Wilkie, who had moved from Sydney to Hobart. In Victoria, former Melbourne candidate Richard Di Natale had top spot. In Western Australia, Jo Vallentine protégé and Jabiluka activist Scott Ludlam headed the ticket and was in with a chance. In Queensland, with little prospect, there was young environmental lawyer Larissa Waters. One name on the New South Wales ticket was curious: Green Bans hero Jack Mundey was running in the (totally unwinnable) fourth place on the party's ticket.

Heading up the South Australian ticket was a new name: Sarah Hanson-Young. She was just 25, and came with the greenest log-cabin story imaginable. Hanson-Young had grown up in country Victoria, and her parents were dedicated green activists who moved from Melbourne to East Gippsland to fight against logging. The family bought 60 acres in the middle of cool temperate rainforest and lived in a solar-powered bark hut, off-grid before it was cool, with water pumped from a creek, a gas bottle fridge, and no TV or phone reception. Hanson-Young was home-schooled through her primary years. Every summer Goongerah would see an influx of protesters from Melbourne, coming up for the 'Forests Forever' campaign, and as a young girl Hanson-Young would run around welcoming everyone and making cups of tea.

But Hanson-Young was no softy, and moved out to go to high school in the timber town of Orbost, an hour's drive away. There were three groups at her high school: kids of loggers and sawmillers, kids from dairy farms, and kids who were second- or third-generation unemployed. It was a tough environment. 'I was the token greenie,' says Hanson-Young, who remembers dating the son of a logger whose car had a bumper sticker reading 'Help the Environment – Run Over a Greenie'. Hanson-Young was one of only 11 students at her school to graduate that year, and moved to Adelaide to study (she had assumed she wouldn't get into university in Melbourne, and when she did, it was too late to change).

Hoping to become an anthropologist, Hanson-Young studied social sciences, got involved in the student union and helped organise carpools for the five-hour drive out to the rally against mandatory detention at Woomera. Hanson-Young got elected as an independent to the student association, first becoming environment officer and then president, and as a young student activist established a good relationship with Natasha Stott-Despoja, who had held the same position. According to Hanson-Young, the Democrats senator was an early source of advice, encouragement and inspiration.

After the *Tampa* affair, Hanson-Young worked for Amnesty International and joined the Greens. She was a media adviser, loved the fray and, after turning down a staffer's job, put her hand up for preselection for the Senate in her own right. Urged on privately by Bob Brown, she took on older Greens candidates and won. Stott-Despoja, who had announced she would retire at the election, rang to congratulate her – *The Australian* immediately dubbed her the 'Green Natasha' – but Hanson-Young wanted to forge her own path.

A week later she found out she was pregnant – unexpectedly, as she had been told she was unlikely to conceive naturally, as she had polycystic ovary syndrome. As she revealed many years later in her book, *En Garde*, she faced an immediate backlash:

> From the moment I started telling people inside the party that I was expecting, the grumbles started. 'You really should have told people you wanted to have a baby before you contested the pre-selection,' one male party member said to me. It wasn't the reaction I had banked on. My joy at being an expectant mother quickly turned to disappointment when a group inside one of the local branches tried to have my preselection ruled invalid on the basis that I was now pregnant.[98]

The sexist campaign against her was quietly dropped. Hanson-Young gave birth to her daughter in February 2007, and prepared for a long hard fight for what everyone assumed would be an unwinnable Senate seat.

Most Greens thought Hanson-Young's chances of taking the sixth South Australian Senate seat evaporated when, two months out from the election, No Pokies state MLC Nick Xenophon announced he was quitting to run for the Senate. One who did not agree with this assessment was Bob Brown's political adviser, Richard Denniss, who was the first person to call Hanson-Young. 'You're going to win now,' he told her, explaining that Xenophon would knock down enough of the Liberal and Labor vote that they would fall short of a third seat and she would drift up to a quota on their preferences. 'That's exactly what happened,' Hanson-Young says.

In the 2007 federal election, the Greens won a small 1.4 per cent swing towards them in the Senate; the ACT Greens did best, with a 21 per cent first-preference vote, followed by Tasmania (18 per cent) and Victoria (10 per cent). Brown was safe, easily earning a quota in his own right, but he had optimistically tipped the Greens would pick up seats in Victoria, Western Australia and the ACT, and that Kerry Nettle would hold her spot in New South Wales. He would be disappointed.

Sarah Hanson-Young was an upset winner on a primary vote of 6 per cent in South Australia, becoming the youngest woman ever elected to the parliament, and Scott Ludlam was comfortably elected in Western Australia on a primary vote of 9 per cent. Elsewhere the results were bleak. Kerrie Tucker fell short of the difficult task of winning the second ACT Senate seat, and would not try again. In Victoria, despite the high primary vote, Richard Di Natale lost out when Family First preferences flowed back to the major parties. After five election attempts, state and federal, Di Natale was ready to throw in the towel.

It was a similar story in New South Wales, where the party lost its Senate seat – an especially bitter pill to swallow. Kerry Nettle had run a busy campaign. The Greens won 8.4 per cent of the primary vote, up 1 per cent on the previous election, but Nettle was knocked out in the final round when the preferences of the Christian Democrats – bulked up by deals with micro-parties – went overwhelmingly back to the majors.[99] The outcome was an upper house in which the Greens were stronger, with five Senators, but had to share the balance of power with Xenophon and Family First; the Democrats were wiped out. In the lower house, the party's best performance was in Melbourne, where Adam Bandt polled 23 per cent on first preferences, within

600 votes of the second-placed Liberal, which forced Labor's Lindsay Tanner to rely on preferences to win his once safe seat.

From election cycle to election cycle, the pattern was becoming clear. The Greens set themselves optimistic goals – for the balance of power, and one day for government – and Brown, as national leader, would personify these aspirations and carry them on his shoulders. Inevitably, the party fell short, leading to a wave of introspection and division. Each time, however, the party was making gains, growing both in votes and in representation. In 2007, the Greens had won first-preference votes in the Senate from 1.1 million Australians – smashing through the goal Brown had set in 2004.

With five representatives in parliament, the Greens were afforded official parliamentary party status, which meant more staff, resources and legitimacy. Party status was no small thing; it had been 15 years and six federal elections since the Australian Greens had formed, and decades more if the movement were traced back to its roots. Post-war, only two other minor parties had achieved this – the DLP and the Democrats – and both had now lost it. The Greens were, indisputably, the third force in Australian politics.

CHAPTER 9

INTO POWER

Kevin Rudd won a standing ovation at the United Nations Climate Change Conference in Bali in December 2007, when he signed Australia up to the Kyoto Protocol, ending years of recalcitrance under John Howard and increasing the pressure on the United States, which was still holding out under George W. Bush. There was an ominous sign for the Greens, at the Australian reception straight afterwards, when Rudd pointedly snubbed Christine Milne. 'The meanness of spirit of Labor was out for all to see,' she says.

Milne was a veteran of the UN talks. She had spoken at the Montreal conference in 2005, which formally ratified the Kyoto Protocol – for Milne, who had grown up in rural Tasmania, this was one of the proudest moments in her career. More than anyone in the federal parliament, she had made climate action her focus. Ahead of the 2007 election she had released a landmark Greens policy, 'Re-energising Australia', which included an emissions-trading scheme for power stations and heavy industry, a carbon tax for transport and a 25 per cent renewable energy target, and called for emissions cuts of 30 per cent by 2020 and 80 per cent by 2050. In short, Milne had a profile on climate, nationally and internationally, and was one of only a few Australian MPs in the audience at Bali – Peter Garrett and Penny Wong were others – as Rudd thanked everyone for coming. 'So Rudd gets up,' she recalls, 'and he chooses not to acknowledge me, and I just thought, "Well, here we go!"'

According to Milne, Rudd remained hostile to the Greens: 'He never had a meeting with Bob in the last year of his prime ministership. Don't you find that extraordinary? Here's the prime minister, they need the Greens, and yet Rudd would not meet with us, and Penny never met me either.'

Labor was riding high and didn't believe it needed the Greens at all. The end of the Howard era was a huge relief for progressive voters, and it seemed Rudd's honeymoon with the electorate would never end, with the polls heading into uncharted territory. The fiscally conservative Rudd government hit the ground reviewing, however, and consulting – as with the elitist 2020 Summit (to which no Greens were invited). A micromanaging prime minister got bogged down rather than embarking on a big-picture, Whitlamite wave of reform.

Rudd's first decision as prime minister – appointments to his cabinet – stripped his environment minister, Peter Garrett, of the climate portfolio, which was handed to Penny Wong, from the left subfaction led by Martin Ferguson, the new resources minister. Rudd did not want an environmental activist like Garrett in the sensitive climate portfolio as Labor moved to introduce an emissions-trading scheme. A Queenslander, Rudd signalled early on that he would resist the Greens' calls to (as he put it) 'shut down the coal industry overnight'.[1] All Labor's efforts over the next two years would go into designing an ETS that would gain Coalition support. The Greens were sidelined, leaving Milne, as the party's climate spokesperson, arguing strenuously for higher emissions reduction targets and fewer free permits for heavy polluters, and a faster transition away from fossil fuels.

The Labor–Green relationship steadily deteriorated, as the government baulked at the 2020 targets recommended by Ross Garnaut in his interim Climate Change Review, along with a deeper 90 per cent cut by 2050. Bob Brown accused Labor of backpedalling:

> Penny Wong has reduced Ross Garnaut to input. That sounds to me like the Rudd government is subject to coal capture. There are huge vested interests at play here: the coal industry, the aluminium industry, the forest logging industry, and it's up to the Rudd government to put this country ahead of those vested interests.[2]

Meanwhile, the conservative side of politics was buoyed by a big swing against the government in the Gippsland by-election of June 2008. Liberal leader Brendan Nelson began to take a tougher line on climate change, arguing that Australia should not pass an ETS until its major trading partners acted. He was rolled on the policy in shadow cabinet, and soon rolled as leader by Malcolm Turnbull.[3] But inside the Coalition the seeds of doubt were sown about the wisdom of bipartisanship on the ETS. The climate wars were in the skirmish phase.

Labor's employment and workplace relations minister, Julia Gillard, started on the rollback of the hated WorkChoices regime. The Greens' Rachel Siewert complained that the rollback did not go far enough: 'It's a misnomer to say that Work Choices [sic] is dead, this is dismantling the worst bits of Work Choices but it's not taking us back to pre–Work Choices.'[4] In a prescient speech, Siewert noted that while the profit share of national income was at record highs, the wages share was at the lowest levels since the 1960s, and heading downwards. By limiting the powers of Fair Work Australia to resolve disputes – that is, by restricting arbitration – Labor had turned its back on the fair go. Siewert reiterated the Greens' support for the right to strike. The Greens were able to make some minor amendments, on flexible work for parents and union rights of entry.

Meanwhile, the global financial crisis was gathering, with a worsening credit crunch overseas and at home. The crisis sparked calls for a 'Green New Deal', a concept touted initially by *New York Times* columnist Thomas Friedman, picked up by French president Nicolas Sarkozy, and fleshed out by a group of environmentalists and economists in the United Kingdom, including British Greens member of the European parliament Caroline Lucas.[5] The Green New Deal was promoted as a series of joined-up policies to solve the triple crunch of the credit crisis, climate change and high oil prices; it proposed re-regulating finance (including breaking up the banks), tax reform and tackling unemployment through massive public investment in renewable energy and 'green-collar' jobs. Soon elected leader of the British Greens, Lucas declared the party would put the Green New Deal at the heart of its platform. The UN Environment Programme got on board, as did the governments of Germany and Norway.

In Australia, the GFC took a mounting toll through 2008. Woodchipper Gunns Ltd began to look shaky. When Lehman Brothers collapsed in September, panic struck. Christine Milne took up the Green New Deal rhetoric enthusiastically in a speech to the Sydney Institute the following month:

> The idea that is swirling around the planet right now is that the solution to the financial collapse is the same as the solution to climate change. To rescue ourselves socially, politically and economically, we need to invest heavily in healing and repairing the Earth's ecosystems and in the transition to a net carbon zero economy. As Sir Nicholas Stern said last Thursday, 'Now is the time to lay the foundation for a world of low carbon growth' ... No less than a change to the economic system is needed, and the current financial crisis is the opportunity to do it.[6]

The debate was hardly academic. As Prime Minister Rudd himself recognised in a long essay for *The Monthly*, the crisis marked the beginning of a fundamental, worldwide re-evaluation of the neo-liberal orthodoxy of the past 30 years – what he called 'free-market fundamentalism, extreme capitalism and excessive greed'.[7]

The Rudd government's response to the GFC is well known, with two massive fiscal stimulus packages worth $53 billion in total, based on the famous advice of then treasury secretary Ken Henry: 'Go early, go hard, go households.' Less well understood is the role the Greens played in passing the two packages – and of course neither Rudd nor the treasurer, Wayne Swan, credited the minor party in their memoirs. For Bob Brown it was a defining moment in the history of the Greens, however, which demonstrated their responsible economic credentials and showed they could be trusted to act sensibly at a time of crisis. As he told the Senate, the tense negotiation with the government during the global meltdown 'was not an easy process for the Greens ... [but] we came into this constructively minded. We wanted to improve this package. We have improved this package. We now support this package.'[8]

In return for supporting the stimulus package, the Greens negotiated relief for pensioners, which was incorporated, and sought $5 million salary caps for banks that were deemed 'too big to fail'. 'The Greens will be looking at this legislation to see if we can't sensibly clip the wings of some of those fly-out-the-door payments to the CEOs of these banks which are now being guaranteed by the Australian taxpayer,' Brown told the ABC.[9] The salary caps were voted down in the Senate, however. Still, Rudd commended the

Greens and crossbenchers Nick Xenophon and Steve Fielding for acting responsibly.[10]

After the first stimulus package, with his ear for a slogan, Brown said: 'Greed got the world into this crisis, green will get it out of this crisis.'[11] Brown was less happy about the prime minister urging people to go out and spend their cash splashes before Christmas:

> What he should be saying to the pensioners and the carers is perhaps invest it in some energy efficiency in the household so that you keep getting a bonus over the months and years ahead, and make sure you keep a little aside for the unforeseens that are coming down the line in a time of global financial crisis.[12]

The environmental movement slammed the absence of green initiatives, and Christine Milne in the Senate mourned the lost opportunity for a Green New Deal:

> Wouldn't it have been better to direct that stimulus to those things that are necessary to address the vulnerabilities of climate change, peak oil, resource dependence, lack of education and the hollowing-out of the manufacturing sector? Wouldn't it have been better to direct the stimulus in that kind of way?[13]

When the Rudd government shortly afterwards proposed a $5 billion nation-building plan, including funding for rail to boost the capacity of the Hunter Valley Coal Chain from 70 million to 200 million tonnes a year, the Greens were horrified. 'Once again the government is using taxpayer funds to help the coal industry, despite the industry being past its used-by date and environmentally unsustainable,' said transport spokesman Scott Ludlam.[14] Rudd soon announced a billion-dollar Renewable Energy Fund, and a new billion-dollar Global Carbon Capture and Storage Institute, meant to catalyse worldwide investment in clean coal. Rudd also rejected calls to defer the planned 2010 start date of the ETS on GFC grounds. Rudd's second, even bigger stimulus package, included a new scheme to install energy-efficient pink batts in half a million homes. If the Rudd stimulus packages were not green, they were at least green-tinged.

There was bitter disappointment, however, at the end of 2008, when Rudd announced the final policy position on his Carbon Pollution Reduction Scheme: a 5 per cent emissions reduction target, rising to 15 per cent if there were strong commitments overseas. The targets were right at the bottom of the range recommended by the UN at Bali and Garnaut in the Climate Change Review, and inconsistent with keeping global warming to 2 degrees Celsius. The Greens, and the scientific community, wanted deeper cuts of between 25 per cent and 40 per cent. A furious Bob Brown was heard to say to Rudd, after he dropped his bombshell, 'Prime Minister, congratulations on your failure.'[15] Federally, Labor and the Greens were on a collision course.

*   *   *

On a national basis, the Greens' polling had jumped straight after Rudd's election, and it remained high through 2008, with primary support bouncing between 9 per cent and 11 per cent in the Newspoll. The tide was coming in for the party. The support reflected early disenchantment with the new Labor government on the left – just as, in 1984, the Greens and the NDP were spurred by disappointment with Hawke – as well as rising public concern about climate change.

An early setback, however, came in mid-2008, when Andrew Wilkie quit the party, which made the front page of the Hobart *Mercury*.[16] Blaming the 'baggage, strictures and difficulties of party politics', Wilkie left the door open to running as an independent in state and federal elections. A prominent Green told the newspaper, off the record, that Wilkie was 'never a tree-hugger'.

Looking back, Wilkie agrees that this perception of him did not help:

> The Tassie Greens are first and foremost an environment party, whereas first and foremost the NSW Greens are a social justice party. Here I was, a high-profile person, *no* environmental activism history – in fact a security services history, which straight away made some people suspicious of me, because there's no shortage of conspiracy theorists in the Greens.

Wilkie's resignation had actually been a while coming: he felt stranded without support from the party during the 2007 campaign, having to fund everything himself, and believes in hindsight that his high profile made him a threat to Christine Milne, who hoped to succeed Brown one day. 'Christine clearly saw me as a threat to her taking over the Greens,' he says, 'because I was close to Bob Brown – he was a friend – and some in the party saw me as a future star.' With Milne's supporters offside, Wilkie realised he was going nowhere inside the party. 'I didn't fall out with the membership,' Wilkie says. 'I fell out with the leadership, and even then it was half-half.' Both Brown and Milne reject this, saying that Wilkie had been told in advance that the party's resources in Tasmania would be thrown behind Bob's campaign, and his demands were unreasonable. 'Andrew is quite wrong about Christine,' says Brown. 'He was second on my Greens Senate ticket and arrived at home one morning close to the election to say if he didn't get a big slice of our campaign funds he would resign from the ticket. I complied but campaign organisers, knowing that only one Green could be elected, were horrified. His stranding was of his own making.' Brown does suggest Wilkie was not a good fit for the party, pointing to an interview Wilkie later gave to *The Mercury*, in which he said, 'The Greens are dominated by people who will always oppose any dam or any pulp mill, no matter where it is. That is not my position – I am not anti-development. For me, the pulp mill is on the table and so too are dams and even canal estates like Ralphs Bay.'[17]

In September 2008, the ACT went to an election and returned a hung parliament: seven Labor, six Coalition and four Greens – a big jump up for the party. Its one current sitting member, Deb Foskey, was a conservationist who had moved to an alternative land co-op in Victoria's East Gippsland region, and then to Canberra to do a doctorate at the Australian National University. As an MLA, she successfully badgered Jon Stanhope's majority Labor government into adopting a number of progressive policies. Early in her term, however, she was criticised for failing to move out of public housing, even though she was on an MLA's salary of $100,000 a year. Eventually Foskey capitulated, but the scandal hardly endeared her to the electorate, with the *Canberra Times* editorialising against her and a public perception forming, fairly or unfairly, that she was not the representative Kerrie Tucker had been.

The Greens acted, quite clinically, to unseat her. Shane Rattenbury, a Greenpeace activist then working on climate change in Europe, got a call out of the blue from Bob Brown's chief of staff, Ben Oquist, asking whether he would be interested in preselection for Foskey's seat of Molonglo – one of the safest Green seats in the country. Rattenbury was interested and agreed to challenge, yet feels uncomfortable about it to this day, as he knew Foskey wanted to stay on. 'Deb was very hurt by that,' he says, 'and that's … you know, politics is nasty sometimes, and for me it certainly remains a painful point as I always liked Deb, I thought she was a good person, I never had a bad thing to say about her.' Rattenbury won, after a rigorous interview process and a ballot of party members, even though he'd been out of the country for five years.

Rattenbury was an interesting character, a man who had grown up in a humble fibro shack in Batemans Bay, on the NSW South Coast, the elder child of a single mum. His mum was not into politics, but his uncle was the Liberal-leaning mayor of the Eurobodalla Shire Council. Extremely bright, Rattenbury won a full scholarship to Canberra Grammar, and the family moved to the capital; he turned up to school in his mother's old bomb, alongside the BMWs and Mercs, wearing a second-hand uniform. Rattenbury did well, and majored in environmental law at ANU. He joined the ACT Greens as soon as they formed in 1992, got the first job at the new Environmental Defenders Office, and was putting his hand up as a candidate as early as 1995, when he met Bob Brown, who has mentored him ever since. Meanwhile, Rattenbury was hired to the industry department under the Commonwealth Graduate Program, and was then recruited to Greenpeace in 1998, where he spent the next ten years.

In 2008 Rattenbury expected to win his own seat in the Molonglo electorate, but it was a real shock when the Greens won two, as well as seats in both the Ginninderra and Brindabella electorates. The result was a real setback for Labor, which now held seven seats; the Liberals had six. Not only did the four Greens suddenly have the balance of power, but it was a genuine toss-up which side they would back to form government, and on what terms.

The four MPs held meetings with both sides, and talks dragged out as the party deliberated. Being Canberra, it was possible to bring almost the whole Greens membership together, and some 400-odd members were invited to decide which issues should be prioritised and which side to back. 'It was an animated discussion, people were excited by the enormous opportunity we'd never had before,' says Rattenbury, and he adds that there were no leaks even as talks dragged on. 'It was very disciplined – because I think the members knew they were being respected.' It took weeks for the Greens to make their decision: taking advice from Brown and Milne, Rattenbury and the Greens negotiated a written agreement with the Stanhope Labor government, and Rattenbury became the first Greens speaker of any parliament in the world. It was the beginning of a decade of the balance of power for the Greens, which would bear fruit as the ACT became the nation's climate leader, setting a goal of 100 per cent renewable energy by 2020.

In September 2008 Western Australia went to a surprise election called by Premier Alan Carpenter, who lost to new Liberal leader Colin Barnett. The WA Greens got a 4 per cent swing towards them and recorded their highest statewide vote, before or since, with 12 per cent in the lower house and 11 per cent in the upper house. For all their regathered strength, though, the WA Greens lost the balance of power in the upper house. The Barnett Liberal government would prove hostile to the party's agenda (though not as hardline or climate-denying as the conservative Coalition regimes soon to follow around the country).

After the election, former attorney-general Jim McGinty retired, opening up his seat of Fremantle, the Greens' spiritual home in Western Australia. The Liberals declared they would not run, giving the Greens a very real chance of winning. The party had a strong candidate in Adele Carles, a local solicitor who had fought to stop Stockland's South Beach residential tower from being built on an old industrial site on the coast south of Fremantle. Carles made history for the party, beating Labor's Peter Tagliaferri, the local mayor, in a seat the party had held for 85 years, to become the Greens' first member of the state's lower house.

What was more, in what ABC election analyst Antony Green remarked was a first for the Greens at either state or federal level,

Carles trounced her Labor opponent on the primary vote, 44 per cent to 39 per cent.[18]

On election night, 16 May 2009, Carles said the ALP had moved too far to the right. 'This is a victory for the people of Fremantle and for democracy,' she said. 'We have forever shattered the two-party myth in Australia. People have dared to look beyond the old parties that have continually let us down.'[19]

Bob Brown said the by-election result sent a message to federal Labor on climate change, and predicted that more seats could fall to the Greens. 'The message to Kevin Rudd is clear: green up the weak, polluter-friendly climate change bill now before federal parliament or suffer the consequences at next year's election.'[20] Treasurer Peter Costello warned that Labor was in trouble in its inner-city heartland, while conservative commentator Gerard Henderson posited that the Greens' win only came with help from the Liberal Party, which would be 'well advised to re-consider its preferences strategy in inner-city electorates' like Fremantle, Melbourne, Sydney and Grayndler.[21] That would come later.

In her first speech, Carles pushed for a ban on live sheep exports out of Fremantle, and spoke of her hope in US President Barack Obama and the planned Green New Deal.[22] In a hung parliament, Carles would prove an influential member of the three-strong cross-bench, who, while generally voting with Labor, occasionally sided with the government. After Carles supported one government gag motion, Labor leader Eric Ripper called her a 'Liberal in a Green suit'. At her Christmas drinks that year, journalists were surprised to find that Premier Barnett and treasurer Troy Buswell were invited, but no one from Labor. Carles explained that her relations with the Labor leader were frosty.

With 12 per cent statewide support in the lower house, and 11 per cent in the upper house, Greens WA had won their strongest vote ever and, like their federal colleagues, achieved parliamentary party status with five members. Adding in the two senators, Siewert and Ludlam, Western Australia now had more Greens MPs than any other state. Party status brought extra resources – although the party had to threaten to sue the government to get them – but the parliament also required the Greens to nominate a leader. The West Australian branch opposed leaders, but Giz Watson was universally recognised as its unofficial leader and was designated as such for the purposes of the parliament.

The Greens' triumph in Fremantle did not last a year. In April 2010 reports surfaced online that Carles and Treasurer Buswell, both married, had been having an affair for months. Carles initially responded it was scurrilous rumour-mongering by Labor, and Buswell would not comment, but behind the scenes her colleagues had known about it since February. A week later Carles gave an interview to Perth's *Sunday Times* confirming the 'stupid' affair; she said it was over, apologised to Buswell's family and to her fellow Greens, and insisted she had neither sought nor obtained any political favours from the treasurer. Buswell's career unravelled and he went to the backbench. Greens upper-house member Robin Chapple said the affair had 'nothing to do with politics. Look at the way Adele has voted on almost every issue – it has been with Labor. It's been a relationship issue and needs to be kept as that.' But the disloyalty was too much for many Greens members, who pushed to expel her, although the party stopped short of demanding her resignation.

Carles quit the party within weeks of confirming the affair, claiming she had been bullied into going public, particularly by Watson. 'I could see no other way forward given my breakdown in relationship with Giz,' Carles said.[23] She sat as an independent and retired from politics at the next election.

The scandal, on such fertile electoral ground for the Greens, was a massive own goal, and a decade later the party's primary support had still not recovered in Fremantle. Watson, looking back, is not sure how the party could have handled things differently – Carles was a popular, longstanding local Green, and no vetting process would have picked up such an improbable affair.

The Queensland Greens got a shot in the arm in October 2008, when the Labor member for the inner-Brisbane lower-house seat of Indooroopilly, Ronan Lee, a committed environmentalist, defected over the Bligh government's inaction on climate change and failure to protect the state's wild rivers. As with Kris Hanna in South Australia, however, the Greens' win was relatively short-lived; Lee was voted out in a general election six months later.

*   *   *

Through 2009 the panic surrounding the GFC eased slowly, although the global political fallout was only beginning. The federal government drafted legislation for the Carbon Pollution Reduction Scheme (CPRS), which, in the view of the Greens' climate spokesperson, Christine Milne, had been progressively 'browned down' with $16 billion in free permits for trade-exposed industries (much of which would head offshore) and compensation for coal-fired power generators. Milne was not alone in her view: at a Senate inquiry, the author of the Climate Change Review, Ross Garnaut, himself expressed disappointment in the scheme's largesse to industry, and said it was a 'line-ball call' whether it would be better to pass the emissions-trading system as it stood or start again.[24]

Labor's hostility towards the Greens was relentless. Penny Wong came to the view in early 2009, as *The Australian*'s editor-at-large Paul Kelly wrote, that the Greens wanted radical differentiation from Labor on climate, and that Bob Brown had 'suffered from too much praise for too long. She was astounded that most of the media took the Greens at face value and suspended criticism when dealing with them.'[25] Martin Ferguson thought Brown's aim was 'to demonise the coal industry in the same way he has sought to demonise the forest industry'.[26] Ferguson, a former ACTU president, would fight the Greens all the way.

Labor's suite of bills for the Carbon Pollution Reduction Scheme were debated through June; the Coalition voted against them on the grounds that Australia should wait until after the United Nations' Copenhagen Summit in December 2009, and after the United States had clarified its intention to introduce a similar cap-and-trade scheme. Debate shifted to the Senate, where the numbers were finely balanced: the Greens plus Labor and Xenophon spoke for 38 seats, and broadly supported climate action, while the Coalition plus Family First's Steve Fielding had exactly the same number, and could block the legislation themselves. Brown flagged that the Greens would oppose it, as did Milne:

> We are not going to accept legislation that is piecemeal, that does
> not give us a whole-of-government approach, that does not look
> at the potential to reduce emissions across the board – particularly
> in land use, land use change and forestry, which go hand in hand –
> that does not go full on with renewables and efficiency and that
> does not get rid of all the subsidies to the fossil fuel sector, which
> undermine the effort.[27]

During the debate, knowing the legislation would fail, Milne moved an amendment to stiffen up the emissions-reduction targets ahead of Copenhagen, committing the government 'to entering the climate treaty negotiations at the end of 2009 with an unconditional commitment to reduce emissions by at least 25 per cent below 1990 levels by 2020 and a willingness to reduce emissions by 40 per cent below 1990 levels by 2020 in the context of a global treaty'.[28] Anticipating defeat, Wong flagged that the government would bring the bills back to the Senate, and the package went down by 42 votes to 30, opposed by the Coalition, the Greens, Xenophon and Fielding.[29]

The Labor government had lost round one, as expected. The pressure on all sides was mounting, backed up by the threat – which Brown acknowledged – that if the legislation was defeated a second time it could serve as a trigger for a double-dissolution climate election, most probably in early 2010. Some, like the former Democrats leader Natasha Stott-Despoja, commenting from the sidelines, thought that was exactly what the Greens wanted.[30]

As yet, there was no great outcry about the Greens' position: they were pushing for tougher action, in line with Garnaut, climate science and the environmental movement, and even sections of the business community, exactly as they had said they would do, yet they had been shut out of the negotiations.[31] Malcolm Turnbull, leader of the opposition, said the Coalition would propose amendments in the coming months; Wong said the government would consider them and try to come to an agreement. But the ground was shifting beneath Turnbull, who was losing authority inside the Liberal Party, and loose cannons like Wilson Tuckey, Cory Bernardi, Julian McGauran and Dennis Jensen were openly decrying the CPRS and climate science, with full-throated support from the Nationals, particularly Barnaby Joyce.[32]

Bob Brown told the ABC that the government should be negotiating with the Greens. 'It's a lost opportunity for the government at the outset because it's putting up a recipe for failure … the Greens have got the formula right.'[33] As a concession, the government split off its Renewable Energy Target legislation, imposing a target of 20 per cent renewables by 2020; this had the support of all sides but had hitherto been packaged up with the CPRS, and it duly passed through the Senate almost without a murmur. It would prove the single most effective legislative response Australia made to climate change.

Under the constitution, Labor had to wait three months to reintroduce its CPRS bills, if it wanted a double-dissolution trigger. In October, before the legislation passed the lower house, the Greens released 22 proposed amendments publicly, with emissions reduction targets of between 25 per cent and 40 per cent, all carbon permits auctioned, trade-exposed industries compensated only for the value of their lost competitiveness (not for their lost profits) and electricity generators receiving no compensation at all.[34] They got nowhere. The next month, Milne released legal advice from Brian Walters SC that the CPRS 'locked in failure', because 'if a government later sought to implement more progressive emissions reductions targets', the Commonwealth would be exposed to compensation claims, 'possibly in the order of billions of dollars'. The CPRS classified emissions units as personal property, the advice explained, so if the government changed its value, 'it must be done on "just terms"'.[35]

In November, with bipartisan talks dragging, the Copenhagen summit fast approaching, the US cap-and-trade scheme bogged down in Congress, and China's position unclear, the CPRS bills came back. Neither the Greens nor the Coalition saw the need to legislate before Copenhagen. What's more, the sceptics within Coalition ranks were growing. Shadow families minister Tony Abbott – who had supported the ETS three months earlier, on the basis that the Coalition could hardly be 'browner than Howard' – told a Liberal Party meeting in the country town of Beaufort that the idea the science of climate change was settled was 'absolute crap'.[36] The CPRS debate was wedging the Liberals hard, and Labor was distracted by the possibility its opponents might split. Government business manager Anthony Albanese marvelled at a caucus meeting: 'We've now got the Libs on the canvas and they are more internally split than any major political party since the great Labor split of the 1950s.'

Turnbull's resources spokesperson, Ian Macfarlane, tried valiantly to come up with a scheme acceptable to his colleagues and the government. An exasperated Wong fronted the deputy prime minister, Julia Gillard: 'I'd like to know if I'm supposed to be negotiating this deal or crashing this deal?' Gillard confessed, 'Well, Penny, I don't bloody know.'[37] Wong feared a repeat of the Republican referendum debate a decade earlier, when reform failed due to opposition on left and right, for entirely different reasons. She was dead right.

For Milne, Labor chose hardball politics rather than the best path to an outcome for the planet: 'They had the choice: they could have held it over post-Copenhagen; instead of that they decided to wedge the Liberals.' But if Labor was indeed hoping to split the Liberals, they failed. Instead, the day before the final vote, Abbott rolled Turnbull and took over the leadership. With the Liberal Party in shock, only two senators, moderate backbenchers Judith Troeth and Sue Boyce, crossed the floor to support the scheme. With the Greens, Xenophon and Fielding opposed, it still went down solidly, 41–33. Cynics wondered whether Troeth and Boyce would have shown quite the same courage if they thought their votes may have clinched it. '[Labor's] strategy failed completely,' says Milne. 'They fell flat on their face.'

Straight after the Abbott coup, two crucial byelections showed a huge surge in Greens support. Former treasurer Peter Costello and former opposition leader Brendan Nelson had resigned, and with no Labor candidates running, the Liberals were pitted against the Greens in the safe seats of Higgins and Bradfield, respectively. In Higgins, the high-profile academic and director of the Australia Institute Dr Clive Hamilton won 32 per cent of the primary vote – up 21 per cent – although Kelly O'Dwyer easily took the seat. In Bradfield, the Greens' Susie Gemmell came second with 25 per cent of the vote – a 14 per cent swing – although Paul Fletcher nevertheless won the contest. The Liberals' well-to-do heartland was sending a message about the leadership coup, it seemed.

The chaotic Copenhagen summit failed to deliver anything binding, or much more than an aspirational communique, despite a last-ditch effort led by US President Obama, and Kevin Rudd came home in a funk. After Christmas the Greens worked hard to come up with a compromise that Labor might be able to live with, taking an idea from Garnaut that a fixed price at the outset could transition into a floating price down the track. The Greens got the backing of peak environmental NGOs, and announced the new proposal in February 2010 outside Parliament House.

Brown and Milne invited Penny Wong down to Hobart. At their meeting, says Milne:

> [Wong] took one look at it and said, 'I'm not even going to show this to the prime minister.' We couldn't have known at that point that the gang of four [Rudd plus Gillard, Wayne Swan and Lindsay Tanner] had already decided to dump the carbon price and go with the mining tax.

For Milne, looking back, there is no other possible explanation. The government had reintroduced the CPRS legislation, as amended by the Coalition under Turnbull's leadership, to the House of Representatives for a third time. Turnbull crossed the floor to vote for it. At the end of April, *The Sydney Morning Herald*'s Lenore Taylor wrote a bombshell story: the government planned to defer the scheme for three years. Rudd's memoir, published many years later, attributed that leak to a staffer in Gillard's office, and claimed it was designed to kill off the scheme altogether, as the deputy prime minister had urged.

In the public mind it was untenable for Rudd, who had described climate change in 2007 as the 'great moral challenge of our generation', to suddenly walk away. His popular support, in all three major opinion polls, dropped suddenly and did not stop falling. As the *Herald*'s political editor, Peter Hartcher, observed:

> Rudd's commitment to action on climate change was a deep part of his political persona. By so easily abandoning it, he raised an existential question in the public mind – if he doesn't stand for this, what does he stand for? If we can't believe his commitment to this, which commitment can we believe? This would help explain why only one in 10 of Labor's lost votes has moved to the

Coalition, which is even more climate-sceptic than Rudd. And why the Greens' share of the vote has surged to a record high of 15 per cent in today's poll. It's entirely possible that Rudd's ETS decision is as fundamental as John Howard's WorkChoices.[38]

In a Newspoll at the end of May, the Greens hit an all-time national peak, with primary support at 16 per cent, the highest vote any third party had ever achieved.[39] Rudd was suddenly vulnerable. Much of the blame for the failure of the parliament to legislate action on climate change, however, would fall on the Greens.

The most stinging critique (although it was not explicitly directed at the Greens), stemmed from a warning made by Garnaut himself, in a public lecture at ANU just before the second vote on the CPRS, that there was 'a danger that the best has become the enemy of the good, and the friend of the bad'.[40] After the CPRS went down, this theme would be prosecuted with particular vigour by many in Labour, from government business manager Albanese to former NSW premier Bob Carr.[41] It was elaborate face-saving. Over the years, the idea has been taken up with increasing vehemence, acquiring a ring of truth it does not deserve. In 2016, former assistant climate change minister Greg Combet even blamed the Greens' decision on the CPRS for Labor's leadership coup:

> It was a major call and it was a major fuck-up. How stupid. They've put action on climate change in Australia back many, many years. They could have voted for it then, and I think Kevin Rudd would probably still be prime minister, and the carbon price would have been in place for seven years by now, and the world would have kept going but our emissions would be going down. That was an unforgiveable act of bastardry. There's no two ways about that.[42]

Brown, Milne and the rest of the party were unrepentant and have remained so, notwithstanding the debilitating climate wars of the decade that followed. The party's position was vindicated at the time, at least according to the two leaders, by a spectacular showing in the Tasmanian election of March 2010. The Greens won 22 per cent of the statewide vote in the House of Assembly, getting up a candidate in all five seats for the first time since 1989. As in that year, the party now held the balance of power. The two major parties held ten seats each, but the Liberals' Will Hodgman refused to talk with the Greens, who therefore wound up in negotiations with Labor's David Bartlett. Unlike 20 years earlier, and due partly to the smaller parliament, which leaves little room for a backbench, the Greens took on ministerial portfolios in the resulting minority government. Tasmanian Greens leader Nick McKim wound up with the portfolios of education, public transport and corrections, while his partner, Cassy O'Connor, took human services, Aboriginal affairs and climate change. (There was no way Labor would let the Greens handle environment or water or forestry policy; climate at a state level was a token concession.) Between McKim and O'Connor, the Greens were responsible for half the state's budget.

With his government in turmoil, Rudd announced the Resource Super Profits Tax, recommended by the Treasury secretary, Dr Ken Henry, in his landmark review of taxation. The government's prosecution of the mining tax debate was badly mishandled, triggering a fierce campaign by the mining industry, which proved to be the final nail in Rudd's coffin. Gillard took over in June 2010, and resources minister Martin Ferguson watered down the tax in private talks with the big three miners, BHP, Rio Tinto and Glencore, until it was so loose that the industry believed they would never have to pay a cent.

Interestingly, in a sign that the pain of the CPRS debate was lingering, the Greens passed Gillard's new Minerals Resource Rent Tax despite some misgivings. The Greens were all for a mining tax, and a sovereign wealth fund, to reinvest the fruits of the commodities boom for the long term, but it was clear the MRRT would achieve none of that. South Australian senator Penny Wright described it as a 'wasted opportunity', but, as Senator Scott Ludlam conceded years later, 'it was a choice between a piss-weak mining tax or nothing at all'.[43]

*   *   *

Rushing straight to an election, Gillard not only eschewed support for an ETS, she also promised there would be 'no carbon tax under the government I lead'. Instead, she announced an execrable policy – a 'citizens' assembly' to debate climate change – which was lampooned on all sides and sank without trace.

Milne recalls that the Greens went into the 2010 election as 'the only party still with a very strong commitment on global warming'. There was fresh wind in the party's sails, too. Behind-the-scenes rich-lister Graeme Wood, founder of accommodation website Wotif, had approached Bob Brown out of the blue in May about donating to the party. Genuinely worried about the future of the planet, and aghast at the failure of the country's politicians to tackle climate change, Wood had been the principal funder of a new group, the Melbourne-based Beyond Zero Emissions, which was determined to focus on solutions commensurate with the climate emergency. This emergency was laid out in stark terms in the landmark 2008 book *Climate Code Red*, by Philip Sutton and David Spratt, an awakening for many people.

Over dinner with Brown and Ben Oquist in Canberra, Wood said the Greens needed to run a professional advertising campaign this time around, and he wanted to help fund it.[44] Wood expected to be one of a handful of wealthy businesspeople prepared to put their money into the cause. He rang around, but struck wariness about donating publicly to the Greens. The Gillard coup had changed everything, forcing Wood's hand. He bore the whole cost himself, forking out $1.6 million in what was then the largest individual political donation Australia had seen. (It would be topped in 2016 by Malcolm Turnbull's $2 million donation to the Liberal Party as he sought re-election as prime minister.) Asked at the time what Wood had sought in return for his donation, Bob Brown said: 'There's nothing Graeme could possibly gain personally out of this … and certainly none's been discussed. Not ever has Graeme said, "Oh, I'd like you to do such and such." Not ever.'

Wood's donation remained secret for months. The Greens chose a Melbourne agency, Cyclone Advertising, which had a long political pedigree – its managing director, Rod Fuller, had worked on the original 'Keep the bastards honest' campaign for the Democrats. The strategy this time was clear: target the balance of power in the Senate and go for maximum reach, pitching to mainstream voters rather than preaching to the converted. New ads were made in two and a half weeks. The key message – 'This time I'm voting Green in the Senate' – came straight from focus group research with former Labor voters, according to Fuller. For the first time the Greens could afford to advertise on the commercial TV networks, though Fuller reckons the bigger parties would still have outspent the Greens by at least ten to one.

Julia Gillard's coup delivered her a poll bounce at first, knocking support for the Greens back down, which prompted Brown to say a big Green vote was temporarily 'parked' with the country's first female prime minister. He was right: the bounce didn't last, and the Greens' poll performance recovered to around 13 per cent. Labor's election campaign was marred by a wooden performance from Gillard, and by sabotage from Rudd. The Greens and Labor did a comprehensive preference deal: the Greens supported Labor in 54 marginal lower-house seats, while Labor's preferences went to the Greens in the Senate in all states and territories. There were no policy trade-offs.[45] Nevertheless, Brown urged voters to ignore all the parties' recommended tickets and to vote for themselves, and called again for above-the-line voting and the abolition of preference deals, along the lines of the upper-house reforms enacted in New South Wales.[46] At the branch level, many Greens were unhappy at the top-down deal.[47]

Gillard declared early on that she could work with the Greens if they had the balance of power, and that in the lead-up to the campaign Brown had sent her a five-point climate action plan, including a carbon tax of $23 a tonne; Labor briefed journalists that the Greens were 'kidding themselves'. Brown had also called for the return home of Australian troops in Afghanistan, after a string of casualties, and flagged that his party would try to increase the mining tax in the next parliament.

Quelling speculation that he would not see out his parliamentary term, Brown said he had no plans to retire: 'I have never not only been happier but felt more on top of [and] confident about … this political life. I'm very well aware that people can overstay their time. If in 10, 20, 30 years down the track, someone taps me on the shoulder, I'll listen.'[48]

All the polls showed the Greens were on track for the balance of power, and in the final days of the campaign Brown was given a prime speaking slot at the National Press Club. He outlined a heavily redistributive platform, which *The Sydney Morning Herald*'s Peter Hartcher described as not just red inside like a watermelon, but red all the way through like a tomato.[49] Brown talked up visionary policies like high-speed rail, 'denticare', marriage equality, abolishing ATM fees, reviewing our defence treaty with the United States, and introducing a national integrity commission. He also proposed a new top marginal tax rate of 50 per cent for the highest 2–3 per cent of income earners, raising the company tax rate to 33 per cent, taxing trusts like companies, raising an extra \$2 billion from a higher mining tax, and – after a robust internal debate – imposing a death tax on estates worth more than \$5 million.[50]

The red-baiting kicked up a notch in the 2010 campaign, as conservative journalists zeroed in on Lee Rhiannon, who had nominated for Senate preselection in 2009; she announced that she would stand down from the NSW Legislative Council if she was successful. Once again, when told of Rhiannon's decision, Bob Brown and Ben Oquist flew up to Sydney to urge her not to run. This time she took a staffer into the meeting, and recalls that 'they put the very strong case that I shouldn't run and, you know, I'm old and I should know I've got this wonderful legacy and just move on'. Rhiannon stood her ground, and was successful in the preselection; looking back, though, she says, 'I would call it bullying.' Brown denies it was bullying, but there is no doubt the preselection marked a new level of conflict inside the party. Cate Faehrmann, who had moved to New South Wales to run the Nature Conservation Council, stood against Rhiannon with the tacit support of Brown, who was openly calling for generational change. Ahead of the contest, Faehrmann met with John Kaye, by then shaping up to be the unofficial leader of the party in New South Wales. He encouraged her to run in the next state election as part of his team, and gently warned her against nominating for the Senate. Faehrmann recalls that when she confirmed she would run against Rhiannon, Kaye told her: 'Right! This. Is. War!' Although she was beaten squarely, Faehrmann says the preselection contest 'was the beginning of everything, in my opinion'.

A month out from the election, state Labor attorney-general John Hatzistergos insinuated Rhiannon was using her New South Wales parliamentary office improperly as a contact point for her Senate campaign. Someone had put Rhiannon's office number on a media release, rather than the Greens campaign office number. Rhiannon apologised, but Brown called publicly for her to resign her seat, so she could focus entirely on the federal election. It was a storm in a teacup, but triggered a run of stories in print and on the ABC about divisions in the Greens.

Hatzistergos followed up with attacks on Rhiannon's use of the Democracy4Sale website, which was part-funded by parliamentary money, to promote her Senate campaign. In *The Australian*, Imre Saluszinsky wrote that 'a red-diaper baby could spell trouble for Bob Brown'. In *The Sunday Telegraph*, AWU national secretary Paul Howes wrote that the NSW Greens were 'being infiltrated by many whose commitment to the environment is questionable, and who are more focused on turning the Greens into a left-wing, socialist-style party'. On Sky News, Howes claimed Rhiannon's family were 'lifelong members of the pro-Stalinist Socialist Party'.[51] Rhiannon dismisses Howe's comments as the same old 'reds under the bed' scare tactics which have been used against her over the years, both outside and inside the Greens.

Come election day, 21 August 2010, there was a historic election result for the party, and one that remains its high-water mark. In both houses of parliament the Greens secured the highest vote ever for a third party, topping the Democrats' best result, in 1990, and that of the DLP, decades earlier. For the first time in Australian history a third party won a Senate seat in each state, taking the Greens' total representation to nine senators, giving the party the sole balance of power in the upper house. The national vote was 13 per cent, up 4 per cent, and Christine Milne in Tasmania and Richard Di Natale in Victoria achieved quotas in their own right, polling first-preference votes of 19.7 per cent and 14.5 per cent respectively. Rachel Siewert was easily re-elected in Western Australia, Penny Wright was successful in South Australia, on 13.2 per cent, and the party won its first Queensland Senate seat, for Larissa Waters, on 12.6 per cent. It had taken 25 years to break through in Queensland, the toughest state for the party, since Drew Hutton founded the Brisbane Greens in 1985. Waters, a solicitor for the state's Environment Defenders Office on the frontline of the anti-fossil fuels 'lawfare', had succeeded at her second attempt. Seasoned environmental activist Sam La Rocca, who had run Waters' campaign, encountered a branch that not only expected defeat, but rejected the idea of planning to win.

Lee Rhiannon was the last to be elected, with a primary vote of 10.6 per cent. Rhiannon says her below-average first-preference vote became the pretext for an argument, led by Brown, that New South Wales had underperformed electorally – an argument she rejects, given the sheer size of the state, the number of parties running, its highly multicultural make-up and the size of the regional vote.

Significantly, the gap between the upper-house and lower-house vote – 13.1 per cent versus 11.8 per cent – was wider than ever, according to Ben Oquist, which suggested the Senate-focused TV ads funded by Wood had made a difference. In New South Wales, there was anger that the state had not seen its fair share of the advertising spend – just $80,000 out of $1.6 million, which funded some ads on SBS. Was there a deliberate attempt to suppress the Greens vote in New South Wales? Why had the branch been kept in the dark about the donation? Rhiannon concedes the state branch policy to limit the size of donations from individuals may have been a factor. 'We may have knocked it back,' she says, 'but they never asked us and they never shared it with us.' The acrimony was temporarily buried under the 'Greenslide' of 2010, however.

Most spectacularly, perhaps, the Greens achieved the dream of breaking into the lower house in a general election, winning the seat of Melbourne from Labor, which had held it since 1904. A victory had been on the cards since Lindsay Tanner had announced his retirement mid-year. The Greens' successful candidate was Adam Bandt, who had gone quite close in 2007 and had run for the party in Melbourne's Lord Mayoral elections the following year. Originally from Perth, Bandt had joined the ALP briefly at high school before diving into radical politics at Murdoch university, where he was a member of the so-called 'Left Alliance' of socialist, feminist and progressive students. After graduating, Bandt had moved to Melbourne, spending a decade as a solicitor at Slater & Gordon – developing close ties to the union movement – and completing a doctorate at Monash university on Marx and the law. Bandt nearly beat Labor's Cath Bowtell on primary votes, polling 36 per cent – just 2 per cent, or 1700 votes, short. The largest share of Family First preferences and 78 per cent of Liberal preferences went to Bandt, helping him glide past Bowtell to victory on the night. Conservative commentators like Gerard

Henderson, who had warned it was a grave mistake for the Liberals to put the Greens ahead of Labor in winnable seats like Melbourne, were proven right, and the Liberals would soon change course.[52]

In the lower house, the Greens vote topped 20 per cent in seven other electorates around the country: Batman, Melbourne Ports and Wills in Victoria; Sydney and Grayndler in New South Wales; Brisbane in Queensland; and Franklin in Tasmania. Much to the Greens' chagrin, Andrew Wilkie was elected in the prize Hobart seat of Denison, easily beating the party's candidate, Dr Geoff Couser, who polled 19 per cent.

The overall result, however, was on a knife-edge: both Labor and the Coalition had 72 seats in the lower house, meaning Australia was facing its first minority government since 1940.[53] Bandt had already committed to supporting a Labor government during the election campaign, and Julia Gillard was the first to make contact with the Greens, calling Bob Brown on election night and meeting him the next day in an effort to gain crucial momentum. As Brown recounted in his memoir, *Optimism*, Gillard had to swallow some pride: she had previously described him as

> … pretty much the most calculating politician in Canberra … not an archangel of moral force. He's a bloke who wakes up every day and says, 'How can I chisel a bit of political advantage today?'

In a chance encounter outside Rudd's office in 2008, Gillard asked Brown what he was 'doing to damage the Labor Party today?'[54]

Nonetheless, at a Sunday meeting in her Melbourne office, a businesslike Gillard sat down with Brown and asked for guarantees of supply and confidence. Brown said he would need to consult his party room and also to speak with the other side, the Coalition, as he had done in Tasmania in 1989. The key to Gillard's forward approach, Brown readily acknowledged in his diary notes, was Bandt's win in Melbourne, which would take Labor to 73 seats and potentially unlock the votes of NSW country independents Tony Windsor and Rob Oakeshott.

Tony Abbott, by contrast, did not contact Brown until Thursday, and they did not meet until the following Tuesday – ten days after the election. Abbott was prepared to talk about anything except a carbon tax, but did not seriously engage.

Meanwhile, talks with Gillard were progressing, and the next day, 1 September, Labor and the Greens signed a five-page agreement with the stated purpose of establishing 'a basis for stable and effective government', including express undertakings on supply and confidence.[55] The agreement was signed by Gillard and Swan for Labor, by Brown and Milne for the Greens, and by Bandt as member-elect for Melbourne, whose win had put the party in such a powerful position.

Asked if there was any tension between him and Brown during the negotiations, Bandt says:

> The opposite … going into a situation where you're sharing power in the country's parliament, you couldn't imagine anyone better than Bob leading you at that point … [He had] managed to lead the build-up to the point where we can talk about getting 10 per cent, then breaking through to the next level in our vote. Yes, it was significant that we broke through in Melbourne, but you stand on the shoulders of people like him.

Nonetheless, Bandt is crystal clear about the significance of his one lower-house seat:

> If Melbourne hadn't elected a Greens MP in 2010, we wouldn't have had a price on [carbon] pollution, the Climate Change Authority, [the] Clean Energy Finance Corporation … had there been another Labor person elected in Melbourne in 2010, we would've had a citizens' assembly on climate change – that was Labor's policy going into the election. It was because they needed the Greens' support to form government that we could negotiate a carbon price.

The Labor–Greens agreement was historic, and the crowning achievement of the national Greens' 18-year history – not to mention the two decades of party activism and grassroots development before 1992. The Greens now were supporting a minority Australian government, and in a position to make serious inroads on policy.

The party did not overplay its hand. Unlike the Greens had in minority governments in Tasmania and Canberra, Brown and Milne did not seek ministries. On the Greens' top priority, action on climate change, Milne insisted that carbon price be legislated by 1 July 2012, and urged the creation of a cabinet subcommittee to come up with a price on carbon. The Multi-Party Climate Change Committee included Labor, the Greens, Windsor and Oakeshott, as well as eminent climate scientist Will Steffen, consultants Rod Sims and Patricia Faulkner, and economist Ross Garnaut, who updated his landmark review. The committee worked well, and within ten months had a comprehensive package of legislation ready to go.

In his memoir, *Fights of My Life*, climate minister Greg Combet speaks highly of Milne, who had carriage of the policy work for the MPCCC, but expresses deep antipathy for the Greens, including over the 2009 rejection of the CPRS. Combet says the major difference between Labor and the Greens was over emissions-reduction targets, and the key breakthrough was to come up with an ETS with a three-year transition from a fixed price to a floating price, which meant that in the early years there was no need for the two parties to agree on the cap on emissions. Unfortunately, in what she later admitted was a terrible error of judgement, Prime Minister Gillard agreed on the ABC's 7.30 that the new carbon price was a form of carbon tax, opening up the government to the accusation she had broken her pre-election promise. Combet writes that his 'greatest regret is I did not provide more fearless advice to Julia to avoid this error'.[56]

The overall Labor–Greens agreement was a visionary document that set out a farsighted reform agenda, much of which was implemented, and some of which remains unfinished business. The agreement called for thorough political donations reform – and preferably, from the Greens' point of view, full public funding of elections – plus above-the-line voting, a truth-in-electoral-advertising law and a leaders' debate commission. It called for the creation of a parliamentary budget office, and for the appointment of a parliamentary integrity commissioner who would enforce a code of conduct for MPs, among other things. It called for a referendum on Indigenous constitutional recognition, as well as national dental care, high-speed rail and a parliamentary debate on the war in Afghanistan. One commentator hailed the advent of a 'whole new way of governing' in Australia – diffuse government by coalition, rather than by rotation between two dominant parties, as had been the case since World War II. It could be revolutionary, or it could mark the infection of Australian politics with the 'European disease'.[57]

Coalition leader Tony Abbott's reaction to the formation of the Gillard minority government was to reprise the tactics used by former state Liberal leader Robin Gray in the years of Tasmania's Labor–Green Accord. He sought to constantly destabilise the government, repeatedly moving censure and no-confidence motions to create a sense of crisis. In this Abbott was aided by the Murdoch media, in particular the national broadsheet *The Australian*, which shocked readers by declaring an openly partisan, anti-Green position in an editorial published on the day the new government was sworn in:

> Greens leader Bob Brown has accused *The Australian* of trying to wreck the alliance between the Greens and Labor. We wear Senator Brown's criticism with pride. We believe he and his Green colleagues are hypocrites; that they are bad for the nation; and that they should be destroyed at the ballot box ...[58]

When proprietor Rupert Murdoch tweeted his free advice soon afterwards – 'whatever you do, don't let the bloody Greens mess it up!' – it was clear the assault would be relentless.[59]

In the wake of their election triumph and the successful negotiations to form minority government, the Greens had their first contested leadership spill. Even with a ten-strong party room – quite big enough for factions to emerge – the result was assumed to be a foregone conclusion. Sure enough, Bob Brown was elected unchallenged as leader, but eyebrows were raised when Sarah Hanson-Young, whom Brown had mentored and who was close to his right-hand man, Ben Oquist, put up her hand for the deputy leadership. There was logic behind her push: if she won as deputy, the leadership team would be a mix of experience and youth, and would broaden beyond Tasmania. Milne was shocked, and won the deputy position with a clear majority, but was put on notice that her eventual succession would not be automatic.

Hanson-Young was appointed chair of the party room and, when news of her challenge broke, pledged full support to the party's leadership. Brown said all his colleagues were potential leaders of the party, and suggested a bit of competition was healthy: 'I encourage it.'[60] Traditionally ambivalent at best about leadership, the Greens were now indulging in leadership intrigue, just like the other political parties.

*　　*　　*

The surge of support for the Greens, along with the hit to the Labor brand from a combination of leadership instability and minority government, put the minor party in a strong position heading into elections in Victoria and New South Wales. In Victoria, based on the 12 per cent statewide primary vote in the federal poll, the Greens were suddenly in contention to win up to 12 seats – one in each of the eight upper-house regions, and four in the lower house, all inner-city seats held by Labor: Melbourne, Brunswick, Richmond and Northcote.

The *Herald Sun* reported that Liberal opposition leader Ted Baillieu was refusing to rule out a preference deal with the Greens.[61] Unofficial Victorian Greens leader Greg Barber left the door open to helping Baillieu form government in the event of a hung parliament, and flagged that his party would want the transport portfolio, mimicking the arrangement in Tasmania.[62]

The possibility of a Liberal preference deal with the Greens put the Nationals mightily offside, however, and a growing backlash saw farmers, the building industry and trucking billionaire Lindsay Fox urge the Liberals to put the Greens last.[63] The Liberals faced a dilemma, and the Victorian election quickly became the 'national test bed' of how the major parties approached the Greens, as former Democrats staffer Christian Kerr wrote in *The Australian*:

> Liberal preferences handed the Labor stronghold of Melbourne to the Greens at the federal election on August 21, but new federal MP Adam Bandt immediately threw his support behind the ALP ... A significant and influential section of the Liberals say they gained nothing by preferencing the Greens. Influential Coalition strategists believe that if the Greens ran split tickets in the seats of La Trobe and Corangamite in the federal poll, giving

voters a choice of directing their preferences to either of the main parties rather than favouring the ALP, Liberal Jason Wood would have held La Trobe and Labor would have lost Corangamite. The two seats would have delivered Tony Abbott a slim majority in the House of Representatives and government.[64]

At the same time, Labor operatives were quietly urging business-people, including in the coal industry, to press the Liberals not to preference the Greens, and were talking with Liberals and Nationals about setting up a bipartisan body, based on 'Tasmanians for a Better Future', which had campaigned against the Greens in 2006.[65] Despite the two-party assault – or perhaps because of it – a Newspoll in October 2010 put the Greens support at a stunning 19 per cent.[66]

The pressure on Baillieu increased, including from former prime minister John Howard, opposing any Liberal preference deal with the Greens. The Greens played their cards close to their chest, refusing to sign up to the usual preference deal with Labor and dangling the prospect of issuing split tickets in key marginals the Liberals hoped to win. Two weeks out from the election, it was still clear as mud: both Liberal and Labor accused the Greens of doing a deal with the other side. One key decision had been made, however: the Liberals' campaign director, Tony Nutt, had snapped, deciding the Greens were double-dealing and would be put last in all lower-house seats.[67] It was a knockout blow to the Greens' chances of holding the balance of power; ABC election analyst Antony Green declared the Greens' lower-house hopes were a 'lost cause'.[68]

Describing a Coalition–Labor alliance to shut out the Greens, Barber said the 'old order has run into each other's arms and if you clearly want to get change to their old failed policies you can't vote for either of them'.[69] In a blow-by-blow analysis, *The Australian* reported that the 'green sweep of the nation ... had come to a grinding halt', adding that Bob Brown had given the Victorian party a spray: "'You think Bob Brown is joking when he says voters should make up their own minds," says a Greens insider. "Well, we just got off the phone from Brown, who delivered a very angry 'I told you so.'"'[70]

On election day, the Greens did not deliver on the promise held out by the surge in support federally, or by the early polling: a small

1.4 per cent swing in the upper house failed to result in any extra seats. A 1 per cent swing in the lower house, to 11 per cent, also delivered nothing. The Baillieu government won a single-seat majority in both houses, leaving the Greens powerless. The week after the poll, the Victorian Greens' party room decided to officially appoint Barber as leader.[71] Victorian Liberal federal MP Andrew Robb said the election marked a turning point:

> Life is about to get a lot more difficult for the Greens politically. They will now be judged not as a vehicle to keep the major parties honest. They will be looked at more closely as to what they stand for – a party with such a left-wing agenda that people did not worry about before.[72]

In New South Wales, as in Victoria, the federal result put the Greens on track to break into the state's lower house. The Labor-held inner-west seats of Balmain and Marrickville were vulnerable. In power for 16 years, the ALP had turned toxic after a string of leadership changes – from Bob Carr to Morris Iemma to Nathan Rees to Kristina Keneally – and scandals concerning factional powerbrokers Eddie Obeid, Joe Tripodi and Ian Macdonald, which would soon lead to sensational hearings at ICAC. A 10 per cent swing against Labor was expected, and Balmain and Marrickville were held on 3.7 per cent and 7.5 per cent margins respectively. The Greens, buoyed by Newspoll showing their primary support at 15 per cent statewide, were considered the favourites to gain them, including by Antony Green.

A generational shift was underway in the NSW Greens: Lee Rhiannon had been elected to the Senate, and replaced by Cate Faehrmann, who was not up for re-election; Sylvia Hale had retired, replaced by barrister and Woollahra councillor David Shoebridge, the lead candidate on the upper-house ticket; Ian Cohen was also retiring. Byron mayor Jan Barham was running in the second slot, and former Orange councillor Jeremy Buckingham was in the third, which the Greens had never won before. After serving two long terms in the state parliament since 1995, Cohen's final years had been plagued by two defamation cases – in one, he was successful against Channel Seven, winning a six-figure payout; in another, he lost to a

North Coast developer whom he had criticised at a private Greens function that was reported in the local paper, the *Byron Echo*. The loss had cost him a fortune, and the stress contributed to the breakdown of his marriage. Coming on top of his estrangement from the Greens' party room, where he was often at odds with Rhiannon, Hale and John Kaye, Cohen was glad to get out.

In her valedictory speech in September 2010, Sylvia Hale spoke of her recent winter trip to Palestine, in the wake of Israel's bombardment of Gaza in retaliation for terrorist attacks, called Operation Cast Lead. Hale accused Israel of 'a policy of ethnic cleansing, of apartheid and of a disproportionate use of force'.[73] They were not idle words: at the December state delegates' meeting, Hale successfully moved, on behalf of her Petersham/Newton Greens branch, a motion calling for support of the Palestinian boycott, divestment, sanctions (BDS) movement against Israel, which passed unanimously, without opposition or dissent – not one speaker against.[74] Looking back, Hale admits she would not have done that if she thought it was going to come up in the looming state election:

> A lot of Greens members aren't aware of foreign policy issues, and so they [may be] inclined to support things without really understanding the ramifications, but can I say there is no way in the world if anyone had thought that the BDS was going to be remotely divisive issue, prior to that [2010] election ... I wouldn't have done that.

Days before Christmas, a Greens councillor in Marrickville, Cathy Peters, moved a motion to support the Israel boycott, and it passed 10–2, with the support of Labor and the Greens, and opposed by the lone Liberal and one independent. Marrickville had become the first Australian council to support BDS, and the story scored a 161-word yarn in *The Sydney Morning Herald*.[75]

Labor frontbencher Anthony Albanese, however, saw an opportunity to skewer the Greens on BDS – he also had a vested interest, given that his wife, Carmel Tebbutt, held the state seat of Marrickville and was fighting to keep it. In the middle of January 2011, Albanese gave an interview to *The Australian* describing the BDS motion as 'self-indulgent', adding that 'foreign policy is a fair way outside the parameters of the role of Marrickville Council'. Behind the scenes, he was pressuring Labor councillor Sam Iskandar, who had supported the BDS motion, to backflip. Soon enough, News Ltd, who never needed much encouragement to hop into the Greens, were piling onto Marrickville Council, lampooning their ambitions to bring peace to the Middle East and exhorting them to stick to local government – 'roads, rates and rubbish'.

All the way to polling day, the barrage did not let up. Premier Kristina Kenneally and opposition leader Barry O'Farrell denounced the boycott; the Coalition even flagged that they would sack the council, if elected. Foreign minister Kevin Rudd slammed the boycott as 'foreign policy made by pre-schoolers'.[76] Marrickville mayor Fiona Byrne was the Greens' endorsed candidate for the state seat, had beat off a late, unexpected preselection challenge from Hale herself. Byrne confessed early on that she was no expert on the Israel/Palestine conflict, but was now thrust into the spotlight to defend a policy that was not her forte. Byrne stumbled in a press conference, saying the party would push for a statewide boycott on Israel: 'It's the NSW Greens' policy to support the boycott, divestment and sanctions movement, which is a global movement. I would suggest that the NSW Greens would be looking to bring that forward at state parliament if we were elected.' Later, Byrne tried to clarify that there were no plans to implement a statewide boycott, but the damage was done.[77]

Another gaffe came when Byrne told one interviewer that the Greens would also consider boycotting China over the occupation of Tibet. Again, the media went wild with reports that the Greens were a threat to Australia's largest trade relationship. Bob Brown distanced the Australian Greens from the whole thing, while continuing to campaign in Marrickville, appearing alongside Byrne and defending her, without supporting BDS.

It was an impossible high-wire act. Labor pulled no punches, running push polls in the final week of the campaign. The media pile-on took a huge toll on the valiant Byrne. By the end of the election campaign, after weeks of relentless pressure, she was a wreck.

The ultimate impact of the BDS debate on the Greens' performance in the election was debatable. Amid a crushing victory that delivered the Coalition a majority in both houses, and relegated Labor to opposition for at least two terms, the Greens got a solid 2.9 per cent swing. Three members were elected to the Legislative Council – Shoebridge, Barham and Buckingham, who just beat Pauline Hanson into the last upper-house seat by 0.04 per cent of a quota – 1300 votes – after a nail-biting count. The Greens now had five seats in the upper house: their best-ever result.

The party also broke into the Legislative Assembly for the first time, with Leichhardt mayor Jamie Parker winning the previously solid Labor seat of Balmain, as polls had predicted. In Marrickville, however, the Greens would be disappointed. Byrne, to her credit, got a record Greens primary vote of 36 per cent, but Liberal preferences flowed to Labor, and Tebbutt was easily re-elected despite a swing against her, in two-party terms, of almost 7 per cent. Two weeks earlier, a Galaxy poll had Byrne the clear favourite, with 44 per cent of the primary vote to Tebbutt's 33 per cent.[78] Even Sylvia Hale concedes BDS had a negative impact: 'Whilst [we] increased our vote, the increase was not as much as would have happened without the BDS – yes, I quite concede that.'

In the days after the election, Bob Brown pointed the finger at the NSW Greens, saying he believed the boycott had had an effect: 'That's my feedback … I'm picking up from the electorate that it's a matter of concern. As I've pointed out through the campaign, it's not national Greens policy.' (The Greens' national council and conference had considered the issue in early 2010, when a comprehensive BDS proposal was allowed to lapse in favour of a more limited boycott of military trade and engagements; the official policy was to 'support the rights of the Palestinian peoples to statehood through the creation of a viable state of Palestine alongside the state of Israel, based on the pre-1967 borders and the right of all peoples in the region to peace'.)

Yet the BDS debate within the party only intensified after the state election. The vexed issue had exposed a deep and growing divide. The day after Parker's win was declared, Cate Faehrmann wrote an op-ed for *The Sydney Morning Herald* titled 'Greens won't get much further if we repeat poll blunders'. The piece became pointed, singling out the BDS policy as an unnecessary distraction. Without naming names, Faehrmann complained: 'Its original proponents within the NSW Greens were nowhere to be seen, and our overwhelmed candidate for Marrickville was left with little support. In any language, it was poor strategy and bad behaviour.' She argued that the Greens should target government in a generation, and offer a progressive alternative to Labor: 'We have no leader in NSW, no shadow cabinet and, therefore, offer no picture of what a Greens government would look like.'[79] It was a searing bit of post-election analysis, and some of Faehrmann's colleagues have never forgiven her.

In May 2011, the state party set up a working group to review the BDS resolution from December. The temperature rose mid-year, as BDS supporters targeted the Israeli-owned Max Brenner chocolate cafés in Melbourne and Sydney; the situation turned ugly, and blew back on the Greens when Lee Rhiannon defended the protests on radio. In the state's upper house, Liberal hardliner David Clarke moved a private member's motion to condemn BDS and the Max Brenner protests, and wedge the Greens. He succeeded. While all Liberal and Labor members voted for the motion, the Greens split. John Kaye and David Shoebridge voted against it. Kaye spoke powerfully, comparing BDS with the movement against apartheid and denying the boycott was anti-Semitic:

> As an Australian Jew I find the exploitation of false accusations of anti-Semitism particularly obnoxious … one might not like that it targets Israel or that it targets shops that are owned by Israelis, but it does not target shops that are owned by Jews. It has no connection to the appalling tactics implemented by the Nazis during the Holocaust.

Faehrmann sought to soften the motion – from 'condemns' BDS to 'notes with concern' – but indicated she would support it. So did Jan Barham, who told the chamber that 'many of my Jewish friends have raised their concerns about where this might go if left unchecked and the types of people it is attracting – extremists from the Right or the Left'. On the voices, the motion was overwhelmingly supported.

Afterwards, there was bitter recrimination. Kaye wrote a memo spelling out the disloyalty of Faehrmann, Barham and Buckingham, who had breached the party's constitution by failing to vote in line with policy, and the Cessnock Kurri Greens moved a motion calling for the three MLCs to resign. At the crucial meeting of the peak state delegates council (SDC) in December, the motion failed and a compromise policy on BDS was passed by modified consensus. The NSW Greens resolved instead to recognise BDS as a 'legitimate, non-violent political tactic seeking to alter the policies and actions of the government of Israel', but also to recognise that there were a variety of views on it within the Greens. It was a fudge, in other words. Open hostilities had broken out in the Greens' own culture war, and the internal effort to censure or oust Faehrmann and Barham dragged on for years.

*   *   *

The BDS debate did not help the Greens' relationship with Labor at the federal level. In the inaugural Whitlam Oration in April 2011, Prime Minister Julia Gillard lashed out at her junior partner in government. Gillard described Labor as 'a party of government and proud of it', and continued with a critique portraying the Greens as anti-growth, anti-jobs, out-of-touch elitists:

> We happily leave to the Greens being a party of protest with no tradition of striking the balance required to deliver major reform ... the differences between Labor and the Greens take many forms but at the bottom of it are two vital ones. The Greens wrongly reject the moral imperative to a strong economy. The Greens have some worthy ideas and many of their supporters sincerely want a better politics in our country. They have good intentions but fail to understand the centrepiece of our big picture – the people Labor strives to represent need work. And the Greens will never embrace Labor's delight at sharing the values of everyday Australians, in our cities, suburbs, towns and bush, who day after day do the right thing, leading purposeful and dignified lives, driven by love of family and nation.[80]

Although her final flourish was gratuitous, Gillard's sharp distinction between the party of protest and the party of government hit a raw nerve inside the Greens.

Relations between Labor and the Greens were further strained as Gillard tried desperately to stop the flow of asylum seekers arriving by boat. On coming to office, Labor's immigration minister, Chris Evans, had dismantled Howard's Pacific Solution, closing detention centres on Nauru and Manus Island and abolishing temporary protection visas. The first year was quiet, but boat arrivals started to increase in 2009, particularly from Sri Lanka, and a turning point came with the November standoff over the MV *Oceanic Viking*, an Australian customs vessel that had rescued 78 Tamil refugees in Indonesian waters; the asylum seekers refused to get off at Bintan Island, where there was an Australian-funded detention centre, fearing they would be returned home. The Greens' immigration spokesperson, Sarah Hanson-Young, recalled that Rudd had ramped up the anti–people smuggler rhetoric: 'Labor was scrambling and trying to speak out both sides of their mouth from the moment of the *Oceanic Viking*.' Labor began to switch from compassion to deterrence, which was reinforced when Gillard appointed Chris Bowen as immigration minister. Boat arrivals tripled in 2010, and there were more deaths at sea, culminating in the Christmas Island tragedy in December.

The government negotiated the so-called Malaysia Solution, a swap of up to 800 refugees intercepted en route to Australia for 4000 refugees waiting in Malaysia to be resettled. Bob Brown immediately denounced the Malaysia Solution as a 'dog's breakfast of a refugee policy', saying it was cruel to send people to Malaysia, which was not a signatory to the United Nations' convention on refugees, and where 'the cane is in frequent use'.[81] A High Court challenge was mounted by refugee advocates, and succeeded. The government sought to amend the *Migration Act* to make the Malaysia Solution work, but was blocked by the Greens and Liberals. Bowen, as minister, was more disappointed in the Liberals, whose opposition was cynical:

> On that issue I am more critical of the Liberals than the Greens, because I accept that the Greens believed in their vote. I disagree with it profoundly, but I accept that their world view led them to that vote ... they just couldn't compute that, that we could actually save a lot more people, we could have a rational policy, and the outcome would be better.[82]

Five years later, Coalition leader Tony Abbott conceded he may have done the wrong thing.[83] The Greens have made no such admission, but given that half the 1200 people who died at sea drowned *after* the Malaysia Solution was rejected, there is no doubt it was a grave decision. In a Senate debate, Hanson-Young did not budge an inch:

> We know that the government has a bad plan when it comes to dumping vulnerable people in Malaysia. We know it contravenes the 1951 Refugee Convention ... it is absolutely paramount that we do what it is we have signed up to do: assess the claims of asylum seekers here on the Australian mainland. It is what the majority of Australians want; it is the cheapest option; it is the most humane one; and, above all else, it is legal. We should just get on with it.[84]

Throughout 2011, the Multi-Party Climate Change Committee thrashed out the details of a new legislative package to put a price on carbon. There were furious disagreements between Labor and the Greens, particularly over the extent of compensation for coal-fired power stations, but the dirty secret of the MPCCC process was that it worked. Combet – who described himself as 'a coalmining engineer, supported by the coalminer's union, representing a coalmining electorate' – finished up with a high regard for Milne, who led the negotiations for the Greens, although the business community regarded her as the devil incarnate. Milne was all over the detail, and a scourge of vested interests resisting change.

As well as fighting for higher ambition at every step, the Greens pushed for the creation of a new Australian Renewable Energy Agency, to invest in research and development, and a new $10 billion Clean Energy Finance Corporation, to give cheap loans to commercially viable renewables projects. A Carbon Farming Initiative was set up to cover the agriculture sector, which was not covered by the carbon price. At the Greens' insistence, the Australian Energy Market Operator was tasked with studying the feasibility of Australia going 100 per cent renewable, and found there was no fundamental obstacle. An independent Climate Change Authority was set up to take the politics out of emissions-reduction targets once and for all, as the Reserve Bank has done for monetary policy. More than compensating for the impact on electricity bills, the tax-free threshold was lifted from $6000 to $18,200, relieving a million low-income earners from paying tax or filing a tax return; Combet hailed this as a major Labor reform.[85]

Both sides put their own spin on the final Clean Energy Future package, which passed into law in November 2011. For Penny Wong, by then finance minister, the Greens' support for the CEF package was proof that their decision to block the CPRS in 2009–10 was cynical politics. The dollar amount of compensation on offer to big polluters in 2011 was higher in than in 2009, Wong argued; she concluded that the Greens had recognised their earlier mistake and backflipped.[86]

Milne never conceded that point, and for her own part criticised Gillard for selling the package poorly – firstly by failing to understand the difference between a carbon tax and an emissions-trading scheme with a fixed price, and secondly by talking too much about prices and compensation and not enough about climate science. '[The prime minister] was not a climate champion and she didn't understand the urgency of acting on climate change,' Milne wrote in her memoir.[87] Nonetheless, the final package was comprehensive, hailed by the International Energy Agency as 'template legislation' for the introduction of a carbon price in developed countries. 'The only criticism they made was that there was too much money for the coal industry, and I couldn't have agreed more,' Milne says. The package came into effect in July 2012, so Milne points out that the Greens' fateful decision of 2009–10 had only cost the country a year of emissions reduction (given that the CPRS would've come into effect in July 2011). In her memoir, Milne records that, on her retirement, she presented a signed set of the *Clean Energy Acts* to the Democracy Museum in Canberra to mark her legacy, and was surprised to be told that Julia Gillard had done the same thing.

*   *   *

At the end of 2011, the Greens' Christmas drinks were a happy affair after what was described as the party's most successful year in politics. Tony Abbott – for his own political purposes, of course – labelled

Brown 'the real prime minister of Australia'. Brown refused to comment on his retirement plans. On 23 March 2012 Brown gave a landmark 'Green Oration' at the Hobart Town Hall, opening with a killer greeting – 'Fellow Earthians' – which got enormous attention. The significance of the date was lost in the ensuing coverage, but it marked 40 years since the United Tasmania Group had formed to run candidates in the state election to save Lake Pedder.

Brown called for a global parliament, picking up on a proposal he and Kerry Nettle had moved in the Senate in 2003 after the invasion of Iraq. The global parliament would be bicameral, based on one vote, one value, but with the house of review having equal representation from every nation. Global democracy, he said, was the only alternative to plutocracy. Brown flagged that he would move for a global people's assembly at the Global Greens' third conference, to be held in Senegal the following week:

> The political debate of the twentieth century was polarised between capitalism and communism. It was about control of the economy in the narrow sense of material goods and money. A free market versus state control. Bitter experience tells us that the best outcome is neither, but some of both. The role of democracy in the nation state has been to calibrate that balance. In this twenty-first century the political debate is moving to a new arena. It is about whether we expend the Earth's natural capital as our population grows to ten billion people in the decades ahead ...[88]

Days later, in the middle of a tiring session at the Global Greens' Congress in Dakar, Brown passed a handwritten note to his partner, Paul Thomas, saying simply, 'Time's up.'[89]

Brown's last speech to the Senate was a tribute to two Tasmanians: David Walsh, the founder of MONA, completed the previous year, which had put Hobart 'on the world map' and would help transform the state's economy, and schoolteacher Miranda Gibson, an activist for Still Wild, Still Threatened who was holding the world's highest tree-sit, alone, 60 metres up a giant eucalypt in the forests of Tasmania's World Heritage Area, from where she blogged and skyped the world with a solar-powered laptop.

In a deal urged on by the Tasmanian Greens to end the state's forest wars once and for all, Tasmanian premier Lara Giddings and Prime Minister Gillard had signed an intergovernmental agreement to stop logging of high-conservation-value forests. Contravening the so-called 'peace deal', Forestry Tasmania had continued logging, and Gibson had been up there since Christmas. 'She is there through rain, snow, hail and storm,' Brown said.

> If you are 60 metres up in a 80-metre or so tree and you are hit by one of those squalls from the south-west – these great trees are the biggest living things on earth, along with the redwoods – the tree responds to those storms not just by bending and swaying but by twisting and turning. The experience of being up there during such a tempest can only be thought about, but Miranda stays there ... I would appeal to the Prime Minister, I would appeal to the Premier, and I would appeal to every one of my fellow senators and fellow parliamentarians to visit Miranda. If you cannot go there and have a cup of tea, then visit her blog site and see what this marvellous citizen of the planet is doing in defence of the planet and in respect of our own humankind species and its future.

Brown clearly identified with Gibson, whom he joined for 'high tea'; he recorded in his memoir that her lone protest reminded him of his fast on Mount Wellington 35 years earlier. Brown left politics in the same spirit as he'd gone in.

CHAPTER 10

MILNE REBUILDS

From the day she became leader in April 2012, Christine Milne knew she would cop the brunt of a looming electoral backlash, after holding the balance of power. Bob Brown had timed his departure well, and commentators almost universally assumed the Greens would go backwards at the next election without their charismatic founder. Opposition leader Tony Abbott predicted the Greens would struggle, comparing them to the Democrats without Don Chipp – which was either ignorant or misleading, because the Democrats' peak came years after Chipp's retirement. Nevertheless, Brown's departure posed a fundamental challenge for the Greens: could anyone fill the gap he left behind, either inside the party or in the minds of the voting public?

Although Milne was a known quantity, Brown's natural successor as deputy, and had been voted up unanimously by the party room, the media reaction to her succession to the leadership was wary. Her fierce advocacy on climate had sharpened perceptions, particularly in the business community, that she was more hardline than Brown. From the get-go columnists described Milne as 'boring', 'shrill' or 'no Bob Brown' – *The Daily Telegraph* even called her a communist.[1] There was a fair degree of sexism mixed in with the commentary, even as the country suffered a bout of introspection over the treatment of its first female prime minister, Julia Gillard. 'I have been criticised from day one – and I regard it as a sexist criticism – for being too strong, too uncompromising and not smiling enough,' Milne says.

> I couldn't tell you how many millions of times over the years I have had people come up to me and say, 'Christine, you need to smile more on TV.' If a male leader comes on TV and is strong and

emphatic and articulate, people go, 'Wow, that's leadership.' But if a woman comes on TV and do that they go, 'Why don't you just smile more, be a bit more feminine, soften it a bit?'

As a veteran politician in her own right, Milne was determined not to become a celebrity, and to lead on her policy substance. As the Australian Greens' first female leader, she made an effort to reach out to all sides of the party at a delicate time. Initially at least, they rallied around her, as if to prove the party was indeed bigger than one man.

Gillard and Milne confirmed that Brown's retirement did not affect the Greens' agreement with Labor, but it was nonetheless a delicate time for the federal government. Gillard was flagging in the face of the remorseless negativity of Abbott, and white-anting by Kevin Rudd, who had challenged unsuccessfully for the leadership in February 2012 and resigned as foreign minister, returning to the backbench: the Gillard government was besieged. Never comfortable in partnership, Labor and the Greens were now borderline hostile to each other, and searching for a way to extricate themselves from their agreement without bringing down the government. Milne commented:

> We mostly end up holding the balance of power in those scenarios when a government goes from majority to minority because they're on the nose for one reason or another ... So when you take over the balance of power in that arrangement, the voters actually meant to get rid of that government and didn't quite make it, and so it's very hard to build from there ... it's always a really hard dynamic.

Milne spelled out that her first priority as Greens leader would be to approach new constituencies in regional areas and in business. 'I come from the country,' she told the ABC.

> My very first campaign was leading the Wesley Vale farmers and fishermen against the pulp mill, and I think this is a century where food security is going to be a big issue globally. And in Australia

we need to link hands with the rural community, particularly farmers, to talk about how Australia might address that. So that's one constituency, and another is progressive business. I've been working a lot with them as a result of the clean energy package, and I think there is a big opportunity there to create jobs and really build the forefront of the new economy, rather than constantly listening to the carping from the old economy.[2]

In the small party room of ten, there was a three-way contest for the deputy leadership, with Sarah Hanson-Young again putting up her hand, as did Scott Ludlam and Adam Bandt. Bandt – who was also described as a Marxist in the News Corp tabloids – won it comfortably, and there was a certain logic to having a leadership team that was balanced across the upper and lower houses, female and male. Ben Oquist took over as chief of staff in Milne's office – and that was where tensions first emerged.

Oquist was the consummate political insider. He and Brown had formed a double act – the Bob and Ben show – for the best part of two decades. Once they had agreed on something, as a rule they could get what they wanted, both in the parliamentary party and with the membership. Milne, as a new leader, did not have the same authority as Brown, and was determined to consult more widely. The relationship between Milne and Oquist was uneasy.

On the other hand, Milne says she put a lot of effort into fixing the relationship between the Australian Greens and the NSW Greens. And in Queensland, Drew Hutton backed Milne's calls to build new constituencies in regional Australia, urging the Greens to 'stop holding focus groups in the inner suburbs of Melbourne and Sydney' and to move towards the centre on economic issues. 'Their reflexes need to be less anti-business and they need to start reaching out to business,' Hutton said, 'especially areas like manufacturing, tourism, agriculture, those sectors that have gone at least partly down the road to sustainability.'[3]

Brown's replacement in the Senate, Peter Whish-Wilson, was hand-picked to boost the party's economic credentials. Whish-Wilson was a Tamar Valley winemaker and surfer who had campaigned against Gunns' pulp mill, and had joined the Greens in 2008. Before moving to Tasmania, he had been a merchant banker for a decade, working around the world for Merrill Lynch and Deutsche Bank. A Duntroon graduate, Whish-Wilson's politics had started right of centre – he voted for Howard in 2001 as a younger man, when, as he now says, he 'had his head up his arse' – and shifted gradually towards the left, accelerating in the wake of the financial crisis. Although he was viewed with some suspicion on the left of the Greens, given his background in high finance and the military, Whish-Wilson argued that it was being a merchant banker that had turned him into a socialist. He started out as the Greens' spokesperson on trade, competition policy and small business.

In her first interviews as leader, Milne flagged she would be taking on the mining industry, but the long investment boom ended in 2012 as prices for key export commodities like coal and iron ore dropped sharply. Labor cut hard in the 2012–13 budget, deepening a policy rift with the Greens by extending the Howard-era 'Welfare to Work' reforms, which forced single parents off the pension and onto Newstart. Howard's 2006 reform had been prospective, but Gillard's reform removed the 'grandfathering', hitting 100,000 sole parents, most of them women, very hard. The change passed through the Senate on 10 October, the same day that Gillard unleashed her celebrated 'misogyny' speech on Tony Abbott. For Milne, it was a galling hypocrisy that left a sour taste in her mouth. Gillard was posing as a defender of women while depriving thousands of single mums of pension payments. In the Senate, the Greens' community spokesperson, Rachel Siewert, fired up, warning that Labor's cuts would drive already vulnerable people further into poverty.

All through 2012, the conservative shift in the electorate became more evident. In March, the stunning victory of former Brisbane mayor Campbell Newman at the Queensland election left Labor with just seven seats in the unicameral parliament, and saw the Greens' statewide vote drop for the first time by a percentage point, to 7.5 per cent. There were swings against the party in local government elections in New South Wales, and they fell short of an expected victory in the Melbourne state by-election mid-year, where Cathy Oke had hoped to replicate the success of Adam Bandt. At the ALP's national conference in Sydney, right-faction powerbrokers Sam Dastyari and

Paul Howes ripped into the Greens as extremist populists, comparing them with One Nation and calling for Labor to stop preferencing them. Victorian opposition leader Dan Andrews described the intervention from New South Wales as unhelpful, saying he wanted to beat the Greens, not belt them.[4]

In October, the Greens got a real shock in the progressive ACT, when a big swing to the Liberals saw their vote drop 5 per cent, causing the loss of three seats, including that of leader Meredith Hunter. With Liberal and Labor winning eight seats each, the decision on who to support fell to the Greens' sole survivor, Shane Rattenbury, who had been speaker in the Legislative Assembly. After consulting with the membership, Rattenbury once again backed Labor, led by Katy Gallagher, and this time he joined the government, emulating his party colleagues in Tasmania and picking up a swag of ministerial portfolios. Another shock loomed for the party in the West Australian election of March 2013, where Premier Colin Barnett was returned with an expanded majority, while the Greens copped swings against them in both houses and lost two seats, including that of unofficial leader Giz Watson.

*   *   *

Ever since the 2010 election, the Greens' leader had met weekly with Prime Minister Gillard in Canberra, but Milne's first meeting for 2013 was perfunctory, box-ticking. It was clear to Milne that Labor was not going to deal with any of the unfinished business under their original agreement with the Greens. Consumed by fending off Rudd, Gillard had started the year by nominating the September federal election date nine months out. Milne records in her memoir that she decided to acknowledge the reality that the two parties' working relationship had broken down – in fact, was at risk of becoming an abusive relationship. Just before her own National Press Club address to kick off the election year, Milne called Gillard to say she was about to declare the Labor–Greens agreement dead – although the minor party would still guarantee confidence and supply. Gillard's only response was to ask whether Milne intended to 'attack her trustworthiness at a personal level'.[5] She did not. In a repeat of the termination of the Labor–Green Accord in Tasmania in 1992, Milne announced that it was Labor, not the Greens, who had walked away from the agreement. Milne's main accusation was that the government had rejected a Greens proposal to improve the 'dud' mining tax, which was failing to raise any money. 'Let's call a spade a spade,' Milne told the Press Club:

> By choosing the big miners, the Labor government is making it clear to all that it no longer has the courage or the will to work with the Greens on a shared agenda in the national interest. By choosing the big miners, the Labor government is no longer honouring our agreement to work together to promote transparent and accountable government and the public interest or to address climate change. Labor has effectively ended its agreement with the Greens. So be it.

Journalists pointed out that the Greens could force Labor to amend the mining tax if they wanted to, by making it a condition of any further legislative support, and reminded Milne that her party had in fact voted for the watered-down mining tax. Milne was less than convincing about the reasons for the sudden termination of the agreement, until she explained:

> [T]hey have ended it. We haven't ended it. They have walked away ... there's no point in having meetings if the meetings are only there to be told what the Labor Party has already decided to do. I can read that in the paper or get it by letter ... there is no point in trying to pretend that something is working when it's not. Let's just be upfront, and I think people are going to be actually really happy with that because the community are now clear. We've got a clear run to the election.[6]

A few months later, in late June, Rudd retook the leadership. For Milne, the change at the helm was a tragedy in hindsight, because Rudd refused to acknowledge, let alone campaign upon, the achievements of the Labor–Green agreement in the Gillard years, 'the most progressive, reformist period of government for decades – something few people knew'. Milne wrote:

I think the reason Rudd Labor loyalists see the CPRS as the be-all and end-all is that it is Rudd's and not Gillard's policy ... when he overthrew Prime Minister Gillard in 2013 he ignored all she had achieved, especially the Clean Energy package. Secondly, Labor refuses ever to talk about its successes in minority government with the Australian Greens in balance of power. That would give credit to the Australian Greens and normalise minority or multi-party government when Labor wants to go to elections reinforcing the two-party system with messaging that says 'majority government is good', 'minority government is bad'.[7]

There was certainly no love lost between Rudd and Milne, who wrote of the 'icy' meeting in which the prime minister asked her for confidence and supply over the weeks to the election. In his book *Whitlam's Children: Labor and the Greens in Australia*, Shaun Crowe interviewed dozens of MPs on both sides about the relationship between the two parties, focusing on the Rudd–Gillard–Rudd years, and found that while the Greens were proud of the achievements of the minority government, the same was much less true of Labor, and there was no appetite for a repeat performance. Adam Bandt told Crowe that for the ALP's Green critics, a successful left-wing alliance was worse than an unsuccessful one:

I think part of the untold story is how much of the right wing of the Labor Party sabotaged it internally. I think there were many people who did not want Labor and the Greens working together – because they'd much rather work with the Liberals than the Greens, and consider themselves closer politically to the Liberals than to the Greens.[8]

Heading into the 2013 election, Milne knew the tide was going out for the Greens and for progressive politics generally, and saw her job as trying to 'put down the anchor, hold all our seats and try and pick up one more'. In the party's favour was the fact that six of its senators were continuing, which meant the Greens did have a chance of picking up seats. Only Sarah Hanson-Young in South Australia, Scott Ludlam in Western Australia and Peter Whish-Wilson in Tasmania were up for re-election. The most promising states were Victoria, where party veteran Janet Rice was preselected, and the ACT, where a star candidate was picked: Simon Sheikh, director of activist group GetUp. Sheikh's candidacy came with a bonus – after a meeting between Ben Oquist and CFMEU secretary Michael O'Connor, the union donated $50,000 to the ACT Greens, in an effort to keep the hard-right Canberra politician Zed Seselja out of the Senate.[9] Sheikh hired an Australian Youth Climate Coalition activist, Ellen Sandell, a former official from the Victorian Department of Premier and Cabinet, to run his campaign. Their shared goal, Sandell recalls, was to wrest a Senate seat off the Liberals and save the carbon price.

Not helping in 2013, by contrast with the previous election, was the absence of any major private donations. Graeme Wood had stressed from the beginning that his 2010 donation was a one-off, but although the uplift in the Greens' vote had been gratifying, the whole experience turned sour when the Liberal Party made a series of spurious allegations against him, Brown and Milne that were referred to the privileges committee.

In 2011–12, as part of the forestry restructure and peace deal in Tasmania, Wood and fellow conservationist Jan Cameron had bought the Triabunna woodchip mill from Gunns Ltd for $10 million, with the intention of closing it down and perhaps turning it into a tourist development. The Greens had publicly supported the deal, and Senate leader Eric Abetz argued their support was corruptly linked to the donation – that Wood was seeking a private benefit in exchange for a donation. It defied logic – Wood and Cameron were bound to lose money at Triabunna – but the privileges committee inquiry could, if it went against Brown and Milne, have seen them jailed. He got expensive legal representation, which he paid for out of his own pocket, and was cleared by the committee. Brown denounced the whole process, which had arguably defamed Wood, as an abuse of the Senate.

Worse, the Wood donation fed the Greens' internal tensions. The NSW Greens had always been wary of the donation on principle, while also being unhappy that hardly any of the Wood donation had been spent there. In a *Crikey* article, journalist Paul Barry accused Lee Rhiannon of hypocrisy. Rhiannon fired back. An op-ed appeared in *Crikey* under the byline of volunteer Norman Thompson, rejecting the accusation against her and criticising the Greens for accepting the huge donation in the first place. 'We need to closely consider what taking this big donation says about the Greens,' it wrote, 'now it appears the Greens are in the same league as the old parties.'[10] Three months later, Thompson wrote that he regretted submitting the article and that Rhiannon had written it; the media pounced. Rhiannon thought it would be in the best interests of the party if she apologised, but regrets it now. Rhiannon and Thompson fell out, and he left the Democracy4sale project soon afterwards. There was a push for an internal investigation into Rhiannon's conduct but it did not proceed. The whole thing was a mess, and a turnoff for any wealthy individuals who may have contemplated giving.

The Greens headed into the 2013 election with their first fully costed platform, with all policies submitted to the Parliamentary Budget Office, which had been established under the agreement with Labor. Neither of the major parties followed suit; Tony Abbott simply insisted the Coalition's policy costings were 'bulletproof'. The Greens had made some hard calls to ensure there was no repeat of the last-minute tabloid beat-ups that had plagued them in previous elections: at the 2012 national council, Bob Brown had prevailed and the party had dumped its perennially controversial policy to impose death duties on estates worth more than $5 million.[11] In its place were a swag of what *The Australian* described as 'soak-the-rich' policies, raising $43 billion, including a so-called Buffett tax (a higher marginal rate on incomes over $1 million), a 0.2 per cent levy on bank assets over $100 billion, a tightened mining tax and the abolition of fossil-fuel subsidies. The funds would be used to raise Newstart by $50 a week, introduce universal dental care, boost funding for the Gonski school reforms by $2 billion, and triple the size of the Clean Energy Finance Corporation to $30 billion.[12] In its post-election report, the PBO found that the total combined impact of the party's pre-election commitments would cost the Commonwealth's cash balance $4 billion, while the Coalition's platform would improve it by $7 billion. Given the size of the national budget, the difference was marginal; after decades of policy development, the Greens' platform had been given a thumbs-up, of sorts, for fiscal responsibility.[13]

None of it mattered. The election was an overwhelming rejection of years of division and instability under the Rudd–Gillard–Rudd governments, and there were big swings away from the Greens in every state, both in the Senate and the House of Representatives. Nationally, some half a million voters deserted the party in the upper house, with primaries falling from 1.7 million to 1.2 million, and the vote falling by 4 per cent to 9 per cent. Worst of all was Milne's home state of Tasmania, where the party's primary vote halved, falling almost 9 per cent to 12 per cent in the Senate and 8 per cent across the lower-house seats – including the heartland seat of Denison, where Andrew Wilkie triumphed as an independent.

Despite the gloom, Peter Whish-Wilson was comfortably re-elected in Tasmania with the help of Labor preferences, Sarah Hanson-Young coasted home on the back of preferences from the Palmer United Party and Labor (and then helped elect Family First's Bob Day with her surplus), while Scott Ludlam scraped into the sixth seat in Western Australia on the back of PUP preferences, pipping Labor's Louise Pratt in a count that was soon voided. Julian Assange's WikiLeaks Party didn't help: against a directive from its national council, in Western Australia and New South Wales the party sent preferences to right-wing candidates, away from the Greens.[14] The ACT was a bright spot: the party polled 19 per cent in the Senate, its best primary vote in the country, which was still 4 per cent down on 2010 but vindicated Sheikh's candidacy.

New South Wales was disappointing: the Senate vote dropped 3 per cent to under 8 per cent, with state MP Cate Faehrmann missing out in her tilt at the Senate, and the party went backwards in its best two lower-house seats, Grayndler and Sydney. In Grayndler, party co-founder Hall Greenland suffered a 3 per cent swing, falling to a 23 per cent primary. A frustrated Bob Brown would later recall Anthony Albanese stopping him in a Senate corridor to thank the Greens for preselecting Greenland to run against him. In Sydney, up against Tanya Plibersek, the Greens' result was even worse, dropping from 24 per cent to 17 per cent. Tanya and Albo had the Greens' measure, it seemed.

Despite the heavy swings everywhere, Victoria's results pointed the way forward, consolidating the branch's power base in the party.

The Greens polled 11 per cent in the Senate – Janet Rice reached a quota easily, helped by Labor preferences – and got positive swings and more than 20 per cent of the primary vote in its four key seats, Melbourne, Batman, Wills and Melbourne Ports. The best result of the night, countrywide, was the upset victory of Adam Bandt, who defied the national trend with a primary vote that jumped seven points, to 42.6 per cent, and maintained his lead over the second-placed Labor candidate despite 63 per cent of Liberal preferences going to Labor in the final round of counting. As Guy Rundle subsequently wrote, the gallery journalists at the post-election party in West Melbourne 'believed, to a man and woman, that they were there to document the noble failure and concession speech of Adam Bandt, the man who had taken Labor's premium and previously very safe seat for a cheeky one-term tenure'.

The stunning win did not come out of nowhere. After working on Larissa Waters' successful 2010 campaign, Sam La Rocca had joined Bandt's office as chief of staff, before winning a political exchange scholarship to join US president Barack Obama's 2012 re-election campaign. He brought back a sophisticated approach, based on organising and consumer data analysis, which helped revolutionise the Greens' approach to campaigning. As he wrote in *Green* magazine:

> We're organising a solid people-powered grassroots effort, in true Greens tradition, to counter the deep pockets and big advertising spends of the old parties. We're building a team of 360 volunteers to make sure we've got polling day totally covered. If each of those people can do just 10 hours over the course of the final 10 weeks of the campaign, we'll have surpassed the 3250 volunteer hours we need to knock on the thousands of doors and make the thousands of calls to reach enough of the voters of Melbourne to shift the 5,000 new votes we need to win this campaign. That will go a long way in inoculating our campaign from the impact of the old parties colluding on preferences and the media locking us out of debate.[15]

The result proved, as Bandt would say later, that the only sure way for the Greens to gain and hold lower-house seats was to beat the major parties at their own game, winning the primary vote rather than relying on coming second and getting over the line with preferences from one of the majors.

Despite Bandt's stunning win, the Greens' remarkable run of growth was over. No party in federal politics had ever before increased its vote in five successive elections, as the Greens had done from 1998 to 2010. Now political analysts pondered whether the party's vote had peaked. Academic Narelle Miragliotta, for example, wrote:

> Without a major realignment of the party system, it will be difficult for the Greens to diversify their base of support beyond their natural 'post-materialist' constituency (estimated by some scholars to be around 10 per cent of the electorate). The Greens vote, it seems, may have reached its natural plateau.[16]

Compounding the electoral pain, the 2013 election marked the rise of new micro-parties, including mining mogul Clive Palmer's Palmer United Party, which won Senate seats in Queensland and Tasmania, and the Sunshine Coast seat of Fairfax, helped by Greens preferences. The preference deal negotiated by Palmer and Ben Oquist helped elect Hanson-Young and Ludlam, but was hugely controversial among Queensland Greens, who felt that they had launched the career of a charlatan. The party's candidate for Fairfax resigned in protest, and the deal rankled for years. As well as PUP, the 2013 election was a win for randoms like the Liberal Democrats in New South Wales, who got the donkey vote, the Australians Sports Party in Western Australia, and the Australian Motoring Enthusiasts Party, whose candidate, Ricky Muir, was elected in Victoria on just 0.5 per cent of the primary vote as a result of Glenn Druery's preference deals. The Greens' primary vote also suffered from the rise of micro-parties on the left, including the Animal Justice Party, which was contesting its first federal election campaign on a live export ban, putting up Senate candidates in Queensland and the ACT.

A fortnight after the disappointing election, Milne was re-elected leader unopposed at the first party room meeting in Canberra, and Bandt returned as deputy. Di Natale was poised to take over from Sarah Hanson-Young as party room chair, but she decided to force a ballot. She got one vote – her own. Storming out of the meeting, Hanson-Young walked past a table of journalists at Aussies Cafe at Parliament House and told them that, under Milne's leadership, the party was 'marching to a slow death' – comments that found their way straight into *The Age*. Rumours that Bandt had sounded out his colleagues for a challenge, in which Hanson-Young would have been his deputy, were denied on all sides, but they were true.[17]

Two days after the party room meeting, Milne's chief of staff, Ben Oquist, issued a public statement citing 'fundamental differences of opinion [between him and Milne] about strategy'. Behind the scenes, Milne had told Oquist she would not be renewing his contract – she wanted a flatter, more collegiate structure. Oquist was furious and, Milne believes, told *Lateline* host Tony Jones that there had been a resulting walk-out of staff from the leader's office. It was true that five staff were leaving – including policy director Clare Ozich, the communications director, and senior economics, climate and campaigns advisers – but that is normal post-election, when political staff often take advantage of generous redundancies, and the departures had nothing to do with Oquist. Ozich, for example, had long been planning to leave and remained extremely loyal to Milne. But when Jones put it to Milne on air that night, she felt ambushed and unable to respond without breaching the privacy of her employees, some of whom were being let go involuntarily. That day, as it happened, Oquist was leaving the country for Germany and so there could be no follow-up queries on his story. 'It was a terrible fabrication,' says Milne, 'to suggest, as many did, that he had led a walk-out of senior staff. Nothing could be further from the truth. Ben doing that to me was just disgraceful, and especially as he was about to get on a plane to Germany, on a trip to Europe, which I had authorised. He basically stabbed me in the back.' Milne's relationship with Oquist has never recovered. The media smelt blood, and there was soon a swirl of speculation that her leadership was terminal. Pushed by reporters, Bob Brown refused to take sides between two of his staunchest friends and allies, and declined to defend his successor when media asked him whether he thought Milne was doing a good job as leader. 'Sorry, I just have no comment,' Brown told *The Mercury*.[18] Brown says now he thought that Milne *was* doing a good job, adding 'she is the finest parliamentary companion I ever had'. But Milne was hurt, and to the public it certainly looked as though the writing was on the wall for her.

Of all in the party room, it was Lee Rhiannon who came out and defended Milne publicly, saying she had not been canvassed, there was no challenge and everyone was responsible for the election result, not just the leader. While backgrounding against Milne continued, the party set about its election review ahead of the national conference, to be held in two months' time.

*   *   *

In Tasmania, the tide was also going out on the Labor/Green government of Premier Lara Giddings. The Greens' historic achievement of taking ministries in the minority government of Premier David Bartlett, then of Giddings after he resigned early on, had proved a mixed blessing. In a repeat of the experience under the Labor–Green Accord 20 years earlier, Tasmania's financial situation turned parlous as state revenues dived by $1.5 billion in the wake of the GFC. When Bartlett resigned unexpectedly at the end of 2010, Giddings took over as premier and treasurer, and it was clear the 2011–12 budget would be austere. 'The state was going broke,' McKim recalls, 'there was no doubt we needed a tough budget.' Just as in the Accord years, education came in for spending cuts, with budget papers flagging the closure of up to 20 local schools.[19] After consulting experts and local communities, McKim took the view that some school closures were justifiable on educational grounds. Tasmania tended to languish at the bottom of league tables on educational outcomes, partly for socioeconomic reasons, but also because there were too many tiny schools, McKim says – including one high school with just 16 students. In the end, no closures were forced, but seven agreed to close. 'The simple fact is if you consolidate your schools, more children get access to highly trained and expert teachers in the area of their expertise,' he says. 'It was politically toxic, but justifiable on merit.'

McKim's approach was much more pragmatic than the over-her-dead-body stand Christine Milne had taken in defence of small country schools two decades earlier – and was emblematic of the compromises inherent in going into government. 'The problem, in hindsight, was that it was done as a budget measure,' McKim says. 'It should have been an education measure.'

Another fraught area was prison reform, which fell to McKim as corrections minister. He wanted to run a human rights–based prison system, and commissioned a ground-up review by former Australian Federal Police commissioner Mick Palmer. McKim wound up clashing with the unions representing prison wardens and other staff, chiefly United Voice and the Community and Public Sector Union. 'I inherited an absolute basket case where the unions were absolutely running the joint,' says McKim. 'They were acting illegally on a daily basis, by putting people in solitary confinement. There was one guy that was in solitary confinement for 13 days, and the prison management didn't even know about it – it was the people on the shop floor that were doing it.' A showdown loomed when McKim removed the heavy-handed Tactical Response Group from Risdon Prison, triggering an escalating industrial dispute in which 56 staff were stood down. McKim took the extraordinary step of requesting correctional services staff from Western Australia be put on standby, leading to accusations he used scab labour, which he denied.[20]

By far the most difficult issue of the Tasmanian Greens' four years in government, however, was the forestry peace deal, which divided the environmental movement and the party itself. After Gunns sued for peace in 2010, the forestry industry, unions and environmental NGOs had spent three years hammering out a compromise, the Tasmanian Forest Agreement, which was then put to parliament to be enacted in legislation. In exchange for ongoing subsidies of $350 million, the TFA expanded the Tasmanian World Heritage Area by 170,000 hectares, and stopped construction of a loop road that would have carved a swathe through the Tarkine, conditional on an end to substantial active protests against logging under a 'durability clause'.

The five Greens MPs were united when the bill was first introduced, and fought to ensure that Labor did not erode any of the environmental gains. 'Then it went upstairs,' recalls McKim, 'and the upper house took a chainsaw to it …'

They basically carved out the reserves into two tranches [and] said the second tranche you have to wait for a few years. So that was when the legislation changed so that it no longer totally reflected the agreement that had been struck between the NGOs, the unions and the timber industry. That made it difficult for us.

Bob Brown objected both to the forest concessions and to the durability clause that silenced protesters – he considered it fundamentally undemocratic – and called on the Greens to block the revised TFA, saying the party and the NGOs had been 'outmanoeuvred'. In a May 2013 essay for the *Tasmanian Times*, so did author Richard Flanagan:

> I lived with the silence of Tasmania for too many years. And now the leaders of The Wilderness Society, Environment Tasmania, the Australian Conservation Foundation and the Tasmanian Greens have signed up to a deal that seeks to achieve what even Gunns failed in doing: silencing the rage Tasmanians felt with the destruction of their land and the corruption of public life that for a time became its necessary corollary. It is perhaps the greatest own goal in Australian political history.[21]

McKim and O'Connor, as cabinet ministers, made the difficult decision to support it, and were supported by Paul O'Halloran and Tim Morris. Kim Booth crossed the floor, voting with the Liberal opposition, saying the bill 'went too far in terms of undermining the fundamental principles of free speech, democracy and protection of parks and conservation reserves'. The Tasmanian Greens maintained that their decision had been the right one, and even now both McKim and O'Connor say that if the party hadn't been in parliament, and sitting in cabinet, the Tasmanian World Heritage Area would not have been extended by 170,000 hectares. But they also acknowledge the damage. 'It did cause serious fractures within the party and the conservation movement down here,' says O'Connor, 'and they haven't been entirely healed, [but] I wouldn't change a thing.'

A day before calling the 2014 election, Premier Giddings called in McKim and O'Connor and sacked them, citing fundamental philosophical differences, in what the opposition called a 'fake divorce'.[22] With the loss of two seats, the Greens' vote plunged from 21 per cent to 12.7 per cent. Labor was thrown out, and the Liberals'

Will Hodgman swept to power on a 12 per cent swing, winning 15 seats out of 25. 'As always we got a touch-up after balance of power, it's happened every time down here,' says McKim. 'It happened when Bob was leader. It happened when Christine was leader, and it happened when I was leader.' Which was true, although the 8 per cent swing against the Greens in 2014 was much worse than the party had suffered in either 1998 or 1992.

At the 2014 South Australian election, Jay Weatherill's first as premier, there was a small swing against the Greens but leader Mark Parnell scraped back into the Legislative Council. The Greens were on the back foot everywhere, it seemed.

*   *   *

Milne tried to turn the Greens' disappointing election results to her advantage by pressing for a radical overhaul of the party. She hoped to resolve the long-running problems she and Brown believed were inherent in the Greens' structure as a confederation, and the financial strength of the larger state branches compared to the smaller state branches. The reform push had its genesis in mid-2013, when Labor proposed that public funding from federal elections would go straight to the national party organisations. The Australian Greens jumped at the chance to take control of this major funding stream. Election funding from the AEC went to the state parties, and in New South Wales was further divided between the state organisation (for every Senate vote cast) and the local branches, which received funding for each vote cast in their electorate.[23] Rhiannon, as the party's democracy portfolio holder, had carriage of the bill and was negotiating with the government for the administration funding to go to state parties, with some to the national level, consistent with a previous decision of the Australian Greens conference, when ABC's *7.30* program revealed Milne had been secretly negotiating with the Labor government for the funds to be paid entirely to the national level. Milne persuaded the party room that she should handle negotiations herself. Rhiannon says the NSW Greens prepared for battle, 'incensed by the attempt to change the party's structure through legislation, rather than through party decisions'. The crisis was averted when the Coalition dropped its support for Labor's bill and the government dumped the reforms.[24]

Labor's electoral reforms were dumped after Tony Abbott reneged on a promise of bipartisan support, but the Greens' federal parliamentary party room had prepared a three-page discussion paper setting out an ambitious overhaul of the party's constitution. Included on the to-do list were items that had been bugbears for Milne and Brown since the beginning: an online strategy to allow direct communication between the Australian Greens and members, unmediated by the state branches; a national membership, and member referendums; a national registration with the federal electoral commission (doing away with registrations in New South Wales, Queensland and Western Australia); a new funding model to give more money to smaller state branches; a restructured national conference and national council, with a trebling of representation from the parliamentary party room; all MPs to have a conscience vote; constitutional recognition of the leader of the Australian Greens, elected by the MPs; more latitude for delegates to national council or conference to make decisions; and no term limits for office bearers.[25] Milne took up the cudgel – and as with the constitutional debates a decade earlier, and a decade before that, when the party was first forming, there was immediate pushback from the larger states, not just New South Wales but also Queensland and Western Australia.

In February 2014 the High Court ordered a fresh half-Senate election be held in Western Australia, after a disastrous bungle by the Australian Electoral Commission saw more than a thousand ballot papers lost. At risk was Scott Ludlam, who had just scraped in in 2013 but was seen as a potential leader, having established something of a cult following among Greens nationally. Ludlam was a bridge between the more radical and mainstream wings of the party, and had built a new constituency for the party among tech-savvy millennials through his staunch advocacy of digital rights. A deft social media campaigner backed up by loyal and talented staff, Ludlam had defeated Labor communications minister Stephen Conroy's proposed internet filter. Now he was fighting for his political life. Happily, he had plenty of material to work with: new prime minister Tony Abbott's electoral honeymoon had soured in record time.

In an electrifying adjournment speech to a near-empty Senate chamber in March, Scott Ludlam looked to the fresh Senate election as an early opportunity for West Australians to send a message to Canberra. Ludlam's speech was squarely addressed to a WA audience, but it was not parochial. It was steeped in Greens history and was a powerful expression of Green values, but it was not partisan. It tapped into the popular backlash against the Abbott government and the prime minister personally. Temperamentally shy and softly spoken, Ludlam delivered his speech carefully and precisely, and with all due respect to the Senate president. But his well-crafted sentences were savage. Ludlam showed that, when backed into a corner by Abbott's relentless denialist right-wing assault, the Greens would not cower but fight.

Ludlam invited the prime minister to come campaigning in Western Australia with his 'excruciatingly boring three-word slogans' and his east-coast caricature of West Australia as a redneck backwater. 'Every time you refer to us as the "mining state",' Ludlam warned, 'as though the western third of our ancient continent is just Gina Rinehart's inheritance to be chopped, benched and blasted, you are reading us wrong.' To be blunt, Ludlam continued, 'the reason that I extend this invitation to you, Mr Prime Minister, to spend as much time as you can spare in Western Australia is that every time you open your mouth the Green vote goes up'.

Ludlam reached back to his mentor and predecessor in the Senate, Jo Vallentine, who 30 years earlier had been elected for the Nuclear Disarmament Party, becoming the 'first representative of what was to become the Greens'. He went on:

> She came into this place as a lone Western Australian representative speaking out against the nuclear weapons that formed the foundations of the geopolitical suicide pact we dimly remember as the Cold War. Since the first day of Senator Vallentine's first term, the Greens have been articulating a vision of Australia as it could be – an economy running on infinite flows of renewable energy; a society that never forgets it lives on country occupied by the planet's oldest continuing civilisation; and a country that values education, innovation and equality. These values are still at the heart of our work …

Ludlam called on all West Australians – not just Greens voters – to think carefully about the balance of power in the Senate:

> What is at stake here, in the most immediate sense, is whether or not Prime Minister Tony Abbott has total control of this parliament in coming years. But I have come to realise that it is about much more than that. We want our country back. Through chance, misadventure and, somewhere, a couple of boxes of misplaced ballot papers, we have been given the opportunity to take back just one seat on 5 April, and a whole lot more in 2016. Game on, Prime Minister. See you out west.

In just over seven and a half minutes, Ludlam had spelt out exactly what the Greens were about – marking himself out as a future leader – and had drawn a line in the sand against the Abbott government, which he predicted would be short-lived. The heartfelt speech took off on social media – within weeks it had been watched by 850,000 people on Facebook and YouTube – and lit a fire under the Greens' campaign in the Western Australia. The party rallied to save Ludlam, hurling nationwide resources at the state campaign, harnessing thousands of volunteers to hand out how-to-vote cards, knock on 20,000 doors and call 50,000 voters directly from phone banks. The result was a massive 6 per cent swing and a primary vote of 15.6 per cent – the highest statewide vote the Greens have ever achieved on the mainland.

In the lead-up to the Abbott government's first budget, it flagged a deficit levy on high-income earners. Christine Milne joined Labor in opposing a broken promise not to introduce new taxes, but internally the Greens were divided. 'Senator Milne's been out since day one saying she doesn't support [the tax], despite the fact it is Greens party policy,' a party source told one newspaper, pointing out that the tax was progressive. 'Her response hasn't gone down well with a number of key people in the party and the membership. She's now trying to work out what to do as she is set to be rolled in party room on it.'[26]

Milne prevailed, however, and the party confirmed its opposition on budget day, on the basis that it was a temporary levy, while the cuts to welfare were not. Paradoxically, on budget eve, when the government flagged it would seek to reintroduce fuel excise indexation – a regressive change – Milne supported it on environmental grounds, causing the party more consternation. The Greens were also at odds over Abbott's signature plan for paid parental leave, which was comparable with the party's own policy. When the budget was handed down, however, it was brutal, and the room for negotiation all but disappeared.

For starters, the budget simply axed $80 billion of health and education spending over a decade, sending the states and territories towards a fiscal cliff. Other blunt measures included a $7 Medicare co-payment, full university fee deregulation, lifting the pension age to 70, and welfare cuts particularly for the young, who would have to wait six months before they could get Newstart payments. 'Big business is quarantined completely as the community pays,' said Milne. 'And in particular it is young people and sick people who are going to pay the most.'[27] There were also cuts to the ABC, SBS and the CSIRO, and the Clean Energy Finance Corporation and the Australian Renewable Energy Agency (known as ARENA) were to be abolished. Simultaneously, in line with Abbott's predilection for road funding, and a step up from his pre-election commitments, the budget also announced extra billions for three contentious tollways: Sydney's WestConnex, Melbourne's East West Link and the Perth Freight Link. A public backlash against each project would drive successful state Greens campaigns in coming years.

In her budget statement, Milne said that in her 25 years of politics, the Abbott budget was 'in a category of its own … the nation is reeling as people come to terms with the extent to which the Prime Minister has shafted and lied to people and led those who believed in him like lambs to the slaughter'. Still wielding the balance of power until the new Senate sat from 1 July 2014, the Greens proposed to block a raft of measures and, like opposition leader Bill Shorten, dare Abbott to call a double-dissolution election. The Abbott government warned the incoming crossbenchers that if they obstructed the budget, they would be wiped out in a double-dissolution that would be held in 2015, after mooted electoral reform to abolish group voting tickets.

Anger mounted around the country as the implications sank in, with thousands rallying in major capitals the next weekend. In

Melbourne, deputy Greens leader Adam Bandt called on Labor and Palmer United to ally with the Greens to force a new election and 'have Tony Abbott out of office by Christmas'.[28] The government's polls collapsed and never recovered in what was reportedly the worst reception of a federal budget in decades.[29]

Milne's budget reply had cited analysis by the architect of the HECS student loans program, Bruce Chapman, which showed that, after deregulation, the fees for a nursing degree would jump from $18,000 to $89,000, and for an engineering degree from $26,000 to $106,800. It would take students 43 years to pay off their debt and their interest bill, compared to an average of ten years currently. Within a few weeks, the Greens' education spokesperson, Lee Rhiannon, had launched a new website, whatwillmydegreecost.com.au, which was accessed a million times on its first day, and showed the average fee increase was $44,500 and the average increase in HECS repayment time was five years.[30] A colossal fightback was ramping up – but there were soon internal arguments as to how the Greens should go about opposing the budget.

In New South Wales, Rhiannon and John Kaye proposed an 'emergency grassroots members consultation' to discuss whether the Australian Greens should block supply. In *Green Voice*, Hall Greenland wrote that after 1 July the non-government senators could combine and refuse to pass the budget. 'This is constitutional and has been done before,' he wrote, 'in 1975 when it was used to bring down the Whitlam government ... By blocking the budget, we will be saying that democracy cannot be treated with such contempt.' New South Wales MP David Shoebridge argued that contrary to public opinion, 'blocking supply' was not an all or nothing tactic. The Senate could oppose specific measures, whether or not they were contained in the budget's appropriation bills, either by amending them or by requesting amendments and refusing to pass them unless they were agreed to in the House.[31] Milne said the idea was 'awesomely stupid politics', and that the party could 'block this brutal budget without creating dangerous unintended consequences'.[32] It raised a very real question: how far would the Greens go to stop hated budget measures? Would the party provoke a constitutional crisis, comparable with 1975?

For Bob Brown, looking back, talk of blocking supply was simply beyond the pale:

We had a group of NSW parliamentarians who were publicly campaigning for the Australian Greens to block the budget, to bring down a government that had been elected for less than a year, for what purpose? It would have been a disaster. This was the same group of people that have always said the Australian Greens should not comment on NSW affairs, but when it comes to Australian Greens affairs, were publicly running a campaign which wasn't responsible [and] which was not what the leader, Christine Milne, at the time was saying.

The Greens' public wrangling over the budget worsened over the party's opposition to fuel excise indexation, which would have cost average households an extra 40–60 cents a week. After initially supporting the change, Milne had later made it conditional on hypothecation of the revenue to fund public transport, after a heated party-room debate in which her deputy, Bandt, along with Peter Whish-Wilson and Scott Ludlam, had prevailed, arguing it was regressive. Now Rhiannon was pushing back on it too, writing to New South Wales members ahead of a national council meeting, and flagging that she may be bound by policy to cross the floor.[33] The government decided to sidestep the Senate by regulating the indexation, deferring the need for legislation for a year. Brick by brick, however, the first Abbott budget was crumbling, leaving a gaping hole with what would be called 'zombie measures' – savings held up in the Senate.

A week before the sitting of the new Senate, in which Palmer United's three senators would wield the balance of power, another of Abbott's policies tanked when former US vice-president Al Gore joined Clive Palmer himself at an unlikely press conference in the federal parliament's Great Hall. The billionaire coalminer announced that although his party would vote down the emissions-trading scheme, it would try to reintroduce something similar later, and would in the meantime save the Clean Energy Finance Corporation, the Climate Change Authority and the Renewable Energy Target.

It was a bolt from the blue, engineered by the former ACF chief Don Henry, who was close to Gore, and Ben Oquist, who had become executive director of the Australia Institute and an adviser to former independent Tony Windsor.[34] For the country's climate policy, it was a huge win as both the CEFC and the RET in particular would go on to deliver millions of tonnes of greenhouse-gas emissions reductions.

For many Greens, however, Oquist's collaboration with Palmer was the last straw, ending his decades-long relationship with the party and killing off any prospect he could come back as a staffer or a candidate. Milne was completely blindsided, and wrote in her memoir that it was the most bizarre event of 2014. She could understand the tactical motives of Henry and Oquist, but could not believe that Gore would 'give credibility and political cover to a coal baron who had stood for election to destroy carbon pricing ... [Gore's] credibility in Australia was all but destroyed in a single day.'[35]

*   *   *

There is no doubt the growing backlash against the right-wing extremism of the Abbott government – an Australian prefiguring of US president Donald Trump – re-energised the Greens and progressive politics more broadly. At a Greens Political Education Trust meeting in Sydney's inner west, on a panel alongside Lee Rhiannon and Adam Bandt, soon-to-be preselection candidate and staunch unionist Jim Casey welcomed the new activism, saying he would:

> ... prefer to see Tony Abbott returned as prime minister, with a labour movement that was growing, with an anti-war movement that was disrupting things in the streets, with a strong and vital women's movement, indigenous movement, and a climate change movement that was actually starting to disrupt production of coal. I'd prefer to see Abbott as prime minister in that environment, than Bill Shorten as prime minister without it.[36]

When Gough Whitlam died that October, the NSW Greens' Hall Greenland provoked the righteous fury of Labor heavies, including left luminary Anthony Albanese, by claiming the Greens were 'Gough's children', and that it was the party that 'takes up where

Gough left off' in espousing free education; Lee Rhiannon posted a Greens logo under an image of Whitlam to Facebook. As Shaun Crowe's *Whitlam's Children* recounts, Albanese called a press conference to denounce the Greens' cheap shot, describing Whitlam as 'a Labor man his entire life'; Bill Shorten phoned Milne to demand the image be taken down.[37] It was more than a spat: Labor, too, was re-energising in opposition and rediscovering its policy courage. The contrast between Whitlam the visionary – the founder of Medicare and so much else – and Abbott the wrecker was plain for all progressive voters to see, and intensely painful. On Whitlam's death, Australians were reminded what politics was supposed to be about.

After November's national conference in Canberra, Milne emerged with an announceable party reform: a new 25-person national council, made up of representatives from the party room, state and territory branches and office bearers, which would meet ten times a year rather than two to streamline policymaking and campaigning. Milne hailed the new council as a cabinet-style structure that would 'professionalise how we work and make us much quicker and more effective'.[38] To this day she counts the reform as one of the most significant parts of her legacy as leader, and believes it is changing the culture of the party over time.

Hall Greenland, however, points out that the new national council fell far short of the constitutional overhaul Milne had touted a year earlier – in fact, the constitution was hardly changed. He wrote in a blog post that the 'tension between federalists and centralisers, between a bottom-up and a top-down concept of the party, has a long history in the Australian Greens. For the most part, the former have prevailed.' The reform did nothing to stop leadership speculation around Milne, which had flared sporadically since the response to the budget. In an op-ed, the Australia Institute's chief economist, Richard Denniss, wrote that under Milne the party's strategy of 'voting against virtually everything the Abbott government announces, including things they actually support, has made them largely irrelevant since the last election'.[39]

The party got a boost from the Victorian election. There was no swing to the Greens to speak of – in the lower house the party's primary vote was steady at 11.5 per cent, and in the upper house it dropped slightly to 11 per cent, with primary votes leaking to the Animal Justice Party, the Cyclists Party, Voluntary Euthanasia and the Basics Rock'n'Roll Party, which took a combined 3 per cent. Otherwise, Green voters may also have backed the Sex Party, whose founder, Fiona Patten, was elected on a 2.6 per cent primary vote. Nonetheless, the left micro-parties fed preferences back to the Greens, whose representation in the state parliament jumped from three to seven.

The key breakthrough was winning the inner-city lower-house seats of Melbourne, which sat wholly within Bandt's federal electorate but had been Labor for a century, and trendy Prahran, in the inner south-east. In Melbourne, the party had preselected climate activist and former CSIRO scientist Ellen Sandell, who campaigned hard against the East West Link, which would carve up several inner suburbs, as well as Royal Park and the Melbourne Zoo, and had a negative benefit–cost ratio of an 80-cent return for every dollar invested. For Sandell, the East West Link campaign was a perfect example of how the Greens could drag Labor to the left by threatening their hold on inner-city seats. The party was able to force Labor to shift its position – from initial support, to support only if contracts were signed, to tearing up contracts and stopping the project dead, which is what ultimately happened. Sandell won a 9 per cent swing, topping the primary vote with 41 per cent, even though two-thirds of Liberal preferences went to the second-placed Labor candidate.

Although the Melbourne victory was not unexpected, the win in Prahran was hugely significant: for the first time in the country, the party had taken a lower-house seat off the Liberals, showing that the Greens were not simply going to cannibalise the progressive vote and eat away at Labor's parliamentary representation. It was a close-run thing. The Greens' candidate, Sam Hibbins, a Stonnington councillor for the party, came third despite a 5 per cent swing, but scraped together enough preferences to sneak into second place by just 31 votes, and then won on Labor preferences by a narrow margin of just 0.4 per cent. Victorian Greens leader Greg Barber's 'bite and hold' strategy was vindicated.

The 2014 breakthrough result was also credited to a ground-up constitutional review started in the wake of the disappointing state election result four years earlier. Engagement and coordination between local branches and the Victorian Greens had been clogged by a middle layer of regional groups, which had to be abolished, turning the state office into an organising, campaigning power-house. Then state director Samantha Ratnam, a Sri Lanka–born aid worker and doctoral candidate in social science, who was heavily involved in the consultation through 2011, recalls that the constitutional changes had to be approved by 90 per cent of members. When they got up overwhelmingly, Ratnam recalls, 'it was a really big moment' that laid the groundwork for the later electoral success. With the Tasmanian Greens faltering and the Victorian Greens surging ahead, the party's centre of gravity was shifting from Hobart to Melbourne.

The Greens' momentum carried through to the New South Wales election of March 2015. Liberal premier Mike Baird was campaigning on an unpopular $20 billion privatisation of the state's electricity networks, which the NSW Greens' unofficial leader, John Kaye, opposed relentlessly. Kaye was easily re-elected to the upper house, along with number two Mehreen Faruqi. Balmain MP Jamie Parker was comfortably returned, making his electorate a safe one, and in Newtown Jenny Leong, inspired partly by the success of her Melbourne colleagues, ran hard on opposition to the giant WestConnex tollway, which would cut through Sydney's inner west. She was elected with the highest primary vote recorded by any Green in the country: 45 per cent.

It was the fight against coal seam gas that spurred the Greens' most surprising success of the 2015 election, however, which came from the Northern Rivers seats of Ballina and Lismore. Firebrand Jeremy Buckingham was the face of the Greens campaign, working with Justin Field of the loose 'Lock the Gate' network, which urged farmers to resist the gas fracking industry that had taken off in Queensland, posing a risk to groundwater and threatening to turn some of the state's most fertile farmlands into a pin-cushion of wells and access roads and pipelines. Buckingham was a tattooed, sweary, pot-smoking anti-politician, a former stonemason and musician who could talk to farmers and whose tireless on-the-ground campaigning built up the fourth-biggest social media profile of any Greens MP in the country, posting stunt videos that regularly went viral, like sitting in a dinghy on a creek bubbling with methane from a riverbed cracked by fracking, and lighting the gas on fire.

Buckingham used the coal seam gas issue to drive a stake into the heart of the Nationals in northern New South Wales, exposing their sellout of agriculture in favour of mining interests. The 'Stop CSG' campaign culminated in the Bentley blockade of 2014, at which thousands of protesters rallied to stop approved exploratory drilling by Metgasco. Supported by feral greenies and conservative farmers alike, the Bentley blockade was to the anti-fossil-fuels campaign what Jabiluka was to the anti-nuclear movement, or the Franklin was to the 'No Dams' campaigners, or Terania Creek was to the anti-loggers before that: an epic, euphoric victory against a powerful opponent, in the Greens' best protest tradition, which would inspire future campaigners to action.

On the back of the campaign, the Greens surged in the two Nationals-held seats of Ballina, won by Tamara Smith, whose primary vote jumped 5 per cent to 27 per cent, and Lismore, where candidate Adam Guise got a swing of 7 per cent, placing him second on primaries with 26 per cent, and in the running to win it. On the night of the election, at the Grandstand at the Sydney University Oval, Greens supporters were ecstatic at the swag of lower-house seats, chanting 'Four, four, four, four!'[40] The next day, with the Greens still ahead in Lismore, commentators called it the party's best result in any state or territory, and deputy Liberal leader Gladys Berejiklian put the boot into the ALP, saying, 'I think it demonstrates [that there are] question marks over what people think Labor stands for.'[41] John Kaye told *The Australian* the results boded well for the party in the federal seats of Sydney, Grayndler, Richmond and Page, and said Labor had 'taken its progressive voters for granted for too long and now we think they've lost them'.[42] Asked whether the Greens would appoint a leader – which they would have been forced to do, had they finished with ten MPs – Kaye said the party rejected the idea. 'We have run a flat structure since there was one of us in 1995,' he said. 'We want to continue to do that ... we don't need fancy titles.'[43]

By the end of the count, however, the Greens had fallen just short in Lismore, and had not won a third upper-house seat, leaving them with a party room of eight MPs – three in the Legislative Assembly and five in the Legislative Council. Despite the Greens' surge, and the Animal Justice Party winning its first seat, the balance of power in the upper house was in the hands of the Shooters and Fishers Party and the two Christian Democrats seats controlled by the 80-year-old Fred Nile, whom Kaye called the 'pilot fish of the lunar right'.[44]

*   *   *

Within weeks of the New South Wales result, federal Greens leader Christine Milne decided it was time to move on after 25 years in state and federal politics. As she wrote later, she was approaching her 62nd birthday, had a grandchild about to be born and knew she could not serve a third six-year term, particularly knowing there would be no progress in climate policy for the foreseeable future. There had been speculation within the party about whether she would hand over after the 2016 election. Confiding only in her family and closest staff, Milne planned the most clinical of exits ahead of the May 2015 budget: there would be no valedictory speech, only a final appearance at the National Press Club.

Who would succeed her as leader? Milne's memoir is silent on the preparatory talks that took place, but there are persistent suggestions that she quietly sounded out Scott Ludlam for the role, yet he didn't feel ready. Neither Ludlam nor Milne will talk about their private discussions, although both confirm that they did speak before her announcement, and he subsequently became co-deputy leader. Adam Bandt, Milne's deputy, was not told.

On the morning that Milne announced her departure to her colleagues in the party room, at 11.30 a.m., there was shell-shock, and then a moment of uncertainty: who would put their hand up? According to Lee Rhiannon it was soon very clear what was going on. 'At the start of a scheduled party room meeting Christine announced that she was resigning as leader and that the party room would adjourn for about an hour for the MPs to discuss the matter and then we would meet again for the ballot,' she noted. Before adjourning, Di Natale indicated that he would nominate for the position of leader. It was also widely assumed that Bandt, then the deputy leader, would most likely nominate to be leader. Rhiannon observed:

In that one hour when people like Scott and Larissa would not return calls some of us concluded that the change over to the new leadership team had been agreed to by an inner circle. That was confirmed when the party room reconvened. It was clear Adam did not have enough support and he chose not to nominate, leaving Richard as the only nominee. Larissa and Scott then put their hand up for co-deputies. Now, you're only going to put your hand up to be co-deputies if you've already worked it out together. That doesn't just happen when you're sitting in a meeting. The impression was that Christine, Richard, Larissa, Scott and Rachel (who retained the position of whip), had it all worked out. It was already signed off. In the end there was only a single nomination for each position.

Straight after the meeting, Lee Rhiannon went on Sky News and complained that she 'personally would have liked more time', and said the party had 'learned some lessons today'.

That afternoon, at his first press conference as leader, Di Natale told journalists who pressed him repeatedly: 'Someone may have been disappointed with the outcome ... surprise, surprise. That's politics, right?' Bandt, who was dumped as deputy, tweeted bravely: 'Congrats Richard & new team! V happy to hand over Deputy to focus on new baby (due in few wks!) & winning further Reps seats in Vic & NSW.' Ludlam, asked in subsequent days why he didn't want the top job, said only: 'I think Richard is a better bet, to be honest.'[45]

For the most part, the media was content to move on, marvelling at the minor party's bloodless coup, and the absence of backgrounding and intrigue. Commentators paid tribute to Milne, including her former chief of staff Ben Oquist, who graciously described her on ABC Radio as a 'colossus of Australian politics' who had achieved a great deal for the Greens and the country, and was 'going out on a high'. Milne's voice nearly cracked during her final speech as leader as she thanked her Tasmanian supporters, after railing against the periods of neoliberalism that had bookended her political career. 'It is a humbling experience to carry the hopes of people for a more caring society and a life-sustaining planet on my shoulders,' Milne said, and finished by quoting a few famous lines from Thoreau. The 'cabin passage' was not for her or the Greens, Milne claimed, urging her party to 'enjoy this moment in Australian politics when the old neoliberal order is crumbling and what replaces it is being actively imagined in order to give our planet and people a safe climate and future'.[46]

CHAPTER 11

THE REAL OPPOSITION

The rise of Richard Di Natale represented a new era for the Greens. A medical doctor who had worked in Aboriginal communities and in India, Di Natale was not an activist, was not of the environmental movement and was not from Tasmania. A former footballer from a working-class migrant family, Di Natale's extended family had voted Labor, and as a 12-year-old he had idolised Bob Hawke for saving the Franklin. But his faith in the ALP was shaken as economic rationalism took a toll on migrant communities. After reading Bob Brown and Peter Singer's *The Greens* – picked up by chance – he had joined the party. When he took over the leadership, Di Natale told journalists he was no ideologue, and that in his view the Greens were 'the natural home of progressive, mainstream Australian voters'. In his view, there was majority support for many of the Greens' key policy positions – tougher action on climate change, humane treatment of asylum seekers, marriage equality: areas where both the old parties were actually lagging behind the electorate. He set a target for the Greens to lift the party's primary vote to 20 per cent within a decade. The Greens could draw support from disappointed Labor and Coalition supporters, he said. 'I think there are a lot of people who are small-L Liberal voters who have got strong concerns about the direction of the country and I want to say to them as well that you can trust us with your vote.' It was a centrist pitch, more like the proposition put to voters by the Democrats than by the radical left. For a party full of activists, however, the word 'mainstream' was challenging, and it would dog Di Natale's leadership of the Greens in the years to come. The Australia Institute's Ben Oquist endorsed Di Natale as a new type of activist, pointing to his recent trip to Liberia during the ebola crisis. 'Richard represents a great "generation next" for the Greens,' he said.[1]

On day one, Di Natale signalled that he would be open to dealing with the Coalition if it delivered policy outcomes, which was a nod to critics of his predecessor Christine Milne's intransigence. But the Greens were already heading in that direction: before she resigned, Milne had signalled that she would soften her stance against talks with Prime Minister Tony Abbott.[2] Supporting fuel excise was seen as an early, obvious move. Within a month of Di Natale taking over the leadership, the Greens did a deal with the social services minister, Scott Morrison, on the assets test for the aged pension. Labor cried foul, claiming the Greens had been dudded, and would accuse them of a 'filthy deal' for years to come, but the policy increased pensions for 170,000 poorer full-pensioners by $30 a fortnight and reduced them for 330,000 wealthier part-pensioners who had healthy super balances and owned their own homes. The reform was in line with Greens policy, and that of the Australian Council of Social Service, but nonetheless represented a welfare cut. The Greens also secured a commitment to review retirement incomes, which would later result in significant reform of superannuation concessions. Morrison was duly grateful for the party's support, putting out a press release: 'I commend the Australian Greens, and their new Leader, Senator Di Natale, supported by Senator Siewert, for their constructive engagement with the government.'[3] There would be more deals with the government to come.

One of Di Natale's first decisions was to appoint former New South Wales MP Cate Faehrmann, then chairing Sea Shepherd Australia, as his chief of staff. After battling the left of the NSW Greens for years, as they sought to censure her and Jan Barham for failing to vote in support of party policy on Israel in 2011, Faehrmann was a hardened factional warrior. Now ensconced in the leader's office, she would give no quarter to the 'watermelons' in New South Wales. In July, South Australian senator Penny Wright announced she would resign after four years, to care for her ill son. In her valedictory speech, she looked back over the 20 years since she and her partner, Mark Parnell, had founded the South Australian Greens in 1995, and was encouraged by the 'mature, collegiate' state of the party and the calibre of the people available to fill her position.[4] The party chose political scientist Robert Simms – another man, following Milne's replacement by

Nick McKim, leading to criticisms the gender balance was shifting.

Wright's resignation forced a Greens reshuffle, which Di Natale announced to the party room under the cover of Malcolm Turnbull's coup against Abbott on 15 September 2015. Both Lee Rhiannon and Janet Rice lost some portfolio responsibilities that were given to Simms: Rhiannon lost higher education and water, and Rice lost LGBTI issues and marriage equality. Also under the reshuffle, schools went to Nick McKim, who was controversial inside the party given his record as education minister in Tasmania.[5] The reshuffle outraged the NSW Greens, who took it as a factionally inspired demotion of Rhiannon that was both unfair and unwise, given her profile and connections in the education sector, and her strong track record fighting against $100,000 degrees. Some in the NSW Greens were so furious that they threatened to withhold funding from the Australian Greens for the forthcoming federal election. When the idea came up at the following month's State Delegate Council, it was soundly defeated, but the tensions lingered and spread interstate, with a Melbourne city branch meeting passing a motion that the leader's right to allocate portfolios was inconsistent with the consensus decision-making model of the Greens.[6]

The end of 2015 was the height of the new prime minister Malcolm Turnbull's electoral honeymoon, reflected in stratospheric approval ratings that gave rise to a general assumption that the Coalition would be returned at the next election, whenever it was held. Obstructing Turnbull was a different proposition, politically, than obstructing Abbott had been. Another deal with the government loomed. Starting in early 2015, a Senate committee had held hearings into corporate tax avoidance, grilling executives of giant multinationals from 'big oil' to 'big pharma' to the 'tech majors', exposing how little tax they paid in Australia. It was not just foreign companies, either: BHP Billiton was avoiding tax by running its marketing operations out of Singapore, and the ATO identified Rupert Murdoch's home-grown News Corp as its biggest tax risk. The inquiry had been initiated by Christine Milne the previous year, and was a textbook example of how the party could usher in positive reform even without the balance of power. Labor senator Sam Dastyari, who chaired the inquiry, later acknowledged Milne's 'incredible work' on the committee.[7]

The hearings helped pressure the government to include a series of anti-avoidance measures in the 2015–16 budget.[8] The Coalition and Labor disagreed, however, on how many companies should be subjected to the new reporting requirements. Labor wanted to subject some 900 companies with a turnover above $100 million to the new regime, but as the end of the year neared, the Greens did a deal with the government to raise the threshold to $200 million, allowing two-thirds of those companies off the hook for reporting purposes. 'If we hadn't got this bill passed today,' Di Natale explained when the deal was announced, 'multinational companies would have enjoyed another full year of not having to disclose their tax on a country-by-country basis ... The Greens chose action.'

Labor cried foul, believing that the government would have caved if the Greens had held out. Dastyari said Di Natale had 'sold out a two-year community campaign' for tax transparency, and Senate leader Penny Wong ramped up the partisan rhetoric: 'In the dead of night the Australian Greens sat down with the Treasurer and cut a deal to sell out the crossbench and the Labor Party, cut a deal to sell out Australian taxpayers ... All so they could show that they are players.'[9] When the ATO put out the first disclosures the following March, the information was so opaque, the *Australian Financial Review*'s Neil Chenoweth wrote, that 'it looks like the Greens were dudded ... outplayed'.[10] In later Senate estimates testimony, however, the ATO commissioner Jeremy Hirschhorn described the laws as a 'fantastic success', saying they had raised billions in extra tax revenue.[11]

As all sides geared up for an election in early 2016, an even more fateful decision loomed for the Greens. The powerful Joint Standing Committee on Electoral Matters had unanimously recommended the abolition of the group voting tickets that allowed micro-parties on tiny primary votes – like Ricky Muir's Australian Motoring Enthusiasts Party – to get above a quota through political horse-trading or preference swaps (so-called preference whispering). Abolishing group voting tickets was long-standing Greens policy, and Lee Rhiannon, as the party's democracy spokesperson, sat on the JSCEM, which held an exhaustive inquiry into Senate voting reform, taking more than 200 submissions.[12] Labor's Gary Gray and John Faulkner had backed the reform when it was proposed in 2014, but Tony Abbott had done nothing about it for fear of antagonising the Senate crossbench.

Debate simmered through 2015, and as the possibility of an early election loomed, Labor withdrew its support, leaving the Greens to deal with the government. Right-wing powerbrokers Stephen Conroy and Sam Dastyari went on the attack, accusing the Greens of wanting to disenfranchise small parties. Rhiannon says Labor knew the bill would pass without them, so it took the opportunity for some political point-scoring. She pointed out Labor had no plans to repeal the legislation. The Greens released research from the Parliamentary Library showing that, if recent elections had been held without group voting tickets, and results had instead been based on first preferences, fewer micro-party candidates from the right would have been elected – no Jacqui Lambie, Ricky Muir, Wayne Dropulich or Bob Day in 2013, and no John Madigan in 2010. The upshot was that Labor and the Greens would have controlled the Senate.[13]

When he took over the prime ministership, Turnbull was determined to push the reform through, and was mulling a double-dissolution election. After a sham half-day parliamentary inquiry into the reforms, it came to a crunch in March 2016, in a marathon parliamentary debate that turned into a circus, culminating in a Labor filibuster and an all-night sitting; Senator Nick Xenophon entered the chamber in his pyjamas. Labor's accusations grew ever more shrill, and Scott Ludlam took them head-on:

> One thing that we have been asked a lot, though, over the last few weeks – and I have a bit of sympathy for this question – is: why are the Greens supporting the Turnbull government on anything, let alone a question as sensitive as Senate voting reform? The answer is reasonably simple. We are supporting it because it is substantially our bill. It is a proposal that we championed since well before the geniuses in the Labor Party accidentally elected Senator Steven Fielding to this place in 2004 on a tiny fraction of the vote. Here is the thing: henceforth you, the voter, will decide where your preferences go; not the Sussex Street hacks, who have been screaming the loudest this week. You decide. Candidates are going to have to work for your vote instead of trusting the secret deals done in secret meetings …[14]

Strenuously opposing the reform was the Australia Institute's Richard Denniss, a former party adviser and experienced preference negotiator, who warned Di Natale in a heated exchange that by abolishing group voting tickets, and enabling a double dissolution election, the Greens were opening the door to Pauline Hanson. Nevertheless the reform passed, with the support of the Greens and Xenophon, and most of the ensuing commentary was supportive. Gallery doyen Laurie Oakes wrote that the Senate voting system 'needed to be cleaned up'.[15] When the bill finally came back into the House from the Senate, Labor's Anthony Albanese hit back that the Greens' deal was not so much about high-minded Senate voting reform as it was about preference deals ahead of the coming election:

> We had the prime minister come in here ... He said that he was indebted to the Greens. We know he is indeed indebted on the basis of this legislation. But that is not all, because his Victorian party president, Michael Kroger, has given up details of where he also is indebted, because a part of this arrangement is this bloke and the Greens securing preferences from the Liberal Party in seats that they believe that they can win, and in return the Greens issuing open tickets in marginal seats that the Liberal Party either hopes to hold onto or hopes to win. That is the game here that is really on.[16]

There was a grain of truth to this. The Victorian Greens were negotiating with the Liberal Party, proposing to issue split tickets in suburban marginals in exchange for Liberal preferences in a handful of inner-city seats – Melbourne, Batman and Wills – and there was speculation about Sydney and Grayndler in New South Wales – although if it was happening, it was without any endorsement or authority from the local campaigns, which would have been horrified. Michael Kroger had confirmed the speculation on Sky News:

> You've got a doctor [Di Natale] who owns a farm who doesn't come from this mad environmental background. He's helped the government get legislation through the Federal Parliament. So you look at the Greens through a slightly different lens these days because they're not the nutters they used to be.[17]

This was a significant concession coming from Kroger, who had backed the Liberals' decision in 2010 to preference the Greens behind Labor, but for many on the left it was the kiss of death. Greens convenor Giz Watson insisted there was no deal, and NSW Greens campaign director James Ryan said Albanese's accusation was a 'Labor Party dirty trick', but Victorian Greens director Larissa Brown confirmed talks had been held. 'We won't be preferencing the Liberals,' Brown told the *Herald Sun*; 'an open ticket is asking voters to have a think about who they'd like to vote for.'[18] To help ward off the Greens' threat, Sydney's *Daily Telegraph* soon launched its famous front-page campaign to 'Save Our Albo'.

As they prepared to do battle in the inner cities, the Labor–Greens animus would only intensify. Labor frontbencher Andrew Leigh told researcher Shaun Crowe later that year:

> My guess is that at some stage in my lifetime, the Greens will over-compromise, be electorally wiped out, and the deals they've done in the Senate will prevent them from returning. Effectively the deal they've done in the Senate pulls up the drawbridge on any small parties. They themselves could not have come into existence under the voting laws they've now supported.[19]

There was an element of self-interest for the Greens, vulnerable to the rise of micro-parties like Animal Justice on the left as well as those on the right. A subsequent analysis of the 2016 election results, however, found that smaller parties were not disenfranchised; instead, voters were quick to catch on to the new system.[20]

Regardless of their merits, accusations that the Greens under Di Natale had done a string of dirty deals with the Liberals – on pension cuts, on tax avoidance, on Senate voting reform – were useful ammunition for Labor. Yet beneath all the political sparring, Labor went into the 2016 federal election having lifted key planks of the Greens' policy platform – particularly in its calls for a banking royal commission, and its embrace of reforms to negative gearing and the capital gains tax, designed to improve housing affordability.

The former had been championed by the Greens' treasury spokesperson, Peter Whish-Wilson, who in June 2015 had introduced a motion calling for a royal commission into misconduct in the financial services sector, which the government and Labor had voted down, although Nationals senator John Williams (who had been calling for a royal commission into white-collar crime for years) crossed the floor to support it.[21] As the banking scandals mushroomed, Labor capitulated in the face of white-hot community anger. Ultimately, opposition leader Bill Shorten found the royal commission to be a useful wedge between the Liberals and Nationals in parliament, and a handy debating point during the 2016 election campaign.

The Greens' housing affordability platform had been developed by spokesperson Scott Ludlam, grounded in the experience of Western Australia's boomtime two-tiered market, which pushed rents and prices beyond the reach of most people, especially the young. Negative gearing and capital gains tax concessions that favoured property investors over owner-occupiers – and over first-home buyers in particular – were recognised as unsustainable by many economists, but were assumed to be politically untouchable. Labor did not go as far as the Greens, proposing only to restrict negative gearing to new homes, and to halve the 50 per cent capital gains discount for housing – but it was a concrete example of policy leadership by the minor party, dragging Labor to the left. Speaking after the 2016 election, Di Natale said that when a major party stole the Greens' policies, 'that's a sign of us being successful ... what you are seeing is a huge challenge to the consensus that emerged in recent decades on trickle-down economics, and the Greens have led the charge on that issue'.

In the lead-up to the 2016 election, however, the Greens commissioned focus group polling, which, to the consternation of some on the left of the party, recommended against campaigning on economic issues at all. Lonergan Research had found that the party was not believed when it was talking about the economy, as though it was going beyond its area of expertise. The Greens were becoming a mainstream party, a realistic third choice, but there was a recurring, nagging doubt about their policy platform: *How are they going to fund it?* So in the 2016 election the Greens went to extraordinary lengths to present a fully costed policy platform, submitting 100 confidential policies to the Parliamentary Budget Office.

Turnbull called the election immediately after the May budget, in which he unveiled plans to cut company taxes to 25 per cent. Turnbull's electoral honeymoon had soured spectacularly when he baulked at GST reform in February, and the contest between him and Shorten turned out to be surprisingly competitive. Polling showed the vote for minor parties was heading for an all-time high – even as the Greens' primary vote had slipped from 11 to 10 per cent.[22]

The ABC's Vote Compass online survey suggested Di Natale was performing well as leader: he outranked Bill Shorten on competency and matched Turnbull on trust.[23] In a May interview to mark his first year in the job, Di Natale spelt out the Greens' ambition to serve in cabinet in a future coalition with Labor, and nominated eight lower-house seats the party hoped to hold by 2026: Melbourne, Melbourne Ports, Batman and Wills in Victoria; Sydney, Grayndler and Richmond in New South Wales; and Fremantle in Western Australia.[24]

Di Natale's leadership style was starting to make an impression: early in the year he had done a profile piece for *GQ* magazine, inevitably involving a fashion shoot, and was ribbed mercilessly by Labor's Stephen Conroy about the black skivvy and check pants he wore – was he the 'black Wiggle'? The interview was thoughtful, canvassing Di Natale's pro-science position as a medical doctor – he questioned party shibboleths like the health risks of genetically modified organisms – and his 'never say never' approach to dealing with the Liberals. But the medium was the message: amid *GQ*'s glossy ads for luxury brands, Di Natale came across as a slick pragmatist, not a firebrand radical.[25]

Midway through the campaign, Di Natale suffered a burst of negative publicity when *The Age* ran an erroneous story that he was underpaying a live-in au pair at his family's Otway Ranges farm. All context was left out: having moved from Melbourne, and with her partner away half the year in a demanding new role, Di Natale's wife Lucy was suddenly isolated with two young kids and no family support. Having done everything by the book, Lucy was devastated to see the au pair story wind up in the news – by the end of the campaign she had pneumonia, which Di Natale was convinced was caused partly by the stress. The Greens had no doubt the Labor dirt unit had swung into action. The smear was obvious: a hypocritical yuppie politician exploiting workers. Nine months later, the Press Council ruled the paper had no reasonable basis for claiming the au pair earned as little as $3.75 an hour, but it was too late – some mud had stuck, and Di Natale was forced to field questions about it for months.[26]

One bomb let off during the campaign clearly didn't help: the Greens' long-time NSW treasurer, Chris Harris, and deputy convenor, Carol Vernon, both resigned over the treatment of executive officer Carole Medcalf, who had made a complaint to Fair Work Australia and was dismissed. ABC reporter Conor Duffy broke the story on 7.30, portraying the state branch as 'plagued by animosity and division'. When questioned about it at a press conference, Di Natale stayed cool and batted it off to the state. But to judge by the look on his face, he was enraged.

Although they lobbied for it, the Greens were unable to join one of the leaders' debates with Turnbull and Shorten. Instead, in a first for the party, Di Natale was invited to a regional debate alongside the Nationals' Barnaby Joyce and Labor's regional spokesperson, Joel Fitzgibbon. Held at Goulburn and broadcast on the ABC, the debate was moderated by Chris Uhlmann, who was determined to put the tough questions to Di Natale, just as he had done to Bob Brown years earlier.

> UHLMANN: Can I put a practical point to you, Richard Di Natale? I was in the Northern Territory in 2011 when they shut down the live cattle exports, and at least two land councils had bought into cattle stations and had their investments and their jobs destroyed. They were connected to the real economy. Would you do that to them again?
>
> DI NATALE: What we'd do with live animal exports, let's accept that...
>
> UHLMANN: They were real jobs...
>
> DI NATALE: They were absolutely real jobs, and what we need to do is make sure that if we're going to, when we transition from the live animal export trade we've got to provide real opportunities

for people. They would be ideal to be employed in the Indigenous rangers program, to give them a pathway to long-term jobs …

UHLMANN: Who pays for that? That's a government program, isn't it, you're talking about?

DI NATALE: Absolutely, it's a government program …

UHLMANN: … a kind of welfare as opposed to a job that comes from …

DI NATALE: … hang on, a government program's not welfare, I mean, you know, let's be clear about that, there are many valuable public servants …

UHLMANN: Absolutely …

DI NATALE: … who aren't on welfare, they're doing really important, meaningful work – a teacher who works at a public school is paid for by the government …

UHLMANN: That was not the point …

It was a revealing exchange, betraying deep-seated fears that the Greens were job-destroyers, and suspicion that the party's plans to 'transition' away from industries deemed unsustainable or unacceptable was really code for welfare. When a question about fracking came up, Di Natale hit back at both parties, attacking the 'revolving door' of donations from the fossil-fuel industry to the Coalition and Labor, and questioning whose interests they were really serving. He got rousing applause, his best of the night. Whether Joyce or Fitzgibbon liked it or not, the debate was livelier and more substantial for the Greens' presence.[27]

The Greens' campaign launch, attended by Brown and Milne, was a showy affair, around the theme 'Standing Up for What Matters'. Despite losing a quarter of their public funding as a result of the lower vote at the last election, the Greens were reasonably well funded in 2016. The party had resolved to go into deficit, chewing up half its reserves, and a huge fundraising effort attracted $4.5 million, including 20,000 small donations of under $100. The final campaign budget of $7 million was comparable with the 2013 election, including some half a million dollars for advertising.[28] In the double-dissolution of 2016, however, the Greens had a record ten Senate seats to defend – including the half-dozen senators elected in 2010 – and were also spending up big on a handful of lower-house seats in Melbourne and Sydney. The budget, which was still dwarfed by the spending of the Liberals and Labor, was spread quite thin, and weighted towards the lower-house campaigns rather than the Senate.

*　　　*　　　*

Two seats told the story of the Greens' 2016 campaign: Batman and Grayndler. Batman, immediately to the north of Bandt's seat of Melbourne, was a red-hot chance for the Greens – Labor power-brokers thought it was a write-off. The incumbent, David Feeney, a right-faction Shorten ally, lived outside the electorate and had a clumsy campaign marred by the revelation that he had failed to disclose a $2.3 million investment property he owned in Northcote.[29] The Greens' candidate, Alex Bhathal, by contrast, was a social worker active in the local community, and known to voters – this was her fifth campaign. A self-described '*Tampa* Green' and a Sikh with the firm backing of the seat's large ethnic Indian community, Bhathal was a conviction candidate who had lifted the party's primary vote steadily, from 12 per cent on her first go, in 2001, to 14 per cent (2004), to 24 per cent (2010), and finally to 26 per cent in 2013, making Batman one of the very few seats that still swung to the Greens that year. She was now within striking distance. Campaigning primarily against the country's indefinite detention of asylum seekers on Manus and Nauru, Bhathal was a prolific fundraiser – pulling in a reported half-million dollars, and a massive volunteer effort. The Greens, in short, threw absolutely everything at the seat.

The Greens also heavily targeted Anthony Albanese's seat of Grayndler, in Sydney's inner west; Di Natale even kicked off his campaign there. Albo approached the contest like the scrapper he was, pointing out that the Greens' candidate, Jim Casey, had 'spent more time in the International Socialist Organization than he has in the Greens political party, and if he was fair dinkum he'd run as an international socialist and see how many votes he got there'.

Casey was no shrinking violet – he had led a 2012 firefighters' strike over WorkCover, in which dozens of fire engines had surrounded the NSW parliament, turning their hoses on it – and he hit straight back: 'I make no apologies for my socialist ideals. It is a bit sad [Albanese] is running away from this; he's happy to DJ songs by Billy Bragg for his mates, but when it comes to a political context he's channelling Joe McCarthy.' Casey's support for BDS was wheeled out against him too. In his only public appearance of the campaign, former prime minister Paul Keating spoke at a Petersham Town Hall rally and launched into the 'pathetic' Greens, calling them a 'bunch of opportunistic Trots hiding behind a gum tree trying to pretend they're the Labor Party'.[30] When talk turned to the giant WestConnex toll road, Casey flatly rejected the idea that nothing could be done to stop it because contracts were signed and work had started. 'All of those conditions were exactly the same with the East West Link in Melbourne, and they stopped that,' said Casey. He continued by nodding to the Green Bans: 'There's a proud history in the inner west of actually stopping projects like this. Annandale would have been wiped out in the '70s with the freeways they were planning then.'

As the Greens' threat to Labor in the inner city sharpened, Tanya Plibersek turned her fire on the party in a major speech to the McKell Institute. Plibersek argued that the Greens could serve to keep Labor out of power nationally, just as the DLP had done between 1955 and 1972 – even though most Greens went to Labor, unlike the DLP. The Greens were no longer just a protest party on the fringes, she argued, but 'a positive danger to the progressive political cause'. Noting that Di Natale refused to rule out forming a coalition with the Liberal Party, and that Jim Casey had said he would rather see the re-election of Tony Abbott if it led to stronger protest movements, Plibersek said: 'The political reality is that, far from making more progressive change possible, the Greens are more likely to prevent real change from happening – because their electoral strategy now relies on preventing the election of a Labor government.' She mocked a tweet by a Victorian Greens MP saying the party had a huge week in parliament:

They 'led calls for ... condemned ... pushed for ... and questioned something else'. That's the problem. Because that's all they can do.

But in a way, that's fortunate, because if they really had any power, what would they do? We actually don't know. Inner-city Greens' candidates are opposed to higher density, and regional Greens are opposed to urban sprawl. Some NSW north coast Greens are opposed to fluoridation of drinking water, but their leaders are in favour of it, at least when the north-coasters aren't listening. Some are for compulsory vaccinations, others are against. Some want a population halt; others want much higher levels of immigration. And at the centre of their policies lies a disregard for the jobs and futures of people not fortunate enough to be their target voters.

More tendentiously, Plibersek took a shot at an Adam Bandt poster claiming 'Denticare – brought to you by the Australian Greens'. Ignoring that the Greens had been pushing for Denticare for more than a decade, Plibersek said:

> Kids' dental care as part of Medicare wasn't brought to you by the Greens, it was brought to you by a Labor government when I was health minister, building on the health policy gains made by previous Labor governments, hard won through negotiation with the crossbench in a minority government. And I had to work out how to structure the system responsibly and how to pay for it too. And the Liberals have now killed it off. And that's what it takes to actually deliver dental care – it's more than a poster.

Normally, heavy hitters from either side of politics declined to engage with the Greens, except in passing, as though the party was a joke or beneath them. Dedicating a whole speech to the difference between Labor and the Greens, Plibersek went further than Gillard had gone three years earlier, giving them both barrels.[31] For Milne, who negotiated directly with Gillard over Denticare, Plibersek's attack was simply nasty.

Three weeks out from the election, Malcolm Turnbull announced the Liberals would put the Greens last in all lower-house seats, in one fell swoop making it very difficult for the minor party to win anywhere. As the polls tightened, Di Natale used his final appearance at the National Press Club to have a go at the two-party system, saying multi-party governments were increasingly common around the world and the incumbent 'old parties' in Australia (and sections of the media) would have to 'get used to it'.[32]

On election night, at the Greens' function in Melbourne, it soon became clear that despite big swings there would be no thumping victories in the inner city, although five seats now had primary votes above 20 per cent. Adam Bandt got a 1 per cent swing towards him to hit a 44 per cent primary vote, and increased his two-party margin to 18 per cent. Bhathal got a swing of 10 per cent to top the primary vote in Batman with 36 per cent, but fell some 1800 votes short and Feeney squeaked back in. Much closer, in an upset, was the vote in Melbourne Ports, where the Greens' Steph Hodgins-May came within 500 votes of second place, from where she would almost certainly have won on Labor preferences. In Grayndler, Casey came third and his primary vote was steady on 22 per cent: there was no swing at all, either for or against Labor or the Greens, and Albanese held the seat easily. The NSW Greens were not as flush as the Victorian branch, as they had rules prohibiting both corporate and union donations, but the party had spent roughly $230,000 on the Grayndler campaign, so the result was disappointing.[33] Outside Victoria and New South Wales, there were encouraging results in Western Australia's Fremantle and Perth, and in Queensland's Brisbane and Griffith, and the party's overall lower-house vote rose 1.6 per cent to 10 per cent, topped by the ACT on 15 per cent. South Australia was the only state to cop an adverse swing, dropping to 6 per cent.

In the Senate, despite a high-profile campaign, the Greens went backwards nationally by 0.6 per cent, to 8.65 per cent. The adverse swing was partly explained by stripping out the one-off boost the party had received in the 2014 West Australian by-election campaign. Now the party's West Australian vote dropped, but it was enough to re-elect both Ludlam and Siewert. The Greens won a small 0.9 per cent swing in Queensland, returning Larissa Waters on a primary vote of 6.9 per cent – an encouraging performance, given the 9 per cent swing to One Nation. Victoria held its ground, with Di Natale and Janet Rice both returned on a primary vote of 10.9 per cent.

Elsewhere, it was grim. The vote in New South Wales went back 0.4 per cent to 7.4 per cent, enough to re-elect Lee Rhiannon in either a full- or half-Senate election. In Tasmania the vote dropped 0.5 per cent to 11.2 per cent, returning both Peter Whish-Wilson and Nick McKim (just). In South Australia the vote dropped 1.2 per cent to 5.9 per cent – the party's worst result in the country, enough to re-elect Sarah Hanson-Young but not Robert Simms, who went out of the Senate after a brutally short nine-month term.

With two senators in each of Victoria, Tasmania and Western Australia, and one each in New South Wales, Queensland and South Australia, the result was not disastrous for the Greens, who still had a ten-person party room, including Bandt in the House of Representatives. But it was the first time the federal party had gone backwards in terms of Senate representation since 1998, and there were none of the gains Di Natale needed if he was to stamp his authority as leader. The protest vote was certainly won: in the lower house, a record one-quarter of Australians voted for anyone but Labor or the Coalition. Explaining why there was a swing to the Greens in the lower house and a swing against them in the upper house, Di Natale said one possibility was that 'we are now regarded by some people as a major party, and they're voting for us in the House of Reps, and they're voting for other micro-parties in the Senate'. If correct, this meant the Greens had become a major party in the eyes of voters just when a backlash against the major parties was peaking.

Before counting was even finished, recriminations within the party spilled over into the public arena. One set of criticisms attacked the party's drift to the centre. Former national convenor Christine Cunningham said:

> In a world desperate for change and hope, we offered a centrist position summed up in a vague slogan. We can continue to be led by a nice-guy, mainstream footy-playing doctor and negotiate incremental change ... Or maybe as a party of really smart, but often too-privileged-to-quite-get-it members, we should take a long hard look at ourselves and make some radical changes.

In the same vein, another former convenor, journalist Osman Faruqi, son of the Greens' NSW MP Mehreen, wrote that the Greens' problem was that 'they have pursued a "steady as she goes" approach over the past decade while the Australian public has been simultaneously losing its faith in politics and rejecting the whole concept of political stability and business as usual'.[34]

From the other direction, Bob Brown gave a series of interviews in which he pointed the finger of blame at the NSW branch. 'NSW should be the strongest Greens state in Australia,' said Brown.

> The Greens were established there 10 years before the Victorian Greens and yet their vote almost went backwards in some electorates ... you can't have people who are still doing things the way we did them in the 70s and 80s still in control. They need to give way to modern young people, including young people in professions like business and law who are keen on changing society for the better.[35]

A week later, Brown went even further in an interview on the ABC's *7.30* program, calling explicitly for his old foe Lee Rhiannon – who had just been re-elected – to step down:

> BOB BROWN: Lee's given long service to the Greens, but it's time for a renewal. We didn't get a quota, a single quota, for the Senate in New South Wales, whereas we got well over a quota in Western Australia and Tasmania and Victoria. Something's missing there ... [T]he incumbents in New South Wales – certainly that's Lee, in the Senate – have given great service, but are not hitting a chord with the voters at the moment. And we need to move on.
>
> MATT WORDSWORTH: So Lee Rhiannon should step aside for new blood?
>
> BOB BROWN: Well, that would be my advice.[36]

Brown had thrown down the gauntlet. Among many NSW Greens, there was outrage. Mehreen Faruqi wrote that she had joined the Greens because of Bob Brown, but he had now 'broken her heart'.[37] Even outside the state, many hoping to heal the party's internal divisions viewed Brown's intervention as unhelpful, given that it was guaranteed to provoke retaliation from Rhiannon and her supporters.

Was Brown's attack warranted? Other states like Tasmania and South Australia had seen worse falls, in proportional terms, and it was much harder to get a Senate quota in New South Wales, representing almost a third of the country in population terms. On the other hand, there is no question that New South Wales had underperformed: the state branch's own election review noted that the lower-than-expected primary vote would mean the party would receive $315,000 less in election funding than it had budgeted for.

Brown was unrepentant, insisting in 2016 that the NSW branch had been a drag on the party nationally for many years:

> [W]ithout the delaying and blocking of the growth of the Greens, we would now have 20 senators and half a dozen people in the Lower House. I'm referring there to the NSW Greens refusing and doing everything they could to stop the Australian Greens getting a leader. We'd still have none if it had been left to this small group from the NSW Greens.[38]

The left of the NSW Greens were incredulous at Brown's finger-pointing, believing his vision of dozens of federal MPs to be fanciful, and the link with the debate over leadership to be tenuous at best. The gloves were off.

*   *   *

Days from the start of the federal election campaign, NSW Greens veteran John Kaye died of cancer. As the unofficial leader of the state's eight Greens MPs, he had been a stalwart of the party's hard left, but also had enough authority to keep the factional brawling within limits. Kaye stood against Bob Brown's view that the Greens were there to 'replace the bastards' and should aim for government. In a video from his deathbed, Kaye told members that 'the critical outcome for the Greens is to not be caught into parliamentarianism, to not be caught into the trappings of power. This isn't and never has been about changing government, that's what Labor, the Liberals and Nats do. This is about changing what people expect from government.' As his widow, Lynne Joselyn, explained, Kaye's view was that 'a constant quest for lower house seats ... and having that as a measure of success, would actually result in a conservatising influence on the Greens'.

Kaye's passing unleashed a storm of controversy over the direction of the party, played out through a bitter preselection battle to fill his upper-house seat. The contest was won easily by former military officer Justin Field, who had fought in the 'Lock the Gate' campaign against coal and coal seam gas, and was a staffer to Jeremy Buckingham, Kaye's main rival in the NSW Greens' party room. Things turned vicious on closed party Facebook pages, with left-aligned Greens denouncing Field as a 'careerist leech', while Joselyn herself told *The Sydney Morning Herald* that Kaye would not have wanted Field to succeed him.

The preselection was the first in which factionally aligned Left candidates, described as the 'watermelons' or the 'Eastern Bloc', recommended preferences be swapped among themselves, and those on the right, dubbed the 'Tree Tories', who launched their own secret 'No nastiness' Facebook page, did the same. Even the bitterly divided NSW Greens had never had formal factions, which were fundamentally inconsistent with the idea of consensus, and Buckingham denounced the emergence of group voting tickets as 'the antithesis of participatory democracy'. In his *7.30* interview, Bob Brown did too, although he subsequently told the ABC that if formal factions were to emerge in the Greens, 'so be it'. For Brown, if the old guard in control of the NSW Greens wanted to become 'a minor entity within the party into the future, that's their right. That's how all other parties function. The Liberals have got that. Labor's got it. The National Party's got it. So I don't fear it.'[39]

Field's preselection win was followed up with another victory by the right wing over the left, when former Richmond candidate Dawn Walker narrowly beat former Kaye staffer Kelly Marks in a controversial preselection to replace Jan Barham, who had resigned, exhausted by factional warfare, which had taken a toll on her mental health.

The left wing of the NSW Greens determined it would not take the successive defeats lying down. On 21 December 2016, a bunch of young NSW Greens activists launched a new group, Left Renewal, with their own logo, intending to work as a formal faction within the Greens. They published an explicitly socialist manifesto, recognising in a statement of principles that 'our struggle for social justice brings us into irreconcilable conflict with the capitalist mode of production, and all other forms of class society'. The Greens' four pillars were recast in terms of the fight against capitalism. Under social justice: '[W]e must create alternatives to and challenge all authoritarian and exploitative economic models, which ultimately requires socialising the means of production.' Under peace, the manifesto rejected the legitimacy of the state and the police, holding 'that capitalism is a violent and antagonistic relation between workers, and those who exploit them … we therefore fight to bring about the end of capitalism'. Under sustainability, the manifesto rejected green–capital partnerships and market solutions such as consumer taxes, arguing that 'the interests of the environment, and the working class, should never be pitted against one another. This means working toward a "just transition" in collaboration with and alongside the working class in order to uncover a renewable world.' The 'participatory democracy' pillar became a call for factional solidarity, 'a degree of tactical unity in order to have real collective influence in the society that we live in. Once a decision has been taken by our organisation [Left Renewal] in a participatory democratic fashion, it is required by members that they respect, implement and where necessary, bind on the organisation's democratic decisions'.[40]

Left Renewal was student politics, basically – an early meeting in Darlington, near the University of Sydney, was full of radical young activists, venting at the party's drift to the centre – but the kicker was that the Greens had always attracted and relied upon students, and the emergence of an organised faction for the first time posed a new challenge for the party.

The mainstream media pounced on the Left Renewal manifesto, confronting Di Natale, who disavowed it completely, saying if the group wanted to end capitalism they were in the wrong party. 'Of course the Greens do not support the overthrow of capitalism or any other ridiculous notions of the sort,' he told *The Sydney Morning Herald*. 'If the authors of this ill-thought-through manifesto are so unhappy with Greens policies, perhaps they should consider finding a new political home.'[41]

Pressure came on both Lee Rhiannon and David Shoebridge to clarify their position on Left Renewal – particularly since a young staffer to Shoebridge, Tom Raue, was one of the instigators. In a jointly written op-ed, they defended Left Renewal as a legitimate contribution to party debate, and supported the right of grassroots members to self-organise. Stressing that neither MP was a member of Left Renewal, or had anything to do with its formation, they clarified their views on capitalism itself:

> Of course capitalism has an extraordinary capacity to organise resources and innovate. Whether it is delivering the iPhone or Facebook, cornflakes or solar panels, there is an energy and creativity in capitalism that anyone can see and we support. But capitalism has also put our planet in danger, as the conditions for life are degraded by an economy in which fossil fuels, profit and the market reign supreme.[42]

By explicitly embracing socialism, Left Renewal had forced the Greens leadership and representatives to declare their hand. In an organisational sense, Left Renewal soon faded away, amid criticisms that the explicitly Marxist language of the manifesto was outdated. Debate on Facebook accused the organisers of entryism, the old Trotskyist tactic. Nobody was kicked out of the party, however, and the organisers got more active inside the Greens, not less. Bob Brown kept up his attacks on Rhiannon, blaming the 'radical agenda' in New South Wales for dragging the party down in the polls nationally, and telling Fairfax Media that 'when it comes to political white-anting, Lee is the Greens' version of Tony Abbott'.[43]

The re-evaluation of capitalism inside the Greens was part of a global phenomenon marked by the rise of UK Labour leader Jeremy Corbyn and the US Democratic presidential candidate Bernie Sanders, both avowed socialists especially popular with young voters who rejected austerity and the dominance of 'the 1 per cent'. While the success of the Leave campaign in the Brexit referendum in June 2016 had barely interrupted the federal election that was underway in Australia, the shock victory of billionaire Donald Trump in November rocked the political class everywhere.

On the left of politics there was despair at the frankly elitist, uninspiring campaign of Hillary Clinton. Trump's populism was quickly aped in Australia by the likes of Pauline Hanson, demanding a response from the left. Led by Di Natale, all nine Greens senators had stood up and walked out when Hanson made her first speech in the new Senate; 'I'm back,' she declared, and warned that Australia was in danger of being swamped by Muslims – a shameless throwback to the warning about Asian immigration she had sounded in her maiden speech in the House of Representatives 20 years earlier. Walking out on Hanson was a purely symbolic gesture, but a strong one, and although commentators were sceptical, the Greens were deluged with fan mail.[44]

Shunning a single speech was one thing, but Hansonism – or Trumpism, for that matter – could not be so easily dismissed. The broad combination of anti-immigrant racism and economic nationalism posed a challenge for the left, as it spoke to many of those left behind by neoliberalism, who were opposed to free-trade agreements like the Trans-Pacific Partnership, also opposed by the Greens. To the extent that right-wing populists snared the anti-establishment protest vote, they could filch from the Greens' support, too. So when Senator Jacqui Lambie declared she was in favour of a tax on speculative financial transactions, a so-called Tobin tax, as well as an estate tax, there was a worried scramble to play political catch-up inside the Greens, although such a tax had been party policy for years. Di Natale also made waves by calling the United States a 'dangerous ally' and the alliance a security threat to Australia that must be re-evaluated; foreign affairs spokesperson Scott Ludlam described President Trump as a 'man-baby' and warned of 'fascism in larval form'.[45]

Least suited to the times was the pragmatic centrist, professional politician. Labor under Shorten had already recognised this, and was busy tacking left, developing a policy platform from opposition that would be described as the most adventurous since Whitlam. The Greens could only move further left. At the party's national conference in Perth at the end of 2017, Di Natale signalled a willingness to revisit difficult policy areas, like the estate tax that had been abandoned in 2012, and drug-law reform, including the potential legalisation of marijuana.[46] In his plenary speech, Di Natale also called for an internal debate on alternative methods to electing the leader of the Australian Greens, potentially including a member plebiscite. Months later he ran some new ideas up the flagpole at his first National Press Club address for 2017, touting a four-day week and a universal basic income, which got some laughs on breakfast television for a couple of days. Di Natale was becoming braver on policy, while remaining open to sensible deals with the federal government, including helping broker a last-minute solution to a silly impasse over the 'backpacker tax' just before Christmas, which saw an extra $100 million funding injected into Landcare.

In the ACT election in October 2016, Shane Rattenbury was returned to the Labor/Greens cabinet as climate and energy minister, and economist Caroline Le Couteur fought her way back into the parliament after a four-year absence. In the West Australian election in March 2017, the government of Premier Colin Barnett was thrown out in a landslide after the Liberals did a preference deal with the resurgent One Nation. Labor's Mark McGowan won a huge majority and the Greens won two extra upper-house seats, campaigning hard against the Abbott-inspired 'Roe 8' section of the Perth Freight Link, which had seen the state government thumb its nose at the community and send bulldozers into the Beeliar wetlands, clearing 300-year-old Jarrah trees weeks before the election.[47] In a post-election analysis for *Green* magazine, long-time party donor Chilla Bulbeck wrote:

> [T]he most pervasive external predictor of the Greens vote in any electorate or region appears to be the extent of the One Nation vote. The lowest Pauline Hanson One Nation (PHON) quota is in North Metro where the Greens quota was the highest. There is almost an inverse relationship between the two quotas.[48]

In the May federal budget, the Turnbull government confirmed its plans to restore some $18 billion of Gonski school funding, which the Abbott government had cut in its 2014 budget, and also to take some money away from 24 overfunded private schools.[49] The new funding package was not sector-blind, however, and was still $22 billion short of the Gonski deal struck by the Gillard government. Labor opposed it and, in the lower house, so did the Greens, with Adam Bandt attacking both major parties in a damning history lesson:

It should not be beyond the wit of this place to return to David Gonski's original idea of a needs-based, fully funded, transparent and sector-blind model that ends the overfunding of wealthy private schools and results in a well-resourced public school sector. But neither Labor nor the coalition has put this on the table.[50]

The real action would be in the Senate, where Sarah Hanson-Young now had the schools portfolio for the Greens, following a bruising reshuffle in the wake of the 2016 election. Having spent nine years leading the charge to close the camps on Manus and Nauru, Hanson-Young had fought to keep her high-profile role, telling journalists she did not understand the change and was 'disappointed'. Di Natale talked about the need for a refresh and denied that there would be any softening of the party's policies on asylum seekers under the new spokesperson, Nick McKim.[51] The Gonski funding bill was Hanson-Young's first test in her new education role, and she was determined to make her mark. She led negotiations with the Liberals' education minister, Simon Birmingham, a fellow South Australian senator.

The Greens were divided on whether to negotiate with the government at all, given there was staunch education union opposition to the new funding model, which they described as a 'con job'. The broader strategy was unclear: why compromise on public education? Why help a dysfunctional, divided Turnbull government? Former education spokesperson Lee Rhiannon was particularly vocal in her opposition to the deal, and started campaigning against it in her home state.

In the final week of the Gonski negotiations, there was a telephone hook-up between the party room and the national council to decide the party's position. One of the national councillors for New South Wales announced that Rhiannon was bound to vote against the final package – effectively, she would cross the floor. This was perfectly in line with the federal party's policy, and the NSW Greens do not allow MPs to exercise a conscience vote against policy. But notice of Rhiannon's position had come very late in the day for her colleagues, including Di Natale and Hanson-Young, who had been negotiating with Birmingham on the basis that they could deliver nine votes in the Senate. Now they were down to eight. This was still a crucial bloc, but from the government's perspective, negotiating with other crossbenchers was suddenly more appealing.

The Guardian now reported that the NSW Greens had directed Rhiannon to vote against the package. It was not enough to kill off talks with the government – Di Natale and Hanson-Young were still at the negotiating table – but when Jacqui Lambie backed the reform, Birmingham had the crossbench votes he needed and the Greens were sidelined. Hanson-Young had been instrumental in securing an extra $5 billion in funding, an independent school resourcing body and more besides, but the Greens could claim no credit – they ended up voting against the legislation on the basis of relatively minor reservations about a $50 million sop to the Catholic sector.

At the next day's party room meeting, Hanson-Young confronted Rhiannon. She had found out via Twitter about an A5 leaflet authorised by Rhiannon and distributed in a handful of NSW electorates, which called for support of the full Gonski package the previous Labor government had agreed on with the states. If it was a hanging offence, it was an unusual one, but for the party room it was the last straw. As Rhiannon tells it, Hanson-Young was 'clearly furious … she and Richard said what I had done had undermined negotiations. I found it ludicrous.' Not all her party colleagues spoke against her, says Rhiannon, but quite a few did. 'More than I'd expect.' As she tells it, Di Natale was especially grave. 'It reminded me of being back at school. We were told my actions had to be reported to the national council [and] "there will be consequences".'

Consequences there were: on the Friday, the nine other Greens in the party room signed a letter to the national council, drafted by Di Natale's chief of staff, Cate Faehrmann, complaining about the leaflet and Rhiannon's failure to tell Hanson-Young or any other federal colleagues about it while negotiations with the government were underway.

The letter was soon leaked, and from that point, the dispute played out all over the media. The national council refused to endorse the letter, batting it straight back to the party room. After a marathon five-hour meeting in Melbourne the following Wednesday, the party room passed two resolutions: one, unanimous, calling for an end to the practice of NSW parliamentarians being bound to vote against the party room if the state branch directs them to do so (even though this had never occurred); and another, to suspend Rhiannon from the party room while 'contentious' issues were being discussed. Significantly, Bandt abstained from the second one.

An #IStandWithLeeRhiannon campaign took off. Rhiannon turned the tables, going on ABC-TV's *Insiders* to express her 'disappointment' in Di Natale's leadership. Di Natale declined to retaliate, but in an interview for *The Monthly* said that Rhiannon 'was disappointed in Bob Brown's leadership, she was disappointed in Christine Milne's leadership, so it's no surprise she's disappointed in mine, especially as she doesn't even believe the party should have a leader'.

In the middle of this all-out brawl, a mysterious Perth lawyer discovered that co-deputy leader Scott Ludlam, born in New Zealand, had dual citizenship and was thus ineligible to be an Australian senator. He resigned almost immediately, in a major blow to the party. Within days, Queensland senator Larissa Waters also resigned, revealing she was born in Canada and had dual citizenship. Having lost both his co-deputies, Di Natale was floored. The Greens were mocked as incompetent, and Di Natale announced a 'root and branch' review of the party's governance and processes. On *7.30* that evening, host Leigh Sales summed it up:

> LEIGH SALES: You've lost your two co-deputy leaders. You've got your New South Wales senator Lee Rhiannon out in the cold, you've got the New South Wales Greens at odds with the federal party. Can you understand why voters may feel that party looks to be in disarray?
>
> RICHARD DI NATALE: It's been a shocking few weeks, no sugar-coating it, Leigh. It's been shocking.

Sales then asked how confident Di Natale was about holding onto the Greens' top job. 'Very confident,' he answered, but the ensuing weeks saw a spate of articles questioning his leadership and the party's direction. The ABC's *Four Corners* program began trailing both Di Natale and Rhiannon, and would soon beam a picture of dysfunction and disunity into hundreds of thousands of Australian homes.

It became clear that the Greens were not the only political party whose MPs were ineligible to sit in parliament, as the dual citizenship saga worsened and spread to other crossbenchers, then to the Nationals and then to both major parties, causing a string of byelections and occupying the federal parliament for much of the ensuing year. Paradoxically, the Greens' handling of Ludlam's and Waters' ineligibility – a forthright announcement and apology, followed by an immediate resignation – came to look increasingly principled as MPs from other parties ducked and weaved and had to be prised from the parliament by the High Court. A column in the notoriously hostile *Australian* ran with the headline 'Are the Greens the only adults in the room?'.[52]

Following normal practice in the event of a casual Senate vacancy, Ludlam and Waters were set to be replaced on a countback by the next person on the Senate ticket at the previous election, disability activist Jordon Steele-John and former Democrat Andrew Bartlett in Western Australia and Queensland, respectively. Bartlett's return to the Senate, this time as a Green, was not uniformly welcomed inside the party room. Bartlett had increasingly aligned himself with Queensland's more radical left, and in a confidential email, inadvertently sent by 'reply all' to the entire national council list, Janet Rice confided to outgoing secretary Rebecca Galdies that she was 'quite worried about the prospect of having [Andrew] as a party room colleague'. Steele-John was wary of a backlash if he was seen to be pouncing on the seat vacated by the popular Ludlam, declaring he wanted the support of the members. There was a path back to the Senate for Ludlam, if Steele-John immediately resigned and was replaced by himself. Ludlam prevaricated, but nine months earlier he had taken leave to treat anxiety and depression and now decided a decade in the Senate was enough – he would return to activism, and writing. Steele-John would become the first senator in a wheelchair. Waters had a young daughter – only a month earlier she had become the first female MP to breastfeed while moving a motion in parliament, causing a media sensation and inspiring women around the country.[53] She decided to spend some time at home, hoping to return to the parliament in due course.

In New South Wales, upper-house MP Mehreen Faruqi announced she would contest the looming Senate preselection, setting up a head-to-head contest with Rhiannon. Faruqi had cross-factional support, represented the kind of generational change Bob Brown was calling for, and as a Pakistani-born Muslim would answer criticisms that the all-white federal party room lacked diversity. The federal Greens MPs came up with a clumsy compromise, allowing Rhiannon back into the party room but setting up a special subcommittee to meet whenever the party held the balance of power and contentious legislation arose, to exclude MPs who were bound by their state party's position or who intended to exercise a conscience vote. Rhiannon replied with a provocative Facebook post welcoming the party room's backdown and saying the new subcommittee was unnecessary and 'sets a bad precedent, but I am pleased it does not have the power to make decisions'. It has never met.

The Greens' handling of the Gonski stoush was diabolical – messy, public and fruitless. If it had been intended to solve the problems in the NSW branch once and for all, it achieved exactly the opposite. For some, the expulsion of Rhiannon from the party room was the 'original sin' that set off a vicious cycle of revenge and retaliation, from which the party has not recovered. At least one member of the party room, speaking off the record, regrets ever signing the letter against Rhiannon, and a few say in hindsight the whole thing was a mistake. On policy grounds, Rhiannon was vindicated, as the implications of Turnbull's Gonski 2.0 deal became clearer and community opposition grew. The Greens were soon glad they had never voted up the deal.

The *Four Corners* story, when it aired, pulled no punches, with Brown, Milne, Di Natale, Ian Cohen, Nick McKim, Jeremy Buckingham, Justin Field and Chris Harris all giving interviews denouncing Rhiannon in particular, and the NSW Greens hierarchy more broadly. Brown's comments were perhaps most damaging: he called Rhiannon a 'team wrecker'. Milne chimed in: 'I think that the current behaviour in New South Wales is actually the death throes of that small cabal. I say that because Lee has burnt her bridges with her parliamentary colleagues, she's burned her bridges with the Australian Greens.'[54] Rhiannon, David Shoebridge and Hall Greenland spoke in her defence.

Two months later, in the preselection ballot, Faruqi defeated Rhiannon solidly, by 1032 votes to 742.[55] Rhiannon knew she had little chance of winning but ran to make a statement that Brown and his colleagues should stop trying to dictate to the NSW Greens. Given the campaign of vilification against her, Rhiannon said, she was 'damaged goods'.

*   *   *

In early 2017 the Global Greens held their fourth congress in Liverpool, and it signposted a shift in European politics – a reaction to the advent of Brexit and Trump. The congress was to be the last organised by stalwart Margaret Blakers, who would step down as convenor of the Global Greens. Since it was born in Canberra in 2001, the Global Greens had been permanently hamstrung by a lack of money and staff, but it had survived near-death experiences to become the world's largest Greens gathering, with more 2000 delegates from more than 90 countries. The Australian presence was strong, with Global Greens ambassador Christine Milne giving a plenary address, harking back to the United Tasmania Group's call in 1972, in the New Ethic, for 'a global movement for survival … which unites humans with nature to prevent the collapse of life support systems on earth'. Sweden's Green climate minister, Isabella Loevin, since elected the deputy prime minister, spoke to the challenge of the Trump era, drawing parallels with the rise of fascism on the continent almost a century earlier. She pointed to recent successes: her own red–green coalition formed in Sweden in 2014, billed as the world's first feminist government and that passed a law binding all future parliaments to a goal of net zero emissions by 2045; or the appointment of Europe's first Greens president, Austria's Alexander van der Bellen, after the dramatic 2016 election, or the rise of the Netherlands' GroenLinks, on a crystal-clear platform: 'Stand for your principles. Be straight. Be pro-refugee. Be pro-European.' As Loevin said, 'We can stop populism, right-wing extremism and nationalism. We greens are a counterweight to them. When they see the world in black-and-white, we see it in all the colours of the rainbow. When they stand for fear, we stand for hope. When they stand for hatred, we stand for love!'[56] Loevin looked ahead to the coming European elections of 2019, and with hindsight it is clear a groundswell was beginning to build. On the other side of the world, at the end of the year, the election of Labour's Jacinda Ardern, in partnership with New Zealand First, marked a milestone for the Greens.

They were part of the government for the first time, after 45 years, striking a confidence and supply agreement that gave them three ministries outside cabinet, including the climate portfolio, and set out a wide-ranging policy programme including a Zero Carbon Act, a climate commission and a welfare overhaul.

For Richard Di Natale, by the end of 2017, after what would be known as the Greens' 'winter of discontent', things were also starting to look up. At the national conference in Hobart, the Australian Greens celebrated the 25th anniversary of their founding. The party's three leaders – Brown, Milne and Di Natale – all spoke to the faithful, and Di Natale painted a picture of how the Greens might evolve over the next 25 years. By 2042, he suggested, the party would control 25 lower-house seats, climbing from a balance-of-power player to a major party that could govern in coalition with either Labor or the Liberals. This would not mean a shift to the centre, however, as Di Natale briefed Fairfax, arguing that voters wanted government to have a strong role in the economy, including active wealth redistribution:

> People were told this lie for decades that if only we supported business, if only we gave tax breaks to the rich and powerful, if only corporate Australia has a free pass, then everyone else will benefit, and there is now a global reaction against that, something that the Greens have been leading in Australia. You see stagnant wage growth, a shrinking middle-class and what you're seeing is a response to that from people right across the globe and it's because they don't buy that line anymore.[57]

Meanwhile, in Di Natale's home state the Greens appeared to be surging ahead. Victorian leader Greg Barber had stunned outsiders by resigning at the end of September, effective immediately. Months earlier he had signalled he would not stand for the upper house at the 2018 election (as had his long-time colleague Colleen Hartland), but he had flagged a possible lower-house tilt. Now he ruled that out, telling the media he would go fishing. The suddenness of Barber's announcement raised a few questions. His seat was taken by popular Moreland councillor Samantha Ratnam, who had been the candidate for Wills in the recent federal election.

At the same time, the party was contesting a by-election in the heartland seat of Northcote. The Greens had preselected Lidia Thorpe, a firebrand Gunnai-Gunditjmara businesswoman and activist who had stormed out of the talks leading to the Uluru Statement from the Heart. Thorpe was a close ally of Alex Bhathal. A single mum who had left school at 14, she had defied discrimination and survived a violent relationship. A Labor dirt campaign targeting her as a former bankrupt backfired when Thorpe explained how her experience of domestic violence had ruined her business. Thorpe won a huge vote, storming the seat with 45 per cent of the primary vote and a 12 per cent swing, and became the first Aboriginal woman to sit in the Victorian parliament.

The by-election was held on the same day as the Hobart national conference, and at about 9 p.m. there was a cross to Northcote workers via Facebook Live. Given the mic, an exhausted Thorpe spoke slowly and without affectation – for all the clichés about the Greens vote in inner Melbourne, there was nothing hipster about this candidate. Draped in a huge land rights flag, in the style of Cathy Freeman, Thorpe recounted attending her first meeting of the Darebin Greens, where she had to make a decision about whether or not to join up. 'They were such wonderful people I knew I'd found a home.'

With party-balloon icons bursting across the screen, and bouquets and brickbats scrolling down the feed bar, the ageing Tassie greenies, who had gathered in a drab conference room to hear speeches about the Greens' past, peered in on the booming atmosphere at a Melbourne nightclub packed with young members, cheering and drinking as the music pumped. It seemed a perfect illustration of the contrast between the old party and the new. The future, it seemed, was over in Melbourne.

A week later, the Greens had a breakthrough in Queensland, finally winning their first seat in the state parliament more than three decades after the party was formed by Drew Hutton. Success did not come entirely out of the blue. In March 2016 a street poet and housing activist, Jono Sri, had been elected to the Gabba ward of the Brisbane City Council, the most powerful local government in the country, with more than a million ratepayers spread over most of the metropolitan area. The Gabba ward covered almost exactly the same inner-city suburbs as the state seat of South Brisbane, and, as was the case so often in the Greens' history, the local council proved to be a beachhead for the party's push into parliament. The Greens mounted a huge campaign to elect young social scientist Amy McMahon, who was doing a PhD on community responses to climate change, but Labor fought equally hard to defend the seat held by deputy premier Jackie Trad, who clung on narrowly despite a 12 per cent swing.

In an upset, the Greens broke through in the Liberal-held seat of Maiwar, won by environmental lawyer Michael Berkman. The Queensland Greens had defied expectations and, although Adani was possibly the number-one issue in the campaign,[58] ran hard on a solid left platform promising affordable homes for all and $1 tickets on public transport. The Queenslanders hoped their win might serve as a template nationally – a more radical alternative to the 'progressive mainstream' model coming out of Melbourne.

Queensland's new Greens senator, Andrew Bartlett, delivering his first speech in the Senate, dispelled any idea that his party was having a 'Democrats moment':

> My experience with the Democrats obviously makes me very conscious of certain failures and very conscious that a political party or any other social organisation is not automatically guaranteed to survive, let alone thrive. Part of why I am very confident that the Greens can continue to build and genuinely transform politics in Queensland and around the country is that the party has such a strong foundation – and, genuinely, a much stronger foundation than the previous party I was involved in – and a much clearer idea of what it stands for and what it is seeking to achieve.

The last fortnight of parliamentary sittings for 2017 were tumultuous. The Greens chalked up a big win when Turnbull saw the writing on the wall and – for fear of losing a vote on the floor of the House – appointed a commission of inquiry into the banks. In all but name, this was the royal commission for which Peter Whish-Wilson had been campaigning for more than four years. In fact, it had been Whish-Wilson's own staff who, after trawling through old parliamentary records, had dredged up the commission of inquiry mechanism, which had last been used 30 years ago by Bob Hawke to investigate criminal allegations against then High Court chief justice Lionel Murphy. The inquiry had the same powers as a royal commission – to compel witnesses, for example, and to recommend prosecutions – and there was crossbench support for the idea. Assistant treasurer Kelly O'Dwyer, when it was put to her, jumped on it. The terms of reference were almost a replica of those proposed by the Greens: in a phone conversation with Whish-Wilson, O'Dwyer implied the government had pretty much copied them. Not that the mainstream media coverage reflected any of this.

By the end of the week, the focus of the parliament had shifted to the lower house, where diehard opponents of marriage equality were moving last-ditch amendments designed to protect religious freedoms, trying to hold back a rising tide of support for Liberal Dean Smith's marriage equality bill, already passed by the Senate. Any change could delay the passage of the legislation until 2018. The public gallery was bursting like a rainbow itself, with celebrity campaigners Magda Szubanski, Alex Greenwich, Christine Forster and the legendary Rodney Croome clapping, laughing, but most of all *waiting* for the parliament to do what the people had a month earlier commanded it to do via postal survey. Every time a conservative amendment went down, the crowd knew, the final moment drew closer, and they cheered. Senators drifted in to watch the historic moment: half the Greens, Dean Smith, Penny Wong, George Brandis, more. When the last amendment failed and speaker Tony Smith put the question that the bill be agreed to, and then declared that the ayes had it, there was spontaneous applause – the gallery applauding MPs, and MPs applauding the gallery.

In a booming voice, Turnbull, whose heart had been broken in 1999 when the country said no to a republic, moved the third reading with an affirmative fist-pump: 'Let's finalise this bill, right now.' Shorten got to his feet: 'Australia, we are going to make marriage equality a reality in minutes …' The applause built again, and the speaker called the member for Melbourne.

Unbelievably, there was a collective eye-roll, muttered jeers and groans, at the idea that Adam Bandt might want to speak on this historic occasion. Here was the sole lower-house representative of the party that had championed the rights of LGBTIQ Australians for decades. Wiped for a moment was the party's proud history: the story of Bob Brown coming out in 1976, when homosexuality was illegal in Tasmania, and later becoming the country's first gay MP; Christine Milne's successful push for decriminalisation in 1997; Giz Watson, the country's first lesbian MP; the Greens' steadfast opposition to John Howard's 2004 amendment to the *Marriage Act*, backed by Labor. The Greens had voted for equality at every step, when it was not only unfashionable but also politically risky. Bandt would not remain quiet on this historic occasion. Graciously, feeling the happy impatience of the gallery, he said less than 60 words declaring that after years of bigotry and hate, it was 'time to pop the bubbly … because love has won'. The Greens had done the hard yards, and served its purpose.

*   *   *

Momentum from wins at the end of 2017 did not carry over into the new year. Tasmania and South Australia went to the polls in March, and the results were not good. Most upsetting was the poor showing in Tasmania, the spiritual birthplace of the party, where the Greens were now suffering an identity crisis.

The setback in 2014 could be explained away as the natural backlash from the experience of governing with Labor. That defeat had spurred party reform, including the introduction of member ballots for preselection contests at last. In September 2015, the outgoing state convenor Austra Maddox called for a re-examination of how the party chose its leader, and said too much weight was given to the opinions of well-paid MPs elected on the basis of hard work by members. Relations between sections of the party and its three MPs remained testy. In the 2018 state election, the Liberal government of Will Hodgman was returned with a diminished majority, having defeated a reinvigorated Labor Party under fresh leader Rebecca White, who had campaigned on banning pokies in pubs and clubs. It was a clear and determined policy commitment – and a reform for which the Greens had called for 20 years. While they supported Labor's policy – in fact, they would have implemented a total ban, including in casinos in Hobart and Launceston – the Greens became a sideshow in the election, and had to compete for airtime with two new entrants: the Jacqui Lambie Network and the Shooters, Fishers and Farmers party, which both failed utterly.

Greens leader Cassy O'Connor's campaign was not helped by occasional salvos from Geoff Holloway, convenor of the re-formed United Tasmania Group, who was threatening to stand candidates under the banner of 'the original Greens'. Holloway and a handful of other UTG veterans believed the Tassie Greens, under the leadership of McKim and O'Connor, had lost their bearings, abandoning the commitment to wilderness. The Greens had their worst election result in Tasmania for 20 years, with the party's primary vote halving from its 2010 peak, falling by almost 4 per cent to around 10 per cent. The result meant they lost Andrea Dawkins in Kim Booth's old seat of Bass. In the fallout, Dawkins quit the party and was elected as an independent to Launceston City Council; Hobart mayor Anna Reynolds and successful candidate Holly Ewin quit too and stood successfully as independents. O'Connor faced a huge challenge rebuilding the Tasmanian Greens' fortunes.

A fortnight later in South Australia, the Greens copped negative swings in both the upper and lower houses as Nick Xenophon, who had resigned from the Senate to make a quixotic tilt at state politics under the moniker SA Best, sucked up votes and oxygen. The biggest blow for the Greens that month, however, was in the party's Melbourne stronghold, during the crucial Batman by-election. Candidate Alex Bhathal, who had been preselected to stand for a sixth time, needed only a 1 per cent swing to take the seat off Labor, and the media expected it was in the bag for the Greens, particularly as the Liberals were unlikely to run. That was until Labor announced its star candidate, former ACTU president Ged Kearney. An ex-nurse, Kearney had been mooted for a state seat, but got a phone call from Labor's head office, which had got wind of trouble in the Greens branches.

The story soon broke: in January, 18 disaffected Greens from Bhathal's Darebin branch had lodged a 101-page bullying complaint against her with head office, seeking her deselection as candidate. The party dismissed the complaint, but it was leaked to *The Australian*'s

Chip Le Grand, who wrote that it did 'not contain grievous instances of bullying or harassment'; he described it as 'frivolous'. Damaging leaks against Bhathal continued throughout the campaign, including to ABC Radio and *The Age*. By the end of the campaign, hundreds of Bhathal's posters had been defaced with 'bully' stickers. For the campaign workers, and for Bhathal herself, it was utterly devastating to be undermined by their own people.

Kearney was formidable, even wooing a thoroughly green audience at the Darebin Climate Action Forum on her opponent's turf, and attracted a parade of Labor luminaries to her campaign from all round the country, including Plibersek and Albanese. When Labor announced its policy to abolish cash refunds for unused franking credits, the Greens tried to play to Liberal supporters, worrying about the impact on self-funded retirees. Bhathal's support for the BDS movement against Israel came into question after Victorian Liberal Party president Michael Kroger told ABC Melbourne's Jon Faine it would be a factor in whether the Liberal Party decided to run a candidate. He would feel bad if the Liberals helped elect Labor, he conceded, but 'I'd feel worse if we didn't run and our preferences were then not directed against Greens and we elected a Greens member who had a record of anti-Semitism'. At a press conference in Canberra, a confident Bhathal found a form of words that suggested a way forward for the party on what had been a vexed issue:

> I've been terribly concerned about the actions of successive Israeli governments. I look at the great leadership of [former prime minister Yitzhak] Rabin as my hope for the state of Israel. I believe that the BDS was very all-encompassing and I disagreed very strongly with the academic and cultural boycott aspects of that campaign.

In the end the Liberals didn't run, and their voters fanned out everywhere: Kearney got an 8 per cent swing, much bigger than the 3 per cent which went to Bhathal. Once again, Animal Justice and other parties on the left detracted from the Greens' primary vote. It was a historic defeat: far from being on an inevitable rising trajectory, due to internal sabotage the Greens had blown their chances in another of the half-dozen winnable lower-house seats in the country. First

Denison, now Batman. With the right candidates, Labor realised, it could hold off the Greens in their inner-Melbourne stronghold, just as Plibersek and Albanese had done in inner Sydney. The win put paid to any argument that Labor should abandon the inner city to the Greens and become a hip-pocket-driven suburban vote-winning machine. One Labor source said that proposition was now regarded as 'fuckwitted to the point of heresy'.[59] The fallout dragged on for months, roiling the party's biggest branch. Bhathal was slowly but surely forced out of the party for talking to the media, unlike those who sabotaged the Batman campaign. The saga was turned into a full-length documentary, *The Candidate*, meant to chronicle a great Greens victory but capturing instead a distressing party train wreck.

At the National Press Club in April, Di Natale tacked further left, flagging policies to set up a publicly owned energy retailer and a new 'People's Bank' – oddly enough, sitting within the Reserve Bank.[60] The next day, David Shoebridge released an alternative manifesto, which went even further, borrowing Jeremy Corbyn's slogan 'For the many, not for the few', and complaining the Greens were not capturing an increased share of the vote despite polls showing growing popular dissatisfaction with democracy and a desire for major change. Shoebridge contrasted the disappointing result in Tasmania with the success of the more radical campaign in Queensland, and criticised the 'growing tendency within the Greens to take a cautious approach to social reform, casting the party as part of the political mainstream seeking achievable reforms'. The manifesto set out a much more radical set of policies: a billionaire's tax; caps on CEOs' salaries; returning the Commonwealth Bank to public ownership; an end to privatisation; and so on.[61]

Amid this internal battle of ideas, two crucial preselections were underway in New South Wales. Cate Faehrmann had resigned as Di Natale's chief of staff, hoping to win the party's nomination to fill the vacancy left by Faruqi when she went to the Senate. During her stint in the leader's office Faehrmann had joined the Victorian Greens, and assumed her membership would now be automatically transferred to NSW. Instead, in a bit of factional game-playing, the branch counted her as a new member, which meant she was ineligible to run for preselection for three months. With the deadline for nominations closing,

Faehrmann went straight to the Supreme Court, with an urgent application to have her membership transferred immediately. She won with costs, and went on to successfully contest the preselection.

The do-or-die preselection battle was between Jeremy Buckingham and David Shoebridge, in a contest for first place on the party's upper-house ticket for the 2019 state election. Under the zipper principle, which was designed to ensure equal representation, the loser would be relegated to third place on the ticket, considered unwinnable. Given that the so-called right of the party had won three successive preselections – Field, Walker and Faruqi – the battle was seen as a final showdown between the warring factions. Shoebridge was unofficial leader of the 'left' of the NSW party room, and had racked up substantial wins, including working with Hunter Valley police whistleblower Peter Fox to push for the Royal Commission into Child Sexual Abuse, moving for the NSW parliamentary inquiry into the Bowraville murders, campaigning for gun control by taking on the shooters lobby and launching the toomanyguns.org public database, and fighting forced council amalgamations. If Shoebridge lost to Buckingham, many of the party's left-wing stalwarts were ready to quit.

The left of the party had already lodged a belated complaint against Buckingham, seeking to suspend or even expel him for his comments to *Four Corners* in 2017. The complaint was dropped only after Buckingham ally Justin Field went public and denounced the tactic on Facebook. The right accused the left of branch stacking, recruiting members of the Socialist Alliance to the Greens. The left of the party say these allegations have never been substantiated. Shoebridge beat Buckingham comfortably, by 1161 to 780 votes.[62]

Lee Rhiannon soon announced her resignation, after more than 18 years in state and federal parliament for the Greens, giving Faruqi time to establish a national profile. At the party's national conference in Brisbane in May, glass-half-full types argued that the result of the two key preselections was ideal: nobody got everything they wanted, and a balance had been struck with Shoebridge and Faehrmann. The members had voted for unity, and for moving on from the wars of the past. These optimists would prove sadly mistaken.

*   *   *

The Greens aim to do politics differently. Those differences include a lack of hierarchical structure and a diffuse and consensus-based decision-making process – both of which befit a small political party made up of like-minded people. But as the party has grown, these free-wheeling notions have been severely tested. Ironically and shockingly, given the high level of feminist membership, it would be issues of sexual misconduct that exposed the lack of internal coherence of the party's structures.

In June 2017 a freelance writer, Lauren Ingram, went public on Facebook with a sensational allegation that a Greens staffer, whom she named, had raped her two years earlier.[63] In her thread, Ingram detailed the assault, her admission to hospital and disappointment with the police investigation. She also accused the Greens of failing to act although four other women had made complaints about the same man, including one rape accusation almost identical to hers. 'The Greens claims to be against violence against women, but don't act when one of their office holders is a serial abuser,' Ingram said. 'So yeah, fuck the NSW Greens and how they pretend to care about women.' Ingram's accusation went off like a grenade, and became national news when she did an interview with ABC Radio National's *Background Briefing*, along with other women who corroborated her story.[64] The man, who had worked for state MPs and on the 2016 federal election campaign, was finally suspended. Until Ingram's complaint the NSW Greens had no policy on sexual assault and harassment. The party, which prided itself on an inclusive and safe culture, had been caught napping, to say the least. Was it an isolated incident, or was there a systemic or cultural issue at play?

Around the same time, the ABC reported that on the night of the 2016 federal election a young female volunteer for the ACT Greens had been sexually assaulted by a man, also a Greens volunteer. The woman, who wished to remain anonymous, had a sympathetic witness who told the female campaign manager what had happened. The victim had not gone to the police until the following February, because she didn't want to disrupt the party's ACT election campaign in October. The police told her too much time had elapsed. Like Ingram, the woman was bitterly disappointed by the party's response to her complaint. The ACT Greens tried to keep a lid on the whole thing, but it snowballed. Another volunteer, Zach Ghirardello, stepped in as the young woman's advocate and told the ABC the Greens had handled the whole thing 'really poorly ... I would say the culture in the party was poisonous, it was toxic'. Aggravating the situation, the Greens leader in the territory, Shane Rattenbury, told the ABC he thought the 'distressing' claims had been dealt with by the party's management committee, when they hadn't.[65]

The #MeToo movement exploded in October 2017. On the cover of its Christmas issue, under the headline 'Exclusive: How the Greens failed me over rape', *The Saturday Paper* published the anonymous woman's story, in her own words. She was utterly scathing of the party's response. Her assailant was stood down from volunteering duties, but was not told it was for misconduct, and he had been invited to a Greens function. He was thanked in the post-election review, and she wasn't, and the report was sanitised to remove 'damning' references to the assault. She wrote:

> The ACT Greens have consistently sought to delegitimise me and my story, adopting the rhetoric of victim blaming ('we can't help someone that doesn't want to co-operate', 'you were flirting with him before the election night'), institutional unaccountability ('it's an issue between two third parties', 'we have no responsibility') and outright denial ('there's two sides to every story'). I am not paraphrasing this: every quote here, and those that follow, is pulled from correspondence between myself, other members and party leaders. ... you've seen the billboards, placards and stickers: 'Standing up for what matters.' How cruel and cynical that representation seems to me now in hindsight, how dangerous and misleading to the hordes of young people searching for a safe community to call their own.

The paper's next issue had a letter from Bob Brown describing the incident as 'a violent, predatory rape' and criticising the victim for failing to report the incident to the police immediately. 'The ACT Greens could not and should not have been expected to substitute for the criminal justice system,' he wrote, defending Rattenbury and suggesting the paper should have a look at the journalists' code of ethics.[66] Brown's letter caused uproar. Lauren Ingram tweeted: 'This is disgusting from Bob Brown. He is defending a man as "decent and considerate" and giving no thought to a victim of sexual assault. He should also be well aware that the justice system doesn't work for most victims of rape.'[67] She posted a response from the victim, who said that a man 'who I looked up to my whole life' was 'paving the way for progressive people, Greens members, voters and environmentalists to adopt his cause and defile women and their supporters who stand up for their rights to bodily autonomy and freedom from institional [sic] neglect'.[68] David Shoebridge, at this time a state MP, accused Brown of 'appalling disrespect to a victim of sexual abuse'.[69]

Richard di Natale, trying to control the situation, told *The Australian*: 'I recognise how difficult it is for the victims of sexual assault to take action and have their voices heard within the legal system and we must do better if they are to receive justice.'[70] If any Australian political party was going to take a hit from the #MeToo movement, the Greens might at first have seemed the most unlikely – but as a party with a strongly feminist tradition and membership, it was also logical that any sexual misconduct would be vigorously debated. The next allegation did not take long to surface, and the rancour threatened to split the party irrevocably.

Ella Buckland was a young Greens activist from the Northern Rivers who had worked for the NSW MP Jan Barham in 2011–12. Five years later, still doing occasional volunteer work for the party, Buckland bumped into David Shoebridge at Nimbin's Mardi Grass festival. Shoebridge mentioned that there could be work coming up in his office, and she should apply. In early 2018, after seeing Shoebridge's post attacking Bob Brown over the ACT Greens case, Buckland got in touch and told him that Jeremy Buckingham – who was about to go up against him in a federal preselection – had assaulted her at an after-work drinks in 2011. Shoebridge offered his support and suggested Buckland get legal advice. She did, and complained to the party in April, which was referred to external firm WorkDynamics for independent investigation. Someone leaked the Buckland allegation to the ABC, which began to investigate.

As yet, Buckingham knew nothing about Buckland's allegation, but the preselection contest between him and Shoebridge was already getting ugly. At the end of April, a phone picture of Buckingham making a 'lewd gesture' at a pub trivia night to raise funds for the party – apparently simulating cunnilingus – was posted on social media and someone tipped off the *Daily Telegraph*, which pounced.[71] Over April and May, *New Matilda* published half a dozen stories attacking Buckingham or his colleagues on the right of the party. Some were written by a Greens member, Michael Brull, who had nominated Shoebridge for preselection, and another was by Shoebridge staffer Lauren Gillin – these connections were only partly disclosed. Shoebridge won the preselection comfortably, but the battle was far from over.

The ABC's *7.30* contacted Buckingham armed with Buckland's allegation, saying they planned to air a story in two or three days. The substance of the allegation was that Buckland, Buckingham and another woman had gone back to his home in inner-city Newtown. Buckland had taken some video on her phone, showing Buckingham drunk and partying in his kitchen, and apparently flirting with the other woman, a party volunteer. After that, Buckland said, she and Buckingham and the other woman had headed out, back towards King Street. On the way, she alleged, Buckingham had grabbed at her crotch, to which she said 'no' loudly and walked off. Buckingham denied the alleged assault occurred – in fact he denied that the three had ever left the flat together. He was backed up by the other woman present, which the ABC neglected to mention. The *7.30* story, when it went to air, including the messy video shot in his home, and pre-recorded interviews with Buckland and Shoebridge, was extremely damaging to Buckingham – although it did include a reference to his denial. It was also damaging to the Greens because it suggested that Buckland had been fobbed off by a staffer when she contacted the office of leader Richard Di Natale and because it harked back to the two earlier incidents with Lauren Ingram and the ACT Greens. Di Natale's office was dumbfounded at the suggestion the complaint had been fobbed off, given his chief of staff Rod Goodbun had engaged directly with Buckland, explaining that the federal parliamentary party leader was explicitly excluded from having a role in sexual harassment complaints and obtaining her permission to refer the matter to the party's national co-convenor. Goodbun had tried to check in with Buckland about progress through July on a number of occasions but she did not respond to those contacts.

Lee Rhiannon called on Buckingham to stand aside, pending the external investigation, but he refused, insisting the allegations were false and part of a factional attack on him. When WorkDynamics had finished its investigation, a draft report was circulated to the party, Buckingham and Buckland. Buckingham, desperate to clear his name, went public with the findings straightaway. The investigator was 'not satisfied that there is sufficient evidence on the balance of probabilities that an incident of sexual harassment as defined by the legislation occurred' and had recommended the party 'resolve the matter with no adverse finding against you [Buckingham] with respect to sexual harassment and inappropriate behaviour'. Buckingham and his supporters thought he was cleared. Buckland was devastated.[72]

In the immediate aftermath of the 7.30 report, on a sunny winter's day at Sydney's Opera House bar, Bob Brown sat down with half the Greens MPs in the NSW parliament. The four state upper house MPs were Jeremy Buckingham, Cate Faehrmann, Justin Field and Dawn Walker – dissed as 'tree tories' or simply 'the right' by their factional opponents NSW Greens. They were talking about the future of their party and, specifically, whether to keep working within the troubled state branch, or split off completely. Brown's view was that the party's name was too important to leave to the old guard of New South Wales, whom he'd fought on and off for decades. Nonetheless, according to those present, Brown said quite clearly: 'If you go, I'll stand with you.' A photo shows the Greens founder and the four MPs, hand-over-outstretched-hand in a kind of pact.

Things went from bad to worse. Three times, motions to remove Buckingham from the upper house ticket or expel him from the party were put to the state delegates council but failed to secure enough support. By now, hard-left candidates were refusing to stand on a Greens ticket that included Buckingham. It had become a fight to the political death, and there was no end in sight.

On 8 November, New South Wales Labor leader Luke Foley resigned after ABC reporter Ashleigh Raper went public with a groping allegation dating back two years. On Facebook, Lee Rhiannon pointed out that the Greens could learn from Labor: 'A very similar allegation of indecent assault has been made by a former staffer against the Greens upper house MP Jeremy Buckingham. Jeremy Buckingham has threatened defamation proceedings against some of those who have discussed the matter.'[73] Two days later, fully three months after the *7.30* story, Greens MP Jenny Leong told the parliamentary party room enough was enough. She insisted that Buckingham resign from parliament, there and then, or she would go into the chamber and denounce him under privilege. It was an extraordinary threat against any sitting MP, let alone a party colleague. Buckingham refused, on principle, but Leong was not bluffing and carried through immediately. In a terse, six-minute speech, she apologised for failing to act sooner and, addressing herself to Buckland, said of her accusation of an 'act of sexual violence' by Buckingham: 'I believe you … our party has failed you'. Leong continued, indicating that there were further outstanding allegations against him: 'Jeremy's actions and behaviour – some widely reported and documented, and some still held in confidence, which must be respected – have had real and lasting consequences for individual women and members and former members of our party, as well as active volunteers in our party.'

Leong said Buckingham, a former friend, had twice behaved aggressively towards her – once in parliament and once on the street in Newtown – and added: 'I am sharing this information because I think it goes to character.'[74] In short, it was the most comprehensive denunciation Leong could muster.

In Canberra, the federal party room was taken by surprise – both by Leong's dramatic intervention, and by an accompanying joint statement by Leong and Senator Mehreen Faruqi. They felt there was no option but to support the call by both women for Buckingham to stand aside. Buckingham was furious and told Di Natale so. In the New South Wales party room, the split was deepening. The next day, Buckingham's long-time factional ally, Cate Faehrmann, wrote a piece for *The Sydney Morning Herald* defending him. Faehrmann explained she had suffered sexual harassment herself, but:

> … it is extremely distressing for me as it is for many women and
> Greens members to see allegations of sexual harassment and
> assault, including the party's handling of these, being used as a

political weapon. … I urged my colleague Jenny Leong to make a complaint via formal party processes if she has new allegations following her speech in Parliament this week using parliamentary privilege. Should an investigation commence, I have asked Jeremy Buckingham to stand aside from formal duties while this takes place. And I will be the first to call on him to resign should a complaint of unacceptable behaviour be upheld. Right now, however, we have a complaint which has been independently investigated, resulting in no adverse finding, being used to bring down a member of Parliament by his opponents within his own party.[75]

Buckingham refused to stand aside or resign, telling the *Herald* he had been 'democratically elected to the parliament and to the NSW Greens Legislative Council ticket by a ballot of all members'.

*   *   *

As the NSW Greens were exploding, in Victoria the Greens were in the final two weeks of a state election campaign. The run-up had not been good, starting with the shock resignation of Greg Barber a year earlier, under a cloud, and the bitter fallout from the Batman by-election. The relatively unknown Samantha Ratnam, vaulted straight from local council into the leadership of an eight-strong parliamentary party, now faced her first state campaign. In April, *The Age* ran an article by former Greens councillor for Casey, Lynette Keleher, warning there was a bullying and abusive culture in the Victorian Greens and a cover-up was underway over the takedown of Alex Bhathal: 'The leakers will not be found. The bullies will continue their careers in the party, and nothing will change.'[76] Days later, the paper reported the circumstances behind Barber's resignation seven months earlier: he had quit after reaching a $56,000 confidential settlement with a former staffer, who alleged sex discrimination, bullying and victimisation during her five-year stint in his office.[77]

The confidentiality did not last long. Soon after the settlement was reached, the woman's partner sent an email to 22 senior Victorian Greens, and Barber resigned two days later. A few months later, the complainant, Liz Ingham, broke her silence. Ingham told the ABC her experience working for Barber caused work-related depression for many years: 'The Greens don't care what happens to women within the party. What they care about is their public image,' she said. Ingham's husband, Trevor Coon, told the ABC that Barber had constantly referred to women in the workplace as 'fat, hairy lesbians', 'power pussies' and 'hairy-legged feminists', and accused him of having a 'men's room' in his office. Barber refused to discuss the complaint or defend himself, citing the confidentiality agreement.[78] Barber told *The Age* the ABC had material from at least one other staffer refuting Ms Ingham's allegations, but had not included that interview in its reporting.[79] Three former Barber staffers later wrote complaints to the ABC about the way the story was covered, contradicting Ingham's claims.

Meanwhile, a Labor dirt unit set about researching the party's candidates and soon drip-fed a series of shitposting scandals into the media. Some were funny but some very serious, like the stories about Footscray candidate Angus McAlpine, a pierced and tattooed plumber, originally from Ballarat, who was also a rap singer for a hip-hop band Broken Aesthetiks. Some of his lyrics were offensively misogynist, including references to the date-rape drug Rohypnol. McAlpine fronted a press conference, standing next to Ratnam, and explained he was deeply apologetic about the 'reprehensible' lyrics; he had fallen into a culture of toxic masculinity as a 'moronic' young man and was trying to change. It didn't stop the stories, however, as a more recent video surfaced in which McAlpine appeared to rap about how it was nothing for him to 'choke a bitch', although he insisted the lyric was a reference to smoking marijuana.[80] The Greens and leader Ratnam stood by McAlpine, but some senior women inside the party were agog that he had ever been preselected. Premier Daniel Andrews did not waste the opportunity, saying the Greens had a 'toxic cultural problem around women' and ruling out any negotiations or alliance with them, should they win the balance of power.[81]

Despite a shocking run of bad news, and notwithstanding a huge swing to Labor, the Greens' statewide vote did not collapse in Victoria: the primary vote fell by roughly 1 per cent in the lower house, to 10.7 per cent, and by 2 per cent in the upper house, to 9.3 per cent. This translated to a shellacking after preferences, however, with the Greens losing four of their five upper house MPs as a result of back-room preference deals. Ratnam herself, in the safest northern metropolitan region, was the only upper house MP re-elected, and the loss of her four colleagues in one fell swoop was a heavy blow for the party. In the lower house, there was no doubt the fallout from the Batman by-election took a heavy toll on the campaign by North-cote's Lidia Thorpe, an ally of defeated Bhathal. A year after her historic victory, Thorpe was out. Ellen Sandell was returned comfortably in Melbourne, and Sam Hibbins clung on in Prahran after another drawn-out count. The only bright spot in the state election was doctor Tim Read's win in Brunswick – another incursion into Labor's old inner-city heartland. When the counting was finalised, however, the party room had been cut in half, from eight MPs to four. The Andrews government had a huge majority in the lower house, and Ratnam – who remained as leader – was sidelined in the upper house.

It was not long before former MP Nina Springle quit the party, arguing there had been no accountability for the outcome. Springle wrote in her resignation letter: 'If it happened in any other party it would be considered a wipe-out ... the party establishment continues to stumble from one train wreck decision to the next, leaving a wake of destruction behind it, blatantly disregarding the human toll, all in the name of something I cannot even name anymore.'[82]

*   *   *

In New South Wales, just three months out from the state election in March 2019, the Greens were in the process of splitting. Jeremy Buckingham refused to stand down, and the MPs who continued to support him – Cate Faehrmann, Justin Field and Dawn Walker – issued an open letter to party members, calling for signatures to support the removal of destructive left forces within the party:

> The NSW Greens is at a crossroads and urgent action is necessary to prevent an irrevocable split of the party. The NSW Greens have been undermined by a deliberate and systematic effort by a small group of members motivated by extreme left ideology. Theirs is a deeply divisive form of politics that poisons goodwill and destabilised our core principles as Greens. Left Renewal was formed almost

two years ago and since then a large group of people from the entry-
ist 'revolutionary socialist' organisation Solidarity have joined and
become active in the NSW Greens. Their involvement and combat-
ive approach to the party has been endorsed and encouraged by
a few current and recent Greens MPs and senior party officials.

The open letter called for a recount of the upper house preselection,
with redistribution of the votes for Buckingham, should he stand aside.
In reply, the party hierarchy argued that if Buckingham was dropped
from the ticket, the next-placed candidate should simply be bumped
up into the winnable second place.[83] But the 'right' argued that this
would disenfranchise members who had voted for Buckingham – if
those votes were redistributed, sitting MP Dawn Walker would have
won. With an eight-year term in the upper house up for grabs, it was
another struggle to the end.

Finally in December 2018, after a motion calling on him to stand
down passed the state delegates council, Buckingham quit the party,
calling a press conference out the back of state parliament and ripping
up a piece of paper reading 'Toxic NSW Greens'.[84] He announced
he would run as an 'independent real Green', challenging the state
party's Marxist agenda.[85] On the ABC's Radio National *Breakfast*
next morning, Buckingham took a shot at the left of the party for
wanting to distance itself from the founder: 'If you think that ...
one of the most successful progressive politicians in Australia's history, Bob Brown, is a right-winger, you've got to be pretty extreme.'
Buckingham said the NSW Greens were now 'uncontrollable'[86] and
subsequently unveiled a credible 15-strong upper house ticket, of
which ten candidates were ex-Greens.

With Buckingham out, and Faehrmann and Field threatening to
follow, the party was on the brink. Behind the scenes, the right was
pushing for a conflict resolution process that would trigger provisions
in the Australian Greens constitution allowing for member bodies
such as the NSW Greens to be expelled. Di Natale warned his NSW
colleagues that if an agreement to mediation could not be reached,
Faehrmann and Field would quit, adding, 'If Bob is out there publicly
supporting the MPs who resign there's a risk that the party will split.'
Privately, after months of dealing with factional brawling in Victoria

and then in New South Wales, Di Natale was himself on the edge of quitting, and contemplated walking away from the leadership. A compromise was reached, and the national council ultimately resolved to support an independent 'root and branch' review of the NSW Greens, headed by former Tasmanian MP Paul O'Halloran. Looking back, Di Natale says, 'I spent weeks negotiating with people from all sides in NSW to broker an agreement that would keep the party together and it remains one of my most important achievements.'

Amazingly enough, given such a dire lead-in, the Greens' vote held. In the lower house, the state-wide vote dropped by 0.7 per cent to 9.6 per cent, but all three sitting members were returned. In Balmain, Jamie Parker won a third term with a 5 per cent primary swing towards him. Jenny Leong, in her first re-election campaign, also got a small swing towards her in Newtown. One disappointment for the party was in Lismore, where lawyer Sue Higginson, who ran the New South Wales Environment Defenders Office for 15 years and whose campaign was launched by Brown, was in with a real chance to take the seat off the Nationals, a win that never materialised.

In the upper house the Greens dropped by a tiny 0.2 per cent, to 9.7 per cent, but the party easily won two quotas. Although Shoebridge and Boyd were comfortably re-elected, the party quickly lost representation when Justin Field decided to quit and sit out the next four years as a lone independent. Overall the Greens had gone backwards – from eight to six MPs – but after the poll, all members committed to mediation and the public brawling stopped, pending the outcome of the review. Without his name above the line, Buckingham was doomed and none of his candidates elected.

*　　*　　*

Buoyed by the Liberal triumph in his home state, Scott Morrison called the federal election a few weeks later. After the bitterly fought campaigns in Victoria and New South Wales, the Australian Greens went into the May poll with a grim goal: defend, defend, defend. In the first half-Senate election since group voting tickets had been abolished in 2016, the higher 14 per cent quota spelled trouble, as polls showed the Greens' primary support had flatlined at around 9–10 per cent. A year out, senior party sources had been speculating that the

Greens could lose half their Senate seats if they got the same vote as in 2016. New South Wales, Queensland and South Australia were vulnerable. Diabolically, all three seats were held by women, meaning defeat would change the Greens party room fundamentally: Mehreen Faruqi, contesting her first federal election, Larissa Waters, only recently back in the Senate after the dual citizenship imbroglio, and Sarah Hanson-Young.

Adding to the tension was the general expectation of a Labor victory, following the replacement of Malcolm Turnbull with Morrison. Historically the Greens vote suffers when the Coalition is in power and a swing is on, and progressive voters worry their vote will be wasted. What's more, the CFMEU and Electrical Trades Union had swung in behind Labor's heavily union-backed campaign. This would hit Adam Bandt, in Melbourne, particularly hard, as the ETU alone had donated more than $780,000 to his campaigns since 2010.

The Greens also faced a policy challenge heading into 2019: under Bill Shorten, Labor had tacked left, in many cases adopting the minor party's policies – a national integrity commission, reform of discretionary trusts, negative gearing and capital gains tax concessions.

Notwithstanding the fractured state of the party in Victoria and New South Wales, the Australian Greens had gathered momentum in the federal parliament. Di Natale had called time on the Coalition in a withering speech at the height of the August coup against Turnbull, labelling the government a 'national embarrassment ... so focused on yourselves that you have forgotten what the country elected you to do, and that is to govern – for them, not for you. You don't deserve to govern; you deserve to be turfed out.' It was watched almost two million times on Facebook generating interest from international media like the BBC but, as usual, almost nothing in Australia. After intense negotiations, the crossbench and Labor had agreed to back laws to evacuate sick asylum seekers to the mainland, to get them the medial treatment they needed. The key was a strategy cooked up in Adam Bandt's office: to amend a dormant government bill in the Senate, which could then pass the House on a simple majority without suspending standing orders – skirting the Greens' usual problem where a private member's bill languished indefinitely. It was not only the first time in 90 years that a government had been defeated on the floor of the House, it was also the first time since 2010 that Labor had stared down the possibility of a Coalition scare campaign on border protection. The Greens' senator Jordon Steele-John, in barely a year in parliament, had spoken passionately on behalf of people with a disability who suffered abuse at the hands of carers and others, and in February succeeded succeeding in getting up a referral for a royal commission. He was then unafraid to wheel himself into the House of Representatives and, literally shouting at the chamber, call on the government to commit to a timetable and funding.[87]

More than anything else, however, 2019 was billed as a climate election. The Greens renewed their call to phase out coal exports, and made the Adani's Carmichael coal mine the centrepiece of their messaging on climate and a clear point of difference between themselves and Labor. During the campaign, a 'Stop Adani' convoy organised by the Bob Brown Foundation left Hobart, to drive all the way up the east coast of Australia to Queensland and then inland to the town of Clermont – a coal town in the Bowen basin, 160 kilometres from where the Carmichael mine would be built, but still the nearest town. 'To address climate change you've got to have a plan to address coal,' Di Natale said, 'and that's why I'm joining the Adani convoy in a few days' time.' The debate about the Stop Adani convoy, and the Coalition's scramble to finalise outstanding approvals before going into caretaker mode, would have a decisive impact on the election, alienating regional Queensland voters, with the Murdoch press beating the story up every step of the way. Inside Labor, the Stop Adani convoy was seen as a political stunt to boost the Greens vote. Felicity Wade, a former campaigner for The Wilderness Society and the Labor Environment Action Network, says the Greens perpetuate conflict over the environment for electoral gain, and draws a parallel between the convoy and the 2012 Tasmanian Forest Agreement. 'Brown and Milne tried to kill the TFA with all their might,' says Wade. 'Part of it is perfect over the good, but why is perfect over the good so important to them? Because Labor being crap and failing is essential to them keeping up their vote. And you see the Green vote collapse when the Tasmanian forest issue is no longer a hot political issue.'

By and large, the Greens struggled for attention in an election that was dominated by a Coalition scare campaign about Labor's tax plans, and dubbed 'Australia's first post-truth campaign'. One of the most misleading claims stoked fears that a Labor government had done a deal with the Greens and the unions to introduce a 40 per cent 'death tax' if elected.[88] This was an old bogey for the Greens, which had adopted an ambiguous position of supporting an inheritance tax in principle but not including one in its official pre-election platform. The party's star candidate for the blue-ribbon Liberal seat of Kooyong, celebrated human rights lawyer Julian Burnside, told ABC Melbourne that some form of inheritance tax 'makes a whole lot of sense when you think about it'.[89] It was grist for the mill, and the Liberals, One Nation and others continued to push the idea that Labor would bring in the inheritance tax 'with the help of the Greens'. In the wake of the campaign, there were renewed calls for legislation to require truth in election advertising – just as Bob Brown had urged decades earlier.

Although the main focus was to hang on to sitting MPs, in Melbourne the party's attention had shifted south of the Yarra, given the inner-north remained cauterised by the Batman disaster. The party set its sights on the Liberal seats of Higgins, where Kelly O'Dwyer was resigning, and Kooyong, held by treasurer Josh Frydenberg. None of it was to be: Jason Ball for the Greens in Higgins actually went slightly backwards; Burnside got a swing towards him, but Frydenberg remained safe. Could the Greens ever win wealthy Liberal seats running on a left-wing platform? More tantalising was Canberra, where former Milne staffer Tim Hollo won 24 per cent of the primary vote, but still ran third. At least Bandt held Melbourne – a foregone conclusion. The Greens' sole lower house seat, now ultra-safe on a margin of more than 20 per cent, was beginning to look more exceptional, and less like a beachhead into the lower house.

Most importantly, the Australian Greens had held on to all their Senate seats, with a swing to the party of 1.6, lifting the national vote to 10.2 per cent after three difficult years in which hard-won gains on legislation and policy were marred by party room brawls and organisational toxicity and failure. In both houses it was the best result since 2010. There were some big swings, too: in South Australia, where the Xenophon phenomenon had fizzled, the party's first preference vote jumped by 5 per cent; in Queensland, where the

Stop Adani convoy had rolled through, the party got a swing of more than 3 per cent. The Greens may not have surged forward dramatically, but the result showed that the base level of support of 10 per cent was solid. If the same results were repeated in 2022, the party could gain another two or three seats in a half-Senate election – perhaps even take the sole balance of power in the upper house. A week after Australia went to the polls, a 'Green wave' surged through European elections, with Die Grünen emerging as the most popular party in Germany for the first time in the country's history, taking 27 per cent of the vote. In a backlash against the populist right, which had been building since Brexit and the Trump election of 2016, Green parties also did well in France and the United Kingdom, Belgium and Ireland. The school strikers, and Extinction Rebellion, had put climate back on the agenda. A surge of left populism, a push for a Green New Deal – was this just the beginning? As one of *The Guardian*'s correspondents observed, 'once seen as fringe idealists, the Greens have obtained credibility after serving as part of coalitions in several countries ... they are a party of government, and not just a home for disconcerted protest voters'.[90]

While a European-style 'green wave' is unlikely in Australia given our voting system, a sharp post-election analysis by commentator Greg Jericho posed a challenge to the Greens and Labor: after a quarter-century of policy failure, the parties should join forces and work together, for the climate's sake.[91] Labor's apparent drift to the right under Anthony Albanese may well suit the Greens. In a cheeky reshuffle announcement following the election, Richard Di Natale described his party as the 'real opposition', styling his spokespeople as shadow ministers for the first time. 'Someone needs to stand up against Scott Morrison's regime of failed trickle-down economics,' he said, 'or we'll end up living in a dog-eat-dog society like Trump's America.'[92] The story of the Greens in Australia – always over-reaching, always close to splitting, always at a crossroads – is far from over.

The Challenge Ahead

CHAPTER 12

CONFRONTING THE CLIMATE EMERGENCY

At a Stop Adani rally in leafy Parramatta Park, in the heart of Sydney's western suburbs, Bob Brown took the stage and told the little crowd of a few hundred dedicated activists (who else would turn out on Easter Saturday?) that it reminded him of a rally at Hyde Park in 1983 to save the Franklin. The protesters won that time, and they would again, Brown said to cheers of 'Good on you, Bob'. This time, however, the cause was different. Conservative estimates put the number of dead due to global heating in 2018 at 150,000 worldwide, Brown said, and worse was to come. 'There are scientists who predict that the population at the end of this century won't be 12 billion, it'll be 1 billion, and between us and that prediction is unimaginable human suffering.' If the crowd understood, it did not dampen their mood.

Brown continued: if Australia, the world's richest-per-capita country ever, couldn't do its own bit to turn that situation around, 'Who can we ask to do it?' After some more rousing speeches, Brown and another 180 vehicles continued on their trip from Hobart to Clermont, in central Queensland, near where Adani's Carmichael coalmine would be built. The mine, which received its last federal approval just days before the election was called, would be served by a rail line to the coast and would open up the Galilee Basin, a whole new coal province 400 kilometres inland. A study for Greenpeace in 2013 listed the Galilee as being among 14 'carbon bombs' globally that, combined, would lock in more than 2 degrees of warming if they went ahead.[1]

If the Franklin campaign was to save a wild river, the Stop Adani campaign was a fight for the planet itself. (Like the Franklin campaign, which predated the Greens, the Adani rally was not meant to be a party-political event, but Greens leader Richard Di Natale was there, as was Senator Mehreen Faruqi and a string of the party's candidates.) Brown was not misrepresenting the science: considered estimates of the carrying capacity of a planet that is 4 degrees warmer – with the tropics uninhabitable, and food chains in collapse – are as low as half a billion people. As of the start of 2019, the national commitments pledged after the 2015 Paris Agreement have the world on course for warming of 3–4 degrees, and emissions are still rising.[2]

*   *   *

The Greens have four pillars, but there is one pillar that distinguishes them from all previous political parties, and without which the party would not exist. It is, of course, a commitment to ecological sustainability. In the Australian Greens' charter, the first of the party's general principles is 'to ensure that human activity respects the integrity of ecosystems and does not impair biodiversity and the ecological resilience of life-supporting systems'.

The twenty-first-century climate emergency, anticipated as early as 1972 in *The Limits to Growth* and flagged by scientists decades before that, puts every other ecological challenge in the shade and will do so for decades. All the gains of the environmental movement are jeopardised by climate change, as Christine Milne realised in 1990 when she was appointed to Australia's first Greenhouse Council, alongside former Victorian premiers Rupert Hamer and Joan Kirner, and went to a briefing on climate science in Melbourne:

> I realised then – which I've argued ever since, and which is why I've made climate my thing – that no matter how many areas we get protected – reefs and forests and everything else – it's going to be a Pyrrhic victory unless we win on the climate. Because ultimately you're going to lose your biodiversity, everything, if we can't constrain global warming.

Milne made climate her mission. After losing her seat in the Tasmanian parliament in 1998, she started attending the United Nations Framework Convention on Climate Change's annual 'Conference of Parties' talks. She was 'absolutely plugged in' to what was happening on climate internationally, and her prime motivation for going into federal politics was 'to actually try and convince the Australian Parliament that we had to act on global warming'. Surveys repeatedly show that most Greens members agree the fight to stop climate change should be the party's number-one priority: in a 2016 survey of 9000 members, 90 per cent said so, and a smaller survey in 2018 was similarly emphatic.[3] Voters, too, expect that of the party, with polls showing the Greens are most trusted on the issue of climate change.[4]

The science of climate change is terrifying, once the risks of unstoppable, runaway warming are understood. As Bill McKibben writes in a recent essay on how human extinction may be about to play out, 'it could get *very* bad'.[5] Climate scientists themselves say the public has no idea of the danger the planet is in, because the message is muffled by layers of effective censorship – some of it self-censorship, some imposed. What climate scientists say privately is scarier than what they publish in peer-reviewed journals. What gets published in peer-reviewed journals is scarier than what gets collated in the reports of the Intergovernmental Panel on Climate Change, which represent a lowest-common-denominator consensus watered down by scientists from powerful UN members like Saudi Arabia and Russia. The United Nations process relies on the IPCC, but the targets set at meetings like 'COP 21' in Paris are not reflected in the actions of member nations. And finally, of course, these commitments are subject to the haphazard domestic politics of each country, filtered through an often actively denialist media – especially in the Anglophone nations dominated by Rupert Murdoch's Fox-ified news organisation.

In Australia, the most coal-dependent rich country, and the highest per-capita emitter, the debate is especially surreal, and completely divorced from the challenge that climate science presents. As David Spratt, co-author of the groundbreaking *Climate Code Red*, wrote in a 2012 critique of the persistent 'bright-siding' embodied in official and NGO campaigns around the carbon price, which emphasised the 'win-win' of clean energy and barely mentioned climate risks: 'It is astounding that neither the prime minister nor any leader of either major party anywhere in Australia can say in public what most already know: that global warming is making high-profile extreme weather events worse.'[6]

The Greens understand all this, and their climate policy platform is the most ambitious, and therefore the most closely attuned to the science, of any of the major parties. As climate science and solutions technology have evolved, so have the Greens' policy commitments strengthened and broadened – in effect, chasing the science. The Greens' first platform, in 1992, anticipated a carbon price by arguing for the externalities of pollution to be internalised. This was not especially radical: former Labor science minister Barry Jones had backed a carbon tax in 1989, so did the Democrats' Senator John Coulter, it was the official policy of Irina Dunn's 'Environment Independents' in 1990, and it was widely debated and ultimately rejected by the Hawke government's Ecologically Sustainable Development Working Groups in November 1991.[7] In 1996 Bob Brown and Peter Singer, in *The Greens*, called for a $5-a-tonne carbon tax, a call which Brown built upon in his early years in parliament, hiking the price to $25 a tonne; he also proposed a public 'Sun Fund' in 1997 to invest in renewables, supported Howard's 2001 mandatory Renewable Energy Target of 2 per cent by 2010, and put forward a 2004 plan called 'Renew Australia' to raise Green Bonds to fund infrastructure, mainly transport.[8]

Climate change really came to the fore in Australian politics in the lead-up to the 2007 election, however, as the millennium drought bit hard, Howard dragged his heels on signing up to the Kyoto Protocol, and *An Inconvenient Truth* and the Stern Review on the Economics of Climate Change ramped up the worldwide debate about climate science and economics. Christine Milne's economy-wide Re-Energising Australia policy, launched ahead of what was dubbed the first climate election, proposed an emissions-trading scheme, a Renewable Energy Target of 25 per cent by 2020 (which is likely, by the way, to be achieved), and overall emissions-reductions targets of minus 30 per cent by 2020, compared with 1990 levels, and minus 80 per cent by 2050. Again, while the targets were aggressive, the ETS mechanism was not especially controversial in 2007: both Liberal and Labor supported just such a scheme as the most cost-effective way of cutting emissions.

Momentum gathered with the release of the IPCC's fourth assessment report in 2007, which sparked controversy by warning that

Himalayan glaciers 'are receding faster than in any other part of the world and, if the present rate continues, the likelihood of them disappearing by the year 2035 and perhaps sooner is very high' (a warning later criticised as unsubstantiated).[9] US president-elect Barack Obama, in his December 2008 victory speech, acknowledged a 'planet in peril'. The 2009 Copenhagen Summit was now or never for the planet. In Australia, the publication of the landmark Garnaut Review in 2008, and more alarming works like *Climate Code Red*, framed the decade to 2020 as the last chance for decisive action, when global emissions must start to fall. The Greens got their best-ever vote in 2010 as the Labor Party, led by Julia Gillard, and the Coalition, under Tony Abbott, vacated the climate policy field altogether.[10] An official plan to achieve 100 per cent renewables was one product of the ensuing Labor/Greens Multi-Party Climate Change Committee. Nonetheless, the Greens' Renew Australia policy document, launched at the end of 2015 under Richard Di Natale's leadership, only had a target of 90 per cent renewables by 2030, and stopped short of calling for the reintroduction of a carbon price, while pushing for zero emissions by 2040.

It was the Greens' achievements in the Gillard minority government that drew young climate activist Ellen Sandell to join the party, when she decided after all that going into politics offered the biggest 'bang for buck'. Sandell had grown up in country Victoria, and won a scholarship to study science at the University of Melbourne, where she was lectured on climate by the likes of David Karoly. Sandell started a campaign to get the university to divest from fossil fuels, and joined the Australian Youth Climate Coalition. After graduating, she worked for a brief time at the CSIRO, then joined the Office of Climate Change inside the Premier's department under Steve Bracks and then John Brumby. The Garnaut Review team was housed just down the corridor, and Sandell had been part of a Victorian delegation to the Bali COP in 2007, full of optimism.

She did 18 months of policy work for the Premier's department and grew progressively disillusioned. A draft carbon sinks forestry policy, based on rigorous consultation with the best experts in the field, came back covered in red ink, with all the science taken out and replaced by forestry industry spin. A policy to put solar panels on schools was dumped – and air-conditioners installed instead – after a single day of hostile callers on talkback radio. All the time, Sandell says, the 'elephant in the room' was brown coal in the Latrobe Valley. 'We were trying to get people to drive more smoothly, to reduce emissions,' she says, 'but when it came to brown coal, it was always too hard.' Vested interests had a stranglehold on the Labor Party, preventing it from taking the necessary action on climate. Sandell quit, and went off to work full-time for the AYCC.

The youth coalition, with 100,000 members, was among the many environmental groups that backed the Greens' decision to vote down the CPRS, and applauded when the Greens signed the agreement with the Gillard government. At the 2013 election, with the tide going out for Labor, Sandell ran the ACT Senate campaign for GetUp! director Simon Sheikh. 'That was a very strategic decision for both of us,' says Sandell. 'We were hoping to protect the carbon price but we just missed out by 0.6 per cent. In the end it was only a couple of votes in the Senate that did it, so if we had been able to win the ACT we could have saved it.' Soon afterwards, she won preselection for the state seat of Melbourne, and went on to win the seat for the Greens in the 2014 election.

As a Greens MP, Sandell has been a staunch advocate for a properly planned and funded transition away from coal-fired power in Victoria; she has visited the Latrobe Valley many times, but found that her pleas fell on deaf ears. In the end, when the French-owned Hazelwood power station shut suddenly in the wake of the Paris climate agreement, workers were given six months' notice and electricity prices spiked through the National Electricity Market as generators gamed the system. Many blamed the Greens for the disruption, leaving Sandell utterly frustrated:

> I'm not a sociopath – maybe don't use the word sociopath – but, you know, I want people to have good lives, I want people to have sustainable jobs. I don't want to screw people over. But we have to think about the big picture, which is that people in Bangladesh are dying, climate change is going to hurt all of us, coal has to close – it already is closing – and absolutely we need to protect people while we do it, but we also need to talk about climate change.

The global energy industry, of course, is transforming regardless of anything the Greens do or don't do. In the decade Australia has lost to the climate wars, technology has advanced so spectacularly that much of the downside to climate action has disappeared, particularly on energy. Renewables plus storage is now cheaper than new coal-fired power – and certainly cheaper than nuclear or carbon capture and storage – and so the dynamic has shifted such that a move to renewables has become inevitable. The future direction of energy markets is also becoming clearer, and it is evident that renewable energy will ultimately power electrified transport. The focus should soon shift to emissions-reduction solutions for the next-most-polluting industries, particularly agriculture, and to the urgent challenge of drawdown technologies that might quickly lower carbon dioxide concentrations in the atmosphere and reverse climate change.

In the energy industry, says Richard Di Natale, the coal industry is 'on the way out – what we're arguing about is a timeframe'. Arguing that the transition should be properly planned for, Di Natale makes the comparison with the demise of the manufacturing and textiles industries as a result of tariff cuts in the 1980s. 'That transition wasn't managed, a lot of people were just left out.' A similar comparison could be made about the demise of the car-manufacturing industry under the Abbott government.

From 2016 to 2019, the Greens' climate change spokesperson was Adam Bandt, who argues, like Di Natale, that the shift to the right over the past three decades has turned 'plan' into a dirty word, as though it's a throwback to a command-and-control economy. Bandt overhauled the party's Renew Australia policy and shifted the focus to a steady phase-out of coal exports over the 12 years to 2030. This is an ambitious goal, which departs from the normal practice under the UN framework, which only counts domestic emissions towards each country's total. That means Australia is only responsible for reducing the emissions from the fossil fuels it burns at home. Yet Australia is the world's largest exporter of coal, and, as Bandt explains when he outlines the policy, if the emissions from burning that coal overseas are included, the country becomes the sixth-largest greenhouse-gas emitter in the world. Effectively, by phasing out coal exports, Australia would be intervening in the energy policy of other countries.

It is not clear whether this would reduce emissions – the world is not short of coal – but, all else being equal, the withdrawal of the Australian supply would push up prices, stimulating more production elsewhere. On the other hand, an export ban would be politically potent. In 2006, when Newcastle City Council passed a motion moved by Greens councillor Michael Osborne, calling on the state government to cap coal exports at existing levels and impose a moratorium on new mines, the story went around the global industry like wildfire: the world's biggest coal port, banning coal.[11]

The Greens' new push to tackle coal exports took cognisance of a crucial development in 2018, when the CSIRO announced a breakthrough that allowed the safe transport of hydrogen, converted to ammonia, opening up the potential that Australia could become a renewable energy superpower by exporting a carbon-free fuel.[12] Finally, the Greens had an answer to the question former ABC political editor Chris Uhlmann had confronted Bob Brown with when he first proposed a coal phase-out in 2007: how would you replace the billions of lost export earnings? The technological breakthrough created a vast possibility for Australia, which Atlassian founder Mike Cannon-Brookes realised when he proposed a 200 per cent renewables target or higher: Australia should install enough renewable generation capacity not just to power its electricity grid, but to electrify its transport, and chase an enormous export market in Asia. The Greens' updated Renew Australia 2030 policy pointed to the potential not just for hydrogen exports, but for direct exports of solar energy via undersea cables – such as the Macquarie-backed Australian Renewable Energy Hub, which proposed to take solar power from the Pilbara, via undersea cables, to Indonesia and Singapore.

After vacillating in the Abbott–Turnbull years over whether or not to back an economy-wide carbon price, in late 2018 the Greens finally confirmed they would once again push for the revival of an emissions-trading scheme.[13] The resulting policy stuck with the 2040 decarbonisation goal, and proposed a carbon price of $32 a tonne – which is where it would have been, had the original ETS never been abolished – to raise $66 billion over a decade. It was the centrepiece of the Greens' policy, funding all the other proposals, but it was hardly mentioned in the document; there is no prospect of an ETS being implemented, after all, unless one of the major parties proposes it.

*   *   *

Should the Greens' climate policy line up with the best science, or should it have a realistic chance of being adopted? It is a genuine conundrum, because even if the Greens were catapulted into government tomorrow, the most urgent action Australia could take would not by itself solve global climate change.

The problem is encapsulated in the party's constant refrain that Australia must take urgent action on climate change to save the Great Barrier Reef. As Climate Extremes Research Fellow at the University of Melbourne Andrew King told ABC's Radio National *Earshot* program in late 2016, after the reef had suffered the first of back-to-back bleaching events that would kill half its coral, 'to be honest, even with very strong action now, even if we really reduce our greenhouse-gas emissions very quickly, we're probably not going to save the reef'.[14] The Greens' environment spokesperson, Larissa Waters, conceded at the time that this presents a diabolically difficult communication challenge for a political party:

> PADDY MANNING: The reef's done for, isn't it? Done for.
>
> LARISSA WATERS: If I was a reef scientist I would have to say that's the inevitable conclusion, but because I'm not, and because I refuse to give up hope, then I think we will change it incredibly significantly, but I will not give up on it. At 2 degrees [global heating] we lose 100 per cent of global coral reefs, and at one and a half [per cent] we lose 90 per cent, and we're on track for 4 [per cent], so at the moment the prospects are not good …
>
> PADDY MANNING: … The Greens' messaging is 'we have to save the reef', but the science is, it can't be saved?
>
> LARISSA WATERS: No, the science is 'we've got to move bloody fast or we will lose it all' … If the message was 'the reef's fucked', what's the point? No one would do anything, and then it really would be fucked.

False hope or not, Waters was absolutely right that urgent action remains necessary even if it is too late to save the reef. As former Greens candidate Clive Hamilton argued in *Requiem for a Species*, helplessness is indeed 'immiserising', and although it is too late to prevent climate disruption, 'any success in reducing emissions is better than doing nothing, because warming and its effects can at least be slowed down'.[15] The difference between a world that is 2 degrees, 3 degrees or 4 degrees hotter is enormous.

The following year, in a meeting at the Newtown Neighbourhood Centre as part of a nationwide listening tour, Richard Di Natale posed this same conundrum to an audience of a hundred or so party members:

> I just want to see a show of hands: who thinks it's really important that we focus primarily on the impacts of climate change: increased risk of fire, coastal inundation and so on? The other [option] is to talk about the opportunities that come from making the transition, the economies we can create, the jobs that come from that, cleaner air and so on.

The highly engaged audience could not make a choice; someone called out, 'Both.'

Climate activist David Spratt says even scientists themselves, not to mention NGOs or the Greens, are guilty of 'bright-siding'. An honest climate policy, he says, would make clear that climate action must take precedence over every other objective this decade: 'Climate change is now an existential risk, one that will annihilate intelligent life or permanently and drastically curtail its potential development. If we do not solve the climate issue, all the other things we care about and campaign about will simply become irrelevant in a world of outright chaos.'

In a seminal *Crikey* article on the future of the Greens, author Guy Rundle wrote that 'there's no point securing same-sex marriage if its beneficiaries will celebrate their 50th anniversaries on a fire-ravaged, climate-war-scarred hellhole'. Rundle argued that the Greens, like all transformative parties, faced a paradox:

Do you insist on your cause as primary and eschew day-to-day government, or try to combine the two? If the cause is sufficiently pressing, you avoid the latter. The African National Congress, before the end of apartheid, did not have an arts policy or a position on the siting of the new Pretoria airport. Its position on everything was 'end apartheid'. The Greens, part of a movement that insists – correctly – that a planetary crisis is imminent and urgent, could take the position that they should just strive for election, to insist upon that and treat everything from tax regimes to same-sex marriage as a fatal distraction. In the early days, the party had more than a flavour of that.[16]

Some committed climate activists have opted against joining a party that has to juggle priorities from asylum seekers to public education to banking royal commissions to raising Newstart and changing the date of Australia Day, in favour of something 100 per cent climate-focused. So, for example, Philip Sutton, co-author of the landmark *Climate Code Red*, has supported the Independents for Climate Action, who fielded Senate candidates in five states in 2019, or former Greens candidate Adrian Whitehead's Save the Planet party, which has contested state elections in Victoria.

Other dedicated activists eschew party politics altogether. Jonathan Moylan, for example, mounted a lone protest against the Maules Creek coalmine in the Liverpool Ranges of New South Wales, camping out in the Leard State Forest, and caused a national outcry in 2013 when he put out a fake press release from ANZ saying the bank had decided not to fund the mine. For 20 minutes, the share market was misinformed, hundreds of millions of dollars were wiped from the value of the miner Whitehaven Coal, and a small number of investors who sold on basis of the announcement would have lost about half a million dollars combined (but might have been glad of it later, as Whitehaven's value continued to fall). In the financial pages, there was outrage. In a stirring op-ed, Bob Brown defended Moylan as a hero in the civil disobedience tradition of Gandhi and Mandela.[17] Moylan had put a lot on the line, suffering national opprobrium and risking prison for his beliefs (although he was given a bond), but he was not interested in going into politics. 'I'm a big believer in the power of independent, nonpartisan movements and willing to work with any communities affected by extractive industries,' he says. 'What we need is a movement powerful enough that it can't be ignored by any politician.'[18]

But Greens MPs must juggle their own priorities with those of their electors. As NSW Greens MP Jenny Leong told *The Sydney Morning Herald*'s Nick O'Malley, much of her time is spent working on behalf of public housing residents in need of immediate assistance to secure not only basic maintenance but also long-term mental health and drug and alcohol support. 'You can't tell someone you are not going to help them get their intercom fixed because climate change is the most pressing global issue,' Leong said.[19]

Adam Bandt has his own view of the best way forward for the party, arguing that a relentless, single-minded focus on climate change can be counterproductive:

> There are a lot of old left groups who say, 'I want to convince everyone that the problem is capitalism, and that means any time someone tells me there is a problem or that they are experiencing a problem, I'll tell them the answer is to smash capitalism.' So that hasn't proved very successful in building movements for social change in the last hundred years ... and I think we've got to make sure we don't fall into a similar trap of saying, 'Well, the answer to everything is to convince you about how important climate change is.'

Bandt looks to the success of the anti-austerity and anti-capitalist political parties overseas, such as the 'red–green–purple' Syriza, now in government in Greece, or Podemos, now the third-largest party in the Spanish parliament. Rather than lecturing voters on climate, he says, Greens politicians should do more listening, and take on board their concerns about unaffordable housing, the high cost of university degrees, and insecure work.

> It's time to take those issues and treat them with the respect that they deserve ... And then you work out a way of linking those various campaigns, to the point where people are more willing

to hear your message about climate change because they know that you're fighting for affordable housing. We've done a micro version of that in Melbourne over the last six years, to the point where people who never would have thought about voting for the Greens now see us as the people that are there campaigning with them and so they're more prepared to trust us or work with us come election time.

An extension of Bandt's view is that capitalism is the fundamental problem, and that fixing capitalism is the only way to tackle climate change. That's the line taken by Naomi Klein in *This Changes Everything*, for example, and it has been reflected in firebrand US Democratic senator Alexandria Ocasio-Cortez's calls for a Green New Deal, which would guarantee clean industry jobs for all, as part of a nationwide effort comparable with a wartime mobilisation.

At a Young Greens conference in Canberra in 2017, delegates heard a rousing talk from Lily Matchett, president of the Australian Students Environmental Network. Matchett was not a member of the Greens, and argued the party was not being radical enough:

> I feel our responses to climate change should be anti-capitalist or at least sharply challenge the capitalist mode of production ... [we should not] fall into a trap of green capitalism, carbon trading schemes, offsets and other market solutions to climate change, which have absolutely failed to bring down average temperature increases. These approaches must be entirely thrown in the bin.

There was plenty of applause for that one. Matchett cited Klein's argument that if an economic justice agenda can be married with climate action, 'then you create a constituency of people that will fight for that future because they directly benefit from it'. Matchett railed against the revolving door of politicians and fossil-fuel interests and called for young Greens to blockade fossil-fuel projects. Matchett had campaigned for her own University of Sydney to divest from fossil fuels, and argued that restoring a safe climate meant leaving fossil-fuel reserves unburned, causing huge writedowns for business. The revolutionary demand worth fighting for, Matchett said, was for 'energy democracy' – a class-based approach proposing socialised production of distributed, 100 per cent renewable energy. 'I'm confused as to why it's easier for us to envisage the end of the human race through catastrophic climate change than to envisage a not-for-profit sustainable energy system or an end to capitalism if it is our will,' she said.

The Greens have responded to these calls for energy democracy: at the National Press Club, Di Natale called for the establishment of a publicly owned energy retailer, and the Renew Australia policy calls for public investment in new transmission lines to renewable energy zones, which are to be created where the wind and solar resources are optimal. NSW Greens MP David Shoebridge, releasing his own manifesto, called on the Commonwealth to 'renationalise the energy grid and commit our common wealth to building a nationwide energy grid powered by renewables'.

Matchett's fiery talk raised a critical issue that is often overlooked by so-called conservatives who deny climate change and resist action: the longer they obfuscate and delay, the greater the crisis, and the more drastic the solutions need to become. Bandt, like Klein, believes in private property and democracy, fearing that the right's climate denialism belies an unspoken agenda:

> The only thing that will get us out of our current predicament is more democracy, not less. There's a real risk of that – that the right takes control of either dealing with climate change or dealing with its effects. And you can very easily imagine a very authoritarian response to the catastrophes of climate change … and I have to wonder whether the immigration politics that we've witnessed in Australia over the last 15 to 20 years is about getting us ready for something even more brutal that's about to come when people in our neighbourhood all of a sudden don't have a home to go to because sea levels are rising, or when people in Africa can't grow crops on their lands anymore, and everyone starts to move – what are they going to do? Well, we've put the walls up and we've learned to turn a blind eye to what happens to them.

In mid-2019, the UN's special rapporteur on extreme poverty said the world was heading towards 'climate apartheid', as the impacts of global heating undermined not only basic rights to life, water, food and housing for hundreds of millions of people, but also democracy and the rule of law:

> The risk of community discontent, of growing inequality, and of even greater levels of deprivation among some groups, will likely stimulate nationalist, xenophobic, racist and other responses. Maintaining a balanced approach to civil and political rights will be extremely complex ... We risk a 'climate apartheid' scenario where the wealthy pay to escape overheating, hunger, and conflict while the rest of the world is left to suffer.

The climate debate is ratcheting up. In the wake of the IPCC's landmark October 2018 report on the impacts of global warming of 1.5 degrees, even the language has shifted, with *The Guardian* announcing in early 2019 it would thenceforth report on the 'climate crisis' and 'global heating'.[20] Swedish schoolgirl Greta Thunberg's climate strikers, the Extinction Rebellion, the Green New Deal and the climate emergency declarations proliferating in cities and states around the world are the new hallmarks of climate action, and half-measures will not suffice. The Greens will either lead this debate, or drown in it.

*   *   *

Radical policy prescriptions like renationalising the electricity grid, let alone smashing capitalism, are in the realms of political fantasy in the wake of a federal election that returned a Coalition government on an explicitly pro-coal platform. Serious climate action will probably wait on the next Labor government, but after its May 2019 defeat the former environment minister Tony Burke flagged that the party could face reality and drop its support for unpopular market-based solutions in favour of a more interventionist 'Green New Deal' approach.

Wherever the ALP lands, it remains implacably hostile to dealing with the Greens, as was clear from a Twitter spat just before the election, when Di Natale told *The Guardian*'s Katharine Murphy that, if elected, Prime Minister Bill Shorten should recognise it was 'important to have a constructive relationship with the Greens', who would urge that 'now is the time to base a policy on science'. Di Natale said one of the tests would be whether the policy included a plan to phase out coal – and the Greens were not going to give Labor a blank cheque, warning there could be a repeat of 2009: 'If it's going to lock in failure, then we won't support it.'[21]

Deputy Labor leader Tanya Plibersek dismissed the Greens' offer to work with Labor, tweeting: 'Yeah, nah. Do you think people have forgotten your party worked with Tony Abbott to stop action on climate change last time? Don't need that kind of help.'[22]

Scott Ludlam posted an angry thread:

> This labor trope that we should have voted for the garbage CPRS just because it had the word 'carbon' in the name is well past its use-by date ... here's a quick refresher. back in 2009, greenpeace called the CPRS a 'monumental fraud'. rudd wanted a 'bipartisan' bill. so he designed the CPRS to appease the coal and gas industries and the climate denialists within the LNP. and when it all went to shit and abbott took the leadership, rudd demanded the greens pass his monumental fraud, without amendments. so if you read this guardian piece and your first instinct is to say 'the greens and other crossbenchers should just pass whatever labor bowls up', respectfully, no. signalling that we would do that simply guarantees mediocrity. and it is way past time for that.[23]

Soon afterwards, Bill Shorten declared Labor would not replicate Gillard's joint policy process with the Greens in any minority government scenario, rebuffing Di Natale's overture.[24]

While federal politics has been marked by dysfunction on climate since 2010, the Greens have been able to make progress at state, territory and local levels. The standout has been the ACT, where Shane Rattenbury became climate minister in a Labor minority government, and has provided the best example in the country of the difference the Greens can make when holding the balance of power. In the Abbott years, when the renewables industry was under assault, the ACT propped it up almost single-handedly with its target of 100 per cent renewables by 2020, on which the Greens agreed with Labor. Rattenbury explains:

> [O]ne of the things we insisted on was a legislated greenhouse-gas
> reduction targets … so I take what had been signed up to [in] Bali,
> which was that developed countries should reduce their emissions
> by 25 to 40 per cent below 1990 levels by 2020. I bring that to the
> negotiating table here and say, 'This is what we, the Greens, want.'
> Jon Stanhope is chief minister, he says, 'No way,' right. He says,
> 'We'll have a legislated target, but there's no way I'm committing
> to a number,' right. The outcome was we would have a legislated
> climate target, and it would be [up to] a committee to determine
> what the number should be … the committee comes back and
> says 25 to 40 per cent, and through campaigning and cajoling we
> end up signing up to 40 per cent reduction below 1990 levels by
> 2020. That policy has now rippled through, and that's what then
> drove the Renewable Energy Target and a bunch of other things
> to meet that target.

Given that two-thirds of the ACT's emissions came from the electricity
sector, going 100 per cent renewable by 2020 was the most effective
way to hit the 40 per cent emissions-reduction target, which the ACT
is on track to do. 'We are a world-leading jurisdiction,' says Rattenbury.

> We were the only people buying in the country in that 2013–2015
> period. And you speak to people in the wind industry, they will
> say it's the ACT that kept us going – this tiny little jurisdiction.
> My view has been we are a small jurisdiction but what we can
> do is because we are progressive and we're small and we can get
> things done. We have a duty and a moral obligation in the climate
> space to do our part, [and] in doing it we can also demonstrate to
> others what's possible.

The ACT has pioneered in other areas, too, with its reverse auction
feed-in tariff strategy to encourage solar energy being copied in
Victoria and Queensland. None of it would have happened without
the legislated target, says Rattenbury, which created 'an authorising
environment for those policies to go through'. When the Coalition's
then energy minister, Josh Frydenberg, was trying to negotiate the
National Energy Guarantee with state and territory energy ministers

through the Council of Australian Governments in 2017–18, Rattenbury was the one Green at the table, and the key dissenting voice, constantly arguing to lift the ambition and threatening to scupper the scheme altogether. In 2019 the ACT became the first Australian jurisdiction to declare a climate emergency.

In New South Wales, to take another example, the Greens were extremely effective as part of a national campaign to roll back the coal seam gas industry, which overran Queensland after three enormous coal seam gas and liquid natural gas projects worth some $60 billion in Gladstone were given rushed approvals by federal energy minister Martin Ferguson in 2010–11, as part of a major boom that will turn Australia into the world's largest LNG exporter. Both Labor and the Coalition were eager supporters of the new industry, leaving only the Greens to campaign for restrictions to protect groundwater and prime agricultural land from fracking. Greens co-founder Drew Hutton formed the nonpartisan 'Lock the Gate' grassroots alliance of farmers and environmentalists to challenge the industry; as the movement gained traction in 2012, he says, it was without doubt 'the biggest thing I've ever done'.

It was vital work: the climate implications of methane emissions from Australia's giant LNG industry – and the east coast CSG industry, in particular – are profound. Australia has benefited, in a sense, from not having to take responsibility for the emissions from its coal exports. The LNG industry flips that equation on its head: our export customers will benefit from reducing emissions by switching from coal to gas, while Australian emissions rise as a consequence of the energy-intensive liquefaction, or 'chilling', process.

The Bentley blockade, which stopped the Metgasco CSG development on the Northern Rivers, was a key moment, and the anti-CSG campaign was part of the worldwide anti-fossil-fuel 'Blockadia' phenomenon, which featured in Klein's *This Changes Everything* documentary. In a 2016 interview, Buckingham drew on his experience campaigning against CSG in an interview with the ABC: 'The Greens need to get radical, we need to get out there, be on the blockades, blockade those coal ports, get arrested. Keep saying it until people are absolutely sick to death of it because that's our job, to defend the planet and put ecology first.'[25]

It is an approach that is thoroughly in keeping with the Greens' origins as a party of protest, although it did not result in them winning a swag of country seats off the back of farmers' support. An alternative approach was to work for a 'Just Transition' for workers and communities affected by responses to climate change, pioneered by the Canadian Labour Congress in 2000 and embraced by the ACTU in 2007.[26] At the Young Greens conference in Canberra in 2017, NSW senator Lee Rhiannon recalled that she and former colleague John Kaye had opened up discussions with the president of the CFMEU, Tony Maher. 'When an industry is in transition,' she said, 'you see unions often becoming blocks on change, because they want to keep their members.' According to Rhiannon, she and Kaye had argued that the CFMEU could shift workers from coal to renewables – effectively from the 'M' for mining to 'E' for energy. 'You can transfer workers from one industry to another, you know you can still keep your members, and we're addressing climate change.'

Rhiannon said the discussions took a long time to set up, and 'being frank didn't go very far', but the encounter bore fruit in a subsequent Senate inquiry into the closure of coal-fired power stations. The CFMEU argued that Australia's coal industry could learn from Germany, where in under three decades some 130,000 coal workers moved out of the industry in an orderly fashion, through sector-wide voluntary redundancy offers, with only a few hundred people finishing up jobless.[27] The experience underscored the vital importance of a large, healthy, publicly funded TAFE system that can retrain workers transitioning to new industries, Rhiannon said.

Ultimately, however, there are large institutional, social and cultural barriers between the CFMEU and the Greens that limit the extent of real collaboration. Most often, the debate falls back on the 'jobs versus environment' binary. On the Adani mine, for example, the CFMEU in Queensland was asking federal election candidates to sign pledges to support the project – a pro-coal tactic that posed a threat to Labor's campaign, and arguably undermined it. The union opposed the Stop Adani convoy, which, when it reached Clermont, got a hostile reaction from coalminers incited by the Murdoch media and plenty of free beer. There were ugly scenes as the convoy passed drunken crowds, with big blokes in high-vis surrounding and hurling abuse at cars, some with kids in them – one had its mirrors ripped off – and all of it was egged on by a far-right circus of federal resources minister Matt Canavan, Clive Palmer, Pauline Hanson and Bob Katter. The convoy was widely interpreted to have backfired, causing swings across Queensland away from Labor and towards One Nation and the Palmer's United Australia Party. Bob Brown blamed the CFMEU, which he said had reprised its role campaigning against Labor leader Mark Latham over forests in the 2004 election. 'And what they got, within months of that election,' he continued, 'was WorkChoices, which hit workers right across Australia, and a number of their own members going to jail, after Howard set up the commission of inquiry into the building industry. They are very slow learners. Here they are doing it again.'[28]

After the forest wars, and now in the climate wars, many greenies see the unions, particularly the CFMEU, as the enemy. Green Bans hero Jack Mundey views this as a wasted opportunity on both sides. 'It concerns me that the union movement hasn't moved with the times,' he said in 2016.

> The union movement now could be a real, important instrument in the whole ecological struggle, because the whole question of global warming, the whole question of the environment, is on the agenda forever more, it's not going to go away, and I believe that the union movement should become more and more involved.

Mundey links the failure to falling union membership, and a lack of grassroots organising by union activists, but says a more proactive stance on the environment could be a real driver of growth for the movement, agreeing that ultimately clean air, clean water, a safe climate and safe planet for their kids to inherit is in the interests of workers:

> JACK MUNDEY: [T]hey're vital to the role of the union movement, they're vital to the future of humanity, so really there's no argument against the union being more involved in ecological and social issues, no argument at all. And it is, I wouldn't say depressing, but it's unfortunate, that the union movement has fallen behind on this area …

PADDY MANNING: Do you think you could imagine a Green Ban that blocked the construction of a new mine in the Galilee Basin, in Queensland, for example, by the Indian company called Adani, that wants to build the world's biggest coalmine, the Carmichael mine, in the Galilee Basin ... not that far from where you grew up? Do you think you could see a Green Ban to block that mine?

JACK MUNDEY: I think it's, first of all, it's convincing the workers themselves. I think there is a need for that sort of action to take place. And if workers could be motivated along those lines, I could see there'd be a great benefit to the whole workers' movement.

The union movement is no monolith and, following the federal election disappointment, there were green shoots, with a senior CFMEU Queensland official warning the state government not to fall for inflated job promises and calling Adani a 'corporate carpet-bagger'.[29] The National Union of Workers issued a statement calling on the union movement to 'think big and take the lead' on the climate emergency. Representing tens of thousands of manufacturing workers whose jobs were directly threatened by heating and drought, the NUW called for a broad social movement to propose solutions and build hope: 'Workers in the food supply chain and workers in the Galilee Basin region should not be divided against each other in order to increase the profit of a mere few.' Bandt tweeted his whole-hearted endorsement: 'This. This is where we need to go next.'[30]

The Greens are at their best when they take a stand apart from the two major parties. The Greens exist in Tasmania because, in 1972, both major political parties were committed to flooding Lake Pedder, and the United Tasmania Group formed to save it. The Greens exist in Western Australia because, in 1984, both major parties were committed to uranium mining, so the Nuclear Disarmament Party took off. The Greens exist in New South Wales, at least in part, because Labor's embrace of economic rationalism under Hawke and Keating left a political vacuum on the left of politics.

So it is now on climate change: if there was not a Greens party, one would have to be invented to speak for the majority of the population which wants the mine stopped, just as there was majority opposition to the woodchip industry throughout the long forest wars. Lawyer Sue Higginson, a Greens candidate in the 2019 New South Wales election, was for 15 years 'at the coalface' of the fight against fossil-fuel projects, as principal solicitor then CEO of the Environmental Defender's Office. EDOs have been extremely effective at so-called 'lawfare', but Higginson realised that 'all you can do is work with the laws you currently have':

> The problem is our parliamentarians are sitting in the bear pit, not passing the laws we need. The large environment NGOs had trapped themselves in the two-party system ... [but] when it comes to climate right now, the one thing that is needed is legislative action. The Greens are the only party that a) is not taking donations [from fossil-fuel interests], and b) is taking advice from the policy experts.

It's not just a party line. As a former editor of *The Australian*, Chris Mitchell, wrote in a recent column: 'And here is the rub. Labor and the Coalition federally and in NSW and Queensland depend heavily on revenue from coal.'[31]

Ultimately, the Greens is a party peopled with climate activists like Higginson in a way that the other parties are not. Driving the climate debate, however, is one thing; winning it is another. Greens environment spokesperson Larissa Waters – herself a former EDO lawyer – says the way to win the climate debate is to link it to inequality, and her party is the only one that can mount that argument. 'It's a take-our-democracy-back kind of argument, and I think that works because people get that,' she says. 'The system is meant to be about them, it's not meant to be held hostage by big business and donors and vested interests, and they know that.' In an important 2014 speech reflecting on the loss of the carbon price, then leader Christine Milne made the same point, arguing the Greens could not win on the climate or social justice until democracy was restored. 'We need to face the shocking fact that Australia is no longer a democracy but has morphed into a plutocracy: government by the wealthy, in the interests of the wealthy. We want it back from the wealthy individuals and corporations who now not only own it, but govern it as well.'[32]

For the vast majority of Australians, a rapid response to the climate emergency is all upside. In the middle of a longwinded workshop session at the Greens' national conference in Perth, a heavily tattooed bloke with piercings spoke up. Young and with a broad Aussie accent, Angus McAlpine was a tradie from Ballarat, in country Victoria – 'I've got a PhD in plumbing,' he joked – who'd watched the blue-collar work dry up in his home town as manufacturers quit. He had an electrifying, three-word explanation for why he'd joined the Greens, which could stand as the party's entire policy platform: 'Renewables equals jobs.'

Who could possibly disagree?

CHAPTER 13

TACKLING INEQUALITY IN THE ASPIRATIONAL ERA

The United Tasmania Group, and the Australia Party before them, envisioned a new political force that was 'neither left nor right but out in front'. Put that proposition to a room full of Greens nowadays and reactions will range from puzzlement to laughter. On the traditional political spectrum – from bigger to smaller government, from greater to lesser redistribution of wealth, from labour to capital – the Greens are unequivocally a party of the left in both membership and policy, although its representatives in state and federal parliaments may waver from time to time. When it comes to achieving social justice, the party's second pillar, and the key challenge of tackling rising inequality, the party is united around a rejection of neoliberal, trickle-down economics, if not an explicit rejection of capitalism. Internal differences are more often about means than ends, political strategy and tactics rather than policy objectives. For many, the party continues to play out the 'realos vs fundis' struggle of Die Grünen.

For former Victorian Greens leader Greg Barber, the increasing polarisation of Australian politics opens up an opportunity. Tony Abbott, first as opposition leader and then as prime minister, took an uncompromising, Tea Party–style approach: 'Blow up the middle ground, destroy it, salt the earth so that no one can live there. There is this huge space now in Australia in the middle ground, and the Greens are just taking bits of it – the sensible centre. It's easy.' Barber's approach is in line with the philosophy of Bob Brown, a 'realo' whose political rhetoric is generally anti-materialist, rather than anti-capitalist. Brown sees much commonality between the platforms of the Greens and the Democrats, who started out at least as centre-right, very supportive of small business, as well as pro-environment, and who insisted that a party aspiring to government should be economically responsible – and who, when holding power, put that philosophy into practice. Contra the idea that the Greens can't manage the economy, Brown says the Greens' critical role in passing the Rudd government's emergency stimulus packages during the financial crisis has never been recognised. 'Why did Australia survive when every other OECD nation went into recession?' he asks. 'Because the Greens were in the national parliament. Who has recognised that? No one, not a soul.'

A more 'fundi' approach is that of Adam Bandt, who argues the Greens should stay true to their roots:

> I think embedded in our principles and in our charter is a pretty coherent critique and program, and it says that inequality is a threat to human life and natural life. It says that unchecked exploitation of resources is wrong and needs to be reined in. It says that the common human project, of which government is part, can be a very strong force for good.

As the neoliberal consensus has broken down in the wake of the financial crisis, Bandt says the Greens may be about to come into their own:

> I think if you look around the world – you look at Greece, you look at Spain to a lesser extent, but even look at Germany – I don't think the path to government is through the centre. That's not saying ... it's necessarily by being radical, either, but I think that the mission that we set ourselves 40 years ago is still the right mission, and I think increasingly people are warming to it, and it would be a mistake to think that now is the time to ditch it or to soften it.

Bandt says neoliberalism has never been popular, either overseas or in Australia:

> Labor and Liberal, for 30 or 40 years, have been telling everyone that 'if it moves, lock it up, if it doesn't, sell it off' is enough of a basis for government philosophy, and people have always been sceptical of it. Every opinion poll will come back and show you that people like the idea of government being involved in ownership of essential services.

Where Bandt and Brown line up is in seeing the potential for Liberal and Labor to eventually coalesce – as their equivalent parties did in Germany's 'grand coalition' – leaving the Greens as the real opposition on the left. Brown says the media struggle with the concept, which he used to bring up at press conferences outside parliament. 'I used to talk about this at the doors quite a lot,' says Brown. 'The natural progression in Australia, as in Germany, is for a Labor–Liberal get-together, with the Greens on the other side. They [journalists] would always put their pencils down.' In a 2016 essay, Bandt drew on the experience of power-sharing under the Gillard government in 2010–13, which he believed was undermined by the right of Labor. 'Labor may in fact prefer to jump to the right,' wrote Bandt.[1] This looks prescient in the aftermath of the 2019 defeat, when new Labor leader Anthony Albanese insisted the party had to focus not only on the distribution of wealth but also on 'the creation of wealth'.

Economic growth has been the undisputed goal of both major parties since World War II, and the Greens, from their earliest days – and before, right back to the Australia Party and the United Tasmania Group, which espoused a steady-state economy – have challenged the assumption that there can be infinite growth on a finite planet. The critique is central to Bob Brown's anti-materialist, anti-greed philosophy, as he wrote in 1990: '[T]he insistent question is whether the planet can withstand human society consuming, as it has, more and more natural resources. The answer is "No – it cannot!" Earth is finite.'[2] In his maiden speech to the Senate, Scott Ludlam gave a passing nod to the same idea: 'When our economy fails to grow we call it a recession; but an entity that knows only blind growth we call a cancer.'

Labor MP Andrew Leigh, a former economics professor, retaliates that 'a party that compares economic growth to cancer is one that deliberately places itself outside the important economic debates that Australia faces'. Leigh challenges the argument made by Clive Hamilton in *Growth Fetish*, that wealth beyond a certain point does not make people happier, citing international happiness surveys that show the opposite: increasing wealth correlates with less worry, pain, depression and anger, rising life expectancy, and higher levels of enjoyment and love. Leigh argues the idea that the economy will eventually 'use up all the stuff in the world is based on a static view about where our GDP comes from', and is dependent on a manufacturing/agricultural economy, whereas 'three-quarters of Australians work in the services sector, where our output is basically weightless'.[3]

In 2019 the Greens' pre-election platform was silent on the desirability of economic growth, and the party's position broadly is unresolved, but settles back on a long-standing critique of GDP, most famously articulated by US senator Robert F. Kennedy back in 1968: that GDP measures everything except what's important. Five decades later, New Zealand's Ardern government announced that in 2019 it would become the first country in the world to hand down a 'Wellbeing Budget', incorporating social, environmental and economic measures, and the ACT's Labor/Greens government has flagged it will look to follow suit.[4] The Greens' federal Treasury spokesperson, Peter Whish-Wilson, has used Senate estimates hearings to chase up the Australian Bureau of Statistics' own Wellbeing Index, and he describes New Zealand's Wellbeing Budget as 'a brilliant idea – imagine if we could have that'. For Whish-Wilson, a wellbeing budget moves 'away from the classic Marxist, labour–capital stuff, to talking about us as human beings: how we live, how we interact with nature, how we interact with each other – it's a whole new set of platforms'.

The Australia Institute's chief economist, Richard Denniss, a former adviser to the Greens who developed a 'Genuine Progress Indicator' for Australia more than two decades ago, says the party's critique of GDP is confused. 'On the one hand the Greens often argue that renewable energy, early childhood development and paid parental leave are "good for the economy",' he says, 'but then they argue that the pursuit of GDP is unsustainable.' Denniss says the focus should be on the shape of the economy (more renewables are good, more coal mines are bad), not the size of the economy (growth in GDP is bad). 'If big investment in renewables and public transport infrastructure fuels GDP growth, that would be good, wouldn't it? I think so, but if you say, "GDP growth is unsustainable on a finite planet," then you can't make those points and you make yourself irrelevant in many important economic debates.' Similarly, he says, the Greens' higher taxes would boost growth, by redistributing income from those less likely to spend it, to those who are more likely to spend it:

[But] the Greens can't trumpet the economic benefits of their tax and spending policies because they don't want to explain that some GDP growth is good. This means that the Greens can't sell the redistributional benefits of their tax policy – which is exactly what the Liberals then criticise them for – only caring about redistribution, not growth … The Greens' fight against all GDP growth, rather than growth in things we want less of, holds them back and boxes them in.

If the Greens are not on the same page as the major political parties when it comes to prioritising economic growth, can they be trusted with the keys to the economy? Surveys consistently show that punters do not rate the Greens highly on economic credibility, says Whish-Wilson, who, as a trained economist and former merchant banker, was preselected to replace Brown precisely in order to boost the party's credentials in this area:

This word 'credibility' is really important, because what we've found is that it comes up consistently in our focus groups and our discussions, that we lose votes because people may scare away from us at the end of the day because they don't trust us on economics. But it's highly subjective – what is economic credibility? It's different things to different people. Is it about economic management and balancing budgets? Is it about understanding business, what businesses need to keep employing people? Or is it actually about challenging and changing the system, and providing a clear alternative? It's difficult to know which one to focus on if you're actually just focused on growing votes, but I don't think that's what we're actually focused on, to be honest … our principles and our aims aren't based on winning votes.

The most politically potent question is how growth is distributed, amid concern about rising inequality, which has dramatically worsened in recent decades on both income and wealth measures. For the Greens, the answer lies in more progressive taxation. As Dutch economic historian Rutger Bregman argued in a celebrated presentation at the Davos World Economic Forum in 2019, solving inequality is about one thing: 'Taxes, taxes, taxes. All the rest is bullshit in my opinion.'[5]

The Greens have proposed new measures like the so-called 'Buffett rule', limiting tax deductions for the very wealthy, as well as the closure of loopholes that benefit the rich – from family trusts to superannuation concessions, refundable franking credits to negative gearing and capital gains tax reform. On business taxes, the party was first to propose a bank levy, continues to support reintroduction of a carbon price and a mining tax, and wants to see a crackdown on multinational tax avoidance and the removal of lurks like the diesel fuel rebate for miners. The party also took a determined stand against tax cuts, and opposed the radical flattening of the income tax system put forward by the Turnbull and Morrison governments, as well as the company tax cuts for businesses with a turnover of more than $10 million (though the party did support lowering the rate for smaller businesses from 30 per cent to 25 per cent). When Labor supported the government's tax cuts for low-income earners in the 2018 budget, the Greens opposed that too.

As a doctor, Di Natale wielded a powerful argument:

> When I hear tax cuts, I hear crowded emergency departments. I hear people having to pay more to go and see their GP. That's what I hear. Could you imagine that instead of this bidding war on tax cuts, we invested that money in our health system so that people didn't have to wait for years to have their hip replaced? Or so that they didn't have to spend a night in an emergency department waiting for their child to be seen?[6]

It was policy bravery.

The Greens reject the idea of artificially restricting total taxation as a proportion of the economy – what Scott Morrison as treasurer decided should be a 'speed limit' of a maximum ratio of tax to GDP of 23.9 per cent. Whish-Wilson says 'these are arbitrary numbers that really have no significance, they're symbolic. Our tax-to-GDP is still one of the lowest in the world.'

Ahead of the 2016 election, the Greens' platform proposed a return to the same level of taxation under John Howard, which was

26 per cent of GDP. The extra couple of per cent roughly translates to an extra $30 billion a year of revenue, which turns out to be enough to fund expensive Greens promises like incorporating dental care into Medicare, or increasing the unemployment allowance. Extra revenue also helps balance the books, of course, and the Greens formulate economic policy with the aim of maintaining a budget surplus through the course of the economic cycle. It is a dilemma for the minor party, however, as Whish-Wilson explains:

> Do we really need to have a balanced election platform going into an election – because we always do, we never get any credit for it – so everything can be paid for? If you're a party of change, a part of big ideas, driving change in parliament, is it really necessary to go to that level of saying the Greens are going to balance the budget when we're never going to be in government to do it, or not in the immediate term?

Where the Greens have been in government – in Tasmania and the ACT, and in local councils around the country – they have proved responsible economic managers when it comes to budgeting, practising fiscal restraint and taking tough decisions as necessary. In fact, argues Richard Denniss, despite constantly attacking neoliberalism the Greens have taken plenty of neoliberal positions, including support for emissions trading, maintaining a budget surplus over the cycle (which he describes as 'a crazy policy'), limiting the tax-to-GDP ratio, or flirting with a debt ceiling. Then, the party has had populist policy wobbles over dividend imputation, or small business tax cuts, or fuel excise indexation, often enough landing on the right of the debate. 'I don't think that the Greens' opposition to "neoliberalism" does much to explain their economic philosophy or goals,' says Denniss. 'I'm not saying that the Greens are "neoliberal" – they are not. But neither are the Liberals or the ALP. All parties support markets-based mechanisms sometimes and government intervention sometimes … the Greens don't make that clear and [therefore] allow their opponents to define them as hostile to markets when in reality, like all parties, they are simply hostile to markets for some things.' Likewise, economist John Quiggin cautions it would be wrong to interpret the Coalition's narrow victory in 2019 as a win for neo-liberalism, which has been abandoned by both major parties – most clearly, in the government's case, in energy policy. The collapse of establishment parties taking the middle ground of market-oriented reform continues around the world, he argues, and the Greens should persist with an unqualified left-alternative platform that allows them to 'say stuff that Labor can't say, but the Greens can. I bet Andrew Leigh would like to be able to support an inheritance tax, for example, but he can't.'

The Greens threw off the fiscal straitjacket in 2018, embracing the radical idea of a universal basic income – an idea that has a long lineage, right back to the guaranteed minimum income proposed by the Australia Party and adopted in the landmark Henderson review of poverty in Australia, which was presented to the Whitlam government in 1975. The debate has new urgency in the twenty-first century as automation threatens up to 40 per cent of future jobs, including in the services sector.

In the United Kingdom, Paul Mason argued in the influential book *PostCapitalism* that computerisation threatened not only jobs, but the entire market system. Reviewing the book, Scott Ludlam wrote:

> If technology, public policy and economic incentives are aligned to sharply reduce the essential costs of living, a postcapitalist world as Mason conceives it invites you to work in the market economy as much or as little as you'd like. The single neoliberal command-ment to work longer hours to consume more stuff and pay off more debt, even as our jobs are being automated or casualised out of existence, is shown a big postcapitalist finger.[7]

In 2016, think tank the Green Institute published a paper titled 'Can Less Work Be More Fair?', which examined different models for a UBI that could be applied in Australia. The institute's director, Tim Hollo, a former adviser to Christine Milne, wrote that a UBI could be an answer not only to rising inequality, but also to the social dislocation driving right-wing populists here and overseas. UBI had appeal on both the left and the right: on the one hand offering a post-work society and 'fully automated luxury communism', and on the other being embraced by the techno-libertarian right, who argued it was 'not socialism': 'Basic income provides a floor, and then people can get as rich as they want.'[8]

In a major speech to the National Press Club at the start of 2018, Di Natale ran it up the flagpole:

> [O]ur current social security system is outdated ... We need a universal basic income. We need a UBI that ensures everyone has access to an adequate level of income, as well as access to universal social services, health, education and housing. A UBI is a bold move towards equality. It epitomises a government which looks after its citizens, in contrast to the old parties, who say 'look out for yourselves'. It's about an increased role for government in our rapidly changing world ... We should begin to imagine a future where our needs are met more and more through universal services and exchange, where everybody having a full-time job may not be possible or indeed desirable. Everyone gets this, including rich people.[9]

The reaction was instructive: *The Australian* ran modelling suggesting the cost of paying every adult the equivalent of the aged pension, $23,000 a year, would be a staggering $254 billion and would jack income tax rates up to 50 or 60 per cent. Independent economist Saul Eslake said the policy was 'an extraordinarily expensive way of seeking to address what may well be a few cracks through which a limited number of people fall'.[10] Conservative Liberal senator Eric Abetz described the plan for universal taxpayer handouts as 'economic lunacy' which would bankrupt the country 'in a matter of years'. 'Di Natale must explain ... who will pay for this regressive agenda when he runs out of other people's money,' Abetz said.

On the Labor side, Andrew Leigh weighed in, pointing out that Australia had one of the best-targeted welfare systems in the world, and replacing it would actually *increase* inequality. 'Why give the same amount to billionaires as battlers?' Leigh tweeted.[11] It was a fair question. In response, Hollo wrote that 'this fetishisation of paid labour strikes me as fundamentally anti-labour. A true labour party would see UBI as perfectly aligned with the eight-hour day, paid holiday and sick leave, the right to collectively bargain, the welfare state, and other successful efforts to improve the lot of workers.'[12] But as trials of UBI faltered overseas – in Finland, and Ontario, Canada – the debate subsided. In the Greens' 2019 pre-election platform, the party proposed an independent Future of Work Commission that would explore the prospect of a UBI.[13]

Similarly, the Greens have allowed themselves to be shouted down on the question of inheritance taxes, which are well established in the United Kingdom, Germany, the United States and Japan, and which conservative institutions like the OECD recommend to reduce wealth inequality.[14] Renowned French economist Thomas Piketty, on a 2016 tour to promote his book *Capital*, expressed his amazement that Australia did not impose an inheritance tax.[15] Until 2012, it was the Greens' stated policy to impose a duty on estates valued at more than $5 million, but Brown prevailed in an internal party debate, arguing that the policy should be dropped as it provided easy fodder for pre-election tabloid scare campaigns over 'death taxes'. Under Di Natale the party has vacillated, reintroducing the principle of dynastic wealth taxes as official policy in 2017 – a move Brown supported as timely – but leaving it out of the the independently costed platform taken to the 2019 election. Needless to say, the scare campaigns continued.

The rather impoverished policy debate in Australia is not the only limitation on the Greens, however. The party's membership itself is spread across a broad spectrum, Whish-Wilson says:

> We still have a lot of members who are relatively economically conservative, and they're members because they're environmentalists and conservationists. The point is, we're not the socialist alliance. If we were, we probably would be going out with a strong policy to nationalise the banks ... but a lot of our members aren't that way inclined.

When Whish-Wilson talks about 'post-capitalism', it is rooted in what is politically possible. Whish-Wilson points to a recent archaeological dig that showed trade was occurring in Africa some 500,000 years ago: the idea of markets and exchange is 'part of us, it's inherent in who we are'. Around the world, there are few, if any, examples of purely socialist or communist countries. 'Every economy's got a form of social security there and government funding for schools and hospitals, and what we fight over is the mix of that economy.'

Among mainstream political commentators, any talk of overthrowing capitalism is 'fringe stuff from the Cold War', as *The Sydney Morning Herald* political editor Peter Hartcher wrote, adding: 'If these views prevail in the Greens, or even look like they might prevail, it's a ticket back to the 3 per cent share of the vote that the Greens attracted in 1998.'[16] Nevertheless, Whish-Wilson himself is attacked from the left, both inside and outside the Greens. High-profile commentator Van Badham has pointed out that Whish-Wilson once described penalty rates as 'outdated', and was described by one Liberal senator as someone who would 'fit squarely in the Coalition with a lot of his positions'. Whish-Wilson points to the UK Greens, who turned sharply left – 'and what happened? It threw the Labour Party into disarray.'

> Corbyn got the ascendancy, then the Labour Party ran really hard to the left, and then look at what happened to the Greens in the last election – they got decimated. Now, we're in the same situation here. I understand the desire to move to the left but once Labor come in and occupy that space, in a way you feel like you've got an outcome because you've got a major party that's adopting your policies and at least in theory is talking up change to the system, but they've got a much bigger megaphone. A lot of ex-Labor voters that have come to us in the past – the term I've heard used is that our support is a mile wide and an inch deep – sometimes they want to go back and reward Labor. You can try and outcompete Labor on what is essentially their turf, but any rules of conflict and war will tell you, you never fight your opponent on their strong ground.

None of this is good enough for those on the left of the Greens, particularly in New South Wales but also increasingly in Queensland, who worry that their party is being overrun by post-materialist yuppies. Hence the formation of the short-lived Left Renewal grouping, which did not last long as a formal faction but which has had a continuing influence. A standard-bearer for the leftmost tendency in the party is NSW upper-house MP David Shoebridge, who released his own 46-page Greens manifesto for 'radical fairness', arguing the party needs to 'think big', offer more than 'technocratic tinkering' and openly challenge the current system:

> Why stop at abolishing negative gearing and no-fault evictions, why not universal housing and unlimited leases? Why just demand more renewable energy, why not commit to a national emergency public infrastructure plan to build and own it? Why not demand an end to all public money for private schooling and a universal right to free TAFE and university? Why not say it loud and proud, that we will 100 per cent restore the right to strike as a basic freedom for working people?

Shoebridge argues that the Greens are limiting their electoral appeal by concentrating on just one pillar – the environment – and need a new strategy which shuns the mainstream. In Europe, he writes, 'Green parties that have strayed towards the centre have been punished with electoral insignificance.'[17] The Shoebridge manifesto strongly backs a universal basic income, plus free and universal healthcare, childcare, schooling, higher education and public transport, funded partly by a new billionaires' tax, 5 or 10 per cent of a billionaire's accumulated wealth each year, which he reckons would raise between $5.5 billion and $11 billion a year. All privatisation is opposed, and he floats the idea of renationalising the Commonwealth Bank, which alone has a market value of $130 billion. No one has to work, in short, and everybody gets just about everything free by taxing the rich and corporations. 'The only thing that holds us back from greater success is lack of imagination to stand by all four of our pillars,' Shoebridge concludes. When it was released, in the same week that Di Natale was proposing a UBI in Canberra, *The Australian* opined that the Shoebridge manifesto would undermine the national leader and 'expose the party to ridicule'.[18]

Asked whether such a manifesto is a pipe dream, Whish-Wilson responds, somewhat surprisingly, that 'pipe dreams are important in politics'. As a party of the left, he says, the Greens will take a view on inequality that 'might appear to be utopian to some people, but if you don't take that approach to begin with, then you'll never achieve anything'.

The truth is probably that the Greens need both their 'realo' and 'fundi' wings, and their culture and platform are stronger for the tension between them. The grand left–right ideological arguments inside the party should not cloak the fact that there is enormous agreement on a range of achievable reforms that would raise revenue to increase the progressivity of the tax system, reduce inequality and fund better services.

A 2015 campaign led by Ludlam as housing spokesman, working with Bandt as Treasury spokesperson, identified $7 billion in extra revenue to be gained by winding back the negative gearing and capital gains tax concessions – a policy that appealed to the younger generation of voters, locked out of the housing market by older, baby-boomer property investors.[19] The policies were adopted by opposition leader Bill Shorten but, after a formidable scare campaign about Labor's 'housing tax' helped the Coalition to an unlikely victory in May 2019, they are unlikely to make it into law. Perhaps less divisive is an overhaul of the Petroleum Resources Rent Tax, which allows oil and gas companies to compound their expenditure on exploration and offset it against tax liabilities. The result has been an incredible tax-free ride for some of the world's largest companies on a multi-decade boom in LNG exports. Whish-Wilson has described it as 'the most egregious rort in the Australian tax code',[20] and says 'there are tens of billions of dollars in that [reform], if you did it properly'.

There is also spirited agreement across the Greens for an end to the punitive government approach to welfare, from income management to drug testing of welfare recipients to programs like Robodebt. The Greens' family and community services spokesperson, Rachel Siewert, says the problem began under John Howard's Welfare to Work program, which took away single-parenting payments once the youngest child turned eight, forcing parents onto Newstart. Things got worse under Labor, says Siewert, when Julia Gillard transferred all of the previously 'grandfathered' single parents onto the dole.

'You can directly now see the impact,' Siewert says, 'by the increase in the number of people that live in poverty.'

Under the Abbott–Turnbull–Morrison governments, the cruelty has been turbocharged and automated. Siewert put questions in Senate estimates which revealed that 2030 had people died in the two years after receiving a Robodebt letter, and files showed that 663 of them were marked as vulnerable, with the suggestion being that the extra stress could be pushing people over the edge, potentially triggering suicides.[21] The Greens stood alone against the targeted compliance framework (TCF) introduced in 2018, which gives private 'service providers' the power to suspend welfare payments to people who have no other source of income. 'TCF needs to go,' says Siewert, adding that 'Robodebts need to go too. There is already a system that addresses deliberate fraud. Robodebt has an unfair impact on people that have done nothing wrong.'

The crowning example of the Greens' staunch advocacy on behalf of the poor is Siewert's campaign to raise Newstart, which had been frozen in real terms for 25 years and is below $40 a day, by at least $75 a week. Welfare and business groups alike supported the increase, and even former prime minister John Howard conceded that Newstart was too low. Labor, nonetheless, ducked and weaved in the lead-up to the 2019 federal election, promising only to review the level of Newstart if elected.

Siewert tells a story about convincing ordinary voters out in the suburbs of Perth that the Greens really did care about social issues. During a campaign against the introduction of income management trials to Western Australia, the Greens:

> … did some letterboxing in some of the lower socio-economic areas in Perth … We didn't put the [Australian Greens] triangle on the front, we put it on the back … people opened it, read it, then turned over the back and saw it was us. People literally rang and – we had a bit where you could tear off and send it in – but people rang the office too and said, 'I got this leaflet, I didn't know you were working on that. It was only when I saw on the back that it was you.' So in other words we got over their objection to the Greens because they thought we were inner-city latte-sippers

or whatever, and actually realised that we're talking about issues that they care about. And realising … you know, we've got four pillars, and one of them is social justice.

Winning votes in the suburbs of Australia's capital cities, from ordinary working-class voters – the Green battlers? – is perhaps the final frontier. Right back to the 1990s, when the party resisted the Keating-era shift to enterprise bargaining, moving through the waterfront disputes and WorkChoices under the Howard government, the Greens have a history of sticking up for workers that is not widely appreciated. The party has consistently supported the right to strike, for example, and was quick to criticise the abolition of weekend penalty rates by the Fair Work Commission in 2017. Former Victorian Greens MPs Sue Pennicuik came into politics via the union movement, working as the first environment officer for the manufacturing workers union and later writing the first environment policy for the ACTU, as well as the early industrial relations policies for the Greens back in the 1990s. She does not see a gulf between Green values and working people, or the union movement for that matter. 'The party isn't anti-union, the party is very pro-union and it's always had a very progressive industrial relations policy … for a long time it has been better than Labor Party policy, in my opinion, on industrial relations'. When she was an active Greens member working at the ACTU, Pennicuik recalls, her colleagues would often confess they were intending to vote for the party rather than Labor. She believes the Greens do appeal in the suburbs, but the vote will grow slowly, not overnight: 'So if you go back 20 years our vote in the suburbs was virtually nil – partly because we didn't run any candidates because we were so small.' Once the party began fielding candidates in every electorate in Victoria, says Pennicuik, it got support everywhere, to varying degrees, including in the suburbs, and it has kept growing: 'People say, "We're not reaching out to them," and I'm like, "We are … if you look at the growth over the last 20 years, we are." But we're not doing it immediately. We're not going from nothing to 30 per cent. So we're going progressively from, you know, two to four to six to eight [per cent] and I think it's better, it's more sustainable that way. And, you know, I have people come to me and say, "I had a look at your policies and I thought, *Oh, I didn't realise,*" you know, "*you had all these policies I agree with.*" Because they saw something in the *Herald Sun* telling them that we were mad.'

Fellow ex-Victorian MP Colleen Hartland came from a deeply Catholic Labor family, growing up in Morwell in the Latrobe Valley. Her father was a staunch unionist who worked for the State Electricity Commission, and she saw how the heart had been ripped out of that community by electricity privatisation. Moving to the industrial suburb of Footscray in Melbourne, and getting a job in state parliament as a cook, Hartland was of and from the working class and identified with it totally. 'I'm quite privileged and quite comfortable now,' she told me in an interview in her office in the Victorian parliament before she retired, '[but] yeah, it is that odd thing, that I feel real pride in the fact that I managed to get here from there'.

For Hartland, the Greens' overt commitment to the environment was, if anything, a barrier to her joining the party. But she was outraged at the chemical pollution of the western suburbs, and when the Coode Island refinery exploded, she took on her first high-profile environmental campaign, motivated as much by class consciousness as anything else. 'Look at the kind of campaign that I've been involved in,' she says, 'pokies in working-class communities … drugs tend to be much more [in working-class communities], our local hospital has one of the worst emergency rooms in the state … a lot of my campaigns have been very much around neglect, and I think that's one of the reasons why having the Green voice in the west has been really important.' That western suburbs seat was lost in the 2018 state election, of course.

Similarly, at the federal level, one of Adam Bandt's first acts as a federal MP was to introduce a 'Fair Protection for Firefighters' bill, which subsequently passed through the Senate, to ensure that firefighters who contract cancer are better able to access compensation and rehabilitation. There are many similar examples of such low-profile advocacy that contradicts ready stereotypes of Greens MPs as inner-city elites.

After nearly 30 years of unbroken growth, Australia remains something of a 'Goldilocks economy', and it may take some kind of downturn to trigger a shift to a genuine economic alternative. Bandt describes neoliberalism as a social project:

It's about government going to great lengths to separate people from each other and to turn people into competitors, and it's about breaking apart social bonds and saying the only way you can live your life is by being fully responsible for everything that happens to you. It's all up to you, and if you succeed you succeed and if you fail you fail and it's no fault of anyone else's. But that takes a lot of work because that's not the natural human condition, and so governments have had to spend 30 years dismantling many of the public projects that sort of held people together or provided a bit of support for people.

It was a chat with a constituent at a stall at Ascot Vale that, for Bandt, crystallised the role of the Greens in reversing three decades of neoliberalism and rebuilding support for people: 'You know, I'm all for the creation of private wealth,' said the constituent, 'but what about the creation of public wealth?'

After the 2019 federal election, Bandt warned that Labor was taking all the wrong lessons from its defeat, turning its back on the left-leaning platform it took to the election. When parliament returned, and the Coalition's tax cuts legislation was introduced, Labor voted with the government to pass the centrepiece legislation – a radical rewrite of the income tax scales, staged over five years, which would see the Commonwealth forego revenue of $158 billion by the end of the decade, with most of the benefit going to higher-income earners. The new, flatter tax system would be more regressive; inequality would worsen. The Greens Treasury spokesperson, Peter Whish-Wilson, delivered one of his best speeches, saying the tax cuts bill debated in the new government's first week was 'very likely to be the most significant piece of legislation that we will see in this 46th Parliament'. With the Australian economy extraordinarily weak, and stormy seas ahead, Whish-Wilson said the tax cuts would hamstring future governments and their ability to pay for essential services. 'It irks me,' he said, 'that this government and this parliament, if it passes these tax cuts, have failed to properly respond to the message of the global financial crisis and have failed to overthrow the shackles of neoliberalism.' Attacking Labor's flaccid response, Whish-Wilson said the Greens would continue to be the real opposition.[22]

If Labor does return to the middle ground, focussing less on tackling inequality and more on becoming a party of aspiration, opening up more room on the left, the best way forward for the Greens may be to stay the course, continuing to advocate – loud and proud – on behalf of the poor and disadvantaged, for higher taxes and more public ownership and investment, better workplace laws and a less punitive welfare regime. A left-wing populism, where justified, in answer to the populist right.

CHAPTER 14

PURSUING PEACE IN THE AGE OF THE STRONGMAN

From Lee Rhiannon rallying against LBJ and the Vietnam War in the streets of Sydney, to Bob Brown fasting on the side of Mount Wellington in a protest against the visit to Hobart of a US nuclear warship, to Jo Vallentine getting arrested at Pine Gap, to Scott Ludlam reading out an anti-war manifesto on the back of a moving aircraft carrier in Perth, the Greens have always been a party against war, and steadfastly opposed to nuclear weapons. Yet it is not a pacifist party, but one that wants to promote peace and non-violence. Heading into the 2020s, this is getting harder. The rules-based international order is being challenged and the world is a less stable place than it was even a decade ago, with trade wars, cold wars or even hot wars on the cards, including in our part of the world.

The first responsibility of a government in any nation is to protect its people, and if the Greens aspire to be a party of government, it behoves them to have well-thought-out positions on foreign affairs and defence. As things stand, there are real questions about how the party plans to keep Australia safe in the era of escalating tensions and 'strongman' leaders, climate crisis and mass migration. Cutting defence spending, renegotiating the US alliance and opposing foreign wars may be an uncertain formula for national security, particularly when combined with antagonising our two most powerful neighbours in the region – Indonesia and China – by supporting the independence of West Papua and Tibet. For many voters, the idea of a 'Greens defence policy' simply would not compute – it would be laughable, even. Yet if the Greens' advice had been followed, Australia would have avoided the disastrous Iraq War, which made the country less safe and led to the rise of ISIS. Australia would not have embarked upon a $195 billion, decade-long spending spree to buy US fighter planes of doubtful quality and French submarines that are already facing blowouts. Australia, in short, would be safer and richer. The building blocks of a truly independent foreign and defence policy, which may even enjoy the support of a majority of Australians, are there.

In theory, the tradition of bipartisanship in Australian foreign policy should make it easier for the Greens to carve out a niche in opposition to the consensus position of the two sides of politics – which is often when the party is at its best. In practice, it doesn't. As academic Andrew Carr wrote in an influential paper, the tendency for the Coalition and Labor to interpret bipartisanship as a process, rather than an agreement on policy, means that when legislation appears before the parliament, there is generally speedy passage and a minimum level of debate. Even parliamentary committees on national security issues are characterised by consensus, rather than by dissent or rigorous questioning. 'Without a partisan spark to motivate scholarship and public engagement,' Carr writes, 'bipartisanship becomes an enveloping blanket which smothers the analysis and creation of Australian defence policy.'

According to one expert Carr cites, this nodding consensus extends to the biggest defence spending program Australia has embarked upon since World War II: '[P]erhaps the most remarkable feature of the defence debate is that there isn't one. Despite the eye-watering sums involved ... there's been next to no discussion of their actual necessity or the circumstances in which the planes, subs and other assets might actually be used.' Over the years, the absence of politicking and media attention has made it harder for the Greens to get noticed. 'While minor parties can stand outside the norm,' writes Carr, 'they are often criticised and delegitimised for their unwillingness to be bound by the norm's conventions for how to approach, discuss and resolve policy concerns.'

Until 2011, of course the Greens had five or fewer members of parliament, arguably resulting in a tendency to neglect foreign and defence policy, or concentrate on where it intersects with human rights, as in East Timor, West Papua, Tibet or Palestine. But this neglect has gone on too long: in a survey sent after the 2019 election, asking which of 18 issues the members would like the party to campaign most strongly on, peace and disarmament did not even rate a mention. ACT member Sue Wareham, a retired doctor who is also a member of the Medical Association for the Prevention of War and a director of the International Campaign to Abolish Nuclear Weapons, wrote in a recent speech: '[O]ne of our four Greens pillars – peace and non-violence – is slipping. When Greens priorities are listed or ranked, and when our vision for Australia is laid out, peace issues often fail to even rate a mention … It is time for this to change.'

That is easier said than done: the Greens are always stretched, even with a ten-member party room. Defence spokesperson Peter Whish-Wilson, who is ex-army, has tended to concentrate on his Treasury portfolio. The foreign affairs spokesperson, Richard Di Natale, is also leader, and inherited the portfolio in the wake of Scott Ludlam's shock resignation. If there are any shortcomings in the party's foreign affairs platform, Ludlam blames himself: when he was given the portfolio in 2015, the party room told him, in as many words, 'we need to be better at this stuff'.

The Greens took a commendable three-page 'peace and demilitarisation' policy to the 2019 election, but predictably it got little attention in a campaign dominated by climate and tax, even as war clouds gathered overseas. The Greens want to renegotiate the US alliance and close all foreign military bases. They also want the parliament to authorise any decision to wage war, to ratify the Treaty on the Prohibition of Nuclear Weapons, to cut military spending and to establish a parliamentary office to oversee procurement. The Greens would abandon the plan to make Australia a top-ten arms exporter and pass laws to stop weapons sales to countries that abuse human rights. Lastly, the Greens would boost foreign aid to 0.7 per cent of gross national income – in line with the UN's sustainable development goals.

These policies have a long lineage and, if implemented, would transform Australia. But the Greens have not made their case to the Australian people for radical change, nor fleshed out what that might mean. In a 2016 interview after the election of Donald Trump, Jo Vallentine said there was support for a re-evaluation of the US alliance across the political spectrum, from former Labor prime minister Paul Keating, who said Australia should 'cut the tag',[1] to the late Liberal prime minister Malcolm Fraser, whose 2014 book

Dangerous Allies argued that the likely threats to Australia would be triggered by the alliance itself. 'It's one area I would like the Greens to be more proactive,' Vallentine says. 'I think the leader – and I have said this to Richard directly – I'd love him to say more about the alliance.' She questions whether Australia could ever pull out of the alliance, however – by removing US bases, for example. 'It's like a major uprising is needed and I don't think that is ever going to happen.'

Vallentine says former foreign minister Bill Hayden admitted as much three decades ago, when he told her Australia was in too deep. 'He was right then,' she says, 'and it's even more so now.'

*   *   *

The Greens do not oppose the use of military force, but have fought a long campaign to democratise the decision to go to war. Bob Brown led calls for Australia to send troops to East Timor in 1999, on humanitarian grounds, and in 2001 backed the invasion of Afghanistan in the wake of the September 11 attacks. Then prime minister Howard reflexively said Australia would stand shoulder to shoulder with the United States in the War on Terror, and a week later Brown, along with Labor and the Democrats, supported the government's motion formally invoking the ANZUS Treaty and committing to 'support within Australia's capabilities United States-led action against those responsible'. Brown acknowledged that 'the villains must be found and brought to justice', but stressed:

> [T]he suffering of more innocent people must not be entertained in the course of that goal – not least the suffering of the already downtrodden, humiliated and mistreated powerless masses of Afghanistan and its neighbours. There is a great duty of care on President Bush and his administration to ensure that only the guilty are punished.

Brown said it would be 'judicious for this nation to take part as warranted according to our own judgement and not to be in the business of transferring that judgement to Washington', and warned against giving the government a blank cheque. He proposed an amendment that called for the 9/11 perpetrators to be brought to justice immediately, but 'through the United Nations, including military action as necessary'.[2] The amendment was not supported.

A week later, in the last sitting week of parliament before the looming federal election, Brown moved a motion, backed by the Democrats, which called on the government to commit to a recall of parliament before any troops were committed.[3] It also failed. The Greens' support for the Afghanistan invasion, in short, was qualified and far from unanimous. In Perth, peace activist Scott Ludlam helped organise a thousand-strong rally to oppose the war. The US-led invasion was not necessary to capture Osama bin Laden, he says now. 'The Taliban actually were prepared to negotiate handing him over if the States would provide some evidence that he was responsible.'

The disastrous invasion of Iraq strengthened calls for the parliament to be given war powers, particularly after Labor, the Greens and the Democrats in the Senate passed a motion condemning the Howard government's commitment of troops in March 2003. The following week, then Democrats senator Andrew Bartlett introduced a bill. 'I know that, over current events, many Australians have been shocked to discover that the Prime Minister has the power to send our troops to a conflict without the support of the United Nations, the Australian Parliament or the Australian people,' he explained. The bill allowed the government to deploy troops in an emergency, provided that parliament debated the decision within two days. Bartlett outlined the long history of the Democrats' efforts to introduce war powers legislation, right back to 1981, and pointed out that the Hawke government had recalled parliament to debate the deployment of Australian troops in the original Gulf War (which was opposed by the Democrats and the lone Greens senator, Jo Vallentine). 'The Howard government has been the first government in our history to go to war without majority Parliamentary support,' Bartlett said. 'It is time to take the decision to commit troops to overseas conflict, out of the hands of the Prime Minister and a subservient cabinet, and place it with the Parliament.'[4]

Five years later, Scott Ludlam reintroduced the same bill, pointing out that the US constitution gave Congress the power to declare war, and that the United Kingdom, in the aftermath of the Iraq invasion, had transferred that power from the executive to the parliament.

Countering arguments that it would be impractical, restrictive and inefficient to use democratic structures to deploy troops, Ludlam insisted that 'parliaments can and do make complex and nuanced decisions, and rapidly when necessary'.[5] The bill was sent to the Senate Standing Committee on Foreign Affairs, Defence and Trade, which declined to hold a public hearing into it because the major parties believed nothing new would come of a debate. The Greens held their own hearing, attended by every member of the inquiry staff, and appended a transcript to their dissenting report. Ludlam concluded that the bill's chances 'may appear to be slim at present, but its time will come'.[6]

In 2010, as part of the Greens' agreement with the Gillard government, the party was finally able to force a full parliamentary debate on the war in Afghanistan. By this time the Netherlands had pulled out, and Canada was set to follow suit. Brown was unequivocal: the Greens believed it was time to withdraw. He spelled out his defence philosophy: 'Except in very extraordinary cases – and Afghanistan in 2010 is not one of them – our troops should be available for Australia's immediate regional security, stability and welfare. We do not underestimate the need for armed services to defend this nation and its neighbourhood.'[7] Britain had resisted pressure to join the Vietnam War without damaging its relationship with the United States, Adam Bandt noted, and Australia too should pursue a more independent foreign policy. In 2011, nonetheless, the Greens voiced their support for the imposition of a UN-backed no-fly zone over Libya, enforced by the United States. Bandt released a statement arguing that 'a no-fly zone would enable the Libyan people to have a fighting chance of ending the Gaddafi dictatorship'.[8]

As Syria's civil war intensified in 2013, opposition leader Tony Abbott said it should be up to parliament to decide whether to send Australian forces to war, but he backed away from the idea when in government. The question keeps arising. In 2014, as Australia joined a US-led coalition to defeat ISIS in Syria and Iraq, Milne opposed it in the absence of a UN resolution and attempted to suspend standing orders in the Senate to force a debate, asking, 'Have we learnt nothing?'[9] Ludlam reintroduced the war powers bill, reminding the Senate that it had spent three decades 'languishing in plain sight while Liberal and Labor prime ministers alike reserve this power to themselves, plunging Australia into a tragic series of overseas expeditionary wars that have had little or nothing to do with the defence of Australia or collective security'.[10] After the United Kingdom's Chilcot Inquiry in 2016 released the findings of its seven-year investigation into the Iraq War, the Greens renewed their call for a similar inquiry in Australia and reintroduced the War Powers Bill again.[11] Milne noted that Australian media coverage of the Chilcot report passed over its mention of the role of John Howard, tweeting: 'Murdoch press will ignore #ChilcotReport, so too Lib/Lab establishment, Howard has never been held to account.'[12] Although the 2019 federal election concentrated overwhelmingly on domestic issues, the war powers question will become vitally important if the United States goes on the warpath – against Iran, North Korea or even China. After the G20 summit in Osaka in mid-2019, Prime Minister Scott Morrison refused to rule out Australian participation in potential military action in Iran, saying any US request for assistance would be considered seriously.[13]

In a 2017 essay for *Green Agenda*, Sue Wareham wrote that Australia had been constantly at war for an unprecedented 16 years and was becoming a 'warrior nation'. She continued: 'The Greens are the only party to be questioning Australia's addiction to US wars, our lack of an independent foreign policy, the anti-democratic nature of our decisions to go to war and our increasing war profiteering.'[14]

Throughout the long wars in Afghanistan and Iraq, and despite accusations to the contrary, the Greens have supported the troops. In 2012, for example, Ludlam went to Afghanistan on a parliamentary delegation and came away impressed with the professionalism of the military but concerned about the changing scope of the mission. Ludlam pressed the government for more transparency, asking for disclosure of details about wounded soldiers, and putting questions in Senate estimates about the incidence of mental-health problems among returning troops and the associated costs from treatment and time off work. On the margins of one hearing, a defence force chief took Ludlam aside and quietly told him: 'What you do here is important. Keep asking the kinds of questions you do, because they are appropriate. It is noticed that you care about the welfare of veterans.'[15]

In 2015 the Greens initiated a Senate inquiry into the mental health of defence force members and veterans, which reported the following year. In his additional comments, Peter Whish-Wilson (who took over from Ludlam) highlighted that the government was skimping on veterans' support services and payments, which had fallen more than 20 per cent in five years to their lowest level since the turn of the century. After being discharged, many veterans found themselves homeless.[16] Defence force personnel were somewhat surprised to find the Greens, of all parties, on their side.

*   *   *

In his first major foreign policy speech, six months prior to the election of Donald Trump, Di Natale slammed the US alliance, telling the cognoscenti at the Lowy Institute that Australia was 'complicit in the terrible consequences US foreign policy has wrought'. Joining the United States in air strikes in Syria was making Australia less safe, he warned: 'We've followed the US into yet another conflict, again with no clear strategic objective.'[17]

After his speech, Di Natale was told it was a common criticism that the Greens 'don't take realpolitik seriously enough'. The institute's research director, Alex Oliver, commented that over 12 years, the Lowy survey had consistently showed very strong public support for the US alliance, which was seen as a cornerstone of Australia's security:

> In any one year we find that more 90 per cent of Australians are overall in support of the alliance, and if you drill down further into the reasons for that, they say that paradoxically we would have to spend more on our defence without the alliance and that the alliance makes us safer from pressure from countries like China.

In response, Di Natale ducked the issue: 'It's just remarkable you can't debate this stuff anymore; there is this stifling bipartisan consensus that simply to even raise questions about the nature of our relationship with the US – the current terms of the alliance – is somehow, it's heresy! Well, it wasn't always that way …'[18]

The Greens' critique of the US alliance only sharpened with Trump's victory six months later. In the Senate, Di Natale pointed out that Australia was the only country to have fought alongside the United States in every major conflict since World War I, and asked the defence minister, Marise Payne, whether she would 'continue this policy and deploy Australian troops, and risk Australian lives, simply on the judgement of President Trump?' Payne played a dead bat in response.[19]

In early 2017, amid the mayhem following Trump's inauguration, including his abortive ban on Muslim immigration, Di Natale tried again:

> The bottom line is that a Trump presidency has dangerous consequences in Australia, and they are especially dangerous because we have in the US alliance a one-way relationship with that nation that is a millstone around our neck and endangers the lives of Australian people and people right across the world ... I look at those opposite. I see the sycophants and the toadies, within both the government and, indeed, the opposition – the doormats over there who are lickspittles and sycophants to the US and refuse to stand up and say, 'This is a relationship that needs to be renegotiated because it is no longer in our national interest.' Now is not the time for appeasement. Now is the time for this country to take a stand. The Greens have long argued, well before the election of President Trump, that we need to review the US alliance, but there has been no more important time to do it than since the election of this dangerous, unhinged, divisive and hateful President. It is time we had this debate in this parliament.[20]

For his part, Scott Ludlam went into the chamber for a speech that described the Trump administration as 'fascism in a larval form' but stressed the continuities in US foreign policy:

> We are one of the unblinking electronic eyes of the Five Eyes mass surveillance driftnet, helping the United States government hack commercial phone and internet providers in Indonesia and Malaysia and throughout South-East Asia. We routinely play

diplomatic lapdog for the US government at the United Nations. In practice, that means that we undermine arms control treaties, nuclear weapons resolutions and attempts to de-escalate the horrific and one-sided conflict between Israel and the people of Palestine. We buy their F35 Joint Strike Fighter aircraft – the ones that cannot go anywhere near a conflict because they are a $1½ trillion piece of flying garbage. We let Australian citizen Julian Assange and his courageous colleagues hang out to dry for disclosing war crimes in Iraq and more conventional crimes revealed in the state department cables. When the United States government says jump, then, if we are lucky, our Intelligence and Security Committee will do a rapid bipartisan inquiry into how high. But inevitably, we jump ...[21]

Australia plays a critical role in the Five Eyes network – particularly through the American base at Pine Gap, which controls geostationary military satellites covering the entire eastern hemisphere. Although the Greens and their political forebears have long called for the base to be closed, since the revelations of National Security Agency whistle-blower Edward Snowden it has been known that Pine Gap provides geolocated, time-sensitive information used in active military conflict such as missile attacks, special forces operations and drone targeting in the Middle East and Africa, implicating Australia in extrajudicial killings in countries such as Yemen and Somalia, with which neither the United States nor our country is at war.[22]

The base's battle-fighting role would be central to any US conflict with North Korea or in the South China Sea, and a leaked review from 2012 confirmed that Pine Gap would be a military target: 'Defence thinking is that in the event of a conflict with the United States, China would try to destroy it.'[23] Pine Gap is the first and last problem for anyone advocating a more independent foreign policy for Australia, but, as former Greens staffer Felicity Ruby suggests, 'it's also a major point of leverage when it comes to a changed meaning and terms of the relationship with the United States'.

As Australia continues paying its 'alliance dues' to the United States, the country has been somewhat insulated from the terrible human and economic consequences of its warring in the Middle East until now, instilling a false sense of security. That may change as tensions rise between the United States and China, our two biggest trading partners, raising the prospect of an hitherto unthinkable military conflict; in May 2019, Australian naval helicopters in the South China sea were attacked by lasers from suspected Chinese militia vessels.[24] A recent seminar on China pitted academic and former Greens candidate Clive Hamilton against defence analyst Hugh White, who complained that, without much debate, in our biggest rearmament since the World War II, 'Australia is building a force whose primary function is to support the US in a war with China'.[25] Prime Minister Turnbull's attempted 'reset' of Australia's relations with China – banning telco Huawei from working on the 5G mobile network, and introducing a suite of laws designed to prevent foreign espionage and interference in the political system – has only exacerbated tensions. White went further in his recent book, *How to Defend Australia*, arguing for a near-doubling of defence spending, and even a debate about whether Australia should develop its own nuclear arsenal. On the last point, White was slapped down by politicians on all sides, who pointed out Australia remained committed to the Nuclear Non-Proliferation Treaty.[26]

The Greens have had a fitful internal debate on Australia's relationship with China and the extent to which it represents a military threat. Hamilton, author of the controversial *Silent Invasion*, attacked White's counsel of defeat on the inevitability of American decline in the Asia-Pacific – based on economic determinism – and the resulting need for Australia to compromise its values and come to terms with China in a gradual process of 'Hong Kong-isation'. Hamilton said the debate in Australia was clouded, however, because any discussion of China's threat to Australia was viewed as xenophobic, including (or perhaps especially) in the Greens. NSW MP David Shoebridge pulled out of hosting a discussion of *Silent Invasion* in the state parliament, Hamilton said, with a group of pro-democracy Chinese-Australians.

It was the far-left, Lee Rhiannon faction of the Greens that attacked me and my book as anti-Chinese and xenophobic and so on, but mainstream Greens, including all of them down in Tasmania, including Christine Milne, thought it was fantastic because it's all about dark money and foreign political interference in our political system, so there is a very broad concern about this across the political system and it breaks all kinds of factional/political divisions.[27]

Then Greens MP Justin Field stepped in to host the forum, was himself called racist, and in a later speech to mark the 30th anniversary of the Tiananmen Square massacre, said the reaction was an effort to shut down debate. 'We are now censoring ourselves, including in our own parliaments,' said Field. Field, a former army intelligence officer stationed in the Pilbara, joined the Greens in disgust at the Iraq war. Now an independent MP, he says too many people in the party take an ideological position on defence issues, without knowing what they're talking about. 'It's all very well to criticise America,' he says, 'but we're pretty exposed down here as a country.'

For her part, as a Greens MP Milne condemned China's human rights abuses against Tibetans and the Uighurs, meeting with activist Rebiya Kadeer when she visited parliament house in 2011. Milne was later refused a visa when she wanted to visit solar technology facilities in China. Then as Greens leader, when President Xi Jinping began his soft power charm offensive, Milne was offered an official visit but declined. 'Human rights cannot be so easily swept under the carpet,' she says now.

The Greens have continually objected to the enormous cost of rearming Australia – a stupendous $195 billion over the decade to 2025, according to the 2016 Defence White Paper, even though it observes there is 'no more than a remote prospect of a military attack on Australian territory by another country in the period to 2035'. That sum accounts for the cost of the three of the most expensive and controversial procurement decisions in our history: the $50 billion deal to buy twelve Shortfin Barracuda submarines from the French, to be built in Adelaide along with nine new ships under the $30 billion Future Frigate program, and the $20 billion purchase of 72 F-35 Joint Strike Fighters from the United States.[28]

The Greens' objections to the JSF program are economic – the US contractor, Lockheed Martin, was effectively given a blank cheque – while they oppose the submarine program on strategic grounds, claiming the case for doubling the size of the existing fleet from six to 12 subs has not been made. In 2016 the Greens latched onto a suggestion by former army officer and academic James Brown, writing in Quarterly Essay that 'it might prove necessary to create a parliamentary defence office, which seeks to improve the security debate in the same way as the Parliamentary Budget Office, established in 2012, has in the area of economics'.[29] The Greens' proposed Parliamentary Defence Office would provide independent advice to parliamentarians and report annually on international threat levels, defence preparedness and defence procurement, and would be funded from redistribution of the defence budget allocation. In a statement, Di Natale said:

> The Liberals and Labor have formed a dangerous consensus to increase defence spending and embark on large and risky acquisition programs that could lock our defence forces into big, heavy and potentially outdated equipment. In doing so, the major parties have also sought to politicise and conflate industry policy and defence policy. There is no guarantee – and very little political or public debate – on whether spending hundreds of billions of dollars on major defence projects will deliver a more peaceful and secure future.[30]

In a March 2019 report the Commonwealth auditor-general was highly critical of the defence department's handling of troubled procurement programs, finding it was 'not able to demonstrate the effectiveness of its regime in managing the recovery of underperforming projects'. Whish-Wilson staffer Fraser Brindlay explains why James Brown's idea of a PDO was so attractive: 'His beef is the same as our beef, and it is that our parliament doesn't do defence scrutiny well, in either of the chambers or through the committee systems, and particularly in relation to procurement.'[31]

Ahead of the 2019 election, the Greens were budgeting to reduce defence spending to historical peacetime levels, from the Coalition's targeted 2 per cent of GDP to 1.5 per cent, freeing some $35 billion to $50 billion in the four years to 2022–23 – although they did not spell out where the cuts would be made. The policy envisages a defence force that is commensurate with our size and location, and that is light, readily deployable and highly mobile.

According to party advisers, this doesn't mean more submarines or frigates, but amphibious craft that can land on the beaches of a Pacific island when climate-related natural disasters occur or insecurity raises its head. They question the $5 billion being spent on the army's new amphibious combat reconnaissance vehicles, which are twice as heavy as the old ones: this 'will only make it harder to put them on a boat or plane into the Pacific; but it does make them much more suitable to rolling down the highways in Mesopotamia. In other words, let's get the kit we need for the Asia Pacific, not the Middle East.'

A key problem is that, in the 2016 White Paper and ahead of the federal election that year, defence policy was turned into a proxy for industry policy, particularly in South Australia, where the new ships and submarines will be built. The Turnbull government adopted a target of turning Australia into one of the world's top ten defence exporters; we currently sit in 19th place. This aim, and the billions in cheap finance made available to defence exporters, were heavily criticised by the Productivity Commission, which wrote that the 'justification for assistance appears to be simply about a desire to sustain and grow an industry that has historically been an expensive failure in Australia'.[32]

It has also led to accusations that Australia is war profiteering. Sue Wareham wrote in 2017 that then defence industry minister Christopher Pyne was 'spruiking sales to outright human abusers such as Saudi Arabia, whose bombing and blockade of Yemen has created a dire humanitarian emergency'. The Greens pursued the matter in parliament, with Di Natale grilling defence officials, who confirmed there was no guarantee that Australians arms exports were not being used in the Yemen conflict.[33] The hearings revealed that one Australian remote weapons systems exporter to the United Arab Emirates, also embroiled in the Yemen conflict, had been given a $36 million government loan, which led to the following heated exchange with acting deputy defence secretary Tom Hamilton:

DI NATALE: Can you state categorically that those weapons will not be used in Yemen?

HAMILTON: Senator, I can state categorically that our assessment process is followed for each and every permit and that includes an assessment of the overriding risk that they will be used to commit human rights abuses.

DI NATALE: I'm asking a specific question.

HAMILTON: Senator, if we assess that they would [be used to commit human rights abuses] we would not approve the permit.

DI NATALE: Will they be used in Yemen?

HAMILTON: Senator, I refer you to our process, we take a very robust and vigorous ...

DI NATALE: I'm not interested in the process, I'm interested in an answer as to whether these weapons will be used in the conflict in Yemen. So you can't give me a no?

HAMILTON: Senator, I'm giving you an answer around the process that we follow to assess ...

DI NATALE: I don't want an answer on the process, I want an answer on whether these weapons will be used in Yemen. I mean, I'm sure you're aware that according to a number of reports, indeed the UK House of Lords have said that these are highly likely to be the cause of significant civilian casualties in Yemen, the arms sales from the UK to Saudi Arabia, so I'm asking you for just a simple yes or no answer: Will these weapons be used in Yemen?

HAMILTON: Senator, I refer you to my answer to your earlier question.[34]

Effectively, instead of the US alliance, the Greens would have Australia adopt a position of armed neutrality, which defence experts like Peter Stanley say would be 'neither easy nor cheap'.[35] There is an unresolved dilemma here: most experts say abandoning the US alliance and adopting an independent foreign policy would mean Australia would have to spend *more* on defence, yet the Greens propose to both renegotiate the alliance and cut spending.

Armed neutrality also raises the question of whether Australia would step out from under the US nuclear umbrella, an issue that arose in a fascinating joust in Senate estimates in 2012 between Scott Ludlam and the then foreign minister, Senator Bob Carr:

BOB CARR: We are strongly committed to a world without nuclear weapons, as we on this side of politics have been since the initiative of the Canberra Commission.

SCOTT LUDLAM: Which was an extremely welcome initiative.

BOB CARR: We remain committed to that.

SCOTT LUDLAM: While still supporting the existence of nuclear weapons in Australian security policy. Perhaps I am the only one in the room who sees the essential contradiction in that.

BOB CARR: I am just asking you to follow through on branding it a contradiction and say that you favour a policy of armed neutrality for Australia – because that is the alternative to the American alliance ... Australia, while nuclear weapons exist, has got to accommodate the possibility that we might one day be threatened by a state that has nuclear weapons. If you want to abrogate the possibility of us falling under the American nuclear umbrella in respect of a nuclear attack – not a conventional attack on Australia – you must follow through on that logic. That logic mandates abandoning the ANZUS Treaty, withdrawing from the ANZUS Treaty.

SCOTT LUDLAM: Or renegotiating it.

...

BOB CARR: How would you word that? This is an interesting exchange, a very important one, because I have never had a Greens party senator spell this out. How would you word that modification in the ANZUS Treaty?

Ludlam declined to answer Carr's question, turning the tables on him in an estimates hearing. In 2017, representing the Australian Greens,

Ludlam appeared at a landmark session of the United Nations that adopted a nuclear weapons ban, on behalf of the International Campaign to Abolish Nuclear Weapons. 'Madame President, you will understand I am not here to represent the Australian government,' he told the General Assembly. 'They have made those views clear by their absence.'[36] Shamefully, Australian diplomats were busy undermining the negotiations on behalf of the United States, and Australia has not signed up to the ban. The Greens are the only party that consistently promotes as party policy the need for Australia to sign and ratify the Treaty on the Prohibition of Nuclear Weapons.[37]

NSW Greens MLC Mehreen Faruqi, who was born in Pakistan and emigrated in 1992, says Australia has really only known war from afar, and there is a vast difference between reading about conflict in the media, or watching it on television, and experiencing it personally. In 2014, at the height of fears over ISIS, Faruqi drew on the experience of Pakistan, which had suffered successive foreign interventions and decades of military rule, to argue that Australians had been conditioned into thinking that armed intervention may be necessary and effective, when in fact 'it's not a way of resolving conflict – in fact it makes things worse'.

> When the debate moves in this direction, we are seen as the procrastinators, maybe the weaklings and the gutless, not wanting to act, and I think that's what really narrows down the choices for our society, to just two … military action or no action … whereas we know that there are many options in between.[38]

Faruqi connected the too-ready acceptance of a need for military intervention by Australians to the country's response to refugees through Operation Sovereign Borders – 'the most secretive, racist and cruel application of Australian immigration policy'. Asylum seekers in boats were 'turned back in dead of night by armed forces [while] the rest are sent off to military-style camps to rot indefinitely. I think we've been kind of conditioned to think the military are useful in these situations when actually their presence is not required at all.' Then she called for the removal of US military bases, including the controversial 1500-strong contingent of marines stationed at Darwin under a 2012 agreement with the Gillard government.[39] 'Nothing good has ever come from their presence here,' she said. 'They only add to the vagueness of a perpetual military threat. And serve no real purpose other than the pursuit of US interests.'

The Greens try valiantly to inject some accountability into parliamentary debates affecting the US alliance, as, for example, when the government sought to amend the war crimes provisions of the criminal code to clarify the legal position of the Australian Defence Force when engaging non-state actors like ISIS. The problem? Australia was a signatory to the Rome Statute and a member of the International Criminal Court, while the United States was not. According to Greens attorney-general spokesperson Nick McKim, '[I]n seeking to provide clarity for the ADF, the government has, as it often does, gone too far. Backed by the ALP, it is proposing to weaken safeguards that protect civilians when our forces are involved in overseas conflicts.'

There were few submissions in a rushed and secretive hearing by the Joint Committee on Intelligence and Security, which included the major parties only. McKim went on the attack:

We need to ask ourselves why the coalition and Labor closed the door on the crossbench. Might it be so that we can unquestioningly follow the US into whatever battle it wants us to, even though it is not a signatory to key international humanitarian law treaties like the Rome Statute?

The problem was how to distinguish ordinary civilians from members of organised armed groups like ISIS. McKim complained that the bill reduced protections for civilians and could very well result in greater civilian deaths perpetrated by the ADF:

This bill gets to the very heart of this government's secrecy around our military operations overseas, and it is quite clearly aimed at our participation in drone strikes. Here in this chamber, we may – and I am sure most of us do – feel very removed from what is happening in the far-flung corners of the globe, but right now in Syria, Iraq, Somalia, Pakistan and, frankly, who knows where else, lethal drones are homing in on people. They are homing in on and killing civilian people. In Syria and Iraq, Australia is involved in at least supporting this mission. Don't you think, Attorney, the Australian people deserve to know what our forces are doing as part of Operation Okra against IS in Syria and Iraq, and any other similar operations for that matter? The Australian Greens say they do. They do have a right to know that. For that reason, we are moving a second reading amendment calling on the government to release a monthly report on the ADF's involvement in military operations involving drones or autonomous weapons which result in civilian casualties.

The amendments were voted down by both major parties, as usual.[40]

For all the Greens' huffing and puffing, Australia remains welded to the United States, even as the relationship increasingly becomes a liability in terms of our relationship with China. What is the alternative? Felicity Ruby says the Greens have never sought to burn Australia's relationship with the United States. Rather, they have posed the question: what would it take for Australia to have a genuinely independent foreign policy? 'We don't know, we've never had one as a nation,' says Ruby. 'Ever.'

Ludlam says the Greens' vision of an independent Australia is not of an isolationist country – a lone, nude, expensively armed outpost – but of a constructive middle power like New Zealand or Costa Rica, working through the United Nations and speaking for common humanity. 'Let's be one of those countries that get together and try to solve stuff … be in the world, not under someone's foot.'

The Greens have the latitude to champion a truly independent foreign policy for Australia, and have done so for decades, from East Timor to West Papua, from David Hicks to Julian Assange, from cluster munitions to drone warfare – but the party gets little credit for it. Could they go harder? Diplomacy dictates: not always. Much of the Greens' foreign policy work goes completely unacknowledged, says Ruby, in part because 'to parade it is to lose it'.

Scott [Ludlam]'s most effective efforts often required invisibility. You could be forgiven for thinking, 'Nothing is happening,' but in fact Christine has been talking to Julie Bishop about Peter Greste, or Bob has been talking to DFAT as well as Dick Smith about freeing the hostage [Nigel Brennan], or Scott gets a concession from the foreign minister on our approach to Burma, or Julian Assange's passport, but only because they're not making a song and dance about it.

The Greens' calls for peace will only get more important as climate change multiplies security threats, geopolitical tensions rise and weapons technology gets ever more destructive. Does the answer for Australia lie in bigger and better weapons systems, and ever-tighter national security laws? In a 2016 paper, Scott Ludlam outlined a vision for the Greens' approach to international affairs that spoke to the rising security threats with multiple arms races on a 'troubled, overcrowded and rapidly overheating planet'. Ludlam cited researcher Christian Parenti, whose work *Tropic of Chaos* outlined how climate change was exacerbating conflicts from Mexico to East Africa to the Golden Crescent in Asia. Parenti coined the term 'armed lifeboat' to describe how places of privilege respond to these conflicts with militarisation and increasing mass surveillance of civil society. According to Ludlam:

> In the armed lifeboat world, the pinchpoints and edge places of global inequality are places of intense misery and perpetual conflict; whether in occupied Palestine, occupied Tibet, on the Mexican border with the United States or our own benighted prison islands … We cannot seriously believe that the struggling, fragile states around the Tropic of Chaos and elsewhere in the Global South will collapse politely, without consequence for the rest of us.

Ludlam joined calls for far-reaching UN reform, particularly the abolition of the veto power of the security council or an amendment to limit vetoes where mass atrocity crimes were being committed, to stop situations where repeated Russian and Chinese vetoes prevented action against the Assad regime in Syria, or where repeated US vetoes prevented action against Israeli bombardments in Gaza or the expansion of illegal settlements. 'As an activist middle power, Australia could be leading these debates,' Ludlam wrote. 'Instead, we're nowhere.' The Greens would make the case that human rights should stand front and centre in Australia's foreign policy, and that 'mass surveillance and global militarism are two sides of the same coin, and that no one survives if the lifeboats are armed'.[41]

CHAPTER 15

CLEANING UP AUSTRALIA'S DEMOCRACY

In her memoir, former Greens leader Christine Milne tells how Bob Brown once bought her an artwork called 'Conspiracy' after she spotted it at a party fundraiser:

> I suggested to Bob that a dark, close sculpture of two men standing huddled together stitching things up perfectly personified the relationship between the Liberals and the Wesley Vale pulp mill proponents North Broken Hill. Bob generously bought the sculpture for me as a present, and it has sat on my bookshelves ever since.'[1]

From the very beginning, the Greens have sought to improve the transparency and accountability of government in Australia, attacking the cosy deals of the two-party system, and the vested interests that work against the will of the people. This agenda – to fix what Bob Brown, in his first major pre-election speech, called the 'machinery of government' – is perhaps the most important legacy of the party's first four decades in politics.

That legacy is felt at federal, state and local government levels: with considerable success, the Greens have almost always pushed for more representative and cleaner politics. They have pushed for donations reform, anti-corruption bodies, freedom-of-information laws, protection of whistleblowers, truth in election advertising, disclosure of donations. Paradoxically, however, although the Greens have undoubtedly been a good thing for Australian democracy, the party's attempt to 'do politics differently' is failing. They preach cleaner politics, but over the years have been less and less successful at practising it themselves. Consensus decision-making turns out to be a poor way of resolving internal disputes that are the inevitable result of heated political debate – particularly in the pressure cooker of social media. The Greens' closed conferences, hit-and-miss pre-selection processes, dispute resolution fails, toxic feuds, declining or stagnant membership and resistance to grassroots engagement in referenda or election of the parliamentary leader – all are hallmarks of a party organisation and culture in need of renewal. As the saying goes: physician, heal thyself.

*   *   *

Bob Brown's first major stump speech as a 'No Dams' independent, written largely by United Tasmania Group founder Dick Jones, included a declaration that 'the machinery of government needs to be improved in Tasmania to streamline decision making and enhance democratic participation'. Brown was picking up on an agenda that UTG had championed through the 1970s.[2] In a speech during his contest for the Senate in 1975, outlining why 'moderate' voters should back neither Whitlam nor Fraser, Jones spelled out the role he saw for UTG: 'By all means elect a majority to govern – in the House of Representatives. But put on the brake in the Senate.' UTG had become a political party, he said, precisely because 'the two major parties were putting aside democratic principles' by denying citizens the right to legally challenge the flooding of Lake Pedder.[3]

Likewise, a decade later the Franklin Dam was, as well as an environmental travesty, fundamentally undemocratic: 45 per cent of voters marked 'No Dams' on their ballot papers in the 1981 referendum because they were only given two pro-dam alternatives; the Hydro Electric Authority was unaccountable to the parliament. The closed, stitched-up character of Tasmania's state government, and the bipartisanship around the policy of hydro-industrialisation, was the essential context of the rise of the Green Independents through the 1980s. In Brown's maiden speech as a state MP, he called for the Hydro to open its books to the public: 'We call ourself a free society; we should be a freely informed society.' As Brown spelled out in a challenge to Liberal premier Robin Gray: 'A democracy is a society in which a government defends the right of all to their most strongly held devotion in life, to jobs and to a fair hearing ... Mr Gray has spearheaded an unprecedented abuse of those within this State who do not agree with him.'[4] Eighteen months later, Brown moved to introduce Tasmania's first Freedom of Information Bill, mirroring the federal provisions passed in the last year of the Fraser government. Brown acknowledged a decade of campaigning for FOI laws in Tasmania, back to the Democrats' Norm Sanders and the UTG before him. It would take another seven years for FOI laws to pass, as part of the Labor–Green Accord struck in 1989.

In the 1980s, the corruption and fraud of the boom and bust ushered in a wave of reform, from the creation of the first Independent Commission Against Corruption in New South Wales in 1988, to Queensland's Fitzgerald Inquiry in 1989 and the 'WA Inc.' royal commission in 1990. In the federal parliament, while there was not yet a push for a dedicated anti-corruption agency, West Australian Greens senator Jo Vallentine moved a private member's bill in 1991, telling the Senate:

> The scandals relating to State Government corruption in New South Wales, Queensland and Western Australia may have never occurred had individuals been empowered to blow the whistle on corrupt practices. In all cases, some Government employees knew what was going on, but kept quiet. Had they felt protected by law, some of them may have been encouraged to tell the truth, saving taxpayers millions of dollars and preventing political and private sector practices from becoming so debased that the public, to a large degree, lost confidence in the political process.[5]

The bill went nowhere, but Vallentine's cause was taken up by her successor, Christabel Chamarette, who sat on the Senate inquiry that in 1994 recommended the Commonwealth pass a form of whistleblower law and set up a protected disclosures agency. The recommendations lay fallow for another decade, until the Democrats' West Australia senator Andrew Murray reintroduced a similar bill and succeeded in getting some protections for private-sector whistle-blowers put into the corporations law. A Protected Interests Disclosure Bill covering the public sector was not passed until 2013, after independent (and one-time Green) Andrew Wilkie put in private member's bills, and the whole area was reviewed by a Senate committee that included Greens senator Peter Whish-Wilson in 2017. Whistleblower protections are still inadequate, but not for a want of effort by the Greens and others on the crossbench.

The Greens, written by Bob Brown and Peter Singer in 1996, imagined a 'new politics' in Australia, based on the principles of grassroots democracy. Parts of the agenda required far-reaching constitutional change, such as replacing the monarchy with an Australian head of state or replacing colonial state boundaries with 'bio-regions' chosen by the locals, like the Murray–Darling Basin or the Wet Tropics. Some of it was more mundane: *The Greens* railed against career politicians, noting that Brown himself had retired from the Tasmanian parliament after a decade (although he would go on, of course, to serve another 16 years in the federal parliament). In the same vein, the Greens have always opposed politicians' perks and entitlements, from unjustified pay hikes to overly generous pension schemes.

Pregnant with significance for the new party, Brown and Singer acknowledged New Zealand's adoption of German-style proportional representation, saying it would break down the two-party system. Proportional elections, they argued, were fairer, resulted in wider political choice, and meant significant debates were played out in the parliament, 'rather than in the closed caucus rooms of the dominant parties themselves'.[6]

In some ways the story of the Greens, in Australia and worldwide, is all about proportional representation. Here, the Greens have done well in jurisdictions or legislatures that have it – like Tasmania's House of Assembly, the ACT parliament and the Senate federally – and badly everywhere else. But proportional representation is not just a question of advantaging the Greens or, for that matter, other smaller parties. It is about restoring a politics that properly represents the views of most Australians, who have moved ahead of the country's parliament. Far from leading debate, the political class in Australia has become a handbrake on it.

In her 2019 Quarterly Essay, Rebecca Huntley wrote that for some decades the country's politicians have failed to listen to the people she describes as the 'un-silent majority'. Far from being poll-driven, political parties have ignored 'all the available surveys', which show, year in and year out, 60 per cent or higher support for big investments in social housing and renewable energy, political dona-tions reform, marriage equality, euthanasia, restrictions on negative gearing, a properly funded Medicare and NDIS, the Gonski reforms, a world-class NBN, and the Uluru Statement from the Heart. These topics attract 'a basic agreement crossing party lines, stretching from soft Liberal and Labor to Green and independent voters – and even (on some issues such as euthanasia and donation reform) to One Nation voters.'

Richard Di Natale made this point in 2015, when he told a com-munity forum in Newtown:

> When I took the leadership, by the way, I said something about 'we represent progressive mainstream values' and people said, 'Oh, I don't want to be mainstream.' What that was saying is, actually, there's a big group in the community who believe what we believe … there are people who want decent public schools, who want Medicare enhanced so that we've got Medicare dental, who actually want to see their environment protected rather than just exploited … who actually believe in income redistribution, who like the idea that if they find themselves in a difficult position, they'll be looked after … the biggest barrier we've got is actually communicating with them unfiltered.

The 2019 election disappointed progressives, but though Huntley conceded her analysis may have been too reliant on polls, causing her to miss the meta-sentiment, she argued the country was hardly trend-ing to the right, either. 'The conclusion to draw is not that Australia is no longer progressive or no longer cares about equality or is becom-ing like America … [it] is that the lack of trust the electorate has in politics has undermined its belief that structural reform – whether that be economic, social or environmental – is something that can be delivered by politicians running the show.'[7]

Restoring trust in politics is imperative, and the Greens' agenda to clean up political donations is at the heart of the challenge. *The Greens* pointed out that the major parties, like their American counterparts, were succumbing to the influence of money in poli-tics, selling access through corporate dinners or observer tickets at conferences. '"Who pays the piper calls the tune" is as true in politics as everywhere else,' Brown and Singer wrote, adding that 'neither party is truly independent: both have to be careful not to offend their corporate backers'. The Greens, by contrast, were financially independent, were not supported by big business, and so were free to 'develop policies and take decisions that are in the interests of Australia and the planet as a whole. We aren't beholden to anyone.'[8]

The NSW Greens went earliest and hardest, reacting against the building boom around the Sydney Olympics. As a newish state MP, Lee Rhiannon was tipped off early on that Labor powerbroker Eddie Obeid was corrupt, and set about pursuing the state government – in the words of later ICAC counsel Geoffrey Watson, she was 'tireless in attempting to expose problematical characters on both sides, especially Obeid and his cronies'.[9] Rhiannon recalls how the progressive weakening of New South Wales' planning laws – particularly the infamous part 3A, which gave politicians discretion over development approvals – was accompanied by a rise in developer donations. 'It got to the point that in some years Labor is taking more donations from developers than they are from unions ... we started using the term "the corrupting influence of political donations".'

The Greens launched their database of political donations, Democracy4Sale, in 2002 as part of a long and ultimately successful campaign to cap corporate donations and ban them altogether from industries such as property, gambling, liquor and tobacco. The database won support across the political spectrum. The Greens' argument was ultimately backed by the High Court in the case of *McCloy v NSW*, in which the former mayor of Newcastle and property developer Jeff McCloy, who had been investigated by ICAC, sought to challenge the 2009 state laws capping developer donations at $5000, on the grounds that they limited a right to free speech in politics, implied in the constitution. Rhiannon says the court's judgement underlined that donations were corrupting, not just because they represented 'money in a paper bag for [one particular] development [but] because politicians start to realise they know what they have to do – they have to change the laws, and they did, to keep their donors happy'. The NSW campaign fed into a national campaign, partly because the ICAC showed how developer donors were circumventing the state bans by funnelling money through the federal parties. 'It just reinforced why you need national uniform laws,' Rhiannon says.

Today, the Greens can claim to be the only political party that does not take donations from the fossil-fuel industry, for example. Since 2012, according to the Greens, the Labor and Liberal parties have taken more than $100 million from the mining, gambling, banking and property industries. By contrast, analysis of donations data shows that all branches of the Greens have received corporate donations of just under $500,000, of which two-thirds was in-kind services like printing, advertising or legal advice, since the party was formed. Unions have donated more than $2.1 million. Individuals have been the greatest financial supporters, with donations above the disclosable threshold totalling at least $8 million. By comparison with the major parties, the Greens have survived on a shoestring. The Greens' policy proposes to ban donations from those industries, place an unspecified cap on all other donations, and ensure that every donation over $1000 is disclosed publicly, in real time. The policy also proposes to end the revolving door between politics and the lobbying industry by banning MPs and senior staff from accepting lobbying jobs after they retire. 'People often ask me why politicians won't take the action on climate change we so desperately need,' Di Natale said at the National Press Club in May 2019. 'The answer is that Australia's coal, oil and gas industry has bought our political system. We have no hope of cleaning up our environment until we clean up politics.'[10]

The Greens' push to get corporate donations out of politics altogether is ongoing. By contrast, the party's long campaign to establish a federal anti-corruption agency has been won, after a decade, with the Coalition government moving to establish a new Commonwealth Integrity Commission in its third term. Bob Brown called for a national integrity commission in 2010, citing the 'powerful and effective work' of state anti-corruption agencies.[11] During the sensational NSW ICAC hearings in 2014, Christine Milne again moved for a national integrity commission, imploring: 'Corruption is serious. It distorts our democracy and it hurts communities … let's get a national ICAC for Australia and let's do it in this parliament to restore and maintain our reputation.'[12] The Greens will fight to ensure the Morrison government's new integrity commission is no toothless tiger.

As in climate policy, a high-water mark for the Greens' influence over the workings of the federal parliament came with the 2010 deal to support the minority government of Julia Gillard.[13] The agreement included more opportunities for independents and minor parties to ask questions or have private member's bills debated. A key measure adopted was a proposal first put by then backbencher Malcolm Turnbull in 2010 to establish a parliamentary budget office providing independent pre-election policy costings for all designated parliamentary parties.

Success of the PBO has not been assured – it was shunned by both major parties in the 2013 election, and in 2016 they only provided a list of policy commitments the day before the poll. By 2019, however, the PBO was becoming part of the furniture, costing the pre-election platforms of the Coalition, Labor and the Greens. The 2010 agreement also proposed a Parliamentary Integrity Commissioner, overseen by the privileges committees of both houses, to handle MPs' entitlements – a constant source of stupid scandals that undermine public confidence in politicians – and to police a Parliamentary Code of Conduct. It is an idea whose time has not yet come, and may never come: a code of conduct has been debated back and forth by the federal parliament for almost half a century, but is always kicked into the long grass.

After sexist abuse was hurled at the Greens' Sarah Hanson-Young in 2018, Richard Di Natale moved a draft code of conduct for senators.[14] The debate assumed new force in March 2019 when former One Nation senator Fraser Anning exploited the Christchurch massacre, making inflammatory anti-Muslim comments that led to calls for his expulsion. Di Natale wrote to the leaders of both major parties, again seeking support for the Greens' code of conduct: 'Too often, fellow MPs have fostered division when they should have been seeking to bring our nation together ... Friday's attack makes it painfully clear that we must no longer allow hateful and divisive rhetoric to find a home in our nation's parliament.'[15]

The Greens have consistently pushed for fairer, more democratic elections. In New South Wales, where the 'preference whisperer' Glenn Druery started out, state MP Lee Rhiannon was a member of the inquiry that recommended the abolition of group voting tickets in the wake of the 1999 election, with its infamous 'tablecloth' ballot paper. Some 15 years later Rhiannon played a key part in a similar federal reform, after the 2013 victory of Ricky Muir's Australian Motoring Enthusiasts Party – engineered by Druery – on 0.5 per cent of the primary vote.[16] Bob Brown has been a consistent advocate for above-the-line voting, and most states are gradually moving to abolish the group voting tickets, which make preference harvesting possible. (Victoria is a notable exception, contributing to the Greens' very disappointing result in the 2018 election.)

The party was pursuing its own electoral advantage, of course: both Liberal and Labor accused the Greens of shutting out smaller rivals like the Animal Justice Party. But the reform does take the power of preference allocation away from backroom players and places it squarely in the hands of voters. Similarly, the Greens' agenda to lower the voting age to 16 is both pro-democratic and self-interested – polls show that the party's support is higher among the young – and springs partly from the party's success in encouraging younger voters to enrol during the same-sex marriage survey in 2017. The Greens' idea for an independent leaders' debates commission may finally become a reality after both Scott Morrison and Bill Shorten appeared to endorse it in the final debate of the 2019 election.

*   *   *

In line with their grassroots philosophy, some of the Greens' best work happens at the local level, where the party has had hundreds of councillors elected over the last 25 years. The Greens have a long-standing policy in favour of constitutional recognition of local government, and have generally resisted forced amalgamations across the country, from Tasmania to New South Wales. Much of the work goes unacknowledged, and there is no room to canvass it here, but occasionally it assumes national prominence. Jan Barham, who was elected to Byron Shire Council in 1999, became the country's first popularly elected Greens mayor in 2004, and fought a high-profile battle – including a string of expensive court cases – to defend a controversial moratorium on new sewerage works that all but stopped property development for more than nine years, but retained the low-scale character of the town and its natural environment, rather than becoming another Gold Coast. Barham stared down the wealthy residents of Belongil, north of Byron, who wanted the council to build retaining walls to protect their multi-million-dollar beachfront properties, threatened by erosion. Barham successfully fought for a long-standing council policy of 'planned retreat', which became a test case for coastal communities in the climate era. She was supported by councils all round the country, and appointed to the National Sea Change Taskforce under the Rudd–Gillard governments, and finished an expert on how local communities around the world are managing sea level rise. Barham came under enormous personal pressure: 'It's different at local level, when you're constantly under attack in the media or in a social or community setting. It's not easy … it gets vicious … I got abused and threatened – in 2008 you know there were full page ads against me.' Barham was re-elected, and went on to become a state MP, and Byron shire recently elected its fourth Greens mayor.

Local government has been fertile soil for the Greens over the decades, nurturing political talent like Jonathan Sri, the young lawyer and musician elected to Brisbane's Gabba ward in 2016. Son of a Tamil refugee, Sri used his seat on the country's most powerful council to trial participatory budgeting by giving residents control of a discretionary public works budget of $400,000. After a series of workshops to identify and cost projects, the Gabba ward used online voting to choose the winners, with more than 600 residents participating. It was a stunning success, which for Sri points a way forward for the Greens nationally, getting back to the grassroots and tapping into the anti-establishment, anti-politician mood of the electorate. Sri's campaign was conducted out of cool basement parties, and he gets around in everything from garish tracksuits to a kurta to T-shirt and shorts.

> What we decided was that there's an important distinction between being a well-organised political force, and a *professional* political force, because we are very cynical of career politicians, very cynical of guys in suits talking down to people, and didn't want to come across that way. In recent years the Greens have been working very hard to position themselves as a serious,

mainstream political party at the very time when voters are sick of serious mainstream political parties ... so there's a huge cynicism towards establishment politics and the Greens have made the mistake of capitulating to that.

Sri is trying to put into practice an alternative vision of democracy:

> My theory of change is very much that rather than focusing on seizing power we need to focus on decentralising power, and at the moment that does mean winning lots of federal seats, because you want a more diverse parliament and that's one way to decentralise power, but for me the long game is to give more decision-making power back to individual communities.

Sri distinguishes his vision from the neoliberal right, which says it wants to decentralise power but simply hands it to corporations, and the socialist left, which wants to centralise power by nationalising everything and letting government decide who gets what. His insurgent campaign was heavily focused on the cost of housing, and his core demand was for 20 per cent of new development to be social or affordable homes. 'Why is it we have thousands of apartments sitting empty in the city, but still have people sleeping rough on the street?' Sri has campaigned for renters' rights – even getting investigated by the council for taking up the tenants' cause with one real estate agent – and he believes housing should not be a commodity for investors. 'I'm definitely anti-capitalist,' he says. 'I think the system is broken and unjust.' Sri thinks the Greens have become too risk-averse:

> We shouldn't be afraid of idealism and we shouldn't be afraid of articulating a positive radical alternative vision for the world. The conservative media is always going to attack us for being the loony left and having these sort of pipe dreams about how society should work ... so what? Those people are never going to vote for us any time soon, they stand to gain from preserving the status quo and our goal is to change the status quo.
>
> Take Larissa Waters, she was the only Green [in Queensland] for six years and was constantly being attacked by the

Courier-Mail, and it made her quite risk-averse. Still around the country the Greens apply what we in Queensland call the *Courier-Mail* test: 'Look, if the *Courier-Mail* got hold of this story and took it out of context and stripped all the good bits away, could they make a scandal out of it?' Whereas we don't apply that test in this office. We're very much like, 'Look, let the *Courier-Mail* write whatever they want. We have direct access to our voters through social media and door-knocking and through on-the-ground political forums, so it doesn't really matter.'

This extends all the way to Sri's anti-capitalist agenda:

I think for the last ten years the Greens have been so afraid of being called socialists that they don't sort of dare criticise capitalism in any form – whereas we put it on our flyers ... We can win seats *and* get elected on a radical platform. It's not a binary choice between being a party of protest and being a party that win seats and then can reform government – you can do both.

*　　　*　　　*

Most participation in Australia's democracy takes place between elections and outside the confines of the nation's parliaments or council chambers, of course, and the Greens have been generally protective of the rights of civil society and the freedom of the press. In the wake of the United Kingdom's phone-hacking scandal, Bob Brown pushed for the first major media inquiry in Australia in 20 years, although he was careful not to make it an inquiry simply into News Corp, which he had branded the 'hate' media.[17] Brown argued that 'the profession's ethics are, in important aspects, undermined, that the public esteem for the news media is depressed and that the concentration of ownership, at least of the print media, is corrosive of the fabric of Australian democracy and ought to be remedied'.[18] When the ensuing Finkelstein Inquiry reported, Brown welcomed the recommendation for a News Media Council to set journalistic standards and handle complaints, and claimed vindication for the inquiry in a cheeky article for *Green*:

They, who inquire into everyone else, can't stand the spotlight on themselves. Here's a fraction of the insults these papers have disgorged against the inquiry or the Greens in recent times: Brown's call is 'disgraceful and opportunistic slander' (*Herald Sun*), 'an attempt to limit public scrutiny of the privileged few who strut the halls of power' (*Adelaide Advertiser*), a 'first step to totalitarianism' (*NT News*) ... 'You'd think you were in the Soviet Union. Truly' (*Herald Sun*) ... and 'This is the green face of fascism' (*The Australian*).[19]

In the end, the Finkelstein recommendations were shelved. At the same time, the Greens pushed for the new arms-length process for recruitments to the ABC and SBS boards, meant to preserve the independence of the two public broadcasters and stop them being stacked with political appointees, only to watch the process be relentlessly undermined by Liberal communications minister Mitch Fifield.

Heading into the 2019 federal election, the party was as unhappy as ever with its media coverage, with Di Natale complaining of a fixation by the news media on the Greens' internal feuds and a failure to cover the party's positive achievements: '[S]ome of the more reasonable outlets seem to criticise the Greens just to show they're balanced, which of course is itself a form of bias.'[20] As for News Corp, in an appearance on ABC-TV's *Q&A*, Di Natale described the company as a 'malignant influence on our democracy'.[21]

As wave after wave of national security–inspired anti-terror legislation has passed since 2001, the Greens have constantly defended civil liberties and resisted new laws that enabled mass surveillance. For Scott Ludlam, later dubbed 'the senator for the internet', a high point was the successful campaign against Labor communications minister Stephen Conroy's mandatory net filter, proposed in 2007 and intended to protect kids from sex and violence online. A whole new constituency opened up for the Greens. 'I can remember when the penny dropped,' recalls Ludlam.

It was my first budget estimates session, September–October 2008, when I'd received two or three emails or Twitter DMs from a couple of concerned randoms, saying, 'What the hell is the story with this quiet little net-filtering announcement of Stephen Conroy?' So I went in there with a handful of articles and just asked him about it and that kind of lit the fuse on Twitter. That transcript [was] quite heavily propagated because I got accused of being pro-paedophile, which was Conroy's style at the time, but ... I thought, 'Right, this is kind of what my job is at the moment, and sure as hell nobody else is going to do it.'

A self-confessed geek, Ludlam got a following in the tech community – which he says would never normally have voted Green – as a defender of digital rights. Next, Ludlam took on the Coalition's mandatory data-retention laws introduced by then attorney-general George Brandis. The campaign failed, and it remains one of the biggest regrets of Ludlam's decade in parliament. 'Instead of them rolling it out as a kind of a child safety initiative, they rolled it out as a national security initiative, which has completely different political resonance,' Ludlam recalls. With hindsight, he believes it may have been possible to mount a successful campaign against the laws by campaigning alongside blue-collar unions like the CFMEU and MUA and AWU, which were put under surveillance.

> The [Australian Building and Construction Commission], when it was afoot, was using warrantless metadata to spy on union organisers. And for me that's a perfect example of a measure that's being introduced notionally as a national security issue that's then being used to spy on and disrupt civil society organisations.[22]

Within weeks of the federal election, Australians had a rude awakening about the cumulative impact two decades of draconian, national security–inspired legislation had had on protection for journalists, whistleblowers, civil society and ordinary citizens, when the federal police launched two raids on News Corp journalist Annika Smethurst and the ABC, over stories that were patently in the national interest. 'The sad truth is that most of Australia's media have been asleep at the wheel when it comes to this ongoing shuffle down the road to an authoritarian regime and a police and surveillance state,' said justice spokesman Nick McKim, who pointed to more than 200 pieces of security legislation that have been passed at state or federal level since 9/11. Although it got little coverage, because the media lose interest when legislation has bipartisan support, McKim said the Greens had 'fought this erosion of rights and freedoms every step of the way in the parliament. We have not supported any of this legislation.' The Greens support a review of national security laws, and have a ready formula for what needs to happen to restore those freedoms that have been wound back: finally introduce a charter of human rights; break the bipartisan lock on national security legislation, for example by allowing crossbenchers onto JCIS; and break up the all-powerful Home Affairs department.[23]

As a protest party, the Greens have consistently fought to defend the rights of protesters, from the Gunns 20 case to Bob Brown's landmark successful High Court action, *Brown v Tasmania*, to strike down his home state's strict anti-protest laws. Many occasions they have exercised those rights themselves, with former Greens MPs Jeremy Buckingham and Dawn Walker both arrested at the site of Adani's Carmichael mine in 2017. When the Turnbull government unveiled a sweeping overhaul of the nation's counterintelligence laws, the Greens were again at the forefront of the resistance, arguing for the rights of civil society in the face of a bipartisan consensus, since the Labor opposition did not want to rock the boat on national security. The bills contained an extremely broad catch-all definition of 'national security' – anything that affects political, military or economic relations between Australia and another country – so anyone blockading a road to protest a live sheep export shipment, for example, or reporting on a breach of human rights at an offshore immigration detention centre by Australian armed forces, could face up to 15 years' jail. Unusually, the entire Senate crossbench – from the Centre Alliance to One Nation – backed the Greens' motion for a Senate inquiry, but the two major parties voted it down.[24]

*   *   *

If the Greens have correctly diagnosed many of the faults in Australia's democracy, which has seen an increasing proportion of voters reject the two-party system, they are yet to identify what is going wrong within their own party. Since the beginning, the Greens have tried to 'do politics differently', aspiring to a gentler, more consensus-driven style of politics. In New South Wales, the party was born in Sydney's inner west, among a bunch of alternative-lifestylers revolted at the behaviour of the ALP's factions and its embrace of blokey machine politics dominated by the right wing of the party. In Western Australia, the Greens grew out of the peace and anti-nukes movement, heavily influenced by Quakers like Jo Vallentine, and the examples set at Greenham Common or Pine Gap. In Tasmania, too, the party was grounded in the non-violent direct-action philosophy of the Franklin blockade.

Consensus may have been achievable when the stakes were lower and the memberships small, but today the party's meetings groan under the strain of accommodating differing and entrenched points of view. This situation is not a new one for the Greens – often disputes revolve around personal and factional fiefdoms at state or local level, and the original cause is obscured, forgotten or irrelevant. Asked to point to policy differences between two factions, even longstanding members sometimes struggle. When a decision is required, the ability of small minorities (generally a quarter of those present) to block consensus means that, very often, discussion drags on interminably and nothing is resolved. As Bob Brown told journalist Guy Rundle in 2014, 'the hardest bums win the battle' – which is to say, those who can sit out the meeting will get their agenda up in the end. Brown pointedly blamed endless obstructive committees run by people like NSW convenor Geoff Ash, partner of Lee Rhiannon. In response, Ash told Rundle: 'Bob's tried to centralise power. We've defended grassroots democracy. It's not an obstacle, it's the foundation on which the Greens' success has been built.'[25]

When the ALP's factions do battle – at the National Conference, for example – there will be a winner and a loser on the numbers: a result. A fundamental problem for the Greens is the failure to recognise that the party has grown to the point that there *are* opposing factions, to accept this as natural, if not inevitable, and change the party's decision-making process accordingly. In a 2016 interview, Brown said he had no problem if a group within the Greens, like Left Renewal, wanted to form a faction. Clinging to a lost ideal of consensus is a type of procedural fakery, a formula for reviews and workarounds that sweep problems under the carpet. The upshot is prolonged disputation: informal factions fight to evict opponents from the party, rather than come to an accommodation with them. Procedural mechanisms, such as complaints or censure motions, are misused to try to resolve political disputes. The incentive created is to lodge ever-worse complaints – a surefire way to turn a culture toxic.

When Bob Brown was leader, he could rally the party, if not unite it, at least while the momentum was sustained. And it was: Brown was always striving to grow the party, and although it constantly fell short of his outsized expectations, under his leadership it did manage the unprecedented feat of lifting its vote in five successive federal elections. Brown was uniquely Green – a personification of his party. He was a fervent environmentalist with jail time to show for it, a gay man who embodied the newer identity politics, and, as an intensely proud resident of a tiny town in Australia's poorest state, had an asceticism that radiated integrity. There was never any question that Brown was an inner-city latte-sipper, nor a careerist after the perks of office – he gave money away at the drop of a hat.

It is no criticism of Christine Milne or Richard Di Natale that they have not been able to rally the party in the same way. Brown himself cannot unify the party now. Party elders say that the Greens have never been united, but by most accounts the level of internal acrimony – and bitter disputes that spill into the public arena – is today worse than ever. Part of the problem may be that the process used to select the leader until now has been opaque. Lee Rhiannon says the Greens have done it the wrong way twice now: successions to Milne and Di Natale were undemocratic stitch-ups. At the party's Perth national conference in 2016, Di Natale flagged a willingness to consider member involvement in electing the party's leader.

Since that time, Jonathan Sri and others have launched an online petition campaigning for direct member election of the leader – one member, one vote. 'If you had a democratic process, prospective leaders would present their strategy and vision for the party and argue for it,' Sri told *The Guardian*. 'It gives the democratically elected leader a much stronger mandate, the fact they're voted in by the members gives the direction they are taking a lot more legitimacy.'[26] A year later, not much has come of it, and the automatic leadership spill after the federal election was conducted by the old rules of the parliamentary party and was uncontested. After the leadership was resolved, and ahead of the party's July national conference, the Greens released results of a member survey that showed just 30 per cent of members supported the status quo. Fully 70 per cent of members supported some form of vote to decide the federal parliamentary leader, but they were split four ways between options including one member, one vote; or a weighted combination of member vote with a vote of MPs, similar to the reform adopted by the ALP after the 2013 election. NSW Greens senator Mehreen Faruqi came out in support of a directly elected, one vote, one value model, and backed the appointment of co-leaders, as occurs in New Zealand, for example, tweeting: 'It's something we should be weighing up as part of this process.'[27] Meanwhile, there is little doubt who is resonating with the public. Half a dozen star Greens have social media profiles to rival any major-party politician: Sarah Hanson-Young tops the current list with 134K friends on Facebook, followed by Adam Bandt (126K), Richard Di Natale (115K) and Larissa Waters (83K), while former Greens MPs Scott Ludlam and Jeremy Buckingham have another 143K and 98K followers respectively.

Something needs to reinvigorate the Greens' membership, which has fallen by roughly a third in Victoria and a tenth in New South Wales, and is skewed towards older retirees and semi-retirees who have more time on their hands. The diversity of the party's representatives and activists has come under question. Women have taken prominent roles through the history of the party, often as accidental entrants to green politics. In the 1970s, Hobart's Brenda Hean, for example, fronted the Save Lake Pedder campaign. In the 1980s, Jo Vallentine stood for NDP in Western Australia, blazing her trail into the Senate, and in the same election Daphne Gollan ran as the very first Greens candidate for the Sydney Greens, while Christine Milne stormed the Tasmanian parliament as the face of Concerned Residents Opposed to Pulpmill Siting and would later become the party's first female leader. In the 1990s, Janet Rice helped form the Victorian Greens and then moved into local government, Christabel Chamarette and Dee Margetts flew the flag for the WA Greens in the Senate, and Kerrie Tucker pioneered Green politics in the ACT.

Giz Watson broke new ground for gay women in Western Australia, becoming the unofficial party leader, and Lee Rhiannon won her way into the NSW parliament in 1999. The strength of women's representation in the party has continued in this century: 45 of 79 of the party's MPs have been female.

Former Greens convenor Osman Faruqi launched a stinging critique of the party in 2016 after his term as office-bearer expired, saying it was 'too white'. The charge was not without justification: at that time, for example, all ten of the federal parliamentary party room were from Anglo-Saxon backgrounds, excepting leader Richard Di Natale. But the party has responded: at the national conference in Perth, Faruqi's mother, then an MLC in New South Wales, convened a session for people of colour, which led to a National Multicultural Greens Group being set up in 2017, based on the model existing in Victoria that had successfully installed candidates Huong Truong, whose parents were Vietnamese; Samantha Ratnam, whose family fled Sri Lanka; and Aboriginal woman Lidia Thorpe as state MPs.[28] Since then, there has been a deliberate effort to check white privilege inside the party and put up a more diverse field of candidates, including in winnable seats.

So it was no accident that, as the Senate sank into the racist mire in the wake of the Christchurch shooting in early 2019, it was the Greens who had a Muslim senator to hold a mirror up to Australia and lead the fight against race hatred. Likewise, it was no accident that after the Lindt café siege it was a candidate for the Greens in Brisbane, Rachel Jacobs, who launched the hashtag #illridewithyou.[29] Again, it was no accident that it was the Greens who fielded a disabled candidate in Western Australia, Jordon Steele-John; when Ludlam resigned suddenly and Steele-John was appointed to the casual Senate vacancy, he became the first senator in a wheelchair, meaning the chamber had to be modified. In his first year in office, Steele-John played a critical role in establishing a royal commission into the abuse of people with disabilities. Nor was it an accident that the Greens stood the first openly intersex candidate, Tony Briffa, in the Melbourne seat of Lalor in the 2001 federal election, or that at a party function in Sydney's Redfern in 2016, the first transgender candidate for the NSW Southern Highlands electorate of Hume,

Michaela Sherwood, was moved to tears of gratitude for the party's endorsement. These were all examples of a party walking the talk on diversity, or starting to.

A possible critique is that the party is not open enough to ordinary working-class Australians from the suburbs. Greens co-founder Drew Hutton believes the party needs a 'bogan revolution', so that it is normal and acceptable for a very un-PC gun owner, for example, to come along to a Greens meeting, along with the inner-city types. Former leader Christine Milne's strategy – to first take the inner city, then the bush, then come back for the suburbs – was a tacit acknowledgement that this is the toughest nut for the party to crack. Yet recent elections suggest her strategy is not working, except in alternative lifestyle enclaves such as the Northern Rivers district of New South Wales. Despite movements to support farmers in their struggle against gas fracking, for example, rural and regional electorates have not swung to the Greens – instead, they have supported centre-right independents like Tony Windsor or Cathy McGowan, or switched to the Shooters, Fishers and Farmers party, or stuck with the Nationals. If the Greens cannot break into the suburbs in a meaningful way, they will remain a party stuck on 10 per cent primary support, pitching to the educated middle and upper classes and 'boxed in' to the inner cities of the capitals.

*　　　*　　　*

In an important 2018 essay, 'Towards Ecological Democracy', Tim Hollo, director of party think tank the Green Institute, analysed why green politics had stalled not just in Australia but around the world, and fascism was again on the rise.[30] With the dominance of neoliberal capitalism faltering, in a Gramscian moment of 'interregnum' or flux, Hollo argued, green politics is still the answer to climate change, and war, and inequality, but it is 'torn between those who see it as a form of social democracy and those who see it as a form of liberal democracy – caricatured as "watermelons vs neoliberals-on-bikes".' The former veer towards centralised state control, the latter to corporate control, and neither is the answer.

Seeing politics through the prism of class conflict is reductive, Hollo argued, as 'there are many inequalities across our society, such as gender, race and sexuality'. Ecological democracy is intrinsically 'intersectional', recognising the interplay between these inequalities, without getting caught up in an identity politics that pits one inequality against another. 'At the simplest conceptual level,' Hollo wrote, 'we do not face a binary choice between the invisible hand of the market and the dead hand of centralised control. We can use our own hands, and get them dirty.'

Hollo was not arguing for a new version of the old Greens slogan 'Neither left nor right but out in front'. Rather, he sought to redefine green politics by returning to the ancient but newly fashionable idea of the commons – both physical and virtual, understood as a resource and a community and a set of social protocols. As a post-capitalist model, Hollo wrote, 'this is, of course, a left politics', but one that goes beyond class by emphasising the solidarity of all beings. 'A commons-based ecological democracy will help us embrace and respect internal diversity and pluralism, as well as external,' he argued. 'It will help us re-learn our agonistic, consensus-based approach, not allowing ourselves to fall into antagonistic patterns of behaviour.' Admitting that this philosophy is open to the criticism that it is utopian, and without pretending to write a manifesto, Hollo instead asked: '[W]hat does it look like? How does it translate into policy and how we do politics? How do we build a politics of full franchise, institutionalised stewardship, de-institutionalised selfishness, interconnection, and reclaimed commons?' His answers pulled together many of the strands that run through the Greens' history.

Hollo acknowledged moves to participatory budgeting, for example, and experiments with a 'citizens' jury' model, which empowers a selection of citizens to make recommendations to government about major issues, from what to do with nuclear waste to the regulation of cycling, for example, in South Australia and the ACT. He pointed to the rise of co-operatives – literal commons, such as community gardens, buy-nothing groups, repair cafés, Linux, Wikipedia – and examples where co-ops are making incursions into the political sphere.

In Spain, for example, in the wake of the financial crisis, and revolting against the ensuing austerity politics, the *indignados* corralled co-ops in childcare, heathcare and housing to launch a political movement, Barcelona en Comú, which won minority government in 2016. Similarly, London's Participatory City project is building community at the local level through cooking co-ops to knitting groups to creative cafés. Reclaiming public space is part of restoring the commons, through protest movements like Occupy or 'subvertising' – which throws back to the BUGA-UP campaigns of the 1980s, led by the likes of Greens stalwart Ian Cohen. The campaigns to defend net neutrality and roll back mass surveillance of domestic populations for government and corporate purposes are another example, as are calls to socialise giants like Facebook and Google, or to create non-profit models of sharing apps such as Airbnb and Uber.

Hollo argued that a new Green politics would rebalance the rights of corporations, people and nature. This does not just mean defending existing democracy by rolling back political donations or closing the revolving door, but positively restoring rights. An Australian bill of rights, for example, is a fundamentally Green project. The legal definition and structure of corporations should be radically altered, stripping them of the fiction of personhood. Conversely, nature should be accorded legal rights, and examples are emerging around the world, from New Zealand to India to Bolivia, which issued a Draft Universal Declaration of the Rights of Mother Earth. 'Why should BHP Billiton have legal rights but the Great Barrier Reef should not?' asks Hollo. 'In an ecological democracy, the concept that the natural world has rights should be embedded at each level, from the local to the global.'

Finally, as a response to the challenges of overheating and war and fascism, Hollo wrote:

> We must also begin to grapple properly with the path towards global democracy, challenge the idea of borders which allow free movement of capital but not of people, and, at the deepest level, question the future of the nation state. Models of regional governance have changed dramatically over human history. Surely we can do better than the post-imperial model we have today, and develop commons-based polycentric governance from the local level through to the global.

With a nod to Bob Brown's vision of a world democracy, Hollo's paper argued that a new ecological politics still has much to offer the future. The Green fire still burns.

*   *   *

The Greens have undoubtedly been the most successful minor party in Australia's post-war political history – certainly in terms of getting members elected to Commonwealth, state and territory parliaments. As the charts on pages 479 and 480 illustrate, by 2019 the Greens had contested 11 federal elections starting from 1990, when the state-based parties in New South Wales, Western Australia and elsewhere, combined with the United Tasmania Group, polled 1–2 per cent of the national primary vote and Jo Vallentine officially became the Greens' first senator. The party has already outlasted the ten elections contested by the Democratic Labour Party from 1955 to 1980 and will certainly outlast the Democrats' 13 elections from 1977 to 2010, given sitting senators will contest the next two federal elections as Greens. At 79 current and former Commonwealth, state and territory MPs, they have achieved almost double the number of the Democrats (42), and more than double the DLP (35) or Pauline Hanson's One Nation (36). The comparison with One Nation, which has never hit the five-MP threshold for being considered a parliamentary party, underlines the Greens' achievement. Apart from fanning racism and anti-immigrant sentiment, One Nation has unpredictable and often incoherent policy positions. Two-thirds – 22 out of 36 – of Hanson's MPs have resigned, been disqualified or expelled; in the case of former senator Fraser Anning, before he even took his seat. The difference between a true political party and a personality-driven electoral vehicle has been rammed home in recent years as Clive Palmer, Cory Bernardi, Jacqui Lambie and others have launched eponymous outfits that quickly flamed out. Even political veterans of decades' standing, such as Nick Xenophon and Bob Katter, have failed to extend their franchise beyond their home state. It is one thing to share or control the balance of power, as most of these individuals have done at some point, and another thing to know what to do with it and to use it for the lasting betterment of the nation, rather than a series of ad-hoc deals.

There are signs the public appreciates the difference, and has begun to bracket the Greens as a major party. In the 2016 election, for the first time in the party's history, the Greens vote in the Senate dropped substantially below its vote in the House of Representatives, as the party pushed hard to clinch lower-house seats in Melbourne. South Australian senator Robert Simms, who lost his seat that election, said it was a great irony for the party: 'We've spent the last twenty years fighting this narrative that we are this kind of fringe group, and then this election, which was sort of an anti-establishment election, people saw the Greens as being part of the furniture, part of the political establishment, and we were kind of lumped in with the big parties.' He suggested Labor's shots at the Greens over dealing with the Liberals on Senate voting reform helped create the perception they were now a major player. The Greens are both major and minor, or somewhere in between.

One thing is clear: the Greens are no longer new. More than 25 years since the Australian Greens were formed in 1992, and almost half a century since the beginnings of the UTG in 1972, the Greens' policy platform is itself an enduring achievement, which stands up to comparison with that of both major parties and has many threads going back to the Democrats, UTG and Australia Party on the one hand, and underpinned by key tenets of democratic socialism on the other, with plenty of economic redistribution, regulatory intervention and an emphasis on public ownership. The platform is credible and robust, and disagreements are most often at the margins, on vexed questions such as fuel excise indexation or a sugar tax or an estate tax, or drug decriminalisation, or domestic gas reservation, which are generally not the subject of mainstream political debate.

*　　*　　*

There is a fair degree of Greens unity around the policy platform; factional disagreements are often personal as much as political. Even among the NSW Greens, where factional differences are most pronounced – Eastern Bloc versus Tree Tories, inner-Sydney Greens versus the Northern Alliance – grassroots members are sometimes unable to identify the policy argument at the heart of a long-running feud. Quite often there is a generational divide among the members.

One older party member from a Sydney branch, whom I met at the Stop Adani rally in the Queensland suburb of Clermont but who did not want to be identified, told me he was amazed to jump online and discover the socialist background of the domineering young branch secretary who started turning up at local meetings full of enthusiasm, but was soon pushing his own version of identity politics so as to get onto the state delegates council, where most of the factional warring takes place. Online, the party culture quickly degenerates into abuse, with obsessives trolling one another on social media. A product of this whipped-up toxic culture is the 101-page internal complaint filed against Alex Bhathal, which in fact says nothing of significance. On a blunt assessment, Bhathal was a high-profile victim of a long-running feud between two Melbourne branches, the Darebin and Moreland Greens – hardly anyone knows where it started, or what it's about. A clue comes when Bhathal talks of her reaction when a Greens candidate for preselection to the Darebin Council got up and said in passing, 'You know we can't wait for Preston and Reservoir to become gentrified'. Bhathal was horrified: 'There was something in me that just went, "Fuck! That's the last thing we want!" Like, you know, everyone's going to lose their houses, their rental properties are going to be completely out of range, elderly migrants won't be able to afford their rents … it's self-centred. She was prioritising the sort of narrow, lazy, demographic, riding-on-the-coattails approach to green politics. I never wanted us to be that sort of party – a party of gentrification, what a sad thing to have to be.'

The drawn-out, toxic internal wars that saw Alex Bhathal and Jeremy Buckingham ousted from the Greens in Victoria and New South Wales in 2018–19 have undoubtedly marked an ugly new low for the party, and it would be wrong to imagine such brawls are confined to the larger states, and that the party is harmonious everywhere else. In Queensland, for example, the recent federal election was marred by internal dispute – pitting Jonathan Sri and his supporters against Senator Larissa Waters – over whether the Greens should campaign on climate change. National Council had resolved that a key component of the campaign would be to focus on the urgent need to end coal and transition to renewables. Remarkably, the Queensland branch opted out, deciding not to run ads relating to climate change, and climate was conspicuously absent from the state launch. The national campaign team had to organise separate advertising on climate to support Waters, and she was re-elected with a healthy swing towards her. After the election, there was heated debate about whether the strategy had worked – and on the left of the party there was deep concern about the impact of the Stop Adani convoy, construed as 'yelling at working people'. Likewise, in Tasmania, the party's 2018 election campaign pitch was blurred by the on-again, off-again reformation of the United Tasmania Group, billing itself as the 'original Greens'. Almost every state branch appears to have its own long-running problems, and an inability to resolve them.

The Greens generally lack power, but this does not make their internal disagreements any less intense – quite the opposite. It sometimes feels as though the party combines the worst of the two old parties: all of the factionalism, and none of the power. The apparently lower stakes can make disputes nastier. *The Saturday Paper*'s Martin McKenzie-Murray diagnosed an 'almost obscene triviality' in the tips he'd received about corruption or mendacity in the Greens: 'The real corruption to be found in these voluminous records of micro-aggression is of language. Disagreement becomes abuse. Debate is violence. Ordinary requests are bullying. Frivolity is recklessness. Jocularity is harassment. I have encountered sensitivity so pronounced, so easily disturbed, that it resembles madness. And I detect in this hypersensitivity an imperious individualism, an almost hysterical primacy of one's feelings – impractical in a political party and disastrous for the communal value of debate.'[31] Politically correct safe meeting practices turn into weapons. Discussion quickly veers away from substantial issues and into personal attack. Off the record, the left says the right is lazy and shirks the hard work of political organisation. The right says the left is dogmatic and process-obsessed, setting up endless committees in a throwback to the Soviet era. As former MP Ian Cohen describes his long-time factional opponents in the NSW Greens: 'They are full-time hardcore political activists who eat, sleep and shit the mechanisms of maintaining power. So you either drop out or defeat them – or you drop out and defeat them, I don't know – but you don't change them.'

It would be wrong to reduce all the Greens' internal conflict to left versus right. For former Democrat Norm Sanders, the country's first environmental MP, the Greens have lost focus. In an unpublished letter to *The Australian*, he wrote:

> I was once a Green voter, but never again. The Greens have drifted more and more rapidly from their environmental base ever since Bob Brown left the helm. It has become so bad that the Greens have shunted the environment off into a corner handled by a 'Spokesperson on the Environment'. Think about it! Not long ago, the environment was their entire reason for being. Now there is only a 'Spokesperson' while the Green Party concentrates on urban social issues … this has left the environmental movement without a voice in Parliament. We feel betrayed.

Yet a younger generation of potential Greens activists may feel exactly the opposite. After the federal election, as Labor under 'left' leader Anthony Albanese caved in to support the Coalition's radical tax-cut agenda, disappointing many progressive voters, Australian Unemployed Workers Union spokesman and freelance journalist Jeremy Poxon – who had campaigned effectively against the Coalition's punitive welfare regime – tweeted sharply: 'ok, so now the labor-bashing is well underway, i can pivot to asking when the Greens are gonna finally dump RDN, & all their other climate neoliberals, so they can become a genuinely socialist, class-oriented party.'[32]

Through it all, the Greens have survived, withstanding hostility from the incumbent major parties, beat-ups and neglect from the media, toxic internal factional brawls and feuds, and all while taking on the country's most powerful vested interests directly. Decade after decade, the Greens have done that on a tiny fraction of the donation income of Liberal and Labor. They have racked up substantial progressive achievements in our federal, state and territory parliaments: from the landmark Clean Energy Future package including a carbon price in 2011, to dental care for kids; from a feasibility study for high-speed rail to abolishing sniffable fuel; from electoral reform to donations reform to protection of territory rights; from drug-law reform to euthanasia laws; from workers comp for firefighters to the push for a rise to Newstart; from a parliamentary budget office to a national integrity commission to a banking royal commission. Over and over, the Greens have led debates – on marriage equality, animal welfare, the war in Afghanistan, or compassion towards asylum seekers. All the while the Greens have fought to stop environmental destruction or save precious places, from halting whaling in the Antarctic to ensuring the preservation of ancient rock art in the Pilbara, from the Gunns pulp mill to the Margiris super trawler, from logging in the Tarkine to Victoria's central highlands. And of course the party has consistently opposed fossil fuel developments from LNG on the Kimberley Coast to CSG at Bentley, from oil drilling in the Great Australian Bight to Adani's giant coal mine in central Queensland. If the Greens were to go the way of the Democrats and the DLP, voters would be entitled to conclude the Coalition and Labor – the 'Coles and Woollies' of Australian politics, as leader Richard Di Natale often says – have a lock on our democracy. Given a record one in four Australians cast their vote elsewhere at the recent federal election, that would be a poor reflection of the will of the people. By dint of idealism rather than opportunism, and hard work not money, the Greens have earned their place in parliaments and councils across Australia and – love them or hate them – the country's democracy is healthier for it.

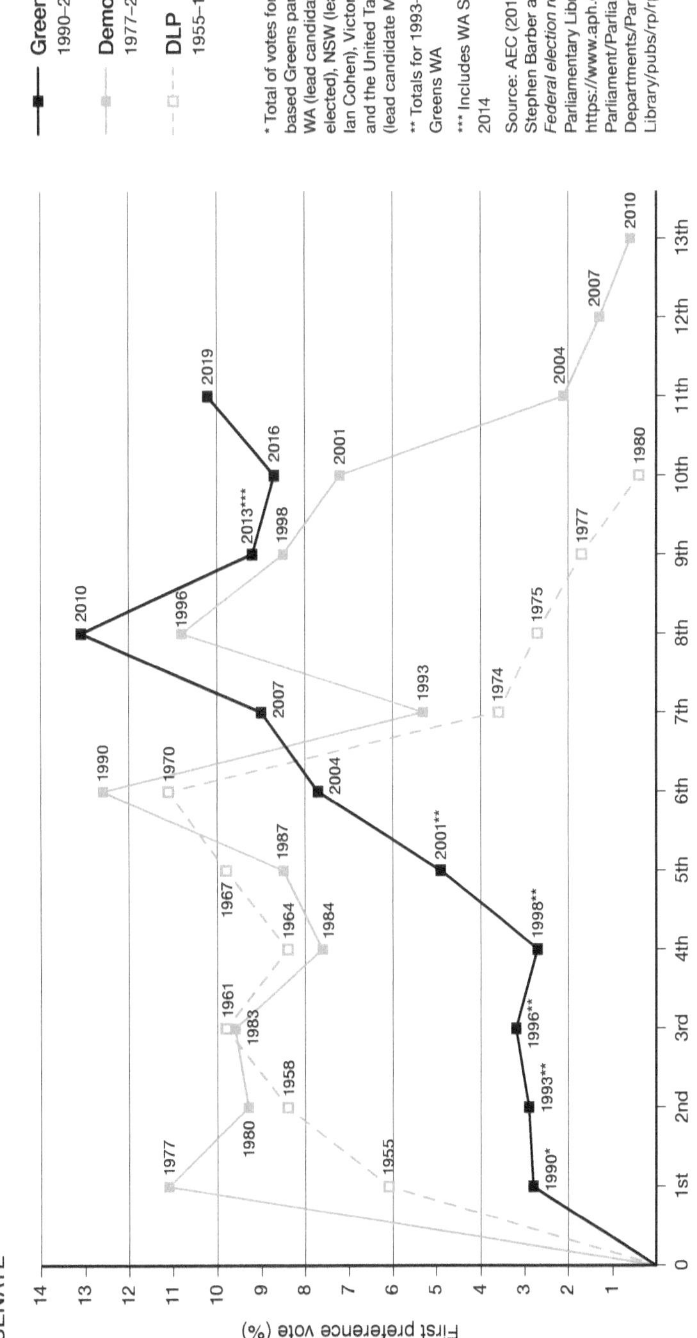

THE SLOW AND STEADY RISE OF THE GREENS' PRIMARY VOTE
VS THE RISE AND FALL OF THE DEMOCRATS AND THE DLP (1955–2019)
SENATE
Greens
1990–2019+
Democrat
1977–2010
DLP
1955–1980
First preference vote (%)
Election contested
* Total of votes for various state-based Greens parties including in WA (lead candidate Jo Vallentine, elected), NSW (lead candidate Ian Cohen), Victoria, SA, ACT and the United Tasmania Group (lead candidate Michael Lynch)
** Totals for 1993–2001 include Greens WA
*** Includes WA Senate byelection 2014
Source: AEC (2016–2019); Stephen Barber and Sue Johnson, Federal election results 1901–2014, Parliamentary Library, 17 July 2014, https://www.aph.gov.au/About_Parliament/Parliamentary_Departments/Parliamentary_Library/pubs/rp/rp1415/FedElect
2019
2016
2013***
2010
2007
2004
2001**
1998**
1996**
1993**
1990*
2010
2007
2004
2001
1998
1996
1990
1987
1984
1980
1977
1975
1974
1967
1964
1961
1958
1955
1983
1970
1980
1977
0
1
2
3
4
5
6
7
8
9
10
11
12
13
14
1st
2nd
3rd
4th
5th
6th
7th
8th
9th
10th
11th
12th
13th

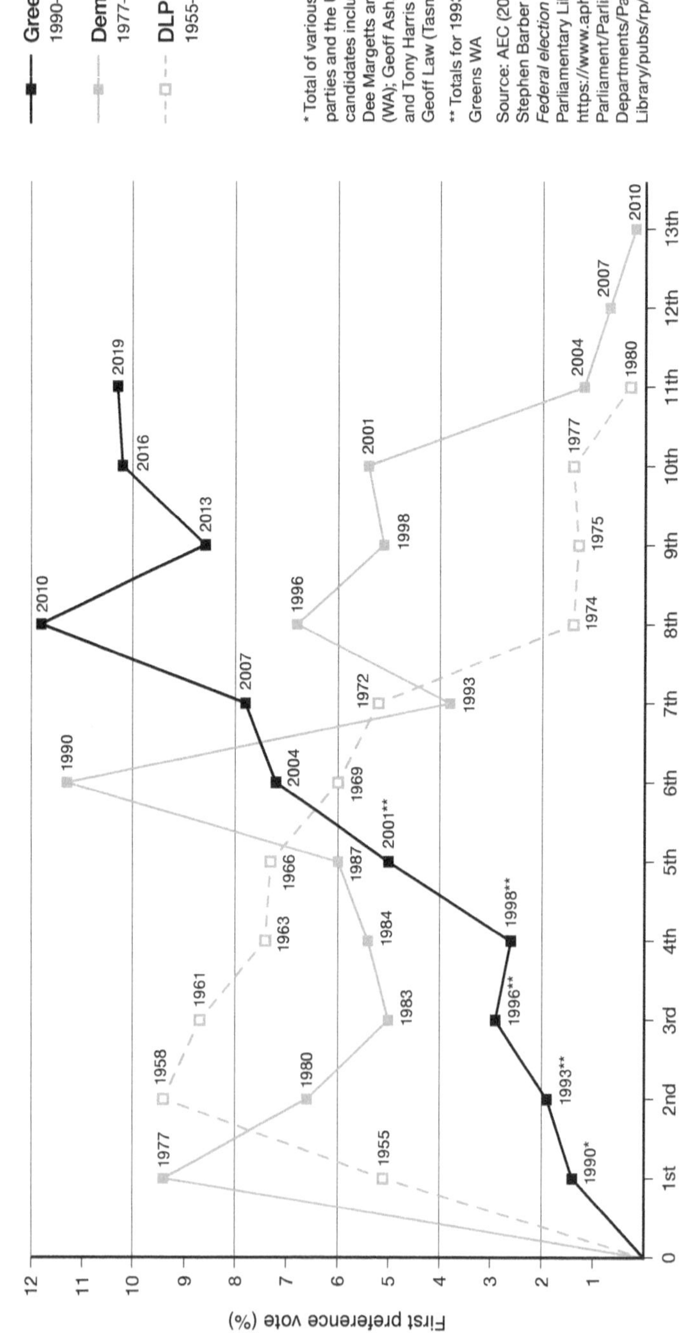
THE SLOW AND STEADY RISE OF THE GREENS' PRIMARY VOTE
VS THE RISE AND FALL OF THE DEMOCRATS AND THE DLP (1955–2019)
HOUSE OF REPRESENTATIVES
Greens
1990–2019+
Democrat
1977–2010
DLP
1955–1980
*Total of various state Greens
parties and the UTG with
candidates including: Giz Watson,
Dee Margetts and Robin Chapple
(WA); Geoff Ash, Steve Brigham
and Tony Harris (NSW); and
Geoff Law (Tasmania)
** Totals for 1993–2001 include
Greens WA
Source: AEC (2016–2019);
Stephen Barber and Sue Johnson
Federal election results 1901–2014
Parliamentary Library, 17 July 2014
https://www.aph.gov.au/About_
Parliament/Parliamentary_
Departments/Parliamentary_
Library/pubs/rp/rp1415/FedElect
First preference vote (%)
Election contested
12
11
10
9
8
7
6
5
4
3
2
1
0
1st
2nd
3rd
4th
5th
6th
7th
8th
9th
10th
11th
12th
13th
1990
1977
1958
1961
1963
1966
1980
1955
1983
1984
1987
1969
1972
1974
1975
1977
1980
1990*
1993**
1996**
1998**
2001**
2004
2007
2010
2013
2016
2019
1996
1998
2001
1993
2004
2007
2010

NOTES

This book draws on interviews with more than 110 current or former Greens, including 47 past or present Greens MPs – most interviewed on multiple occasions between 2016 and 2019 – as well as numerous people outside the party. Unless otherwise referenced, quotations in this book are sourced from these interviews. I am extremely grateful for the goodwill and cooperation of all those who took the time to be interviewed. Correspondence has been referred to as such in the notes.

PROLOGUE: FOREBEARS

1   Hall Greenland, 'LBJ – our part in his downfall', *Watermelon Papers*, 24 October 2016.

2   Gregg Borschmann, 'Recorded interview with Bob Brown (b. 1944–)', National Library of Australia Oral History Section, 19 March 1994, p. 43.

3   Clive Hamilton, *What Do We Want? The Story of Protest in Australia*, NLA Publishing, 2016, p. 10.

4   Sam Everingham, *Gordon Barton: Australia's Maverick Entrepreneur*, Allen & Unwin, Sydney, 2009, Kindle location 1801–1823.

5   Tony Blackshield, 'The Australia Party', *Current Affairs Bulletin*, vol. 49, no. 2, July 1972, p. 35.

6   'Australia Party: principles and policies', authorised by W. K. F. McPherson, Fergus McPherson private papers, no date.

7   No author, 'Senator seeks new party', *The Age*, 23 June 1969; see also no author, 'A Brief History', 6 pp., Fergus McPherson private papers, undated.

8   Tony Blackshield, 'The Australia Party', p. 40.

9   'Australia Party', Fergus McPherson private papers.

10 Alan Marshall, *The Great Extermination: A Guide to Anglo-Australian Cupidity, Wickedness and Waste*, William Heinemann, Melbourne and London, 1966, p. 216.

11 Judith Wright, *The Coral Battleground*, Thomas Nelson, Melbourne, 1977, Kindle location 2438.

12 Libby Robin, *Defending the Little Desert: The Rise of Ecological Consciousness in Australia*, Melbourne University Press, 1998, p. 54.

13 No author, 'Questions put to the prime minister at the National Press Club Luncheon – Canberra – 1971', Press release, Canberra, 15 April 1971.

14 Mungo MacCallum, 'Peter Howson, minister for "trees, boongs and poofters"', *Crikey*, 5 February 2009.

15 Lisa Milner, *Swimming Against the Tide: A Biography of Freda Brown*, Ginninderra Press, Canberra, 2017, p. 47.

16   ibid., p. 51.

17   ibid., p. 140.

18   ibid., p. 141.

19   Wilton John Brown, *The Communist Movement and Australia: An Historical Outline – 1890s to 1980s*, Australian Labor Movement History Publications, Sydney, 1986, pp. 267–72.

20   Hall Greenland, *Red Hot: The Life and Times of Nick Origlass*, Wellington Lane Press, Sydney, 1998, pp. 202–3.

21   ibid., p. 244.

22   Jack Mundey, *Greens Bans and Beyond*, Angus and Robertson, Sydney, 1981, p. 6.

23   ibid., p. 22.

24   ibid., pp. 61–2.

25   Richard Roddewig, *Green Bans: The Birth of Australian Environmental Politics*, Hale & Iremonger, Sydney, 1978, p. 8.

26   Jack Mundey, *Greens Bans and Beyond*, pp. 81–2.

CHAPTER 1: THE WORLD'S FIRST GREEN PARTY

1   There is a fitful debate about whether the United Tasmania Group is the world's first Green party. The 'Movement Populaire pour l'Environnement' (MPE) was formed earlier, in December 1971, in the Swiss canton of Neuchâtel, but did not contest an election until May 1972. See Sara Parkin, *Green Parties: An International Guide*, Heretic Books, London, 1989, p. 203 but note a typographical error: Parkin writes that MPE was formed in December 1972, and received 18 per cent of the vote and 8 of 41 seats in the May 1972 elections. See also Andreas Ladner and Michael Brändle, 'Switzerland, the Green Party, alternative and liberal greens', in E. Gene Frankland, Paul Lucardie and Benoît Rihoux (eds), *Green Parties in Transition: The End of Grassroots Democracy?*, Ashgate Publishing, Farnham, 2008, p. 110. Pamela Walker describes UTG as 'the first political party based on an environmental platform to contest elections within any parliamentary system in the world' in 'The United Tasmania Group', Thesis submitted to the University of Tasmania, 1986. The Global Greens' website states the world's first Green parties began in 1972 and 'These were in the Australian state of Tasmania (the United Tasmania Group) and in New Zealand (the Values Party)'; see 'Who We Are', *Global Greens*, 2019. The website links to the terrific 1999 doctoral thesis of New Zealand activist and author Christine Dann, 'From earth's last islands: the global origins of Green politics', Thesis submitted to Lincoln University, 1999, which explores how two new Green parties were formed so close together in Tasmania and New Zealand.

2   See Richard Jones (ed.), *Damania: The Hydro-Electric Commission, The Environment & Government in Tasmania*, Fullers Bookshop, Hobart, 1972, p. x.

3   Bill Lines, *Failing Nature: The Rise and Fall of the Wilderness Society*, Envirobook, Sussex Inlet, 2019, p. 2.

4   No author, 'Petition pedder – by the yard', *The Mercury*, 5 July 1967.

5   For Angus Bethune's quote, see his interview in the two-part 1972 documentary 'The Last Summer', telerecordings, YouTube, 15–6 March 2009, www.youtube.com/watch?v=xYEb08HVFxg (Part 1) and www.youtube.com/watch?v=dhvfJGHI16o 9 (Part 2, at the seven-minute mark).

6   All members of the upper house in Tasmania are nominally independent but Michael Hodgman was later a federal MP for the Liberal party and Liberal member of Tasmania's lower house.

7   telerecordings, 'Lake Pedder The Last Summer Pt 2', YouTube, 16 March 2009.

8   Pamela Walker, 'The United Tasmania Group', p. 35. It was Des Shield who dubbed them the 'Laborials'.

9   Brian Proudlock, written notes of 2015, provided by Geoff Holloway.

10 telerecordings, 'Lake Pedder The Last Summer Pt 1', YouTube, 15 March 2009.

11 Lake Pedder Action Committee, 'Minutes of meeting held March 23, 1971 at the home of Mrs B. Hean', Tasmanian Archives and Heritage Office, NS591/1/4.

12 No author, 'The struggle to save Pedder', *UTG Extra*, United Tasmania Group, Hobart, April 1972, p. 2.

13 Max Angus, *The World of Olegas Truchanas*, Olegas Truchanas Publication Committee, Hobart, 1975, p. 54.

14 After meeting with Tasmanian premier Angus Bethune on 22 November 1972 (presumably with Dick Jones, who describes the meeting to Milo Dunphy), Brenda Hean wrote back to him that day. She had believed he was a conservationist at heart, and felt that the conservation vote had helped him 'considerably' to gain office, but if he would not agree to a twelve-month delay in the flooding of Lake Pedder, then 'I, like many thousands of others who have always voted for the Liberal Party, and people who have "swung over to give it a go", emphatically state that nothing will restore our faith in your leadership, nor that of your party.' See United Tasmania Group Papers, Tasmanian Archives and Heritage Office, NG2412.

15 Anna Grieve and Steve Best (dir.), *Lake Pedder*, Film Australia, 1997.

16 Patsy Jones, 'The Ecology of Conservation', July 1971, Patsy Jones private papers. See also Peter Hay, *Main Currents in Western Environmental Thought*, UNSW Press, Sydney, 2001, p. 25.

17 Richard Jones, 'Preface', *Damania*, p. iv.; see also the editorial in *Search*, journal of the Australian and New Zealand Association for the Advancement of Science, April 1971.

18 Milo Dunphy in a letter to Brian Proudlock dated 25 January 1972, in 'Milo Dunphy', Dunphy Papers Mainly Relating to the Bushwalking Conservation Movement, 1905–1984 (Dunphy Papers), Mitchell Library, State Library of New South Wales, MLMSS 4457, Box MLK3345, Item 37.

19 Richard Jones, *Damania*, pp. 17, 20.

20 Milo Dunphy in a letter to Kevin Kiernan dated 3 March 1972, Dunphy Papers.

21 Richard Jones, *Damania*, p. 18.

22 Dick Jones in a letter to Milo Dunphy dated 7 December 1971, Dunphy Papers.
23 Record of conversation on 10 February, Dunphy Papers.
24 Federal Hotels had secretly lent Lyons $1000 to make a deposit on a home in Melbourne's Camberwell. Lyons had also been offered a hefty retainer in PR, with Federal as a client, and British American Tobacco had paid Lyons a huge sum – $25,000, worth ten times that in today's money – allegedly by way of an advance for his memoirs, which were never written. Bribery allegations would soon be flying thick and fast, leading to a police investigation and calls for a royal commission. It was not until the publication of James Boyce's groundbreaking *Losing Streak* in 2017, which uncovered the police report, that it was confirmed: Lyons was almost certainly on the take. See James Boyce, *Losing Streak: How Tasmania Was Gamed by the Gambling Industry*, Black Inc., Melbourne, 2017.
25 Dunphy Papers.
26 Peter Meredith, *Myles and Milo*, Allen & Unwin, Sydney, 1999, p. 246.
27 James Boyce, *Losing Streak*, pp. 28–9.
28 *The Mercury*, 23 March 1972, p. 13.
29 Lake Pedder Action Committee, copyright of G. L. Bugg, Jones Family Papers, Tasmanian Archives and Heritage Office, NTG2668.
30 ibid.
31 'United Tasmania Group submission to the federal inquiry into Lake Pedder', United Tasmania Group Papers.
32 Pamela Walker, 'The United Tasmania Group', pp. 11–12.
33 Milo Dunphy in a letter to Rod Broadby, circa early 1972, Dunphy Papers.
34 See cover letter for news release dated 3 April 1972, United Tasmania Group Papers.
35 Christine Dann, 'From earth's last islands', p. 245 and Appendix D.
36 Kevin Kiernan in a letter to Milo Dunphy dated 23 February 1972, Dunphy Papers.
37 Christine Milne, *An Activist Life*, University of Queensland Press, St Lucia, 2017, pp. 22, 24.
38 No author, 'Tasmania party sees its main plank sink', *The Australian*, 21 April 1972.
39 Letter dated 10 April 1972, enclosing $300 cheque from Mrs D. Knight on behalf of Mr J. Medwin, for the Australian Centre Party State office, to the chairman of the United Tasmania Group, United Tasmania Group Papers.
40 Pamela Walker, 'The United Tasmania Group', p. 50, citing conversations with Bob Brown and Hugh Dell, and citing Phillip Lowe and Jane Goyder, *Environmental Groups in Politics*, Allen & Unwin, London, 1983.
41 ibid., p. 50.
42 M. Haward and P.R. Hay, 'Tasmania's greening: eco-politics and the electorate 1972–1986', Paper presented to the Eco-Politics Conference, Griffith University, 1986, p. 2.
43 Sara Parkin, *Green Parties*.

44   Undated letter from Dick Jones to Mr N.R.M Mackerras, Wentworth
     Chambers (in reply to a letter from Mackerras, a member of the NSW
     state executive of the DLP), dated 29 March 1972, which enclosed a $50
     cheque and included a request: 'I will send a further and larger donation
     if you can assure me that ZPG [zero population growth] will not be a part
     of your Group's platform at this election.' See Jones Family Papers.

45   K.F. Febey, *Report on Parliamentary Elections 1973*, Parliament of
     Tasmania, p. 3.

46   Christine Dann, 'From earth's last islands', p. 252.

47   ibid., p. 261.

48   Christian Parenti, '"The Limits to Growth": A book that launched a
     movement', *The Nation*, 5 December 2012.

49   'Preface', Edward Goldsmith et. al., *A Blueprint for Survival*, Penguin
     Books, London, pp. 12–13.

50   Pamela Walker, 'The United Tasmania Group', p. 58.

51   News release, 21 January 1973, Fergus McPherson private papers.

52   Laurie Oakes, '"Inquest" to learn Pedder's lessons', *The Sun*, 31 January
     1973, no page number.

53   Email correspondence with author, 8 March 2017. Asked whether 'it
     was simply too late to save the lake by the time the Whitlam government
     was voted in and you were appointed?' Cass replied, 'That is true. The
     Burton Inquiry proposal, if accepted, would hopefully have restored the
     appearance but not the unique flora and fauna.'

54   *Togatus*, University of Tasmania Student Union, Hobart, 1977, p. 5.

55   Dick Friend cited in Martin Mulligan and Stuart Hill, *Ecological
     Pioneers: A Social History of Australian Ecological Thought and Action*,
     Cambridge University Press, Melbourne, 1997, p. 248.

56   See *UTG Extra*, United Tasmania Group, Hobart, November 1972, p. 2.

57   Richard Flanagan, 'Return the people's Pedder', in Cassandra Pybus and
     Richard Flanagan (eds), *The Rest of the World Is Watching: Tasmania
     and the Greens*, Pan Macmillan, Sydney, 1990, p. 199.

58   Narelle Miragliotta, 'One party, two traditions: radicalism and
     pragmatism in the Australian Greens', *Australian Journal of Political
     Science*, vol. 41, no. 4, 2006, p. 586 (cited in Shaun Crowe, *Whitlam's
     Children: Labor and the Greens in Australia*, Melbourne University
     Publishing, Melbourne, 2018, p. 54).

59   Dick Jones, 'Does UTG align with the left or with the right?', *UTG Extra*,
     United Tasmania Group, Hobart, June 1974, pp. 1–2.

60   Christine Milne, *An Activist Life*, p. 293.

61   Sara Parkin, 'Degrees of green: an international perspective on green
     political parties', Richard Jones Memorial Lecture, University of
     Tasmania, Hobart, 1990.

62   Peter Thompson, *Bob Brown of the Franklin River*, Allen & Unwin,
     Sydney, 1984, p. 39.

63   Bob Brown in a letter to Arnold Rowlands dated 15 December 1975,
     United Tasmania Group Papers.

64   Bob Brown in a letter to Peter Blackwell, quoted in Richard Flanagan,
     'Return the people's Pedder', p. 198.

CHAPTER 2: DEMOCRATS, BLOCKADERS, DISARMERS

1   Christian Gillitzer, Jonathan Kearns and Anthony Richards, *The Australian Business Cycle: A Coincident Indicator Approach*, Reserve Bank of Australia, October 2005, p. 27.

2   See 'Dinner in honour of the Honorable the Prime Minister of Australia and Mrs Fraser', Sheila Weidenfeld Files at the Gerald R. Ford Presidential Library, Box 34, folder 'State Dinners – 7/27/76 – Australia'.

3   See Don Chipp and John Larkin, *The Third Man*, Rigby in association with Beckett Green, Adelaide, 1978, p. 187. Although a later section of the book does cover environment policy, it does not seem to have been a motivating factor in the formation of the Democrats.

4   No author, 'Australia Party Tip', *Central Western Daily*, 25 September 1973.

5   Fergus McPherson, 'Report to the NSW Executive and State Council', Fergus McPherson private papers, 4 June 1974.

6   Rod Myer, 'What made John Siddons one of Australia's most unusual and enigmatic politicians', *The New Daily*, 29 September 2016.

7   'Environment priorities of the Australia Party', Fergus McPherson private papers, January 1973.

8   Undated draft copy for election leaflet, addressed at 1 Arundel Street, Glebe, 6 pp., in Fergus McPherson private papers. Correspondence with former Australia Party members including McPherson suggests this pamphlet is from 1973, when the party was based at Arundel Street.

9   Lyn Allison, 'Condolences: Hon. Leslie Chipp AO', *Senate Hansard*, Parliament of Australia, Canberra, 4 September 2006, p. 42.

10 Peter Thompson, *Bob Brown of the Franklin River*, pp. 43–4.

11 ibid., pp. 54–5.

12 Bob Brown, *Optimism: Reflections on a Life in Action*, Hardie Grant Books, Melbourne, 2015, pp. 26–7.

13 Norman Sanders, 'Who saved the Franklin?', draft of unpublished chapter, author copy, p. 7.

14 Hamish Sewell, 'Norm Sanders interviewed by Hamish Sewell in the Old Parliament House', Political and Parliamentary Oral History Project, National Library of Australia, 24 November 2011, p. 123.

15 Bill Lines, *Failing Nature*, p. 20.

16 Gregg Borschmann, 'Recorded interview with Bob Brown', p. 109.

17 Hamish Sewell, 'Norm Sanders interviewed by Hamish Sewell in the Old Parliament House', p. 154.

18 Bob Brown, speaking at the 25th anniversary of the Australian Greens in Hobart, 18 November 2017, author recording.

19 Peter Thompson, *Bob Brown of the Franklin River*, p. 157.

20 ibid., p. 156.

21 Hamish Sewell, 'Norm Sanders interviewed by Hamish Sewell in the Old Parliament House', p. 156.

22 Norman Sanders, 'Who saved the Franklin?', draft of unpublished chapter, author copy; see also Lyn Allison, 'Democrats' role in saving the wilderness has been sold down the river', *The Sydney Morning Herald*, 31 December 2002.

23   Christine Milne, 'Condolences: Hon. Donald Leslie Chipp AO', p. 60.

24   Harsha Prabhu (ed.), *Rainbow Dreaming: Tales from the Age of Aquarius,* Rainbow Collective, Nimbin, 2013, p. 58.

25   Peter Meredith, *Myles and Milo*, pp. 273–4.

26   The exact quote 'there had always been a light green tinge to Labor politics' is from the author's copy of a draft chapter of the subsequently published memoir, Bob Carr, *Run for Your Life*, Melbourne University Press, Melbourne, 2018. The quote does not appear in the published book, but similar sentiments are at pp. 228, 237–8.

27   Ian Cohen, *Green Fire: An Account of the Australian Environmental Protest Movement*, Angus and Robertson, Sydney, 1997, p. 48.

28   Tony Stephens, 'Joe Glascott 1931–2016: journalist who saved rainforests', *The Sydney Morning Herald*, 21 January 2016.

29   Geoff Law, *The River Runs Free: Exploring and Defending Tasmania's Wilderness*, Penguin Books, Melbourne, 2008, p. 198.

30   Ian Cohen, *Green Fire*, p. 74.

31   Hamish Sewell, 'Norm Sanders interviewed by Hamish Sewell in the Old Parliament House', p. 158.

32   Gregg Borschmann, 'Recorded interview with Bob Brown', p. 98.

33   Benjamin Weinthal, 'The Nazi roots of the German Greens', *The Jerusalem Post*, 7 July 2013.

34   Sara Parkin, *Green Parties*, p. 120.

35   Per Gahrton, *Green Parties, Green Future: From Local Groups to the International Stage*, Pluto Press, London, 2015, p. 163.

36   ibid.

37   Gregg Borschmann, 'Recorded interview with Jo Vallentine (b. 1946–)', National Library of Australia Oral History Section, 15 December 1993, pp. 61, 211.

38   ibid., pp. 78–9.

39   Peter Garrett, *Big Blue Sky: A Memoir*, Allen & Unwin, 2015, p. 141.

40   Drew Hutton and Libby Connors, *A History of the Australian Environment Movement*, Cambridge University Press, Melbourne, 1999, p. 224.

41   Gregg Borschmann, 'Recorded interview with Jo Vallentine', p. 112.

42   Peter Garrett, *Big Blue Sky*, pp. 138–9.

43   Greg Adamson, 'The rise and undermining of anti-nuclear political action', *Green Left Weekly*, no. 361, 19 May 1999.

44   Geraldine Brooks, 'New senator's disarming style', *National Times*, 23 August 1985.

45   Barbara Kearns, *Stepping Out for Peace: History of CANE and PND (WA)*, People for Nuclear Disarmament, Marylands, 2004, p. 9.

46   Tony Harris, 'Social chauvinism: an analysis of the "new order" in the ALP branches of the inner city of Sydney', September 1983, Tony Harris Further Papers Relating to Activity in the Australian Labor Party and The Greens in the Municipality of Leichhardt, ca. 1973 – ca. 1992, Together with a Background Paper by Tony Harris (Tony Harris Papers), 2008, Mitchell Library, State Library of New South Wales, MLMSS 9583.

47   Paola Totaro, 'ALP vote to expel seven "Greens"', *The Sydney Morning Herald*, 9 July 1984.

CHAPTER 3: GREEN INDEPENDENTS

1   Anonymous handwritten message scrawled on a press clipping, Bob
     Brown, Parliamentary and Political Papers (Bob Brown Papers),
     Tasmanian Archives and Heritage Office, NS2029.
2   Phil Beck, 'Lowe decision to quit Assembly was no surprise', *The
     Examiner*, 20 July 1986.
3   Bob Brown, 'Cannabis – time for a change', Speech given at Hobart Town
     Hall meeting, 11 August 1993, Bob Brown Papers.
4   Bob Brown, 'Natural Death Bill 1986: Second Reading', Tasmanian
     House of Assembly Hansard, Hobart, 29 October 1987, pp. 4715–6.
5   Bob Brown, 'Speaking on the Consolidated Fund Appropriation Bill
     1987–88', in ibid., 1 October 1987, p. 3403.
6   Bob Brown, Title unsourced, in ibid., 27 October 1987, p. 4522.
7   ibid., p. 4523.
8   Bob Brown, 'The winning formula', Paper for the green independents by
     the Gay Law Reform Group, no date, Bob Brown Papers.
9   Rodney Croome, Open letter to Green Independents dated 20 October
     1990, ibid.
10   Christine Milne, *An Activist Life*, p. 95.
11   Mary-Louise O'Callaghan, 'The greening of the ALP', *The Sydney
     Morning Herald*, 22 March 1986.
12   ibid.
13   Patsy Jones, four-page undated brochure, Richard Jones Memorial
     Lecture Appeal, University of Tasmania, Patsy Jones private papers; also
     Bob Brown, 'Dick Jones Tribute', *Togatus*, Tasmania University Union,
     Hobart, vol. 57, no. 2, April 1986, Patsy Jones private papers.
14   Bob Brown, *Memo for a Saner World*, Penguin Books, Melbourne, 2004,
     p. 179.
15   Gregg Borschmann, 'Recorded interview with Bob Brown', p. 125.
16   ibid., p. 63.
17   ibid., p. 74.
18   ibid., pp. 56–7.
19   ibid., p. 142.
20   ibid., p. 141.
21   Christine Milne, *An Activist Life*, p. 127.
22   Bob Brown and Peter Singer, *The Greens*, Text Publishing, Melbourne,
     1996, p. 77.
23   Bob Brown, 'The federal election result and the future', Agenda for a meeting
     held at the Methodist Hall, Launceston, 5 May 1990, Bob Brown Papers.
24   Memo from Michael Lynch circa 1990, Bob Brown Papers.
25   Sara Parkin paper, p. 3, in ibid.
26   Bob Brown and Peter Singer, *The Greens*, p. 33; Bill Lines describes
     Keating as 'unendingly hostile' to conservation in *Failing Nature*, p. 98.
27   Gregg Borschmann, 'Recorded interview with Bob Brown', p. 145.
28   Katrina Bolton, 'The Australian Greens: getting real', *Sunday Extra*,
     ABC Radio National, 1 June 2003.
29   Gregg Borschmann, 'Recorded interview with Bob Brown', p. 132.

30 Jane Sullivan, 'Parliament's pursuer of peace finds a little of her own on the lawns', circa 1985 and 'Vallentine Days', *The Age*, 21 December 1985.

31 Jo Vallentine and Peter Jones, *Quakers in Politics: Pragmatism or Principle?*, The Religious Society of Friends, Brisbane, 1990, p. 26.

32 Paul McGeogh, 'Nuclear accident plan attacked', *The Sydney Morning Herald*, 20 May 1986.

33 No author, 'N-disaster planning urged', *The West Australian*, 27 May 1986.

34 Standing Committee on Foreign Affairs and Defence, 'Safety procedures relating to nuclear powered or armed vessels in Australian waters', Parliament of Australia, Canberra, 1986.

35 Jo Vallentine and Peter Jones, *Quakers in Politics*, p. 26.

36 Kent Acott, 'Vallentine thrown out of chamber', *The West Australian*, 18 July 1986 and Sean Murphy, 'Inquiry fails to satisfy senator', *The West Australian*, 11 October 1986.

37 Ian Holland, 'Crime and candidacy: current issues brief no. 22, 2002–03', Parliament of Australia, Canberra, 24 March 2003.

38 Jo Vallentine and Peter Jones, *Quakers in Politics*, p. 24.

39 Luis M. Garcia, 'Stay in touch', *The Sydney Morning Herald*, 13 May 1987.

40 Tracey Aubin, 'Party's over but the cause lingers', *The Sydney Morning Herald*, 15 June 1987.

41 Gregg Borschmann, 'Recorded interview with Bob Brown', p. 184.

42 Advertisement for the Vallentine Peace Group, *The West Australian*, 26 June 1987, p. 12.

43 Gregg Borschmann, 'Recorded interview with Bob Brown', p. 181.

44 Peter Bowers, 'February 1988: Bob's date with death or glory?', *The Sydney Morning Herald*, 17 January 1986.

45 Kent Acott, 'Final victory – Vallentine', *The West Australian*, 4 August 1987.

46 Jo Vallentine and Peter Jones, *Quakers in Politics*, p. 32.

47 ibid., p. 38.

48 Jane Sullivan, 'Parliament's pursuer of peace …' and 'Vallentine Days'.

49 Staff reporters, 'Vallentine arrested at Pine Gap rally', *The Australian*, 19 August 1987.

50 Keith Scott, 'Vallentine invokes Nuremberg principles to back peace action', *The Canberra Times*, 22 October 1987.

51 See Sylvia Cyclone, 'Vallentine interview with Stuart Reid re Miles and Vallentine families Marble Bar "Redlands" politics', October 1995 and April 1996, Battye Library, Western Australia, p. 22.

52 Fred Chaney, Pine Gap Defence Space Research Facility: discussion of matter of public importance, procedural text', *Senate Hansard*, Parliament of Australia, Canberra, 21 October 1987, p. 1047.

53 Gregg Borschmann, 'Recorded interview with Jo Vallentine', pp. 172–3.

54 Mark Irving, 'Vallentine free of protest charge', *The Australian*, 18 April 1989.

55 No author, 'Disgrace to the Senate', *Sun-Herald*, 2 October 1989.

56 Jo Vallentine and Peter Jones, *Quakers in Politics*, p. 80.

57 Deanie Carbon, 'Senator plagues nation's conscience', *The West Australian*, 22 December 1988.

58 Gregg Borschmann, 'Recorded interview with Jo Vallentine', p. 196.

59 Jo Vallentine and Peter Jones, *Quakers in Politics*, p. 36.

60   Judith Whelan, 'Most leaks should not be a crime, govt told', *The Sydney Morning Herald*, 6 January 1992.

61   House of Representatives Standing Committee on Legal and Constitutional Affairs, 'Whistleblower protection: a comprehensive scheme for the Commonwealth public sector', Report of the Inquiry into Whistleblowing Protection within the Australian Government Public Sector, Parliament of Australia, Canberra, February 2009, p.viii.

62   Senator John Coulter, 'Vallentine must take credit for Antarctic mining ban: Democrats', Media release, 30 April 1991. See also Vallentine: 'I mean, this is what is so fascinating about politics. You cannot pigeon-hole people. It was like Michael Hodgman from Tasmania, "the mouth from the south", was fantastic on East Timor. Always was strong on the issue of supporting the East Timorese push for independence. And then here was Noel Crichton-Browne saying, "If you've ever been there, you couldn't even countenance the idea of mining being allowed. No exploration. No mining. Antarctica is special."' Gregg Borschmann, 'Recorded interview with Jo Vallentine', p. 207.

63   Brendan Nicholson, 'Feisty campaigner will not go quietly', *The West Australian*, 17 September 1991.

64   No author, 'Senator arrested', *The Sydney Morning Herald*, 17 August 1990.

65   Jeremy Thompson, 'Vallentine to retire: "time for a new voice"', *The Canberra Times*, 17 September 1991; see also Paul Chamberlin, 'Protests close Senate gallery', *The Sydney Morning Herald*, 22 January 1991.

66   Stephen Bevis, 'Vallentine waits for word on pension', *The West Australian*, 1 February 1992.

67   Brendan Nicholson, 'Vallentine to quit Senate', *The West Australian*, 17 September 1991.

68   Jo Vallentine and Peter Jones, *Quakers in Politics*, p. 41.

69   ibid., p. 48.

CHAPTER 4: GETTING TOGETHER

1   Paddy Manning, 'No love lost in the Greens', *Background Briefing*, ABC Radio National, 11 September 2016.

2   Bob Brown and Peter Singer, *The Greens*, p. 83.

3   'The inaugural meeting of the Liffey Group Steering Committee – minutes', Greens New South Wales Inc. Records, ca. 1980–2014 (Greens NSW Papers), Mitchell Library, State Library of New South Wales and courtesy The Greens NSW, 1194792, 15 May 1985.

4   Kristine Taylor, 'Lock me away', *Australian Story*, ABC, 8 October 2014.

5   'Preconference newsletter, March 1986, Getting Together conference (Sydney, Easter, 1986)', p. 15, Greens NSW Papers.

6   The Greens, 'Draft manifesto: workshop October 5–6–7, Glebe Town Hall', 1985, Tony Harris Papers.

7   David Leser, 'Towards the birth of a Green Party', *The Australian*, 27 March 1986, p. 12.

8   'Getting Together: transcripts, outcomes and contacts from the Easter Conference 1986', Greens NSW Papers, p. 9.

9   ibid., p. 24.

10   ibid., p. 40.

11   Bob Brown and Peter Singer, *The Greens*, p. 84.

12   Drew Hutton (ed.), *Green Politics in Australia: Working Towards a Peaceful, Sustainable and Achievable Future*, Angus and Robertson, Sydney, 1987, pp. 83–4.

13   See Tim Doyle, 'The green elite and the 1987 election', *Chain Reaction*, no. 63/64, 1987, pp. 26–31.

14   Ian Cohen, *Green Fire*, p. 142.

15   Jack Mundey, Stacey Miers and Bill Whiley, 'NSW Upper House Election Review – a few unanswered questions', no date, Milo Dunphy Papers.

16   No author, 'A green independents get-together, Hobart, 9 and 10 December 1989', Bob Brown Papers.

17   Jim Collins in an undated letter to Bob Brown, ibid.

18   Milo Dunphy in a letter to Bob Brown, dated 23 November 1989, four pp., Bob Brown Papers.

19   Ean Higgins, 'Red faces over green ballot', *The Australian*, 9 November 1989.

20   Sue Quinn, 'Anti-green thugs force candidate to quit election', *The Sunday Telegraph*, 11 March 1990.

21   Robert Haupt, 'Why no-one is nailing the big green lie', *The Sydney Morning Herald*, 17 March 1990.

22   Tony Harris in a letter to green parties dated 5 November 1990, Greens NSW Papers.

23   Danny Bessel, 'Towards the Australian Greens', no date, ibid.

24   Undated and unsigned five-page letter addressed 'Dear Member or Branch Convenor', which begins, 'The 5 Green Independents think that a national Greens party should be based on a get-together with the Democrats. But read on …', Bob Brown Papers.

25   Bob Brown and Peter Singer, *The Greens*, p. 80.

26   Lenore Taylor, 'Democrats propose merger with Greens', *The Australian*, 17–18 August 1991.

27   Tony Harris in a letter to all green parties dated 10 April 1991, Greens NSW Papers.

28   Tony Harris in a letter to all green parties dated 29 April 1991, ibid.

29   Tony Harris in a letter to all green parties dated 15 April 1991, ibid.

30   Bob Brown in a letter to Sue Arnold dated 14 April 1991, ibid.

31   Drew Hutton in a memo to Karen Alexander dated 7 November 1990, regarding the attendees and agenda for a meeting on 18 November at the Australian Conservation Foundation in Fitzroy, attaching a five-page summary of the meeting, ibid.

32   Ian Cohen, *Green Fire*, p. 168.

33   Cassandra Pybus, 'Greens and Democrats out to strike a deal', *Australian Society*, June 1991, page number not recorded.

34   'Report, National Greens Meeting, 17–18 August 1991', Greens NSW Papers.

35   Karen Fletcher in an undated letter to all green parties, ibid.

36   Steve Brigham, 'Progress towards the formation of a national green party', 28 January 1992, ibid.

37 Janet Rice, 'Green State Election Strategy', no date, Victorian Greens archives, Melbourne, access provided by Colin Smith.

38 Bob Brown in a letter to Christabel Chamarette dated 8 July 1992, Bob Brown Papers.

39 *Christopher Paul Williams vs. Australian Electoral Commission and The Greens (1995), 21 AAR 467.*

40 Christine Milne, *An Activist Life*, pp. 300–1.

41 Bob Brown and Peter Singer, *The Greens*, pp. 84–5.

42 See The Greens, Media release, 30 August 1992; Robert Garran, 'National greens are banking on grass-roots disenchantment', *Australian Financial Review*, 31 August 1992; Ann-Maree Moodie, 'Budding Greens sound a warning', *The Australian*, 31 July 1992; 'Greens get ready for election', *The Sydney Morning Herald*, 31 August 1992; also 'Australian Greens founding conference', *Greenline: Newsletter of the Queensland Greens*, no. 5, October 1992.

CHAPTER 5: BREAKING THROUGH

1 Petra Kelly and Gert Bastian, open letter dated 18 December 1990, Bob Brown Papers.

2 Petra Kelly, 'Open letter to the Green Party', attached to postcard to Bob Brown dated 10 September 1992, ibid.

3 Tony Catterall, 'Petra: suicide or murder?', *The Observer*, 25 October 1992.

4 Sara Parkin, *Green Parties*, p. 124.

5 Joachim Jachnow, 'What's become of the German Greens?', *New Left Review*, no. 81, May–June 2013.

6 ibid.

7 Afterword by Petra Kelly in Gail Chester, *Articles of Peace: Celebrating Fifty Years of Peace News*, Prism Press, Bridport, 1987.

8 'Matters of public importance: unemployment', *House Hansard*, Parliament of Australia, Canberra, 13 May 1993, p. 788.

9 The Australian Greens, 'Federal election program 1993: summary of principles and policies', Australian Greens archives, Melbourne, access provided by Colin Smith.

10 David Mussared, 'Voters confused by "econobabble"', *The Canberra Times*, 20 February 1993.

11 Andrew Darby, 'Memoirs a matter of profit from crime', *The Sydney Morning Herald*, 1 December 1993.

12 The Australian Greens, *Annual Report 1993*, Australian Greens archives.

13 The Australian Greens, 'Minutes of the Greens National Council Meeting 1–2 May 1993', Australian Greens archives, p. 5.

14 David Mussared, 'Greens to contest ACT Senate seats', *The Canberra Times*, 30 January 1993.

15 The Australian Greens, 'Minutes of National Council, 24–25 October 1992', Australian Greens archives, p. 5.

16 ibid., Appendix 5, p. 2.

17 Danielle Cook, 'Greens: we'll win four Senate seats', *The Sydney Morning Herald*, 9 February 1993, and No author, 'Environment will be

an issue: Brown', *The Canberra Times*, 9 January 1993.

18   James Norman, *Bob Brown: Gentle Revolutionary*, Allen & Unwin, Sydney, 2004, p. 170.

19   See for example the profile by Simon Kent, 'A quiet warrior fights for the planet', *The Sydney Morning Herald*, 22 November 1992.

20   James Norman, *Bob Brown*, p. 157.

21   Andrew Darby, 'Brown to stand for federal seat', *The Sydney Morning Herald*, 12 February 1993.

22   Anne Davies, 'Brown, Greens add colour to seats in Tassie', *The Sydney Morning Herald*, 2 March 1993.

23   Robert Garran, 'Discover Brown, PM tells Greens', *Australian Financial Review*, 23 December 1992.

24   James Norman, *Bob Brown*, p. 168.

25   David Mussared, 'Kelly courts green vote', *The Canberra Times*, 12 February 1993.

26   No author, 'Democrats, Greens plan merger,' *The Canberra Times*, 13 February 1993.

27   David Mussared, 'Greens' exciting direction: Brown', *The Canberra Times*, 23 February 1993.

28   Peter Walsh, 'Snake oil patent-sharing', *Australian Financial Review*, 9 February 1993.

29   Christine Milne, *An Activist Life*, pp. 107–8.

30   Peter Boyle, 'Victorian Green Alliance to stand for Senate', *Green Left Weekly*, 17 February 1993.

31   Mike Taylor, 'ALP snares three Tasmanian seats', *The Canberra Times*, 14 March 1993.

32   Judy and Geoff Lambert, *The Future is Green: A Report on the Federal Election Campaign of The Australian Greens*, March 1993, Australian Greens archive, p. 3.

33   Undated media release, attached to The Australian Greens, 'Minutes of the Greens National Council, 1–2 May 1993', Australian Greens archive.

34   James Norman, *Bob Brown*, p. 169.

35   Philip Ruddock, 'Matter of public importance: immigration', *House Hansard*, 5 May 1992, pp. 2358–9.

36   ibid., p. 2376.

37   ibid., p. 2373.

38   Christabel Chamarette, Parliamentary Debates, *Senate Hansard*, Parliament of Australia, Canberra, no. 152, 5 May 1992, p. 2245.

39   Christabel Chamarette, Parliamentary Debates, *Senate Hansard*, Parliament of Australia, Canberra, no. 152, 7 December 1992, p. 4304–6.

40   Christabel Chamarette, 'Is detention justified?' in Mary Crock (ed.), *Protection or Punishment: The Detention of Asylum Seekers in Australia*, Federation Press, 1993, p. 56.

41   ibid., p. 58.

42   Dee Margetts, 'Governor-general's speech address-in-reply', *Senate Hansard*, Parliament of Australia, Canberra, no. 152, 18 July 1993, p. 255.

43   David Hardaker, 'Balance and power', *Four Corners*, ABC-TV, 10 February 1996.

44 Dr Liz Young, 'Minor parties … major players? The Senate, the minor parties and the 1993 Budget', Department of the Parliamentary Library Parliamentary Research Service, Australian Government Publishing Service, Canberra, 1997, pp. 78–9.

45 Dee Margetts, 'Address-in-reply debate, legislative council, Wednesday 23 May 2001', Western Australia Legislative Council, Parliament of Western Australia, p. 2.

46 Christabel Chamarette, *Greens*, https://greens.org.au/wa/people/christabel-chamarette.

47 David Forman, 'Green Menace', *Business Review Weekly*, 19 February 1996.

48 Dee Margetts, 'IR Reform Bill 2R', *Senate Hansard*, Parliament of Australia, Canberra, 7 December 1993, p. 3982.

49 Lucinda Schmidt, 'Family trusts under the hammer', *Business Review Weekly*, 26 February 1996.

50 Gregg Borschmann, 'After 20 years of uneasy peace, the forest wars are back', *The Guardian*, 20 March 2018.

51 Andrew Darby, 'Moving to greener electoral pastures', *The Sydney Morning Herald*, 7 January 1995.

52 Tim Colebatch, 'Labor should take heed of the word around town', *The Age*, 2 March 1995.

53 Kerrie Tucker, *Legislative Assembly Hansard*, ACT Legislative Assembly, Canberra, 1995, Week 1, p. 10.

54 Farah Farouque, 'Keating shrugs off poll result', *The Age*, 20 February 1995.

55 Bill Lines, *Failing Nature*, p. 123.

56 Matt Peacock, 'Australian Greens', *Background Briefing*, ABC Radio National, 3 September 1995.

57 Mark Baker, 'Nappy Valley shouts but does anyone listen?', *The Age*, 27 March 1995.

58 Frank Walker, 'Labor, Greens talk a deal', *Sun-Herald*, 19 February 1995.

59 Antony Green, 'NSW elections 1995', *Background Paper*, NSW Parliamentary Library Research Centre, July 1995, pp. 18, 22.

60 Greg Sargent in a memo dated 5 July 1995, Australian Greens archive.

61 James Norman, *Bob Brown*, p. 170.

62 Bob Brown and Peter Singer, *The Greens*, pp. 90–1.

63 ibid., p. 55.

64 Memo from Chris Harries to Margaret Blakers dated 14 July 1995, Australian Greens archive.

65 Chris Harries, 'Bob's election campaign: nipping problems in the bud', undated, ibid.

66 Pamela Williams, *The Victory: The Inside Story of the Takeover of Australia*, Allen & Unwin, Sydney, pp. 152–5, 209–11; also Bill Lines, *Failing Nature*, p. 220.

67 Katharine Murphy and Louise Dodson, 'Qualified support for environment policy', *Australian Financial Review*, 1 February 1996.

68 Gerard Henderson, 'Greens' fiscal agenda a recipe for economic blues', *The Sydney Morning Herald*, 27 February 1996.

69 Clare Kermond, 'War of words between Greens and Democrats at Telstra rally', *The Age*, 16 February 1996.

70 Gareth Boreham, 'Insults fly as Democrats, Greens see red', *The Age*, 29 January 1996.

71 Michael Dwyer, 'It's a game of musical chairs for the Senate outcome', *Australian Financial Review*, 29 January 1996.

72 James Norman, *Bob Brown*, p. 177.

CHAPTER 6: PICKING FIGHTS

1 'Transcript of the Prime Minister the Hon. John Howard, MP interview with Neil Mitchell', Radio 3AW, 22 March 1996.

2 Bob Brown, 'Natural Heritage Trust of Australia Bill 1996: in committee', *Senate Hansard*, Parliament of Australia, Canberra, 24 February 1997, p. 862.

3 Greg Barber, ANU analysis, Attachment 6, no date.

4 Christine Milne, *An Activist Life*, pp. 83–4.

5 Geoffrey Barker, 'Discord Mark I', *Australian Financial Review*, 19 April 1996; see also Katharine Murphy and Stephen Long, 'Reith deals with Kernot on IR', *Australian Financial Review*, 15 May 1996.

6 No author, 'Australian govt accepts Telstra opposition – Greens', Reuters, 13 August 1996; Hans van Leeuwen and Louise Dodson, 'Overhaul the tax system, Greens senators tell PM', *Australian Financial Review*, 14 August 1996.

7 Jacqueline Dickenson, 'Mal Colston: the worst rat of the lot?', *Australian Society for the Study of Labour History*, 2007.

8 Dee Margetts, 'Deputy president and chairman of committees: election', *Senate Hansard*, Parliament of Australia, Canberra, no. 179, 20 August 1996, p. 2693.

9 Bob Brown, 'Governor-general's speech: address in reply', *Senate Hansard*, Parliament of Australia, Canberra, no. 179, 10 September 1996, p. 3158.

10 Greg George, Greg Barber, Jo de Silva, et. al., 'A ten-year strategy for the Australian Greens: a discussion paper' (draft), 1997 (no month, but from its contents written between June and October), Australian Greens archive.

11 Bob Brown, 'Order of business: Workplace Relations and Other Legislation Amendment Bill 1996', *Senate Hansard*, Parliament of Australia, Canberra, 29 October 1996, p. 4665.

12 Nina Field, 'PM to seek support on greenhouse', *Australian Financial Review*, 29 April 1997.

13 Bob Brown, 'Sun Fund Bill 1997: second reading', *Senate Hansard*, Parliament of Australia, Canberra, 25 June 1997, p. 5146.

14 Stephen Lunn, 'US juggernaut swamps small beer at Kyoto', *The Australian*, 9 December 1997.

15 Clive Hamilton, 'Australia hit its Kyoto target, but it was more a three-inch putt than a hole in one', *The Conversation*, 16 July 2015.

16 Bob Brown, 'The Republic', transcript of media conference, 28 August 1997.

17   Catherine Moore, 'A brave move by Bob in the Senate', Letters, *The Australian*, 1 September 1997.
18   Christine Milne, 'Constitutional Convention 25', 2 February 1998.
19   Sarah Hanson-Young, Twitter post, 5 April 2018.
20   No author, 'Australia Greens criticise ERA plan', Reuters, 11 October 1996.
21   No author, 'Senate vote condemns Jabiluka mine', Reuters, quoted on *ABC Morning Update*, 21 October 1997, and No author, 'Protest underway at ranger mine site', *ABC Midday Update*, 5 November 1997.
22   Anne Yardley, 'Transcript of an interview with Hon. Giz Watson (b. 1957 –)', Parliamentary History Advisory Committee and State Library of Western Australia, p. 143.
23   No author, 'Thousands protest against Australian uranium mine', Reuters, 5 April 1998.
24   Karl-Erik Paasonen, 'Between movements of crisis and movements of affluence: an analysis of the campaign against the Jabiluka uranium mine, 1997–2000', PhD thesis, School of Political Science and International Studies, University of Queensland, 2007.
25   Nick Hordern, 'Labor "unclear" about Jabiluka', *Australian Financial Review*, 10 June 1998.
26   Wayne Howell, 'NT – ALP will stop Jabiluka mine if no contracts signed – Beazley', AAP, 11 June 1998.
27   Stuart Rintoul and Stephen Lunn, 'The thinning green line', *The Australian*, 6 July 1998.
28   Steven Luntz with Geoff Lambert, 'Discussion paper on electoral prospects', undated, Australian Greens archive.
29   The Open Mind Research Group, 'The Greens (a qualitative study)', May 1998, Australian Greens archive.
30   Sarah Dent, 'Greens target Hanson', *Herald Sun*, 3 August 1998.
31   'Black Green joins blockade of North Ltd at Jabiluka protest in Melbourne', Media release, *The Greens*, 9 September 1998.
32   AAP General News, 'Fed – Greens say green products to rise in price', AAP, 14 August 1998.
33   Charmaine Clarke, 'Greens seek union support', Media release, *The Greens*, 30 September 1998.
34   AAP General News, 'Fed – Greens present parties with preferences wish list', AAP, 3 September 1998.
35   Bruce Montgomery, 'Green party turns out to be a fizzer', *The Australian*, 14 August 1998.
36   Crispin Hull, 'Feds may follow Tasmania's lead', *The Canberra Times*, 1 September 1998.
37   Gordon Feeney, 'Vic – Bob Brown wins again over anti-logging charges', AAP, 23 October 1998.
38   Matthew Franklin, 'Flesh gets pressed a little too hard', *The Courier-Mail*, 9 September 1998.
39   Don Woolford, 'Fed – "men in black jackets" squashed protest child', AAP, 9 September 1998.
40   Heather Kirkpatrick, 'Greens federal election report 98', 1998, Australian Greens archive.

41   Bob Brown, 'Life beyond the tax package', Letters, *The Australian*,
      18 September 1998 (in response to Stephen Lunn, 'Environment dries up',
      The Australian, 16 September 1998).

42   AAP General News, 'Fed – Greens distance themselves from Jabiluka
      siege', AAP, 21 September 1998; Peter Johnston, 'ERA office firebombed',
      Green Left Weekly, 30 September 1998; No author, 'Bombs fail to win
      support for cause', *The Australian*, 22 September 1998.

43   Don Woolford, 'Fed – Greens unveil election manifesto', AAP,
      22 September 1998.

44   AAP General News, 'Fed – Brown says Aussie Greens celebrating German
      win', AAP, 29 September 1998.

45   Don Woolford, 'Fed – Smith, Harradine face extinction in Tasmania',
      AAP, 4 October 1998.

46   Greens post-election review, p. 5, Australian Greens archive.

47   ibid., p. 15.

48   ibid., p. 16.

49   ibid., p. 29.

CHAPTER 7: TURNING THE CORNER

1   Sam Byrne, 'Council needs its Greens', *Australian Greens*, Spring 2000,
      p. 26.

2   Joy O'Brien, 'A first for South Australian Greens', *Green*, Autumn 2001,
      p. 26.

3   Stewart Smith, 'Forests in NSW: an update', Briefing Paper no. 2/99,
      NSW Parliamentary Library Research Service, February 1999, p. 7.

4   'Forestry Revocation and National Park Reservation Bill: second
      reading', *Legislative Council Hansard*, Parliament of New South Wales,
      28 November 1996.

5   Ben English and Rachel Morris, 'Taking a pot shot: MPs admit – we get
      high, but you lot get drunk', *The Daily Telegraph*, 22 November 1997.

6   'M2 Motorway', *Legislative Council Hansard*, Parliament of New South
      Wales, 22 September 1996.

7   Simon Benson and Mark Robinson, 'Carr splits logs: forests traded for
      jobs and votes', *The Daily Telegraph*, 13 November 1998.

8   Trudy Harris, 'Forests decision angers all sides: Greens declare war on
      Carr', *The Australian*, 13 November 1998.

9   No author, 'Obituary: John Kaye', *The Sydney Morning Herald*, 6 May
      2016, and Paddy Manning, 'No love lost in The Greens'.

10   Rod Donald, 'Greens in the balance', *Green*, Autumn 2001, p. 16.

11   Christine Dann, '*Te tangi o te kakariki* (the call of the green parakeet)',
      Green, Spring 2000, p. 17.

12   No author, 'Global Greens to visit Australia', *The Daily Telegraph*,
      11 August 1997.

13   'Minutes of the 4–5 December 1999 National Council meeting, Sydney',
      Australian Greens archive.

14   AAP General News, 'Global greens conference on network against
      corporate globalization', AAP, 19 March 2001.

15   Michael Elliott, 'The new radicals', *Newsweek*, 13 December 1999, pp. 26–9.

16   Christine Milne, 'From birth scream to global government', *Green*, Winter 2000, p. 8.

17   Kirsten Lawson, 'Green MP in forum blockade', *The Canberra Times*, 11 September 2000.

18   AAP General News, 'Greens' Brown accuses court of baiting WEF protesters', AAP, 11 September 2000.

19   Ben Oquist, 'A people's globalisation', *Green*, Spring 2000, p. 19, and Bob Brown, 'Bob's back page', *Green*, Spring 2000, p. 28.

20   Andrew Clennell, 'Nader may have cost us Kyoto Protocol, says Swiss delegate', *The Sydney Morning Herald*, 16 April 2001.

21   Nicholas Confessore, 'Green Herring', *American Prospect*, 1 March 1992.

22   Megan Saunders, 'It ain't easy being Green in politics', *The Australian*, 17 April 2001.

23   Margaret Blakers (ed.), *The Global Greens: Inspiration, Ideas and Insights from the Rio+10 International Workshop and Global Greens 2001*, The Australian Greens and The Green Institute, Canberra, 2001, p. 15.

24   Mark Ludlow, 'Global push to lift Green poll chances', *The Mercury*, 17 April 2001.

25   Stewart Jackson, 'WA election: Greens and Forests sweep Libs from office', *Green*, Autumn 2001, p. 6.

26   Email from Ben Oquist to Kerrie Tucker dated 7 March 2001, Australian Greens archive.

27   Sean Curley, 'Queensland Election', *Green*, Autumn 2001, p. 7.

28   'Minutes of the National Council', Brisbane, 29–30 April 2000, Australian Greens archive.

29   'Minutes of the National Council', Canberra, December 2000, ibid.

30   No author, 'Green Party Highlights', *Green*, Spring 2000, p. 13.

31   Amanda Lohrey, *Groundswell: The Rise of the Greens*, Quarterly Essay 8, Schwartz Publishing, Collingwood, 2007, p. 208.

32   'Minutes of the National Council', Brisbane, 29–30 April 2000, ibid.

33   'Minutes of the National Council', Melbourne, 19–20 May 2001, ibid.

34   'Australian senate votes in favour of East Timor self-determination', Agence France-Presse, 16 October 1996.

35   Bob Brown, *Optimism*, pp. 90–1.

36   'West Papua: suspension of standing orders', *Senate Hansard*, Parliament of Australia, Canberra, 23 November 1999.

37   'East Timor: international war crimes tribunal', *Senate Hansard*, Parliament of Australia, Canberra, 21 August 2001.

38   'Boat arrivals and boat "turnbacks" in Australia since 1976: a quick guide to the statistics', Research Paper Series 2016–17, Parliament of Australia, Canberra, 17 January 2017, p. 2.

39   David Marr and Marian Wilkinson, *Dark Victory: How a Government Lied Its Way to Political Triumph*, Allen & Unwin, Sydney, 2003, p. 45.

40   Michael Perry, 'Asylum seekers on hunger strike in Indian Ocean', Reuters, 28 August 2001.

41 Ben Oquist, 'Greens in the Senate', *Green*, Spring 2001, p. 10.

42 Bob Brown, *Memo for a Saner World*, p. 2.

43 'United States of America: terrorist attacks', *Senate Hansard*, Parliament of Australia, Canberra, 17 September 2001.

44 'Matters of urgency: United States of America terrorist attacks', *Senate Hansard*, Parliament of Australia, Canberra, 24 September 2001, and AAP General News, 'Fed – army expert, Brown warn signed blank cheque for military', AAP, 23 September 2001.

45 Editorial, *Herald Sun*, 26 October 2001.

46 AAP, 'Murphy's exit will change balance of power: Brown', 3 October 2001.

47 Penelope Debelle and Sophie Douez, 'Greens fuming over preferences', *The Age*, 22 October 2001.

48 The Australian Greens, 'Political party annual return form, 2001–2002', Australian Electoral Commission, 2002, Australian Greens archive, and Dinesh Mathew, 'The Australian Greens: national campaign coordinator 2001 election report', December 2001, Australian Greens archive.

49 Glenn Milne, 'Voters see a true representative in Green', *The Australian*, 21 October 2002, p. 15.

50 Hugh Mackay, 'Comfort and the Green vision', *The Sydney Morning Herald*, 10 August 2002.

51 Dinesh Mathew, 'The Australian Greens: national campaign coordinator 2001 election report', Australian Greens archive, December 2001.

52 No author, 'Australia Greens to mull Telstra-for-trees deal', Reuters, 31 May 2002.

53 AAP General News, 'Fed – Greens council blocks Telstra sale 2', AAP, 1 June 2002.

54 Christine Milne, 'Structure of Australian Greens', submission to review panel, 28 February 2002, Australian Greens archive.

55 Australian Greens Review Panel, *Review Paper No. 2*, 11 April 2002, ibid.

56 Margaret Blakers, 'Minutes of the Australian Greens National Council, 8–9 December 2001, Hobart', Appendix 3, Green Institute discussion paper, December 2001, ibid.

57 Margaret Blakers, 'Australian Greens review report', 21 August 2002, ibid.

58 Victorian delegates, 'Report from the National Council meeting in Hobart, 1–2 March 2003', ibid.

59 Stewart Jackson, *The Australian Greens: From Activism to Australia's Third Party*, Melbourne University Press, Melbourne, 2016, p. 84.

60 ibid., p. 154.

61 ibid., p. 225.

CHAPTER 8: TAKING A STAND

1 Matt Price, 'Forget the ranters, ask hard questions – terror hits home', *The Australian*, 19 October 2002.

2 Rick Wallace, 'Australian troops to leave for Gulf, Howard denies war inevitable', *Herald Sun*, 11 January 2003.

3 Andrew Greene, 'Australian Defence Force's Iraq war secrets revealed in newly declassified report', *ABC News*, 26 November 2018.

4   AAP General News, 'Brown says Greens have good prospects in
     Cunningham', AAP, 27 September 2002.
5   Brad Norington, 'Cunningham by-election attracts analysts from US',
     The Sydney Morning Herald, 17 October 2002.
6   Brendan Nicholson, 'News – a slap in the face for Crean', *The Sunday
     Age*, 20 October 2002.
7   Mark Skulley, 'Green power: the threat to Labor in Victoria', *Australian
     Financial Review*, 9 November 2002.
8   Mark Latham, *The Latham Diaries*, Melbourne University Press,
     Melbourne, 2005, pp. 210–1.
9   Carmen Lawrence, 'This is why I've resigned', *The Australian*,
     6 December 2002.
10   No author, 'It's not that easy to be Green, Mr Hanna', *The Age*,
     3 February 2003.
11   Alan Ramsey, 'Little men in a coward's castle', *The Sydney Morning
     Herald*, 22 February 2003.
12   No author, '150,000 rally against Iraq war in Australia', 14 February
     2003, Agence France-Presse; d0ct0r0ct0pUs, 'Stop the War in Iraq
     Rally – 15 Year Anniversary', YouTube, 11 February 2013.
13   Lee Rhiannon, 'Limited terms – nothing new for Greens NSW but should
     it apply to our MPs', letter to members dated February 2001, author copy.
14   Clause 10.7, 'Constitution of the Greens NSW', *The Greens*, adopted
     October 1993 (amended to December 2017; confirmed February 2018;
     registered April 2018).
15   Peta Donald, 'Bob Brown on the NSW Greens' drug policy', *The World
     Today*, ABC Radio, 3 March 2003.
16   Annabel Hepworth, 'Storm over Greens donor reform plans', *Australian
     Financial Review*, 4 March 2003.
17   Robert Wainwright, 'ALP opens lead on the final turn', *The Sydney
     Morning Herald*, 10 March 2003.
18   Nick O'Malley, 'Timing helps Greens', *The Sydney Morning Herald*,
     21 March 2003.
19   Lee Rhiannon, 'Parliamentary electorates and elections amendment bill,
     second reading', *Legislative Council Hansard*, Parliament of New South
     Wales, Sydney, 9 November 1999.
20   AAP General News, 'Greens the new third force in politics', AAP,
     23 March 2003.
21   No author, 'Brown slams Labor's support for ASIO bill', *ABC News*,
     17 June 2003.
22   Bob Brown, 'Bob's back page', *Green*, Summer 2003, p. 24.
23   Bob Brown, *Memo for a Saner World*, p. 222. Also cited in Bob Brown,
     'Bob's Back Page', *Green*, Summer 2003, p. 24, which includes the last
     line and has a slightly different version of the middle sentence: 'Respect
     the world's laws and the world will respect you.' Journalist Margo
     Kingston records the interjection as 'Respect Australia. Return the
     Australians to this nation for justice. If you respect the world's laws, the
     world will respect you.' See Margo Kingston, *Still Not Happy, John!*,
     Penguin Books, Melbourne, 2004, p. 191.

24 Margo Kingston, *Still Not Happy, John!*, p. 194.

25 'Bob's Back Page', *Green*, Summer 2003, p. 24.

26 Margo Kingston, *Still Not Happy, John!*, pp. 194–5.

27 Peter Garrett, *Big Blue Sky*, p. 276.

28 Bob Brown, 'Garrett, the ALP and the Greens', *Green*, Winter 2004, p. 2.

29 Peter Garrett, *Big Blue Sky*, p. 281.

30 Mark Latham, *The Latham Diaries*, p. 306.

31 Lenore Taylor, 'Major parties' Tassie hopes pulped', *Australian Financial Review*, 30 June 2004.

32 Mark Riley, 'Former spy eyes greener pastures', *The Sydney Morning Herald*, 10 December 2003.

33 Karen Middleton, *Albanese: Telling It Straight*, Vintage, Sydney, 2016, pp. 279–81, and Anthony Albanese, 'Adjournment – superannuation: same sex partners', *House Hansard*, Parliament of Australia, Canberra, 10 December 1996, p. 8174.

34 See for example Lane Sainty, 'These gay couples might be why Howard banned same-sex marriage: here's how it all went down in 2004', *BuzzFeed*, 4 November 2016.

35 Deirdre McKeown, 'Chronology of same-sex marriage bills introduced into the federal parliament: a quick guide', Research Paper Series 2017–18, Parliamentary Library, updated 15 February 2018.

36 No author, 'Brown says spring poll may turn votes green', *The Canberra Times*, 30 August 2004.

37 Matthew Denholm, 'Omens look good for rising Greens star – election 2004', *The Australian*, 17 September 2004.

38 John Quiggin, 'Don't fear a Greens senate', *Australian Financial Review*, 29 July 2004.

39 No author, 'First salvos fired in election ad campaign', 13 September 2004, *B&T Weekly*, and Sheena MacLean and Lara Sinclair, 'Small player, big budget', *The Australian*, 7 October 2004.

40 AAP General News, 'Fed – Labor prone to Greens' kooky policies, says Howard', AAP, 30 August 2004.

41 Ben Oquist, 'The *Herald Sun* attacks the Greens', *Green*, Autumn 2005, p. 7.

42 Sally Jackson, 'Press council rap for attack on Greens', *The Australian*, 10 March 2005.

43 Saffron Howden, 'Fed – misleading story cost Greens seats: Brown', AAP, 4 March 2005.

44 Dr Sarah Miskin and Dr Richard Grant, 'Political advertising in Australia', Parliamentary Library Research Brief, 29 November 2004, no. 5, 2004–05, p. 7.

45 Michael Bachelard and Michelle Wiese Bockmann, 'Greens object to Family First "dirty work" – election 2004', *The Australian*, 29 September 2004; Ben Oquist, 'We are all Americans now', *Green*, Summer 2004, p. 18; Sheena MacLean and Lara Sinclair, 'Small player, big budget'.

46 Ben Oquist, 'We are all Americans now', p. 18.

47 Andrew Darby, 'Brown's fears for a nastier Australia', *The Age*, 11 October 2004.

48   Heather Low Choy, 'Democrats spiteful, says Milne', *Sunday Tasmanian*, 19 September 2004.
49   Michael Bachelard and Matthew Denholm, 'Greens eye the balance of power – election 2004', *The Australian*, 1 September 2004.
50   See Matthew Denholm, 'Latham's ghost haunts Labor's forest policy', *The Australian*, 28 May 2011.
51   Matthew Denholm, 'October revolution: workers join capitalists', *The Australian*, 7 October 2004.
52   Malcolm Farr, 'PM: I didn't buy off union – Howard denies $4 million deal with CFMEU', *The Daily Telegraph*, 6 October 2005.
53   Bernard Lane and Matthew Denholm, 'Greens intend to paint broader political picture – minor parties', *The Australian*, 11 October 2004.
54   AAP General News, 'Fed – Milne star in gloomy night: Brown', AAP, 9 October 2004.
55   AAP General News, 'Fed – Greens win seats but fail to nab balance of power', AAP, 10 October 2004.
56   Aban Contractor, 'Preference call compromises Greens' Tasmania bid', *The Sydney Morning Herald,* 16 October 2004.
57   Scott Emerson, 'Is it 10th time lucky for perennial loser? – election 2004', *The Australian*, 12 October 2004.
58   No author, 'Nationals highlight ballot bungle woes', *ABC News*, 13 October 2004, and Greg Roberts, 'Row may force new Senate poll – election 2004', *The Australian*, 13 October 2004.
59   Greg Roberts, 'Nats "offered" reef review for preferences', *The Australian*, 26 October 2004, and Mark Horstman, 'Fishermen attempt to overturn reef bans', *ABC News*, 26 October 2004.
60   Tim Colebatch with Josh Gordon, 'Anglers to clinch majority for PM', *The Age*, 28 October 2004.
61   Narelle Miragliotta, 'One party, two traditions', p. 585.
62   No author, 'I'll wear ovaries T-shirt again: Nettle', *The Sydney Morning Herald*, 11 February 2006.
63   Department of Parks and Wildlife (WA), Department of Agriculture, Fisheries and Forestry (Cwth), 'A report on progress with the implementation of the *Regional Forest Agreement for the South-West Forest Region of Western Australia*', Department of Parks and Wildlife, Perth, July 2013.
64   Jim Scott, *Legislative Council Hansard*, Parliament of Western Australia, Perth, 2013.
65   Paul Jarvis, 'Greens threaten to use gag in one vote debate', *The Countryman*, 28 April 2005.
66   Ron Chapman, 'Transcript of an interview with Christine Sharp (b. 1947–)', State Library of Western Australia, Parliamentary History Advisory Committee, 31 August 2006 – 1 September 2006, item OH 3597, p. 80.
67   ibid.; see also Antony Green, 'The growing bias against Perth and the South West in WA's Legislative Council', *Antony Green's Election Blog*, 20 March 2018; Adrian Beaumont, 'Electoral system flaws deny Labor and the Greens WA upper house majority', *The Conversation*, 31 March 2017; Norm Kelly, 'Western Australian Electoral Reforms: Labor

finally succeeds', *Australian Journal of Political Science*, vol. 41, no. 3, September 2006, pp. 419–26.

68 Jacob Kagi, 'WA Greens offer to work with government on any upper house reform', *ABC News*, 3 April 2017.

69 Paddy Manning, 'The felling of Gunns', *The Sydney Morning Herald*, 12 March 2011.

70 Annie Guest, 'Gunns to sue conservationists', *PM*, ABC Radio National, 15 December 2004.

71 Editorial, 'Threat to freedom of speech', *The Mercury*, 4 April 2006.

72 No author, 'Environmentalists seek donations to fight Gunns suit', *ABC News*, 15 January 2005.

73 'Private members' business: strategic lawsuits against public participation', *House Hansard*, Parliament of Australia, Canberra, 10 October 2005.

74 *Gunns Limited v Marr [2005] VSC 251*, Supreme Court of Victoria, 18 July 2005.

75 Danny Rose, 'Vic – Gunns to fight on despite judge's "chainsaw" mauling', AAP, 28 August 2006.

76 No author, 'Gunns 20 becomes Gunns 15', *ABC News*, 17 November 2006, and No author, 'Gunns abandons legal action against Greens leaders', *ABC News*, 13 December 2006.

77 No author, 'Tas logging operations breach RFA, court rules', *ABC News*, 19 December 2006.

78 Christine Cunningham and Stewart Jackson, 'Leadership and the Australian Greens', pp. 496–511.

79 Per Gahrton, *Green Parties, Green Future*, p. 90.

80 Adam Bandt, 'Making progressive government happen', in Dennis Altman and Sean Scalmer (eds), *How to Vote Progressive in Australia: Labor or Green*, Monash University Publishing, Melbourne, p. 190.

81 Andrea Humphreys, 'The German red–green coalition', *Green*, Summer 2005, p. 7; see also Simone Peter in *Global Greens 2017*, Global Greens, 2019, p. 38.

82 AAP General News, 'Fed – Donald a "magnificent Kiwi and great humanitarian": Brown', AAP, 6 November 2005, and Bob Brown, 'A tribute to Rod Donald', *Green*, Summer 2005, p. 18.

83 Christine Cunningham and Stewart Jackson, 'Leadership and the Australian Greens', pp. 496–511, and AAP General News, 'Fed – Bob Brown elected Greens leader', AAP, 29 November 2005.

84 The peak Democrats representation was between 1998 and 2001, when the party had fifteen MPs around the country: nine senators plus three MPs in South Australia, two in Western Australia and one in New South Wales. After the New South Wales election of March 2007, the Greens had nineteen MPs: four senators, four Tasmanian Members of the House of Assembly (MHAs), four New South Wales Members of the Legislative Assembly (MLCs), three Victorian MLCs, two Western Australian MLCs, one South Australian MLC and one Australian Capital Territory MLA. See 'Table 2: Democrat state and territory representation 1979– 2008' in Cathy Madden, *Australian Democrats: The Passing of an Era*, Research Paper

no. 25, 2008–09, Parliament of Australia, Canberra, 27 March 2009.
85 No author, 'Logging breaches', *The Age*, 2 August 1991.
86 Jean Kennedy, 'NSW Greens outraged by withheld Snowy Hydro documents', *ABC News*, 1 June 2006.
87 Alan Ramsey, 'Here we go again – sold down the river', *The Sydney Morning Herald*, 1 April 2006.
88 AAP General News, 'Costello declares Snowy hydro sale legal', AAP, 24 May 2006, and Bob Brown, 'Selling the Snowy – or rescuing the Senate', *Green*, Winter 2006, p. 23.
89 Michael Duffy, 'Payola: a state-sanctioned business model', *The Sydney Morning Herald*, 12 August 2006.
90 Ben Cubby, 'Slow but steady rise for Greens', *The Sydney Morning Herald*, 26 March 2007.
91 'Inaugural speech of Dr John Kaye', Parliament of NSW, Sydney, p. 453.
92 David Marr, 'Where art thou, brethren?', *The Sydney Morning Herald*, 20 January 2007.
93 Christopher Rootes, 'The first climate change election? The Australian general election of 24 November 2007', *Environmental Politics*, June 2008, vol. 17, no. 3, pp. 473–4.
94 John Howard, *Lazarus Rising*, HarperCollins, Sydney, 2010, p. 552.
95 Christopher Rootes, 'The first climate change election?', pp. 473–80.
96 Debra Kilsby, 'Voter perceptions of the Greens: a qualitative research report', DDR Strategic Research, Australian Greens archive, June 2007.
97 Ben Packham, 'Greens tone down election policies', *Herald Sun*, 13 April 2007.
98 Sarah Hanson-Young, 'Sarah Hanson-Young: "I was told having a baby was a mistake"', *news.com.au*, 14 October 2018.
99 Joe Hildebrand, 'Senate deal good news only for Nile', *The Daily Telegraph*, 8 November 2007.

CHAPTER 9: INTO POWER

1 Prime Minister of Australia, 'Transcript of doorstop inteview: Bendigo, Victoria', Media release, 11 December 2008.
2 AAP General News, 'Fed – Greens savage Labor's Garnaut backpedalling', AAP, 21 February 2008.
3 Paddy Manning, *Born to Rule*, Melbourne University Press, Melbourne, 2015.
4 No author, 'Govt moves to abolish WorkChoices', *The Sydney Morning Herald*, 25 November 2008, and Bernard Keane, 'CPRS bills slip to a quiet defeat to yawning voter non-interest', *Crikey*, 13 August 2009.
5 Thomas Friedman, 'A warning from the garden', *The New York Times*, 19 January 2007; No author, 'Sarkozy's Green New Deal', *The Australian*, 27 October 2007; Green New Deal Group, 'A Green New Deal: joined-up policies to solve the triple crunch of the credit crisis, climate change and high oil prices', New Economics Foundation, on behalf of the Green New Deal Group, 2008.
6 Christine Milne, 'The Greens, balance of power and climate politics', Speech to the Sydney Institute Greens MPs, 28 October 2008.

7   Kevin Rudd, 'The global financial crisis', *The Monthly*, February 2009.

8   Commonwealth of Australia, Parliamentary Debates, *Senate Hansard*, 12 February 2009, p. 901.

9   Alexandra Kirk, 'Govt considers using Budget surplus to stimulate economy', ABC Transcripts, 13 October 2008.

10   Michael Brissenden, 'Pensioners and carers big winners in Rudd's rescue package', ibid., 14 October 2008.

11   Peter Martin, 'Songs of praise from all parties', *The Age*, 15 October 2008.

12   No author, 'Families urged not to blow $1000 government bonus', *ABC News*, 8 December 2008.

13   'Social security and other legislation amendment (Economic Security Strategy)' and 'Appropriation (Economic Security Strategy) Bill 2008–2009 (no. 1, 2)', *Senate Hansard*, Parliament of Australia, Canberra, 24 November 2008.

14   AAP Bulletins, 'Govt unveils $4.7b nation building plan', AAP, 12 December 2008.

15   No author, 'Meet our Mr Five Per Cent', *The Daily News*, 17 December 2008.

16   Sue Neales, 'Wilkie walks away from Greens', *The Mercury*, 30 May 2008.

17   Sue Neals, title unsourced, *The Mercury*, 20 March 2009.

18   No author, '2009 Fremantle by-election results', ABC Elections, updated 26 May 2009.

19   Stephen Luntz and Mike Feinstein, 'Historic Green win to lower house of Western Australia state parliament', *Green Pages*, The Green Party of the United States, Washington, DC, 17 July 2009.

20   AAP General News, 'Fed – more ALP seats at risk with Greens win: Brown', AAP, 17 May 2009.

21   AAP General News, 'Fed: Costello says Labor in trouble', AAP, 18 May 2009, and Gerard Henderson, 'AAP Greens profit from Liberal largesse', *The Sydney Morning Herald*, 18 May 2009.

22   'Loan Bill 2009', extract from *Legislative Assembly Hansard*, Parliament of Western Australia, Perth, 9 June 2009.

23   Joe Spagnolo, 'I have caused great pain to many people', *The Sunday Times*, 25 April 2010, and Nicolas Perpitch, 'Sniffer's affair with Greens MP puts career as Treasurer in doubt', *The Australian*, 26 April 2010.

24   Jacob Saulwick, 'Garnaut's climate change agonising', *The Sydney Morning Herald*, 17 April 2009.

25   Paul Kelly, *Triumph and Demise: The Broken Promise of a Labor Generation*, Melbourne University Press, Melbourne, 2014, p. 198.

26   Paddy Manning, 'Strolling towards the jaws of death', *The Age*, 10 July 2010.

27   Bob Brown (p. 3939) and Christine Milne (p. 3925), 'Carbon Pollution Reduction Scheme Bill 2009', *Senate Hansard*, 22 June 2009, Parliament of Australia, Canberra.

28   Christine Milne, 'Carbon Pollution Reduction Scheme Bill 2009', *Senate Hansard*, 11 August 2009, Parliament of Australia, Canberra, p. 4422.

29   Penny Wong in 'Carbon Pollution Reduction Scheme Bill 2009', *Senate Hansard*, 13 August 2009 and division 42–30, p. 4832, Parliament of Australia, Canberra.

30 Natasha Stott Despoja, 'Dinosaur fun is just beginning', *The Advertiser*, 11 August 2009.

31 Kenneth Davidson, 'Polluters win no matter who is in power', *The Age*, 31 August 2009.

32 Stephanie Peatling, 'It's D-day for Turnbull over climate change', *Herald Sun*, 18 October 2009.

33 Emma Rodgers, 'Wong talks tough on "day of reckoning"', *ABC News*, 13 August 2009.

34 AAP General News, 'Fed – Greens release ETS amendments', AAP, 12 October 2009, and Emma Rodgers, 'Greens unveil emissions scheme amendments', *ABC News*, 12 October 2009.

35 No author, 'Legal advice show billions more could flow to big polluters', Targeted News Service, 22 November 2009.

36 Stuart Rintoul, 'Town of Beaufort changed Tony Abbott's view on climate change', *The Australian*, 11 December 2009.

37 Albanese and Wong in Paul Kelly, *Triumph and Demise*, p. 21.

38 Peter Hartcher, 'How Rudd lost his nerve on an ETS election', *The Sydney Morning Herald*, 15 May 2010.

39 See Andrew Bartlett, *Green*, Winter 2010, p. 5.

40 Ross Garnaut, 'One year after the Garnaut climate change review', University of Melbourne, 14 September 2009.

41 Bob Carr, 'Greens put purity before carbon-cutting cap and trade', *The Australian*, 8 May 2010, and Matthew Franklin and Lanai Vasek, 'The Greens won't beat us, Labor insists', *The Australian*, 29 April 2010. The latter article includes the text: '"The fact is that if the Greens had supported our legislation along with the two Liberals who crossed the floor, we would have a CPRS in operation today," said a Labor strategist. "I don't believe anyone who voted Labor in 2007 is going to vote Greens on this issue. In fact, there's an opportunity for us to engage with Greens voters and ask them why the Greens rejected our scheme."'

42 Shaun Crowe, *Whitlam's Children*, p. 131.

43 ibid., p. 195, and Paddy Manning, 'The fraught history of Labor and the Greens', *The Australian*, 16 November 2018.

44 Paddy Manning, 'What makes someone give $1.6m to a political party?', *The Sydney Morning Herald*, 8 January 2011.

45 Phillip Coorey, 'Greens–Labor preference deal', *The Sydney Morning Herald*, 19 July 2010, and AAP General News, 'Fed – No policies for preferences: Brown', AAP, 19 July 2010.

46 Leigh Sales, 'Brown argues for abolishing preferences deals', ABC Transcripts, 19 July 2010.

47 Paul Austin, 'Greens fury at Labor deals', *The Age*, 13 August 2010.

48 AAP General News, 'Fed – Indigenous singer new Greens star', AAP, 14 July 2010.

49 Peter Hartcher, 'The Greens are actually more like tomatoes – red all over', *The Sydney Morning Herald*, 19 August 2010.

50 Steve Lewis, 'What a vote for Greens really means – election 2010', *The Daily Telegraph*, 19 August 2010.

51 Gerard Henderson, 'Radical roots seep through at the heart of Greens',

The Sydney Morning Herald, 27 July 2010.

52   Gerard Henderson, 'Hung parliament would be a pain in the neck for everyone', *The Sydney Morning Herald*, 17 August 2010.

53   Dr Nicholas Horne, 'Hung parliaments and minority governments', Parliament of Australia, 23 December 2010.

54   Bob Brown, *Optimism*, pp. 149–52.

55   Extract of debate on 'The Commonwealth Franchise Bill 1902', House of Representatives, Parliament of Australia.

56   Greg Combet, *The Fights of My Life*, Melbourne University Press, Melbourne, p. 252.

57   Geoff Kitney, 'A whole new way of governing', *Australian Financial Review*, 23 August 2010.

58   Editorial, 'Needed: a policy for Julia, direction for Labor', *The Australian*, 9 September 2010.

59   Bob Brown, *Optimism*, p. 152.

60   James Massola, 'Sarah Hanson-Young pledges support for Greens leadership after failed challenge', *The Australian*, 26 October 2010.

61   Stephen McMahon, 'Greens now loom over state poll; swing would deliver 12 seats', *Herald Sun*, 23 August 2010.

62   David Rood, Clay Lucas and Ben Schneiders with Paul Austin, 'Our options are open, say Greens Party quizzed on state poll scenario', *The Age*, 24 August 2010.

63   Ed Gannon, 'Little Green men spook the bush', *Herald Sun*, 29 September 2010.

64   Christian Kerr, 'Liberals' preferential dilemma', *The Australian*, 5 October 2010.

65   Melissa Fyfe, 'Labor plot to crush Greens', *The Sunday Age*, 24 October 2010.

66   Stephen Lunn, 'McKim accuses ALP of "tricks" – Victorian election', *The Australian*, 30 October 2010.

67   AAP General News, 'IC – blue erupts over preference deals', AAP, 14 November 2010.

68   Paul Austin and David Rood with Clay Lucas, 'Libs' preference bombshell', *The Age*, 15 November 2010, and No author, 'Preference snub renders Greens "a lost cause"', *ABC News*, 15 November 2010.

69   AAP General News, 'Vic – Greens refuse to admit defeat after deal', AAP, 15 November 2010.

70   Milanda Rout and James Massola, 'Deal founders on Greens' arrogance', *The Australian*, 20 November 2010.

71   Richard Willingham, 'State Greens vote Barber as leader', *The Age*, 23 December 2010.

72   John Masanauskas, 'Despite leader's spin, an undeniably poor showing Greens' whitewash', *Herald Sun*, 29 November 2010.

73   Sylvia Hale, 'Palestinian refugees and Gaza blockade: valedictory', *Legislative Council Hansard*, Parliament of New South Wales, Sydney, 2 September 2010.

74   Sylvia Hale, 'Setting the record straight: the Greens, the 2011 election, and the boycott of Israel', *Medium*, 17 September 2017.

75   Kelsey Munro, 'Suburb joins Israeli boycott', *The Sydney Morning Herald*, 21 December 2010.

76   AAP General News, 'Fed – Marrickville Israel boycott rankles DFAT', AAP, 24 February 2011.

77   Imre Salusinszky, 'Shameful way with words on display', *The Australian*, 23 March 2011.

78   Josephine Tovey, 'Battle for Marrickville down to the wire', *The Sydney Morning Herald*, 26 March 2011.

79   Cate Faehrmann, 'Greens won't get much further if we repeat poll blunders', *The Sydney Morning Herald*, 7 April 2011.

80   Julia Gillard, 'Walking the Reform Road', Inaugural Gough Whitlam Oration, Whitlam Insitute, 31 March 2011.

81   Alison Rehn and Phillip Hudson, 'Malaysia solution is a huge tax burden: asylum seeker costs to soar', *Herald Sun*, 9 May 2011.

82   Shaun Crowe, *Whitlam's Children*, p. 167.

83   Gareth Hutchens, 'Labor "gobsmacked" by Tony Abbott's U-turn on "Malaysia solution"', *The Guardian*, 14 August 2016.

84   Sarah Hanson-Young, 'Motions: asylum seekers', *Senate Hansard*, Parliament of Australia, Canberra, 21 September 2011.

85   Greg Combet, *The Fights of My Life*, p. 239.

86   Shaun Crowe, *Whitlam's Children*, p. 140.

87   Christine Milne, *An Activist Life*, p. 192.

88   Bob Brown, *Optimism*, pp. 193–208.

89   Sarah Macdonald, 'By my side with Bob Brown and Ben Oquist', *Nightlife*, ABC Radio, 22 April 2017.

CHAPTER 10: MILNE REBUILDS

1   Simon Benson, 'Will Greens turn red now that Brown is down?', *The Daily Telegraph*, 14 April 2012.

2   Emma Alberici, 'Christine Milne to lead Greens', ABC Transcripts, 13 April 2012.

3   Bernadette Habel, 'New era as Greens look to the future', *The Examiner*, 14 April 2012.

4   ABC News (Australia), 'ALP conference witnesses fierce debate', YouTube, 16 July 2012.

5   Christine Milne, *An Activist Life*, p. 259.

6   Christine Milne, 'Christine Milne addresses the National Press Club', *GreensMPs*, 19 February 2013.

7   Christine Milne, *An Activist Life*, p. 327.

8   Shaun Crowe, *Whitlam's Children*, p. 112; see also Paddy Manning, 'The fraught history of Labor and the Greens'.

9   James Massola, 'Behind Greens closed door', *Australian Financial Review*, 16 May 2013, p. 20.

10   Noman Thompson, 'Greens: we are not hypocrites when it comes to donations', *Crikey*, 7 February 2012.

11   Matt Denholm and Christian Kerr, 'Brown welcomes demise of death tax', *The Australian*, 9 July 2012.

12   Christian Kerr with Pia Akerman and Michael Bennet, 'Greens' $43bn hit on business, the wealthy', *The Australian*, 15 July 2013.

13   Commonwealth of Australia, '2013 post-election report', Parliament of Australia, 18 October 2013.

14   Narelle Miragliotta, 'Election 2013 brings a mixed result for the Greens', *The Conversation*, 8 September 2013.

15   Sam La Rocca, 'Grassroots organising wins campaigns: lessons from the US', *Green*, Winter 2013, pp. 8–9.

16   Narelle Miragliotta, 'Election 2013 brings a mixed result for the Greens', *The Conversation*, 8 September 2013.

17   Bianca Hall, 'Milne's Greens "marching to slow death"', *The Sunday Age*, 29 September 2013.

18   Lanai Scarr, 'Pressure on Milne as staff walk out', *The Mercury*, 27 September 2013.

19   Lara Giddings, 'Strong decisions, better future', 2011–12 Budget speech, Tasmania, 16 June 2011.

20   No author, 'I run the prison: McKim', *ABC News*, 21 February 2011, and Josh Jerga, 'WA accused of strike breaking in Tas', *The Sydney Morning Herald*, 9 March 2011.

21   Mel Barnes, 'Conflict over forest "peace" deal', *Green Left Weekly*, no. 965, 11 May 2013.

22   Zoe Edwards, 'Tasmanian premier sacks Greens, visits governor as election date speculation mounts', *ABC News*, 17 January 2014.

23   See Hall Greenland, 'A recurrent danger', *Green Mail*, December 2017, p. 9.

24   Chris Uhlmann, 'Backbench backlash cans electoral funding plans', *7.30*, ABC-TV, 30 May 2013.

25   'Discussion paper for the Australian Greens Constitution Committee', Australian Greens Party Room, 15 May 2013.

26   Jonathan Swan, 'Fate of Abbott's deficit levy hinges on fight within the Greens', *Sun Herald*, 11 May 2014.

27   Naomi Woodley, 'Hockey outlines billions in savings, but critics say it'll divide Australia', ABC Transcripts, 14 May 2014.

28   Pia Akerman and Gina Rushton with Sarah Elks and Sarah Martin, 'Election calls rise as Abbott anger vented', *The Australian*, 19 May 2014.

29   Naomi Woodley, 'Govt defends tough budget in face of falling polls', ABC Transcripts, 19 May 2014.

30   Lee Rhiannon, 'One million hits on Greens new "What will my degree cost?" website while VCs unite against Coalition's reforms', *GreensMPs*, 5 June 2014.

31   Hall Greenland, 'Yes we can (block the budget)', and David Shoebridge, 'How to stop the Abbott budget', both in *Green Voice*, June 2014, pp. 1–2.

32   Sean Nicholls, 'NSW Greens branded "awesomely stupid" over moves to block supply', *The Sydney Morning Herald*, 7 June 2014.

33   Mark Kenny and Lisa Cox, 'Greens face new fuel tax backflip', *The Age*, 3 July 2014, and Lisa Cox and Mark Kenny, 'Greens split over decision to block fuel excise lift', *The Canberra Times*, 8 July 2014.

34   Lenore Taylor, 'Al Gore and Clive Palmer: behind the scenes of an unlikely bromance', *The Guardian*, 26 June 2014.

35   Christine Milne, *An Activist Life*, pp. 265–6.
36   The Greens NSW, '"One Term Tony" Jim Casey, Fire Brigade Employees' Union', YouTube, 3 November 2014.
37   Shaun Crowe, *Whitlam's Children*, pp. 1–2.
38   Shalailah Medhora, 'Greens form new national council to help boost stagnating support', *The Guardian*, 9 November 2014.
39   Sophie Morris, 'Green's hornet's nest', *The Saturday Paper*, no. 36, 1–7 November 2014.
40   Natalie O'Brien and Anna Patty with Jacob Saulwick, 'Four seats in lower house a "seachange"', *Herald Sun*, 29 March 2015.
41   Will Glasgow, 'Greens stun Labor and the Nationals', *Australian Financial Review*, 30 March 2015.
42   Rick Morton, 'Greens "kidding if they want Tanya, Albo",' *The Australian*, 30 March 2015.
43   AAP General News, 'NSW Greens reject leadership concept', AAP, 29 March 2015.
44   Hayden Cooper, 'Fred Nile: controversial Christian Democrat MP poised to hold balance of power in New South Wales parliament', *ABC News*, 16 April 2015.
45   Sophie Morris, 'Milne, Di Natale and Greens' deliberate leadership coup', *The Saturday Paper*, no. 59, 9–15 May 2015.
46   Christine Milne, 'Christine Milne's final press club address as leader of the Australian Greens', *GreensMPs*, 12 May 2015.

CHAPTER 11: THE REAL OPPOSITION

1   Michelle Grattan, 'New Greens leader wants to send a message to those with "mainstream values"', *The Conversation*, 6 May 2015.
2   Sophie Morris, 'Milne, Di Natale and Greens' deliberate leadership coup'.
3   David Crowe, 'Labor's surprise decision to vote against Aged Pension changes', *The Australian*, 16 June 2015.
4   Penny Wright, 'Parliamentary representation – valedictory', *Senate Hansard*, Parliament of Australia, Canberra, 19 August 2015.
5   Josh Taylor, 'Greens' sneaky portfolio reshuffle upsets NSW branch', *Crikey*, 17 September 2015.
6   Josh Taylor, 'Greens kiss and make up but tensions linger', *Crikey*, 13 October 2015; see also that day's 'Tips and rumours'.
7   Sam Dastyari, 'Tax Laws Amendment Bill 2015', *Senate Hansard*, Parliament of Australia, Canberra, 9 November 2015.
8   Les Neilson, 'Tightening anti-avoidance provisions for multinational companies', Budget Review 2015–16 Index, Parliament of Australia, Canberra, May 2015.
9   Heath Aston, 'Greens deal with Scott Morrison on tax shield sparks Labor fury', *The Sydney Morning Herald*, 3 December 2015.
10   Neil Chenoweth, Facebook post, 24 March 2016.
11   Jeremy Hirschhorn, 'Senate Economics Legislation Committee Estimates', *Proof Committee Hansard*, 5 April 2019, Parliament of Australia, Canberra.

12   Lee Rhiannon, 'Senate voting reform is about giving Australians control of their vote', Media release, *GreensMPs*, 28 September 2015.
13   Dan Harrison, 'Labor and Greens would control Senate under proposed reforms, research finds', *The Sydney Morning Herald*, 24 June 2015.
14   Scott Ludlam, 'Reforming Senate voting', *The Greens*, 16 March 2016; see also Scott Ludlam, 'Commonwealth Electoral Amendment Bill 2016, second reading', *Senate Hansard*, Parliament of Australia, Canberra, 15 March 2016, p. 2008.
15   Laurie Oakes, 'Pork chops in pyjamas', *The Daily Telegraph*, 18 March 2016.
16   Anthony Albanese, 'Commonwealth Electoral Bill 2016 – consideration of Senate message', *House Hansard*, Parliament of Australia, Canberra, 17 March 2016.
17   Michael Koziol, '"They're not the nutters they used to be": Liberals open to Greens "arrangement"', *The Sydney Morning Herald*, 10 March 2016.
18   Ellen Whinnett, 'Liberals ready to team with Greens to oust David Feeney from Melbourne seat Batman', *Herald Sun*, 9 May 2016.
19   Shaun Crowe, *Whitlam's Children*, p. 213.
20   Damon Miller, 'The new Senate voting system and the 2016 election', Research Paper 2017–18, Parliamentary Library, 25 January 2018.
21   Adele Ferguson, Sarah Danckert and Heath Aston, 'Senate votes down call for Royal Commission into financial sector misconduct', *The Sydney Morning Herald*, 24 June 2015; see also Peter Whish-Wilson, *GreenMPs*, https://peter-whish-wilson.greensmps.org.au/tags/banks-royal-commission.
22   Charis Chang and AAP, 'Record numbers plan to vote for independent candidates or micro-parties, poll finds', *The Courier-Mail*, 6 June 2016.
23   Clare Blumer, 'Vote compass: Malcolm Turnbull leads Bill Shorten on question of who voters trust', *ABC News*, 16 May 2016.
24   James Massola and Fergus Hunter, 'Election 2016: the eight seats Richard Di Natale plans to turn Green by 2026', *The Sydney Morning Herald*, 5 May 2016.
25   Matthew Drummond, 'GQ&A: Richard Di Natale', *GQ*, March–April 2016, pp. 90–5.
26   James Massola, 'Election 2016: Greens leader Richard Di Natale fails to declare home, pays au pairs low wage', *The Sydney Morning Herald*, 19 May 2016; Vivienne Kelly, 'Press Council rules against *The Age* in article about Greens' leader Richard Di Natale', *Mumbrella*, 19 January 2017; Sarah Martin, 'Au pair wage claim is fake news, says Richard Di Natale', *The Australian*, 15 March 2017.
27   The Australian Greens, 'Richard in the ABC Regional Debate', YouTube, 25 May 2016.
28   Nick Cooper, 'On the shoulders of giants', *The Greens*, 21 November 2016; see also Paddy Manning, 'A good hard look at the Greens', *The Monthly*, August 2016.
29   James Massola, Richard Willingham and Fergus Hunter, 'Election 2016: David Feeney didn't declare $2.3m house and "doesn't know" if it's negatively geared', *The Sydney Morning Herald*, 17 May 2016.

30   Adam Gartrell and National Political Correspondent, 'Federal election 2016: Paul Keating launches withering attack on "pathetic" Greens', *The Sydney Morning Herald*, 25 June 2016.

31   Tanya Plibersek, 'The progressive's case for Labor', speech to the McKell Institute, NSW Parliament House, Sydney, 15 June 2016.

32   Gareth Hutchens, 'Australia destined for minority government, says Greens' Di Natale', *The Guardian*, 23 June 2016.

33   Campaign spending figures in New South Wales sourced from 'Preliminary NSW 2016 federal campaign report', authorised by Ben Moroney, Convenor Election Campaign Committee, 19 August 2016, author's copy.

34   Christine Cunningham quote and figures in Osman Faruqi, 'Without some serious soul searching, the Greens will never move beyond the 10% plateau', *The Guardian*, 5 July 2016.

35   Melissa Davey, 'Behind the "successful" 2016 election: the tension at the heart of the Greens', *The Guardian*, 23 July 2016.

36   Matt Wordsworth, 'Bob Browns calls on Senator Lee Rhiannon to stand down', *ABC News*, 29 July 2016.

37   Mehreen Faruqi, 'I joined the Greens because of Bob Brown, but now he has broken my heart', *The Guardian*, 2 August 2016.

38   Paddy Manning, 'No love lost in the Greens'.

39   Lynne Joselyn and Bob Brown in ibid.

40   Left Renewal, 'Statement of principles', Facebook, 21 December 2016.

41   Heath Aston, 'Hard-left faction forms inside Greens aiming to "end capitalism"', *The Sydney Morning Herald*, 22 December 2016.

42   David Shoebridge and Lee Rhiannon, 'Left Renewal: since when has taxing the rich and saving the planet been so controversial?', *The Guardian*, 12 January 2017.

43   Adam Gartrell, 'Greens descend into public brawl amid doubts over "invisible" Richard Di Natale's leadership', *The Sydney Morning Herald*, 27 January 2017.

44   Tony Wright, 'Pauline Hanson speech: by walking out, the Greens gave the senator exactly what she craves', *The Sydney Morning Herald*, 14 September 2016.

45   Fergus Hunter, 'Richard Di Natale: "United States alliance now represents a security threat to Australia"', *The Sydney Morning Herald*, 21 November 2016.

46   Richard Di Natale, 'Greens announce drug policy reform', Media release, *GreensMPs*, 27 November 2016.

47   Irena Ceranic, 'Roe 8 environmental damage could take decades to restore, according to experts', *ABC News*, 30 March 2017.

48   Chilla Bulbeck, 'Reflections on WA state election 2017: evidence-based campaigning', *The Greens*, 13 July 2017.

49   Malcolm Turnbull and Simon Birmingham, 'True needs-based funding for Australia's schools', Media release, 2 May 2017, and Marilyn Harrington, 'A new plan for school funding', Parliamentary Library, May 2017.

50   Adam Bandt, 'Australian Education Amendment Bill 2017: second reading', *House Hansard*, Parliament of Australia, Canberra, 24 May 2017.

51 Matthew Knott, '"I'm disappointed": Greens leader Richard Di Natale strips Sarah Hanson-Young of immigration role', *The Sydney Morning Herald*, 25 August 2016.

52 The Mocker, 'Are the Greens the only adults in the room?', *The Australian*, 2 November 2017.

53 Melissa Shedden, 'Senator Larissa Waters on the unexpected power of a single act', *news.com.au*, 4 March 2019.

54 Louise Milligan, 'Inside the Greens', *Four Corners*, ABC-TV, 14 August 2017.

55 Liv Casben, Lily Mayers and Stephen Dziedzic, 'Lee Rhiannon loses NSW Greens preselection Senate spot to Mehreen Faruqi', *ABC News*, 25 November 2017.

56 Milne (p. 14) and Loevin (pp. 20–1) in *Global Greens 2017*, p. 14.

57 David Wroe, 'Greens plan 25 seats over the next generation to become major political force', *The Sydney Morning Herald*, 18 November 2017.

58 Sarah Elks, 'Queensland election: how Palaszczuk's Adani veto turned tide for ALP', *The Australian*, 8 December 2017.

59 Paddy Manning, 'The fraught history of Labor and the Greens'.

60 Greens MPs, 'Richard Di Natale – National Press Club 2018', YouTube, 3 April 2018.

61 David Shoebridge, 'Greens Manifesto', *Greens Manifesto*, 2019.

62 Lisa Visentin, 'Cate Faehrmann and David Shoebridge triumphant in Greens preselections', *The Sydney Morning Herald*, 13 May 2018.

63 Lauren Ingram, Twitter post, 18 June 2017.

64 Hagar Cohen, 'Rape shaming: Why some women are naming their alleged attackers online', *Background Briefing*, ABC Radio National, 6 August 2017.

65 Elise Scott and Diana Hayward, 'Greens bungled handling of alleged election night sexual assault, former volunteers claim', *ABC News*, 20 October 2017.

66 Michael Brull, 'Jeremy Buckingham's unacceptable response to Bob Brown's victim blaming', *Medium*, 14 April 2018.

67 Lauren Ingram, Twitter post, 28 January 2018.

68 ibid.

69 David Shoebridge, Facebook, 30 January 2018.

70 Remy Varga, 'Greens condemn Bob Brown for "victim blaming"', *The Australian*, 31 January 2018.

71 Anna Caldwell, 'It's sleazy being Green: MP condemned for lewd gesture', *The Daily Telegraph*, 30 April 2018.

72 Alexandra Smith, '"Claptrap": Greens MP apologises to Buckingham after calling for him to resign', *The Sydney Morning Herald*, 20 November 2018.

73 Remy Varga, 'Former Greens Senator Lee Rhiannon says party could learn lessons from Labor in wake of Luke Foley's resignation', *The Australian*, 12 November 2018.

74 Jeremy Buckingham, *Legislative Assembly Hansard*, Parliament of New South Wales, Sydney, 13 November 2018.

75 Cate Faehrmann, 'I know the horrors of sexual harassment, but mob rule is not justice', *The Sydney Morning Herald*, 14 November 2018.

76   Lynette Keleher, 'Victorian Greens overridden by a bullying and abusive internal culture', *The Sydney Morning Herald*, 11 April 2018.

77   Noel Towell, 'Former Victorian Greens leader hit by sexual discrimination, bullying claims', *The Age*, 10 April 2018.

78   Lorna Knowles, 'Former Victorian Greens leader Greg Barber accused of calling women "fat, hairy lesbians" in workplace', *ABC News*, 6 September 2018.

79   Noel Towell, 'Ex-Victorian Greens leader Greg Barber bites back at Liberal MP, ABC', *The Guardian*, 21 September 2018.

80   Richard Willingham, 'Greens defend rapping candidate Angus McAlpine over another questionable lyric', *ABC News*, 14 November 2018.

81   Michael McGowan, 'Daniel Andrews says Greens have a "toxic cultural problem" around women', *The Guardian*, 18 November 2018.

82   Paddy Manning, 'Whither the Greens? How a reckoning looms for a party fighting to hang on', *The Guardian*, 4 May 2019.

83   Kylar Loussikian, 'Former Greens MP lashes party over fossil fuel links', *The Sydney Morning Herald*, 17 February 2019.

84   Jeremy Buckingham, Facebook, 19 December 2018.

85   Lisa Visentin, '"Ripping up my membership": Jeremy Buckingham quits "toxic" Greens to run as an independent', *The Sydney Morning Herald*, 20 December 2018.

86   Jeremy Buckingham, ABC Radio, 21 December 2018.

87   Paul Karp, 'Coalition backs disability royal commission – but doesn't give green light', *The Guardian*, 18 February 2019, and Lane Sainty, '"We cannot be a minority": there must be people with disability heading royal commission, senator says', *BuzzFeed*, 2 April 2019.

88   See Katharine Murphy, Christopher Knaus and Nick Evershed, '"It felt like a big tide": how the death tax lie infected Australia's election campaign', *The Guardian*, 8 June 2019, and the Hon. Josh Frydenberg, MP, 'Death Taxes – You Don't Say, Bill!', Media release, 24 January 2018.

89   Richard Ferguson, 'Julian Burnside eyes Kooyong, targets wealthy with death taxes', *The Australian*, 5 March 2019.

90   Emma Graham-Harrison, "A new power in Brussels: the Green wall of Europe", *The Guardian Weekly*, 7 June 2019, pp. 18–9.

91   Greg Jericho, 'Labor and the Greens have to join forces – for the climate's sake', *The Guardian*, 2 June 2019.

92   Richard Di Natale, 'Australian Greens announce new shadow ministries for the real opposition', Media release, *The Greens*, 5 July 2019.

CHAPTER 12: CONFRONTING THE CLIMATE EMERGENCY

1   Ria Voorhar and Lauri Myllyvirta, 'Point of no return: the massive climate threats we must avoid', *Greenpeace*, January 2013, p. 41.

2   Climate Action Tracker, 2019, https://climateactiontracker.org/publications/warming-projections-global-update-dec-2018/

3   Susan Griffiths-Sussems, '2018 supporter survey: the results are in!', *The Greens*, 19 October 2018.

4   Sam la Rocca, 'Grassroots organising wins campaigns', p. 10 (references Newspoll since 2008).

5   Bill McKibben, 'This is how human extinction could play out', *Rolling Stone*, 9 April 2019.

6   David Spratt, 'Is all "good news" and no "bad news" a good strategy?', *Climate Code Red*, 21 April 2012.

7   No author, 'Jones backs carbon tax to cut greenhouse gases', *The Australian*, 9 November 1989; 'Environmental and economic management: discussion of matter of public importance', *Senate Hansard*, Parliament of Australia, Canberra, 6 December 1989; Irina Dunn, 'Senator Irina Dunn: Environment Independent Policies for the Federal Election 1990'.

8   Bob Brown, 'Sun Fund Sun', *The Greens*, 2 December 1997, and Bob Brown, 'Greens release $35 billion plan for investing in a sustainable future', Media release, 6 May 2004.

9   Damian Carrington, 'IPCC officials admit mistake over melting Himalayan glaciers', *The Guardian*, 21 January 2010.

10   AAP General News, 'Fed – Greens call for 100 per cent renewables', AAP, 24 July 2010.

11   Joseph Kerr and Dennis Shanahan, 'City puts brakes on coal exports', *The Australian*, 9 November 2006, and Jason Gordon, 'Jobs the price of coal call', *The Newcastle Herald*, 3 February 2007.

12   Lexy Hamilton-Smith, 'Hydrogen fuel breakthrough in Queensland could fire up massive new export market', *ABC News*, 8 August 2018.

13   David Crowe, 'Greens seek to shame Labor by vowing to restore carbon tax', *The Sydney Morning Herald*, 3 November 2018, and Paddy Manning, 'Green backs carbon price', *The Monthly Today*, 17 October 2018. See also Phillip Coorey, 'Greens give up on a carbon price, want government-owned "People's Bank"', *Australian Financial Review*, 3 April 2018, which reported that 'Senator Di Natale will raise the white flag on trying to put a price on carbon because the prospect of an effective price being adopted by Parliament is 'almost non-existent.'

14   Andrew King, *Earshot*, Radio National, 31 October 2016.

15   Clive Hamilton, *Requiem for a Species: Why We Resist the Truth about Climate Change*, Allen & Unwin, Sydney, 2010, pp. 222–3.

16   Guy Rundle, 'Rundle: will the Greens go the way of the Democrats?', *Crikey*, 7 July 2016.

17   Bob Brown, 'It's coalminers, not Moylan, who are costing us the Earth', *The Sydney Morning Herald*, 11 January 2013.

18   Personal communication to the author on Facebook.

19   Nick O'Malley, 'Enemies within as Greens caught in civil war', *The Sydney Morning Herald*, 15 February 2019.

20   Damian Carrington, 'Why the Guardian is changing the language it uses about the environment', *The Guardian*, 17 May 2019.

21   Katharine Murphy, 'Richard Di Natale: Labor should come to negotiating table on climate policy', *The Guardian*, 18 April 2019.

22   Tanya Plibersek, Twitter post, 17 April 2019.

23   Scott Ludlam, Twitter post, 17 April 2019.

24   Katharine Murphy, 'Bill Shorten rules out joint climate policy process with Greens if Labor wins power', *The Guardian*, 26 April 2019.

25   Paddy Manning, 'No love lost in the Greens'.

26   Geoff Evans, 'A just transition to a clean, renewable energy economy is urgent – and possible', Australian Student Environment Network, 2008.

27   Tony Maher, 'Our transition to a cleaner energy future must be just for workers', *New Matilda*, 3 November 2016, and Senate Standing Committees on Environment and Communications, 'Final report: retirement of coal fired power stations', Parliament of Australia, Canberra, 29 March 2017.

28   Paddy Manning, 'The Adani election: a green light for a mega-mine lights up a Green', *The Monthly Today*, 12 April 2019.

29   Sarah Vogler, '"Don't be conned on Adani": Premier warned', *The Courier-Mail*, 23 May 2019.

30   Adam Bandt, Twitter post, 19 May 2019.

31   Chris Mitchell, 'Time for Bob Brown's environmentalists to tell the truth about Adani coal', *The Australian Business Review*, 19 July 2019.

32   Senator Chris Milne, 'Things are crook in Tallarook', *Green Agenda*, 21 February 2015.

CHAPTER 13: TACKLING INEQUALITY IN THE ASPIRATIONAL ERA

1   Adam Bandt, 'Making progressive government happen', in Dennis Altman and Sean Scalmer, *How to Vote Progressive in Australia*, p. 180.

2   Cassandra Pybus and Richard Flanagan, *The Rest of the World Is Watching*, p. 252.

3   Andrew Leigh, 'Why progressives should be pro-growth', in Dennis Altman and Sean Scalmer, *How to Vote Progressive in Australia*, p. 171.

4   Elise Scott, 'Canberra to introduce wellbeing index, as New Zealand bases budget around concept', *ABC News*, 5 May 2019.

5   Martin Farrer, 'Historian berates billionaires at Davos over tax avoidance', *The Guardian*, 30 January 2019.

6   Paddy Manning, 'Calling time on tax cuts', *The Monthly Today*, 6 June 2018; see also Amy Remeikis, 'Greens rule out supporting tax cuts of either major party', *The Guardian*, 21 May 2018.

7   Scott Ludlam, 'What comes next?', *The Monthly*, December 2015 – January 2016.

8   The Green Institute, 'Can less work be more fair?: A discussion paper on universal basic income and shorter working week', December 2016.

9   Luke Michael, 'Greens call for universal basic income', *Pro Bono Australia*, 5 April 2018, and Adam Creighton, 'Greens income plan to cost extra $256bn a year', *The Australian*, 5 April 2018.

10   Adam Creighton, 'Greens income plan to cost extra $256bn a year.'

11   ibid., and Rachel Baxendale, 'Let's have welfare for all, says Di Natale', *The Australian*, 4 April 2018.

12   Tim Hollo, 'UBI, work and Labo(u)r' parties', *The Green Institute*, 6 April 2018.

13   The Australian Greens, 'A future for all of us, the Greens' policy
        platform, election 2019', *The Greens*, May 2019, p. 58.
14   Sean Farrell, 'Use inheritance tax to tackle inequality of wealth, says
        OECD', *The Guardian*, 13 April 2018.
15   Emma Alberici, 'Thomas Piketty suggests Australia introduce inheritance
        tax to address wealth inequality', *ABC News*, 25 October 2016.
16   Peter Hartcher, 'Even bad press is good news for the publicity-hungry
        Greens', *The Sydney Morning Herald*, 13 May 2016.
17   David Shoebridge, 'The Greens Manifesto', p. 14.
18   John Ferguson, 'Greens' agenda targets bosses and billionaires in tax-the-
        rich plan', *The Australian*, 7 April 2018.
19   Scott Ludlam, 'The case for capital gains tax reform: a fairer tax system
        and housing market for all', Analysis and Policy Observatory, 2015.
20   Senate Standing Committees on Economics, 'Treasury Laws Amendment
        (2019 Petroleum Resource Rent Tax Reforms No. 1) Bill 2019
        [Provisions]', *Senate Hansard*, Parliament of Australia, Canberra,
        1 April 2019.
21   Shalailah Medhora, 'Over 2000 people died after receiving Centrelink
        robo-debt notice, figures reveal', *Hack*, Triple J, 18 February 2019.
22   Peter Whish-Wilson, 'Forty-sixth Parliament first session – first period',
        Senate Hansard, Parliament of Australia, Canberra, 4 July 2019.

CHAPTER 14: PURSUING PEACE IN
THE AGE OF THE STRONGMAN

1   Leigh Sales and Myles Wearring, 'Paul Keating says Australia should "cut
        the tag" with American foreign policy', *ABC News*, 11 November 2016.
2   'United States of America: terrorist attacks', *Senate Hansard*, Parliament
        of Australia, Canberra, 17 September 2001, p. 27169.
3   'Matters of urgency: United States of America: terrorist attacks', *Senate
        Hansard*, Parliament of Australia, Canberra, 24 September 2001, p. 27649.
4   'Defence Amendment (Parliamentary Approval for Australian
        Involvement in Overseas Conflicts) Bill 2003, second reading', *Senate
        Hansard*, Parliament of Australia, Canberra, 27 March 2003, p. 10320.
5   'Defence Amendment (Parliamentary Approval of Overseas Service) Bill
        2008 (No. 2), second reading', *Senate Hansard*, Parliament of Australia,
        Canberra, 17 September 2008, p. 4982.
6   Senate Standing Committees on Foreign Affairs Defence and Trade,
        'Australian Greens – dissenting report', Parliament of Australia,
        Canberra, 12 February 2010.
7   Bob Brown, 'Ministerial statements – Afghanistan', *Senate Hansard*,
        Parliament of Australia, Canberra, 25 October 2010, p. 575.
8   Adam Bandt, 'No-fly zone can't wait: Bandt', *The Greens*, 16 March 2011.
9   Latika Bourke, 'Iraq involvement to combat Islamic State "nothing like"
        2003, says Tony Abbott', *The Sydney Morning Herald*, 1 September 2014.
10   'Defence Amendment (Parliamentary Approval of Overseas Service)
        Bill 2014, second reading', *Senate Hansard*, Parliament of Australia,
        Canberra, 17 July 2014, p. 5266.

11 Scott Ludlam, 'Greens to re-introduce War Powers Bill in light of Chilcot review', *The Greens*, 7 July 2016.

12 Kate Lyons, 'Australia can learn from Chilcot report, says ex-Greens leader', *The Guardian*, 7 July 2016.

13 Luke Henriques-Gomes and Katharine Murphy, 'Scott Morrison on Iran: we'll "seriously consider any US request to join military action', *The Guardian*, 28 June 2019.

14 Sue Warenham, 'Time to bump peace up the agenda', *Green Agenda*, 15 December 2017.

15 Felicity Ruby, email correspondence with author, 18 May 2019.

16 Senate Standing Committees on Foreign Affairs Defence and Trade, 'Mental health of Australian Defence Force members and veterans', Parliament of Australia, Canberra, 17 March 2016.

17 David Wroe, 'Richard Di Natale slams US alliance, says Australia is joining "regional arms race"', *The Sydney Morning Herald*, 16 May 2016.

18 Emma Connors, 'Greens call for foreign policy debate', *The Interpreter*, 17 May 2016.

19 'Questions without notice: United States election', *Senate Hansard*, Parliament of Australia, 10 November 2016, p. 2487; 'Motions: suspension of standing and sessional orders', *Senate Hansard*, Parliament of Australia, Canberra, 10 November 2016, p. 2488.

20 'Motions: suspension of standing orders', *Senate Hansard*, Parliament of Australia, Canberra, 22 November 2016, p. 2889.

21 Scott Ludlam, 'Fascism in larval form, and this is why we aim to misbehave', *The Greens*, 7 February 2017.

22 Nick Miller, 'Revealed: the room inside Pine Gap no Australian could enter, bar one', *The Sydney Morning Herald*, 25 April 2018.

23 Peter Cronau, 'The Base: Pine Gap's role in US warfighting', *Background Briefing*, ABC Radio National, 20 August 2017.

24 Andrew Greene, 'Australian military aircraft targeted with lasers during South China Sea flights', *ABC News*, 29 May 2019.

25 Paul Barclay, 'Hugh White and Clive Hamilton discuss Australia's China policy', *Big Ideas*, ABC Radio National, 7 May 2019.

26 Andrew Greene, 'Australia may need to consider nuclear weapons to counter China's dominance, defence analyst says', *ABC News*, 2 July 2019; Hugh White, 'Time to take up arms as Asian power rises?', *The Weekend Australian*, 29–30 June 2019, p. 21.

27 Paul Barclay, 'Hugh White and Clive Hamilton discuss Australia's China policy'.

28 Australian National Audit Office, 'Joint strike fighter – introduction into service and sustainment planning', Parliamen of Australia, Canberra, 5 December 2018.

29 James Brown, *Firing Line: Australia's Path to War*, Quarterly Essay 62, Black Inc., Carlton, 2016, p. 58.

30 Richard Di Natale, 'Peace and security: nonviolent global cooperation', *The Greens*, Parliament of Australia, Canberra, 1 July 2016.

31   Australian National Audit Office, 'Defence's management of its projects of concern', Auditor-General Report No. 31, 2018–19 Performance Audit, Commonwealth of Australia, Canberra, 2019.
32   Australian Government Productivity Commission, 'Trade & Assistance Review 2016–17', Productivity Commission Annual Report Series, Commonwealth of Australia, Canberra, 2018.
33   Lisa Martin, 'No guarantee Australian weapons aren't used in Yemen conflict, government says', *The Guardian*, 20 February 2019.
34   Dylan Welch, Kyle Taylor and Rebecca Trigger, 'Australian government under fire over export of weapons system to war crime-accused Saudi Arabia', *ABC News*, 20 February 2019.
35   Paul Barclay, 'Armed neutrality – an alternative to the US alliance?', *Big Ideas*, ABC Radio National, 11 June 2012.
36   ICAN, 'Senator Scott Ludlam', Vimeo, 6 July 2017.
37   Sue Wareham, 'Time to bump peace up the agenda', *Green Agenda*, 15 December 2017.
38   The Greens NSW, 'ANZAC's long shadow: Mehreen Faruqi, NSW Greens MP', YouTube, 15 Oct 2014.
39   Nick Deane, 'US troops are now in Darwin. But questions remain as to why', *The Guardian*, 27 April 2018.
40   'Criminal Code Amendment (War Crimes) Bill 2016, second reading', *Senate Hansard*, Parliament of Australia, Canberra, 1 December 2016, p. 3966.
41   Scott Ludlam, 'Australian foreign policy: the Greens approach', *Australian Institute of International Affairs*, 3 June 2016.

CHAPTER 15: CLEANING UP AUSTRALIA'S DEMOCRACY

1   Christine Milne, *An Activist Life*, p. 103.
2   No author, 'The UTG and you', *UTG Extra*, April 1972, p. 1.
3   Dick Jones, 'Policy speech Senate elections 1975', Patsy Jones private papers, 1975.
4   Bob Brown, *House of Assemby Hansard*, Parliament of Tasmania, Hobart, 13 April 1983, p. 171.
5   Jo Vallentine, 'Whistleblowers Protection Bill 1991, second reading', *Senate Hansard*, Parliament of Australia, Canberra, 12 December 1991, p. 4695.
6   Bob Brown and Peter Singer, *The Greens*, pp. 101–3.
7   Rebecca Huntley, 'Response', *The Prosperity Gospel: How Scott Morrison Won and Bill Shorten Lost*, Quarterly Essay 74, Black Inc., Carlton, 2016, p. 96.
8   Bob Brown and Peter Singer, *The Greens*, pp. 112–3.
9   Aaron Patrick, 'Bennelong byelection: the case against Kristina Keneally', *Australian Financial Review*, 7 December 2017.
10   David Crowe, 'Greens vow to "clean up politics" in pitch for votes', *The Sydney Morning Herald*, 1 March 2019.
11   Bob Brown, 'Victorian anti-corruption commission highlights need for a national integrity agency', Media release, 2 June 2010, and 'National

Integrity Commission Bill 2010, second reading', *Senate Hansard*, Parliament of Australia, Canberra, 22 June 2010, p. 3907.

12 'National Integrity Commission Bill 2013 – second reading', *Senate Hansard*, Parliament of Australia, Canberra, 15 May 2014, p. 2687.

13 Parliament of Australia, 'Australian Greens, Labor commit to agreement for stable government', Media release, 1 September 2014.

14 'Motions – parliamentary code of conduct', *Senate Hansard*, Parliament of Australia, Canberra, 29 November 2018.

15 Paul Karp, 'Greens demand hate speech by MPs be stamped out after Christchurch massacre', *The Guardian*, 17 March 2019.

16 Kate Legge, 'Canberra's biggest micro player', *The Australian*, 15 March 2019.

17 Katharine Murphy, 'Greens press government to support media inquiry', *The Sydney Morning Herald*, 10 September 2011.

18 Bob Brown, 'Submission to the independent inquiry into media and media regulation', National Library of Australia, Canberra.

19 Parliament of Australia, 'Greens welcome Finkelstein's news media council', Media release, 2 March 2012.

20 Paddy Manning, 'Whither the Greens?'.

21 Anne Davies, 'Q&A: News Corp a malignant influence on our democracy, Richard Di Natale says', *The Guardian*, 14 May 2019.

22 See Sam Vincent, 'Scott Ludlam goes viral', *The Monthly*, April 2016.

23 Paddy Manning, 'Cop it sweet?', *The Monthly Today*, 6 June 2019.

24 Paddy Manning, 'Sabotaging democracy: espionage and foreign interference laws are being rushed through', *The Monthly Today*, 27 June 2018.

25 Guy Rundle, 'The future of the Greens', *The Monthly*, February 2014.

26 Paul Karp, 'Greens MPs cautiously welcome push for members to elect federal leader', *The Guardian*, 11 April 2018.

27 Sarah Martin and Katharine Murphy, 'Greens leadership: less than a third of party's members happy with selection process', *The Guardian*, 28 June 2019; see also Greens for Democratic Leadership, Facebook, 24 June 2019.

28 Huong Truong, 'Multicolouring the Greens', *The Greens*, 25 January 2017.

29 Rachael Jacobs, 'How #illridewithyou began with Rachael Jacobs' experience on a Brisbane train', *Brisbane Times*, 16 December 2014.

30 Tim Hollo, 'Towards ecological democracy', *Green Agenda*, 28 April 2018, Parts 1 and 2.

31 Martin McKenzie-Murray, 'Batman: how it went wrong for the Greens', *The Saturday Paper*, no. 197, 24–30 March 2018.

32 Jeremy Poxon, Twitter post, 2 July 2019.

ACKNOWLEDGEMENTS

This book is not an official history, but I start by thanking the Australian Greens for their cooperation, access to and assistance with the federal party's historical records up until the mid-2000s (when they migrated online). Party veteran Colin Smith, unofficial historian and archivist, was extremely helpful and offered enormous insight. I was also given discounted media access to plenary or non-members sessions of the party's national conferences in Perth, Alice Springs, Hobart and Brisbane, as well as Young Greens and Green Institute conferences in Canberra. The NSW Greens allowed me access to their archives, put up with me hanging around outside a state delegates council meeting in Bowral (and drinking at the pub after), and welcomed me at various talks and workshops.

I'm especially grateful to the many Greens staffers who bore the brunt of the work of dealing with my requests. Particular mention goes to Matt Siegel, Will Kelly, Hilary Miller, Rosie Collins, Rod Goodbun and Cate Faehrmann, Jay Tilley and Larissa Brown in the office of Richard Di Natale, who handled countless queries over the last three years. Also, in no order, Gideon Reisner, Fraser Brindley, Pat Caruana, Adam Pulford, Jennifer Faerber, Clare Ozich, and others who can't be named but whose help has been invaluable.

Special thanks to those Greens who billeted me at party conferences: in Perth, Giz Watson and June Lowe; in Canberra, Dierk and Rosemary von Behrens; in Alice Springs, Steve Ryan and flatmates, who helped me try to recover my stolen mountain bike! Thanks to Richard Di Natale and the Australian Greens federal party room, who passed the hat around and offered to cover the $1000 excess ... even though I couldn't accept.

For access to personal archives I thank in particular Bob Brown, Patsy Jones; Dexter Dunphy; Geoff Holloway, who guided me through the United Tasmania Group archives; and Hall Greenland, who helped me with the papers of Tony Harris. Also, Fergus McPherson approved access to the Australia Party's files. Thanks to Bob Carr, Moss Cass and Lyndon Schneiders for advance copies of unpublished manuscripts.

Thanks to the librarians at the special collections desk at Mitchell Library – particularly, Bruce Carter; to the State Library of New South Wales' Richard Neville, Melissa Brooks and Jenn Bain, who offered advice on transcription, and to librarians working in the manuscript collections at the Tasmanian archives in Hobart, Perth's Battye Library, State Library Victoria and the National Library of Australia. (At the NLA, Kylie Moloney and Megan Williams explained that a trove of Bob Brown's papers, covering more of his time in Canberra, remain unaccessioned; this is a job for future researchers.) Thanks to the National Museum of Australia for access to the private papers of Richard Jones – particularly to Lee Burgess, who dug them out of the system. A special thank you to archivist Ewan Maidment, who photographed a number of documents for me.

Huge thanks to those who read part or all of this book in manuscript: Bob Brown, Christine Milne, Richard Di Natale, Adam Bandt, Peter Whish-Wilson and Fraser Brindley, Scott Ludlam and Felicity Ruby, Drew Hutton, Hall Greenland, Colin Smith, Margaret Blakers, Stewart Jackson, David Spratt, Richard Denniss, John Quiggin, Julie Macken, Jonathan Pearlman, Peter Manning and others who cannot be identified. You have greatly improved the book with your feedback, which I have tried to incorporate. Errors remain mine alone.

Although I hope to provide a definitive account of the life of the party, it is not possible to do justice to every theme, twist or turn in the story. Perforce I have dealt sparingly with the role of the Greens in local government, or the intricacies of the party's story in Queensland, South Australia and the Northern Territory. Similarly, I conducted interviews with as many key people in the Greens story as possible, but there are absences. In some cases, individuals were unwilling to speak; in other cases, I ran out of time and/or space. I'm eternally grateful to everyone who has supplied me with leads and angles, advice or information: this book could not have happened without you.

Thanks also to my mother-in-law, Maureen Wimborne, who compiled a spreadsheet of the Greens primary vote in every federal electorate back to the beginning, and my son Jude Manning, who did similar for disclosed donations to the Greens and the data for the charts on pages 479–80. Thanks to my mother, Maria Manning, for supporting me with the cost of transcribing hundreds of hours of tape (and thanks to Trint for extending my account).

This project began more than three years ago. Over its course I have published two essays on the Greens for *The Monthly*, pieces for *The Guardian* and *The Sydney Morning Herald*, and a documentary for ABC Radio National's *Background Briefing*. Thanks to the producers and editors who have taken an interest in this project or made allowances as I juggled along the way, particularly: Nick Feik, Natalie Book and Kate Greenwood; Wendy Carlisle, Tim Roxburgh and Suzanne Smith; Lucy Clark; Julie Lewis; and Ben Raue. Thanks to Roberta Ivers and Dan Ruffino at Simon & Schuster, for holding on my next book, and to Louise Adler and Sally Heath for being accommodating as the update of *Born to Rule* was in planning. Thanks to Tara Wynne at Curtis Brown for bearing with me. Thanks to Morry Schwartz, Erik Jensen and Nick Feik for the steady gig at *The Monthly Today*, which has informed this book. Most of all, heartfelt thanks to my publisher, Chris Feik, who waited and waited, and cut and cut, and whose insight and wisdom I trust completely; Julian Welsh, who paid incredible attention to detail in copyediting; and Julia Carlomagno, who remained encouraging and worked a deadset miracle to get this book over the line in time.

Heartfelt thanks to the friends I have bored rigid by no-showing so often, to the family I have missed, and especially to my two sons, Jude and Milo, and my wife, Melinda.

Lastly, I would like to recognise those thousands of Greens members over the decades who get no mention here but who have worked tirelessly – almost always, without reward or prospect of election – to make the Greens what it is: the most successful third party in Australian history, and a great Australian story.

INDEX

1951 Refugee Convention 295
1975 Henderson review of poverty 418
1992 Earth Charter 196
1992 Mabo decision 140
2015 Paris Agreement 388
2016 Defence White Paper 440–2
2019 Davos World Economic Forum 415

Aarons, Laurie xvi, 98
Abbott, Tony (prime minister) 224–5,
    236, 272–3, 282–3, 285, 287, 295–7,
    299, 300, 302, 307, 316–23, 319,
    332–4, 343, 351, 402, 411, 424, 434
ABC (Australian Broadcasting
    Commission) 5, 7, 37, 77, 128, 146,
    180, 216, 221–2, 242, 246, 262, 272,
    280, 300, 319, 328, 366, 371, 375–6,
    381, 404, 464
ABC 7.30 247, 284, 315, 340, 347, 349,
    356, 372–4
ABC Four Corners 356, 358, 368
ABC Insiders 356
ABC Lateline 311
ABC Q&A 463
ABC Radio National 369–70, 378, 395
ABC This Day Tonight 33, 35
ABC Vote Compass 339
Abetz, Eric 306, 419
Aboriginal Driver Training Program 135
Aboriginal Treaty Support Group 50
Abrahams, Georgine 93
ACT Greens 132, 145–6, 256, 265–7,
    306, 369–72
Administrative Appeals Tribunal (AAT)
    116–17
Afghanistan war 138, 205, 248, 278,
    284, 432–5
AID/WATCH 190
Ajani, Judith (The Forest Wars) 145
Albanese, Anthony 229, 272–3, 275,
    289, 308, 322–3, 336–7, 342–3, 345,
    366–7, 413, 476
Allison, Lyn 40, 158

Alternative Coalition 86
Amalgamated Engineering Union xiv
American Prospect 'Green Herring' 195
Amnesty International 204, 231, 255
Andren, Peter 241
Andrew, Neil 223–4
Andrews, Daniel (Vic premier) 303,
    376–7
Animal Justice Party 310, 324, 327, 337,
    366, 459
Anning, Fraser 458, 473
anti-terrorism laws 218
ANZUS Treaty xii, 81, 432, 444
Ardern, Jacinda (NZ prime minister)
    414, 359
Armstrong, Rev. Lance (Good God, He's
    Green!) 70, 75, 154
Arnold, Sue 109
Ash, Geoff 101, 112–13, 116–18, 125,
    190, 209, 466
Asia-Pacific Economic Cooperation
    (APEC) 152, 157
Askin, Bob (NSW premier) ix, xx–xxi
Assange, Julian 438, 447–8
asylum seekers 135–7, 201, 205–6, 218,
    232–3, 294–5, 331, 342, 354, 380,
    397, 478
Australia Institute 155, 273, 322–3, 414
Australia Party xii, xv, 18, 23, 30–1, 98,
    118, 125–6, 163, 189, 411, 413, 418,
    468, 474
Australian Conservation Foundation
    (ACF) xiv, 66, 96, 98, 103–5, 134,
    148, 161, 177, 226, 314
Australian Council of Social Service 332
Australian Council of Trade Unions
    (ACTU) xiv, 405, 425
Australian Cyclists Party 324
Australian Democrats 30–2, 36–7, 41,
    45, 51, 65, 70, 75, 102–3, 105, 115,
    131–4, 138, 155, 157, 159, 161, 163,
    168, 170, 173, 180, 185, 197–8, 206–7,
    211, 233, 248, 473–4, 476

Australian Electoral Commission 86,
112–16, 208, 232, 315–16
Australian Energy Market Operator 295
Australian Financial Review 217, 334
Australian Greens x–xi, xvi–xvii, xxii,
30, 31, 59, 108, 125–8, 139–40, 151,
156–7, 160, 165–6, 183–4, 199, 237–9,
243–4, 250, 285, 302, 339, 390–1,
427, 458, 465, 468
  170-page policy platform 231
  the 1990 'Green election' 75, 101–3,
  119
  the 1997 ten-year strategy 167–9
  the achievements 451, 474–6
  Bob Brown as leader 91, 242–4,
  285, 467
  Christine Milne as leader 299–302,
  311–13
  culture renewal 452
  the demographic 179–80, 250–3
  the formation 111–12, 118–20, 474
  fundraising and contributions 126–8,
  153, 186, 249, 277, 306–7, 315
  the logo 40
  the 'new moral compass' 207
  an overhaul 315–16, 323
  Richard Di Natale as leader 331–2,
  334, 339–40, 356
  the trailblazers of 143
Australian Greens conferences 194, 196–7,
201, 213, 243, 312, 323, 360–1, 467
Australian Greens Coordinating Group
213
Australian Greens elections 77, 102,
128–34, 129, 129–34, 147–9, 153–9,
162–3, 178–9, 181–2, 200, 206, 208,
230–7, 249, 256–7, 277, 280–2,
305–10, 334–2, 344–6, 379
Australian Greens Local Government
Network 188
Australian Greens Quick Decision-
Making Group 171
Australian Greens Steering Group 117
Australian Industrial Relations
Commission 165
  Australian Manufacturing Workers'
  Union (AMWU) 207, 245, 250,
Australian Motoring Enthusiasts Party
310, 334, 459
Australian Renewable Energy Agency
(ARENA) 295, 319
Australian Republic Movement (ARM) 172
Australian Security Intelligence
Organisation (ASIO) 216, 222
Australian Students Environmental
Network 399

Australian Tax Office (ATO) 334
Australian Unemployed Workers Union
476
Australian Union of Students 14–15
Australian Workers' Union (AWU) 280,
464
Australian Youth Climate Coalition
(AYCC) 306, 391–2
Australians Against Further Immigration
157
AWB Ltd (Australian Wheat Board) 236

Bacon, Jim (Tas premier) 181, 228
Badham, Van 421
Bahro, Rudolf (*Socialism and Survival*)
54
Baillieu, Ted (Vic premier) 286–8
Baird, Mike (NSW premier) 325
Baldwin, Peter 54–5
Ball, Jason 382
Bandt, Adam 219, 256, 281–3, 286,
301–2, 305, 309–11, 320–2, 324,
327–8, 344–6, 353–5, 364, 380, 382,
393, 398–400, 407, 412–13, 423,
426–7, 434, 468
Barber, Greg 22, 162–3, 187, 244–6,
286–8, 324, 360, 375–6, 411
Barham, Jan 288, 291–3, 332, 349, 371,
459–61
Barnett, Colin (WA premier) 267–8, 303,
353
Barnett, Mike 79
Barry, Paul (journalist) 306
Bartlett, Andrew 204, 206, 234, 357,
362, 433
Bartlett, David (Tas premier) 276, 312
Barton, Gordon x–xii, 23, 30
Bastian, Gert 121
Batchelor, Noreen (UTG) 16
Bates, Dr Gerry (lecturer) 65, 69, 70
'Battle for Kelly's Bush' (1971) xx–xxi
'Battle of Farmhouse Creek' 59, 66–68,
79
'Battle of Seattle' protests (1999) 194
BDS (Palestinian boycott, divestment,
sanctions) 289–3, 343, 366
Beazley, Kim 82, 89, 176, 203, 206,
214–15
Beirne, Greg 249
Bell, Robert 102, 158, 184
Bellamy, David 44
Bennett, John (attorney-general) 63
Berejiklian, Gladys (NSW premier) 326
Berkman, Michael 362
Bernardi, Cory 271, 473
Berriman, Mark 102

Bessel, Danny 104
Betancourt, Ingrid (Colombian Greens) 196
Bethune, Angus (Tas premier) 4–6, 9–11, 13
Beyond Zero Emissions 277
Bhathal, Alex 203–4, 342, 345, 361, 365–6, 375, 377, 475
BHP 136, 198, 276, 333, 472
Bicycle Victoria 245
Birds and Animals Protection Bill (1910) 42
Birmingham, Simon 354–5
Bjelke-Petersen, Joh 81, 147
Blair, Tony (UK prime minister) 156
Blakers, Margaret 115, 194, 199, 211–13, 359
Bligh, Anna (QLD premier) 269
'Blockade Handbook' 43
Blue Mountains National Park xiv, 41
'Blueprint for Survival' (Ecologist UK) 19, 31
Bob Brown Foundation 381
Bogong newsletter 132
Bolt, Andrew 215
Bolte, Henry xiv
Bongiorno, Justice Bernard 241–2
Booth, Kim 210, 365
Borbidge, Rob 147, 149–50
Border Protection Bill 204
Borschmann, Gregg 53
Boswell, Ron 235
Bourne, Vicki 207
Bowen, Chris 294
Bowtell, Cath 281
Boyce, Sue 273
Boyle, Peter 101
Bracks, Steve (Vic premier) 217, 244–5, 391
Braid, Harry 39
Brandis, George 226, 363, 464
Bregman, Rutger (historian) 415–16
Brenner, Max cafés 292
Brereton, Laurie 102, 206
Brexit 351, 359, 382
Briffa, Tony 469
Brigham, Steve 107, 113, 115–16, 119, 129
Brindlay, Fraser 441
Brisbane Greens 91–2, 280
Broadby, Rod (UTG) 13
Brogden, John 221–2
Brooks, Geraldine (author) 40
Brown, Bill xvi–xvii, 191
Brown, Bob ix, x, 57, 79, 87, 98–9, 107–10, 115, 117–18, 122–3, 146, 152, 154, 159, 181–3, 187, 193, 199–200, 207, 211, 253–4, 267–8, 272, 287, 306, 314, 321, 358, 370–1, 406, 413, 431–2, 459, 462, 466
    Australian of the Year 44
    becoming politically active 32–33
    and the fiscal stimulus packages 262–3
    and the five-point climate action plan 278
    and George W. Bush (US president) 224–6
    on a global parliament 297
    and The Greens 150–2, 155, 390, 435–5
    his 'Green Oration' 297
    his *USS Enterprise* protest 34–5, 429
    and *The Human Tragedy* 129
    and *Memo for a Saner World* 223
    'the most credible politician' 186
    and newspaper ad 20–1
    and *Optimism* 201, 282
    resigning politics 297
    resigns from Tasmanian parliament 129
    speech to the Senate 166
    on the *Tampa* crisis 203–4
Brown, Freda x, xvi, 191
Brown, James (Quarterly Essay) 441
Brown, Larissa 337
Brown, Ron 6, 13, 15–16
Browne, Sally-Anne 200
Brull, Michael 372
Brumby, John 391
Brunt, Tony 17
Buckingham, Jeremy 288, 291–3, 325–6, 349, 358, 368, 371–5, 377–8, 404, 465, 468
Buckland, Ella 371–4
Buckman, Greg 198, 208–9, 213
BUGA-UP (Billboard Utilising Graffitists Against Unhealthy Promotions) 97, 472
Builders Labourers Federation (BLF) xix–xxii, 24
Bulbeck, Chilla 353
Burke, Brian (WA premier) 79
Burke, Tony 401
Burnie *Advocate* 60, 132
Burnside, Julian 381
Burton, Bob (journalist) 39
Burton inquiry 24
Bush, George W. (US president) 195, 204, 216, 223–6, 249
Buswell, Troy 268–9
Butler, Kevin 147
Button, John 105

Byrne, Fiona 290–1
Byrne, Sam 187
Byron Echo 289

Cairns, Jim xvi, 79
Caldicott, Dr Helen 98, 106
Call to Australia Party 97, 109, 157
Calwell, Arthur xi
Cameron, Jan 306
Camilleri, Joseph 105
Campaign Against Nuclear Energy
  (CANE) 50
Campaign to Save Native Forests 50
Campbell, Mary (National Trust) xx
Canavan, Matt 406
Canberra environment centre 132
Canberra truckers' blockade 1995 145–6,
  233
Cannon-Brookes, Mike (Atlassian
  founder) 394
Cape York wilderness area 148–50
Carbon Farming Initiative 295
Carbon Pollution Reduction Scheme
  (CPRS) 264, 270–2, 274–6, 284,
  296, 305, 392, 402
Carles, Adele 267–9
Carmichael coal mine (Adani) 177,
  381, 387, 406–7, 465
Carnell, Kate 145
Carpenter, Alan (WA premier) 267
Carr, Andrew 430
Carr, Bob (NSW premier) 42, 66, 98,
  146, 188–9, 192, 221, 226, 247, 275,
  288, 444
Carson, Rachel (*Silent Spring*) xiii
Casey, Jim 322, 342–3
Cass, Dan 180, 216
Cass, Moss 24, 180
Cassidy, June 102
Cassola, Arnold 197
Centre Alliance 465
Centre Party 5, 10, 15
centrist policies 30, 331, 346, 352
Cessnock Kurri Greens 293
CFMEU (Construction, Forestry,
  Maritime, Mining and Energy Union)
  144–5, 189, 206, 228, 233–4, 250,
  306, 380, 405–7, 464
Chaelundi State Forest 188
Chamarette, Christabel 86–7, 116, 129,
  133, 135–43, 156, 158, 166, 453, 468
Chaney, Fred 77, 84
Chapman, Bruce (HECS architect) 320
Chapple, Robin 102, 197, 239, 269
Chernobyl 78, 122, 124
Chilcot Inquiry 2016 (UK) 435

Chipp, Don (*The Third Man*) 29, 36, 40,
  96, 106
Christian Democratic Union CDU
  (Germany) 47–8, 242
Christian Democrats 256, 327
Christmas Island 138, 202, 294
Christoff, Peter 115
Clarke, Charmaine 180–1, 185
Clarke, David 292
Clean Energy Acts 296
Clean Energy Finance Corporation
  (CEFC) 283, 295, 307, 319, 321–2
Clean Energy Future 296
Cleary, Phil 180
Climate Action Forum 366
climate change 249, 253, 268, 271–2,
  274, 276, 284, 388–90, 396, 400–1,
  448
Climate Change Authority 283, 295, 321
Climate Change Review 260, 264,
  270–1, 274–5, 284, 391
climate commission (New Zealand) 360
Clinton, Bill (US President) 195
Clinton, Hillary 351
Club of Rome (*The Limits to Growth*)
  18–19, 31, 388
Coalition for Gun Control 190
Cohen, Ian (*Green Fire*) 42–4, 96–8,
  102, 109, 146–7, 188–90, 220, 222,
  288–9, 358, 472, 475
Collins, Jim 99
Colong Committee xv, 10
Colong wilderness area 39, 41
Colston, Mal 90, 165
Combet, Greg (*Fights of My Life*) 275,
  284, 295–6
Commonwealth Integrity Commission
  457
Communist Party of Australia (CPA)
  x, xvi, xviii, 96, 98, 191
Community Aid Abroad 50, 129
Community and Public Sector Union 313
'Community Independents' 98
Concerned Residents Against Moral
  Pollution (CRAMP) 64
Concerned Residents Opposed to
  Pulpmill Siting (CROPS) 68–9, 468
'Conference of Parties' talks 388
Conroy, Stephen 316, 335, 339, 464
Conservation Council of Victoria 104,
  115, 244
Constitutional Convention 170–2
Cook, Peter 77
Cook, Stuart 199
Coolungubra Forest, NSW 43
Corbyn, Jeremy (UK) 351, 367, 421

Corr, Gary 141
Costello, Peter 176, 233, 268, 273
Coulter, John xv, 31, 89, 106–7, 390
Council of Australian Governments 404
Country Liberal Party (NT) 181
Country Party 5, 8, 32
Courier-Mail 253, 461–2
Court, Charles (WA premier) 50
Court, Richard (WA premier) 144, 173, 195
Court of Disputed Returns 235
Couser, Dr Geoff 282
Cowles, Chris (LPAC) 12
Cox, Jim 71
Crean, Simon 215–17, 223, 226
Crichton-Browne, Noel 89
Crikey 306–7, 396
Croome, Rodney 64–5, 363
Crosby, Lynton 207
Crossley, Louise 178, 183–4, 196
Crowcher, Trish 49
Crowe, Shaun (*Whitlam's Children: Labor and the Greens in Australia*) 305, 323, 337
CSG (coal seam gas) industry 326, 404
CSIRO (Commonwealth Scientific and Industrial Research Organisation) 8, 319, 391, 394
Cundell, Peter (ABC host) 43
Cunningham, Christine 346
Cunningham, Liz 148–9
Cyclone Advertising 277

Daily Planet magazine 198
Daintree Rainforest 43, 96
Damania 9
Dangerous Weapons Bill (1987) 62–3
Dann, Christine (author) 18
Dastyari, Sam 302, 334–5
Dawkins, Andrea 365
Dawkins, John 138, 140
Day, Bob 308, 335
Debnam, Peter 247–8
Dell, Hugh (UTG) 22–3
Democratic Labor Party (DLP) xi, 23, 217, 257, 280, 343, 473, 476
Democratic Socialist Party (DSP) 100–4, 107, 109–11, 113–14, 116
Denborough, Dr Michael (NDP) 50, 54
Denison Greens 76
Denniss, Richard 256, 323, 336, 414, 417
Di Natale, Richard 217, 254, 256, 280, 310, 327–8, 336–9, 345, 352–3, 358, 360, 367, 371, 401–2, 421, 431, 455, 457, 467, 468, 469, 476
    on the coal industry 393–4

on defence 441–3
    the draft code of conduct for senators 458
    his speech to the government 380
    and the sexual harassment cases 372, 374
    on social security and taxes 416, 419–20
    on the verge of quitting 378–9
Direct Action (journal) 101
Doctors for Forests 197
Doctors for Native Forests 240
Dombrovskis, Peter 40–1
Donald, Rod (Green Party New Zealand) 194, 243
'Doubts Removal' Bill 17
Douglas-Apsley National Park 72
Downer, Alexander 201
Draft Universal Declaration of the Rights of Mother Earth 472
Druery, Glenn 191, 310, 458
Duffy, Conor (ABC reporter) 340
Dunn, Irina 98–9, 102, 390
Dunphy, Milo xiv–xv, 8–11, 13–14, 24, 39, 41, 93, 98–100, 186, 188
Dunstan, Don (SA premier) 63
Durack, Peter 80
Dutton, Peter 225
Duxbury, Louise (environmental consultant) 81, 86

'Earth First' eco-terrorist group (US) 132
East Gippsland forest 104
East Timor 32, 142, 201–2, 430, 432, 447
East West Link (Melbourne) 319, 324, 343
'eco-human centred' 93–4
ecological sustainability 56, 134, 388
Ecologically Sustainable Development Working Groups 1991 390
Ecology Party (UK) 19
'eco-tage' 41
eco-tax package 183
Electrical Trades Union 249–50, 380
Electrona zinc works 65
Elix, Jane (Women's Electoral Lobby) 93
Ellis, Bob 98
emissions-trading scheme (ETS) 169–70, 260–1, 263, 272, 284, 296, 321, 390, 394–5
Energy Resources Australia (ERA) 173, 176–7, 183
Environment Commissioner 126
Environment Planning and Assessment Act 42, 189

Environment Tasmania 314
Environmental Defenders Office 158, 266, 280, 379, 408
Environmentally Sustainable Industries Commission 126
'Envirovote' 98
Eslake, Saul (economist) 419
'Eurocommunism' xvi
European Federation of Green Parties 197
European Greens Party conference (1998) 194
Evans, Alan 72
Evans, Andrew (Assemblies of God) 232
Evans, Chris 294
Evans, Gareth 138–9
Evans, Harry 225
Everett, Merv 17
Everingham, Sam (biographer) x–xi
Evers, Diane 197
Exclusive Brethren 248
Extinction Rebellion 383, 401
Extremely Greedy 40% Extra Party 154

Faehrmann, Cate 200, 279, 288, 291–3, 308, 332, 355, 367–8, 373–4, 377–8
Fahey, John (NSW premier) 146
'Fair Protection for Firefighters' Bill 426
Fair Work Australia 261, 340
Fair Work Commission 2017 425
Family First 232–5, 256, 270–1, 281, 308
Faruqi, Mehreen 325, 347, 357–8, 367–8, 374, 380, 387, 445–6, 468
Faruqi, Osman (journalist) 346, 469
Faulkner, John 334
Faulkner, Patricia 284
Federal Hotels' casino development 4, 10
Feeney, David 342, 345
Ferguson, Martin 260, 270, 276, 404
Field, Justin 325–6, 349, 358, 368, 373, 377–9, 440
Field, Michael (Tas premier) 71–4, 76–7, 154, 163
Fielding, Steve 263, 270–1, 273, 335
Fifield, Mitch 463
First Australian 171
Fischer, Joschka (Germany) 124, 184, 193, 205, 242–3
Fisher, Gillian 53
Fishing Party 235
Fitzgerald Inquiry (1989) 453
Fitzgibbon, Joel 340–1
Fitzsimmons, Jeanette (Green Party NZ) 193
Flanagan, Richard (author) 26, 182, 240, 314

Fletcher, Karen 114
Fletcher, Paul 273
Foley, Luke 373
For a Caring Tasmania (FACT) 64
Ford, Gerald (US president) 29
Forestry Commission NSW 41
Forestry Tasmania 298
'Forests Forever' campaign 254
Foskey, Deb 236, 241, 265–6
four pillars policies 22, 46, 100, 106, 122, 388, 425, 429–31, 448, 466
Fox, Lindsay 286
Fox Ranger uranium inquiry 30
Franklin River dam 32–4, 37, 59–61, 70, 131, 145, 452
Franklin River dam blockade 39–41, 53, 66, 68, 79, 91, 96, 129, 154, 326, 387, 466
Fraser, Malcolm (*Dangerous Allies*) 29–30, 34, 39, 135, 431–2, 452
Freedom of Information Bill 452
freedom-of-information laws 60–1, 132, 166, 452–3
Freight Link (Perth) 319, 353
Fricker, Ally 96
Friedman, Thomas 261
Friend, Dick 20
Friends of the Earth 280
Frydenberg, Josh 382, 403
Fuller, Rod 277–8
'fundis' fundamentalists 49, 107, 123–4, 411–12, 423
Future of Work Commission 420

Galdies, Rebecca 357
Gallagher, Katy 303
Gallop, Geoff (WA premier) 237
Garrett, Peter (*Big Blue Sky*) 51, 53–4, 81, 104, 108–9, 119, 177, 226–8, 259–60
Gay, John 241
Gay Law Reform Group 64
GDP (gross domestic product) 414–17, 441–2
Gemmell, Susie 273
Georges, George 49, 79
German Greens ('Die Grünen') xxii, 22, 26, 47–8, 56, 106, 122, 184, 382
    'fundis' and 'realos' 49, 107, 123–4
    the Offenbach conference 46
    the red–green coalition 123–4, 193, 242
'Getting Together' conference (1986) 91–4, 105
GetUp 306, 392
GFC (global financial crisis) 2008 261–2, 270, 312

Ghirardello, Zach 370
Gibson, Miranda 297–8
Giddings, Lara (Tas premier) 298, 312, 314
Gillard, Julia (prime minister) 71, 73, 253, 261, 273–4, 276–8, 282–5, 293–6, 298–300, 302–5, 353, 391–2, 423, 434, 457
Gillin, Lauren 372
Glencore 276
Global Carbon Capture and Storage Institute 263
Global Greens 194–7, 199, 204, 212, 297, 359
Gollan, Daphne 54, 56, 97–8, 468
Gonski school reforms 307, 353–5, 358, 455
Goodbun, Rod 372–3
Goolengook forest 182
Gore, Al (*An Inconvenient Truth*) 195, 249, 321–2
Gorton, John (prime minister) 39
Goss, Wayne (QLD premier) 147–50
Gough, Andy 201
GQ magazine 339
Grand Green Tour 212–13
grassroots democracy 46, 56, 118, 122–3, 187, 455, 466
Gray, Gary 334
Gray, Robin (Tas premier) 38–9, 61, 65, 67, 69, 70–1, 73, 285, 452
Great Barrier Reef xiii, xx, 29, 472
Greble, Ruth 249
Green, Antony (ABC election analyst) 267, 287
Green Alliance 100–4, 109, 113–14, 132
Green Bans xviii, xxii, 24, 41–2, 48, 192, 254, 343, 406–7
'Green Democrats' 106
Green Development 86
Green Earth Alliance 87
Green Electoral Network (GEN) 99
Green Independents Business and Industry Strategy 75
Green Independents (Tas) 59–62, 65, 70–7, 87, 98–100, 103, 109, 105, 452
Green Institute 212–13, 418, 470
Green Left Weekly (DSP) 101, 108, 110
Green magazine 198, 211, 243, 309, 353, 462
'Green Manifesto' 92
Green New Deal 261–3, 268, 383, 399, 401
'Green not Greed' slogan 97
Green Party (NZ) 18, 193–4
Green Party UK 19

'Green Political Network' conferences 100
Green Registration Committee 113
'Green State Election Strategy' (Vic) 115
Green Voice 320
Greenhouse Council 388
greenhouse-gas emissions 126–7, 161, 166, 169, 249, 322, 393, 395, 403
Greenland, Hall xvii–xviii, 55, 93, 95, 101, 103, 107, 112, 147, 190, 322–3, 358
Greenpeace 266, 387
'Green Politics Network' 115
Greens in Lowe 114
Greens Political Education Trust 322
Greens SA 158–9, 200, 206, 244
Greens WA 52, 86–7, 102–3, 133, 173, 197–8, 200, 206, 213, 237, 265–7
'Greenslide' 2010 281
Greig, Brian 184, 233
Greiner, Nick (NSW premier) 98
GroenLinks (Netherlands) 359
Groom, Ray (Tas premier) 77, 132, 153–4
GST (goods and services tax) 133, 138, 156–8, 178, 180, 184, 199–200, 206, 208, 210, 339
Guantanamo Bay 223–4, 248
Guaranteed Adequate Income (GAI) scheme 126
Guise, Adam 326
Gun Control Australia 164
gun law reform 153, 163–4
Gundjehmi corporation 173
Gunns 20 case 240–2, 249, 465
Gunns Ltd 228, 240, 261, 306

Habib, Mamdouh 223
Habibie, B.J. (Indonesian president) 201–2
Habitat (ACF) 94, 124
Haines, Janine 96, 103
Hale, Sylvia 147, 220, 222, 246, 288–91
Hamer, Rupert 388
Hamilton, Dr Clive 155, 273
  and *Growth Fetish* 413
  and *Requiem for a Species* 396
  and *Silent Invasion* 439
Hamilton, Tom 442–3
Hand, Gerry 135
Hanna, Kris 218–19, 244, 269
Hanson, Pauline 141, 157, 166–7, 180, 185, 202–3, 235, 291, 303, 336, 352–3, 381, 406, 473
Hanson-Young, Sarah (*En Garde*) 172, 254–6, 285–6, 294–5, 301, 305, 308, 310–11, 346, 354–5, 380, 458, 468
Hare-Clark system 45, 59, 145, 166

Harradine, Brian 24–5, 77–8, 132,
136–8, 165, 170, 184, 204, 228
Harris, Chris 340, 358
Harris, Tony 54–6, 94, 100–1, 103–4,
107, 116, 190
Hartcher, Peter (political editor) 274–5,
278, 421
Hartland, Colleen 115–16, 245, 360, 426
Hatton, John 98
Hatzistergos, John (attorney-general)
279–80
Haupt, Robert (journalist) 103
Haussleiter, August 46
Hawke, Robert 'Bob' (prime minister)
xiv, 40–1, 50, 68, 76, 89, 97, 102–5,
114, 135, 264, 363
Hawke government 43, 45, 56, 66, 85,
100, 142, 150–1, 390, 407, 433
Hayden, Bill 84–5
Hazelwood power station 392
Hean, Brenda (LPAC) 7, 9, 13–14, 21, 468
Henderson, Gerard 155–6, 268, 281–2,
418
Henderson, Judy 129, 130–2, 150
Henry, Don 322
Henry, Dr Ken 262, 276
Henty, Jenny 162
Herbert, Kim 86, 159
Heritage Commission 29
Hewson, John 101, 125, 127, 130, 138
Hibbins, Sam 324, 377
Hicks, David 223, 248, 447
Hickson, Jill 41
Higginson, Sue 379, 408
Hill, Robert 161, 170, 176
Hine, Doug 113, 119
Hirschhorn, Jeremy (ATO commissioner)
334
HMAS *Jervis Bay* 201
HMAS *Manoora* 202
HMS *Edinburgh* 85
Hodgins-May, Steph 345
Hodgman, Will 276, 315, 364
Holgate, Harry (Tas premier) 38
Hollister, Di 62, 70, 73, 154
Hollo, Tim ('Towards Ecological
Democracy') 380, 382, 418–19, 470–2
Holloway, Geoff (UTG) 16, 34, 365
Holt, Harold (prime minister) ix, xi
Home Affairs 465
homosexuality decriminalisation xiii,
63–4, 154, 364
Horodny, Lucy 145
Howard, John (prime minister) 81, 97,
140–1, 145, 155, 157–8, 164–6, 169–
70, 176, 183, 207, 209, 219–20, 225–6,

229–31, 233–6, 247–9, 287, 416, 424
Howard government 88, 127, 161,
172–3, 178, 180, 184–5, 198–9, 201–5,
215–16, 222–3, 259, 425, 432–3, 435
Howes, Paul 280, 303
Hu Jintao (Chinese president) 223, 225–6
Human Rights and Equal Opportunity
Commission 141
Hunter, Meredith 303
Hunter Valley Coal Chain 263
Hunters Hill Trust xx
Huntley, Rebecca (Quarterly Essay) 454–5
Huon Defenders 240
Huon Forest Products 72
Hutton, Drew 91–2, 94, 98, 102, 105–11,
114, 116–17, 119–20, 129–30, 147–50,
155, 199–200, 230, 235–6, 280, 301,
361, 404, 470
Hydro Electric Commission (the Hydro)
3–5, 8–10, 12, 15, 24, 33, 37, 39, 43–4,
63, 66, 73, 452
Hydro Employees Action Team (HEAT)
39
'hydro-industrialisation' 4, 60, 452

Iemma, Morris (NSW premier) 247–8,
288
Illawarra Greens 107
Independent Commission Against
Corruption (ICAC) 247, 288, 453,
456–7
Independents for Climate Action 397
Ingham, Liz 375–6
Ingram, Lauren 369–72
Intergovernmental Panel on Climate
Change (IPCC) 389–91, 401
International Campaign to Abolish
Nuclear Weapons 445
International Covenant on Civil and
Political Rights 142
International Energy Agency 296
Iraq War 215–19, 222, 229, 233, 429,
433–5, 440
Iskandar, Sam 290

Jabiluka anti-mine campaign 30, 173–7,
180, 183, 326
Jabiluka uranium mine 161, 178
Jackson, Stewart (political scientist) 75,
213–14
Jacobi, Carrie 184
Jeanes, Mark 250–1
Jenkins, Jean 81
Jensen, Dennis 271
Johnson, Lyndon 'LBJ' (US president)
ix–x, 32, 226, 429

Johnston, Hetty 235
Joint Committee on Foreign Affairs,
  Defence and Trade 82
Joint Committee on Intelligence and
  Security 446, 465
Joint Standing Committee on Electoral
  Matters 334
Jones, Barry (*Sleepers, Wake!*) 54, 390
Jones, Dr Richard (LPAC) 7–13, 15, 17,
  22, 24–8, 35–6, 45, 60, 66, 98, 189, 452
Jones, Malcolm (Outdoor Recreation
  Party) 191
Jones, Patsy 11, 24–5, 66
Jones, Peter 47, 93
Joselyn, Lynne 348
Joyce, Barnaby 235, 271, 340

Kaiser, Mike 148
Kakadu National Park 131, 161, 173
Kangaroo '89 operation 82
Katter, Bob 406, 473
Kaye, John 192, 230, 246, 248, 279, 289,
  292, 320, 325–7, 348–9, 405
Kearney, Ged 365–6
Keating, Paul (prime minister) 68, 76,
  117, 125, 127, 130, 134, 138–9, 144–6,
  157, 343, 431
Keating government 88, 105, 140, 142–3,
  149–51, 161, 407, 425
Keleher, Lynette 375
Kelly, Petra (*Fighting for Hope*) xxii,
  46–9, 91, 121–4
Kelly, Ros 76, 128, 130–1
Keneally, Kristina (NSW premier) 288,
  290
Kennett, Jeff (Vic premier) 115, 162
Kernot, Cheryl 107, 139, 156, 158, 165,
  169, 172, 184, 210, 218
Kerr, Christian 286–7
Kerr, Duncan 130, 133, 170
Kiernan, Kevin (geomorphologist) 3, 7,
  9, 12–14, 21, 24–5, 34, 39, 66
King River scheme 59
Kinnear, Scott 200
Kirner, Joan 115, 388
Kissinger, Henry (US) 32, 86
Klein, Naomi (*This Changes Everything*)
  399–400, 404
Kosciuszko National Park 42
Kroger, Michael 336, 366
Kyoto climate talks (1997) 161, 169–70
Kyoto Protocol 195, 206, 233, 249, 259,
  390

La Rocca, Sam 280, 309
Labor Greens 55–6

Labor Party (ALP) xi–xii, xvii, 4, 22–4,
  26, 32, 37–9, 55–7, 68, 70, 84, 89, 99,
  115–16, 130–3, 142, 146, 157, 163,
  165, 179, 181–2, 185–6, 217–18, 233
Labor–Green Accord 59, 61, 64, 72–3,
  75–7, 129, 153, 285
Labor–Greens agreement 283–4, 293,
  303–5
Laird, Norman (UTG) 13, 15–16
Lake Manapouri hydro scheme 17
Lake Pedder 3–4, 10, 15, 32, 34, 36, 41,
  60, 70, 297, 407, 452
Lake Pedder Action Committee (LPAC)
  5–6, 8–9, 11–14, 17, 20, 27, 32
Lake Pedder 'Blue Ban' proposal 25
Lamb, Bob 96, 116
Lambert, Judy 128
Lambie, Jacqui 335, 352, 355, 365, 473
Landa, Paul 41
Landcare 353
Lang, Jack (NSW premier) 217
Lapthorne, Nadine 86
Latham, Mark (*Diaries*) 217, 226, 228,
  233–4, 406
Law, Geoff (TWS) 43
Lawrence, Carmen 144, 217–18
Lawson, Damien 219
Lawyers for Forests 197
Lazarus Rising (John Howard) 164, 249
Le Couteur, Caroline 353
Lee, Ronan 269–70
Lees, Meg 178, 181, 199, 210
'Left Alliance' 281
Left Renewal 349–51, 377, 422, 466
Lehany, Kath xx
Leigh, Andrew 337, 413–14, 418–19
Lemonthyme Forest, Tasmania 43, 66,
  68
Lennon, Paul (Tas premier) 228
Leong, Jenny 231, 325, 374–5, 379, 398
Liberal Democrats 310
Liberals for Forests 197
Liberal Party 23, 26, 38, 133, 143, 147,
  163, 179, 197–8, 210, 227, 232, 257,
  266, 294, 303, 342, 343, 365, 381, 441
Liberal Reform Group xi–xii
Lightfoot, Ross 225
Little Desert National Park xiv
Llewellyn, Paul 86, 239
LNG (liquefied natural gas) 237, 404
'Lobby for Peace' network 80
'Lock the Gate' network 325, 349, 404
Loevin, Isabella (Sweden) 359
Lonergan Research 338
Lowe, Doug (Tas premier) 37
Lucas, Caroline (Green Party UK) 261

Ludlam, Scott 175–8, 254, 263, 268,
276, 301, 305, 308, 321, 327–8, 335,
338, 345, 352, 356–7, 402, 413, 418,
423, 429, 431, 434–5, 437–8, 444–5,
447–9, 468
    and 'Atomic Oz' 174
    digital rights defender 463–4
    elected in WA 256
    his address to Canberra 316–18
Luntz, Stephen 162, 178
Lynch, Michael 76, 102
Lyons, Kevin 5, 10–11, 15, 26–7

Macdonald, Ian 288
Macfarlane, Ian 273
Mack, Ted 98
Madigan, John 335
Maher, Tony (CFMEU) 405
Malaysia Solution 294–5
Manly Dam 190
Mansell, Michael 141
Margarula, Yvonne 175
Margetts, Dee 86, 102, 129, 133,
138–44, 156, 165, 169–70, 178, 184,
198, 209, 238–9, 468
Maritime Union of Australia (MUA)
172–3, 190, 464
Marks, Kelly 349
Marr, Alec (TWS) 66–7, 146, 155
Marr, David (*Dark Victory*) 202, 248
Marriage Act amendment (2004) 364
Marshall, Alan (*The Great
Extermination*) xiii
Mason, Colin 32, 40
Mason, Paul (*PostCapitalism*) 418
Masters and Servants Act 22
Matchett, Lily 399–400
Matson, Murray 44
Maules Creek coalmine 397
McAlpine, Angus 376, 409
McCloy, Jeff 456
McCullough, Jill (TWS) 40
McDonald, Kevin 62
McGauran, Julian 271
McGinty, Jim (attorney-general) 239,
267
McGowan, Cathy 470
McGowan, Jim (NSW premier) 42
McGowan, Mark (WA premier) 239, 353
McHugh, Jeanette 102
McKell, Bill (NSW premier) 42
McKell Institute 343
McKibben, Bill 389
McKim, Nick 67, 210, 241, 276, 312–15,
333, 346, 354, 358, 365, 446–7, 464–5
McLeay, Leo 89

McMahon, Amy 362
McMahon, Les 55
McMahon, William 'Billy' (prime
minister) xv, 39
McMullan, Bob (Labor) 66
McPherson, Fergus 23, 30
Medcalf, Carole 340
Medical Association for the Prevention of
War 431
Medicare 29, 134, 232, 319, 323, 344,
417, 455
Melbourne City Council 187
Melbourne Group 105–6, 108–9, 114
Melzer, Jean 53
Member of Legislative Council (MLC)
86, 98, 115, 147, 188, 191, 197, 238–9,
245–6, 293
Menzies, Robert (prime minister) x–xi,
4, 32, 118
Merkel, Angela (German chancellor) 242
Metgasco CSG development 326, 404
#MeToo movement 370–1
Middle Australia Project 167
Middle Gordon Hydro-Electric Scheme
4, 17, 24, 36
Mighell, Dean 250
Migration Act 136, 294
Milne, Christine 14–15, 26, 69, 70,
73–4, 77, 118, 145, 153–4, 181–2, 194,
199, 228–30, 233–4, 265, 267, 280,
283–4, 300–1, 306, 310–12, 318–20,
358, 360, 388–9, 408, 434, 440, 451,
457, 467, 470
    on a federated Australian Greens
        structure 211–12
    her resignation from politics 327–9
    leader of Green Independents (Tas)
        129
Milne, Ian (UTG) 13
Minchin, Nick 246
Minerals Resource Rent Tax 276
Miragliotta, Narelle (political scientist)
26, 310
Mirarr people 173–6
Mirvac 192
MIT 'world model' of five factors 18–19
Mitchell, Alex 148
Moles, Sarah 200
Moore, Catherine 171–2, 199
Moore, Clover 98
Moore, Michael 145
Morris, Tim 210, 314
Morrison, Scott (prime minister) 332,
379, 380, 416, 424, 435, 459
Mosley, Geoff (cowriter *Outline for a
Bushland Magna Carta*) xiv, 186

Movement Populaire pour l'Environment (Switzerland) 18
Moylan, Jonathon 397–8
Muir, Ricky 310, 334–5, 459
Multi-Party Climate Change Committee (MPCCC) 284, 295, 391
Mundey, Jack xviii, xix, xx–xxii, 24–5, 48, 57, 98, 109, 192, 254, 406–7
Murdoch, Rupert 232, 285, 333, 389
Murdoch media 210, 285, 381, 405, 435
Murphy, Lionel (chief justice) 363
Murphy, Shayne 132, 206, 209
Murray, Andrew 158, 207, 453
MV *Oceanic Viking* 294
Myall Lakes Committee 8

Nader, Ralph (US activist) 13, 18, 156, 195, 234
National Biodiversity Act 126
National Election Campaign Committee 129, 252–3
National Electricity Market 392
National Energy Guarantee 403–4
National Farmers Federation 172
National Firearms Agreement 164
National Integrity Commission 379, 457
National Multicultural Greens Group 469
National Party 8, 149, 151, 162–4, 189, 235, 239, 271, 286–7, 326, 338, 340, 349, 357, 379, 470
National Press Club 47, 156–7, 219, 278–9, 303–4, 327, 344, 353, 367, 400, 419, 457
National Sea Change Taskforce 460
National Tertiary Education Union 186, 192, 230
National Trust xx
National Union of Students 186
National Union of Workers (NUW) 407
Native Title Act 1993 140–2
Native Title Tribunal 141
Natural Death Bill (1986) 62
Natural Heritage Trust 155, 161, 170
Nature Conservation Council 99, 279
Nature Walkabout (TV series) xiv
NDIS (National Disability Insurance Scheme) 455
Neilson, Bill (Tas premier) 34
Nelson, Brendan 260–1, 273
neoliberalism 352, 412, 417–18, 426–7
Nettle, Kerry 177, 200–1, 207, 209, 215, 220, 223–5, 230, 236, 249, 254, 256–7, 297
New England New State Movement 32
'New Ethic' statement 21–3, 196, 359
New Housewives Association (1946) xvi

New Left Party 98
New Liberal Movement 30
New Matilda 372
New Movement 80
New South Wales Aboriginal Land Council 141
New South Wales Legislative Council referendum 146–7
New Zealand First 360
Newbury, Annabel 52, 86
Newman, Campbell 302
News Corp 231, 301, 333, 462–4
News Ltd 290
News Media Council 462
Newspoll 210, 264, 275, 287–8
Newstart 302, 307, 319, 397, 423–4
Nightcap National Park blockade 42–3, 96
Nile, Elaine 97
Nile, Fred 109, 232, 327
Nitschke, Dr Philip 159
No Aircraft Noise party 147, 220
'No Dams' 37–8, 326, 452
No Pokies 256
Noranda 69
Norman, James (biographer) 129, 134, 158
North Atlantic Treaty Organization (NATO) 48
North Broken Hill 68–9
North Forest Products lawsuit 240–1
North Ltd 161, 173, 180, 241
North West Cape communications base 82
Northern Land Council 173
NSW Greens 76, 98, 107, 109, 111–13, 118, 146, 188, 190–2, 199–201, 207–9, 216, 219, 220–1, 243, 247–8, 286, 288–92, 306, 325–7, 333, 347–9, 351, 373, 377–9, 476
NT Greens 201
NT News 463
Nuclear Disarmament Party (NDP) xvii, 50–4, 56, 77–8, 81, 92, 97–8, 101–2, 106, 110, 119, 135, 264, 317, 407, 468
Nuclear Non-Proliferation Treaty 439
Nutt, Tony 287

Oakes, Laurie 24, 139, 336
Oakeshott, Rob 282, 284
Obama, Barack (US president) 268, 274, 309, 391
Obeid, Eddie 288, 456
O'Brien, Joy 188
Ocasio-Cortez, Alexandria (US Democrat) 399
Occupy movement 194

O'Connor, Cassy 276, 365
O'Connor, Michael (CFMEU) 145, 228, 233–4, 306
O'Connor, Rod 10
Odgers' Australian Senate Practice 78
O'Dwyer, Kelly 273, 363, 382
O'Farrell, Barry (NSW premier) 290
Office of Climate Change 391
O'Gorman, Paddy 189
O'Halloran, Paul 314
Oke, Cathy 302
Oliver, Alex 436
Olympic Dam 50, 174
One Nation 167, 180–2, 184–5, 197, 207, 239, 248, 303, 345, 353, 381, 406, 455, 465
'Open Council' xviii
Oquist, Ben 128, 134, 152, 158, 195, 198, 201, 203, 220–1, 233, 246, 266, 277, 279, 281, 285, 301, 306, 310–11, 322, 328, 331
Organ, Michael 216, 223, 229–30
Origlass, Nick xvii–xviii, 54–5
Osborne, Michael 394
Osborne, Paul 145
Owens, Joe xix
Ozich, Clare 311

Pablo, Michel (Fourth International) xvii
Pacific Solution 138, 204, 294
Palmer, Clive (Palmer United Party) 308, 310, 320–2, 406, 473
Palmer, Mick (AFP commissioner) 313
Parenti, Christian (*Tropic of Chaos*) 448
Parer, Warwick 173
Parker, Jamie 159, 221, 291, 325, 379
Parkin, Sara (*Green Parties*) 27, 46, 76, 123–4
Parliamentary Budget Office 307, 338, 441, 458
Parliamentary Code of Conduct 458
Parliamentary Defence Office 441
Parliamentary Integrity Commissioner 458
Parliamentary Salaries and Allowances Amendment Bill 61
Parnell, Mark 158–9, 244, 315, 332
Parratt, Andrew 153, 159–60
Patmore, Peter 72, 74
Patrick Stevedores 172
Patten, Fiona (Sex Party) 324
Payne, Marissa 437
Peace and Nuclear Disarmament Action Group 54
'Peace Squadron' 96
Peace Trust Fund 88

Peacock, Andrew 102–3, 150
Pennicuik, Sue 245, 425–6
People for Nuclear Disarmament (PND) 49
People party (UK) 19, 46
'People's Party' (US) 18
Percy, Jim (SWP) 100–1, 110–11, 116
Percy, John (SWP) 100–1
Perth *Sunday Times* 269
Peters, Cathy 289
Petroleum Resource Rent Tax 423–4
Petrusma, Jacqui 235
Picton Valley blockade 66, 128
Pieman River scheme 34, 66
Piketty, Thomas (*Capital*) 420
Pine Gap 47, 49, 82–4, 86, 122, 429, 438, 466
Pinnell, Gemma 230–1
Plibersek, Tanya 231, 308, 343–4, 366–7, 402
populist 112, 303, 352, 382, 383, 418, 428
Port Arthur massacre 154, 163
Powell, Janet 106, 115, 129
Poxon, Jeremy 477
Pratt, Louise 308
Precipitous Bluff, Tasmania 34
Press Council 232, 340
Price, Max (Tiger Moth pilot) 21
Protected Interests Disclosure Bill 2013 453
Protection of Public Participation Bill 241
Proudlock, Brian (LPAC) 5
Pusey, Michael 167
Putt, Peg 129, 154, 182, 210, 240–2
Pybus, Cassandra 110
Pyne, Christopher 442

Quakers 43, 54, 80, 466
Queensland Greens 117, 147, 149, 151, 198, 200, 206, 244, 310
Quiggin, John (economist) 231, 417–18

Racial Discrimination Act 143
Rainbow Alliance 87, 105, 115
Rainforest Information Centre 190
Rann, Mike (SA premier) 218
Raper, Ashleigh (ABC reporter) 373
Ratnam, Samantha 325, 361, 375–7
Rattenbury, Shane 159, 266–7, 303, 353, 370, 402–4
Raue, Tom 351
Read, Mark 'Chopper' (*Hits and Memories*) 127
Reagan, Ronald (US president) 29, 47, 81
'realos' realists 49, 107, 122–3, 411–12, 193, 423

Reece, Eric 'Electric' (Tas premier) 4, 15, 17, 23–4, 34, 36
Re-Energising Australia policy 390
Rees, Nathan (NSW premier) 288
Refugee Week (1992) 137
Regional Forest Agreements (RFA) 143–4, 237
Reith, Peter 169, 172
Renew Australia policy 390–1, 393–4, 400
Renewable Energy Act 2000 243
Renewable Energy Fund 263
Renewable Energy Hub 394
Renewable Energy Target (RET) 272, 321–2, 390, 403
Republic Advisory Committee 134
Resource Super Profits Tax 276
Reverberi, Daniela 102
Rhiannon, Lee ix–x, 49, 198, 209, 220, 222, 243, 248, 279, 281, 288, 306, 312, 315, 321, 327–8, 333–5, 345, 347, 350–1, 354–5, 358–9, 373–4, 405, 456, 458, 467–8
    and #IStandWithLeeRhiannon 356
    and democracy4sale.org 221, 247, 280, 307, 456
    her resignation 368
    and whatwillmydegreecost.com.au 320
    joining the Australian Greens 189–92
Rice, Janet 44, 104–5, 115, 306, 309, 333, 345, 357, 468
Richardson, Dennis (ASIO director-general) 216
Richardson, Graham 40–1, 51, 56, 66–9, 76, 103–5
Richmond Ranges 188
Richter, Judy 53
Rio Earth Summit (1992) 126–7, 194
Rio Tinto 276
Ripper, Eric 268
Risstrom, David 187, 230, 234
Robb, Andrew 146, 155, 158, 288
Roberts Alan (*The Self-Managing Environment*) 92
Robodebt 423–4
Rock Island Bend 40–1
Rocks precinct, Sydney xxii, 192
Rosen Robert 153
Rouse, Ed 71
Roy Morgan poll 134, 211, 249–51
RU-486 abortion drug 236
Ruby, Felicity 438, 447–8
Rudd, Kevin (prime minister) 150, 248–9, 253, 259–60, 262–4, 268, 274–6, 278, 282, 290, 294, 300–1, 304–5, 308, 412, 460
Ruddock, Philip 136
Rundle, Guy (journalist) 309, 396–7, 466
Rundle, Tony (Tas premier) 154, 163
Ryan, James 337
Ryan, Phil 130

'S11' blockade 194–5
SA Greens 219, 244, 315, 365
Sales, Leigh (ABC host) 356
Same Sex Relationships (Enduring Equality) Bill 229–30
same-sex marriage campaign 152, 237, 229–30, 233, 279, 331, 333, 363, 364, 396–397
Sandell, Ellen 306, 324, 377, 391–2
Sanders, Bernie (US Democrat) 351
Sanders, Norm 35, 38, 40, 43–5, 67, 78, 96, 453, 477
Sargent, Greg (TWS) 149
Sarkozy, Nicholas (French president) 261
Saulwick, Jenny 115–16
Save the Planet party 397
SBS (Special Broadcasting Service) 128, 207, 281, 319, 463
Scott, Jim 129, 144, 173–4, 237–9
Scott, Kelvin (UTG) 13
Scotts Peak dam 24
Scullion, Nigel 226
Sea Shepherd Australia 332
Sekhon, Gurm 162, 165, 187, 209
Senate committee into corporate tax avoidance 333–4
Senate inquiry into the closure of coal-fired power stations 405
Senate inquiry into the mental health of defence force members and veterans 436
Senate Standing Committee on Foreign Affairs, Defence and Trade 434–5
Serpentine Dam, Tasmania 10, 21
Serventy, Lyn 86
Serventy, Vincent (*Continent in Peril*) xiv
Seselja, Zed 306
Sharp, Christine 173, 238–9
Sheikh, Simon 306, 308, 392
Sherwood, Michaela 470
Shoebridge, David 288, 291–2, 320, 351, 358, 367–8, 371–2, 379, 400, 422, 439–40
Shoobridge, Louis 6
Shooters, Fishers and Farmers Party 327, 365, 470
Shorten, Bill 319, 323, 338–9, 339, 352, 363, 380, 401–2, 423, 459
Siddons, John 30–1

Siewert, Rachel 200, 207, 230, 234, 236, 244, 261, 268, 280, 328, 302, 332, 345, 423–5
Simms, Robert 332–3, 346, 474
Sims, Rod 284
Singer, Peter (bioethicist) 156, 158, 180
   and *Animal Liberation* 150
   and *The Greens* 150–2, 155, 390, 453–5
Sky News 280, 328, 336
Smethurst, Annika (journalist) 464
Smith, Dean 363
Smith, Paul 33
Smith, Tamara 326
Smyth, Brendan 146
Snowden, Edward (NSA whistleblower) 438
Snowy Mountains hydro scheme 4, 246–7
Social Democratic Party (SPD) Germany 46, 48, 122–4, 193, 242–3
Socialist Alliance 368
Socialist Party of Australia xvi, 104, 190, 280
Socialist Workers Party (SWP) 52–4, 100, 104, 110
South West Committee 6
Southern forests, Tasmania 66
Spratt, David (*Climate Code Red*) 277, 389, 396
Springle, Nina 377
Sri, Jonathon 460–2, 467
St John, Edward 25, 53
Stanhope, Jon 237, 265, 267, 403
Stanley, Peter (defence expert) 443
State Delegates Council 220, 475
State Electricity Commission 426
State Planning Authority (NSW) xx
Steele-John, Jordon 357, 381, 469
Steffen, Will (climate scientist) 284
Stern Review on the Economic of Climate Change (UK) 249, 390
Still Wild, Still Threatened 297–8
Stolen Generations 154, 180
Stop Adani campaign 381–2, 387–8, 405, 475
'Stop CSG' and the Bentley blockade 326, 404
Stott-Despoja, Natasha 199, 204, 206, 210, 255, 271
Strahan, Tasmania 43–4
'strategic lawsuit against public participation' (SLAPP suit) 240–1
Sun Fund 170, 390
Sutton, John 187
Sutton, Philip (*Climate Code Red*) 277, 397

Sutton, Phillip 105
Swan, Wayne 262, 274, 283
Sydney Council 57, 98
Sydney Greens 56, 57, 86, 92–3, 95, 100
Sydney Institute 155–6, 261–2

Tactical Response Group 313
Tagliaferri, Peter 267
Tampa crisis 138, 202–3, 214
'Tampa Greens' 203–4
Tanner, Lindsay 162–3, 230, 257, 274, 281
targeted compliance framework (TCF) 424
Tarkine wilderness, Tasmania 153
Tasmanian Forestry Agreement (TFA) 313
Tasmanian Greens 60–5, 70–1, 77, 112, 117, 153, 198–200, 210, 275–6, 364–5
Tasmanian Times 314
Tasmanian Trades and Labor Council 24
Tasmanian Wilderness Society (TWS) 7, 33–6, 40, 96, 105, 134, 146, 148–9, 157–9, 161, 314
'Vote for the Environment' campaign 103
'vote for the forests' campaign 68
Tasmanian Wilderness World Heritage Area 34, 68, 72, 297, 313
Tebbutt, Carmel 289, 291
Telstra sale 155–7, 165, 209–11
Tenants Union 244
Terania Creek rainforest blockade 41–2, 326
Thatcher, Margaret (UK prime minister) 29, 47
The Advertiser (Adelaide) 463
The Advocate (Burnie) 132
The Age 78, 218–19, 311, 339, 366, 375, 376
The Australian xi, xiv, xxi, 15, 20, 44, 93, 100, 119, 169, 177, 183, 207, 215, 233, 244, 255, 270, 280, 285–7, 289, 307, 326, 357, 365, 371, 408, 419, 421, 463, 475–6
The Canberra Times 181, 265
The Daily Telegraph 247, 253, 299, 337, 372
The Examiner (Launceston) 14, 20, 27, 33, 39, 61, 63
The Franklin Wild River (1980) 44
The Guardian 195, 355, 383, 401, 467
The Herald Sun 205, 231–2, 286, 337, 426, 463
The Mercury (Hobart) 4, 9, 11, 14, 34, 130, 241, 264–5, 311
The New York Times 229, 261
The Northern District Times 229
The Saturday Paper 370, 475

The Sun Herald 85
The Sunday Telegraph 221–2, 280
The Sydney Morning Herald x–xi, xx,
    40, 66, 81, 97, 103, 119, 130, 147,
    219–20, 229, 231, 247, 274, 278, 289,
    291, 349, 350, 374–5, 398, 421
The Telegraph 101–2
Thomas, Paul 152, 187
Thompson, Norman 247, 307
Thompson, Peter (*Bob Brown of the
    Franklin River*) 64
Thorpe, Lidia 361, 377
Thunberg, Greta (the school strikers) 401
Togatus (UTAS) 26
Total Environment Centre 10–11
'Towards the Formation of a National
    Greens Organisation' 108–9
Toyne, Phillip 103–4
Trad, Jackie 362
Transfield 192
Trans-Pacific Partnership 352
Treaty on the Prohibition of Nuclear
    Weapons 431
Triabunna woodchip mill 4, 228, 306
Tripodi, Joe 288
Trittin, Juergen (Germany) 243
Troeth, Judith 273
Truchanas, Olegas 6–7, 40
Truganini statue 13–14
Trump, Donald (US president) 322,
    351–2, 359, 382, 431, 436–7
Tucker, Kerrie 132–3, 145–6, 230, 236,
    256, 266, 468
Tuckey, Wilson 271
Turnbull, Malcolm (prime minister) 134,
    249, 261, 271, 273–4, 277, 333–4, 335,
    339, 340, 344, 353–4, 358, 363, 380,
    394, 424, 439, 442, 458, 465
Turnbull, Reg 'Spot' xii

Uhlmann, Chris (political editor) 340–1,
    394
Uluru Statement from the Heart 455
UN Environment Programme 261
UN Framework Convention on Climate
    Change 126, 388, 393
Union of Australian Women xvi
UN Climate Change Conference 2007
    259
UN Copenhagen Summit 2009 270–4,
    391
UN High Commissioner for Refugees 204
United Tasmania Group (UTG) 13,
    15–18, 25–8, 32–3, 73, 75, 102, 103,
    297, 365, 411, 413, 452, 473–5
    the formation 12, 16, 474

'new deal for Aborigines' 14
the 'new-life economy' 14
and 'Pedder Lives' 21
and *UTG Extra* newsletter 14
and 'Vote for the Survival Group' 19
United Voice 313
Unity Party 181, 185
universal basic income (UBI) 418–20,
    422
University of Melbourne 8, 245
University of New South Wales (UNSW)
    189, 192
University of Queensland (UQ) 8, 231
University of Tasmania (UTAS) 8, 14,
    35, 65
University of Technology (UTS) 130, 177
University of Western Australia 50
University of Wollongong 216
Uren, Tom 23–4, 177
US Alliance 84, 429, 432, 436–7, 443–6
US Nurrungar base 85–6
USS *Oldendorf* 96

Vallentine, Jo 47, 51–4, 57, 77–9, 98,
    102–3, 107–10, 115, 129, 166, 174–5,
    187, 429, 431–3, 453, 468, 473
    her achievements 86–9, 143
    the HMS *Edinburgh* protest 85
    and the 'Just Defence' seminars 84
    resigns from parliament 90, 135
Vallentine, Kate (Gaia Foundation) 174
Vallentine Peace Group 80, 86
Values Party (New Zealand) 18–19
van der Bellen, Alexander 359
Vernon, Carol 340
Victorian Greens 22, 115, 150, 161–3,
    200, 207, 217, 244–5, 286–8, 323–5,
    367, 375–7
Victorian Peace Network 219
Vietnam War ix, xii, 46, 86, 92, 192,
    215, 219, 429, 434
Volmer, Ludger (Germany) 242
Voluntary Euthanasia Party 324

WA Greens 86–7, 112, 178, 197
WA Inc 1990 144, 453
Waldheim Huts, Cradle Mountain 69
Walker, Dawn 349, 368, 373, 377–8, 465
Walker, Pamela 16
Waller, Hazen 119
Walsh, David (MONA founder) 297
Walsh, Peter 105, 131
Walsh Bay, Millers Point 192
Walters, Brian 272
War on Terror 204–5, 222, 432–3
War Resisters' International 86

Warden, James 146
Wareham, Sue (*Green Agenda*) 431, 435, 442
Washpool National Park 42, 188
Waters, Larissa 254, 280, 309, 328, 345, 356–7, 380, 395–6, 408, 461, 468
Watson, Geoffrey (ICAC) 247, 456
Watson, Giz 102, 173, 237–40, 269, 303, 337, 364, 469
Weatherill, Jay (SA premier) 315
Wellbeing Budget (NZ) 414
Welch, Bruce 187
Welfare to Work reforms 302, 423
Wesley Vale pulp mill 59, 68–72, 112, 173, 300, 451
West, Jonathan 96
WestConnex (Sydney) 319, 325, 343
Western Mining's Roxby Downs 50
Western Suburbs Greens 114
Whish-Wilson, Peter 301–2, 305, 308, 321, 337, 346, 362–3, 414–17, 420–3, 427–8, 431, 436, 454
Whistleblower's Protection Bill 88
White, Hugh (*How to Defend Australia*) 439
White, Rebecca 364
White, Sir Alfred (UTG) 13
White Australia policy xiii
Whitehaven Coal 397
Whitehead, Adrian 397
Whitlam, Gough (prime minister) xi–xii, 23–4, 33, 35, 40, 50, 131, 142–3, 322–3, 352, 452
Whitlam government 27, 29, 32, 320, 418
Whitlam Oration (2011) 293
Wigney, Rebecca 133
WikiLeaks Party 308
Wild Rivers National Park 37
Wildlife Preservation Society xiii
Wilkie, Andrew 229, 254, 264–5, 282, 308, 367, 453
Wilkinson, Marian (*Dark Victory*) 202
Willey, Mary 37
Williams, Chris 116, 133
Williams, John 338
Williams, Pamela (*The Victory*) 155
Wilson, Sir Ronald 141
Windsor, Tony 241, 282, 322, 470
Woman's Day 81
Women's International Democratic Federation xvi
Wong, Penny 229, 259–60, 270–71, 273–4, 296, 334, 363
Wood, Graeme (Wotif) 277, 281, 306
Wood, Jason 287
Wood, Robert 97, 102
Woodley, John 132

WorkChoices 248, 261, 275, 406, 425
WorkCover 343
WorkDynamics 371, 373
Workplace Relations Bill 165, 169
World Economic Forum 194–5
World Heritage Area 34, 68, 72, 297, 313–14
World Heritage Committee 177
World Heritage Convention (1974) 32, 40
World Heritage in Danger 173
World Heritage Properties Protection Bill 40
World Trade Organization 194
Wran, Neville (NSW premier) 41–2, 66, 68
Wright, Judith (*Coral Background*) xiii, xiv
Wright, Penny 44, 158–9, 276, 280, 332
Wyner, Issy xviii, 55

Xamon, Alison 239
Xenophon, Nick 256, 263, 270–1, 273, 335–6, 365, 382, 473

Yarran, Gladys 87
Young, Virginia (TWS) 149
Young Greens conference 399, 405

Zero Carbon Act (New Zealand) 360

9 781863 959520